Discoveries and Breakthroughs in Cognitive Informatics and Natural Intelligence

Yingxu Wang
University of Calgary, Canada

INFORMATION SCIENCE REFERENCE

Hershey · New York

Director of Editorial Content: Kristin Klinger
Senior Managing Editor: Jamie Snavely
Assistant Managing Editor: Michael Brehm
Publishing Assistant: Sean Woznicki
Typesetter: Sean Woznicki
Cover Design: Lisa Tosheff
Printed at: Yurchak Printing Inc.

Published in the United States of America by
    Information Science Reference (an imprint of IGI Global)
    701 E. Chocolate Avenue
    Hershey PA 17033
    Tel: 717-533-8845
    Fax: 717-533-8661
    E-mail: cust@igi-global.com
    Web site: http://www.igi-global.com/reference

Library of Congress Cataloging-in-Publication Data

Discoveries and breakthroughs in cognitive informatics and natural
intelligence / Yingxu Wang, editor.
    p. cm.
  Summary: "This book provides emerging research topics in cognitive
informatics research with a focus on such topics as reducing cognitive
overload, real-time process algebra, and neural networks for iris recognition,
emotion recognition in speech, and the classification of musical chords"--
Provided by publisher.
  Includes bibliographical references and index.
  ISBN 978-1-60566-902-1 (hardcover) -- ISBN 978-1-60566-903-8 (ebook) 1.
Neural computers. 2. Cognitive science. 3. Artificial intelligence. I.
Wang, Yingxu.
  QA76.87.D57 2010
  006.3--dc22
                   2009042998

British Cataloguing in Publication Data
A Cataloguing in Publication record for this book is available from the British Library.

All work contributed to this book is new, previously-unpublished material. The views expressed in this book are those of the authors, but not necessarily of the publisher.

Advances in Cognitive Informatics and Natural Intelligence (ACINI) Series

ISBN: 1948-9722

Editor-in-Chief: Yingxu Wang, University of Calgary, Canada

Novel Approaches in Cognitive Informatics and Natural Intelligence
Yingxu Wang, University of Calgary, Canada
Information Science Reference • copyright 2009 • 395 pp • H/C (ISBN: 978-1-60566-170-4)

Creating a link between a number of natural science and life science disciplines, the emerging field of cognitive informatics presents a transdisciplinary approach to the internal information processing mechanisms and processes of the brain and natural intelligence. Novel Approaches in Cognitive Informatics and Natural Intelligence penetrates the academic field to offer the latest advancements in cognitive informatics and natural intelligence. This book covers the five areas of cognitive informatics, natural intelligence, autonomic computing, knowledge science, and relevant development, to provide researchers, academicians, students, and practitioners with a ready reference to the latest findings.

The Advances in Cognitive Informatics and Natural Intelligence (ACINI) Book Series seeks to fill the gap of literature that transcends disciplinary boundaries, and is devoted to the rapid publication of high quality books. In providing a scholarly channel for new research principles, theories and concepts, the book series will enhance the fields of Natural Intelligence, Autonomic Computing, and Neuroinformatics. The development and the cross fertilization between the aforementioned science and engineering disciplines have led to a whole range of extremely interesting new research areas known as Cognitive Informatics and Natural Intelligence. Advances in Cognitive Informatics and Natural Intelligence (ACINI) Book Series seeks to propel the availability of literature for international researchers, practitioners, and graduate students to investigate cognitive mechanisms and processes of human information processing, and to stimulate the transdisciplinary effort on cognitive informatics and natural intelligent research and engineering applications.

Hershey • New York
Order online at www.igi-global.com or call 717-533-8845 x 100 –
Mon-Fri 8:30 am - 5:00 pm (est) or fax 24 hours a day 717-533-8661

Table of Contents

Detailed Table of Contents

Chapter 1

   *Zhiwei Shi, Chinese Academy of Science and Graduate University of Chinese Academy of
      Sciences, China*
   Hong Hu, Chinese Academy of Science, China
   Zhongzhi Shi, Chinese Academy of Science, China

Recent fruitful progresses on brain science have largely broadened the understanding of the cerebrum. These great works led the authors of this chapter to propose a computational cognitive model based on a graphical model that they carried out before. The model possesses many attractive properties, including distinctive knowledge representation, the capability of knowledge accumulation, active (top-down) attention, subjective similarity measurement, and attention-guided disambiguation. It also has "consciousness" and can even "think" and "make inference." To some extent, it works just like the human brain does. The experimental evidence demonstrates that it can give reasonable computational explanation on the human phenomenon of forgetting. Although there are still some undetermined details and neurobiological mechanisms deserving consideration, this work presents a meaningful attempt to give further insights into the brain's functions.

Chapter 2

      Yi X. Zhong, Beijing University of Posts and Telecommunications, China

An attempt was made in this chapter to propose a new approach to the intelligence research, namely the cognitive approach that tries to explore in depth the core mechanism of intelligence formation of intelligent systems from the cognitive viewpoint. It is discovered, as result, that the mechanism of intelligence formation in general case is implemented by a sequence of transformations conversing the information to knowledge and further to intelligence (i.e., the intelligent strategy, the embodiment of intelligence in a narrower sense). It is also discovered that the three major approaches to AI that exist, the structural simulation approach, the functional simulation approach, and the behavior simulation approach, can all be harmoniously unified within the framework of the cognitive approach. These two discoveries, as well as the related background, are reported in this chapter.

Chapter 3

Lisa Fan, University of Regina, Canada
Minxiao Lei, University of Regina, Canada

With the explosion of available data mining algorithms, a method for helping user to select the most appropriate algorithm or combination of algorithms to solve a given problem and reducing users' cognitive overload due to the overloaded data mining algorithms is becoming increasingly important. This chapter presents a meta-learning approach to support users automatically selecting most suitable algorithms during data mining model building process. The authors discuss the meta-learning method in detail and present some empirical results that show the improvement that can be achieved with the hybrid model by combining meta-learning method and Rough Set feature reduction. The redundant properties of the dataset can be found. Thus, the ranking process can be sped up and accuracy can be increased by using the reduct of the properties of the dataset. With the reduced searching space, users' cognitive load is reduced.

Chapter 4

Alberto de la Encina, Universidad Complutense de Madrid, Spain
Mercedes Hidalgo-Herrero, Universidad Complutense de Madrid, Spain
Pablo Rabanal, Universidad Complutense de Madrid, Spain
Ismael Rodríguez, Universidad Complutense de Madrid, Spain
Fernando Rubio, Universidad Complutense de Madrid, Spain

Developing cognitive programs is a complex task. Thus, special purpose languages can help developing such systems. This chapter presents a programming environment to help studying the behavior of cognitive models. This environment allows to easily define new cognitive processes, it simplifies the methods to interconnect them, and it also provides graphical information to analyze how a complex cognitive system is evolving. Moreover, it also includes observation facilities, so that the user can analyze the internal behavior of each of the cognitive entities appearing in the system. The authors illustrate the usefulness of their system by using several examples within the chapter.

Chapter 5

Hélène Hagège, Université Montpellier, France
Christopher Dartnell, LIRMM, France
Éric Martin, University of New South Wales, Australia
Jean Sallantin, LIRMM, France

Old and recent theories stress that any understanding of the processes by which humans can learn requires to fully appreciate the relationships between the "nature of learning" and the "learning of nature." From a constructivist viewpoint, acquiring knowledge is, like any human activity, dissociable neither from its underlying project nor from the knowing subject. The authors of this chapter relate the lessons from philosophy, psychology, didactics and ethics to their work in computational scientific discovery that aims at empowering learning machines with the task of assisting human researchers (Dartnell, Martin, Hagège, & Sallantin, 2008). The chapter concludes with didactical and ethical considerations

Chapter 6

Human factors are the most predominated factors in all systems where humans are part of the systems. Human traits and needs are the fundamental force underlying almost all phenomena in human task performances, engineering organizations, and socialization. This chapter explores the cognitive foundations of human traits and cognitive properties of human factors in engineering. A comprehensive set of fundamental traits of human beings are identified, and the hierarchical model of basic human needs is formally described. The characteristics of human factors and their influences in engineering organizations and socialization are explored. Based on the models of basic human traits, needs, and their influences, driving forces behind the human factors in engineering and society are revealed. A formal model of human errors in task performance is derived, and case studies of the error model in software engineering are presented.

Chapter 7

While many data mining models concentrate on automation and efficiency, interactive data mining models focus on adaptive and effective communications between human users and computer systems. User requirements and preferences play an important role in human-machine interactions, and guide the selection of knowledge representations, knowledge discovery operations and measurements, combined with explanations of mined patterns. This chapter discusses these fundamental issues based on a user-centered three-layer framework of interactive data mining.

Chapter 8

Concepts are the most fundamental unit of cognition that carries certain meanings in expression, thinking, reasoning, and system modeling. In denotational mathematics, a concept is formally modeled as an abstract and dynamic mathematical structure that encapsulates attributes, objects, and relations. The most important property of an abstract concept is its adaptive capability to autonomously interrelate itself to other concepts. This chapter presents a formal theory for abstract concepts and knowledge manipulation known as "concept algebra." The mathematical models of concepts and knowledge are developed based on the object-attribute-relation (OAR) theory. The formal methodology for manipulating knowledge as a concept network is described. Case studies demonstrate that concept algebra provides a generic and formal knowledge manipulation means, which is capable to deal with complex knowledge and software structures as well as their algebraic operations.

Chapter 9
Yingxu Wang, University of Calgary, Canada

Systems are the most complicated entities and phenomena in abstract, physical, information, and social worlds across all science and engineering disciplines. System algebra is an abstract mathematical structure for the formal treatment of abstract and general systems as well as their algebraic relations, operations, and associative rules for composing and manipulating complex systems. This chapter presents a mathematical theory of system algebra and its applications in cognitive informatics, system engineering, software engineering, and cognitive informatics. A rigorous treatment of abstract systems is described, and the algebraic relations and compositional operations of abstract systems are analyzed. System algebra provides a denotational mathematical means that can be used to model, specify, and manipulate generic "to be" and "to have" type problems, particularly system architectures and high-level system designs, in computing, software engineering, system engineering, and cognitive informatics.

Chapter 10
Yingxu Wang, University of Calgary, Canada

Real-time process algebra (RTPA) is a denotational mathematical structure for denoting and manipulating system behavioral processes. RTPA is designed as a coherent algebraic system for intelligent and software system modeling, specification, refinement, and implementation. RTPA encompasses 17 metaprocesses and 17 relational process operations. RTPA can be used to describe both logical and physical models of software and intelligent systems. Logic views of system architectures and their physical platforms can be described using the same set of notations. When a system architecture is formally modeled, the static and dynamic behaviors performed on the architectural model can be specified by a three-level refinement scheme at the system, class, and object levels in a top-down approach. RTPA has been successfully applied in real-world system modeling and code generation for software systems, human cognitive processes, and intelligent systems.

Chapter 11
Yingxu Wang, University of Calgary, Canada
Xinming Tan, University of Calgary, Canada & Wuhan University of Technology, China

Real-time process algebra (RTPA) is a form of denotational mathematics for dealing with fundamental system behaviors such as timing, interrupt, concurrency, and event/time/interrupt-driven system dispatching. Because some key RTPA processes cannot be described adequately in conventional denotational semantic paradigms, a new framework for modeling time and processes is sought in order to represent RTPA in denotational semantics. Within this framework, time is modeled by the elapse of process execution. The process environment encompasses states of all variables represented as mathematical maps, which project variables to their corresponding values. Duration is introduced as a pair of time intervals and the environment to represent the changes of the process environment during a time interval. Temporal ordered durations and operations on them are used to denote process executions. On the basis of these means, a comprehensive set of denotational semantics for RTPA are systematically developed and formally expressed.

Chapter 12

Yingxu Wang, University of Calgary, Canada
Cyprian F. Ngolah, University of Calgary, Canada & University of Buea, Republic of Cameroon

The need for new forms of mathematics to express software engineering concepts and entities has been widely recognized. Real-time process algebra (RTPA) is a denotational mathematical structure and a system modeling methodology for describing the architectures and behaviors of real-time and nonreal-time software systems. This chapter presents an operational semantics of RTPA, which explains how syntactic constructs in RTPA can be reduced to values on an abstract reduction machine. The operational semantics of RTPA provides a comprehensive paradigm of formal semantics that establishes an entire set of operational semantic rules of software. RTPA has been successfully applied in real-world system modeling and code generation for software systems, human cognitive processes, and intelligent systems.

Chapter 13

Yingxu Wang, University of Calgary, Canada
Jian Huang, University of Calgary, Canada

Software patterns are recognized as an ideal documentation of expert knowledge in software design and development. However, its formal model and semantics have not been generalized and matured. The traditional UML specifications and related formalization efforts cannot capture the essence of generic patterns precisely, understandably, and essentially. A generic mathematical model of patterns is presented in this chapter using real-time process algebra (RTPA). The formal model of patterns are more readable and highly generic, which can be used as the meta model to denote any design patterns deductively, and can be translated into code in programming languages by supporting tools. This work reveals that a pattern is a highly complicated and dynamic structure for software design encapsulation, because of its complex and flexible internal associations between multiple abstract classes and instantiations. The generic model of patterns is not only applicable to existing patterns' description and comprehension, but also useful for future patterns' identification and formalization.

Deductive semantics is a novel software semantic theory that deduces the semantics of a program in a given programming language from a unique abstract semantic function to the concrete semantics embodied by the changes of status of a finite set of variables constituting the semantic environment of the program. There is a lack of a generic semantic function and its unified mathematical model in conventional semantics, which may be used to explain a comprehensive set of programming statements and computing behaviors. This chapter presents a complete paradigm of formal semantics that explains how deductive semantics is applied to specify the semantics of real-time process algebra (RTPA) and how RTPA challenges conventional formal semantic theories. Deductive semantics can be applied to define abstract and concrete semantics of programming languages, formal notation systems, and large-scale software systems, to facilitate software comprehension and recognition, to support tool development, to enable semantics-based software testing and verification, and to explore the semantic complexity of software systems. Deductive semantics may greatly simplify the description and analysis of the semantics of complicated software systems specified in formal notations and implemented in programming languages.

Chapter 15

Iterative and recursive control structures are the most fundamental mechanisms of computing that make programming more effective and expressive. However, these constructs are perhaps the most diverse and confusable instructions in programming languages at both syntactic and semantic levels. This chapter introduces the big-R notation that provides a unifying mathematical treatment of iterations and recursions in computing. Mathematical models of iterations and recursions are developed using logical inductions. Based on the mathematical model of the big-R notation, fundamental properties of iterative and recursive behaviors of software are comparatively analyzed. The big-R notation has been adopted and implemented in Real-Time Process Algebra (RTPA) and its supporting tools. Case studies demonstrate that a convenient notation may dramatically reduce the difficulty and complexity in expressing a frequently used and highly recurring concept and notion in computing and software engineering.

Chapter 16

The cognitive processes modeled at the metacognitive level of the layered reference mode of the brain (LRMB) encompass those of object identification, abstraction, concept establishment, search, categorization, comparison, memorization, qualification, quantification, and selection. It is recognized that all higher layer cognitive processes of the brain rely on the metacognitive processes. Each of this set of fundamental cognitive processes is formally described by a mathematical model and a process model. Real-time process algebra (RTPA) is adopted as a denotational mathematical means for rigorous modeling and describing the metacognitive processes. All cognitive models and processes are explained on the basis of the object-attribute-relation (OAR) model for internal information and knowledge representation and manipulation.

Chapter 17

Bing Zhou, University of Regina, Canada
Yiyu Yao, University of Regina, Canada

Granular computing is an emerging field of research that attempts to formalize and explore methods and heuristics for human problem solving with multiple levels of granularity and abstraction. A fundamental issue of granular computing is the construction, representation and utilization of granules and granular structures. Basic granules represent the basic pieces of knowledge. A granular structure reflects the connections between different pieces of knowledge. The main objective of this book chapter is to examine a logic approach to granular computing for combining rough set analysis and formal concept analysis. Following the classical interpretation of concepts that a concept consists of a pair of an extension and an intension, the authors interpret a granule as a pair containing a set of objects and a logic formula describing the granule. The building blocks of granular structures are basic granules representing elementary concepts or pieces of knowledge. They are treated as atomic formulas of a logic language. Different types of granular structures can be constructed by using logic connectives. Within this logic framework, this chapter shows that rough set analysis and formal concept analysis can be interpreted uniformly by using the proposed logic language. The two theories share high-level similarities, but differ in their choices of definable granules and granular structures. Algorithms and evaluation measures can be designed uniformly for both theories.

Chapter 18

Lech Polkowski, Polish-Japanese Institute of Information Technology, Poland
Maria Semeniuk-Polkowska, Warsaw University, Poland

Granular computing, initiated by Lotfi A. Zadeh, has acquired wide popularity as a tool for approximate reasoning, fusion of knowledge, cognitive computing. The need for formal methods of granulation, and means for computing with granules, has been addressed in this work by applying methods of rough mereology. Rough mereology is an extension of mereology taking as the primitive notion the notion of a part to a degree. Granules are formed as classes of objects which are a part to a given degree of a given object. In addition to an exposition of this mechanism of granulation, the authors point also to some applications like granular logics for approximate reasoning and classifiers built from granulated data sets.

Chapter 19

N. Gadhok, University of Manitoba, Canada

W. Kinsner, University of Manitoba, Canada

This chapter evaluates the outlier sensitivity of five independent component analysis (ICA) algorithms (FastICA, Extended Infomax, JADE, Radical, and β-divergence) using (a) the Amari separation performance index, (b) the optimum angle of rotation error, and (c) the contrast function difference in an outlier-contaminated mixture simulation. The Amari separation performance index has revealed a strong sensitivity of JADE and FastICA (using third- and fourth-order nonlinearities) to outliers. However, the two contrast measures demonstrated conclusively that β-divergence is the least outlier-sensitive algorithm, followed by Radical, FastICA (exponential and hyperbolic-tangent nonlinearities), Extended Infomax, JADE, and FastICA (third- and fourth-order nonlinearities) in an outlier-contaminated mixture of two uniformly distributed signals. The novelty of this chapter is the development of an unbiased optimization-landscape environment for assessing outlier sensitivity, as well as the optimum angle of rotation error and the contrast function difference as promising new measures for assessing the outlier sensitivity of ICA algorithms.

Chapter 20

W. Kinsner, University of Manitoba, Canada

R. Dansereau, University of Manitoba, Canada

This chapter presents a derivation of a new relative fractal dimension spectrum, DRq, to measure the dissimilarity between two finite probability distributions originating from various signals. This measure is an extension of the Kullback-Leibler (KL) distance and the Rényi fractal dimension spectrum, Dq. Like the KL distance, DRq determines the dissimilarity between two probability distibutions X and Y of the same size, but does it at different scales, while the scalar KL distance is a single-scale measure. Like the Rényi fractal dimension spectrum, the DRq is also a bounded vectorial measure obtained at different scales and for different moment orders, q. However, unlike the Dq, all the elements of the new DRq become zero when X and Y are the same. Experimental results show that this objective measure is consistent with the subjective mean-opinion-score (MOS) when evaluating the perceptual quality of images reconstructed after their compression. Thus, it could also be used in other areas of cognitive informatics.

Chapter 21

Weiwei Xing, Beijing Jiaotong University, China

Weibin Liu, Beijing Jiaotong University, China

Baozong Yuan, Beijing Jiaotong University, China

This chapter proposes a 3D object classification approach based on volumetric parts, where Superquadric based Geon (SBG) description is implemented for representing the volumetric constituents of 3D object.

In the approach, 3D object classification is decomposed into the constrained search on interpretation tree and the similarity measure computation. First, a set of integrated features and corresponding constraints are presented, which are used for defining efficient interpretation tree search rules and evaluating the model similarity. Then a similarity measure computation algorithm is developed to evaluate the shape similarity of unknown object data and the stored models. By this classification approach, both whole and partial matching results with model shape similarity ranks can be obtained; especially, focus match can be achieved, in which different key parts can be labeled and all the matched models with corresponding key parts can be obtained. Some experiments are carried out to demonstrate the validity and efficiency of the approach for 3D object classification.

Chapter 22

Michael Jenkin, York University, Canada
Andrew Hogue, York University, Canada
Andrew German, University of Ontario Institute of Technology, Canada
Sunbir Gill, York University, Canada
Anna Topol, York University, Canada
Stephanie Wilson, York University, Canada

For systems to become truly autonomous it is necessary that they be able to interact with complex real-world environments. This chapter investigates techniques and technologies to address the problem of the acquisition and representation of complex environments such as those found underwater. The underwater environment presents many challenges for robotic sensing including highly variable lighting and the presence of dynamic objects such as fish and suspended particulate matter. The dynamic six-degree-of-freedom nature of the environment presents further challenges due to unpredictable external forces such as current and surge. In order to address the complexities of the underwater environment, the authors have developed a stereo vision-inertial sensing device that has been successfully deployed to reconstruct complex 3-D structures in both the aquatic and terrestrial domains. The sensor combines 3-D information, obtained using stereo vision, with 3DOF inertial data to construct 3-D models of the environment. Semiautomatic tools have been developed to aid in the conversion of these representations into semantically relevant primitives suitable for later processing. Reconstruction and segmentation of underwater structures obtained with the sensor are presented.

Chapter 23

Zhiwei Shi, Chinese Academy of Science, China
Zhongzhi Shi, Chinese Academy of Science, China
Hong Hu, Chinese Academy of Science, China

Traditionally, how to bridge the gap between low-level visual features and high-level semantic concepts has been a tough task for researchers. In this chapter, the authors propose a novel plausible model, namely cellular Bayesian networks (CBNs), to model the process of visual perception. The new model takes advantage of both the low-level visual features, such as colors, textures, and shapes, of target objects and the interrelationship between the known objects, and integrates them into a Bayesian framework, which possesses both firm theoretical foundation and wide practical applications. The novel model successfully overcomes some weakness of traditional Bayesian Network (BN), which prohibits BN being applied to large-scale cognitive problem. The experimental simulation also demonstrates that the CBNs model outperforms purely Bottom-up strategy 6% or more in the task of shape recognition. Finally, although the CBNs model is designed for visual perception, it has great potential to be applied to other areas as well.

Chapter 24

    Guangzhu Xu, China Three Gorges University, P.R. China
    Yide Ma, Lanzhou University, P.R. China
    Zaifeng Zhang, Lanzhou University, P.R. China

Iris recognition has been shown to be very accurate for human identification. In this chapter, an efficient and automatic iris recognition system using Intersecting Cortical Model (ICM) neural network is presented which includes two parts mainly. The first part is image preprocessing which has three steps. First, iris location is implemented based on local areas. Then the localized iris area is normalized into a rectangular region with a fixed size. At last the iris image enhancement is implemented. In the second part, the ICM neural network is used to generate iris codes and the Hamming Distance between two iris codes is calculated to measure the dissimilarity. In order to evaluate the performance of the proposed algorithm, CASIA v1.0 iris image database is used and the recognition results show that the system has good performance.

Chapter 25

    Yongjin Wang, University of Toronto, Canada
    Muhammad Waqas Bhatti, University of Sydney, Australia
    Ling Guan, Ryerson University, Canada

This chapter introduces a neural network based approach for the identification of human affective state in the speech signal. A group of potential features are first identified and extracted to represent the characteristics of different emotions. To reduce the dimensionality of the feature space, whilst increasing the discriminatory power of the features, the authors introduce a systematic feature selection approach which involves the application of sequential forward selection (SFS) with a general regression neural network (GRNN) in conjunction with a consistency-based selection method. The selected parameters are employed as an input to the modular neural network, consisting of sub-networks, where each sub-network specializes in a particular emotion class. Comparing with the standard neural network, this modular architecture allows decomposition of a complex classification problem into small subtasks such that the network may be tuned based on the characteristics of individual emotion. The performance of the proposed system is evaluated for various subjects, speaking different languages. The results show that the system gives quite satisfactory emotion detection performance, yet demonstrates a significant increase in versatility through its propensity for language independence.

This study demonstrates that the internal structure of the chord classification networks can be interpreted. It reveals the first network classified chord structure first by representing individual notes in terms of circles of major thirds and major seconds, and then by combining these representations to position chords in a three-dimensional hidden unit space. Despite use of a different local representation of input chords, interpretation of the second network reveals a very strong tendency to adopt a transformation of input similar to that observed in the first network. While there is a growing body of evidence concerning specialised neural processing of tones and chords (e.g., Peretz & Zatorre, 2005), this evidence is not yet sufficiently precise to indicate whether distributed representations based on tone circles are used by the brain. A search for examples of an ANN reorganising an input encoding scheme into this type of representation, was not successful. This raises the question of whether circles of thirds and seconds are pertinent to human subjects' representation of musical stimuli.

This chapter introduces basic types of nonconventional neural units and focuses their mathematical notation and classification. Namely, the notation and classification of higher-order nonlinear neural units, time-delay dynamic neural units, and time-delay higher-order nonlinear neural units is introduced. The classification of nonconventional neural units is founded first according to nonlinearity of aggregating function, second according to the dynamic order, third according to time-delay implementation within neural units. Introduction into the simplified parallel of the higher-order nonlinear aggregating function of higher-order neural units revealing both the synaptic and nonsynaptic neural interaction is made; thus, a new parallel between the mathematical notation of nonconventional neural units and the neural signal processing of biological neurons and is drawn. Based on the mathematical notation of neural input inter-correlations of higher-order neural units, it is shown that higher-order polynomial aggregating function of neural inputs can be naturally understood as a single-equation representation consisting of synaptic neural operation plus nonsynaptic neural operation. Thus it unravels new simplified yet universal mathematical insight into understanding the higher computational power of neurons that also conforms to biological neuronal morphology according to nowadays achievements of biomedical sciences.

Chapter 28

J.D. Wang, Asia University, Taiwan
Ka-Lok Ng, Asia University, Taiwan

The maximal repeat distribution analysis is redone by plotting the relative frequency of maximal repeat patterns against the rank of the appearance. In almost all of the cases, the rank plots give a better coefficient of determination values than the authors' previous work, i.e. frequency plot was used. A randomized version is repeated for the maximal repeat study; it is found that rank plot regression analysis did not support scaling behavior; hence, the validity of the findings is not due to an artifact.

Preface

Cognitive informatics is a multidisciplinary field that acts as the bridge between natural science and information science. Specifically, it investigates the potential applications of information processing and natural intelligence to science and engineering disciplines. This collection, entitled *Discoveries and Breakthroughs in Cognitive Informatics and Natural Intelligence*, provides emerging research topics in cognitive informatics research with a focus on such topics as reducing cognitive overload, real-time process algebra, and neural networks for iris recognition, emotion recognition in speech, and the classification of musical chords.

Chapter 1, "*A Computational Cognitive Model of the Brain*" by Zhiwei Shi, Hong Hu, and Zhongzhi Shi, proposes a computational cognitive model based on a graphical model that they carried out before. The model possesses many attractive properties, including distinctive knowledge representation, the capability of knowledge accumulation, active (top-down) attention, subjective similarity measurement, and attention-guided disambiguation. It also has "consciousness" and can even "think" and "make inference." To some extent, it works just like the human brain does. The experimental evidence demonstrates that it can give reasonable computational explanation on the human phenomenon of forgetting. Although there are still some undetermined details and neurobiological mechanisms deserving consideration, this work presents a meaningful attempt to give further insights into the brain's functions.

Chapter 2, "*A Cognitive Approach to the Mechanism of Intelligence*," by Yi X. Zhong, explains a new approach to the intelligence research, namely the cognitive approach that tries to explore in depth the core mechanism of intelligence formation of intelligent systems from the cognitive viewpoint. It is discovered, as result, that the mechanism of intelligence formation in general case is implemented by a sequence of transformations conversing the information to knowledge and further to intelligence (i.e., the intelligent strategy, the embodiment of intelligence in a narrower sense). It is also discovered that the three major approaches to AI that exist, the structural simulation approach, the functional simulation approach, and the behavior simulation approach, can all be harmoniously unified within the framework of the cognitive approach. These two discoveries, as well as the related background, are reported in this chapter.

Chapter 3, "*Reducing Cognitive Overload by Meta-Learning Assisted Algorithm Selection*" by Lisa Fan and Minxiao Lei presents a meta-learning approach to support users automatically selecting most suitable algorithms during data mining model building process. The authors discuss the meta-learning method in detail and present some empirical results that show the improvement that can be achieved with the hybrid model by combining meta-learning method and Rough Set feature reduction. The redundant properties of the dataset can be found. Thus, the ranking process can be sped up and accuracy can be increased by using the reduct of the properties of the dataset. With the reduced searching space, users' cognitive load is reduced.

Chapter 4, "*Analyzing Learning Methods in a Functional Environment*" by Alberto de la Encina, Mercedes Hidalgo-Herrero, Pablo Rabanal, Ismael Rodríguez, and Fernando Rubio, presents a programming environment to help studying the behavior of cognitive models. This environment allows to easily define new cognitive processes, it simplifies the methods to interconnect them, and it also provides graphical information to analyze how a complex cognitive system is evolving. Moreover, it also includes observation facilities, so that the user can analyze the internal behavior of each of the cognitive entities appearing in the system. The authors illustrate the usefulness of their system by using several examples within the chapter.

Chapter 5, "*Humans and Machines: Nature of Learning and Learning of Nature*" by Hélène Hagège, Christopher Dartnell, Éric Martin, and Jean Sallantin, relates the lessons from philosophy, psychology, didactics and ethics to their work in computational scientific discovery that aims at empowering learning machines with the task of assisting human researchers (Dartnell, Martin, Hagège, & Sallantin, 2008). The chapter concludes with didactical and ethical considerations

Chapter 6, "*On Cognitive Properties of Human Factors and Error Models in Engineering and Socialization*" by Yingxu Wang, explores the cognitive foundations of human traits and cognitive properties of human factors in engineering. A comprehensive set of fundamental traits of human beings are identified, and the hierarchical model of basic human needs is formally described. The characteristics of human factors and their influences in engineering organizations and socialization are explored. Based on the models of basic human traits, needs, and their influences, driving forces behind the human factors in engineering and society are revealed. A formal model of human errors in task performance is derived, and case studies of the error model in software engineering are presented.

Chapter 7, "*User-Centered Interactive Data Mining*" by Yan Zhao and Yiyu Yao is guided by the concept that while many data mining models concentrate on automation and efficiency, interactive data mining models focus on adaptive and effective communications between human users and computer systems. User requirements and preferences play an important role in human-machine interactions, and guide the selection of knowledge representations, knowledge discovery operations and measurements, combined with explanations of mined patterns. This chapter discusses these fundamental issues based on a user-centered three-layer framework of interactive data mining.

Chapter 8, "*On Concept Algebra: A Denotational Mathematical Structure for Knowledge and Software Modeling*" by Yingxu Wang presents a formal theory for abstract concepts and knowledge manipulation known as "concept algebra." The mathematical models of concepts and knowledge are developed based on the object-attribute-relation (OAR) theory. The formal methodology for manipulating knowledge as a concept network is described. Case studies demonstrate that concept algebra provides a generic and formal knowledge manipulation means, which is capable to deal with complex knowledge and software structures as well as their algebraic operations.

Chapter 9, "*On System Algebra: A Denotational Mathematical Structure for Abstract System Modeling*" by Yingxu Wang presents a mathematical theory of system algebra and its applications in cognitive informatics, system engineering, software engineering, and cognitive informatics. A rigorous treatment of abstract systems is described, and the algebraic relations and compositional operations of abstract systems are analyzed. System algebra provides a denotational mathematical means that can be used to model, specify, and manipulate generic "to be" and "to have" type problems, particularly system architectures and high-level system designs, in computing, software engineering, system engineering, and cognitive informatics.

Chapter 10, "*RTPA: A Denotational Mathematics for Manipulating Intelligent and Computational Behaviors*" by Yingxu Wang, discusses real-time process algebra (RTPA), a denotational mathematical structure for denoting and manipulating system behavioral processes. RTPA is designed as a coherent algebraic system for intelligent and software system modeling, specification, refinement, and implementation. RTPA encompasses 17 metaprocesses and 17 relational process operations. RTPA can be used to describe both logical and physical models of software and intelligent systems. Logic views of system architectures and their physical platforms can be described using the same set of notations. When a system architecture is formally modeled, the static and dynamic behaviors performed on the architectural model can be specified by a three-level refinement scheme at the system, class, and object levels in a top-down approach. RTPA has been successfully applied in real-world system modeling and code generation for software systems, human cognitive processes, and intelligent systems.

Chapter 11, "*A Denotational Semantics of Real-Time Process Algebra (RTPA)*" by Xinming Tan and Yingxu Wang seeks a new framework for modeling time and processes in order to represent RTPA in denotational semantics. Within this framework, time is modeled by the elapse of process execution. The process environment encompasses states of all variables represented as mathematical maps, which project variables to their corresponding values. Duration is introduced as a pair of time intervals and the environment to represent the changes of the process environment during a time interval. Temporal ordered durations and operations on them are used to denote process executions. On the basis of these means, a comprehensive set of denotational semantics for RTPA are systematically developed and formally expressed.

Chapter 12, "*An Operational Semantics of Real-Time Process Algebra (RTPA)*" by Yingxu Wang and Cyprian F. Ngolah presents an operational semantics of RTPA, which explains how syntactic constructs in RTPA can be reduced to values on an abstract reduction machine. The operational semantics of RTPA provides a comprehensive paradigm of formal semantics that establishes an entire set of operational semantic rules of software. RTPA has been successfully applied in real-world system modeling and code generation for software systems, human cognitive processes, and intelligent systems.

Chapter 13, "*Formal Modeling and Specification of Design Patterns Using RTPA*" by Yingxu Wang and Jian Huang reveals that a pattern is a highly complicated and dynamic structure for software design encapsulation, because of its complex and flexible internal associations between multiple abstract classes and instantiations. The generic model of patterns is not only applicable to existing patterns' description and comprehension, but also useful for future patterns' identification and formalization.

Chapter 14, "*Deductive Semantics of RTPA*" by Yingxu Wang presents a complete paradigm of formal semantics that explains how deductive semantics is applied to specify the semantics of real-time process algebra (RTPA) and how RTPA challenges conventional formal semantic theories. Deductive semantics can be applied to define abstract and concrete semantics of programming languages, formal notation systems, and large-scale software systems, to facilitate software comprehension and recognition, to support tool development, to enable semantics-based software testing and verification, and to explore the semantic complexity of software systems. Deductive semantics may greatly simplify the description and analysis of the semantics of complicated software systems specified in formal notations and implemented in programming languages.

Chapter 15, "*On the Big-R Notation for Describing Interative and Recursive Behaviors*" by Yingxu Wang, introduces the big-R notation that provides a unifying mathematical treatment of iterations and recursions in computing. Mathematical models of iterations and recursions are developed using logical inductions. Based on the mathematical model of the big-R notation, fundamental properties of iterative and recursive behaviors of software are comparatively analyzed. The big-R notation has been adopted and implemented in Real-Time Process Algebra (RTPA) and its supporting tools. Case studies demonstrate that a convenient notation may dramatically reduce the difficulty and complexity in expressing a frequently used and highly recurring concept and notion in computing and software engineering.

Chapter 16, "*Formal RTPA Models for a Set of Meta-Cognitive Processes of the Brain*" by Yingxu Wang, describes the cognitive processes modeled at the metacognitive level of the layered reference mode of the brain (LRMB), which encompass those of object identification, abstraction, concept establishment, search, categorization, comparison, memorization, qualification, quantification, and selection. It is recognized that all higher layer cognitive processes of the brain rely on the metacognitive processes. Each of this set of fundamental cognitive processes is formally described by a mathematical model and a process model. Real-time process algebra (RTPA) is adopted as a denotational mathematical means for rigorous modeling and describing the metacognitive processes. All cognitive models and processes are explained on the basis of the object-attribute-relation (OAR) model for internal information and knowledge representation and manipulation.

Chapter 17, "*Unifying Rough Set Analysis and Formal Concept Analysis Based on a Logic Approach to Granular Computing*" by Bing Zhou and Yiyu Yao examines a logic approach to granular computing for combining rough set analysis and formal concept analysis. Following the classical interpretation of concepts that a concept consists of a pair of an extension and an intension, the authors interpret a granule as a pair containing a set of objects and a logic formula describing the granule. The building blocks of granular structures are basic granules representing elementary concepts or pieces of knowledge. They are treated as atomic formulas of a logic language. Different types of granular structures can be constructed by using logic connectives. Within this logic framework, this chapter shows that rough set analysis and formal concept analysis can be interpreted uniformly by using the proposed logic language. The two theories share high-level similarities, but differ in their choices of definable granules and granular structures. Algorithms and evaluation measures can be designed uniformly for both theories.

Chapter 18, "*On Foundations and Applications of the Paradigm of Granular Rough Computing*" by Lech Polkowski and Maria Semeniuk-Polkowska, addresses the need for formal methods of granulation, and means for computing with granules by applying methods of rough mereology. Rough mereology is an extension of mereology taking as the primitive notion the notion of a part to a degree. Granules are formed as classes of objects which are a part to a given degree of a given object. In addition to an exposition of this mechanism of granulation, the authors point also to some applications like granular logics for approximate reasoning and classifiers built from granulated data sets.

Chapter 19, "*Robust Independent Component Analysis for Cognitive Informatics*" by N. Gadhok and W. Kinsner evaluates the outlier sensitivity of five independent component analysis (ICA) algorithms (FastICA, Extended Infomax, JADE, Radical, and β-divergence) using (a) the Amari separation performance index, (b) the optimum angle of rotation error, and (c) the contrast function difference in an outlier-contaminated mixture simulation. The Amari separation performance index has revealed a strong sensitivity of JADE and FastICA (using third- and fourth-order nonlinearities) to outliers. However, the two contrast measures demonstrated conclusively that β-divergence is the least outlier-sensitive algorithm, followed by Radical, FastICA (exponential and hyperbolic-tangent nonlinearities), Extended Infomax, JADE, and FastICA (third- and fourth-order nonlinearities) in an outlier-contaminated mixture of two uniformly distributed signals. The novelty of this chapter is the development of an unbiased optimization-landscape environment for assessing outlier sensitivity, as well as the optimum angle of rotation error and the contrast function difference as promising new measures for assessing the outlier sensitivity of ICA algorithms.

Chapter 20, "*A Relative Fractal Dimension Spectrum for a Perceptual Complexity Measure*" W. Kinsner and R. Dansereau presents a derivation of a new relative fractal dimension spectrum, DRq, to measure the dissimilarity between two finite probability distributions originating from various signals. This measure is an extension of the Kullback-Leibler (KL) distance and the Rényi fractal dimension spectrum, Dq. Like the KL distance, DRq determines the dissimilarity between two probability distibutions X and Y of the same size, but does it at different scales, while the scalar KL distance is a single-scale measure. Like the Rényi fractal dimension spectrum, the DRq is also a bounded vectorial measure obtained at different scales and for different moment orders, q. However, unlike the Dq, all the elements of the new DRq become zero when X and Y are the same. Experimental results show that this objective measure is consistent with the subjective mean-opinion-score (MOS) when evaluating the perceptual quality of images reconstructed after their compression. Thus, it could also be used in other areas of cognitive informatics.

Chapter 21, "*3D Object Classification Based on Volumetric Parts*" by Weiwei Xing, Weibin Liu, and Baozong Yuan, proposes a 3D object classification approach based on volumetric parts, where Superquadric based Geon (SBG) description is implemented for representing the volumetric constituents of 3D object. In the approach, 3D object classification is decomposed into the constrained search on interpretation tree and the similarity measure computation. First, a set of integrated features and corresponding constraints are presented, which are used for defining efficient interpretation tree search rules and evaluating the model similarity. Then a similarity measure computation algorithm is developed to evaluate the shape similarity of unknown object data and the stored models. By this classification approach, both whole and partial matching results with model shape similarity ranks can be obtained; especially, focus match can be achieved, in which different key parts can be labeled and all the matched models with corresponding key parts can be obtained. Some experiments are carried out to demonstrate the validity and efficiency of the approach for 3D object classification.

Chapter 22, "*Modeling Underwater Structures*" by Michael Jenkin, Andrew Hogue, Andrew German, Sunbir Gill, Anna Topol, and Stephanie Wilson, investigates techniques and technologies to address the problem of the acquisition and representation of complex environments such as those found underwater. The underwater environment presents many challenges for robotic sensing including highly variable lighting and the presence of dynamic objects such as fish and suspended particulate matter. The dynamic six-degree-of-freedom nature of the environment presents further challenges due to unpredictable external forces such as current and surge. In order to address the complexities of the underwater environment, the authors have developed a stereo vision-inertial sensing device that has been successfully deployed to reconstruct complex 3-D structures in both the aquatic and terrestrial domains. The sensor combines 3-D information, obtained using stereo vision, with 3DOF inertial data to construct 3-D models of the environment. Semiautomatic tools have been developed to aid in the conversion of these representations into semantically relevant primitives suitable for later processing. Reconstruction and segmentation of underwater structures obtained with the sensor are presented.

Chapter 23, "*A Novel Plausible Model for Visual Perception*" by Zhiwei Shi, Zhongzhi Shi, and Hong Hu proposes a novel plausible model, namely cellular Bayesian networks (CBNs), to model the process of visual perception. The new model takes advantage of both the low-level visual features, such as colors, textures, and shapes, of target objects and the interrelationship between the known objects, and integrates them into a Bayesian framework, which possesses both firm theoretical foundation and wide practical applications. The novel model successfully overcomes some weakness of traditional Bayesian Network (BN), which prohibits BN being applied to large-scale cognitive problem. The experimental simulation also demonstrates that the CBNs model outperforms purely Bottom-up strategy 6% or more in the task of shape recognition. Finally, although the CBNs model is designed for visual perception, it has great potential to be applied to other areas as well.

Chapter 24, "*An Efficient and Automatic Iris Recognition System Using ICM Neural Network*" by Guangzhu Xu, Yide Ma, and Zaifeng Zhang, presents an efficient and automatic iris recognition system using Intersecting Cortical Model (ICM) neural network is presented which includes two parts mainly. The first part is image preprocessing which has three steps. First, iris location is implemented based on local areas. Then the localized iris area is normalized into a rectangular region with a fixed size. At last the iris image enhancement is implemented. In the second part, the ICM neural network is used to generate iris codes and the Hamming Distance between two iris codes is calculated to measure the dissimilarity. In order to evaluate the performance of the proposed algorithm, CASIA v1.0 iris image database is used and the recognition results show that the system has good performance.

Chapter 25, "*Neural Networks for Language Independent Emotion Recognition in Speech*" by Yongjin Wang, Muhammad Waqas Bhatti, and Ling Guan, introduces a neural network based approach for the identification of human affective state in the speech signal. A group of potential features are first identified and extracted to represent the characteristics of different emotions. To reduce the dimensionality of the feature space, whilst increasing the discriminatory power of the features, the authors introduce a systematic feature selection approach which involves the application of sequential forward selection (SFS) with a general regression neural network (GRNN) in conjunction with a consistency-based selection method. The selected parameters are employed as an input to the modular neural network, consisting of sub-networks, where each sub-network specializes in a particular emotion class. Comparing with the standard neural network, this modular architecture allows decomposition of a complex classification problem into small subtasks such that the network may be tuned based on the characteristics of individual emotion. The performance of the proposed system is evaluated for various subjects, speaking different languages. The results show that the system gives quite satisfactory emotion detection performance, yet demonstrates a significant increase in versatility through its propensity for language independence.

Chapter 26, "*An Analysis of Internal Representations for Two Artificial Neural Networks that Classify Musical Chords*" by Vanessa Yaremchuk demonstrates that the internal structure of the chord classification networks can be interpreted. It reveals the first network classified chord structure first by representing individual notes in terms of circles of major thirds and major seconds, and then by combining these representations to position chords in a three-dimensional hidden unit space. Despite use of a different local representation of input chords, interpretation of the second network reveals a very strong tendency to adopt a transformation of input similar to that observed in the first network. While there is a growing body of evidence concerning specialised neural processing of tones and chords (e.g., Peretz & Zatorre, 2005), this evidence is not yet sufficiently precise to indicate whether distributed representations based on tone circles are used by the brain. A search for examples of an ANN reorganising an input encoding scheme into this type of representation, was not successful. This raises the question of whether circles of thirds and seconds are pertinent to human subjects' representation of musical stimuli.

Chapter 27, "*Foundation and Classification of Nonconventional Neural Units and Paradigm of Nonsynaptic Neural Interaction*" by I. Bukovsky, J. Bila, M. M. Gupta, Z-G Hou, N. Homma, introduces basic types of nonconventional neural units and focuses their mathematical notation and classification. Namely, the notation and classification of higher-order nonlinear neural units, time-delay dynamic neural units, and time-delay higher-order nonlinear neural units is introduced. The classification of nonconventional neural units is founded first according to nonlinearity of aggregating function, second according to the dynamic order, third according to time-delay implementation within neural units. Introduction into the simplified parallel of the higher-order nonlinear aggregating function of higher-order neural units revealing both the synaptic and nonsynaptic neural interaction is made; thus, a new parallel between the mathematical notation of nonconventional neural units and the neural signal processing of biological neurons and is drawn. Based on the mathematical notation of neural input inter-correlations of higher-order neural units, it is shown that higher-order polynomial aggregating function of neural inputs can be naturally understood as a single-equation representation consisting of synaptic neural operation plus nonsynaptic neural operation. Thus it unravels new simplified yet universal mathematical insight into understanding the higher computational power of neurons that also conforms to biological neuronal morphology according to nowadays achievements of biomedical sciences.

Chapter 28, "Scaling *Behavior of Maximal Repeat Distributions in Genomic Sequences: A Randomize Test Follow Up Study*," J.D. Wang and Ka-Lok Ng conducts a follow-up analysis of maximal repeat distribution analysis by plotting the relative frequency of maximal repeat patterns against the rank of the appearance. In almost all of the cases, the rank plots give a better coefficient of determination values than the authors' previous work, i.e. frequency plot was used. A randomized version is repeated for the maximal repeat study; it is found that rank plot regression analysis did not support scaling behavior; hence, the validity of the findings is not due to an artifact.

Discoveries and Breakthroughs in Cognitive Informatics and Natural Intelligence examines innovative research in the emerging, multidisciplinary field of cognitive informatics. Researchers, practitioners and students can benefit from discussions of the connections between natural science and informatics that are investigated in this fundamental collection of cognitive informatics research.

Chapter 1
A Computational Cognitive Model of the Brain

Zhiwei Shi
Chinese Academy of Science and Graduate University of Chinese Academy of Sciences, China

Hong Hu
Chinese Academy of Science, China

Zhongzhi Shi
Chinese Academy of Science, China

ABSTRACT

Recent fruitful progresses on brain science have largely broadened our understanding of the cerebrum. These great works led us to propose a computational cognitive model based on a graphical model that we carried out before. The model possesses many attractive properties, including distinctive knowledge representation, the capability of knowledge accumulation, active (top-down) attention, subjective similarity measurement, and attention-guided disambiguation. It also has "consciousness" and can even "think" and "make inference." To some extent, it works just like the human brain does. The experimental evidence demonstrates that it can give reasonable computational explanation on the human phenomenon of forgetting. Although there are still some undetermined details and neurobiological mechanisms deserving consideration, our work presents a meaningful attempt to give further insights into the brain's functions.

INTRODUCTION

The last decades have witnessed an increasingly large effort into the investigation of the brain. No one can deny that research on the brain is now becoming one of the hottest issues in the scientific field. Researchers from various disciplines, including neuroscience, mathematics, psychology, computer science, and so on, dedicate themselves to explore the secrets in the brain, which is considered the most complicated and valuable part of the human being.

Thanks to the higher resolution brain-scan devices, more powerful computers, and fruitful advances in many related areas, such as neuroscience, machine learning, and artificial intelligence, researchers have made significant progress in understanding the structure and function of the cerebral cortex (see Miyashita, 2004, and Wang & Kinsner, 2006, for reviews). Many researchers have developed mathematical models of the neocortex that accord well with experimental results and provide directions for implementation (see, e.g., Elman, 1995; George & Hawkins, 2005; Lee & Mumford, 2003; Rao & Ballard, 1996; Shastri, 2001; Wang, 2006; Wang, Wang, Patel, & Patel, 2006). Although these models vary considerably in details, and some of them just focus on some specific aspects of the brain, for example, the visual system (Lee & Mumford), memory system (Shastri, 2001), or language processing (Elman, 1995), they shed light on the fundamental issues of the cerebrum as well as the corresponding computational cognitive model.

First of all, different from the conventional view that the brain is a passive and stimulus-driven system that simply reacts to outside input, many researchers believe that the brain is an active and adaptive system that interprets external stimuli according to its internal status. Engel, Fries, and Singer (2001) review much evidence demonstrating that "internally generated activity shows distinct temporal patterning against which input signals are matched." Other researchers (Wang, 2003; Wang & Wang, 2006) also indicate that the perceptual result can be determined by both the external stimuli and the internal status.

Additionally, more and more researchers agree that a cognitive model is a dynamic system where the temporal factor plays a significant role in the model. Wang (2002) developed real-time process algebra (RTPA) to formally describe the cognitive system architectures and dynamic behaviors with a set of new mathematical notations. Rao and Ballard (1996) use a form of the extended Kalman filter to dynamically combine input-driven bottom-up signals with expectation-driven top-down signals to predict the recognition state. Elman's (1995) dynamic approach to language processing is another example, where the author utilizes simple recurrent networks to predict the following word according to earlier input accumulation. In his model, the hidden layer also receives input from context units that hold the state of the hidden units from the previous step.

The third issue is about the topological structure of the cognitive model. Many researchers have proposed hierarchical structures to describe a reasonable model. For instance, to explain the fundamental cognitive mechanisms and processes of natural intelligence, Wang et al. (2006) developed the layered reference model of the brain (LRMB), where the model of the brain is depicted with six layers, namely, the sensation, memory, perception, action, metacognitive, and higher cognitive layers. Rao and Ballard (1996) also carry out a hierarchical structure to model visual recognition in the visual cortex. Lee and Mumford (2003) adopt a hierarchical structure to illustrate the Bayesian inference in the visual system as well. Yet, the recent research (Achard, Salvador, Whitcher, Suckling, & Bullmore, 2006) has shown that the topological structure of the cerebrum is a small-world network. As a matter of fact, some previously proposed models, for example, the object-attribute-relation (OAR) model (Wang, 2006; Wang & Wang,

2006), is essentially a network structure. Nevertheless, mathematically, the two styles of structure are topologically isomorphic. The only difference in the implementation is that it is often a tough problem to determine how many layers should be designed in the hierarchical architecture. Therefore, the network topology seems more promising in describing the topological structure in the cerebrum, although the hierarchical approaches provide conceptually more clear expression.

Clearly, the three essential properties mentioned above, namely, the important role of internal status, dynamic process, and network connection structure, are crucial for a successful cognitive model. It is a pity that no existing computational model embodies all these properties. In this article, we extend our previous model (Shi, Shi, & Hu, 2006), globally connected and locally autonomic Bayesian network (GCLABN), which is designed to model visual perception, to attain a computational cognitive mode, connected component network for the brain (CCNB), which from a macroscopic viewpoint provides a highly plausible hypothesis on how the brain functions as a whole. The novel model adopts a network structure, performs dynamic processes on the network, and formally and rigorously describes how internal status affects the perception of external stimuli. Although it seems a fool's game to model the entire cerebrum because the architecture and cellular functions are only partially known, we still believe that even models that are in fundamental respects inconsistent with the known cerebrum can provide meaningful insights into mechanisms that may contribute to actual cortical functioning.

The rest of this article is organized as follows. In the second section, we briefly review our prepetosed model GCLABN, and in the next section, we generalize GCLABN to obtain a novel model, the connected component network (CCN). Then we present how to apply the CCN to model the computational processes inside the human brain and discuss some important issues about the model. The section after that utilizes a classical psychological experiment to lend support to our model, and finally we conclude the article and depict some future work.

RELATED WORK

In this section, we briefly review the GCLABN model that we proposed before. A detailed description can be found in our previous work (Shi et al., 2006).

Before we depict GCLABN, we need to review some related notions.

A directed graph G is a centered graph if and only if it has one center node, denoted $C(G)$, with all the edges pointing to it from other noncenter nodes. A centered Bayesian network (CBN) is a pair (G, P), where G is a centered graph and P is a set of conditional probabilistic distributions (CPDs) of the center node given its parents. Figure 1 gives a sample of a centered graph and a sample of a CBN, where the corresponding center node is n_2.

Now we come to the definition of the GCLABN. A GCLABN is a union, $GCLABN = B_1 \cup B_2 \cup ... \cup B_n$, where B_i ($i = 1, ..., n$) are centered Bayesian networks and are subject to the following constraints:

$$C(B_i) \neq C(B_j) \quad 1 \leq i < j \leq n \tag{1}$$

and

$$C(B_i) \in (\bigcup_{j \neq i} V_j) \quad i = 1, ..., n \tag{2}$$

Figure 1. Samples of centered graph and CBN

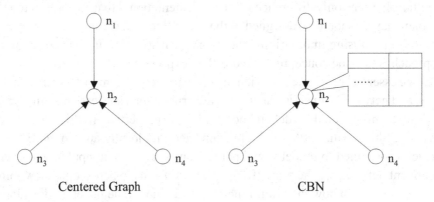

where V_j is the node set of B_j. The first constraint makes every component network unique. The second constraint makes all the component networks connected in terms of center nodes. A GCLABN is illustrated in Figure 2.

From a global standpoint, a GCLABN is a labeled directed graph where the edges encode the direct influence between nodes, and each center node (a node with parents) is tagged with a conditional probabilistic table given its parents, as is shown in Figure 3. The reason that we define it as a union of a set of CBNs is both to make the concept intuitive and to emphasize how a node, from its local standpoint, is affected by its neighbors.

Figure 2. A GCLABN as a union of a set of CBNs

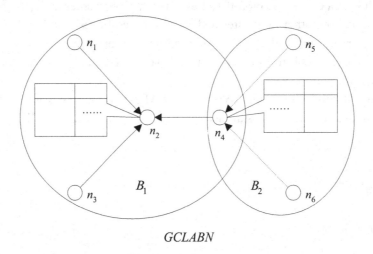

Figure 3. A GCLABN as a labeled directed graph

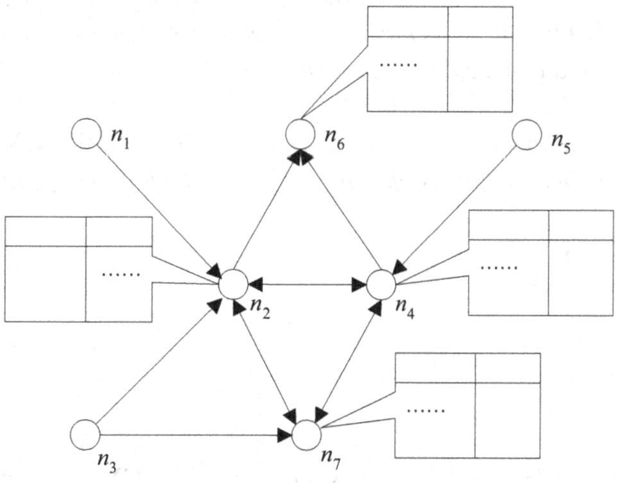

GCLABN

Note: The bidirectional edge in the graph embodies the reciprocal relationship between the center nodes

CONNECTED COMPONENT NETWORK

In following paragraphs, we will generalize the GCLABN to attain a CCN.

As we stated in our previous work (Shi et al., 2006), in a GCLABN, the edges are all predefined. Consequently, the major task of creating and modifying a GCLABN is to construct and refresh the CPDs of the center nodes. According to David Heckerman (1996), the CPD of a node can be viewed as a local distribution function, which is nothing more than a probabilistic classification or regression function. Thus, a GCLABN can also be viewed as a collection of probabilistic classification or regression models organized by the direct relationships between the center nodes. Consequently, all kinds of techniques that produce probabilistic outputs, for example, probabilistic neural networks (MacKay, 1992), probabilistic decision trees (Buntine, 1993), and linear classification methods (Shi & Shi, 2005), can be utilized to determine the probabilistic output of a center node given its parents. In light of this idea, we extend our GCLABN model to a more general model, the connected component network.

To begin with, we replace the CPD in a CBN with a probabilistic function f to get a component network.

Definition 1: *A component network (CN) is a pair (G, f), where G is a centered graph with the center node n_i, and f: $(x_1, ..., x_{i-1}, x_{i+1} ..., x_k)$ -> D_i is a probabilistic function, where k is the number of nodes in G, x_j ($j = 1, ..., k$ and $j \neq i$) is the value of node n_j, and D_i is the distribution of the center node n_i. Here, the node n_i is also the center node of the CN, denoted $C(CN)$.*

Definition 2: *If all the variables corresponding to the nodes in a component network are subject to binomial distributions (namely, each variable will take two values, 1 for active and 0 for inactive), and* *f can deal with the probabilities $f: (p_1, ..., p_{i-1}, p_{i+1}, ..., p_k) \rightarrow p_i$, where p_j (j = 1, ..., k) is the probability that the node n_j is active, we will name the function f as the identification function of the center node for it indicates the probability that the center node n_i is active. Then we can incorporate numerous component networks to form a connected component network.*

Definition 3: *A connected component network (CCN) is a union, $CCN = CN_1 \cup CN_2 \cup ... \cup CN_n$, where CN_i (i = 1, ..., n) are component networks that are subject to the following constraints:*

$$C(CN_i) \neq C(CN_j) \quad 1 \leq i < j \leq n \tag{3}$$

and

$$C(CN_i) \in (\bigcup_{j \neq i} V_j) \quad i = 1, ..., n \tag{4}$$

where $C(CN_i)$ is the center node of CN_i, and V_j is the node set of CN_j. A sample CCN is illustrated in Figure 4.

From the definition and the figure, we can see that a CCN has the same topological structure as a GCLABN, and the only difference is that each node in a CCN is labeled with not just a CPD but instead a more general probabilistic output function.

USING CCN TO MODEL THE BRAIN

In this section, we will demonstrate how we model the cognitive process in the brain with a CCN. To begin with, let us examine the rough information processing in the brain, which is illustrated in Figure 5.

Figure 4. A sample CCN

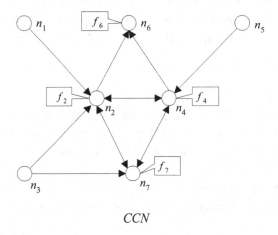

CCN

Figure 5. An illustration of the information processing in the brain

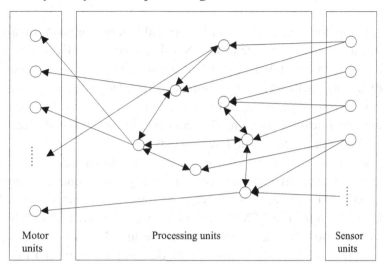

For the sake of conciseness, we divide all the brain units, each of which can be viewed as a neuron, a neural column (Gilbert & Wiesel, 1989), or the like, into three categories. They are sensor units, processing units, and motor units. The sensor units can translate the stimuli outside the brain into a perfect feature representation. The motor units are in charge of sending instructions from the cerebrum to every other part of the body to control the individual's behavior. The processing units are the core part of the brain, and they integrate the information gathered from sensor units with the current state of all the processing units to form control instructions that are sent to the motor units.

From Figure 5, we find that it is very easy to translate the graphical structure of the brain into a CCN. If we regard the sensor units as the noncenter nodes and the motor units and processing units as the center nodes, and attach probabilistic output functions to the center nodes, we can easily get a computational cognitive model as a CCN for the brain (CCNB). Note that in the CCNB, each unit corresponds to a binomial distributed random variable. So, the probabilistic output function tagged to any given unit is its identification function (see Definition 2). In a CCNB, each component network is composed of a center unit, its corresponding identification function, and all of its neighbor nodes.

Note that in Figure 5, there are no links from processing units to sensor units mainly because we adopt the idea that the procedure of conveying external stimuli to the inside of the brain is purely a feed-forward process (Van Rullen & Thorpe, 2001; Wang & Wang, 2006). In addition, there are no links among sensor units as well just because we omit the interactions between sensor units to gain more focus on the process among the processing units.

In the rest of this section, we will discuss some important issues regarding the CCNB, including knowledge representation, how to train a CCNB, the consciousness and subconsciousness of a CCNB, feature selection and attention, similarity and disambiguation, how to "think," and how to make inferences.

Knowledge Representation

The most important issue for a cerebral model is knowledge representation. In spite of the anatomic meaning of a single unit, each center node in a CCNB should semantically be interpreted as a concept that exists in the brain, or an object that exists in the physical world that is learned by the brain. Thus, different from conventional methods in data mining and knowledge discovery, where a concept or an object is represented by a feature vector, in the CCNB, a concept or object is represented by a center node plus a corresponding identification function. The reciprocal influence between the nodes just encodes the interrelationship between the corresponding concepts.

Apart from the superficial formal difference, the new method embraces richer interpretation and carries much more information. At any time instant t, for any given concept or object n_i, its neighbor nodes can be classified into two categories, namely, an external factor set, denoted $EFS_i(t)$, and an internal factor set, denoted $IFS_i(t)$. The $EFS_i(t)$ includes the nodes that are mostly activated by the current external stimuli, such as visual cues, auditory cues, and the like. The $IFS_i(t)$ is composed of the nodes that represent the internal status or the ongoing activities, and are irrelevant to the current external stimuli. Thus, the identification function of a center node can be rewritten as

$$p_i(t+1) = f_i(EFS_i(t+1), IFS_i(t)) \tag{5}$$

where $p_i(t+1)$ is the probability of the activation of the target node n_i at time instant $t+1$, and f_i is its identification function.

Besides its dynamic meaning, Equation 5 suggests that the activation of a processing unit or the emergence of an object or concept in the brain is determined by both the external factors and the internal factors. This is in accordance with the finding that information processing is not purely a passive stimulus-driven process, but also involves active and highly selective control (Engel et al., 2001; Itti & Koch, 2001; Wang & Wang, 2006). Moreover, this formula both largely reduces the information required and improves the accuracy of recognition, especially in the situation that incomplete features are accompanied by a large amount of noise. This is often the case for human beings.

Learning of a CCNB

Regarding the learning of a CCNB, one problem is how to get the identification functions. The primary difficulty in the learning of a CCNB is that the domain contains millions of concepts. In each learning case, however, only an extremely small part is available, and no algorithm can handle the incomplete data with such a large proportion of missing data. Fortunately, like the GCLABN (Shi et al., 2006), the entire learning task of a CCNB can be separated into many tiny tasks, and each task focuses on one component network. Thus, these tiny tasks can be performed separately. Therefore, as we mentioned earlier in this article as well as in our previous work Shi et al. 2006), many algorithms can be utilized to learn each of the component networks.

The other problem of the learning of a CCNB is how to add new concepts and new connections to the CCNB. As is stated in Wang, Liu, and Wang (2003) that not just the neurons themselves but also the interconnections between neurons encode the knowledge in the brain. In a CCNB, besides the sensor units, there are two kinds of units. One category contains the units having relatively firm connections to their neighbors. These units, as well as the related connections, represent the known knowledge stored in the CCNB and can be interpreted as the long-term memory in the human brain. Another category includes the units having relatively temporal connections. They reflect the concepts or objects that have come into the mind, but have not been consolidated yet. These units can be viewed as neurons in the working memory of the human brain. When a CCNB encounters a new concept, an unused unit will be assigned to represent the concept, and all the units that are active contemporarily with this unconsolidated concept will be connected to it. Additionally, if separated units are activated contemporarily, new links between them will be created as well according to Hebbian learning rules. If, in a certain time window, more samples of the temporarily created concepts or connections are encountered, the temporal knowledge will be consolidated. Then this newcomer knowledge, encoded by the new links and/or the new units, will "move" to the first category. In the meantime, learning algorithms are applied to make the identification function produce more precise predictions. On the contrary, if in the certain time window no sample is come across any more, the temporary links will fade out, and if all the links of a newly created unit have faded out, the unit is free and ready to learn some other new concept again. In the process, the size of the time window is a tunable parameter, which may take different values in different CCNBs.

This learning strategy is inspired by and also gives computational explanation to the psychological theory of forgetting. In a study by Jenkins and Dallenbach (1924), participants remembered more of a previously learned list when they slept before taking the memory test than when they remained awake. Because interference is much less likely to be encountered while sleeping, although a natural decay process unfolds whether one is asleep or awake, the author suggests that interference may play an important role in explaining why we forget what we once knew.

Consciousness and Subconsciousness

In this subsection, we will introduce the consciousness and subconsciousness of a CCNB. According to the Merriam-Webster online dictionary[1], consciousness is defined as "the quality or state of being aware especially of something within oneself." Consequently, the consciousness of a CCNB can be viewed as the current state of its processing units, especially the activated ones, for they really represent something (the concepts that they encode) being aware in the CCNB. Also in the Merriam-Webster online dictionary, subconsciousness is defined as "existing in the mind but not immediately available to consciousness." So, we propose the definitions of the consciousness and the subconsciousness of a CCNB as follows.

Definition 4: *For any given time instant t, the consciousness of a CCNB is the set of the k most active processing units, denoted $Con_t(CCNB)$.*

Here, the higher the identification function value is, the more active the corresponding unit is.

Definition 5: *For any given time instant t, the set of the processing units whose identification function values are higher than some predefined threshold th but lower than those of the units in the consciousness is the* **subconsciousness** *of a CCNB, denoted* $SubCon_t(CCNB)$.

The parameters k and th are both tunable, and they may vary in different CCNBs.

Feature Selection and Attention

Another significant issue for a cerebral model is feature selection and selective attention. In the physical world, there is an overload of information that is much more than an individual can handle. So, some feature selection mechanisms must be employed by human beings. Accordingly, a CCNB should also be able to implement these mechanisms.

As we just mentioned, the topological structure of the CCNB is just like the small-world structure in the human brain (Achard et al., 2006). The sparsely linked structure largely reduces the information processed by an individual unit. As we see, the dimensionality of the domain of a CCNB is the number of its units, which may easily reach the order of millions or even billions (Wang et al., 2003). In contrast, except for some hub units, the number of neighbors of any given unit, which may reach the order of thousands or so (Wang et al.), is far less than the domain dimensionality. In a CCNB, although feature selection is not stated explicitly, for any unit, its identification function and its local topological structure implicitly performs the process.

The next problem is how to select the useful information from the large amount of information provided by the sensor units. Human beings, apart from their inherent proper structure, also utilize the attention mechanism to facilitate information selection. As Itti and Koch (2001) stated, the selective attention mechanism can help the individual to focus on a small but crucial part of the information. More concretely, human beings employ a two-component attention framework, namely, top-down and bottom-up, to attain the goal.

According to Equation 5, the identification function value of a processing unit at the next time instant is calculated based on both the internal system state at the current time instant and the external stimuli at the next time instant. On one hand, some units that get more support from the current consciousness and subconsciousness are more possible to get into the consciousness at the next time instant. We name these units consciousness candidates. The external stimuli, which can provide more positive effects on these hopeful candidates, are expected to give more support in the coming time instant. The expectation for some specific external stimuli, including visual cues, auditory cues, and so forth, implements the selective top-down attention mechanism. On the other hand, primarily due to the presence of some extremely prominent external stimuli, some noncandidate units that have much closer relationships with these stimuli defeat the hopeful candidates and come into the consciousness. This process can be interpreted as bottom-up attention. Thus, the top-down and the bottom-up attention mechanisms can both be achieved in the CCNB.

Similarity and Disambiguation

As we have just shown, in our model, a concept or object is merely depicted as a center node with an identification function, but not a vector. As a result, the similarity between two concepts is not determined by the Euclidean distance any more, but instead is measured by the difference between two identification function values on a given scene[2]. For example, $Sim(n_1, n_2, s) = 1 - (f_{n1}(s) - f_{n2}(s))^2$ and $Sim(n_1, n_2, s) = 1 - |f_{n1}(s) - f_{n2}(s)|$ are all reasonable similarity measurements, where s is the given scene, $Sim(n_1, n_2, s)$ is the similarity between node n_1 and n_2 on s, and $f_{n1}(s)$ and $f_{n2}(s)$ are the identification function values of node n_1 and n_2 on the scene s, respectively. Note that if node n_1 and n_2 both respond to the stimuli from the same object, the similarity measurement works; otherwise, the similarity is meaningless.

According to Equation 5, in contrast to the Euclidean-distance-based similarity, the new measurement emphasizes much more on subjective measurement, which enables the prior knowledge and the internal system state to play a significant role in the concept or object recognition.

This similarity measurement will raise a problem; namely, different concepts with high identification function values may compete to explain one object because only a small part of the features of the object is taken into account. So, some disambiguation method should be imported to deal with this problem. As a matter of fact, the attention mechanism we discussed can contribute. According to top-down selective attention, when some concepts are in the consciousness, their related concepts are expected. If two or more concepts compete to explain some certain object, the selective attention mechanism will guide the CCNB to find more discriminative cues of the objects. This process will continue until, eventually, some concept wins the competition due to more support from the new observation, or some other unexpected concepts come into the consciousness so that the disambiguation process is interrupted.

It is important that the attention-guided disambiguation process not only be exploited to distinguish similar concepts, but is also used to explore new properties of a known concept as well. It endows a CCNB with the capability to gain new knowledge on purpose.

"Thinking" in a CCNB

Can a machine think? The idea sounds somewhat striking. Yet, in the following paragraph, we will show that, to some extent, a CCNB can think.

As we defined in the former subsection, at any time instant, the k most active processing units compose the consciousness of a CCNB. Thus, as time goes by, a CCNB will provide a series of concepts that have emerged in the consciousness of the CCNB. At any time instant, its output is caused by both the external stimuli and the CCNB internal states, which, according to Equation 5, can be regarded as the accumulation of previous "experiences." This information processing style is just like the way human beings think: Ideas emerge in our mind one after another; a later idea results from the combination of the very previous idea, the accumulated knowledge structure, and the current sensory stimuli.

Furthermore, at any given time instant, even if we get the same external stimuli as a CCNB does, it is hard for us to exactly predict what will emerge in the consciousness of the CCNB if the CCNB has enough knowledge and has worked long enough for both the knowledge structure and the current internal status are unknown to us. This property also makes the CCNB more like a human being and not an inanimate machine or a nonliving program.

Additionally, as we mentioned in our previous work (Shi et al. 2006), the inference process of a GCLABN may be recursive and may not converge to a stationary point, primarily due to the existence of a directed circle in the model. In a CCNB, the situation is almost the same. However, if we view this recursive process as a thinking process, the problem is not a problem any more for it is unnecessary to require an individual to stop thinking.

As a matter of fact, the thinking process can be viewed as a dynamic process. Let $P(t)$ denote the processing unit state vector at time instant t, and $S(t)$ denote the sensor unit state vector at time instant t. If we adopt a linear system, the state-updating rule for a CCNB can be given as follows:

$$P(t+1) = A(t)P(t) + B(t)S(t+1) + \varepsilon \qquad (6)$$

where $A(t)$ and $B(t)$ are both coefficient matrixes, and ε is a random noise vector.

If we adopt a nonlinear system, the state-updating rule for a CCNB can be depicted as follows:

$$P(t+1) = g(t, P(t), S(t+1), \varepsilon) \tag{7}$$

where g is a nonlinear function.

Although the dynamic system representation is mathematically concise and helps in the understanding of the thinking in a CCNB, its implementation for a super-large-scale problem with numerous variables is usually infeasible, especially for nonlinear cases. So we prefer to employ identification functions, as in Equation 5, to accomplish the computation. The identification functions also have the following merits. First, for any given node, the number of its neighbors is far less than the dimensionality of the entire domain (the total number of the units), and this makes the learning process efficient. Second, the learning process can be performed in a parallel style or even in a distributed way. Third, the identification function makes the corresponding unit work in the manner that a real neuron does. This is very significant because even though we omit most of the biological details, we should still keep in mind that a computational cerebral model, according to David Marr[3], should "place important constraints on what neural circuits might be implementing it" (as cited in Rao, Olshausen, & Lewicki, 2002).

Making Inference in a CCNB

In this subsection, we will focus on the inference in a CCNB. Traditionally, in a probabilistic graph model, a directed edge is interpreted as a causal relationship between the two related nodes, where the parent node is the cause and the child node is the result (Heckerman, 1996). However, in a CCNB, we introduce a different view of causal relationships that accords more with how we as human beings think.

Definition 6: *In a CCNB, a set of concepts **B** is the inferential result of a set of concepts **A**, denoted **A->B**, if and only if **B** appears in the consciousness that follows the one that contains **A**.*

Due to many factors, such as subconsciousness and other ongoing activities that do not enter the sphere of consciousness and subconsciousness, the consciousness of a CCNB is usually unpredictable. So, we import another notion, belief, to indicate the confidence of the inference.

Definition 7: *The belief of an inference A->B, denoted **Be(A->B)**, is the conditional probability of **B** in the consciousness given the concept **A** in the very previous consciousness, namely, **Be(A->B)** = $P(B \in Con_{t+1}(CCNB)|A \in Con_{t}(CCNB))$.*

The inference with high belief encodes another kind of knowledge learned by a CCNB that involves more than one concept or object and reflects the intrinsic connections among them. It can be the order of nature, a series of steps in an operating process, or a snippet of a scenario, for example, as in events or situations. In most cases, it is the refinement of accumulated experiences of the CCNB.

The following is an example. Suppose that A = {"lightning"} and B = {"thunder"}; if the belief of A->B is very high, for example, 90%, and A is in the current consciousness, it is greatly possible that B will appear in the consciousness of the next instant. Of course, it is also possible that some other concept set, for example {"raining"} rather than B, comes into the consciousness in the next instant due to some uncertain causes.

Therefore, the inference in a CCNB provides a reasonable computational explanation of the inference and prediction in the cerebrum. It also gives a plausible explanation for why human beings make mistakes even though they know the right answer.

EXPERIMENTAL EVIDENCE

As we described in the previous section, a CCNB can model the cerebrum meaningfully. Besides this, it also implements many distinctive functions that are crucial to human brains. It has consciousness and subconsciousness, it can learn new concepts, it can make feature selection and form attention, it can disambiguate, and it can even think and make inferences. It presents so much attractive properties that any specific experiment is insufficient to demonstrate all its properties. Alternatively, we borrow a traditional experiment from Wixted (2005) to illustrate part of its capability of giving a computational explanation for forgetting.

One of the widely accepted mechanisms of forgetting is the cue-overload effect (Robinson, 1920; Watkins & Watkins, 1975). Cue overload occurs when more than one concept is associated with one retrieval cue. The most frequently used experiment for investigating this phenomenon is the A-B, A-C paired-associates procedure (Wixted, 2005). In this procedure, three cue-target word-pair lists are used. They are A-B (e.g., *hero-prison, water-valley, tiger-image,* etc.); A-C, which has the same cues as A-B but different targets (e.g., *hero-women, water-salad, tiger-infant,* etc.); and C-D, which contains a completely different set of words from A-B. Two groups of participants are asked to learn these lists. The experimental group learns the A-B list followed by the A-C list, while the control group learns the A-B list followed by the C-D list. Then, both groups are tested by giving them the A cues and asking for the recall of the B targets. Typically, the control group performs better than the experimental group. This indicates that when more targets are attached to one cue, the retrieval based on the cue will become more inaccurate.

Figure 6. After learning different material, two CCNB models face the same stimulation "hero," the unit marked with a grid. In Model A, two units "women" and "prison" compete to be active, while in Model B, only the unit "women" receives information and is ready to be active.

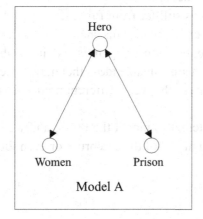
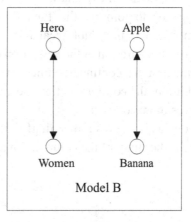

This result can be easily explained by the CCNB model. Suppose that we have two CCNB models. One, denoted Model A, is assigned to learn the pairs *hero-women* and *hero-prison*; the other, denoted Model B, is assigned to the pairs *hero-women* and *apple-banana*. After the learning process, the two models will have the following substructures, which are depicted in Figure 6. Here, we omit the irrelevant units and links.

From Figure 6, we can see that in Model A, when the unit *hero* is activated, the unit *women* and the unit *prison* compete to be active. The current internal system state, which encodes the previous experiences of the model and some uncertain external cues, will dominate the output. So, the output of Model A is, to some extent, unpredictable. On the contrary, in Model B, when the unit *hero* is activated, only the unit *women* receives information; thus, more possibly, the output of Model B is *women*.

The case study illustrates that the CCNB can give satisfied computational explanation to cue-overload forgetting. In addition, it also demonstrates the capability of the CCNB to perform associative memory.

CONCLUSION

In this article, we generalize our previous model GCLABN to gain a computational model for the brain, CCNB. Although the new model omits many neurobiological details to obtain a more concise model, for example, some known hierarchical structures and functional regions, it takes much neurobiological and psychological evidence into account to make itself more reasonable. As we present in previous sections, the CCNB adopts a novel knowledge representation method where a concept or object is represented as a unit plus an identification function, and the interrelationships between concepts are encoded by connections. It is this distinctive representation that leads to a special similarity measurement and makes the selective attention mechanism and attention-guided disambiguation in the CCNB feasible. In addition, the model can learn new knowledge. This feature enables a CCNB to accumulate knowledge, which in turn makes the model more intelligent. In particular, all the accumulated concepts do not stand separately, but are integrated as a whole, where each concept can fertilize the understanding of others. We also demonstrate that the CCNB possesses consciousness and subconsciousness, and can even think and make inferences as human beings do. Yet, performing thorough experimental verification for the model is somewhat infeasible. Alternatively, we review a well-known psychological experiment to lend support to our model in terms of the forgetting mechanism. The experiment shows that our model can provide satisfied computational explanation for the phenomenon.

Meanwhile, we have to point out that the model is still far from fully developed. Some parameters are still undetermined, and more biological and neural mechanisms should be taken into account. For example, a change in the duration of the activation of the processing units and the inhibition of the reactivation of the same unit in a continuous time instant are valuable ideas that may make the model more reasonable. In addition, the communication mechanism between different models is also a significant aspect that deserves more concern.

In summary, our work makes a meaningful attempt to model the brain, and we hope it can open up a new avenue for the study of the computational model of the cerebrum or even for constructing an artificial brain.

ACKNOWLEDGMENT

This work is supported by the National Science Foundation of China (No. 60435010), the 863 National High-Tech Program (No. 2006AA01Z128), and the National Basic Research Priorities Programme (No. 2007CB311004). We would like to thank Professor Yingxu Wang for his valuable comments on an earlier draft of this article.

REFERENCES

Achard, S., Salvador, R., Whitcher, B., Suckling, J., & Bullmore, E. (2006). A resilient, low-frequency, small-world human brain functional network with highly connected association cortical hubs. *Journal of Neuroscience, 26*(1), 63-72.

Buntine, W. (1993). Learning classification trees. In *Artificial intelligence frontiers in statistics* (pp. 182-201). London: Chapman and Hall.

Dean, T. (2005). A computational model of the cerebral cortex. In *The Proceedings of the 20th National Conference on Artificial Intelligence (AAAI-05)* (pp. 938-943). Cambridge, MA.

Elman, J. L. (1995). Language as a dynamical system. In R. F. Port & T. van Gelder (Eds.), *Mind as motion* (pp. 195-225). MIT Press.

Engel, A. K., Fries, P., & Singer, W. (2001). Dynamic predictions: Oscillations and synchrony in top-down processing. *Nature Reviews Neuroscience, 2*, 704-716.

George, D., & Hawkins, J. (2005). A hierarchical Bayesian model of invariant pattern recognition in the visual cortex. In *Proceedings of the International Joint Conference on Neural Networks*.

Gilbert, C. D., & Wiesel, T. N. (1989). Columnar specificity of intrinsic horizontal and corticocortical connections in cat visual cortex. *Journal of Neuroscience, 9*, 2432-2442.

Heckerman, D. (1996). *A tutorial on learning with Bayesian networks* (Tech. Rep. No. MSR-TR-95-06). Microsoft Research.

Itti, L., & Koch, C. (2001). Computational modelling of visual attention. *Nature Reviews Neuroscience, 2*(3), 194-203.

Jenkins, J. B., & Dallenbach, K. M. (1924). Oblivescence during sleep and waking. *American Journal of Psychology, 35*, 605-612.

Lee, T. S., & Mumford, D. (2003). Hierarchical Bayesian inference in the visual cortex. *Journal of the Optical Society of America, 2*(7), 1434-1448.

MacKay, D. (1992). Bayesian interpolation. *Neural Computation, 4*, 415-477.

Miyashita, Y. (2004). Cognitive memory: Cellular and network machineries and their top-down control. *Science, 306*(5695), 435-440.

Rao, R. P. N., & Ballard, D. H. (1996). Dynamic model of visual recognition predicts neural response properties in the visual cortex. *Neural Computation, 9*, 721-763.

Rao, R. P. N., Olshausen, B., & Lewicki, M. (2002). *Probabilistic models of the brain: Perception and neural function.* Cambridge, MA: The MIT Press.

Robinson, E. S. (1920). Studies from the psychological laboratory of the University of Chicago: Some factors determining the degree of retroactive inhibition. *Psychological Monographs, 28*(128), 1-57.

Shastri, L. (2001). A computational model of episodic memory formation in the hippocampal system. *Neurocomputing, 38-40,* 889-897.

Shi, Z., & Shi, Z. (2005). Constructing fast linear classifier with mutual information. In *Proceedings of the Second International Conference of Neural Network and Brain (ICNN&B2005)*, Beijing, China (pp. 1611-1615).

Shi, Z., Shi, Z., & Hu, H. (2006). A novel plausible model for visual perception. In *Proceedings of ICCI 2006*, Beijing, China (pp. 19-24).

Van Rullen, R., & Thorpe, S. (2001). Is it a bird? Is it a plane? Ultra-rapid visual categorization of natural and artificial objects. *Perception, 30,* 655-668.

Wang, Y. (2002). The real-time process algebra (RTPA). *The International Journal of Annals of Software Engineering, 14,* 235-274.

Wang, Y. (2003). On cognitive informatics. *Brain and Mind: A Transdisciplinary Journal of Neuroscience and Neurophilosophy, 4*(2), 151-167.

Wang, Y. (2006, May 8-10). *The OAR model for knowledge representation.* Paper presented at the 19th Canadian Conference on Electrical and Computer Engineering (CCECE'06), Ottawa, Canada.

Wang, Y., & Kinsner, W. (2006). Recent advances in cognitive informatics. *IEEE Transactions on Systems, Man, and Cybernetics (C), 36*(2), 121-123.

Wang, Y., Liu, D., & Wang, Y. (2003). Discovering the capacity of human memory. *Brain and Mind: A Transdisciplinary Journal of Neuroscience and Neurophilosophy, 4*(2), 189-198.

Wang, Y., & Wang, Y. (2006). Cognitive informatics models of the brain. *IEEE Transactions on Systems, Man, and Cybernetics (C), 26*(2), 203-207.

Wang, Y., Wang, Y., Patel, S., & Patel, D. (2006). A layered reference model of the brain (LRMB). *IEEE Transactions on Systems, Man, and Cybernetics (C), 36*(2), 124-133.

Watkins, C., & Watkins, M. J. (1975). Buildup of proactive inhibition as a cue-overload effect. *Journal of Experimental Psychology: Human Learning and Memory, 1*(4), 442-452.

Wixted, J. T. (2005). A theory about why we forget what we once knew. *Current Directions in Psychological Science, 14*(1), 6-9.

ENDNOTES

[1]   http://www.m-w.com/home.htm
[2]   It includes both the internal state of a CCNB and the external stimuli received.
[3]   He is often considered the founder of computational vision.

This work was previously published in International Journal of Cognitive Informatics and Natural Intelligence, Vol. 2, Issue 4, edited by Y. Wang, pp. 85-99, copyright 2008 by IGI Publishing (an imprint of IGI Global).

Chapter 2
A Cognitive Approach to the Mechanism of Intelligence[1]

Yi X. Zhong
Beijing University of Posts and Telecommunications, China

ABSTRACT

An attempt was made in the article to propose a new approach to the intelligence research, namely the cognitive approach that tries to explore in depth the core mechanism of intelligence formation of intelligent systems from the cognitive viewpoint. It is discovered, as result, that the mechanism of intelligence formation in general case is implemented by a sequence of transformations conversing the information to knowledge and further to intelligence (i.e., the intelligent strategy, the embodiment of intelligence in a narrower sense). It is also discovered that the three major approaches to AI that exist, the structural simulation approach, the functional simulation approach, and the behavior simulation approach, can all be harmoniously unified within the framework of the cognitive approach. These two discoveries, as well as the related background, will be reported here in the article.

INTRODUCTION

Artificial intelligence is a branch of modern science and technology aiming at the exploration of the secrets of human intelligence on one hand and the transplantation of human intelligence to machines on the other hand, so that machines are able to perform functions as intelligently as they can. What is the essence of intelligence, as we should understand it in the scientific context, then? What are the parts of human intelligence that can technically be feasible for transplanting to machines? In what ways would humans be able to make machines really intelligent? These are some of the major issues we should make clear in AI research.

Due to the high complexity of the issues, there have been many approaches proposed in history to the research of these secrets. The three dominant approaches are: (1) the structural simulation approach, whose typical representative is neural networks, (2) the functional simulation approach, whose typical representative is expert systems, and (3) the behavior simulation approach, whose typical representative is sensory-motor systems. They study the intelligence, respectively, from different angles of views: (1) the views of the biological neural networks structure in human brain, (2) the views of its logical reasoning processes, and (3) the views of its input-output behavior. They are good approaches to the intelligence research, and therefore have all made certain progresses so far.

Some of the technically well-known contributors of the three approaches to AI can be briefly listed as the following.

A great number of artificial neural network models, algorithms, and applications have been developed in the line of the first approach. The well-known contributions can be seen from, for example, McCulloch and Pitts (1943), Rosenblatt (1958), Hopfield (1982), Rumelhart et al. (1990), and Ruan (2006). Various results in symbolic logic and expert systems with applications in wide areas have been presented in the stream of the second approach. The impressive achievements can be found from, for instance, Feigenbaum and Feldman (1963), Simon (1969), Newell and Simon (1972), Barr et al. (1982), Russell and Norvig (2006), and many more. Quite extractive sensory-motor systems have been designed in the thought of the third approach. The outstanding examples can be seen from Brooks (1990, 1991). Note that the neural networks approach (also called connectionism approach), has been renamed the computational intelligence since the early 1990s through the process of combining fuzzy logic and genetic algorithms.

On the other hand, however, each of the three approaches has also been confronted with respective and critical difficulties.

The neural networks approach faces the dilemma in dealing with the relationship between the structural complexity and the intelligent performance of neural networks. The number of neurons in the human brain is as large as 10^{10}, and the total number of connections among the neurons is in the order of 10^{14}, and the huge number of connections gives the guarantee of high intelligence to the human brain. This scale would be impossible, nevertheless, for artificial neural networks to reach based on industrial capability in modern technology. If the number of neurons and connections in artificial neural networks are reduced to the feasible order for industrial implementation, the performance in intelligence will be severely reduced, too. It is very difficult, even for today and the near future, to find a satisfactory compromise between the complexity in structure and the performance in intelligence.

The expert systems approach is confronted with the difficulty in such issues as knowledge acquisition, representation, and inference. Knowledge is one of the most crucial bases for any expert system, and nonetheless, most of the knowledge bases have been basically built up manually relying on the system designers. It is, of course, hard work with low efficiency. At the same time, the power of the means of knowledge representation and inference based on mathematical logic are also rather limited in expression and operation. This leads to another problem, severe limitation in practical applications. The low efficiencies, as a bottleneck, in knowledge acquisition, representation, and inference make the expert systems approach far from as promising as it was announced and expected in the early days of AI history.

Because the sensory-motor approach does neither simulate the biological neural networks of human brain, nor simulate the process of symbolic manipulation, it therefore does not need knowledge bases as that in expert systems, nor does it suffer from the structural dilemma mentioned before. It seems that it is able to totally avoid such difficulties as that seen either in neural networks or in the expert systems approach. This may be true to a certain extent. However, the sensory-motor approach suffers from another difficulty, the difficulty of having higher-level intelligence. The performance the sensory-motor systems can achieve is relatively simple in general, although useful. It is really difficult for the sensory-motor approach to implement the high level intelligence like thinking, reasoning, and many other complicated features in intelligence.

Moreover, while facing certain critical difficulties, the three approaches seemed not quite harmonious to each other in the history of their development, and it is still difficult to work with them together nowadays. People from the three disciplines sometimes even argued among one another as to which one among the three is the best. This makes researchers re-evaluate the approaches to AI and find some new and more reasonable approaches to the AI research so that the difficulties stated above may either be overcome or be avoided.

Based on his own observations and study, the author of the article would like to propose a new approach to the AI research with the aim of directly touching the essence of intelligence. That is, such an approach that concerns mainly the core mechanism of intelligence formation insight from the cognitive viewpoint, rather than the only observation of the structure, or function, or behavior of the intelligent systems. In other words, this approach is featured with the core mechanism of intelligence formation: how intelligence for problem solving is effectively produced from information? We name it a cognitive approach to the mechanism of intelligence. Due to the space limitation we have for the article, the report made below will have to be, in general, concise and brief.

A DEFINITION OF INTELLIGENCE AND A MODEL OF HUMAN INTELLIGENCE FORMATION

Although there are many definitions of intelligence existing already in literature, it should be necessary to explain the author's own understanding about the concept of intelligence so as to serve as a foundation of the discussions in the article.

For any given problem and its environment, as well as a prescribed goal for the problem solving, **the concept of intelligence is defined as the entirety of the following interrelated abilities,** the ability to acquire the information concerning the given problem and its environment, the ability to refine the information into knowledge, the ability to produce a strategy by activating the knowledge, together with all related knowledge stored in the knowledge bases, under the guidance of the prescribed goal, and the ability to converse the strategy into the corresponding action, so that thereby the problem can be solved, while the constraints given by the environment can be met and the prescribed goal can be reached. In short, intelligence is the ability to solve problems and such factors as problem (**P**) given, the problem's environment (**E**), the prescribed goal (**G**) for the problem solving, the information (**I**) concerning P and E, the knowledge (**K**) produced from the information, the strategy (**S**) based on I, K and G, and the corresponding action (**A**), which are the indispensable elements for forming Intelligence.

Clearly, intelligence, so defined, is a kind of phenomenon that pervasively exists in the real world of living beings. Human intelligence is nevertheless the most powerful and typical one among others on this planet. It would thus be meaningful to take human intelligence as an example in our study below. A general model for describing the process of human intelligence formation is necessarily given as a background of the discussions that will be carried on later in the article.

In Figure 1, we show the model of human intelligence formation process. It consists of eight steps. (1) **Preconditions Setting:** When facing a problem and its environment in the real world, the humans should first be able to set up some prescribed goal in the brain for the problem solving. (2) **Information Acquisition:** The sensing organs are asked by the brain to acquire the information about the problem and the environment in the real world, often called ontological information. Here, it is named Information-1 in Figure 1. The information already obtained by the sensing organs is termed the Information-2. (3) **Information Transferring:** The information-1 should be passed, via the nerve system, to the brain for use, and that becomes Information-3. (4) **Information Processing:** When the information is sufficiently available, the brain will have to process it for convenient use in later stages, and the result is called Information-4. The general term for those from Information-2 through to Information-4 is often termed epistemological information. (5) **Knowledge Producing:** The brain will then refine the epistemological information into the related knowledge. (6) **Strategy Creation:** If the epistemological information and the related knowledge are ready, the brain should, directed by the goal, activate the knowledge and the information to the strategy. As the strategy is the major embodiment of the intelligence for problem solving, it is often called intelligent strategy, here expressed as Intelligence-1. (7) **Strategy Transferring:** The intelligent strategy will have to be passed, also via the nerve system, to the actuators, and thus becomes Intelligence-2. (8) **Strategy Execution:** Intelligence-2 at actuator will finally be conversed into the corresponding intelligent action, that is, the Intelligence-3, through which the problem will gradually be solved if all the steps mentioned above are right.

It is indicated in Figure 1 that there are three categories of goods, or products, produced during the process of human intelligence formation: (a) **information**, including information-1 (ontological information), information-2 (sensed information), information-3 (transmitted and received information), and information-4 (processed information), (b) **knowledge**, and (c) **intelligence**, including intelligence-1 (intelligent strategy created), intelligence-2 (transmitted and received strategy), and intelligence-3 (intelligent action). It is also noted that the strategy is often referred to as **intelligence in the narrower sense,** whereas the ability embedded in the entire process from steps (1) to (8) in Figure1 is referred to as **intelligence in the completed sense**.

What we have to point out here, however, that although the model in Figure 1 clearly shows how the intelligence is formed from knowledge and information through the steps (1) - (8), yet the step (1), how

Figure 1. Model of human intelligence process

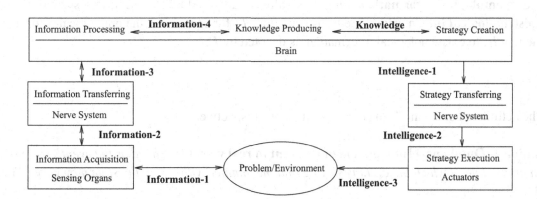

to set up the prescribed goal in the brain for the problem solving, is still mysterious up to now. This will be ignored in the article because of the fact that what we are concerned with is the study of artificial intelligence and that in such cases the prescribed goal will be assigned by the system designer, instead of the system itself. In other words, P, E, and G are supposed to be given beforehand as preconditions. This consideration is well in agreement with the definition of intelligence stated above. Furthermore, it is required that the properties of Information-2 and Information-3 be the same in normal case and so is that of Intelligence-1 and Intelligence-2. Therefore, the attention of the study will be paid to the information acquisition (Transformation 1), knowledge producing (Transformation 2), strategy creation (Transformation 3), and strategy execution (Transformation 4).

CORE MECHANISM OF INTELLIGENCE FORMATION: INFORMATION-KNOWLEDGE-INTELLIGENCE TRANSFORMATIONS

Keeping in mind that the related parts of the transformations to be discussed in this section are the core (not all) processes for the intelligence formation and are characterized by the information-knowledge-intelligence transformation, we now would like to have a brief investigation into each of the core transformations, as follows:

The Transformation 1: From Ontological Information to Epistemological Information

As is shown in Figure 1, the first task for an intelligent system to perform is to get the information from the real world necessary for dealing with the problem to be handled under given constraints (C) given by the environment and with respect to the prescribed goal. The information concerning G will be stored internally within the brain, whereas the information concerning P and C will usually have to be acquired from the outside world, where the problem is presented.

Note that if the information concerning P and C is fully available in database, what is needed is the technology called information retrieval and information extraction using Intelligent Search Engine that would be the story about natural language processing, and will be discussed in another article.

In the present case, the information about P and C are supposed to be acquired from the real world where the problem at hand is defined. In terminology, the information on P and C in the real world is termed as **ontological information** and the one already acquired by a subject, or a system, is called the **epistemological information**. The transformation, T_1, for conversing the ontological information, denoted by I_O, to epistemological information, is denoted by I_E:

$$T_1 : I_O \mapsto I_E \tag{1}$$

The definitions on I_O and I_E in (1) are given below, respectively:

Definition 1: Ontological Information of an event in real world *is defined as the event's self-presentation on its state at which the event is staying and the manner with which the state may vary (Zhong, 2002).*

Figure 2. The transformation from I_O to I_{sy}

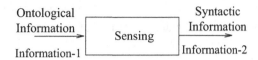

Note that the ontological information, I_O, is the purely objective information about the event itself without any subject's factors interfered, and is thus really the original source of information.

Definition 2: Epistemological Information of an event possessed by a subject *is a description, given by the subject, concerning the state at which the event is staying and the manner with which the state may vary. Due to the fact that the subject in normal cases has the abilities to sense and to understand the event and has a certain goal in mind, his description on the state and the manner of the event should thus be not only concerned with the form and the meaning of the state/manner of the event, but also with their utility with respect to the subject's goal, that are respectively called the Syntactical Information, Semantic Information, and Pragmatic Information while the trinity of the three components is called the Comprehensive Information (Zhong, 2002).*

As mentioned above, the concept of epistemological information may represent information-2, information-3, and information-4. In the case of sensing, however, the function of transformation T_1 in (1) is to converse the ontological information (Information-1) into a special type of the epistemological information, Information-2, the syntactic information, as is shown in Figure 2 and Equation 2.

$$I_{sy} = f(I_O), \qquad I_{sy}, I_O \in R^n \tag{2}$$

where the symbol I_{sy} denotes the syntactic information, f the function mapping I_O into I_{sy}, and R^n the n-dimensional real space. For the sake of good quality in fidelity of the transformation conversing the ontological information into the syntactic information, the property of monotony, or the one-to-one correspondence mapping and sometimes the linearity in transformation, is required for function f within a certain range of the domain of the information in question. The specific requirement for that range depends on the practical problem in hand. Such a kind of transformation is easy to implement.

If, in other cases that are usually more complicated and much more useful than sensing, the comprehensive information, another type of epistemological information, that consists of syntactic, semantic, and pragmatic information, is required as output of the transformation T_1, the sensing system, combined with a proper knowledge base and algorithms in logic, will be needed, as shown below in Figure 3.

In Figure 3 the knowledge and rule bases contain both the knowledge on the relationship between the syntactic information and the goal implementation and the rules that are needed for producing the semantic information based on the related syntactic and pragmatic information. Therefore, the syntactic information in Figure 3 is obtained in the same way as that in Figure 2. The pragmatic information can be obtained as a product of comparing and computing the syntactic information with the goal expression (e.g., both syntactic information and the goal can be expressed in vector form, and the pragmatic information can be calculated as the project of the syntactic information vector on the goal vector). On the other hand, the semantic information that is more abstract than syntactic and pragmatic information can be produced through the logic deduction based on the syntactic information and the related pragmatic information obtained previously. To a certain extent, the function of information processing (i.e., the transformation from information-3 to information-4) may fall into this category.

The Transformation 2: From Information to Knowledge

The next step of the mechanism of intelligence formation is to deal with the transformation that converses the epistemological information to the related knowledge, and the information here must consist of the syntactic, semantic, and pragmatic information. The related concepts in this step are given below.

Definition 3: Knowledge *concerning a certain category of events is the description, made by subjects, on the states at which the objects may stay and the law with which the states may vary. It is noted that the description should first include the form of the states and law that is termed the formal knowledge, and then the meaning of the states and law that is named the content knowledge, and finally the value of the states and law with respect to the subject's goal that is called the value knowledge. All three aspects of the description constitute a trinity of knowledge (Zhong, 2000).*

Comparing definitions 2 and 3 in detail indicates that the difference between the definitions of information and knowledge just lies in the fact that information is directly related to a specific state/manner of each of the events, whereas knowledge is related to the abstract states/law embedded in the collective events. It is well known that any law can only be established through a great number of observations and inductive calculation over the observed samples, and hence the transformation of epistemological information to knowledge can in principle be implemented through inductive-like algorithms over the sample set of epistemological information:

$$T_1 : \cap \{I_E\} \mapsto K \tag{3}$$

Figure 3. Transformation from I_O into I_E

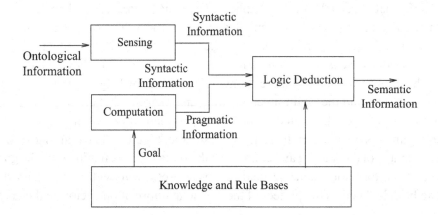

Where the symbol $\cap$ in Equation 3 stands for a class of inductive-like algorithms; $\{I_E\}$ the sample set of the epistemological information, whereas K the knowledge produced from $\{I_E\}$ via induction. In some complicated cases, there may be a need for a number of iterations between induction and deduction within the transformation, and the deduction itself can be expressed as

$$K_{new} \Leftarrow \Re \{K_{old}, C\} \tag{4}$$

Where the symbol $\Re$ in Equation 4 represents the deduction operator, K_{old} the set of knowledge which is already known before the deduction, while K_{new} is the knowledge newly deduced from K_{old} and C, the latter of which stands for the constraints that the deductive operation must follow.

More specifically, the formal knowledge as one of the three components of knowledge can be refined from syntactic information through the inductive operation, and the value knowledge, another component of knowledge, can also be refined from pragmatic information through inductive algorithm, whereas the content knowledge, the third component of knowledge that is more abstract in nature, can only be refined from semantic information through induction/deduction based on formal and value knowledge, as indicated below:

$$K_F \Leftarrow \cap \{I_{sy}\} \tag{5}$$
$$K_V \Leftarrow \cap \{I_{pr}\} \tag{6}$$
$$K_C \Leftarrow \cap \{\Re (K_F, I_{sem}, K_V, C)\} \tag{7}$$

Where the symbols K_F, K_C and K_V in Eqs. (5)-(7) respectively stand for the formal, the content, and the value knowledge, while I_{sy}, I_{sem} and I_{pr} for syntactic, semantic, and pragmatic information as they were before. The detailed description on general algorithms related to Equations 5, 6, and 7 can be referred to Zhong (2000) that can also be explained in Figure 4.

As is seen from Figure 4, both formal knowledge and value knowledge can in principle be produced through inductive algorithm, respectively over syntactic and pragmatic information, while content knowledge should be produced through induction operation over semantic information and deduction operation over the related formal and value knowledge. All the inductive and deductive algorithms are feasible in general.

It is also important to note that knowledge itself, in accordance with the different stages in the process of its growth, can be classified into four categories: the innate knowledge (the primitive stage of

Figure 4. Transformation from I_E to K

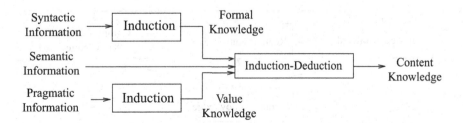

knowledge growth), the empirical knowledge (the first stage of knowledge growth), the regular knowledge (the second stage of knowledge growth) and the commonsense knowledge (the third stage of knowledge growth). The more précised definitions of the four categories of knowledge can be given below.

Definition 4: Innate Knowledge *is the knowledge that humans possessed and inherited from their birth without the learning process. It is the result of human evolution. It is also termed inherent knowledge sometimes.*

Definition 5: Empirical Knowledge *is the knowledge that is produced by inductive procedure, like training and learning algorithms, and yet without verification. The empirical knowledge, denoted by K_E, may also be called the potential knowledge, or preknowledge, sometimes.*

Definition 6: Regular Knowledge K_R, *can be defined as matured knowledge. It is the second stage of knowledge growth. Most of the knowledge produced through deduction can be regarded as the regular knowledge. The empirical knowledge may grow to the regular knowledge if it was positively verified through scientific means.*

Definition 7: Commonsense Knowledge *is the regular knowledge that has been well known and well popularized in society and therefore need not have formal proof process any more for its validity. Commonsense Knowledge in this regard can also be called the popular knowledge.*

The significance of the concept of knowledge categories will be evident later, and the relationships among the four categories of knowledge, pictured in Figure 5, are also clear and easy to understand.

It should be useful to note that the categories of innate knowledge and commonsense knowledge have many properties in common and thus, in many cases when without causing confusion, may be regarded as one big category of knowledge and called the commonsense knowledge for convenience.

Transformation 3: From Knowledge to Intelligence in the Narrow Sense (Intelligent Strategy)

The basic task for strategy creation in Figure 1 is to create an intelligent strategy, based on both the related knowledge and information obtained and directed by the goal given. The strategy serves as the guideline for problem solving successfully.

Figure 5. Four categories of knowledge

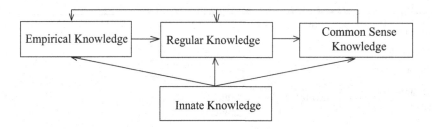

Definition 8: Strategy *for problem solving is a sort of procedure along which the given problem could be satisfactorily solved, meeting the constraints and reaching the goal. The strategy could only be created from the related knowledge and information and directed by the prescribed goal. The strategy is the major embodiment of intelligence for problem solving.*

The transformation from the given knowledge, information, and goal to the intelligent strategy can be expressed as following map

$$T_3 : (P, C, G; K) \mapsto s \in S \tag{8}$$

Where $s \in S$ in Equation 8 denotes a strategy in the space of strategies, P the problem to be handled, C the constraints set up by the given environment, G the goal for problem solving, and K the knowledge related to the problem solving.

Theoretically speaking, for any reasonably given P, C, G, and K, there would exist a group of strategies such that the problem can be solved satisfactorily, and among the strategies there might exist at least an optimal one leading to the optimal solution. The specific implementation of the transformation will be dependent on the properties of the problem faced, the constraints and goal given, and particularly on the knowledge possessed.

In the case that only empirical knowledge, including the incomplete knowledge or uncertain knowledge, is provided, the form of the transformation could be implemented via learning, training, and testing approaches. As is well known in fact, this has been the case widely adopted in artificial neural network's learning [3-5] and fuzzy logic (Zadeh, 1979) as well as rough set methods (Pawlak, 1994).

As for cases where the category of regular knowledge has been available, the transformation could be implemented via a series of logical inferences. Obviously, the typical approach of intelligent strategy formation of this kind is the traditional artificial intelligence, or expert system approach (Barr, 1982; Russell & Norvig, 2006).

In the case of common-sense knowledge, as well as the case of innate knowledge, where the relationships between the input pattern and the output actions have been well established, the mechanism of intelligent strategy formation could be implemented by directly linking the input pattern and the corresponding output actions. As long as the input pattern is recognized, the output strategic action can directly be determined based on the commonsense knowledge related to the problem without any inferences needed. This is the typical feature of strategy formation in sensory-motor category (Brooks, 1990, 1991).

Up to now, all the major transformations from ontological information to epistemological information and further to knowledge and even further to intelligence (intelligent strategy) have been described in brief. The detailed algorithms needed in the transformations are in principle feasible theoretically and technically.

Transformation 4: From Strategy to Action

The final step in the core mechanism of intelligence formation is the transformation conversing the intelligent strategy into intelligent action. This must be again a kind of one-to-one mapping and can then be expressed as below in Equation 9 and Figure 6.

Figure 6. Transformation: From strategy to action

$$T_4 : S \longmapsto A \tag{9}$$

Where S and A in Equation 9 denote the strategy and action spaces, respectively. This transformation can generally be implemented by adopting control system whose input is strategy, while the output is the corresponding action. Due to the fact that control systems have been a kind of conventional technology nowadays, we will not discuss the issues of control systems anymore.

The Mechanism of Intelligence Formation (A Summary)

As it is indicated in Figure 1, there are four categories of transformational units, T_1 (from Information-1 to Information-2 in Figure 1), T_2 (from epistemological information to knowledge), T_3 (from knowledge to intelligence-1), and T_4 (from intelligence-2 to intelligence-3), in the process of intelligence formation. Due to the fact that there should be no change (no distortion, in other words) allowed in information itself in the process of communication, the information at the output of a communication system should be the same as that at its input, we thus ignored the discussions on communication process (the transformation from information-2 to information-3 and the transformation from intelligence-1 to intelligence-2). Due to the similar consideration, we did not discuss the transformation from information-3 to information-4, as the function of information processing may be regarded as parts of the process from syntactic information to epistemological information.

Looking at the entire process shown in Figure 1, it is noticed that both the units of information acquisition and execution are two kinds of interface between the core of intelligent system and the external world: the former transforms the ontological information in the external world to the epistemological information in the system, while the latter transforms the intelligent strategy to the intelligent action to the external world for solving the problem concerned. On the other hand, both the transformational units of knowledge producing (cognition) and strategy-creating, are the two consecutive inner cores of the intelligent system: the former transforms the epistemological information into the corresponding knowledge, and the latter transforms the knowledge, combining with the related information and the goal, into the intelligent strategy.

In any cases as long as the problem, the environment of the problem, and the prescribed goal for the problem solving are given as preconditions, it is the synergetic collaboration among all the four transformations – (1) from the ontological information to the epistemological information, (2) from epistemological information to knowledge, (3) from knowledge to intelligent strategy, and (4) from intelligent strategy to intelligent action – more briefly the "information-knowledge-intelligence transformations" that makes it possible for a system to have the needed intelligence for solving the problem successfully, meeting the constraints from the environment and reaching the goal satisfactorily. In other words, **the information-knowledge-intelligence transformations do formulate the mechanism of intelligence formation.** This is the major conclusion of the article.

A UNIFYING THEORY OF AI

As was mentioned earlier in the article, in a long history of the development of Artificial Intelligence research there have been three major approaches in the area in literature: (1) the structural simulation approach, or neural networks approach, (2) the functional simulation approach, or expert systems approach, and (3) the behavior simulation approach, or sensory-motor system approach. The three approaches seem quite distinctive, and even exclusive, to each other. It was clearly seen in the last section, however, that all of them followed the same core mechanism of intelligence formation, the "information-knowledge-intelligence transformations." That is to say, as far as the mechanism of intelligence formation is concerned, there exists a unique, and unifying, theory of intelligence.

In fact, the three approaches can **work together complementarily** in the following way: (1) when the empirical knowledge is in use, the mechanism will be implemented through the neural network technology; (2) if the regular knowledge is in use, the mechanism will be realized through the expert system technology; and (3) if the commonsense knowledge is in use, the mechanism will be implemented through the sensory-motor system technology. Moreover, they can **work together harmoniously** in the following way: (1) the empirical knowledge obtained from the neural network approach, after verification, can be used as a basis in expert system approach; (2) the regular knowledge obtained from the expert system approach, after popularization, can be used as a basis in the sensor-motor system approach; and (3) the commonsense knowledge is in turn the basis for the other two approaches and the regular knowledge can also provide supports to the work of neural networks approach.. This can be seen in Figure 7.

Note that the symbols 'V.' and 'P.' in Figure 7 stand for 'Verification' and 'Popularization,' while 'E.K.,' 'R.K.,' and 'C.K.' are the Empirical Knowledge, Regular Knowledge, and Commonsense Knowledge, respectively.

Figure 7. Intelligence theory unification

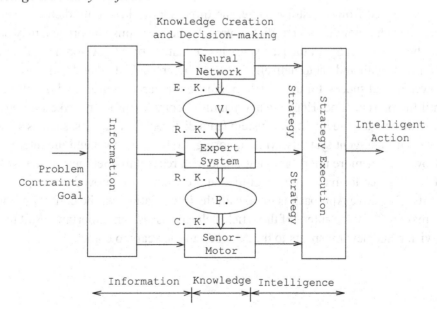

It can be concluded clearly from Figure 7 that the neural networks approach, the expert systems approach, and the sensory-motor system approach all follow the same core mechanism of intelligence formation, the information-knowledge-intelligence transformation, and the difference lies only on the microscopic view, the specific way in implementing the same mechanism.

This can be re-expressed in the following way: (1) if the knowledge to be used in the process of intelligence formation must be refined from information directly and instantly (this is referred to as the category of knowledge, the empirical knowledge), the implementation of the mechanism will have to employ the training and testing procedure by using such approaches as artificial neural networks; (2) if the knowledge to be used in the process of intelligence formation can be obtained from some knowledge bases and not necessary to be refined from information directly (this is referred to the category of knowledge, the regular knowledge), the implementation of the mechanism will have to employ the logic inference by using such approach as expert systems; (3) If the knowledge to be used in the process of intelligence formation is the already known relationships between the input patterns and output actions (this is referred to as the category of knowledge, the commonsense knowledge), the implementation of the mechanism will have to employ the matching procedure by using such approaches as sensory-motor systems.

After all, based on the analyses above, it is clear that the three approaches already existing in Artificial Intelligence research so far are by no means in contradiction to each other as they were during the past. They, Artificial Neural Networks Approach (The Structuralism), Expert Systems Approach (The Functionalism, also often regarded as the traditional AI approach), and Senor-Motor system Approach (The Behaviorism), are well complementary to each other indeed and harmoniously work together. The three approaches, as a trinity, form a unified theory of artificial intelligence within the framework of mechanism approach. No one can take the other's place.

It is the author's belief that the unification of the neural networks approach, the expert systems approach, and the sensory-motor system approach into a harmonic theory of AI based on the same core mechanism of intelligence formation of any kinds of intelligent systems may be of significance to the future development in AI research as the information-knowledge-intelligence transformations are the common roots of AI and are almost always feasible and practical in terms of modern technology.

The lesson we learned from the story above, the three approaches contradictory to each other in the past become now a harmonious and unified approach, the mechanism approach, may be something related to scientific methodology. In the past years in the history of AI development, the methodology we have been familiar with and "automatically" used is the one called "Divide and Conquer" that has been a very powerful and successful methodology during the past centuries and is still very useful in most cases until the present time. Hence, when handling complex problems like intelligent systems, we will naturally investigate the intelligent system from different view angles, such as structure, function, and behavior of intelligent systems, while ignoring the interrelations and the interactions among these angles. However, the more important view angle with respect to intelligent systems should be the mechanism of intelligence formation, the cognitive approach, as was proved in the previous section. The essence of the Cognitive Approach is to take all the interrelations in the entirety of the process of intelligence formation. This, the author of the article believes, is also an important result that may bring about the new vision and new prospects to the AI study in the years to come.

OPEN ISSUES: NEW ROOM FOR DISCOVERIES AND INNOVATIONS

What will be the future of Intelligence research? There have been answers from different views (Hawkins et al., 2004; Shi 2006; Wang, 2003, 2007; Wang & Kinsner, 2006; Yao, 2005; Zadeh, 2001), each of which has proposed good view in this regard. To the author's knowledge, the unified theory of artificial intelligence based on the core mechanism of intelligence formation should be promising because of the fact that all the transformation formulas related to the core mechanism of intelligence formation expressed as T_1, T_2, T_3, and T_4 in the third section can in principle be feasible both in theory and in technology, although there are many problems remaining to be considered.

The Mathematical Dimension

On one hand, all the transformations T_1, T_2, T_3, and T_4 in the third section have clear definition on their input and output and proper requirements on the relation between the input and output. For example, the transformation T_1, conversing ontological information to epistemological information, can be a kind of linear function (ideally) or monotonic and 1-to-1 mapping function (practically) in the case when syntactic information is required as its output (sensing system) while it can be a kind of vector calculation and logic operation when comprehensive information is required as output. The transformation T_2, conversing epistemological information to knowledge, can be a certain kind of logic operation, mainly the induction, analogy, association, and the like, while the transformation T_3, dealing with the conversion from information, knowledge, and the prescribed goal to intelligent strategy, can in simple cases be a kind of mathematical programming or a kind of sophisticated logic operations in complex cases. As far as the transformation T_4, mapping the intelligent strategy into the corresponding action can reasonably be a kind of mathematical treaties, some of which can be found in control theory. Therefore, all the transformations are in principle reasonable and feasible.

On the other hand, there are some mathematical issues related to the information-knowledge-intelligence transformations that are widely open and remain to be developed. This is because of the fact that information, knowledge, and intelligence are abstract in nature as well as complex in properties, and typically associated with many kinds of uncertainties, such as the uncertainty caused by randomness, the uncertainty caused by fuzziness, uncertainty caused by vagueness, uncertainty caused by nonlinearity, uncertainty caused by incompleteness, and so on. For effectively dealing with these uncertainties, the classical mathematical theory, although well matured, is not sufficient. New kinds of mathematical theories are strongly demanded. Some of the new mathematical theories, like probability theory, stochastic (random) process, mathematical statistics, fuzzy set theory (Zadeh, 1965), rough set theory (Pawlak, 991), chaotic theory, and so forth, have been already functioned. However, the information-knowledge-intelligence transformation may need even newer types of mathematics coming up to cope with the uncertainties and complexity. There is thus a conjecture that the beauty of classical mathematical theory, the strictly rigorousness, may need to be loosened to cover more practical and complex phenomena and such kinds of means, like algorithms, logic expressions, and reasoning as well as formal, or even natural, language descriptions, and so forth, may have to be accepted as new components of modern mathematical theories. This might be regarded as a great challenge and a large and open problem.

Another issue related to mathematics is the logic theory. It is a common understanding that there is fundamental demand for logic in the representation and reasoning in information/knowledge/intelligence.

There have been many kinds of logic theory existing in literature in which the proposition logic and the predicate logic are commonly regarded as classical logic theory. However, the power of the classical logic is rather limited in expression and reasoning, particularly in the cases with incomplete information and complicated interrelations. For overcoming or compensating the weakness of the classical logic, a number of new logic systems have been proposed during the past years. To name a few, the many-valued logic, fuzzy logic, nonmonotonic logic, model logic, temporal logic, dynamic logic and intuition logic, and so forth, are some of the examples. Although each of these nonclassical logics, also named nonstandard logics sometimes, is able to provide some potential power for a certain particular need in logic operation, there is a lack of a unified theory of logic. Therefore, we have another conjecture that there should be some universal logic to occur, which should be able to unify all the different logic theoretically, making each of the logics as a component of the universal logic (He, 2006).

It is also necessary to point out that even if the new mathematical theories and the universal logic are available, there is still much work remaining to be done because of the fact that the mechanism of intelligence formation will not act as panacea for all intelligent systems designing in any cases, although it is able to provide the core mechanism as a governing rule for the system designing. Specific algorithms for any specific transformations should be derived and developed for specific problems given in different cases. Therefore, the establishment of unified theory of AI based on core mechanism of intelligence formation will never close the door to the research in AI and rather, it opens up a much wider gate to the vast space for countless and endless creation.

The Biological Dimension

In addition to the open issues in mathematical and logic theories, there seem open issues related to biological science that may be more interesting and meaningful to the understanding of human intelligence. From what we discussed above, the answers to the following queries may really be of significance:

1. Can it be possible to find the apparent evidences in biological systems that can give solid support to the mechanism of intelligence formation we proposed in the article? More specifically, can it be possible to find the organisms and processes within biological systems that perform the information-knowledge-intelligence transformations?
2. If the answer is positive, then how do the information-knowledge-intelligence transformations carry on in human and other biological systems? More specifically, how does the ontological information in the real world become epistemological information including syntactic (form), semantic (content), and pragmatic (value) information in human system, how does the information become the related knowledge, how does the knowledge become intelligent strategy, and how does the intelligent strategy become intelligent action in human systems?
3. How can the specific formal descriptions concerning events acquired by sensing organs and stored in memories become abstract content concerning the same events in the thinking process, both in natural and artificial intelligent systems? And how do the formal perceptions of external events produce the related meaning within human brain as Professor Zadeh emphasized in "Zadeh (2001)?" This is also termed the "Brain and Mind Relation."
4. What hints and clues would the core mechanism of intelligence formation give to cognitive science and brain science for the deeper understanding of human intelligence?

We believe that the generation of content from the formal descriptions must be a central issue in intelligence process and expect to have certain positive responses either from the biological circle or from the cognitive circle, as well as from the circle of information science. That will really be helpful for further research in both natural and artificial intelligence research.

Technological Dimension

We have mentioned the dilemma faced in the structural simulation approach. We have to point out at the stage that the discoveries of Mechanism Approach and the Unified Theory of AI certainly open up promising directions of AI, effectively turning the AI research from a controversial stage to a harmonious stage, but it does not mean the problem of the dilemma in implementation of neural networks has also been solved. In fact, as can be seen from Figure 6, we still need the large-scale neural networks with high complexity for getting empirical knowledge through learning and training procedures. Nanotechnology, quantum technology, and so forth, may provide some of the possible solutions. We expect the progress from these directions.

CONCLUSION

A new approach, namely the Cognitive Approach to the mechanism of intelligence, was proposed in the article that is different from the existing approaches like structural simulation approach, functional simulation approach, and behavior simulation approach. The major discovery reported here is that the nucleus of the Cognitive Approach, or the core mechanism of intelligence formation in intelligent systems, is the information-knowledge-intelligence transformations that are in principle feasible both in theory and technology. It is also discovered that depending on the category of knowledge involved in the process, the Cognitive Approach can be implemented either as Structural Simulation Approach, Functional Simulation Approach, or Behavior Simulation Approach. Therefore, a by-product of the study is obtained in the article, that is, the Structural Simulation Approach, the Functional Simulation Approach, and the Behavior Simulation Approach are special cases of the Cognitive Approach and can harmoniously be unified within the framework of the Cognitive Approach.

The new approach is of course meaningful. But its significance is not to close the door of AI research, but rather, it opens up many interesting opportunities of which researchers must cope. New mathematical theories, new logic theories, new biological theories, and new implementation technologies are the spaces where many new discoveries can be expected. It may be more interesting that this study has very close relation to Cognitive Informatics in nature, as both of them have similar ends and means (Wang, 2003, 2007; Wang & Kinsner, 2006).

REFERENCES

Barr, A. & Feigenbaum, E. (1982). *The handbook of artificial intelligence*. William Kaufmann.

Brooks, R. A. (1990). Intelligence without representation. *Artificial Intelligence, 47,* 139-159.
Brooks, R. A. (1991). Intelligence without reasoning. In *Proceedings of IJCAI'91*, Sydney.

Feigenbaum, E. A., & Feldman, J. (Eds.). (1963). *Computers and thought.* McGraw-Hill.

Hawkins, J., & Blackeslee, S. (2004). *On intelligence.* Times Books. New York: Henry Holt and Company.

He, H. (2006). Principles of universal logic. Beijing, China: Science Press.

Hopfield, J. J. (1982). Neural networks and physical systems with emergent collective computational abilities. In *Proceedings of the National Academy of Science* (Vol. 79, pp. 2554-2558).

McCulloch, W. S. et al. (1943). A logical calculus of the ideas imminent in nervous activity. *Bull. Math. Biophy., 5,* 115-135.

Newell, A., & Simon, H. A. (1972). *Human problem solving.* Englewood Cliffs, NJ: Prentice Hall.

Pawlak, Z. (1991). *Rough sets – theoretical aspects of reasoning about data.* Dordrecht: Kluwer Academic Publishers.

Pawlak, Z. (1994). Decision analysis using rough sets. *International Trans. Oper. Res. ,1*(1), 107-114.

Ren, X. (2006). *Neural computation science.* National Defense Industry Press.

Rosenblatt, F. (1958). The perceptrom: A probabilistic model for information storage and organization in the brain. *Psychology Review, 65,* 386-408.

Rumelhart, D. E. (1990). Brain style computation: Leaning and generalization. *Introduction to neural and electronic networks.* New York: Academic Press.

Russell S., & Norvig, P. (2006). *Artificial intelligence: A modern approach* (2nd ed.). Pearson Education Asia Limited and Tsinghua University Press.

Shi, Z. Z. (2006). *On intelligence science.* Beijing, China: Tsinghua University Press.

Simon, H. A. (1969). *The sciences of artificial.* Cambridge, MA: The MIT Press.

Wang, Y. (2003, August). On cognitive informatics, brain and mind. *A Transdisciplinary Journal of Neuroscience and Neorophilosophy, 4(*3), 151-167. Kluwer Academic Publishers.

Wang, Y. (2007). The theoretical framework of cognitive informatics. *The International Journal of Cognitive Informatics and Natural Intelligence (IJCiNi), 1*(1), 1-27. Hershey, PA: IGI Publishing.

Wang, Y., & Kinsner, W. (2006, March). Recent advances in cognitive informatics. *IEEE Transactions on System, Man and Cybernetics (C), 36*(2), 121-123.

Yao, Y. Y. (2005, May). Web intelligence: New frontiers of exploration. In *Proceedings of the 2005 International Conference on Active Media Technology*, Takamatsu, Japan, (pp. 3-8).

Zadeh, L. A. (1965). *Fuzzy Sets, Information and Control, 8,* 338-353.

Zadeh, L. A. (2001). A new direction in AI – toward a computational theory of perception. *AI Magazine, 22(*1), 73-84.

Zhong, Y.X. (2000). A framework of knowledge theory. *China Engineering Science, 2*(9), 50-64.

Zhong, Y.X. (2002). *Principles of information science* (3rd ed. in Chinese). Beijing. China: BUPT Press.

ENDNOTE

[1]   This work was supported in part by Natural Science Foundation of China (No.60496327 and No.60575034)

This work was previously published in International Journal of Cognitive Informatics and Natural Intelligence, Vol. 2, Issue 1, edited by Y. Wang, pp. 1-16, copyright 2008 by IGI Publishing (an imprint of IGI Global).

Chapter 3
Reducing Cognitive Overload by Meta–Learning Assisted Algorithm Selection

Lisa Fan
University of Regina, Canada

Minxiao Lei
University of Regina, Canada

ABSTRACT

With the explosion of available data mining algorithms, a method for helping user to select the most appropriate algorithm or combination of algorithms to solve a given problem and reducing users' cognitive overload due to the overloaded data mining algorithms is becoming increasingly important. This chapter presents a meta-learning approach to support users automatically selecting most suitable algorithms during data mining model building process. The authors discuss the meta-learning method in detail and present some empirical results that show the improvement that can be achieved with the hybrid model by combining meta-learning method and Rough Set feature reduction. The redundant properties of the dataset can be found. Thus, the ranking process can be sped up and accuracy can be increased by using the reduct of the properties of the dataset. With the reduced searching space, users' cognitive load is reduced.

The explosion in the amount of available data on any given subject has led researchers to the area of knowledge discovery and data mining. The main motivation of these research areas is that humans are not capable of analyzing the current size of the available data either manually or with basic statistical methods. As a result, the technological challenge of performing everything automatically has dominated the interests of researchers and developers. Thus, data mining was established as a methodology for extracting potentially useful information from very large amounts of data.

To deal with different complicated data, scientists have developed numerous data mining algorithms. These different data mining algorithms work well on different kinds of data. For example, Neural Network Algorithms (Wasserman, 1989) can deal with discrete data, Data Association Rule Algorithms

DOI: 10.4018/978-1-60566-902-1.ch003

(Kotsiantis & Kanellopoulos, 2006) can find groups of common items in transactions, and Clustering Algorithms (Kaufman & Rousseeuw, 1900) can both group similar items and deal with discrete data. Not a single algorithm can perform well on different data. As well, when different data mining algorithms are performed on the same data, the outputs are different. Thus, choosing the right algorithm to use for a specific type of data can be a challenge.

The Data Mining algorithm is the mechanism that creates mining models. Extensive research has been performed to develop appropriate machine learning techniques for different data mining problems, and has led to a proliferation of different learning algorithms (Bernstein & Provost, 2001). With the explosion of available data mining algorithms, select appropriate algorithms or combination of algorithms to solve a given problem becomes more important than its availability.

Ideally, there exists a single algorithm that can solve all the problems, or we can try all the algorithms to the problems to find the best algorithms, which can obtain the best accuracy and efficiency balance. Unfortunately, scientists have to develop different algorithms to satisfy different situations. Thus there are large amount of algorithms and models developed. Facing the enormous algorithms, the users can hardly handle all of them, and it is difficult to decide which one or combination of some algorithms is the most fitted for their problems. It shows that for a novice user, the data mining process space is overwhelming. Many novice users simply use the algorithms that they are familiar with (Kirsh, 2000). Consider the 2000 KDDCUP, in which 30 teams of data mining researchers and professionals competed to mine knowledge from electronic-commerce data. Most algorithms were tried by only a small fraction of participants. The only algorithm that was tried by more than 20% of the participants was decision-tree induction.

We can view data mining algorithms overload as information overload or data overload. Cognitive overload is the result of excessive demands made on the cognitive processes, in particular memory (Woods, Patterson, & Roth, 2002). Cognitive load increases with the amount of information to process. People feel information anxiety and suffer. Cognition in principal is mainly a process of information manipulation, according to the point of view of cognitive science. Cognitive Informatics (Wang, 2003) proposed by professor Y.X. Wang investigates the internal information processing mechanisms and process of the natural intelligence. Woods et al (2002) examined three different characterizations capturing the nature of the data overload problem and how they lead to different proposed solutions. Our approach to solve the data mining algorithms overload problem is to use machine intelligence (meta-learning) to cooperatively aid human users in selecting the most appropriate algorithms and assist the users to make decisions.

META-LEARNING BASIC CONCEPT

Meta-learning is an approach to select the appropriate learning algorithms for data mining, and the task of meta-learning is to find functions that can map datasets to the appropriate data mining algorithms. It is a process of learning at meta-level (Dzeroski & Zenko, 2002). It is similar to other machine learning methods in its ability to capture valuable information or knowledge from data. However, it is especially designed to enhance the machine learning process. Meta-learning is acquiring knowledge that can guide users in the application of data mining. It is a way to learn how a data mining system can work in a more effective way. Essentially, it is learning how to learn. The objective of meta-learning is to generate a user support system for selection of the most appropriate supervised learning algorithms for such tasks.

The meta-learning framework is usually based on a classification on the meta-level often disregarding a large amount of information gained during the induction process. Considering only a small subset of meta-attributes may significantly reduce both the time and effort applied for the corresponding process (Peng et al., 2002). The use of meta-knowledge will greatly reduce the amount of experience to be carried out. This also will enhance the performance of data mining and encourage users to work in a comfortable and effective way. Cognitive overload will be reduced. An excellent review of different aspects of meta-learning is given by Vilalta and Drissi (2002).

Previous works show that no one algorithm is generally better than any other algorithm, but rather different algorithms are more suited to different data mining tasks. For example, consider that there are two datasets, D1 and D2 and two algorithms, A and B. For dataset D1, algorithm A might perform better than algorithm B, but for dataset D2, algorithm B might perform better than algorithm A. Thus, scientists have developed many methods to define the learning task to which the learning algorithms will be applied. For example, a variety of data characterization techniques have been developed. These techniques are based on three strategies, including what are known as simple measure, statistical measure, and information theory-based measure. However, the quality of these measures still needs to be improved.

The procedures of meta-learning can be divided into three steps. The first step is to describe the characteristics of a dataset by using a set of meta-attributes. Several techniques have been developed, such as data characterization techniques (DCT), to describe the problem to be analyzed, including simple measures like the number of attributes, classes etc., statistical measures like the mean and variance of numerical attributes, and information theory-based measures like the entropy of classes and attributes. However, not all the meta-attributes are useful, and the data characterization still needs to be improved in terms of correctness and effectiveness by developing more predictive meta-attributes and selecting the most informative ones.

The second step is to develop a correlation between the task description and the optimal learning algorithm. The method to develop correlations between the meta-attributes and the performance of learning is significant. We use Adjusted Ratio of Ratios (ARR) measure (Brazdil & Soares, 2000) to get the correlations.

In the third step, when a new dataset is given, the most similar training datasets were searched; and the meta-knowledge of the similar datasets were used to predict the new one. The most popular method used in meta-learning research is a similarity method like k-nearest neighbour.

EXISTING META-LEARNING METHODS AND ALGORITHM SELECTION SYSTEMS

Data Characterization Methods

Many methods have been developed to solve the problem of how to define a set of descriptors that can be used to describe a dataset in a way that can be used by the meta-learning method. The description methods can be considered *data characterization*. There are three main methods to solve the problem of how to define a set of descriptors. There are information/statistical properties-based data characterization, landmarking, and decision tree-based data characterization.

Information and Statistical Properties Based Data Characterization

The description of a dataset in terms of its information/statistical properties appeared for the first time within the framework of the STATLOG project (Michie & Spiegelhalter, 1996). They extracted 15 characteristics from a set of registered datasets, such as the number of attributes, the number of examples, and the number of classes. One of the contributions of their work is that they divided three categories of dataset characteristics, namely simple, statistical, and information theory-based measures. Statistical characteristics are mainly appropriate for continuous attributes, and information theory-based measures are more appropriate for discrete attributes. The other contribution is that they combine these characteristics with the performance of the algorithms and generate rules to guide selection based on the characteristics of the dataset. This method is based just on the morphological similarity between the new dataset and the existing collection. In addition, it does not classify these datasets. When a new dataset comes, it simply compares the characteristics of the new dataset to all the old datasets.

Lindner and Studer (1999) provide an extensive list of information and statistical measures of a dataset computed for each attribute or pair of attributes. They provide a tool for the automatic computation of these characteristics, which is called Data Characterization Tools (DCT). It uses the STATLOG meta-attributes set as a starting point, and proceeds with careful evaluation of their properties in a statistical framework. One contribution of the DCT is that it discovers some highly correlated characteristics and omits some of the redundant ones from their study.

Landmarking

An alternative approach to characterizing datasets, called landmarking, was proposed in (Papoulis, 1991). It characterizes the datasets by using the performance (e.g. accuracy) of a set of simple learners, called landmarkers. The basic idea of landmarking is to use the performance of a few fast-learning algorithms to characterize the dataset. Each algorithm can perform well in a class of datasets called the area of expertise of a learner. The landmarking approach is that the performance of a learner on a task uncovers information about the nature of the task. A dataset can be described by the collection of areas of expertise to which it belongs. A landmark learner is a learning mechanism whose performance is used to describe a task. Landmarking is the use of these learners to locate the task in the expertise space, the space of all areas of expertise.

In the other words, the landmarking method uses some fast and simple algorithms as the landmarkers and applies these algorithms to the new dataset first. After all the simple algorithms are deployed on the dataset, the performances of each simple algorithm can be obtained. Thus, a ranking of the performances of these simple algorithms can be obtained. In the knowledge base, each simple algorithm represents a complicated algorithm. The landmarking method assumes that if a simple algorithm has the best performance on the dataset, its corresponding complicated algorithm should also have the best performance on the dataset.

Decision Tree Based Data Characterization

Another characterization method for meta-learning is a decision tree-based data characterization, which has been developed by using the characteristics from the structural shape and size of the decision tree induced from the dataset (Peng, Flach, Brazdil, & Soares, 2002). Based on the idea that the same training set always produces a similarly structured decision tree, the complexity of learning is determined by measuring the structure and size of the decision tree and using the measures to predict the model complexity generated by other learning algorithms. Instead of using the meta-attributes, which are generated by DCT, this method uses c5.0 to generate the meta-attributes of a dataset, like the width and height of the tree and number of nodes etc. When a new dataset is acquired, k-NN is used to find a similar training dataset in the training database. The candidate algorithms' performances of the training dataset are also measured by adjusted ratio of ratios (ARR), and a recommendation is given based on the most similar training dataset's ranking algorithms' list. Fifteen new meta-attributes are used to predict the rankings and to compare the results with the ranking generated by DCT (25 meta-attributes) and the ranking generated by Landmarking (5 meta-attributes). The experiment result is that the new decision tree method outperforms the other two methods.

Algorithm Selection Methods

Several meta-learning strategies have been proposed for algorithm selection (Dash & Liu, 2003) (Todorovski & Blockeel, 2002). In general, there are three options in generating the output of the meta-learning method. One of the options is to select a single learning algorithm from an algorithm set. This selected algorithm is expected to create the best model for the dataset. The second option is to select a subgroup of learning algorithms, including not only the best algorithm but also the algorithms that are not significantly worse than the best one. The third is to rank the learning algorithms according to their performance. The ranking will assist the user to make the final decision in the learning algorithm selection. This ranking-based meta-learning is the main approach in the Esprit Project MetaL project. Ranking the preference order of algorithms is performed based on estimating the performance of the algorithms. In data mining, performance can be measured not only in terms of accuracy but also time. In this thesis, we assess the performance with the Adjusted Ratio of Ratios (ARR) measure, which combines accuracy and time. ARR gives a measure of the advantage of a learning algorithm over another algorithm in

Existing Algorithm Selection Systems

Data Mining Advisor (DMA) (Alexandros & Melanie, 2001) also uses the ARR measure. It already has a set of candidate algorithms and a group of training datasets; the performance of the candidate algorithms for each subset in the training datasets is known. When the user gives a new dataset, DMA first uses K-NN algorithm to find a similar subset in the training datasets. Based on this subset, it retrieves information about the performance of candidate algorithms, then ranks the candidate algorithms and gives the appropriate recommendation. DCT tool is used to find the characteristics of the datasets.

Other algorithm selection systems and strategies have been proposed to solve the algorithm selection problem in data mining. An expert system called "Consultant" (Sleenman & Rissakis, 195) presented by Sleenman and Rissakis, is an advisory system. It determines the character of the application by asking users to answer several questions, and helps users select a suitable Machine-Learning tool for their problems. The foundation of this system is a knowledge base. It stores a static rule set obtained by extensive interviewing of the Machine-Learning tool experts and the domain expert who have used the tool to solve their problems. Such a system has two main disadvantages. First, this rule-based system is very difficult to maintain. When a new algorithm is introduced, the system needs to re-compute all the rules to make them consistent with each other. Second, this method depends on just the users' subjective experiences.

This system requires the users to know their problem domain well. If users have limited knowledge and give the Consultant wrong information, the corresponding prediction will not be correct.

Rendell and Seshu in VBMS (Rendell & Seshu, 1987) give a classification of the problem to let the users make a selection and then give a prediction about the corresponding algorithms. VBMS starts with no knowledge of the suitability of biases. Next, it induces relationships between problem classes and biases. It considers the new tasks as new classification tasks, and this slows down the process, particularly if the user is a novice.

Another system based on biased selection methods, called CRL/ISO, is presented by Tcheng and Lambert (1989). It manages a set of diverse inductive biases, builds hybrid concept representation, and searches for an optimum bias in this inductive bias space. It is limited in the categories of bias, and fixes the strategy for searching the bias space.

Bernstein and Provost (2001) present IDEA based on Ontology. This system contains two core components. The first component is called Data Mining Process Planner. It performs a search of data mining processes defined by ontology to enumerate valid data mining processes. The second core component is the heuristic ranker. It ranks the valid data mining processes using one of several possible heuristic functions. This system is used to assist the data mining process.

A ROUGH SET-ASSISTED META-LEARNING METHOD

Previous researchers developed different methods try to solve algorithm selection problem. Some of them applied Meta-learning method to assist selecting algorithms, but they treat all the meta-attributes as the same. None of the previous researchers considered the attributes' importance in their methods. Actually, different sets of attributes have different effect on decision making, some are more important than the others, and also not all of the attributes are useful in making decisions. To find out a smaller set of the important attributes can save lots of time on processing recommendation procedure. In this chapter, we also use the k-Nearest Neighbor (k-NN) algorithm to compare two datasets similarity by using meta-attributes. Since this algorithm is easily affected by the noisy attributes, we propose a Rough Set assisted meta-learning method to help eliminating the redundant part of the meta-attributes and then use the essential part to do the next step calculation. By applying k-NN on the essential part of the meta-attribute, we can avoid this negative effect. Moreover, we can increase the recommendation accuracy and reduce the processing time. Choosing the right algorithm to use for a specific task can be a challenge. We present a hybrid model combining meta-learning method and Rough Set feature reduction to assist users to select algorithms that effectively reduces users' cognitive overload.

Method

In this section, we will give an overview of the theoretical foundation of our approach. The evaluation about how to evaluate one algorithm is better than another is given by calculating the ARR value for a given dataset. In order to increase the speed, we used Rough Set to reduce the meta-attributes. Rough Set reduct and the reason of using Mutual Information to assign weight to the meta-attributes after Rough Set reduct are given in the later section.

The Distance Based Multicriteria Evaluation Measurement

Based on the idea that for similar datasets, algorithms should behave similarly. Statistical properties, such as skewness, kurtosis, and kind of attributes, are defined to describe each dataset. When a new dataset is given, using k-NN (Mitchell, 1997) approach could get k similar datasets from the training datasets. The distance function Dis(DS$_j$, DS$_{new}$) between j-th dataset and new dataset is:

$$Dis(DS_j, DS_{new}) = \sqrt{\left(\sum_i^m weight_1(i) * \left|\frac{DS_j(i) - DS_{new}(i)}{stdev(i)}\right|^2\right)} \tag{1}$$

Where DS$_j$(i) is the i-th attribute value of dataset j from the training datasets stored in the knowledge base. DS$_{new}$(i) represents the i-th attribute of the new dataset. m is the number of attributes. wight$_1$(i) will be defined in the following section. Stdev(i) is the standard deviation of the i-th attribute over all datasets.

Since the evaluation about how to evaluate one algorithm is better than another is mainly based on the accuracy rates and the time rates, the method called Adjusted Ratio of Ratios (ARR) (Soares & Brazdil, 2000) combines the accuracy and the execution time together as a scale to compare two algorithms' performance on the same dataset. (ARR) can be seen as an extension of the success rate ratios (SRR) (Brazdil & Soares, 2000), which aggregates two other basic ranking methods: average ranks and significant wins.

$$ARR_{a_p,a_q}^{d_i} = \frac{\dfrac{ACC_{a_p}^{d_i}}{ACC_{a_q}^{d_i}}}{1 + AccD * \log\left(\dfrac{T_{a_p}^{d_i}}{T_{a_q}^{d_i}}\right)} \tag{2}$$

Where $ACC_{a_p}^{d_i}$ is the accuracy of the algorithm a$_p$ on dataset d$_i$, and $T_{a_p}^{d_i}$ is the time of the algorithm a$_p$ on dataset d$_i$. AccD measures the relative importance of accuracy and time, which is defined by user. The accuracy ratio ($ACC_{a_p}^{d_i} / ACC_{a_q}^{d_i}$) represents the advantage of algorithm a$_p$ over the algorithm a$_q$. The time ratio ($T_{a_p}^{d_i} / T_{a_q}^{d_i}$) represents the disadvantage of algorithm a$_p$ over algorithm a$_q$. Here, log ($T_{a_p}^{d_i} / T_{a_q}^{d_i}$) represents the order of magnitude of the ratio. By multiplying AccD parameter to this expression log ($T_{a_p}^{d_i} / T_{a_q}^{d_i}$), the relative importance between accuracy and time can be taken into account. AccD parameter is given by the user to make ten times speedup or slowdown.

The ranking of a candidate algorithm can be built by computing the geometric mean across all datasets and then the arithmetic mean across algorithms.

$$ARR_{a_p}(j) = \frac{\sum_{a_q} \sqrt[n]{\prod_{d_i} ARR_{a_p,a_q}^{d_i}}}{m} \tag{3}$$

Where n represents the number of datasets, and m represents the number of algorithms. Therefore, the better performance of a_p algorithm for a certain dataset j, the higher ARR it will get.

To compute the new dataset's ARR score, three nearest neighbor datasets are needed. These three most similar training datasets identified by apply 3-NN approach already have the ARR about each candidate algorithms. Thus a new ARR about the new dataset can be calculated by weight mean of the three training datasets' ARR. More details about the reason why we choose 3-NN can be found in (Berrer & Keller, 2000).

$$\text{ARR}_{a_p}(\text{new}) = \sum_{j=1}^{3} weight_2(j) * ARR_{a_p}(j) \tag{4}$$

Here, ARR $_{a_p}$ (new) represents the ranking score of algorithm a_p about the new dataset. The weights are computed as the inverse proportion of the 3-NN distances of each training datasets j to the new dataset. Weight$_2$(j) is calculated as:

$$\text{Weight}_2(j) = \sum_{j=1}^{3} \frac{\dfrac{1}{Dis(DS_j, DS_{new})}}{\dfrac{1}{Dis(DS_j, DS_{new})}} \tag{5}$$

When DS_j is the training dataset j. DS_{new} is the new dataset. $Dis(DS_j, DS_{new})$ is the distance between j dataset and the new dataset.

Feature Selection and Rough Set Assisted Reduction

In a classification problem, the number of features can be quite large, many of which can be irrelevant or redundant. A relevant feature is defined in (Dash & Liu, 2003) as one removal of which deteriorates the performance or accuracy of the classifier, and an irrelevant or redundant feature is not relevant. These irrelevant features could deteriorate the performance of a classifier that uses all features since irrelevant information is included inside the totality of the features. Thus the motivation of a feature selector is (a) simplifying the classifier by the selected features; (b) improving or not significantly reducing the accuracy of the classifier; and (c) reducing the dimensionality of the data so that a classifier can handle large volumes of data. Many approaches as feature selectors have been proposed. In this chapter, we choose rough sets assisted dimensionality reduction method that does not depend on any threshold.

In Rough Set theory (Pawlak, 1982), the reduct of knowledge is the most fundamental part of knowledge. It can help us to reduce the dimensionality of datasets. By getting the reduct of the meta-attributes without losing information, we can make the recommendation procedure fast and efficient. The following paragraph will explain what the reduct is.

An information system S = {U, Q, V, f }, where U is a non-empty and finite set of objects called Universe U = { x_1, x_2, ..., x_n}. Q represents a finite and non-empty set of attributes. Q = C $\cup$ D and C $\cap$ D = φ. C and D are Condition attributes and Decision attributes respectively. V is a set of domains of all attributes Q of S, V = $\cup_{a} \in Q$ V_a. V_a is a domain of the attribute a. f: U$\times$Q $\rightarrow$ V, is a function f(x, a) $\in V_a$, for a $\in$ Q and x$\in$ U. x, y $\in$U are indiscernible if x, y have the same values for a given set of attributes $B(B \in Q)$. Indiscernible objects are elements of an equivalence class $[x]_B$. The set $U/IND(B)$ is the set of all equivalence classes in the relation B. The equivalence relation $IND(B)$ is defined as $IND(B) = \{(x, y) \in U \times U$: for every $a \in B, a(x) = a(y)\}$. An attribute a is said to be dispensable if $IND(B) = IND(B-\{a\})$ in a given subset of attributes $B \in Q$. Reduct can be demonstrate that B is a family of equivalence relations and let $B \in B$. If $IND(B)=IND (B-\{B\})$, B is dispensable in B; otherwise B is indispensable in B. The family B is independent if each B is indispensable in B. $B' \in B$ is a reduct of B if: B' is independent and $IND(B') = IND(B)$. In other words, it must satisfy the following two conditions: First, the original attribute set can be substituted by the reduct while preserving the accuracy of classification. Second, if any one of attributes is removed from the reduct, it will absolutely lead to new inconsistency.

Weight Adjustment by Using Mutual Information

In information theory, the mutual information (Papoulis, 1991) of two variables is a quantity that measures the mutual dependence of the two variables. Here, we use mutual information to measure the dependence of the meta-attributes (MA) and the candidate algorithms (ALG). Therefore, mutual information measures how much information MA contains about ALG. The mutual information can be calculated as follows:

$$I(MA_i, ALG) = \sum_{i}^{m} \sum_{j}^{n} p(MA_{ij}, ALG_j) \log \frac{p(MA_{ij}, ALG_j)}{p(MA_{ij})p(ALG_j)}$$

(6)

where MA_i represents the i-th meta-attribute. There are n training datasets. $p(MA_{ij})$ and $p(ALG_j)$ are the marginal probability distribution functions of MA_i and ALG respectively, and $p(MA_{ij}, ALG_j)$ is the joint probability distribution function of MA_i and ALG. If MA and ALG are independent, their mutual information is zero. This is easy to see in one direction: if MA and ALG are independent, then $p(MA_j, ALG_j) = p(MA_j) * p(ALG_j)$, and accordingly:

$$\log \frac{p(MA_j, ALG_j)}{p(MA_j)p(ALG_j)} = \log 1 = 0$$

(7)

Moreover, mutual information is nonnegative $I(MA;ALG \geq 0$ and symmetric $I(MA;ALG) = I(ALG;MA)$. The larger mutual information is, the larger dependency between the MA and ALG are. Thus, we can give the meta-attribute a weight corresponding to their $I(MA; ALG)$.

$$weight_1(i) = \frac{I(MA_i, ALG)}{\sum_{i}^{m} I(MA_i, ALG)}$$

(8)

EXPERIMENT

Experimental Descriptions

There are two ways to map the datasets' characteristic to the performance of the algorithm. First, capture the knowledge about the algorithms from experts. Second, capture the knowledge about the algorithms from experiments. In this paper, the Adjusted Ratio of Ratios (ARR) method (Soares & Brazdil, 2000) is used to scale the performance of the candidate algorithms by combining the accuracy and time in it. Through experiments, ARR can be obtained by calculating the algorithms' accuracy and time of each dataset. After the experiments, ARR of each algorithm corresponding to every dataset are saved in the knowledge base for future use. The ranking procedure is shown in Figure 1.

We use k-NN (Mitchell, 1997) to find out the most similar dataset in the knowledge base to a given new dataset. 25 characteristics (Todorovski, Blockeel, & Dzeroski, 2002), which are obtained by using the Data Characterization Tool (DCT), are defined as meta-attributes and are used to compare the two datasets' similarities. A distance function that based on the characteristics of the two datasets is used to find the most similar neighbors, whose performance is expected to be similar or relevant to the new dataset. The recommended ranking of the new dataset is built by aggregating the candidate algorithms' performance on the similar datasets.

The knowledge base stores the datasets' characteristics that are represented by meta-attributes and the candidate algorithms' performance corresponded to each dataset. When a new experiment result is generated, it can be added into the knowledge base without re-learning the existing result.

Figure 1. The Ranking Procedure

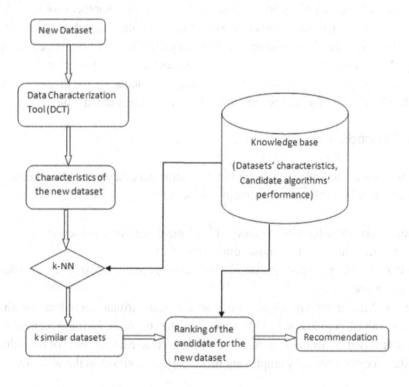

Table 1. DCT Dataset Properties

25 meta attributes (DCT dataset properties)		
Nr-attributes	Nr-sym-attributes	Nr-num-attributes
Nr-examples	Nr-classes	MissingValues-Total
MissingValues-relative	Lines-with-MissingValues-Total	Mean-Absolute-Skew
MeanKurtosis	NumAttrsWithOutliers	MStatistic
MstatDF	MstatChiSq	SDRatio
Fract	Cancor	WilksLambda
BartlettStatistic	ClassEntropy	EntropyAttributes
MutualInformation	JointEntropy	Equivalent-nr-of-attrs
NoiseSignalRatio		

Experimental Setting

Here we choose twenty-one datasets and six algorithms to do the experiment. These datasets are from the UCI repository. First, we use DCT to get the 25 DCT properties (Todorovski et al., 2002) of each dataset. The 25 characteristics are shown in Table 1.

DCT properties contain properties of the individual attribute in the dataset, such as entropy of each symbolic attribute. After we get the 25 attributes' value, we replace the original attribute values of an information table with more general categories (Ziarko & Shan, 1995) in order to abstract knowledge from low-level information. By representing in the less precise representation, the interesting patterns and relationships might appear and easy for us to discover. Therefore, before we apply rough set theory on data, we first transfer the high precise attribute value into the less precise one. At the same time, another problem - how to optimally discrete the attribute values, generates. This is a subject of on going research that not yet settled, and the current solution is that using the domain knowledge to guide the discretization. Here, based on different attributes' property, we use the low-level information to represent the original high-level information. And all of our works, such as comparing the similarity of two datasets, calculating the distance of the two datasets, and computing the weight for ARR, are based on this low-level information table.

Experimental Procedure

In order to find an efficient method to obtain higher prediction accuracy and reduced time, we investigated and conducted four experiments by using different approaches.

- **Experiment 1:** The meta-learning method with 25 meta-attributes is used to give user a recommendation to help him or her selecting most-suited algorithm.
- **Experiment 2:** Based on the first approach, a weight is given to each attribute in order to increase the prediction accuracy.
- **Experiment 3:** After applied rough set theory on 25 meta-attributes, a reduct contained 8 meta-attributes can be obtained. A prediction can be made by using the meta-learning method with the reduct.
- **Experiment 4:** Based on the third approach, a weight is set to each attribute of the reduct. An algorithm recommendation can be given by employing meta-learning method on the weighted reduct.

RESULTS AND DISCUSSION

After implementing the first experiment, we can obtain prediction accuracy of the original method around 54%. Our next three improved methods are compared with this original method. When the weight is being considered, the prediction accuracy of the meta-learning method with 25 weighted meta-attributes increases to 66.7%. After applying rough sct theory, the accuracy of prediction becomes 70.8%. Based on our fourth experiment, the recommendation accuracy is 71.6% which just increases a little compared to the third experiment.

The results show that not all of the 25 meta-attributes are useful. It is necessary to find out the noisy attributes. From the results, we can see that without treating all 25 meta-attributes as the same, a higher accuracy than the original method can be obtained.

If we use rough set theory to get a reduct of 25 meta-attributes, the prediction accuracy is 16.8% higher than the original accuracy and 4.1% higher than the weighted assisted meta-learning method. Although the time used to prepare our knowledge base is increased, the storage space in the knowledge base and the time used to give a recommendation are both reduced. The reason is that we only need to store 8 meta-attributes of each training dataset and calculate 8 meta-attributes to give a recommendation.

The fourth experiment, a weight is added to each attribute of the reduct, but the accuracy did not increase too much. The rough set theory already gives an essential part of meta-attributes -- the reduct, and this reduct is good enough for our algorithms recommendation. Moreover, processing time is sacrificed to set a weight for each attribute in preparing knowledge base. Thus adding weights to the reduct is not necessary when we build a real system. Comparing with the original method (Experiment 1), Table 2 shows the difference between the four experiments.

In Table 2, M.L is the abbreviation of meta-learning. R.S represents rough sets, and M.I is mutual information.

The theory of our recommendation system is based on rough sets assisted meta-learning method. To explain how our system works, we give a detailed explanation of the method as follows.

After we have the low-level information table, we can use rough set theory to find important attributes. The reduct of this information table can be obtained. Those attributes are shown in Table 3.

Table 2. A Comparison of Four Experiments

	Experiment			
	Exp.1	Exp.2	Exp.3	Exp.4
Methods being used	M.L	M.L & M.I	M.L & R.S	M.L & M.I & R.S
Number of methods being used	1	2	2	3
Number of attributes	25	25	8	8
Weight	no	yes	no	yes
Storage space	same	increased	decreased	decreased
Time used for data preparing	same	increased	increased	increased
Time used for ranking	same	same	same	same
Total time used	same	increased	increased	increased
Accuracy	54%	66.7%	70.8%	71.6%
Accuracy increase	/	12.7%	16.8%	17.6%

Table 3. Reduct of the DCT properties

8 meta attributes (DCT dataset properties)	
Nr-sym-attributes	Nr-num-attributes
Nr-classes	NumAttrsWithOutliers
MstatDF	Fract
Cancor	ClassEntropy

Table 4. A comparison between original method and new method

Algorithm	TrueScore	Predicted Score with RS	True Rank	Predicted Rank with RS	Predicted Rank without RS
c50tree	1.024	1.020	1	1	2
c50rules	1.023	1.019	2	2	3
c50boost	1.022	1.018	3	3	1
clemMLP	0.997	0.996	4	4	5
mlcib1	0.967	0.981	5	5	4
lindiscr	0.936	0.968	6	6	6

After delete the redundant attributes, we use the same ranking method to get the new dataset's ranking score. The rough set theory help us to eliminate the redundant attributes, thus the recommend system can use less time to give a ranking score to the users. Moreover, since this method uses distance function, redundant attributes will affect the accuracy when we calculate two datasets' similarity. Here we give an example in Table 4, which gives a comparison between the ranking method with rough sets and the ranking method without rough sets.

Based on our experiment, using the ranking method without rough sets, the accuracy is increased. Moreover, the meta-attributes, which used to compare the two datasets' similarity are reduced from 25 to 8. The time used to calculate two datasets' distance is reduced.

The user interface is illustrated in Figure 2 to demonstrate the rough sets assisted meta-learning algorithm selection system.

CONCLUSION AND FUTURE WORK

In this chapter, we present our research work on using meta-learning method to reduce user cognitive overload during the model building process and help user effectively to select the most appropriate data mining algorithms and give the ranking recommendation automatically. To find a good algorithm selection method, we conducted experiments on four combination methods: the original meta-learning method, meta-learning method combined with mutual information method, meta-learning method combined with rough sets method, and meta-learning method combined with rough set theory and the mutual information method. The results indicate that by using rough sets-assisted meta-learning method, the algorithm recommendation accuracy is high and the recommendation is very useful in helping users select the most appropriate algorithm for their dataset.

Figure 2. System interface based on rough sets assisted meta-learning method.

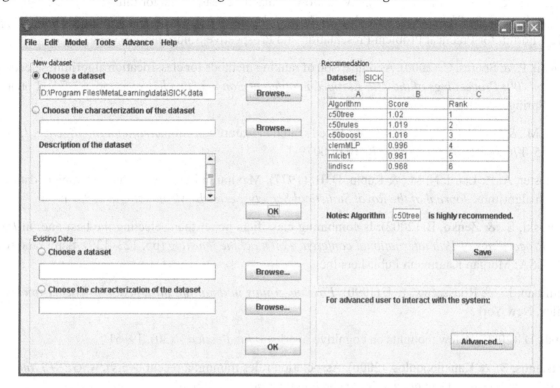

Moreover, a prototype algorithm recommendation system is designed and built using the rough sets-assisted meta-learning method. It can assist both novice and expert users. When the user has little knowledge about the algorithms, this ranking system can reduce the searching space, give him/her the recommendation and guide the user to select the most suited algorithms. For expert users, it could be useful for double-checking his/her thinking. By using the hybrid model combining meta-learning and Rough Set, we can increase the speed and improve the performance.

Examining the algorithm overload problem in the model building process, we found that machine and human user should be tightly coupled to work cooperatively together. System should not solely rely on machine intelligence, nor should solely rely on human users. Machine intelligence is supplemental to human users and assists the users to deal with cognitive overload and make appropriate decisions for the model building process. In the future work, we will investigate more on our proposed model and provide more functions to assist not only the model building process but also the whole data mining process.

REFERENCES

Alexandros, K., & Melanie, H. (2001). Model selection via meta-learning: A comparative study. *International Journal on AI Tools*, *10*(4), 444–455.

Bernstein, A., & Provost, F. (2001). An intelligent assistant for the knowledge discovery process. In *Proceedings of IJCAI-01 workshop on wrappers for performance enhancement in kdd.*

Berrer, H., & Keller, I. P. J. (2000). Evaluation of machine-learning algorithm ranking advisors. In *Proceedings of the PKDD 2000 workshop on data mining, decision support, meta-learning and ilp* (pp. 1-13). Forum for Practical Problem Presentation and Prospective Solutions.

Brazdil, P., & Soares, C. (2000). A comparison of ranking methods for classification algorithm selection. In *Ecml '00: Proceedings of the 11th European conference on machine learning* (pp. 63–74). London, UK: Springer-Verlag.

Dash, M., & Liu, H. (2003). Consistency-based search in feature selection. *Artificial Intelligence, 151*(1-2), 155–176. doi:10.1016/S0004-3702(03)00079-1

Dempster, A. P., Laird, N. M., & Rubin, D. B. (1977). Maximum likelihood from incomplete data via the em algorithm. *Journal of the Royal Statistical Society. Series B. Methodological, 39*, 1–38.

Dzeroski, S., & Zenko, B. (2002). Is combining classifiers better than selecting the best one. In *Icml '02: Proceedings of 19th international conference on machine learning* (pp. 123–130). San Francisco, CA, USA: Morgan Kaufmann Publishers Inc.

Kaufman, L., & Rousseeuw, P. J. (1990). *Finding groups in data: an introduction to cluster analysis.* Wiley, New York.

Kirsh, D. (2000). A few thoughts on cognitive overload. *Intellectica, 1*(30), 19–51.

Kotsiantis, S., & Kanellopoulos, (2006). Association rules mining: a recent overview. *GESTS international transactions on computer science and engineering, 32*(1), 71-82.

Lindner, G., & Studer, R. (1999). AST: support for algorithm selection with a CBR approach. In *Proceedings of the 3rd European conference on principles and practice of knowledge discovery in databases* (pp.418-423).

Michie, D., & Spiegelhalter, D. (1996). Book review: Machine learning, neural and statistical classification (Edited by. Michie, D.J. Spiegelhalter and C.C. Taylor; Ellis Horwood Limited, 1994). *SIGART Bull, 7*(1), 16–17.

Mitchell, T. (1997). *Machine learning.* New York: McGraw-Hill.

Papoulis, A. (1991). *Probability, random variables, and stochastic processes* (3rd ed.). New York: McGraw Hill.

Pawlak, Z. (1982). Rough sets. *International Journal of Computer and Information Sciences, 11*, 341–356. doi:10.1007/BF01001956

Peng, Y., Flach, P. A., Brazdil, P., & Soares, C. (2002, August). Decision tree-based characterization for meta-learning. In M. Bohanec, B. Kasek, N. Lavrac, & D. Mladenic (Eds.), *Ecml/Pkdd'02 Workshop on Integration and Collaboration Aspects of Data Mining, Decision Support and Meta-Learning* (pp. 111-122). University of Helsinki.

Rendell, L., Seshu, R., & Tcheng, D. (1987). Layered concept-learning and dynamically-variable bias management. In . *Proceedings of, IJCAI-87*, 308–314.

Sleeman, D., Rissakis, M., Craw, S., Graner, N., & Sharma, S. (1995). Consultant-2: pre and post-processing of machine learning applications. *International Journal of Human-Computer Interaction, 43*(1), 43–63.

Soares, C., & Brazdil, P. (2000). Zoomed ranking: Selection of classification algorithms based on relevant performance information. In *Pkdd '00: Proceedings of the 4th European conference on principles of data mining and knowledge discovery* (pp. 126–135). London, UK: Springer-Verlag.

Tcheng, D., & Lambert, B. (1989). Building robust learning systems by combining induction and optimization. In *11th International Joint Conference on AI*.

Todorovski, L., Blockeel, H., & Dzeroski, S. (2002). Ranking with predictive clustering trees. In *Ecml '02: Proceedings of the 13th European conference on machine learning* (pp. 444–455). London, UK: Springer-Verlag.

Vilalta, R., & Drissi, Y. (2002). A perspective view and survey of metalearning. *Artificial Intelligence Review, 18*(2), 77–95. doi:10.1023/A:1019956318069

Wang, Y. (2003). Cognitive informatics: a new transdisciplinary research field. *Brain and Mind: A transdisciplinary Jounal of Neuroscience and Neurophilosophy, 4*, 115–127.

Wasserman, P. D. (1989). *Neural computing theory and practice*. Van Nostrand Reinhold.

Woods, D. D., Patterson, E. S., & Roth, E. M. (2002). Can we ever escape from data overload? A cognitive systems diagnosis. *Cognition Technology and Work, 4*, 22–36. doi:10.1007/s101110200002

Ziarko, W., & Shan, N. (1995). Discovering attribute relationships, dependencies and rules by using rough sets. In *Proceedings of the 28th annual Hawaii international conference on system sciences* (pp. 293–299).

Chapter 4
Analyzing Learning Methods in a Functional Environment

Alberto de la Encina
Universidad Complutense de Madrid, Spain

Mercedes Hidalgo-Herrero
Universidad Complutense de Madrid, Spain

Pablo Rabanal
Universidad Complutense de Madrid, Spain

Ismael Rodríguez
Universidad Complutense de Madrid, Spain

Fernando Rubio
Universidad Complutense de Madrid, Spain

ABSTRACT

Developing cognitive programs is a complex task. Thus, special purpose languages can help developing such systems. This chapter presents a programming environment to help studying the behavior of cognitive models. This environment allows to easily define new cognitive processes, it simplifies the methods to interconnect them, and it also provides graphical information to analyze how a complex cognitive system is evolving. Moreover, it also includes observation facilities, so that the user can analyze the internal behavior of each of the cognitive entities appearing in the system. The authors illustrate the usefulness of their system by using several examples within the chapter.

DOI: 10.4018/978-1-60566-902-1.ch004

ANALYZING LEARNING METHODS IN A FUNCTIONAL ENVIRONMENT

The relation between the Computer Science and other older well established sciences is known to be twofold. On the one hand, the Computer Science provides tools, automatic analysis techniques, and even new concepts to other sciences, which enables the construction of new methodologies and theories in these areas. On the other hand, many methods used in Computer Science are inspired in the nature. Examples of this relation are Ants-based Algorithms, Neural Networks, and river formation dynamics (Rabanal, Rubio, & Rodríguez, 2007, 2008). This twofold relation is particularly fruitful in the scope of Cognitive Science, which exploits the similarities between natural and artificial reasoning processes. In particular, the roots of several Artificial Intelligence algorithms are based on the cognitive processes of the brain, while simulating a cognitive process in a computational environment may help to validate/ refute a theory in the field of Neuroscience.

There is a topic that has been typically concerned by informatics scientists that, actually, fits perfectly in the context of Cognitive Informatics (Zhang et al., 2007; Wang, 2002; Wang & Kinsner, 2006; Kinsner, 2008). This is the relation between *artificial* cognitive processes and *human* cognitive processes. This issue has been addressed for years by computer scientists, and it is one of the main topics of interest in Artificial Intelligence. One of the first approaches proposed to relate both concepts was made by Alan Turing and it consists in a nowadays classical test. In brief, the *Turing test* (Saygin, Cicekli, & Akman, 2000; Turing, 1950) says that a system should be considered *intelligent* if its *behavior* cannot be distinguished from that of a human being.

Following this idea, in the long term we are specially interested in being able to compare how both automatic systems and humans learn the rules governing their environment. Let us note that comparing the learning processes of both humans and machines is hard because it requires to compare the cognitive theories each of them builds and refines along time. This enables the comparison of the levels of accurateness of each of them along time.

In this article, we will concentrate on developing an environment to help analyzing the behavior of an automatic system. We will be able to observe its external behavior by recording the relations between its input stimuli and its output responses. However, the most interesting part is that we will also be able to observe its internal behavior. That is, we will observe how the entity *constructs* its responses to the input stimuli.

In order to obtain our objectives, we will consider an specific programming environment. The main part of our programming environment is its core language. Eden (Klusik, Loogen, Priebe, & Rubio, 2001; Loogen, Ortega-Mallen, Pena, Priebe, & Rubio, 2002; Rubio & Rodríguez, 2003; Hidalgo-Herrero, Ortega-Mallen, & Rubio, 2006) is a parallel extension of the functional language Haskell (Jones & Hughes, 1999) which provides 'controlled' parallelism, as opposed both to more implicit approaches such as GpH (Glasgow Parallel Haskell) (Trinder et al., 1996, 1998) and to more explicit ones such as *Concurrent ML* (Reppy, 1991). In this sense, in Eden the programmer decides which expressions are processes and how processes are connected, having explicit control over the communication topology. The remaining aspects such as sending and receiving messages, process placement, data distribution, etc. are implicitly controlled by the runtime system. The parallel constructions of Eden allow to easily specify any topology. This is specially important when simulating the complex topologies that can appear in cognitive models. Moreover, Eden programming has the advantages of functional languages. That is, its high-level constructions simplifies the task of developing programs, and it facilitates the creation of executable templates that reduce the time needed to develop applications.

The structure of the rest of the paper is the following. In the next section we review some basic learning theories. In Section 2 we outline the main characteristic of our language. Then, in Section 3 we show how to implement cognitive models. Afterwards, Section 4 describes the basic details of our observing facilities, while Section 5 contains a detailed description about how to perform observations in a systematic way. Finally, in Section 6 we present our conclusions and some lines for future work.

LEARNING THEORIES

Before describing what kind of learning analysis we will be able to perform with our programming environment, we must remark that we are specially interested in being able to analyze how an automatic system can deduce the rules governing a situation.

We will base our observations and the players tasks on two main learning theories: behaviorism and constructivism. Before explaining how we use these models let us explain them:

Behaviorism: The aim of this theory is to use experimental methods to observe the behavior of the subject. With respect to learning, this premise leads to consider that learning happens just when a correct response is given after the presentation of a stimulus, and the trainer can detect whether the subject has learnt or not by observing his or her behavior over a period of time. Since the subject internal or mental processes cannot be observed directly by an experimental method, this theory does not worry about them. The main tool to motivate the learning is the use of reinforcements of learned behaviors.

Constructivism: This model states that learning takes place when the subject experiments and interacts with the environment. She learns via the action (Piaget, 1973). Thus, knowledge is embedded in the meaningful tasks that the teacher poses to the learner. The latter assembles his or her knowledge by composing and modifying it when he or she has to solve the problem at hand.

With respect to the way of instruction, behaviorism transmits or transfers behaviors representing knowledge. However, constructivism focuses on the building of knowledge from the experience. That is, from a constructivist point of view, learning is a process of building rather than an acquisition of knowledge.

THE PROGRAMMING LANGUAGE

Before describing how to take advantage of our environment, let us sketch the main features of our core language. Eden (Loogen et al., 2002; Rubio & Rodríguez, 2003, 2004) extends the lazy functional language Haskell (Jones & Hughes, 1999) by adding syntactic constructions to explicitly define and instantiate processes. It is possible to define a new *process abstraction* p by using the following notation that relates the inputs and the outputs of the process: p = process x->e where variable x will be the input of the process, while the behavior of the process will be given by expression e. In the general case, where a process has several inputs and also several outputs, each of the communication channels can be named explicitly. For instance, the following process has three inputs and two outputs:

```
p = process (in1,in2,in3) -> (out1,out2)
  where out1 =  ...
        out2 =  ...
```

Note that the only thing the programmer needs to do is to explain how the outputs are to be computed by taking into account the inputs.

Process abstractions are not actual processes. In order to really create a process, a *process instantiation* is required. This is achieved by using #, a predefined infix operator. Given a process abstraction and an input parameter, it creates a new process, and returns the output of the process. Each time an expression c1 # c2 is evaluated, the invoker process will be responsible for evaluating and sending e2, while a new process is created to evaluate the application (e1 e2). In the general case, when a process has several inputs and outputs, we can also name explicitly each of them. For instance, we can instantiate as follows the process p defined above:

```
(realout1,realout2) = p # (realin1, realin2, realin3)
```

By using process abstractions and instantiations we can specify any topology connecting cognitive entities: For each conceptual entity we will define a process abstraction, specifying the number of inputs and outputs that they should have, and specifying how to obtain the outputs by taking into account the inputs. Then, each cognitive entity will be instantiated as many times as needed, specifying the connections that are needed to simulate the real behavior. For instance, in case we have defined the behavior of an agent that is able both to interact with the environment and with another agent, we could connect two agents as follows:

```
(out1ToEnv,out1ToPartner)=agent # (in1FromEnv,in1FromPartner)
(out2ToEnv,out2ToPartner)=agent # (in2FromEnv,in2FromPartner)
in1FromPartner = out2ToPartner
in2FromPartner = out1ToPartner
```

In order to connect the output of one agent to the input of the other, it is enough to specify the correct data dependencies.

In addition to process abstractions and instantiations, Eden provides a predefined function called merge that combines a list of inputs into a single one. This is useful to select from a list of alternatives, and also to take into account several of them to generate a single output. In particular, it can be used as a way to represent free will, because it allows the internal process to select from a list of alternatives without the direct control of the programmer. For instance, let us suppose that in one situation an agent can choose either to try to find food or to try to sleep. In this case, we can use merge2 (a particular case of merge, used to choose between only two alternatives) to join both alternatives, so that the agent can internally decide (randomly) what she wants to do. The source code needed to describe this situation is quite simple. In fact, the only piece of code that need to be used is given below. The first line describes how to call to the function, while the last lines describe the functions.

```
... decision (merge2 eating sleeping)
      ...
decision (Left x: _) = ... {try to find food}
decision (Right y: _) = ... {try to sleep}
```

where function decision can either make pattern matching with the first or the second alternative, as desired.

Basic Environment

Eden's compiler has been developed by extending the most efficient Haskell compiler (GHC (Jones, Hall, Hammond, & Partain, 1992; Jones, 1996)). An important feature of Eden's compiler is that it reuses GHC's capabilities to interact with other programming languages. So, Eden can be used as a coordination language, while the computation language can be, for instance, C. That is, Eden will be used to specify the connection topologies of the cognitive entities, while the behavior of each of them can be implemented in other language: It will only be necessary to provide the corresponding definition relating inputs with outputs.

In order to easily port the compiler to different architectures, Eden's runtime system has been designed to work on top of a message passing library. In the current compiler, the user can choose between PVM (Geist, Beguelin, Dongarra, & Jiang, 1994) and MPI (MPI, 1994).

An important advantage about using Eden to describe cognitive processes is that we have implemented a set of tools that allows visualizing the behavior of the programs. The name of our visualizing environment is Paradise. It can help us to understand the behavior of a specification with graphs like the one presented in Figure 1. In this setting, the y axis represents the number of processes to be studied in the system, while the x axis represents the evolution in time. Two different colors are used for each type of process (in our case, there are two types: *conscious* and *subconscious*). The first color is used to represent how many processes of that type are currently active, while the second one is used to represent how many of them are currently inactive. In the graph, it can be seen that initially there are not many conscious processes active. Then, after some time, conscious activity starts to be more intense. This can be easily seen because the color of the processes change, denoting the transition to an active mode. However, the graph also shows that the intense conscious activity only takes a while, as it suddenly decreases again.

Figure 1. Simulation of a cognitive model

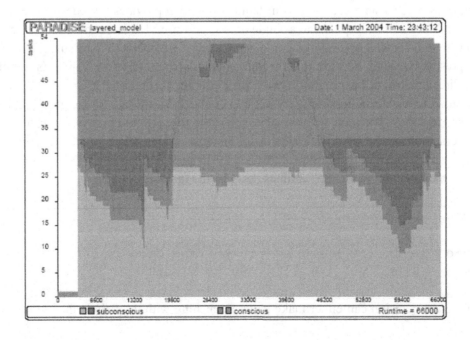

Let us remark that there is a strong similarity between this kind of graphs and the study of cerebral activity with scanners of the cerebral activity. The main difference is that we are not dealing with real systems, but only with simulations. Thus, even though we are not studying the behavior of the actual cognitive entities, we have a powerful tool to test/develop predictions of our cognitive models in a much simpler way.

DEFINING COGNITIVE PROCESSES

Process abstractions in Eden are not just annotations, but first class values which can be manipulated by the programmer (i.e. passed as parameters, stored in data structures, and so on). This facilitates the definition of general schemes by using higher order functions. Moreover, and what is more important, these schemes can be trivially used by anybody to test modifications to cognitive models without needing to know how to define Eden processes. In this section we illustrate, by using simple examples, how these schemes can be written in Eden.

Following the layered reference model presented in Wang, Wang, Patel, and Patel (2006), we can describe the life functions of the brain by decomposing them into several layers. The four layers at the bottom of the hierarchy deal with subconscious tasks, while the top two layers deal with the conscious functions (see Figure 2). Moreover, each of the six layers requires complex internal structures to actually describe them. Thus, it is interesting to be able to obtain an implementation of the hierarchy where the programmer can modify easily the parts that she is interested in, while the rest of the hierarchy is kept unchanged.

Let us comment on how to implement the layered reference model in Eden. First of all, the brain functions can be decomposed into two categories: the conscious and the subconscious. Thus, we can say that a brain process receives two kinds of inputs: conscious inputs (ci) and subconscious inputs (si). Analogously, it also generates two kinds of outputs. Moreover, the internal structure can be described by means of two entities: the one corresponding to the conscious functions, and the one corresponding to the subconscious ones. The Eden program describing this structure is the following one:

```
brain = process (ci, si) -> (co, so)
   where (co, cTOs) = conscious # (ci, sTOc)
          (so, sTOc) = subconscious # (si, cTOs)
```

Notice that conscious and subconscious functions are not completely independent. In fact, there can be information flowing from the conscious to the unconscious and viceversa. This is the reason why the (sub)conscious part has two inputs, and also two outputs: Value cTOs is used as a mechanism to transmit information from the conscious to the subconscious, while sTOc allows transmitting information in the opposite sense. The only thing that we need to do to properly connect conscious and subconscious functions is to use the same name for the output values of one of them and the input values of the other one.

Once the general structure is defined, we can refine each of the processes to better describe the layered model. As described in "Wang et al. (2006)," the conscious functions can be divided into two layers (the higher cognitive functions and the meta cognitive functions). Following the same pattern

Figure 2. Layered reference model of the brain. (See (Wang et al., 2006), for details.)

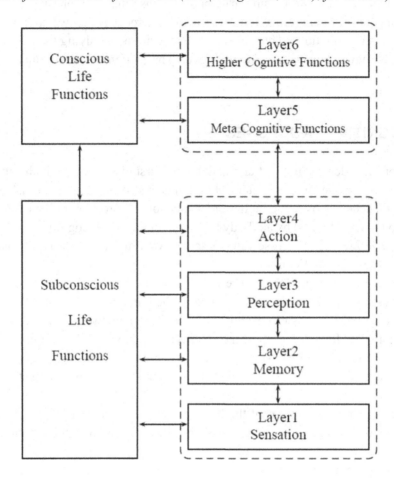

as before, we can easily split the conscious process into two layers. The only thing we need to do is to provide the following source code:

```
conscious = process (ci, sTOc) -> (co, cTOs)
    where (co6,c6TOc5) = layer6 # (ci6, c5TOc6)
          (co5,cTOs,c5TOc6) = layer5 # (ci5, sTOc, c6TOc5)
          (ci5,ci6) = ci
          co = (co5, co6)
```

Note that the idea behind this refinement is the same as when defining the process brain. Each layer makes explicit its list of inputs and outputs, and the proper connections are performed. In this sense, it is worth to point out that the externally visible inputs to the conscious (ci) are internally split into two different inputs (ci5 and ci6), and analogously with the outputs. Let us also note that one of the outputs of layer5 is cTOs, as this layer is the one that interacts with the subconscious functionalities. However, in case layer6 also needs access to the subconscious, layer5 can always retransmit the appropriate information. Following the same ideas as before, we can also define the subconscious process in an analogous way:

```
subconscious  = process (si, cTOs) -> (so, sTOc)
   where (co4, s4TOs3, sTOc) = layer4 # (si4, s3TOs4, cTOs)
           (co3, s3TOs2, s3TOs4) = layer3 # (si3, s2TOs3,s4TOs3)
           (co2, s2TOs1, s2TOs3) = layer2 # (si2, s1TOs2,s3TOs2)
           (co1, s1TOs2) = layer1 # (si1, s2TOs1)
           (si1, si2, si3, si4) = si
           so = (so1, so2, so3, so4)
```

Once we have a general scheme, we can concentrate on the definition of each of the layers. For each of them we can use a completely different topology, following the appropriate cognitive models. The interested reader can find more details about how to define them in Rubio and Rodríguez (2004).

INTRODUCING OBSERVATIONS IN EDEN

Once we know how to develop cognitive entities with our language, let us consider how we can introduce observations. In order to do that, we will extend the Hood system (Gill, 2000; Encina, Llana, & Rubio, 2005, 2006; Encina, Llana, Rubio, Hidalgo-Herrero, 2007; Encina, Rodríguez, & Rubio, 2008). Thus, before describing how we can use it with cognitive processes, we start by illustrating what kind of observations can be obtained by using Hood, and then we will show how to implement it. Let us consider an example. It will be complex enough to highlight important aspects of Hood, but also relatively simple to be easily understandable without requiring knowledge about Haskell. Given a natural number, the following Haskell function returns the list of digits of that number:[1]

```
natural:: Int -> [Int]
natural = reverse
                                    . map ('mod' 10)
                                    . takeWhile (/= 0)
                                    . iterate ('div' 10)
```

That is, natural 3408 returns the list 3:4:0:8:[], where [] denotes the empty list and: denotes the list constructor. Note that, in order to compute the final result, three intermediate lists where produced in the following order:

```
-- after iterate
3408:340:34:3:0:_
-- after takeWhile
3408:340:34:3:[]
-- after map
8:0:4:3:[]
```

Notice that the first intermediate list is infinite, although only the first five elements are computed. As the rest of the list does not need to be evaluated, it is represented as _ (the underscore char).

By using Hood we can annotate the program in order to obtain the output shown before. In order to do that, we have to use the observe combinator that is the core of Hood. The type declaration of this combinator is: observe::String -> a -> a. From the evaluation point of view, observe only returns its second value. That is, observe s a = a. However, as a side effect, the value associated to a will be written, using the label s, in a file that will be analyzed after the evaluation finishes. It is important to remark that observe returns its second parameter in a completely lazy, demand driven manner. That is, the evaluation degree of a is not modified by introducing the observation, in the same way that it is not modified when applying the identity function id. Thus, as the evaluation degree is not modified, Hood can deal with infinite lists like the one appearing after applying iterate(‘div‘ 10).

If we consider again our previous example, we can observe all of the intermediate structures by introducing three observations as follows:

```
natural:: Int -> [Int]
natural = reverse
                        . observe "after map"
                        . map ('mod' 10)
                        . observe "after takeWhile"
                        . takeWhile (/= 0)
                        . observe "after iterate"
                        . iterate ('div' 10)
```

After executing natural 3408, we will obtain the desired result. Hood does not only observe simple structures like those shown before. In fact, it can observe anything appearing in a Haskell program, including functions. For instance,

```
(observe "length" length) (4:2:5:[])
```

will generate the following observation:

```
-- length
  { \ (_:_:_:[]) -> 3 }
```

That is, we are observing a function that returns the number 3 (without evaluating the concrete elements appearing in the list) when it receives a list with three elements. Let us remark that it is only relevant the number of elements, but not the *concrete* elements. That is, the observation mechanism detects that the laziness of the language will not demand the concrete elements to compute the overall output. As it can be expected, higher-order functions can also be observed.

Basic Ideas of our Implementation

In this section we introduce the main details of the implementation of our analysis scheme. Let us note that one of the main difficulties to implement our framework is an intrinsic feature of Eden as well as of any other parallel functional language: The absence of state. Due to this characteristic, tracing issues have to be dealt with in a different manner to that used in other programming paradigms. In particular, our observation mechanism cannot be based on observing how some variables change, because variables do not exist in lazy functional systems. Besides, let us remind that the laziness is locally applied to each process, which means that any computation is executed only if either it is actually required by other computation in the *same* process or it *could* be required by other computations in another process. This means that we have two possibilities to perform an observation in a process: Either the result of the observation is *demanded* by another computation in the process, or the observation is performed in a *new* process, which would allow it to be performed regardless of whether it produces any result that is demanded by other computation. The second solution is not only inefficient but also useless for our purposes: Since we are interested in observing the result of computations *inside* each process, observations have to be performed where the corresponding results are obtained.

So, in order to ensure that the observations are performed, we need the result of each computation to be demanded by other computations in the same process. There is a similar issue in lazy functional programming whose standard solution inspires a customized solution to our problem. Interacting with the input/output (e.g., the screen, the keyboard, a file, etc.) in an Eden program faces difficulties that are similar to those in our problem. This is because the result of writing a text is not demanded by other computations: It just stays in the screen, file, etc. To provide a simple and intuitive notation to interact with the outside world, Eden (as well as its sequential counterpart, Haskell) provides *monads*, which are functions where a parameter is *hidden*. This allows representing the standard output by a parameter that is not explicitly given. By doing so, a sequence of interactions with the outside can be written in a similar way as it is written in an imperative language: Each interaction is written after each other in the order in which they must occur. If the appropriate monadic like notation is used then the output of each interaction (e.g., the *state* of the screen at a given moment) is implicitly assumed to be the input of the next interaction as they are ordered, and so on.

By using monads in our framework, the result of each observation can be properly sent to a log file. This feature is provided by Hood and its function observe, which encapsulates the required interaction with the outside world in a monadic style. Unfortunately, Hood provides us with the required tracing capabilities only in a *sequential* environment, but we need to observe the behavior of each process in a parallel environment. In particular, we need to *independently* observe the information concerning each process in the program. So, we need to take the control over where and when each tracing information is written. This requires to redefine some of the functionalities provided by Hood. In particular, we have modified the (sequential) tracing monad to provide a new parallel version. The aim of this modification is to send the information collected in each processor to a different file. By using a suitable implementation of the observation procedure, the required information is finally collected in the corresponding files. Then, our post-processing functionalities compute and organize the tracing information contained in the files, which concerns the behavior of the program at each point.

OBSERVING ENTITIES

In this section we show how we can use the features presented in the previous section in order to analyze cognitive entities.

Behavioral Observations

If we consider the behaviorism model, an entity can be analyzed by just observing its external behavior. That is, this theory only considers what outputs are produced for each stimulus provided as input. We can easily introduce observations to perform this task. For instance, in the layered reference model of the brain, we can observe the data that is sent to each layer by annotating the second parameter of the # instantiating operator. Following this idea, the conscious process could be rewritten as follows:

```
conscious     = process (ci, sTOc) -> (co, cTOs)
   where (co6,c6TOc5) = layer6 # (observe "in6" (ci6, c5TOc6))
         (co5,cTOs,c5TOc6)
          = layer5#(observe "in5" (ci5, sTOc, c6TOc5))
         (ci5,ci6) = ci
         co = (co5, co6)
```

Moreover, the output of each layer can also be observed by annotating the output of each process abstraction. In particular, we can also annotate the output of the conscious subsystem. This can be done by introducing a new observation in the corresponding process abstraction. Thus, the conscious process could be rewritten as follows:

```
conscious
    = process (ci, sTOc) -> (observe "outConscious" (co, cTOs))
   where (co6,c6TOc5) = layer6 # (observe "in6" (ci6, c5TOc6))
         (co5,cTOs,c5TOc6)
              = layer5 # (observe "in5" (ci5, sTOc, c6TOc5))
         (ci5,ci6) = ci
         co = (co5, co6)
```

Obviously, following a similar approach we can also annotate the subconscious subsystem: the input of each layer can be observed by annotating the second parameter of the # operator, while the output of the processes can be observed by annotating the output of the process abstractions:

```
subconscious
    = process (si, cTOs) ->       (observe "outSubconscious"(so, sTOc)
   where (co4, s4TOs3, sTOc)
             = layer4 # (observe "in4" (si4,s3TOs4,cTOs))
         (co3, s3TOs2, s3TOs4)
             = layer3 # (observe "in3" (si3,s2TOs3,s4TOs3))
         (co2, s2TOs1, s2TOs3)
             = layer2 # (observe "in2" (si2,s1TOs2,s3TOs2))
         (co1, s1TOs2)
             = layer1 # (observe "in1" (si1,s2TOs1))
         (si1, si2, si3, si4) = si
         so = (so1, so2, so3, so4)
```

Notice that it is relatively simple to introduce the appropriate observations. However, it can be time consuming to do it when many processes are available. In this sense, it could be better to provide pre-defined operators including observing facilities. In fact, next we present a redefinition of the basic Eden constructors. This redefinition performs all the required observations in such a way that the user can forget any details concerning observations: He must just instantiate the processes he wants to analyze by calling the functions provided by the new constructors. Then, the system automatically reports any change on both its input and its output. By applying the new observation constructors to both an invoker and an instantiated process, all the needed information will be properly reported. Thus, if we want to observe the inputs and outputs of a process that computes a given function f then, instead of directly using f, we will call the following function processObs using f as parameter:

```
processObs f = process ins -> (observe "outsFromProcess" outs)
   where outs = f ins
```

The previous function defines a process with input ins. After function f is normally applied to the input, the output outs is obtained. The observation of this term (labelled by outsFromProcess) reports the data this process transmits to its creator.

The previous function allows us to observe the treatment of the outputs of the instantiated process. Similarly, we need a new functionality to observe the behavior of the invoker process. Next we redefine the process instantiation operator to include the observation capabilities. The new operator, based on the standard operator #, is ##:

```
p ## actualParameters
   = (p # (observe "outsToProcess" actualParameters))
```

The new operator allows any process to instantiate a new process by using the standard one. Besides, an observation is introduced to report the values that have been sent to the new process. Observations labelled by outsToProcess report the data that is sent from the invoker to the instantiated process (regardless of whether the instantiated process requires them).

Constructivism Observations

In order to perform a behavioral analysis, the previous schemes are enough, as they can be used to obtain both the inputs and outputs of any process appearing in the environment. However, a more complex approach is needed in case we also want to analyze the internal details of the entities. That is, in case we want to know how the entities *construct* their responses by considering their input stimuli. In order to analyze it, we will start with the simplest part of the analysis: Detecting what parts of the input stimuli are relevant and what parts are completely irrelevant for producing their response. In this sense, it is important to remark that we can use basically the same mechanism as before. The only difference is that we have to observe not only the values sent as outputs from one entity to another one, but also the *inputs actually used* by each entity. Notice that the inputs actually used by an entity are not necessarily all of the inputs received. For instance, an entity receiving a list of ten inputs could only need to use four of them to decide how to proceed.

In this sense, it is worth to remind that the observe primitive provides us information about what was really needed to obtain the output. For instance, when writing

```
(observe "length" length) (4:2:5:[])
```

we obtain the observation

```
-- length
  { \ (_:_:_:[]) -> 3 }
```

representing that it was necessary to count all the input values, but it was not necessary to process any particular input value. Analogously, when writing something like

```
(observe "take 2" (take 2)) (4:2:5:3:8:[])
```

we obtain the observation

```
-- take 2
   { \ (4:2:_) -> 4:2:[] }
```

representing that it was necessary to use the first two values, but it was completely irrelevant the rest of the values of the input list.

In order to observe not only the values produced/received by the entities, but also the values actually consumed, we redefine the basic operators by adding two additional observations. In the process abstraction we add an observation insToProcess to detect what values received by a newly created entity are actually needed by the process to obtain its output:

```
processObs f = process ins -> (observe "outsFromProcess" outs)
   where outs = f ins'
            ins' = observe "insToProcess" ins
```

Analogously, when instantiating a new process we need to detect what values sent by the new process are actually required by the invoker entity:

```
p ## actualParameters
   = observe "insFromProcess"
              (p # (observe "outsToProcess" actualParameters))
```

Figure 3 summarizes what is being observed after the redefinition of the two basic operators. By combining the new process abstraction processAbs and ## we obtain the four basic pieces of information we were looking for. For instance, by using insToProcess and outsFromProcess we can analyze the actual relation between the inputs and outputs of a concrete process. That is, we can detect whether a concrete input is relevant or not to obtain the corresponding outputs. Moreover, a simple comparison between

Figure 3. Invoker and Instantiated Processes

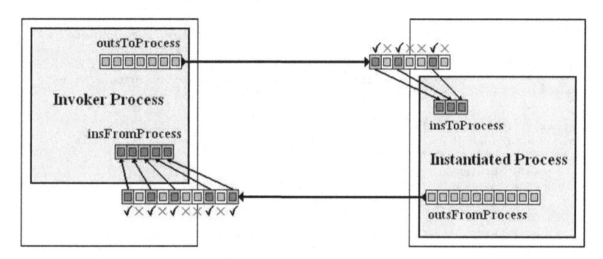

outsToProcess and insToProcess allows to detect the aspects where the new process ignores its relation with its environment.

Although the previous pieces of information are quite relevant, they are not enough to perform a detailed analysis from a constructivism point of view. In order to do that, we need to analyze not only what inputs are really relevant, but also *how* the process *constructs* its decisions by using its input stimuli. Fortunately, our observing facilities do not only observe basic data structures: As we are using a higher-order language, we can also deal with the observation of the functions governing the behavior of the entities. In fact, we can also observe the internal details of the computation, even when the computations require the use of higher-order functions. In order to show a simple example, let us suppose that we are dealing with a simple checkers player. From the behaviorism point of view, we can analyze the checkers-player entity by only analyzing its inputs and outputs. However, in order to analyze how the checkers-player actually plays, we need to observe its internal structure to discover what kind of strategy it uses.

In order to do that, we have to introduce the observe primitive attached to the main function describing the entity, not attached to the inputs or outputs. The following scheme follows this idea:

```
processObs f = process ins -> outs
    where outs = (observe "mainFunction" f) ins
```

However, by only using this scheme we only analyze the toplevel structure. Fortunately, we can nest our observations as needed.

We have already implemented a checkers player in our language. The concrete implementation we have used is based on the minimax algorithm. Minimax is a typical algorithm used in two players games where players perform moves by turns. The aim is to find the best move the computer can perform at its turn.

A search tree containing all possible situations after n moves is generated. Afterwards, each of the leaves is assigned a number representing its valuation: The larger the number is, the better the position is

Figure 4. Minimax in Eden, observing the heuristic method

```
data DataIn = DataIn Int                    -- Number of parallel levels
                    Int                     -- Number of levels to explore
                    (Int -> Int -> Int)     -- Maximize (or minimize) function
                    (Int -> Int -> Int)     -- Minimize (or maximize) function
                    (Board -> Int)          -- Heuristic to evaluate a board
                    Board                   -- State of the game

minimax :: Process DataIn Int
minimax = process (DataIn depth_par depth f1 f2 evaluate state) -> result
    where
      nexts = obtainNexts state
      outs  = [minimax # (DataIn (depth_par - 1) (depth - 1) f2 f1 evaluate next) |
               next <- nexts]
      result
        | null nexts || (depth == 0) = (observe "heuristic" evaluate) state
        | depth_par == 0             = minimaxSeq depth f1 f2 evaluate state
        | otherwise                  = foldr1 f1 outs
```

for the computer. Finally, the internal nodes of the tree are evaluated, using its children values as follows: If the node corresponds to an opponent move, the minimum value of the children is selected; otherwise the maximum is selected. Thus, minimizing and maximizing levels alternate in the tree.

This problem can be easily solved using a functional language, as described by Hughes in "Hughes (1989)". The basic part of the Eden source can be seen in Figure 4, where we have introduced an observation to analyze the heuristic that the system is using to decide how to move. Obviously, it is also trivial to add more observations. For instance, in Figure 5 we have also introduced another observation to analyze the minimax method itself. This second observation allows to observe the depth of the search tree that is being used, the maximizing and minimizing methods, etc. In fact, it is possible to add as many observations as needed. In Figure 5 we have shown how to observe two pieces of information, but we could also introduce observations in any part of the code. For instance, we could also observe how many levels of the search tree is using the program to select its next movement. This piece of information is quite relevant in case we want to know how much effort is being performed by the machine.

We would like to highlight that we can observe systems as complex as desired. That is, we do not only observe deterministic programs where the behaviour is completely defined by the programmer. In fact, we can observe anything. Let us remind that Eden includes facilities for implementing systems where free-will is relevant. As a very short example, let us consider the following piece of code extracted from "López, Nunez, and Rubio (2004)":

```
stabilizer = process restartcs -> (sleeps, crashs)
    where fails = merge [gyro # (restarts,ackss!!i)| i <-[0..5]]
          (sleeps,crashs,restarts,ackss)=ctrol#(fails,restartcs)
```

The only relevant part for our current purposes is that it uses the predefined construction merge for *deciding* dynamically what it should do. Let us remind that function merge takes as input a list of alternatives and it internally selects what to do next. Thus, in case we want to analyse the internal decisions

Figure 5. Minimax in Eden, observing also the minimax itself

```
data DataIn = DataIn Int                        -- Number of parallel levels
                    Int                         -- Number of levels to explore
                    (Int -> Int -> Int)         -- Maximize (or minimize) function
                    (Int -> Int -> Int)         -- Minimize (or maximize) function
                    (Board -> Int)              -- Heuristic to evaluate a board
                    Board                       -- State of the game

minimax :: Process DataIn Int
minimax = process (DataIn depth_par depth f1 f2 evaluate state) -> result
  where
    nexts = obtainNexts state
    outs  = [minimax # (DataIn (depth_par - 1) (depth - 1) f2 f1 evaluate next) |
            next <- nexts]
    result
      | null nexts   || (depth == 0) = (observe "heuristic" evaluate) state
      | depth_par == 0               = (observe "minimax" minimaxSeq)
                                                depth f1 f2 evaluate state
      | otherwise                    = foldr1 f1 outs
```

taken by the system without the direct control of its designer, we can consider the following redefinition of the basic merge function:

```
mergeObs options = observe "outDecisions" (merge obsOptions)
  where obsOptions = observe "inOptions" options
```

By using it, we can trivially rewrite our piece of code to obtain information about the internal decisions taken by the system:

```
stabilizer = process restartcs -> (sleeps, crashs)
  where fails = mergeObs[gyro # (restarts,ackss!!i)|i<-[0..5]]
        (sleeps,crashs,restarts,ackss)=ctrol#(fails,restartcs)
```

As it can be expected, we can also include more detailed information about the internal decisions of the system in case we also observe function merge itself.

CONCLUSION AND CURRENT WORK

We have presented a framework that allows to define and also to analyze cognitive processes. We are specially interested in being able to analyze how a cognitive process learns the rules governing its environment. Thus, we have implemented observation facilities to help analyzing this issue. Our observation facilities do not only provide information about the external behavior of the entities, but also about their internal way of work. That is, we can analyze how they construct their responses to the input stimuli they receive. Obviously, now that we have developed our observation mechanisms, the next step is to use it intensively to analyze concrete problems. In this sense, we must remark that the most interesting example for us will be the one presented in "Hidalgo-Herrero, Rodríguez, and Rubio (2005)".

The overall aim of our line of work is to compare the learning strategies used by humans and by automatic programmed environments. In particular, one of our main running examples is the system we presented in "Hidalgo-Herrero et al. (2005)". This is a friendly model called *Troglodytes*. In this system, we have some troglodytes trying to survive by recollecting bananas, hunting dinosaurs cooperatively, escaping from dangerous cavernous lions, and reproducing themselves to spread all around their world. These troglodytes have to learn what are the rules governing their environment (lions are dangerous, bananas are profitable, etc). Moreover, the same environment is provided to actual persons, and they also have to learn by themselves the rules governing their environment in the game.

REFERENCES

Encina, A., Llana, L., & Rubio, F. (2005). Formalizing the debugging process in Haskell. In *Proceedings of International Conference on Theoretical Aspects of Computing, (ICTAC'05)* (LNCS 3772, pp. 211–226). Springer-Verlag.

Encina, A., Llana, L., & Rubio, F. (2006). Introducing debugging capabilities to natural semantics. In *Proceedings of 6th International Andrei Ershov Memorial Conference, Perspectives of System Informatics, (PSI'06)* (LNCS 4378, pp. 195–208). Springer-Verlag.

Encina, A., Llana, L., Rubio, F., & Hidalgo-Herrero, M. (2007). Observing intermediate structures in a parallel lazy functional language. In *Proceedings of 9th International ACM SIGPLAN Conference on Principles and Practice of Declarative Programming, (PPDP'07)*, (pp. 109-120). ACM Press.

Encina, A., Rodríguez, I., & Rubio, F. (2008). A debugger for parallel Haskell dialects. In *Proceedings of 8th International Conference on Algorithms and Architectures for Parallel Processing, (ICA3PP'08)* (LNCS 5022, pp. 282–293). Springer-Verlag.

Geist, A., Beguelin, A., Dongarra, J., & Jiang, W. (1994). *PVM: Parallel Virtual Machine*. MIT Press.

Gill, A. (2000). Debugging Haskell by observing intermediate data structures. In *Proceedings of the 4th Haskell Workshop*. Technical Report of the University of Nottingham.

Hidalgo-Herrero, Ortega-Mallén, Y., & Rubio, F. (2006). Analyzing the influence of mixed evaluation on the performance of Eden skeletons. *Parallel Computing, 32*, 528–538.

Hidalgo-Herrero, M., Rodríguez, I., & Rubio, F. (2005). Testing learning strategies. In *Proceedings of the 4th IEEE International Conference on Cognitive Informatics (ICCI'05)* (pp. 212–221). IEEE-CS Press.

Hughes, R. (1989). Why Functional Programming Matters. *The Computer Journal, 32*(2), 98–107. doi:10.1093/comjnl/32.2.98

Jones, S. L. P. (1996). Compiling Haskell by program transformation: A report from the trenches. In *ESOP'96 —European Symposium on Programming* (LNCS 1058, pp. 18–44). Springer-Verlag.

Jones, S. L. P., Hall, C. V., Hammond, K., & Partain, W. (1992). *The Glasgow Haskell compiler: a technical overview.* Computer Science Dept., Glasgow University.

Jones, S. L. P., & Hughes, J. (1999, February). *Report on the programming language Haskell 98.* (Tech. Rep.).

Kinsner, W. (2008). Complexity and its measures in cognitive and other complex systems. In *Proceedings of the 7th IEEE International Conference on Cognitive Informatics, (ICCI'08)* (pp.121-123). IEEE-CS Press.

Klusik, U., Loogen, R., Priebe, S., & Rubio, F. (2001). Implementation skeletons in Eden: Low-effort parallel programming. In *Proceedings of the Implementation of Functional Languages (IFL'00)* (LNCS 2011, pp. 71–88). Springer-Verlag.

Loogen, R., Ortega-Mallén, Y., Peña, R., Priebe, S., & Rubio, F. (2002). Parallelism abstractions in Eden. In *Proceedings of the Patterns and Skeletons for Parallel and Distributed Computing* (pp. 95-128). Springer-Verlag.

López, N., Núñez, M., & Rubio, F. (2004). An integrated framework for the performance analysis of asynchronous communicating stochastic processes. In *Formal Aspects of Computing 16*(3), 238-262. Springer-Verlag.

MPI. (1994). A message passing interface standard. *International Journal of Supercomputer Applications, 8*(3) & *8*(4).

Piaget, J. (1973). *Introduction à l'Épistemologie Genetique.* PUF, Paris.

Rabanal, P., Rubio, F., & Rodríguez, I. (2007). Using River Formation Dynamics to Design Heuristic Algorithms. In *Proceedings of the 6th International Conference on Unconventional Computation, (UC'07)* (LNCS 4618, pp. 163-177). Springer-Verlag.

Rabanal, P., Rubio, F., & Rodríguez, I. (2008). Finding Minimum Spanning/Distances Trees by Using River Formation Dynamics. In *Proceedings of the 6th International Conference on Ant Colony Optimization and Swarm Intelligence, (ANTS'08)* (LNCS 5217, pp. 60-71). Springer-Verlag.

Reppy, J. H. (1991). CML: A higher-order concurrent language. In *Proceedings of the ACM SIGPLAN Conference on Programing Language Design and Implementation* (pp. 293-305). ACM Press.

Rubio, F., & Rodríguez, I. (2003). A parallel framework for computational science. In *Proceedings of the International Conference on Computational Science (ICCS'03)* (LNCS 2658, pp. 1002-1011). Springer-Verlag.

Rubio, F., & Rodríguez, I. (2004). A parallel language for cognitive informatics. In *Proceedings of the 3rd IEEE International Conference on Cognitive Informatics (ICCI'04)* (pp. 32-41). IEEE-CS Press.

Saygin, A., Cicekli, I., & Akman, V. (2000). Turing test: 50 years later. *MANDMS: Minds and Machines, 10*, 463–518. doi:10.1023/A:1011288000451

Trinder, P. W., Hammond, K., Loidl, H. W., & Jones, S. L. P. (1998). Algorithm + strategy = parallelism. *Journal of Functional Programming, 8*(1). doi:10.1017/S0956796897002967

Trinder, P. W., Hammond, K., Partridge, A. S., & Jones, S. L. P. (1996). GUM: A portable parallel implementation of Haskell. In *Proceedings of Programming Language Design and Implementation (PLDI'96)* (pp. 79-88). ACM Press.

Turing, A. (1950). Computing machinery and intelligence. *Mind*, *59*(236), 433–460. doi:10.1093/mind/LIX.236.433

Wang, Y. (2002). On cognitive informatics. In *Proceedings of the 1st IEEE International Conference on Cognitive Informatics (ICCI'02)* (pp. 34-42). IEEE-CS Press.

Wang, Y., & Kinsner, W. (2006, March). Recent advances in cognitive informatics. *IEEE Transactions on Systems, Man and Cybernetics. Part C, Applications and Reviews*, *36*(2), 121–123. doi:10.1109/TSMCC.2006.871120

Wang, Y., Wang, Y., Patel, S., & Patel, D. (2006, March). A layered reference model of the brain. *IEEE Transactions on Systems, Man and Cybernetics. Part C, Applications and Reviews*, *36*(2), 124–133. doi:10.1109/TSMCC.2006.871126

Zhang, D., Kinsner, W., Tsai, J., Wang, Y., Sheu, P., & Wang, T. (2007). Cognitive informatics in practice – a report of IEEE ICCI 2005. *International Journal of Cognitive Informatics and Natural Intelligence*, *1*(1), 79–83.

ENDNOTES

[1] The first line of the definition only provides the type declaration of the function: given an integer it returns a list of integers. The other four lines define the sequence of functions to be applied to obtain the overall effect, being reverse the last one to be applied. The higher-order function iterate applies infinite times the first function it receives. For instance, applying iterate (+3) 1 returns the infinite list 1:4:7:10:13:...

[2] Research partially supported by the Spanish MCYT project TIN2006-15578-C02-01, the Junta de Castilla-La Mancha project PAC-06-0008-6995, and the Marie Curie project MRTN-CT-2003-505121/TAROT.

Chapter 5
Humans and Machines:
Nature of Learning and Learning of Nature

Hélène Hagège
Université Montpellier, France

Christopher Dartnell
LIRMM, France

Éric Martin
University of New South Wales, Australia

Jean Sallantin
LIRMM, France

ABSTRACT

Old and recent theories stress that any understanding of the processes by which humans can learn requires to fully appreciate the relationships between the "nature of learning" and the "learning of nature." From a constructivist viewpoint, acquiring knowledge is, like any human activity, dissociable neither from its underlying project nor from the knowing subject. The authors of this chapter relate the lessons from philosophy, psychology, didactics and ethics to their work in computational scientific discovery that aims at empowering learning machines with the task of assisting human researchers (Dartnell, Martin, Hagège, & Sallantin, 2008). The chapter concludes with didactical and ethical considerations.

INTRODUCTION

Reflecting on learning, knowledge and reality is consubstantial with occidental philosophy, from its very origin in ancient Greece, more than two thousand years ago. Since that time and right to the 20th century, philosophy and what we today call "science" – the *phusikè* of Aristotle (384 BC – 322 BC) – were viewed as one and the same activity. Descartes (1596 – 1650), considered as the initiator of modern philosophy, exposed in his *Discourse on the Method of Rightly Conducting the Reason, and Searching for Truth in the Sciences* (1637) a way of considering the relationship between on one hand an agent thinking on reality, and on the other hand the preconditions and actions from which true knowledge

DOI: 10.4018/978-1-60566-902-1.ch005

can emerge. He expressed the need to start from a *tabula rasa* by putting into question any previously constituted knowledge or belief. The only piece of certainty one can start with is one's own existence ("I think therefore I am"). Also one should "divide difficulties into small enough parts to be able to resolve them" and select true statements that appear "clear and sound in the mind" (Descartes, 1637). He so much imprinted our occidental vision of science and our relationship to reality that the inherited "Cartesiano-positivist institutional epistemologies" would constitute the base of "the social contract between science and society, and thus the status of teachable knowledge" (Le Moigne, 1995 p. 8). Paradoxically, such epistemologies are "at the same time individually disputed and institutionally accepted" (Le Moigne, 1995 p. 14). This could be partly explained by the "astonishing lack of epistemological culture of scientific researchers" (Le Moigne, 1995 p. 8) and by the contemporary institutional separation between science and philosophy. It is fair to say that in our work, we attempt to restore this lost unity.

The so-called "Cartesiano-positivist epistemologies", that we will explicit later on, have thus persisted under different forms until now, while interactions between science, technology and society have been shaping our world and our ways of thinking. For instance, with the advent of the industrial revolution, the transformation of matter into energy has been as much of a reality in everyday life as in theoretical physics. More recently, the advent of the information era has also constituted a big revolution and various scientific disciplines have emerged to model the processes that underlie learning (artificial intelligence [AI] and neurosciences). Together with parts of more traditional disciplines (psychology, philosophy and linguistics), they have been grouped under the generic term of cognitive sciences (Vignaux, 1991 p. 9). Different underlying paradigms provide a variety of approaches to learning and help study the relationships between intelligent machines and human beings.

The aim of this paper is to address the following questions. What scientific models do we use to understand human learning and to produce learning machines? Where do these models come from? What are their scopes and limits? How and why do we choose to use those models? What do they tell us is possible or is out of reach?

In the first section, we will overview i) the models that western societies have recently produced in order to explain the nature of learning and ii) the models that they have developed about the learning of nature, particularly through the prism of so-called "scientific discovery." In the second section, we will present the general evolution that occurred in the field of AI about assisting human discoveries with learning machines and then introduce the main aspects of our work in this domain. Finally, we will discuss the didactical and ethical dimensions inherent to discovering how learning of nature is performed, and to using assisting machines.

HUMAN LEARNING

Nature of Learning

After a few preliminary considerations, we review the conceptions on human learning as they evolved in western culture. We then focus on a particular model of the scientific activity, and highlight how the two conceptualisations of "general learning" and of "scientific learning" converge to constructivist paradigms.

Preliminary Considerations: Different Objects of Human Learning, One Fundamental Base

We would like to answer the question: "how do we learn?" But one might preferentially ask "how do we learn what?" It is of striking evidence that we do not learn mathematics the same way as we learn how to ride a bicycle or to be a respectful person. These examples correspond to different categories of knowledge (in the sense of the French word *savoirs*) that have been called in the French curricula *savoirs, savoir-faire* and *savoir-être* (and which could roughly be translated respectively as declarative knowledge, procedural knowledge and self knowledge or as intellectual skills, practical skills and self-management skills). Thus it seems that different processes could underlie different kinds of learning. Can we unravel a common denominator to all human learning activities?

Despite this remarkable heterogeneity, our ontological development consists, from a psychological point of view, in learning to be human and then to be a particular individual in the human community. In fact, soon after birth, the baby is fused to the totality of his environment, encompassing his mother, other living beings and also the surrounding non living things (Searles, 1960 p. 47). Normal development would therefore be firstly to differentiate from the nonliving environment, secondly to recognize oneself as part of mankind, and thirdly to assess oneself as an individual, notably distinct from the mother (Searles, 1960 p. 60). The adolescent has normally become fully aware of being human, has turned away from nonhuman objects, and focuses on humans (Searles, 1960 p. 98). As Piaget (1896 – 1980) remarked, teenagers feel destined to save the world; maybe they want to save other people from the nonhuman experience they just got rid of (Searles, 1960 p. 101).

To answer our preliminary question, we thus need to know what a human is. This is a vast question… Nowadays everyone seems to agree that we are animals with something more. From a biological point of view, and as Darwin stated, this "something" seems to be more quantitative than qualitative (Marchand, & Chaline, 2002). We share similar structures with chimpanzees but some of them, such as the neurological structure, are more developed (for instance, we have a bigger brain). However, a recent study, which has yet to be confirmed, argues that humans may possess particular neurons that would make their frontal neocortex more efficient than the chimpanzees' (Molnar et al., 2008). From a philosophical point of view, this something is often claimed to be qualitative. According to Morin (1921 –), being human is a ternary concept that entwines the individual, the species and society, such that none of these terms can be reduced nor subordinated to any of the other two (Morin, 1973). Along the same lines, Anselme conceives of humans in terms of a tension between a cosmic evolution (our biological dimension, what Morin designed under the term of *species*) and an ethical evolution, which prevents us to be solely "gladiators in the arena" (Anselme, 1989 p. 35). This ethical evolution would have emerged with consciousness, which gave rise to a collective will to refuse, denounce and fight natural injustices to overcome them. The first known writings in human history are indeed descriptions of behavioural norms, meant to keep us away from animality (Anselme, 1989 p. 21).

To summarise, our fundamental learning task would be to first become aware that we are a social being, with a duty by the community, and then to be a singular human in this community. These considerations can offer an interesting angle to analyse any particular object of learning and make up a privileged frame in the present article.

A Little Allegory of the Scientific Models of Human Learning

Chapter 1: In the Light of the Cartesiano-Positivist Epistemologies

We start the story with the neuropsychological studies in the first part of the 20th century. The works of the Russian psychologist Pavlov (1849 – 1936) have been translated in English for the first time in 1927. His experiments with dogs and how they can learn to associate a sound signal with the presentation of food lead to the concept of classical conditioning (a type of associative learning). The dog learns to salivate after repeated association of both signals. Following sufficient training, the dog salivates even when the food is not presented, providing evidence that it has been conditioned to salivate when it hears the sound signal. This form of learning (external stimulus → response) is better described as training and cannot be easily applied to wild animals or young humans who learn a lot through self-initiated exploration (Astolfi et al., 1978 pp. 123-124). Kornoski discovered operant learning in 1928: the stimulus is self-initiated after a self-initiated action (Astolfi et al., 1978 p. 124). These studies, together with philosophical logical positivism, inspired Skinner[1] (1904 – 1990).

In the late 20's in Europe, the philosophical and normative movement dedicated to unifying the various sciences has been constituted. It represents an emblematic "Cartesiano-positivist epistemology" (Le Moigne, 1995, p. 15). The so-called Vienna Circle focused on defining a universal method, primarily following an empirical approach, which could ascertain the constitution of true knowledge. Given this line of ideas, a central point of behaviourism is that the mind, or any related concept, depends on metaphysical considerations and cannot constitute an object of scientific research. The only empirical object worthy of scientific investigation about learning would thus be behaviour – the only empirically observable output of learning. Behaviour is considered as the result of a linear causal process that originates from a stimulus. This stimulus can be either external (Pavlov's dog) or internal (operant conditioning, the second type of associative learning). Skinner is well known for his work on the latter, where the stimulus has an endogen origin (for example when a button, activated by accident, triggers feeding). He also studied classical conditioning and invented famous experimental devices, notably to study associative learning in rodents. The matter was to evaluate how rodents learn to avoid or implement a particular behaviour (depending on the experimental setup) after a particular stimulus. The expected behaviour is rewarded (positive reinforcement) or the behaviour to avoid is penalized (negative reinforcement). For example, in the "shuttle-box" the rodent has to learn to move from one part of the box to the other soon after a light flash has occurred in order to avoid an electric shock from the bottom of the part of the box where it is. Skinner extended his theory to human learning, arguing that positive reinforcement was a key mechanism in education. He also developed a theory about programmed teaching where children learn school contents by themselves, without any teacher intervention, with the help of a protocol support (Astolfi et al., 1978 p. 125).

Nowadays Skinner's radical behaviourism tends to be associated with negative values, emblematic of times when society was an authoritarian patriarchy. However, we should note that reinforcement in human education might not be sufficient, but still seems undisputedly effective.

The field of neuropsychology led to a further categorisation of learning, notably by studying brain areas and neuron connections involved in particular processes and requiring different kinds of memories (from human or animal models). Procedural memory (that deals with the ability to implement particular tasks, for instance, riding a bicycle) has the particularity of being "overconceptual", i.e. people are unable to explain how they did learn or how they performed the task (Vignaux, 1991 p. 205). "Simple learning" (non-associative) can give rise to sensitization or habituation, depending on whether the response increases or decreases with the repetition of a similar stimulus. "Observational learning", or imitation, is considered to be a predominant and ancestral way of human learning. The astonishing recent discovery of mirror neurons, which are activated when one performs a given task or looks at someone who is performing it, suggests that these biological structures play an important role in imitation. However, this is controversial (Dinstein, Thomas, Behrmann, & Heeger, 2008).

Beside these biological approaches, which also fall under the Cartesiano-positivist framework, the Swiss biologist and psychologist Piaget brought a conceptual revolution in the way he modelled learning. Contrary to the behaviourists, he tried to model what happens in the "black-box" and, moreover, he proposed a radically different paradigm to conceptualise learning, as we will explain in the next chapter. To be able to understand this epistemological shift, let us first briefly outline the now common Cartesiano-positivist epistemologies. According to Le Moigne (1931 –), they are based on two related hypotheses that concern the nature of knowledge: i) an ontological hypothesis, which postulates the existence of a reality per se, external to the subject and pre-existing to his learning activity (Le Moigne, 1995 p. 21) and ii) a determinist hypothesis, in relation to this external reality (Le Moigne, 1995 p. 24). The assertion that some domains of reality are not amenable to any deterministic description is also considered a form of determinism – and even chaos is now determinist (Le Moigne, 1995 p. 24). Popper (1902 – 1994) tried to go beyond this notion in *The Open Universe: An Argument for Indeterminism* (1982), but still resorts to an ontological reality (Le Moigne, 1995 p. 26). The knowable reality would have a proper rationale and this rationale would not necessarily depend on observational determinations.

Chapter 2: In the Light of the Constructivist Epistemologies

Piaget defined *epistemology* broadly « in first approximation, as the study of valid knowledge constitution", thus grouping common and scientific knowledge. Let us describe the counterparts to the hypotheses of the Cartesiano-positivist epistemologies. i) The phenomenological hypothesis posits, as Piaget wrote, "the inseparability between the act to know an 'object' and the act to know the 'self'" (Le Moigne, 1995 p. 75). Thus the knowable reality is phenomenological, and it is what the subject experiments. This means that knowledge is at the same time a building process and the result of this process. The learning process is no longer understood as a duality between the knowing subject and the environment, but as a co-construction of both poles of the interaction. ii) The teleological hypothesis underlines the project, the intentionality that underlies any act of knowing (Le Moigne, p.79).

Piaget opposed the methodological postulate of the behaviourists and advocated that non-observable phenomena have to be modelled. He was not interested in individual subjects, but in an epistemic subject "modelled as all the mechanisms common to all subjects of a same level" (Astolfi et al., 1978 p. 133). He made numerous observations on his own children. Thanks to repeated contacts with the environment, a child develops elementary units of intellectual activity, which Piaget called « schemes ». Schemes exhibit a circular causality between an action in the environment and its perception. They can evolve through assimilation (of a novel object to a pre-existing scheme) and accommodation (of a modified pre-existing scheme to a novel object). Conflicts provoked by distortion between representation and perception play a motor role in learning. This theory falls in the realm of structuralism because learning is defined as the reorganisation of pre-existing knowledge (Foulin & Mouchon, 1998 p. 13). To Piaget, this "genetic epistemology" rests on logic (Astolfi et al., 1978 p. 135). In his work *Traité de Logique* (1949), he represents the main conceptual thought processes in the form of symbolic operations, formalised as an algebraic calculation, from the simplest tasks of comparison and ranking to elaborated abstract constructions (Astolfi et al., 1978 p. 136).

The theory of self-organizing systems, which draws from several scientific disciplines (logic, cybernetic, biology, anthropology…), shares common points with Piaget's theory. Both consider the learning system as an open system able to modify the laws that keep it operational and its responses, through interactions with its environment (Astolfi et al., 1978 p. 132). Those theories focus on the scale of the subject (or the learning system), modelled only in his cognitive dimension, and neglecting the roles of symbol manipulation and of social influences (Foulin & Mouchon, 1998 p. 18).

The socio-constructivism of the Russian Vygotsky (1896-1934) was exposed in his major work *Thought and Language* (1934). Whereas Piaget considered mostly intra-individual processes through 2 poles "learning subject"-"object", to Vygotsky, learning is fundamentally a movement from inter-individual to intra-individual processes (3 poles: alter-subject-object, Foulin & Mouchon, 1998 p. 35). Learning would thus consist in the intra-individual reconstruction of tools that have been deposited by others in the underlying culture, with language as the most important of all. Vygotsky insists on the fact that people mostly do not learn alone, but need educators.

Education sciences have promoted a synthesis of these aspects (Doise & Mugny, 1997). The notions of socio-cognitive conflict, of problem based learning and of peer regulation are supposed to guide the implementation of a socio-constructivist way of teaching (Prince, 2004).

Let us go now a little bit further. To Grize (1984), "natural logics" correspond to circular cognitive processes known as "means-ends analysis" (Le Moigne, 1995 p. 89): means give rise to intermediate finalities, which suggest novel means, which evoke other possible ends. The modalities of dialogical reasoning guide the consultation of anterior experiences that constitute a pool of plausible heuristics, selected with the help of a "feasibility" criterion (Le Moigne, 1995 p. 89). Those heuristics do sometimes have a lot in common with what Aristotle called "abduction" (but they are not constrained by a demand of formal truth, as advocated by Pierce, Le Moigne, 1995 p. 89). They can also resort on techniques that play with shape and meaning such as word plays, metaphors and schematisation (Perelman, & Olbrechts-Tyteca, 1970). So the natural logics that underlie the human construction of knowledge and learning are always associated with imagination, poetry, emotions… and proceed through somehow obscure ways. But in cognitive sciences, the computational metaphor has had a strong (and practical) influence on the way human learning is conceptualized. Piaget himself, as we have seen, cast his theory in a formal language. Le Moigne (1995) suggests a slight paradigm shift that we think is of prime significance (p. 80). This shift is prompted by the consideration of the teleological hypothesis, which according to Le Moigne, raises difficulties (Le Moigne, 1995 p. 80). "The meditation of the object by the subject always the takes form of a project", writes Bachelard (1934). Albeit issued from cybernetics, the concept of teleology does not seem to be amenable to a full formal reduction. Is there a cognitive model that captures the notions of will, of motivation, of drive to achieve a goal?

All theories that we have presented until now have in common that they focus on the "cognitive"[2] dimension, which learning and intelligence have long been subordinated to. Piaget explicitly and intentionally excluded the affective dimension; his epistemic subject is ideally motivated. This model does not explain learning failure or difficulty. One learns with one's "intelligence" (pre-existing schemes) and with one's emotions. Even in the context of traditional learning, such as a scientific course at school, there is no doubt that "emotional features" – referred to as *affects* in psychology – play an important role. To dare learn something it is essential to feel secure and not be afraid of failure, error or "mistake" (a term which often has a moral connotation), it is essential to be self-confident (Favre, 2007). But more is needed: learning stems from an impulse, an envy, an aim, what in psychology is called a *motivation*. Affects and motivation are psychological concepts that would help give support to the teleological hypothesis proposed by Le Moigne. They can be considered as motors or brakes, depending on the situation. They depend on our personal history: our ontological development relying on past interactions (not only with other human beings). They correspond to our internal physiological state and reactions (hormonal, cardiac…) when we face a particular situation, and to the associated feelings (pleasure, pain…). In the central nervous system, neural circuits involved in processing this "affective information" are also those that process the "cognitive information"; both dimensions are biologically integrated in learning (Favre, 2006). Affects and motivational factors are difficult to express with words, they are not easily conceptualized, nor formalised with logico-mathematical operations. They seem diffuse and sometimes are overwhelming as we do not have full control over them. In western culture, they are traditionally neither analyzed nor harnessed, contrary to the teachings of oriental culture (through meditation for instance). Research in science education has shown that language can contribute to regulating emotions (Favre, 2007). Transforming emotions into an object of learning is an introspection process that can be called metacognition (Bell, 1991) and that can give rise to valuable skills. These ideas prompted the distinction between several forms of intelligence, such as the intrapersonal and the interpersonal forms of Gardner (1984) and as the emotional form of Goleman (1997), which correspond to being skilful at managing emotions.

Conclusion

The last point is to us a key aspect of an education system that recognizes the complexity of human nature. Emotion management is a tool that, if no better than « traditional knowledge », seems necessary at least "not to be only a gladiator in the arena". The factors that are typically human (as opposed to machines), motivation and affects, have until now been marginalised in our occidental approach and scientific decoding to learning, and are outside the realm of machine learning. The pleasure to learn is an important motivation, but unfortunately school enforces the view that learning is a very serious activity, seldom a game. The last two remarks allow us to make a point that we will later seriously address. Knowledge is a status acknowledged with values (this is the axiological dimension of knowledge). Notably, in western society, scientific, conceptual, academic *etc.* knowledge has a privileged status, that is denied to other forms of knowledge (Fourez, 2002 pp. 115-117); it is considered a better reference and more valid generally. It is widely recognised as "useful", "good" and "beautiful", and associated conception qualifications to these values are "objective", "realistic", "universal" and "issued from reason" (Hagège, 2007). This legitimation of the scientific knowledge originates from the Cartesiano-positivism ambient epistemologies and often gives rise to scientism and technocratism (Le Moigne, 1995 p. 23).

Every sort of human activity would be subsumed by some kind of project, which relies on values. A major point of constructivism is indeed that one cannot separate any knowledge, conception, object… from the human project whose construction has been shaped, individually or socio-historically, by them (Fourez, 2002 p. 37). The "object" of learning[3], once assimilated, is part of the learner and thus contributes to constitute his self. Thus, during learning, the identity of the learner is at stake. In fact, if one follows the phenomenological reasoning right to its end and assumes that no form of reality precedes learning and has an existence per se, then the same position should be adopted for the learning subject who is co-constructed through the learning process. Thus we are sent back to our preliminary considerations, and claim that what is fundamentally at stake, while learning, is learning to be one human self. We have come full circle.

Learning of Nature

At first sight, scientific knowledge seems to be a particularly efficient way to learn about nature. In this part, we will briefly review some prominent theories that aim at explaining scientific discoveries, and also discuss, as we have begun already, the link between learning through scientific discovery and general learning.

A Little Allegory of the Scientific Understanding of Scientific Processes

As has been recalled, Piaget proposed an extensive definition of epistemology, but this term is also used in a narrower sense; it designates the study of science at work. Thus we will here distinguish between "common knowledge" and "scientific knowledge", since science is usually considered to be the (only) enterprise devoted to building valid knowledge. We already evoked positivism and its normative approach to science inherited from the Cartesian occidental philosophy. "Normative" means that the theory is focused on "how science should be." This movement advocated an empirical method based on a principle of verification. Popper was among the first to advocate a descriptive approach to science (Lecourt, 2001 p. 73). I.e., he was mainly interested in "how science really is." He based his reflection on the study of history of physical sciences. If an experiment validates a hypothesis, it just indicates that the latter offers a satisfying model for interpreting reality, relatively to the context of the experiment. Such a model is not the only possible one and cannot be tested in all possible contexts. Thus it may one day happen that some aspects of the model will be refuted in another context (Chalmers, 1976 p. 74). This refutation is the only genuine proof that one can hope for. The decision of whether or not a hypothesis or a theory should be adopted or promoted is regulated by the scientific community. This falsifiability theory has been a big revolution in epistemology and will provide a foundation to our implementation of machine learning paradigms. First the current body of scientific knowledge is no longer viewed as a repository of definite truths, but as a set of tools to solve problems. Second, objectivity in science is no longer a property that emanates from nature or natural objects, which scientists just have to discover (literally "to remove the cover that was hiding them") but it has become an intersubjective construct. Scientific objects do not pre-exist in nature; so one cannot separate which part of the construction comes from humans, and which part comes from nature or reality (Fourez, 2002 pp. 175-177, 254).

Popper's student Lakatos (1922–1974) proposed a more refined theory after applying Poppers' theory to the history of mathematics (1976). One can consider that he refuted his master's theory. He proposed to reconstruct scientific history *a posteriori*, by only considering how scientific ideas evolve, a method related to the internalist approach in history of sciences – this point will oppose him to Kuhn's approach. To him, hypotheses or theories are not independent from each other, which implies that the refutation process is not so simple: some theories are more important than others; they constitute the hard core of a research program on which all the rest is based[4] (Chalmers, 1976 p. 135). Thus they will not be easily refuted. A so called "protective belt" of auxiliary hypotheses preserves them. If those hypotheses are changed, the program can still progress. So if a counterexample arises, *ad hoc* hypotheses will be created and put in the protective belt to protect the core hypotheses. Scientific theories are seen as embedded into structures and research programs are either progressive (enriching the hard core) or degenerative (only creating *ad hoc* hypotheses). This conception changed the previous linear conception (progress through conjectures and refutation) into a vision where both parameters – theories and relations between theories – are taken into account to explain rational advancement in science.

Kuhn (1922 – 1994) studied history of physics and added another dimension to the model of scientific progress: the social dimension (1962). To him, rational considerations only are not sufficient to understand scientific evolution. There are also non-rational factors like confidence or faith in a theory that explain why people trust a theory more than another one. Moreover, "normal science" is hosted in a paradigm (Chalmers, 1976 p. 151). A paradigm is a disciplinary matrix that comprises theories, legitimated questions and panels of admissible responses but also cultural traditions of what is considered a valid method to conduct a proof, that changes over time. For example in molecular biology, in the 70's, one had to do *in vitro* experiments to demonstrate a molecular mechanism – *i.e.*, to purify, isolate components and make them react in a tube. Today this sort of proof is considered accessory, and one needs an *in vivo* argument to convince one's peers (Hagège, 2004). Kuhn emphasized that extraordinary events sometimes happen: a crisis, followed by a paradigmatic revolution, as occurred for the transition between Newtonian and Einsteinian physics. He pointed out that both paradigms, which correspond to non-reconcilable visions of the world, are incommensurable; to judge the validity, the quality or the efficiency of a paradigm, one needs tools that are part of the paradigm. Thus, there is no external tool thanks to which one could rationally (or "absolutely") compare which paradigm would be best.

The study of science has then been enriched with other dimensions, including anthropological and psychological dimensions. For the last thirty years, science has witnessed a major overhaul, becoming a techno-sciences system, encompassing studies about its very nature. The so called "science studies" bring various pictures of scientific dynamics (Pestre, 2006 p. 5). The object called "science" appears to be a protean process and all general assertions about science that we have evoked now seem insufficient, sometimes meaningless. Meaning can only be found in a particular context, at a particular epoch, concerning some singular actors and could be constructed over and over again, depending on our cultural reading (Pestre, 2006 p.7). Those science studies conclude that there is no tangible criterion that demarcates science from other human activities, no proper method that would be intrinsic to the scientific activity. If one wants to characterise the scientific activity, one should study what has been called "science" at a given time, in a given context. Science does not have any substance, any essence, does not exist per se; its meaning is constructed by its actors and by those who relate to it, making it to their own image, given their projects and the way they construct themselves. We can here recognise an important feature of constructivist epistemologies, which naturally embrace the ethical considerations that we will evoke later on. Let us first note that the consideration that science lacks essence puts the Cartesiano-positivist institutional epistemologies into question, as the privileged status of science in the western countries is precisely grounded in the tacit acceptance of a universal proof administration mode, of a proper and undoubted optimal method.

Conclusion 1: Nature of Learning and Learning of Nature

The foundations of constructivism that Le Moigne (1995) proposes can be apprehended intellectually but do not seem easy to instantiate in our everyday acts and thinking, particularly the phenomenological hypothesis. Indeed, those with a western background tend to think on the basis of a duality principle (that opposes the self – a thinking self (*cogito ergo sum*) – to the rest of the world) whose terms i) are kept well distinct and ii) implicitly receive a proper existence, thus a form of permanence[6]. As Descartes illustrated, our stronger belief corresponds to the existence of a self (thus somehow separated from the rest of reality). But is it possible to know without separating[7]? Arguably, this is possible in cultures (see e.g. Scheurmann, 1920 pp. 115-124) that seek a unifying knowledge, not dependent on language and concepts, a form of omniscience as Buddhists attribute to the historical Shakyamuni Buddha (David-Néel, 1977 pp. 240-242).

To Le Moigne (1995), Popper and Kuhn fall under the Cartesiano-positivist epistemologies because of their subscription to the ontological and determinist hypothesis (p. 15). Fundamentally, he blames them for not applying to their own discourse what they apply to others' (p. 14). We notice, in their defence, that such a circular demand rapidly makes head spin, because of the duality principle from which one cannot really escape – except maybe a Buddha. Our natural cultural propensity is to place ourselves outside of discourse or of the "observed reality" and to look at reality and apprehend it "from the outside". Yet other authors qualified Kuhn as a constructivist (Strike, & Posner, 1992) and Popper, because of his clear move from logical positivism, could also be considered as one. Kuhn's and Piaget's conceptions of knowledge construction are indeed comparable – at two different scales, either the scientific community or the individual – with respect to both following features. First, knowledge does not increase through a linear accumulation of "units of information", but consists in a qualitative reorganization of the initial knowledge structure (Lonka, Joram, & Brysin, 1996; Strike, & Posner, 1992). Second, every knowledge depends on a knowing subject (Fourez et al., 1997), so it is subjective by nature. Thus, opinions, points of views and beliefs all belong to science and learning (Bachelard, 1971; Kuhn, 1962). Knowledge then appears to be not dissociable from its sociological, historical and psychological dimensions and therefore its status can only be approximate and provisional. We can add a third common feature to the various facets of socio-constructivism (cf. Vygotsky and Kuhn), namely, the fundamental regulatory role that the community places on learning.

Conclusion 2: Implications for Learning of Nature in the Classroom

Scientific knowledge is often presented as having an intrinsic value, independent of human history and of any context. In fact, science teachers and students do not spontaneously make theirs the conceptions of constructivist science (Boulton-Lewis, Smith, McCrindle, Burnett, & Campbell, 2001; Lemberger, Hewson, & Park, 1999; Waeytens, Lens, & Vandenberghe, 2002). For instance, to future biology teachers, knowledge is an "external truth that can be discovered through observation, discussion, sense-making" and also "a collection of additive facts" (Lemberger et al., 1999). In that sense, experiment can play the role of a supreme referee to verify theories. This naive, positivist labelled epistemology also comes with a realist view, according to which the world is intimately knowledgeable, so that scientific knowledge is all about truth: the world as it is. Experiments are thus presented as proving something absolute and sciences as composed of accumulated knowledge (or facts) that have a stable and universal interpretation. Moreover, teachers often hope that students will be able to rediscover these truths by themselves and will be convinced of their truthfulness by the strength of evidence they contain. In addition, students should acquire a universal scientific method, even though epistemologists agree that no such method exists.

To solve these issues, science education studies suggested that science should be taught in a way that would allow students to gain knowledge they would master a tool that can be usefully applied to one of their own projects (Fourez, 2002 pp. 84-85). That is why Problem Based Learning (PBL) appeared as more efficient than traditional magisterial teaching (Vernon, & Blake, 1993). PBL is mostly practiced in small groups and the teacher only plays the role of an accompanist, and not of a "Nature representative who knows how the world is made" as in traditional courses. These assumptions have several important implications, which we will not discuss here, particularly concerning the attitude of a constructivist teacher and the coherent modalities of evaluation he or she should implement.

Altogether, this presentation implies that it is of utmost importance to form people, notably teachers, to epistemology. For the sake of coherence and efficiency, this can be done neither in a magisterial nor in a dogmatic way. In the next section, we emphasise that the evolution we mentioned has also started to affect machine learning paradigms, and we will present an attempt to bring this evolution one step further. The implementation we propose can serve as a basis for a game that can be taken seriously and fulfils our expectations.

HUMAN AND MACHINE ASSOCIATED LEARNING OF NATURE

Since the inception of artificial intelligence, researchers have aimed at endowing machines with learning and problem solving abilities. "Computational scientific discovery" became an active field of research when machine learning techniques started showing conclusive results in the late 70's. These results motivated the simulation of historical discoveries (Lenat, 1983; Langley, Bradshaw, & Simon, 1981; Langley, Simon, & Zytkow, 1987), and since the beginning of the 21st century, research in this domain has been oriented toward the discovery of unknown rules (Simon, Valdés-Pérez, & Sleeman, 1997). Our main contribution is to define an interaction protocol encompassing both human and machine learning, resulting in a formal foundation for discovery platforms: the machine learns at the same time as the user, and this co-learning leads to a pertinent understanding of the problem and a pertinent modelling of the processes of simulation and prediction. A complete presentation of this work can be found elsewhere (Dartnell, Martin, & Sallantin, 2008; Dartnell, 2008), and we will succinctly synthesise its key aspects in relation to the philosophical, psychological, and didactical considerations discussed in the first part of the present paper.

Since machine learning and problem solving are often associated in literature, for the sake of clarity we will use the term *solver* to refer to an *artificial learner*. Many machine learning methods have been developed, such as neural networks (Haykin, 1998), genetic algorithms, Bayesian networks (Heckerman, Geiger, & Chickering, 1995) or symbolic learning with Galois lattices (Liquière, & Sallantin, 1998) and our point is not so much to discuss their relevance or efficiency than to show the limits of the paradigms to which they correspond in the light of the previous discussion.

The principles of nominalization and reducibility are essential to give a problem solver the ability to adapt. Nominalization is the ability to build an abstraction of an observed phenomenon and reducibility is the ability to instantiate these abstract and symbolic concepts in a concrete way, by means of action or experimentation. Therefore, interaction between the solver and its environment are *sine qua non* conditions of its evolution: by comparing the results of theoretical computations and the results of its interactions with the environment, the solver is able to detect contradictions between "reality" and the formulated theories.

The use of contradictions as a dialectic engine and the revision of a theory imply logical pre-requisites that we will not discuss here. However, these questions correspond to the modelling of logic programs as proposed by Lakatos: how does a logical system deal with contradictions and how could a protective belt be formalized and implemented? Dartnell, Martin, Hagège et al., (2008) proposed to explore the paths of paraconsistent, deontic, and defeasible logics.

We now focus on the main existing machine learning paradigms and outline their evolution, which can be put into correspondence with the evolution of the conceptions on with human learning, as will be highlighted.

A Little Allegory of Learning from Each Other

Several learning paradigms have been proposed to provide frameworks of study and tools of analysis that can qualify and quantify the learning process. Among those, we can cite "identification in the limit" (Gold, 1967), "query learning" (Angluin, 1988), and "PAC-learning" ("Probably Approximately Correct-learning", Valiant, 1984) as having a strong impact on the machine learning community. Each of them proposes a different model of reality, a different form of interaction between the learner and the environment, and different criteria of successful learning. One of the main evolutions concerns the role played by the learner during the learning process, which has evolved from a passive role to a more active one.

We illustrate these differences on several variations of the card game that was used in the experimentations related thereafter. We advocate that the last version is suitable for both human and machine learning and opens a gate to a human-machine collaborative learning/discovery platform.

We first present identification in the limit, which defines an infinite and passive process. Then we present how the use of queries transforms a passive learner into an active one. We do not present *PAC*-learning here since it deals with finite notions whereas we are interested in infinite processes and infinite representations of reality.

Passive Learning

To illustrate the problem of identification in the limit, let us use a simple card game between two players. One of them, the game master, chooses an infinite sequence of cards such that any card can be referred to by its position in the sequence. Suppose the second player, the solver, has a vocabulary V allowing him to describe exactly any card at any position. For example V could consist of the set of unary predicate symbols *{ace, two, . . ., jack, queen, king}* ∪ *{hearts, diamonds, clubs, spades}*, complemented with constants for the numerals and a binary predicate symbol that, applied to pairs of numerals, is interpreted as the usual ordering on the natural numbers. At each step, the game master reveals the next card in the sequence so that the learner discovers them one by one, by using the numeral n to refer to it the nth card in the sequence and using the two unary predicate symbols that determine the card uniquely. For instance, "*queen(0), hearts(0), ace(1), spades(1), queen(2), hearts(2), ace(3), spades(3), ...*" is the beginning of a possible sequence. After it has taken note of a new card, the solver emits a conjecture, in the form of a logical program that *exactly* describes a *unique infinite* sequence of cards. Such a logic program is said to be univocal. Of course, not all sequences of cards can be described by a logic program over V, and not all sequences of cards that can be described by a logic program over V can be described by a univocal logic program. The identification process is considered successful if after no more than a finite number of steps, the solver converges toward a correct conjecture, i.e., if it changes its mind a finite number of times or none at all, and if the program it converges to correctly describes the underlying sequence. Note that since the sequence is infinite, the learner usually cannot know that its current hypothesis is correct or that it has converged to a correct description.

Though it is impossible to know that one's view is correct, an incorrect view cannot be held forever: every conjecture is refutable in the limit. Each new card might invalidate the solver's current conjecture. And in case the conjecture is incorrect, the learner has the guarantee that it will at some point receive the description of a card that definitely indicates that its conjecture is incorrect. But the refutation might occur after a very long time and the solver has no option but passively observe the cards as they are presented to it.

We now describe how the use of queries can open the gate to active learning and the definition of search strategies.

Active Learning

We illustrated passive learning with a game in which a solver has to exactly identify a univocal program, that is, a logic program describing a unique infinite sequence, which is revealed to it one card after the other. We shall now illustrate active learning with a classification game, in which the solver has to exactly identify an equivocal program, that is, a logic program that describes possibly many infinite sequences of cards. In other words, an equivocal logic program describes a set of card sequences that happen to have some property – the property expressed by the logic program –, and the aim of the solver is to determine that property in the limit. We do not only change the nature of the game, but also how the game is played, by allowing the solver to query an oracle for the sake of testing its hypotheses. So instead of being presented with an infinite sequence of cards, the solver can test whether the property it has in mind is correct by asking an oracle, that knows what the underlying property is, whether its current guess is correct. Note that the game is extensional, not intentional: the solver is not requested to discover a particular representation of a given property, but any representation (equivocal program) that correctly captures the extension of the property.

Let W be the set of all infinite sequences, let Ptarget be an equivocal logic program describing a set Wtarget $\subseteq$ W, and let H be a possibly infinite set of equivocal programs representing the solver's hypothesis set.

At each step, the solver is allowed to query an oracle using one of the types of queries introduced and studied in (Angluin, 1988, 2004):

- **Membership:** The input is a possible game X $\in$ W, and the answer is true if X $\in$ Wtarget, or false if X is a counterexample.
- **Equivalence:** The input is a set WH $\subseteq$ W of possible games, and the answer is true if WH $\equiv$ Wtarget, or a counterexample X $\in$ WH Δ Wtarget otherwise.
- **Subset:** The input is a set WH $\subseteq$ W of possible games, and the answer is true if WH $\subseteq$ Wtarget or a counterexample X $\in$ WH $-$Wtarget otherwise.
- **Superset:** The input is a set WH $\in$ W of possible games, and the answer is true if WH $\supseteq$ Wtarget, or a counterexample X $\in$ Wtarget $-$WH otherwise.

The classification is said to be successful if after a finite number of queries and experiments, the solver converges toward a program PH $\in$ H such that PH $\equiv$ Ptarget. Note that contrary to the scenario of identification in the limit, the process just described allows the solver to know that it has found a correct answer. Of course, this is not because the solver is required to be smarter in this version of the game, but because the solver is assisted by an oracle that can have more computing power than a universal Turing machine. Leaving these (essential) considerations aside, this evolution of machine learning paradigms can be put in parallel with the notions of classical conditioning, in which the learner does not have any initiative (passive), and operant conditioning in which it initiates the stimulus (active).

Beside this, we could consider that the oracle plays the role of nature in a "Cartesiano-positivist world" in which nature is a perfect referee. The existence of an omniscient oracle, able to answer the solver's queries, could therefore be seen as "reality's resistance to experiment" and the learner as a purely rational observer.

The following variation, which we developed for our experiments, illustrates how to partly get rid of this limit by introducing pairs as imperfect oracles.

Social Learning

As we mentioned earlier, an important trend in epistemology is to consider that learning proceeds through social interactions and we give room to this important aspect in our game. Inspired by multi-agent systems and game theory (Chavalarias, 1997), we propose to distribute the resolution of equivalence queries on a community of solvers confronted to the judgment of other solvers. Each of them can then publish his or her conjectures and refute existing ones according to a Popperian conception of science. We now drop the term "solver" and switch back to using the term "learner" to emphasise that this transposition of science to machine learning paradigms is, albeit simple, suited to both human and machine learning. It implies individual exploration and learning, social evaluation and institutional accreditation.

We symbolize the product of the social interaction by a gain function. By attributing or deducing points for each query, depending on the answer (refuted or not), we can create competitive or collaborative environment between multiple learners. This prompts for publications to score points and experimentations to corroborate or refute a published theory. The gain function motivates the learners to try and search for counterexamples and ensure that publications will either remain as consensual references and gain credit, or be refuted in the limit.

Implementation of the Last Variation

This distributed learning protocol was developed using the multi-agent system *Madkit* (Gutknecht, & Ferber, 1997), which implements the formalism *AGR* (Ferber, & Gutknecht, 1998). The resulting platform takes the form of a card game: *Eleusis+Nobel*[5] (Dartnell, & Sallantin, 2005). Each learner is an agent, *Learner*, and belongs to a scientific community sharing a set of problems. These problems are implemented as equivocal programs describing sets of infinite card sequences such as "alternation of black and red cards" for instance. An agent "Problem" is created to simulate each problem and can be accessed to validate finite card sequences. Membership queries are co-semi-decidable since they refer to infinite sequences, but restrictions to finite sequences or infinite sequences of a special kind can be decidable and are suitable for simulation and experiments. Dedicated messages corresponding to experimentation, publication and refutation have been defined as speech acts. "Experimentation" messages are synchronized (the sender waits for the answer) and sent directly to the agent in charge of simulating experimentations for the chosen problem. The sender receives the answer "yes" or "no" and the result is displayed as shown on Figure 1. The sequences are built by adding new cards to the existing sequence. Correct cards are displayed at the requested position, circled in green, whereas wrong cards are displayed under the main sequence, and circled in red. This part of the protocol is private, which ensures that each learner has his or her own private experimentation background.

After considering the risk associated with the publication of their conjectures, learners can send a "Publication" message to the community. Since this kind of query is co-semi-decidable, publication

Figure 1. Eleusis + Nobel's Web Display

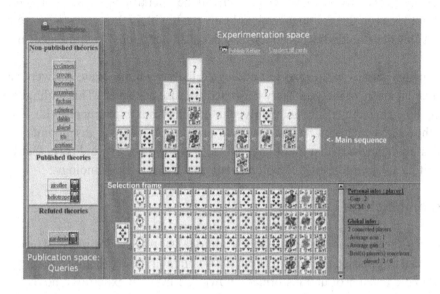

messages are unsynchronized. Each learner receives this public query and can send a refutation message containing a counterexample selected in his or her own experimentation panel. The agents in charge of simulating experimentations simply react to these queries by switching role to *Published* or *Refuted* so that the state of the art is always visible.

Learning Impact of the Game

The first experimentations were designed to quantify the impact of distributing queries among players. The second one, more meticulous, aimed at qualifying the epistemological impact of Eleusis+Nobel. Both of them shared the same set of 33 hidden rules, and the gain function was defined as follows: publishing was rewarded with $P = 1$ point, and refuting (respectively, being refuted) was rewarded (sanctioned) by a gain (a loss) of $R = 2$ points. Subset and superset queries were not implemented in this version of the game.

We wanted to study the impact of the game on students who aspire to become science teachers. Success, to us, would mean that they acquire a vision of science which can be qualified as constructivist. As we already mentioned, several psychosociological studies already showed that pre-service teachers spontaneously adopt a positivist and realistic vision of science (Boulton-Lewis et al., 2001; Lemberger et al., 1999; Waeytens et al., 2002). As reported elsewhere (Hagège, Dartnell, & Sallantin, 2007), we used psychometric tools (answer sheets) to evaluate how science conceptions evolve by querying third year university biology students who aim at becoming teachers. We used "negative controls", in the form of a set of students from the same group who did not play to the game, but who also fulfilled the pre-test and the post-test. In contrast, the "players" played Eleusis+Nobel during two hours between the pre-test and the post-test.

We evaluated several aspects related to constructivism. The aspect that has been recurrently and significantly changed concerns the role of subjectivity in the scientific process. As all observed changes of answers did not focus on themes that were explicitly dealt with in the game, but were just practiced, we inferred that this constructivist conception had been subconsciously assimilated, in the Piagetian sense.

Moreover, open questions in the post-test addressed feelings during play. Answers vastly differed: either players liked it much, or they got "very frustrated because of cheats". This highlights what we also observed during the game: they really got involved into it. Previous experiments with 13 or 20-year-old pupils lead to the same conclusion. When time was over, a majority was disappointed and wanted to continue (that rarely happens with a traditional course!). Altogether, this indicates that Eleusis+Nobel game can constitute a very interesting complementary tool to teach epistemology.

Extensions on Machine Learning

As we mentioned in the previous section, both the traditionalist and the constructivist teaching and learning conceptions can be opposed (Chan, & Elliott, 2004). In the first conception, teaching is considered as a non problematic transfer of untransformed knowledge from an expert to a novice. Learning thus corresponds to absorbing such knowledge. At the other end, learning is the creation and acquisition of knowledge through reasoning and justification. Teaching facilitates learning, and does not consist in knowledge transmission.

The formal learning models presented earlier can be described as the transmission from a teacher to a learner of a program that represents the target concept, either directly or indirectly through examples or queries. Extensions in machine learning, based on the previous cognitive considerations, explore the case where this transmission is impossible. Human learning involves complex agents, who are all different and unique, have limited modelling abilities and have an incomplete knowledge of themselves. Such constraints, which evoke the introduction of *limited rationality* by Simon in economics theory, lead to a change of paradigm since simulation becomes out of reach for agents ignoring the way they operate.

These constraints are clearly illustrated by Angluin (2003) with the example of juggling, for which anyone knowing how to juggle can play the role of a valid teacher (or model) for the learner. However, this learner can learn by imitation, without knowing the involved process, resorting to procedural memory (see "Nature of learning"). In contrast to formal learning models that give the learner the capacity to simulate, Angluin and Krikis (2003) propose to take into account and formalize the fundamental differences between agents and how difficult it is to each of them to achieve a given task.

Conclusion

Machine learning paradigms have evolved from passive learning to active learning. We selected identification in the limit and learning with queries as the most suited ones in the context of scientific discovery, and we used them to formalize the problem of scientific discovery. In this context, conceptions of reality are infinite and as an oracle has to be part of the equation, answering queries is unrealistic, as the oracle needs to be endowed with capabilities that go beyond the power of a universal Turing machine. We proposed to distribute the resolution of queries in a social game of publication and refutation, and we evaluated *Eleusis+Nobel*, an implementation of our protocol, on a human community. This experiment highlighted two important features:

- The protocol is suitable for human learning, since the community was able to find a consensus concerning a set of thirty-three more or less difficult rules in a reasonable time (two hours).
- The protocol is appropriate to teach constructivist conceptions to students, which means that the epistemic notions on which it is founded are acceptable and significant of how science is assumed to be practiced "in reality." Moreover, conceptual changes occurred in a procedural manner, with potentially longer effects than thc kind of learning that requires declarative memory.

Moreover, our natural conception choices of multi-agent systems led us to define an *AGR* model of interactive learning, and the abstraction level of the implementation allows one to adapt the current platform to other contexts than cards. These three points tend to indicate that this protocol is a good candidate to design interactive platforms for assisted science discovery, pedagogic tools, or other "science" games. Inspired by more cognitive considerations and related new work in machine learning, we proposed several extensions to this protocol, among which:

- The introduction of a complexity measure such as time, to introduce a heuristic and restrain co-semi-decidable membership queries to decidable complexity queries;
- The implementation of subset and superset queries to favour the interaction between learners and to favour an increased competition among theories, in a more Popperian conception of science.

GENERAL CONCLUSION

In this paper, we reviewed some models of human and machine learning. We also presented our own conception and our work on machine assisted science discovery for human researchers.

What Can We Expect, or Not, From Machine Assisted Human Learning?

Our conception of human learning is that of a complex process, which cannot be fully understood. The scientific procedures which aim at dissecting "reality" follow an analytic approach that separates entities that are essentially linked together (for instance subject/environment or self/reality as it is, knowledge/affects, human/machine…). Thus, the product of our analytic mind, as learning machines, would never be as complex as their designers. What takes the role of "reality" for the machine is determined and digitalized by the initial input, with separate objects and an associated language to describe them. "The machine simulates the bias of the programmer".

Nevertheless, we can stress some advantages of assistant machines over human tutors. An important advantage concerns the affective dimension of learning. The machine, devoid of value judgment, constitutes an impartial interface, so that shy or aggressive people, for instance, probably would have fewer barriers to interact with a machine. Moreover, the superior computing abilities of a machine could be used as a tool to select and provide relevant information to the user. A protocol such as Eleusis+Nobel could automate the exploration, and help in sorting out and understanding the data via a unified interaction protocol between humans and machines. Machine learning is necessary to have access to the interests and the needs of a user in such a way that the latter does not need to program his assistant. One can imagine that if internet sites implement « Problem » agents corresponding to the information they intend to communicate, then the acquisition of this knowledge could be done via a learning game and no longer through lectures (a magisterial procedure).

What Do We Expect from Machine Assisted Human Learning?

The advent of intelligent machines in western societies changed our ways of thinking, learning and communicating. We face a relationship to our human condition. We already suggested that what is fundamentally at stake in learning is to learn to be human. Integrating the constructivist principles, we update at every moment our definition of humankind and the definition of our individual and collective identities, through every one of our actions. We would claim that humanity does not have a proper existence or essence, but that we give a meaning to the notion of humanity every time we act. It is permanently reconstructed in the underlying co-constructed framework. Thus the question that would ideally guide each one of our actions – and *a fortiori* those of our actions that have important consequences – is: in which world do we want to live? What humanity do we want to defend? What do we want to do? How? And what for? This ethical and pragmatic questions call for an axiological one. What values are important to us? Do we want machines to reinforce competitiveness and individualism? Or do we want them to value equity and solidarity? Listening to Anselme (1989), in order to reinforce our ethical evolution (vs. our cosmologic evolution), we should choose actions that favor cooperation, and are open to others, and promote respect and responsibility. But the ethical process implies that it is up to everyone to choose his actions, in full consciousness, after having thought about the consequences in a discursive way (Simon, 1993 p. 172).

REFERENCES

Angluin, D. (1988). Queries and concept learning. *Machine Learning, 2,* 319–342.

Angluin, D. (2004). Queries revisited. *Theoretical Computer Science, 313,* 175–194. doi:10.1016/j.tcs.2003.11.004

Angluin, D., & Krikis, M. (2003). Learning from Different Teachers. *Machine Learning, 51,* 137–163. doi:10.1023/A:1022854802097

Anselme, M. (1989). *Après la morale, quelles valeurs?* Paris: Privat.

Astolfi, J.-P., Giordan, A., Gohau, G., Host, V., & Martinand, J.-L. Rumelhard, G., et al. (1978). *Quelle éducation scientifique pour quelle société?* Paris: Puf l'éducateur.

Bachelard, G. (1934). *Le Nouvel Esprit Scientifique.* Paris: Broché (2003).

Boulton-Lewis, G., Smith, D., McCrindle, A., Burnett, P., & Campbell, K. (2001). Secondary teachers' conceptions of teaching and learning. *Learning and Instruction, 11,* 35–51. doi:10.1016/S0959-4752(00)00014-1

Chalmers, A. F. (1976). Qu'est-ce que la science? (translated from *What is this Thing Called Science? An Assessment of the Nature and Status of Science and its* []). Paris: La Découverte.]. *Methods (San Diego, Calif.),* 1988.

Chan, K.-W., & Elliott, R. (2004). Relational analysis of personal epistemology and conceptions about teaching and learning. *Teaching and Teacher Education, 20,* 817–831. doi:10.1016/j.tate.2004.09.002

Chavalarias, D. (1997). *La thèse de popper est-elle réfutable?* Unpublished doctoral dissertation, CREA - CNRS/Ecole Polytechnique.

Dartnell, C. (2008). *Conception d'un Cadre Formel d'Interaction pour la Découverte Scientifique Computationelle*. Ph.D. thesis, Université Montpellier 2.

Dartnell, C., Martin, E., Hagège, H., & Sallantin, J. (2008). Human Discovery and Machine Learning. *International Journal of Cognitive Informatics and Natural Intelligence*, *2*, 55–69.

Dartnell, C., Martin, E., & Sallantin, J. (2008). Learning from Each Other. Springer Berlin / Heidelberg: *Discovery science*, 148-159.

Dartnell, C., & Sallantin, J. (2005). Assisting scientific discovery with an adaptive problem solver. Springer Berlin / Heidelberg: *Discovery science,* 99-112.

David-Néel, A. (1977). *Le bouddhisme du Bouddha*. Paris: Pocket (1989)

Descartes, R. (1637). *Discours de la Méthode*. Paris: Maxi-poche (1995)

Dinstein, I., Thomas, C., Behrmann, M., & Heeger, D. J. (2008). A mirror up to nature. *Current Biology*, *18*, 13–18. doi:10.1016/j.cub.2007.11.004

Doise, W., & Mugny, G. (1997). *Psychologie sociale et développement cognitif*. Paris: Armand Colin

Favre, D. (2006). Émotion et cognition: un couple inséparable. *Cahiers Pédagogiques*, *448*, 66–68.

Favre, D. (2007). *Transformer la violence des élèves*. Paris: Dunod.

Ferber, J., & Gutknecht, O. (1998). A meta-model for the analysis and design of organizations in multi-agent systems. In *Third international conference on multi-agent systems (icmas98)* (p.128-135).

Foulin, J.-N., & Mouchon, S. (1998). Psychologie de l'éducation. Paris: Nathan (2005)

Fourez, G. (2002). *La construction des sciences*. Paris: DeBoeck Université.

Fourez, G., Englebert-Lecomte, V., & Mathy, P. (1997). *Nos savoirs sont nos savoirs*. Paris: DeBoeck Université.

Gardner, H. (1984) *Frames of Mind: The Theory of Multiple Intelligences*. Basic Books.

Gold, E. M. (1967). Language identification in the limit. *Information and Control*, *10*, 447–474. doi:10.1016/S0019-9958(67)91165-5

Goleman, D. (1997). *L'Intelligence émotionnelle: Comment transformer ses émotions en intelligence*. Paris: R. Laffont

Gutknecht, O., & Ferber, J. (1997, December). *MadKit: Organizing heterogeneity with groups in a platform for multiple multiagent systems* (Tech. Rep. No. 97188). LIRMM, 161, rue Ada - Montpellier - France.

Hagège, H. (2004). *Emergence et évolution de la notion d'information génétique*. Unpublished doctoral dissertation, LIRDEF – Université Montpellier 2.

Hagège, H. (2007). Jugement de valeurs, affects et conceptions sur l'élaboration du savoir scientifique: la recherche d'obstacles l'enseignement des questions vives. In A. Giordan & J.-L. Martinand (Eds.), *XXVIII^emes journées internationales sur la communication, l'éducation et la culture scientifiques, techniques et industrielles. "Ecole, culture et actualite' des sciences techniques*

Hagège, H., Dartnell, C., & Sallantin, J. (2007). Positivism against constructivism: A network game to learn epistemology. Springer Berlin / Heidelberg: *Discovery science*, 91-103.

Haykin, S. (1998). *Neural Networks: A Comprehensive Foundation*. Upper Saddle River, NJ: Prentice Hall.

Heckerman, D., Geiger, D., & Chickering, D. M. (1995). *Learning Bayesian networks: The combination of knowledge and statistical data*. Springer.

Kuhn, T. (1962). *La structure des révolutions scientifiques*. (Translated from *The Structure of Scientific Revolutions*, 1972). Champs Flammarion.

Lakatos, I. (1976). *Proofs and refutations*. Cambridge University Press.

Langley, P. Simon, H. A., & Zytkow, J. M. (1987). *Scientific discovery: Computational explorations of the creative processes*. Cambridge: The MIT Press

Langley, P., Bradshaw, G. L., & Simon, H. A. (1981). Bacon5: The discovery of conservation laws. *IJCAI'81*.

Le Moigne, J.-L. (1995). *Les épistémologies constructivistes*. Paris: Puf, Que sais-je? Lenat, D. B. (1983). The role of heuristics in learning by discovery. In *Machine Learning: An Artificial Intelligence Approach*.

Lecourt, D. (2001). *La philosophie des sciences*. Paris: Puf Que sais-je? Lemberger, N., Hewson, P., & Park, H.-J. (1999). Relationships between prospective secondary teachers' classroom practice and their conceptions of biology and of teaching science. *Science Education, 83*, 347–371.

Liquiere, M., & Sallantin, J. (1998). *Structural machine learning with galois lattice and graphs*. 5th International Conference on Machine Learning.

Lonka, K., Joram, E., & Brysin, M. (1996). Conceptions of learning and knowledge: Does training make a difference. *Contemporary Educational Psychology, 21*, 347–371. doi:10.1006/ceps.1996.0021

Marchand, D., & Chaline, J. (2002). *Les merveilles de l'évolution*. Paris: Broché.

Molnár, G., Oláh, S., Komlósi, G., Füle, M., & Szabadics, J., Varga, et al. (2008). Complex Events Initiated by Individual Spikes in the Human Cerebral Cortex. *PLoS Biology, 6*, 1842–1849. doi:10.1371/journal.pbio.0060222

Morin, E. (1973). *Le paradigme perdu*. Paris: Seuil (1979)

Perelman, C., & Olbrechts-Tyteca, L. (1970). *Traité de l'argumentation. La nouvelle rhétorique*. Paris: Vrin.

Pestre, D. (2006). *Introduction aux Science Studies*. Paris: La Découverte.

Popper, K. R. (1934). *Logique de la découverte scientifique.* Paris: Broché (2002).

Prince, M. (2004). Does Active Learning Work? A Review of the Research. *Journal of Engineering Education, 93,* 223–231.

Scheurmann, E. (1920). *Le Papalagui, Les étonnants propos de Touiavii, chef de tribu, sur les hommes blancs.* Paris: Pocket (2001)

Searles, H. (1960). *L'environnement non humain* (translated from *The Nonhuman Environment,* 1986). Paris: nrf Gallimard.

Segal, J. (2003). *Le zéro et le un, histoire de la notion scientifique d'information au 20ᵉ siècle.* Paris: Syllepse.

Simon, H., Valdés-Pérez, R. E., & Sleeman, D. H. (1997). Scientific discovery and simplicity of method. *Artificial Intelligence, 91,* 177–181. doi:10.1016/S0004-3702(97)00019-2

Simon, R. (1993). *Ethique de la responsabilité.* Paris: Cerf.

Strike, K., & Posner, G. (1992). A revisionist theory of conceptual change. *Philosophy of Science, Cognitive Psychology, and Educational Theory and Practice,* 147-176.

Valiant, L. (1984). A theory of the learnable. *Communications of the ACM, 27,* 1134–1142. doi:10.1145/1968.1972

Vernon, D. T., & Blake, R. L. (1993). Does problem-based learning work? A meta-analysis of evaluative research. *Academic Medicine, 68,* 542–544. doi:10.1097/00001888-199307000-00015

Vignaux, G. (1991). *Les sciences cognitives.* Paris: La Découverte.

Vygotsky, L. S. (1934). *Pensée et langage.* Paris: La Dispute (1997).

Waeytens, K., Lens, W., & Vandenberghe, R. (2002). Learning to learn: Teachers conceptions of their supporting role. *Learning and Instruction, 12,* 305–322. doi:10.1016/S0959-4752(01)00024-X

ENDNOTES

[1.] Note that Wiener, the father of cybernetics, was together with Skinner a member of the North American Institute for the unity of science. This highlights the links between the initial proposals to model animal and machine learning in terms of circulation of information, even if a theoretical rupture has taken place between Wiener's approach to teleological behaviour and Skinner's radical behaviourism, which keeps *intention* out of the model (Ségal, 2003 p. 183). We will consider later a reduction that is pragmatically operated, even if not necessarily theoretically, by identifying "cognition" with a set of logico-mathematic operations, thus precisely denying the specificity of human learning as opposed to machine learning.

[2.] There are several acceptations of the term "cognitive". Here we take its meaning from psychology, where it is restrained to logico-mathematic operations, to reasoning on linguistic representations or to procedural acquisition… all "traditional 'objects'" of learning which lack any affective dimension. As we will emphasise later, though the "cognitive sciences" are supposed to consider all aspects of learning, their object is actually pragmatically reduced to the same unique dimension as in psychology (Vignaux, 1991 p. 13). The term "cognitive" designates the "form of 'representations' and of 'data processing'" (Vignaux, 1991 p. 198).

3.	In accordance with a constructivist point of view, we consider that there is no "object" of learning that would exist per se, before a learning act, and that would be the same for several individuals. This notion of object is just a practical denotation that facilitates communication.

4.	Note that others argue that some hypotheses or laws, such as the first principle of thermodynamics (energy of the universe is constant), are not falsifiable; one cannot go through it with the fine-tooth comb of experiment (Fourez, 2002 p. 71).

5.	http://www.lirmm.fr/kayou/netoffice/eleusis/

6.	To argue that this is a paramount problem – that only Buddhas could overcome? – it suffices to underline that i) believing that our vision of the world corresponds to the world as it is and ii) adjusting our acts on the basis of this belief is the cause of every war. This belief, this representation is associated with such a strong feeling about reality - from which it is so hard (or impossible?) to distant oneself – and about a somehow permanent self that some people are prompt to kill to defend it.

7.	The idea that we want to advance here is that the primary duality consists in considering the self separated from the rest of the world. Moreover, we mostly act as if this separated self were permanent: as if we were, to ourselves, the most important person on earth. Then, by a mirror effect, as one sees the world as one's own image, one could know by dissecting reality, by "artificially" isolating objects and considering them i) permanent and ii) separated from each other. Yet "objects", such as "the self", are fundamentally impermanent and linked to "the rest of the world"; they do not have a proper existence.

Chapter 6
On Cognitive Properties of Human Factors and Error Models in Engineering and Socialization

Yingxu Wang
University of Calgary, Canada

ABSTRACT

Human factors are the most predominated factors in all systems where humans are part of the systems. Human traits and needs are the fundamental force underlying almost all phenomena in human task performances, engineering organizations, and socialization. This article explores the cognitive foundations of human traits and cognitive properties of human factors in engineering. A comprehensive set of fundamental traits of human beings are identified, and the hierarchical model of basic human needs is formally described. The characteristics of human factors and their influences in engineering organizations and socialization are explored. Based on the models of basic human traits, needs, and their influences, driving forces behind the human factors in engineering and society are revealed. A formal model of human errors in task performance is derived, and case studies of the error model in software engineering are presented.

INTRODUCTION

In many disciplines of human knowledge, almost all of the hard problems yet to be solved share a common root in the understanding of the mechanisms of the natural intelligence and cognitive properties of human factors. Human traits and needs are the fundamental force underlying all the phenomena in human task performances, engineering organizations, and socialization (Eagly & Chaiken, 1992; Embry,

1986; Hull, 1943; Leahey, 1997; Maslow, 1962, 1967; Reason, 1987, 1990; Sternberg, 1998; Wang, 2002, 2003, 2007a, 2007c; Wang, Wang, Patel, & Patel, 2006; Westen, 1999; Wickens, Gordon, & Liu, 1998; Wiggins, Eiggins, & Zanden, 1994).

Because the basic objects under study in sociology are individual human beings and their interactions, social psychology is the key to understand a wide range of complicated social phenomena and the driving forces underpinning them. The study on human traits forms the foundation of sociology because every individual's social behavior is driven and constrained by those axiomatic human traits, characteristics, and the derived needs based on them. The study on human traits also forms the foundation for engineering organization.

This article explores the cognitive foundations of human traits and cognitive properties of human factors in engineering and socialization. In the remaining sections, a comprehensive set of fundamental traits of human beings are identified. A human needs hierarchy (HNH) model is rigorously developed on the basis of Maslow's (1970) model of motivation and personality. The characteristics of human factors in engineering are elaborated, and the influence of the human factors in socialization is formally discussed. Based on the models of basic human traits, needs, and their influences, the driving forces behind the human factors in engineering and society are revealed. A formal model of human errors in task performance is then derived and its applications in work product review, inspection, and quality assurance in software engineering are presented.

COGNITIVE FOUNDATIONS OF HUMAN TRAITS

Studies on human traits form the foundation of sociology because every individual's social behavior is driven and constrained by those axiomatic human traits and the derived needs based on them (Wang, 2002, 2003, 2007a, 2007c; Wang et al., 2006; Wickens et al., 1998; Wiggins et al., 1994). The studies on human traits also form the foundation for engineering organization.

Axiomatic Human Traits

The basic evolutional need of humans is the tendency to maximize the inclusive fitness of both individuals and the whole of mankind. It can be described by the philosophical doctrines of egoism and altruism.

Definition 1. *Egoism is a social behavior of human beings in which individuals put their own interests first in decision making.*

Both sociologists and economists believe that egoism drives most of the behaviors of individuals. However, statistically, all individual behaviors as a whole form the natural force toward the development and welfare of the entire society.

The basic forms of egoism of individuals are to maximize personal life span, profit, pleasure, esteem, and power; to possess information; and to minimize costs, energy consumption, and inconvenience. It is noteworthy that most forms of egoism are dependent on the cooperation or recognition of others collectively known as the society. This basic constraint is the sociological foundation of altruism.

Definition 2. *Altruism is a social behavior in which individuals sacrifice their own interests for the welfare of a group or society.*

Altruism can be explained by the term *inclusive fitness* as defined below (Westen, 1999).

Definition 3. *The inclusive fitness of human beings is their own reproductive success and those of genetically related individuals.*

Lemma 1. *Egoism is constrained by altruism, and the implementation of altruism is dependent on the natural egoism.*

Lemma 1 provides an explanation of the relationship between egoism and altruism. Based on Lemma 1, the following theorem can be derived.

Theorem 1. *The basic evolutional need of mankind is to preserve both the species' biological traits via gene pools and the cumulated knowledge base via various information systems.*

History indicates that evolution favors species like human beings and other organisms that are able to seek the maximum inclusive fitness.

Basic Personality Traits in Engineering

A variety of human personality traits are identified in psychology, social psychology, cognitive science, management science, and cognitive informatics (Leahey, 1997; Maslow, 1962, 1967; Sternberg, 1998; Wang, 2002, 2003, 2007a, 2007c; Wang et al., 2006; Westen, 1999; Wickens et al., 1998; Wiggins et al., 1994). The taxonomy of personality traits of human beings in engineering can be summarized in Table 1. In Table 1, eight categories of personality traits are identified: emotion and motivation, attitude, cognitive ability, interpersonal ability, sociability, rigorousness, creativity, and custom. Attributes for each category of personality traits are provided in Table 1, which form the fundamental internal and personal characteristics of the human factors in engineering and socialization.

The entire set of human personality traits as given in Table 1 can be mapped into different tasks and processes of projects and groups. Based on this, the requirements for personnel at the task and process level and project level can be formally specified.

THE HIERARCHICAL MODEL OF BASIC HUMAN NEEDS

As an individual, the basic biological need of humans is a stable inner environment regulated by a mechanism known as homeostasis.

Definition 4. *Homeostasis is an adaptive biological mechanism of the human body that maintains a relatively constant state in order to live and function.*

Table 1. Taxonomy of personnel traits and attributes

Emotion and Motivation	Attitude	Cognitive Ability	Interpersonal Ability
Comfort/fear	Proud of job	Knowledge	Pleasant
Joy/sadness	Responsible	Skills	Tolerant
Pleasure/anger	Disciplined	Experience	Tactful
Love/hate	Thorough	Instructiveness	Helpful
Ambition	Careful	Learning ability	Scope of contact
Impulsiveness	Assertive	Expressiveness	Variety of contact
Trying in uncertainty	Energetic	Knowledge transfer-ability	Consultative
Following rules	Enthusiastic	Reaction to events	Responsible
Self-expectation	Tolerant	Efficiency	Respectful
	Tactful	Attention	Trustworthy
	Confident	Abstraction	Sympathetic
	Individual	Searching	Modest
	Team oriented	Categorization	Loyal
	Productive	Comprehension	Flexible
	Persistent	Planning	Independent
		Decision making	
		Problem solving	
		Analysis	
		Synthesis	

Sociability	Rigorousness	Creativity	Custom
Collaboration capability	Contingent error rate	Abstraction capability	Exterior hobby
Communication capability	Repeatable error rate	Imagination	Interior hobby
Extroversion	Error-correction capability	Analogy capability	Quietness
Introversion	Pinpoint capability	Curiousness	Activeness
Culture factor	Concentration capability	Design ability	Literature
Leadership	Logical inference capability	Hands-on capability	Vision
Group orientation	Reliability	Broad mind	
Organization capability	Precision		
Concern of others	Perception		
Dependability	Consistency		
Compatibility	System		
	Talent		

At the psychological level, Sigmund Freud (1895/1966) perceived that humans are motivated by internal tension states known as drives that build up until they are released. The basic drives that Freud identified are self-preservation, sex, and aggression. However, he focused only on the last two drives later in his theory. Clark Hull (1943) proposed the drive-reduction theory that states motivation stems from a combination of drive and reinforcement of unfulfilled needs. The primary drives are innate drives such as hunger, thirst, and sex; the secondary drives are acquired drives such as studying, socializing, and earning money.

The hierarchy of human needs is identified by Abraham Maslow (1962, 1970) as five levels known as the needs of physiological, safety, social, esteem, and self-actualization from the bottom up. The five basic levels of human needs are described in Table 2. Except those at Level 5, most needs identified by Maslow as shown in Table 1 are deficiency needs, which are needs generated by a lack of something. The Level 5 needs for self-actualization can be perceived as growth needs.

On the basis of the needs taxonomies of Maslow, Hull, and Freud, a formal human needs hierarchy model is developed in Definition 5, Figure 1, and Table 3.

Definition 5. *The HNH model is a hierarchical model that encompasses five levels of fundamental human needs known from the button up as N_0, physiological needs; N_1, psychological needs; N_2, cognitive needs; N_3, social needs; and N_4, self-expressive needs.*

Table 2. Maslow's hierarchy of needs

Level	Category	Needs	Description
1	Lower order needs	Physiological	Needs for biological maintenance such as food, water, sex, sleep, etc.
2		Safety	Needs for physical and social security, protection, and stability such as shelter
3		Social	Needs for love, affection, socialization
4	Higher order needs	Esteem	Needs for respect, prestige, recognition, and self-satisfaction
5		Self-actualiza-tion	Need to express oneself, to grow, and to fulfill one's maximum potential toward success

Figure 1. The human needs hierarchy (HNH) model

Table 3. The human needs hierarchy (HNH) model

Level	Basic Needs	Description
N_0	Physiological	Needs for maintaining homeostasis, such as food, water, clothes, sex, sleep, and shelter
N_1	Psychological	Needs for feeling safe and comfortable, and for well-being
N_2	Cognitive	Needs for satisfaction of curiosity, knowledge, pleasure, and interaction with the environment
N_3	Social	Needs for work, socialization, respect, prestige, esteem, and recognition
N_4	Self-expressive	Need to express oneself, grow, and fulfill one's maximum potential toward success

The HNH model can be illustrated as shown in Figure 1. Detailed explanations of each of the basic needs are provided in Table 3.

Theorem 2. *The lower the level of a need in the HNH hierarchy, the more concrete or material oriented the need. In other words, the higher the level of a need, the more virtualized or perception oriented the need.*

Definition 6. *The predominate need of an individual is the need at the lowest unsatisfied level of the HNH model.*

Maslow (1970) suggests that human needs should be satisfied level by level. That is, the lower level needs should be satisfied before any higher level needs come into play. This observation leads to the following theorem.

Theorem 3. *When multiple needs of a person are unsatisfied at a given time, satisfaction of the most predominate need is most pressing.*

Understanding of the nature of basic human needs is not only useful in predicating motivations of human beings in a given context, but also important in identifying the driving forces for the approach of engineering organization, the types of societies, and the corresponding economic structures.

The following sections discuss the influence of human factors in engineering and society.

CHARACTERISTICS OF HUMAN FACTORS

Human factors are not only a constantly important constraint in almost all disciplines of science and engineering, but also the most active and dynamic factors to be considered. Nevertheless, human beings themselves are directly the object of study in a number of disciplines such as psychology, cognitive science, ergonomics, sociology, cognitive informatics, medical science, neuroscience, and natural intelligence.

Definition 7. *Human factors are the roles and effects of humans in a system that introduce additional strengths, weaknesses, and uncertainty.*

Properties of Human Factors in Engineering

There are numerous human factors identified in science, engineering, sociology, psychology, and everyday life. The taxonomy of human factors in engineering can be classified into human strengths, weaknesses, and uncertainties, as shown in Table 4.

Widely varying productivities are one of the major factors of human beings, particularly in creative work such as software development. It is found that the productivity of human creative work is conservative. That is, creative productivity is independent of languages, tools, and forms of groups; however, it depends on human cognitive, physiological, and psychological capabilities.

Definition 8. *Conservative productivity is a basic constraint of software engineering due to cognitive complexity and due to the cognitive mechanism in which abstract artifacts need to be represented physiologically in the brain via growing synaptic neural connections.*

The fact that before any program is composed, an internal abstract model must be created inside the brain (Wang, 2007a; Wang, Liu, & Wang, 2003) reveals the most fundamental constraint of software engineering, as follows.

Lemma 2. *Software, as any other creative artifact, is created and grown in the brain first before it can be represented on a medium or transferred to a computer.*

Because the growth of the human neural system is naturally constrained due to the cognitive mechanism in which abstract artifacts need to be represented physiologically in the brain via growing synaptic neural connections, as described by the 24-hour law in Wang (2006) and Wang and Wang (2006), it is very hard to dramatically improve the productivity of software development.

According to the statistics of several sources (Boehm, 1987; Dale & Zee, 1992; Jones, 1986; Livermore, 2005; Wang, 2007b), the average productivity of software development in lines of code (LOC) was about 1,300 LOC/person-year in the 1970s, 2,500 LOC/person-year in the 1980s, and 3,000 LOC/person-year in the 1990s, where management, quality assurance, and supporting activities are consid-

Table 4. Taxonomy of human factors

No	Category	Basic Factor
1	Strengths	Natural intelligence, autonomic behaviors, complex decision making, highly skilled operations, intelligent senses, perception power, complicated human coordination, adaptivity
2	Weaknesses	Low efficiency, slow reactions, error prone, tiredness, distraction
3	Uncertainties	Productivity, accuracy, reaction time, persistency, reliability, attitude, performance, motivation to try uncertain things

ered part of programming. It is obvious that productivity in software engineering has not increased remarkably in the last three decades, despite advances in hardware and programming languages. In other words, no matter what kinds of programming languages are used, as long as they are used for human programming, there is no difference in principle. This assertion is equivalent to the answers for the following questions. Has there ever been a writer who was productive because he or she wrote in a specific language? Would typing speed determine a writer's productivity?

The productivity of software development is key among all the cognitive, organizational, and resource constraints in software engineering. The other constraints may be overcome as a result of the improvement of software engineering productivity. The major approach to improve software development productivity is to explicitly express software architectures and behaviors. Therefore, automatic tools may be developed that are capable to seamlessly generate code based on the explicit specifications.

Human psychology, such as motivations and attitudes, influences human factors very much (Eagly & Chaiken, 1992; Fischer, Shaver, & Carnochan, 1990; Wang, 2007a, 2007c). The great variety of human psychological and cognitive capacity influenced by motivations, attitudes, focus, and attention are the major reasons for human uncertainties in productivity, accuracy, reaction time, persistency, and task performance.

Properties of Human Factors in Socialization

Task performance and engineering organizations are not the only things influenced by fundamental human factors and needs, but the forms of societies and their organizations are indirectly determined by basic human needs as well.

There are various types of societies corresponding to different economic structures and their levels of development. The relationships between the basic human needs, economic structures, and social types can be explained in the following model.

Definition 9. *The formal socialization model (FSM) is a relational model that describes the relationships between basic human needs, economic structures, and social types, as shown in Figure 2.*

Figure 2. The formal socialization model (FSM) of human societies

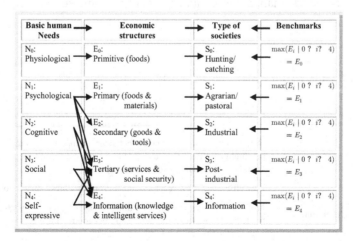

The FSM reveals that natural rules exist between the types of societies, the underlying economic structures, and the dominant sector in the economy because both social architectures and economic structures are driven by the current level of predominately unsatisfied fundamental human needs according to Theorem 4.

Theorem 4. *The type of society* T_{S_i}, $0 \leq i \leq 4$ *is determined by the dominant sector of the corresponding economic structure* T_{E_i}, *which is constituted by the current level of predominately unsatisfied human needs* $\overline{T_{N_i}}$, *that is,*

$$T_{S_i} = \max(T_{E_i})$$
$$= \max(\overline{T_{N_i}}), 0 \leq i \leq 4. \tag{1}$$

It is noteworthy that the trend of socialization according to Theorem 4 may be predicated such that the emerging information-based economy will drive the society into a new era, the information society, where the major sector of the information society will be information-processing related, involving professionals providing intelligent services.

Corollary 1. *The next type of society after postindustrialization is the information society driven by the current level of predominantly unsatisfied social and self-expressive needs and the underlying information-oriented economy.*

The fundamental driving force for this trend is that the higher level human needs built upon the satisfied lower level ones, namely, the cognitive (N_2), social (N_3), and self-expressive (N_4) needs, will be the new focus of postindustrialized societies. Because all N_2 through N_4 needs are based on information and intelligent services, when the material-level needs are satisfied, the form of economy and type of society will be evolved into an information-oriented society naturally.

Social Environments for Software Engineering

According to social psychology foundations discussed in preceding sections, the social environment, such as culture, ethical norms, and attitude, greatly influences people's motivation, behavior, productivity, and quality toward coordinative work. The chain of individual motivation in a software organization can be illustrated as shown in Figure 3.

The cultures and values of a software development organization help to establish a set of ethical principles or standards shared by individuals of the organization for judging and normalizing social behaviors. The identification of a larger set of values and organizational policy toward social relations may be helpful to normalize individual and collective behaviors in a software development organization that produces information products for a global market.

Another condition for supporting the creative work of individuals in a software development organization is to encourage diversity in both ways of thinking and work allocation. It is observed in social ecology that a great diversity of species and a complex and intricate pattern of interactions among the populations of a community may confer greater stability on an ecosystem.

Figure 3. The chain of motivation in a software organization

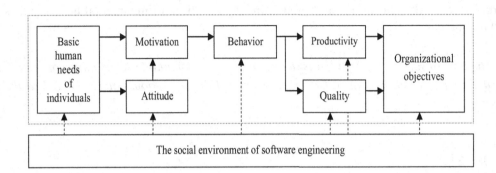

Definition 10. *Diversity refers to the social and technical differences of people in working organizations.*

Diversity includes a wide range of differences between people such as those of race, ethnicity, age, gender, disability, skills, education, experience, values, native language, and culture.

The principle of system mutation indicates that if the number of components of a system reaches a certain level, the critical mass, then the functionality of the system may be dramatically increased, as stated in Theorem 5. That is, the increase of diversity in a system is the condition to realize the system fusion effect, which results in a totally new system.

Theorem 5. *The principle of diversity of system creativity states that the more diverse the workforce in an organization (particularly the creative software industry), the higher the opportunity to form new relations and connections that leads to the gain of the system fusion effect.*

THE FORMAL MODEL OF HUMAN ERRORS

It is a fact that people do make mistakes, and fortunately, most of them may be corrected by additional undo or redo actions. However, in safety- or mission-critical contexts, the impact of human errors can be catastrophic, such as in the nuclear and chemical industries, rail and sea transport, and aviation.

Taxonomy of Human Errors

Definition 11. *A human error is a human operator error caused by wrong actions and inappropriate behaviors.*

Wickens et al. (1998) identified a long list of reasons that cause operator errors, such as inattentiveness, poor work habits, lack of training, poor decision making, personality traits, and social pressure. The systematic human error reduction and prediction approach (SHERPA) proposed by D. Embry in 1986 identifies 16 potential psychological errors. Reason (1987, 1990) developed a similar system known as the generic error modeling system (GEMS). The set of human behavioral errors identified in SHERPA are as follows.

- Action omitted
- Action too early
- Action too late
- Action too much
- Action too little
- Action too long
- Action too short
- Action in wrong direction
- Right action on wrong object
- Wrong action on right object
- Misalignment
- Information not obtained or transmitted
- Check omitted
- Check on wrong object
- Wrong check
- Check mistimed

A comparative study of the above work indicates that there is still a need to seek a more logical taxonomy of human errors, which will be developed in the next section (Wang, 2007; Wang et al., 2006).

The Behavioral Model of Human Errors

A formal behavioral model of human errors (BMHE) is derived in this subsection based on human and system behaviors that explains the fundamental mechanisms of human errors.

Definition 12. *A human behavior B is constituted by four basic elements known as the sets of objects (O), actions (A), space (S), and time (T):*

$$B = (O, A, S, T)$$
$$= O \times A \times S \times T. \tag{2}$$

Any incorrect configuration of any of these four elements results in a human error in task performance. Therefore, there are 16 modes of human errors on the basis of the combinations of these four basic elements. The BMHE is shown in Table 5.

Corresponding to Table 5, a human error tree (HET) is illustrated in Figure 4. It is noteworthy that the identification of the object is the most important task in a chain of actions because it is obvious that a correct action in a correct location at a correct time but on a wrong object is still an error action. Observing Figure 4 and Table 5, it may be found that for a human operator, there is only a 1:16 chance to get a given action or behavior to be correct, but there is a 15:16 chance to get it wrong. That is, the probabilities of human success $p(+)$ and human error $p(-)$ in performing a specific task, respectively, are

Table 5. The behavioral model of human errors (BMHE)

No.	Objects	Action	Space	Time	Error Mode
0	T	T	T	T	Correct action
1	T	T	T	F	Mode 1: Wrong timing
2	T	T	F	T	Mode 2: Wrong place
3	T	T	F	F	Mode 3: Wrong timing and place
4	T	F	T	T	Mode 4: Wrong action
5	T	F	T	F	Mode 5: Wrong action and timing
6	T	F	F	T	Mode 6: Wrong action and place
7	T	F	F	F	Mode 7: Wrong action, place, and timing
8	F	T	T	T	Mode 8: Wrong object
9	F	T	T	F	Mode 9: Wrong object and timing
10	F	T	F	T	Mode 10: Wrong object and place
11	F	T	F	F	Mode 11: Wrong object, place, and timing
12	F	F	T	T	Mode 12: Wrong object and action
13	F	F	T	F	Mode 13: Wrong object, action, and timing
14	F	F	F	T	Mode 14: Wrong object, action, and place
15	F	F	F	F	Mode 15: All wrong

$$\begin{cases} p(+) = \dfrac{1}{16} = 6.25\% \\ p(-) = \dfrac{15}{16} = 93.75\% \end{cases} \tag{3}$$

The BMHE and HET indicate that the natural rate of human errors in performing tasks should be very high. Fortunately, a well-trained human being is fault tolerant when performing tasks and a well-established engineering process is fault tolerant, too. The major means for fault tolerance in task performance is checking and rechecking. By adopting all checking and monitoring techniques in each step of the HET, the error ratio as shown in Equation 3 may be greatly decreased.

The Random Feature of Human Errors

On the basis of various fault-tolerant measures and referring to Figure 4, the following statistical properties of human errors may be observed.

Theorem 6. *The statistical properties of human errors are as follows.*

a. **Oddness:** Although individuals make different errors in performing tasks, the chance of making a single error for a given task is greater than that of making multiple errors.
b. **Independence:** Different individuals have different error patterns in performing the same task.

Figure 4. The model of the human error tree (HET)

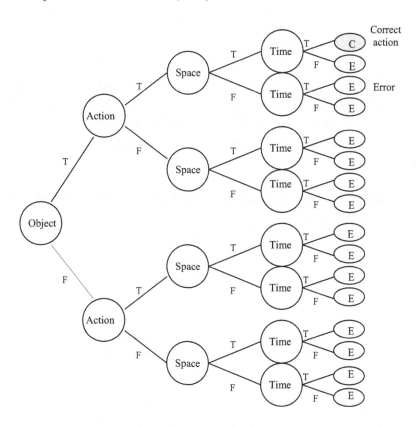

c. **randomness:** Most of the different individuals make the same error at different times in performing tasks.

Properties a through c reveal the random nature of human errors on objects, actions, space, and time in performing tasks in a group.

Corollary 2. *The random nature of human errors during task performance in a group is determined by the statistical properties stating that the occurrences of the same errors by different individuals are most likely to happen at different times.*

The Theoretical Foundation of Quality Assurance in Creative Work

The findings as stated in Theorem 6 and Corollary 2 form a theoretical foundation for fault tolerance and quality assurance in software engineering. They indicate that human errors may be prevented from happening or be corrected after their presence as soon as possible in a coordinative group context by means of peer reviews.

Theorem 7. *The n-fold error reduction structure states that the error rate of a work product can be reduced up to n folds from the average error rate of individuals r_e in a coordinative group via n-nary* *peer reviews based on the random nature of error distributions and independent nature of error patterns of individuals:*

$$R_e = \prod_{k=1}^{n} r_e(k).$$
(4)

Example 1. *A software engineering project is being developed by a group of four programmers. Given the individual error rates of the four group members, $r_e(1) = 10\%$, $r_e(2) = 8\%$, $r_e(3) = 20\%$, and $r_e(4) = 5\%$, estimate the error rates of the final software by adopting the following quality assurance techniques: (a) pairwise reviews between Programmers 1 and 2, and Programmers 3 and 4, and (b) 4-nary reviews between all group members.*

a.   The pairwise reviews between Programmers 1 and 2, and Programmers 3 and 4 will result in the following error rates R_{e1} and R_{e2}:

$$
\begin{aligned}
R_{e1} &= \prod_{k=1}^{2} r_e(k) \\
&= 10\% \cdot 8\% \\
&= 0.8\%
\end{aligned}
$$

$$
\begin{aligned}
R_{e2} &= \prod_{k=3}^{4} r_e(k) \\
&= 20\% \cdot 5\% \\
&= 1.0\%
\end{aligned}
$$

b.   The 4-nary reviews between Programmers 1 through 4 will yield the following error rate R_{e3}:

$$
\begin{aligned}
R_{e3} &= \prod_{k=1}^{4} r_e(k) \\
&= 10\% \cdot 8\% \cdot 20\% \cdot 5\% \\
&= 0.008\%
\end{aligned}
$$

Theorem 7 and Example 1 explain why multiple peer reviews may greatly reduce the probability of errors in program development and software engineering. Theorem 7 is also applicable in academic circles, where peer-reviewed results may virtually prevent any mistake in a final article before its publication.

In software engineering quality assurance, a four-level quality assurance system is needed for certain critical software functions and projects as shown in Table 6.

Example 2. *For a given program reviewed according to the four-level quality assurance system as shown in Table 6, assuming $r_e(10) = 10\%$, $r_e(2) = 5\%$, $r_e(3) = 2\%$, and $r_e(4) = 10\%$, estimate the quality of the final result of this program.*

According to Equation 4, the 4-nary quality assurance system may yield an expected error rate R_{e4}:

Table 6. The four-level quality assurance system of software engineering

Level	Checker	Means
1	Programmer	Self-checking, module-level testing
2	Senior member	Peer review, module-level testing
3	Tester/ quality engineer	System-level testing, audit, review, quality evaluation
4	Manager	Quality review, delivery evaluation, customer survey

$$R_{e4} = \prod_{k=1}^{4} r_e(k)$$
$$= 10\% \cdot 5\% \cdot 2\% \cdot 10\%$$
$$= 0.001\%$$

The results indicate that the error rate of the above system has been significantly reduced from the initial 100 bugs/kLOC to 1 bug/kLOC. This demonstrates that the hierarchical organization form for software system reviews can greatly increase the quality of software development and significantly decrease the requirement for individual capability and low error rates in software engineering.

CONCLUSION

Human factors are the most predominant factor in all systems humans are a part of. This article has explored the cognitive foundations of human traits and cognitive properties of human factors in engineering and societies. The relationship between the fundamental human needs, traits, economical structures, and forms of engineering organizations and societies is established. Based on the models of basic human traits and their influences, the driving forces behind the human factors in engineering and society have been revealed. A formal model of human errors in task performance has been derived. Based on the identification of the random feature of human errors, the effectiveness of review techniques as an important means of quality assurance systems in human creative work, such as in software engineering and journalism, is formally explained.

A number of key findings have been reported in this article: (a) The basic evolutional need of mankind is to preserve both the species' biological traits via gene pools and the cumulated knowledge base via various information systems, (b) the lower the level of a need in the HNH, the more concrete or material oriented the need (in other words, the higher the level of a need, the more virtualized or perception oriented the need), (c) when multiple needs of a person are unsatisfied at a given time, satisfaction of the most predominant need is most pressing, (d) the type of society is determined by the dominant sector of the corresponding economic structure, which is constituted by the current level of predominantly unsatisfied human needs (as a consequence, the next type of society after postindustrialization is the information society driven by the current level of predominantly unsatisfied social and self-expressive needs and the underlying information-oriented economy, and (e) the error rate of a work product can be reduced up to *n* folds of the average error rate of individuals in a group via *n*-nary peer reviews based on the random nature of error distributions and independent nature of the error patterns of individuals.

ACKNOWLEDGMENT

The author would like to acknowledge the Natural Science and Engineering Council of Canada (NSERC) for its partial support of this work. The author would like to thank the anonymous reviewers for their valuable comments and suggestions.

REFERENCES

Boehm, B. W. (1987). Improving software productivity. *IEEE Computer, 20*(9), 43.

Dale, C. J., & Zee, H. (1992). Software productivity metrics: Who needs them? *Information and Software Technology, 34*(11), 731-738.

Eagly, A. H., & Chaiken, S. (1992). *The psychology of attitudes.* San Diego, CA: Harcourt Brace.

Embry, D. E. (1986). *SHERPA: A systematic human error reduction and prediction approach.* Paper presented at the International Topical Meeting on Advances in Human Factors in Nuclear Power Systems, Knoxville, TN.

Fischer, K.W., Shaver, P. R., & Carnochan, P. (1990). How emotions develop and how they organize development. *Cognition and Emotion, 4*, 81-127.

Freud, S. (1966). Project for a scientific psychology. In J. Strachey (Ed.), *The standard edition the complete psychological works of Sigmund Freud* (Vol. 1). London: Hogarth Press. (Original work published 1895)

Hull, C. L. (1943). *Principles of behavior: An introduction to behavior theory.* New York: Oxford University Press.

Jones, C. (1986). *Programming productivity.* New York: McGraw-Hill Book Co.

Leahey, T. H. (1997). *A history of psychology: Main currents in psychological thought* (4th ed.). Upper Saddle River, NJ: Prentice- Hall Inc.

Livermore, J. (2005). *Measuring programmer productivity.* Retrieved from http://home.sprynet.com/~jgarriso/jlpaper.htm

Maslow, A. H. (1962). *Towards a psychology of being.* Princeton, NJ: Van Nostrand.

Maslow, A. H. (1970). *Motivation and personality* (2nd ed.). New York: Harper & Row.

Reason, J. (1987). Generic error-modeling system (GEMS): A cognitive framework for locating common human error forms. In J. Rasmussen et al. (Eds.), *New technology and human error.* New York: Wiley.

Reason, J. (1990). *Human error.* Cambridge, United Kingdom: Cambridge University Press.

Sternberg, R. J. (1998). *In search of the human mind* (2ⁿᵈ ed.). New York: Harcourt Brace & Co.

Wang, Y. (2002, August). Keynote: On cognitive informatics. In *Proceedings of the First IEEE International Conference on Cognitive Informatics (ICCI'02)*, Calgary, Canada (pp. 34-42). IEEE Computer Society Press.

Wang, Y. (2003). Cognitive informatics: A new transdisciplinary research field. *Brain and Mind: A Transdisciplinary Journal of Neuroscience and Neurophilosophy, 4*(2), 115-127.

Wang, Y. (2006). On the informatics laws and deductive semantics of software. *IEEE Transactions on Systems, Man, and Cybernetics (C), 36*(2), 161-171.

Wang, Y. (2007a). Formal description of the cognitive processes of perceptions with emotions, motivations, and attitudes. *International Journal of Cognitive Informatics and Natural Intelligence, 1*(4), 1-13.

Wang, Y. (2007b). *Software engineering foundations: A software science perspective* (Vol. 2). New York: Auerbach Publications.

Wang, Y. (2007c). The theoretical framework of cognitive informatics. *International Journal of Cognitive Informatics and Natural Intelligence, 1*(1), 1-27.

Wang, Y., Liu, D., & Wang, Y. (2003). Discovering the capacity of human memory. *Brain and Mind: A Transdisciplinary Journal of Neuroscience and Neurophilosophy, 4*(2), 189-198.

Wang, Y., & Wang, Y. (2006). Cognitive informatics models of the brain. *IEEE Transactions on Systems, Man, and Cybernetics (C), 36*(2), 203-207.

Wang, Y., Wang, Y., Patel, S., & Patel, D. (2006). A layered reference model of the brain (LRMB). *IEEE Transactions on Systems, Man, and Cybernetics (C), 36*(2), 124-133.

Westen, D. (1999). *Psychology: Mind, brain, and culture* (2ⁿᵈ ed.). New York: John Wiley & Sons, Inc.

Wickens, C. D., Gordon, S. E., & Liu, Y. (1998). *An introduction to human factors engineering.* New York: Addison Wesley Longman, Inc.

Wiggins, J. A., Eiggins, B. B., & Zanden, J. V. (1994). *Social psychology* (5ᵗʰ ed.). New York: McGraw-Hill, Inc.

This work was previously published in International Journal of Cognitive Informatics and Natural Intelligence, Vol. 2, Issue 4, edited by Y. Wang, pp. 70-84, copyright 2008 by IGI Publishing (an imprint of IGI Global).

Chapter 7
User–Centered Interactive Data Mining

Yan Zhao
University of Regina, Canada

Yiyu Yao
University of Regina, Canada

ABSTRACT

While many data mining models concentrate on automation and efficiency, interactive data mining models focus on adaptive and effective communications between human users and computer systems. User requirements and preferences play an important role in human-machine interactions, and guide the selection of knowledge representations, knowledge discovery operations and measurements, combined with explanations of mined patterns. This chapter discusses these fundamental issues based on a user-centered three-layer framework of interactive data mining.

INTRODUCTION

Data mining is featured by applying computer technologies to carry out nontrivial calculations for many important tasks, such as description, prediction and explanation of data. Computer systems can maintain precise operations under heavy information load, and maintain steady performance. Without the aid of computer systems, it is very difficult for people to aware, extract, memorize, search and retrieve knowledge in large and separate datasets, to interpret and evaluate data and information that are constantly changing, and to make recommendations or predictions in the face of inconsistent and incomplete data. It is true that computer technologies have freed humans from many time-consuming and labour-intensive activities. However, full automation of cognitive functions such as decision making, planning, and creative thinking remains human's job. Implementations and applications of computer systems reflect requests and preferences of human users, and contain certain human heuristics. Computer systems must rely on human users to set goals, select alternatives if original approach fails, participate in unanticipated

DOI: 10.4018/978-1-60566-902-1.ch007

emergencies and novel situations, and develop innovations in order to preserve safety, avoid expensive failure, or increase product quality (Elm *et al.* 2004; Hancock and Scallen, 1996; Shneiderman, 1998).

According to the above observations, we believe that interactive systems are required for data mining tasks. Though human-machine interaction has been emphasized for many disciplines, it did not receive enough attention in the domain of data mining until recently (Brachmann and Anand, 1996; Han, Hu and Cercone, 2003; Zhao, 2007; Zhao and Yao, 2005). Generally, an interactive data mining system is an integration of a human user and a computer. They can communicate and exchange information and knowledge. Through interaction and communication, computers and users can divide the labours in order to achieve a good balance of automation and human control. Computers are used to retrieve and keep track of large volumes of data, and to carry out complex mathematical or logical operations. Users can avoid routinized, tedious, and error-prone tasks, concentrate on critical decisions, planning, and cope with unexpected situations (Elm *et al.* 2004; Shneiderman, 1998). Moreover, interactive data mining can encourage learning, improve insights and understandings of the domain, stimulate the exploration of creative possibilities, and help users to solve particular problems. Users' feedback can be used to improve the system. The interaction is mutual beneficial. A foundation of human-computer interaction may be provided by cognitive informatics (Wang, 2002; Wang, 2003; Wang, 2004).

For conceptually modelling data mining, Yao (2003) proposed a three-layered framework consisting of the philosophy layer, the technique layer, and the application layer. The main objective of this chapter is to extend the framework for interactive data mining by introducing the notion of user preference and judgement. Within this new user-centered framework, we revisit and summarize our recent studies on data mining regarding the three layers. The study of different decision logic languages enables the definition of granules and concepts at the philosophy layer (Yao, 2003). The study of rule interestingness measures reveals the relationships among granules and concepts in the philosophy layer, and facilitates the discovery of interesting patterns in the technique layer (Yao, Chen and Yang, 2003; Yao and Zhong, 1999, Zhong, Yao and Ohshima, 2003; Zhong, Yao, Ohshima and Ohsuga, 2001). The study of different knowledge discovery strategies is essential for the technique layer (Yao, Wang, Wang and Zeng, 2005; Yao and Wong, 1992). Finally, the study of explanation-oriented data mining demonstrates the importance of having user involvement before and inside the application layer (Yao, Zhao and Maguire, 2003). The synthesis of the existing results leads to a high-level understanding of interactive data mining, as well as new insights to the potential of human-machine interaction in the design of interactive data mining systems.

A FRAMEWORK OF INTERACTIVE DATA MINING

A three-layered conceptual framework represents the understanding, discovery, and utilization of knowledge, and can be extended to a user-centered conceptual framework for interactive data mining by introducing the notion of user preference.

Modelling User Preference

User preference can be expressed in various forms. Quantitative judgement involves the assignment of different weights to different entities. Qualitative judgement is expressed as an ordering of entities. In many situations, user judgement is determined by semantic considerations. For example, it may be interpreted in terms of more intuitive notions, such as the cost of testing, the easiness of understanding, or the action ability. It is virtually impossible to list all practical interpretations of user judgement. In addition, the meaning of user judgement becomes clear only in a particular context of application. A simple and straightforward way to represent user judgement on entities is to assign them with numerical weights (Krantz *et al.* 1971). Formally, it can be described by a mapping:

$$w : E \to \Re,$$

where E is a finite non-empty set of entities, and $\Re$ is the set of real numbers. For an entity $e \in E$, $w(e)$ is the weight of e. The numerical weight $w(e)$ may be interpreted as the degree of importance of e, the number of occurrences of e in a set, or the cost of testing e in a rule.

A difficulty with the quantitative method is the acquisition of the precise and accurate weights of all entities. On the other hand, a qualitative method only relies on pairwise comparisons of entities. For any two entities $a, b \in E$, we assume that a user is able to state whether one is more important than, or more preferred to, the other. This qualitative user judgement can be formally defined by a binary preference relation $\succ$ on E. For any two $a, b \in E$:

$$a \succ b \Leftrightarrow \text{the user prefers } a \text{ to } b.$$

In the absence of preference, we say that a and b are indifferent. An indifference relation $\sim$ on E is defined as:

$$a \sim b \Leftrightarrow \neg(a \succ b) \wedge \neg(b \succ a).$$

Based on the strict preference and indifference, one can define a preference-indifference relation $\succeq$ on E:

$$a \succeq b \Leftrightarrow (a \succ b) \vee (a \sim b).$$

If $a \succeq b$ holds, we say that b is not preferred to a, or a is at least as good as b.

A user preference relation is asymmetric and negative transitive, so it is a *weak order* on E. A weak order imposes a special structure on the set E of entities. The indifference relation $\sim$ divides the set of entities into disjoint subsets. Furthermore, for any two distinct equivalence classes $[a]_\sim$ and $[b]_\sim$ of $E/\sim$, either $[a]_\sim \succ' [b]_\sim$ or $[b]_\sim \succ' [a]_\sim$ holds. In other words, it is possible to arrange the entities into several levels so that entities in a higher level are preferred to entities in a lower level, and entities in the same level are indifferent. When each equivalence class contains exactly one entity, the preference relation $\succ$ on E is in fact a linear order itself. In general, if we do not care how to order entities in an equivalence class, we can extend a weak order into a linear order such that a is ranked ahead of b if and only if $a \succeq b$. For a weak order, its linear extension may not be unique (Fishburn, 1970).

The quantitative judgement can be easily translated into qualitative judgement. Given the weights of entities, we can uniquely determine a preference relation. Suppose there are two entities a and b, $w(a)$ and $w(b)$ represent the importance of a and b, respectively, a preference relation is defined by:

$$a \succ b \Leftrightarrow w(a) > w(b).$$

When $w(a)$ and $w(b)$ is the cost of entities a and b, the following preference relation should be used instead,

$$a \succ b \Leftrightarrow w(b) > w(a).$$

In general, two entities may have the same weights. The translation to a qualitative preference relation only preserves the ordering of entities implied by the weights. The additional information given by the absolute weight values is lost.

In the reverse process, a user preference relation can be represented in terms of the weights of entities. A rational user's judgement must allow numerical measurement. The following theorem states that a weak order is both necessary and sufficient for a numerical measurement (Fishburn, 1970; Roberts, 1979): Suppose $\succ$ is a preference relation on a finite non-empty set E of entities. There exists a real-valued function $u : E \to \Re$ satisfying the condition:

$$a \succ b \Leftrightarrow u(a) > u(b),$$

if and only if $\succ$ is a weak order. Moreover, u is uniquely defined up to a strictly monotonic increasing transformation. The function u is referred to as an order-preserving utility function. It provides a quantitative representation of a user preference. That is, the numbers of $u(a), u(b), \dots$ as ordered by $>$ reflect the order of $a, b, \dots$ under the preference relation $\succ$. The utility function also truthfully represents the indifference relation, that is,

$$a \sim b \Leftrightarrow u(a) = u(b).$$

According to the theorem, for a given preference relation, there exist many utility functions. The utility functions are in fact based on the ordinal scale. That is, it is only meaningful to examine the order induced by a utility function. Although numerical values are used, it is not necessarily meaningful to apply arithmetic operations on them.

A User-Centered Three-Layered Framework

A three-layered conceptual framework of data mining is proposed by Yao (2003), which consists of the philosophy layer, the technique layer and the application layer. The philosophy layer investigates the essentials of knowledge. One attempts to answer the fundamental question, namely, what is knowledge? There are many related issues to this question, such as the representation of knowledge, the expression and communication of knowledge in languages, the relationship between knowledge in the mind and in

Figure 1. A user-centered three-layered framework of interactive data mining

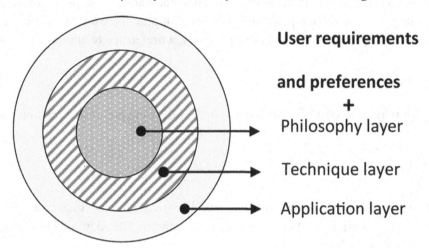

the external real world, and the classification and organization of knowledge. The philosophical study of data mining serves as a precursor to technology and application. It generates knowledge and the understanding of our world, with or without establishing the operational boundaries of knowledge.

The technique layer is the study of knowledge discovery by machine. One attempts to answer the question: how to discover knowledge? In the context of computer science, there are many issues related to this question, such as the implementation of human knowledge discovery methods by programming languages, which involves coding, storage and retrieval issues in a computer, and the innovation and evolution of techniques and algorithms in intelligent systems. The mainstream of research in machine learning, data mining, and knowledge discovery has concentrated on the technique layer. Logical analysis and mathematical modelling are considered the foundations of the study of the technique layer in data mining.

The ultimate goal of knowledge discovery is to effectively use discovered knowledge. The application layer therefore should focus on the notions of "usefulness" and "meaningfulness" of discovered knowledge for the specific domain. These notions cannot be discussed in total isolation without applications, as knowledge in general is domain specific.

The user-centered three-layered framework consists of the philosophy layer, the technique layer and the application layer, and considers one important factor, user requirements and preferences. Figure 1 illustrates this conceptual framework. It is important to note that when user requirements and preferences are interpreted as a general factor, it means multiple views, various choices and judgements. When it stands for a specific requirement, then it is "it." For a certain user coming to an interactive data mining system, if he/she has a vague requirement, then the system should be able to allow him/her to explore the multiple choices and views, even to build up his/her own view and method; while a user proceeds with a clear requirement or preference, then the system should be able to cooperate with this requirement, and try to search for the patterns that fit this preference. That helps a user to form a conceptual model of the nature of the problem, enables the user to solve particular problems, and to understand what the system can and cannot do. It helps a user to establish trust towards the system. More specifically, in the user-centered three-layer framework, the philosophy layer studies and takes on multiple or specific views to perceive the dataset. The technique layer deals with multiple or specific methods to manipulate data sets according to a particular view. The application layer concerns multiple or specific ways for understanding and utilizing the discovered pattern for real-world applications.

MULTIPLE VIEWS IN THE PHILOSOPHY LAYER

Interactive data mining systems provide pertinent and apposite supports regarding a particular view. According to a specific problem, a user may prefer one view to another, one solution to another, one arrangement to another, one attribute order to another, or one evaluation to another.

Languages for Rule Description

An information table represents all available information. Knowledge or rules can be discovered based on information tables. The rows of an information table represent the objects. The columns describe a set of attributes. An information table can be formally defined by a quadruple:

$$S = (U, At, \{V_a \mid a \in At\}, \{I_a \mid a \in At\}),$$

where U is a finite nonempty set of objects, At is a finite nonempty set of attributes, V_a is a nonempty set of values of $a \in At$, any $I_a : U \to V_a$ is an information function. The mapping $I_a(x) = v$ means that the value of object x on attribute a is v, where $v \in V_a$.

To describe the information in an information table, we need to define two decision logic languages L_0 and L_1 (Yao, 2003). The decision logic language L_0 has been studied by Pawlak (1991). Similar languages have been studied by many authors (Demri and Orlowska, 1998; Yao, 2001). In this language, an atomic formula is $a = v$, where $a \in At$ and $v \in V_a$. If ϕ and ψ are L_0 formulas, then so are $\neg\phi$, $\phi \wedge \psi$ and $\phi \vee \psi$. For an atomic formula $\phi = (a = v)$, if an object x has a value v on the attribute a, then we say that the object x satisfies ϕ, denoted as $x \models_{L_0} \phi$. Otherwise, we say x does not satisfy ϕ. The set of objects that satisfy a formula ϕ is denoted as $m(\phi)$. The formula ϕ can be viewed as the description of a set of objects in $m(\phi)$.

The decision logic language L_1 consists of a set of formulas. An atomic formula of L_1 is a descriptor $(a, =)$, where $a \in At$. If ϕ and ψ are L_1 formulas, then so are $\neg\phi$, $\phi \wedge \psi$ and $\phi \vee \psi$. For an atomic formula $\phi = (a, =)$, if an object pair (x, y) has the same value on the attribute a, then we say that (x, y) satisfies ϕ, denoted as $x \models_{L_1} \phi$. Otherwise, we say x does not satisfy ϕ. The set of object pairs that satisfy a formula ϕ is denoted as $m(\phi)$. The formula ϕ can be viewed as the description of a set of object pairs in $m(\phi)$.

It is important to note that both the equality relations $a = v$ in L_0 and $(a, =)$ in L_1 are a special case of the atomic formula. A more general relation R_a can be used to define an atomic formula. Relation R_a may be interpreted as the similarity, dissimilarity, or ordering of values in V_a, which can be either quantitatively or qualitatively defined. In a general sense, R_a can be a quantitative relation $>, \geq, <$ or $\leq$ or a qualitative relation $\succ, \succeq, \prec$ or $\preceq$.

Table 1.

	ψ	$\neg\psi$	Total
ϕ	a	b	a+b
$\neg\phi$	c	d	c+d
Total	a+c	b+d	a+b+c+d=n

Measures of Rules

Knowledge derivable from an information table is commonly represented in the form of rules. A rule can be defined and represented as $\phi \Rightarrow \psi$, where ϕ and ψ are two formulas defining two concepts or granules.

Rule measures can be classified into two categories: objective measures and subjective measures (Silberschatz and Tuzhilin, 1995). Objective measures depend on the structure of rules and the underlying data used in the discovery process. Subjective measures depend on the user beliefs (Liu, Hsu and Chen, 1997; Silberschatz and Tuzhilin, 1995).

Objective Measures

Measures defined by statistical and structural information are viewed as objective measures. For example, Gago and Bento (1998) proposed a measure for selecting discovered rules with the highest average distance between them. The distance measure is developed based on the structural and statistical information of a rule such as the number of attributes in a rule and the values of attributes. A rule is deemed as interesting if it has the highest average distance to the others. One does not consider the application and domain when measuring the discovered rules by using the distance measure. Information theoretic measures are also objective measures because they use the underlying data in a data set to evaluate the information content or entropy of a rule (Lee, 1987; Smyth and Goodman, 1992; Yao, 2003).

For a rule in terms of $\phi \Rightarrow \psi$, the relationship of any two formulas ϕ and ψ of a rule can be characterized by a two-by-two contingency table:

$$a = m(\phi \wedge \psi) \qquad b = m(\phi \wedge \neg\psi)$$
$$c = m(\neg\phi \wedge \psi) \qquad d = m(\neg\phi \wedge \neg\psi)$$

Based on the contingency table, various quantitative measures can be used for rule interestingness evaluation (Hilderman Hamilton, 2000; Yao, Chen and Yang, 2003; Yao and Zhong, 1999).

Two concepts ϕ and ψ are viewed as being non-associative or independent if the occurrence of ϕ does not alter the probability of ψ occurring. In other words, if the occurrence of ϕ can affect the probability of ψ, then we say that the concept ψ is dependent on or associated with the concept ϕ. The degree of concept association can be evaluated by one-way association measures.

Support is a commonly used measure for evaluating the ratio of the generality of a rule $\phi \Rightarrow \psi$. It may be interpreted as a measure of the degree of truth of the formula ϕ in the information table, denoted as:

$$support(\phi \Rightarrow \psi) = \frac{|\, m(\phi)\, |}{|\, U\, |}$$
$$= P(\phi) = \frac{a+b}{n},$$

where $|.|$ is the cardinality of the set. A rule is more general if it has a higher support and thus covers more objects of the universe.

Confidence is a measure for evaluating the probability of the occurrence of a formula ψ given that another formula ϕ occurs (Agrawal, Imielinski and Swami, 1993):

$$confidence(\phi \Rightarrow \psi) = \frac{|\, m(\phi \wedge \psi)\, |}{|\, m(\phi)\, |}$$
$$= P(\psi \mid \phi) = \frac{a}{a+b}.$$

Confidence is one-direction from ϕ to ψ and can be viewed as a one-way association measure (Yao and Zhong, 1999). In other words, the concept ϕ depends on the concept ψ, but ψ may not depend on ϕ. In set-theoretic terms, it is the degree to which $m(\phi)$ is included in $m(\psi)$. A rule with the maximum confidence 1 is a certain rule, otherwise is a probabilistic rule.

Coverage of ψ provided by ϕ is the quantity:

$$coverage(\phi \Rightarrow \psi) = \frac{|\, m(\phi \wedge \psi)\, |}{|\, m(\psi)\, |}$$
$$= P(\phi \mid \psi) = \frac{a}{a+c}.$$

It may be viewed as the conditional probability of an object satisfying ϕ given that object satisfies ψ.

If two concepts ϕ and ψ in a rule have a two-way association relationship, then the concept ϕ must depend on or be associated with the concept ψ, and the converse is also true. Two-way measures are symmetric and viewed as two-way association measures (Yao and Zhong, 1999).

RI is a measure on the evaluation of the association of a discovered rule (Shapiro, 1991). It is defined by:

$$RI(\phi \Rightarrow \psi) = P(\phi, \psi) - P(\phi)P(\psi).$$

The two concepts ϕ and ψ are recognized as being non-associative or independent when $RI = 0$. In fact, this measure determines the degree of association of a rule by the comparison of the joint probability of two concepts $P(\phi, \psi)$ with respect to the expected probability of the non-association assumption

$P(\phi)P(\psi)$. $RI > 0$ represents a positive association from ϕ to ψ. $RI < 0$ represents a negative association, which is from ψ to ϕ.

IND is a measure of rule interestingness (Brin, Motwani and Silverstein, 1997). This measure is defined by:

$$IND(\phi \Rightarrow \psi) = \frac{P(\phi, \psi)}{P(\phi)P(\psi)}.$$

The two concepts ϕ and ψ are recognized as being non-associative or independent when $IND = 1$. This measure is the ratio of the joint probability of $\phi \wedge \psi$ and the probability obtained if ϕ and ψ are assumed to be independent. In other words, the rule has a stronger association if the joint probability is further away from the probability under independence.

IS is another measure of rule interestingness (Tan, Kumar and Srivastava, 2002). It can be defined by:

$$IS(\phi \Rightarrow \psi) = \frac{P(\phi, \psi)}{\sqrt{P(\phi)P(\psi)}}.$$

The basic notion of the *IS* measure is similar to the measure of independence. Furthermore, it is equivalent to the geometric mean of confidences of the rule. However, its range is between 0 and 1 instead of *IND*'s range, between 0 and ∞.

Subjective Measures

Although statistical and structural information provides an effective indicator of the potential effectiveness of a rule, its usefulness is limited. One needs to consider the subjective aspects of rules. Subjective measures consider the user who examines the rules. For example, Silberschatz and Tuzhilin proposed a subjective measure of rule interestingness based on the notion of unexpectedness and in terms of a user belief system (Silberschatz and Tuzhilin, 1995; Silberschatz and Tuzhilin, 1996). The basic idea of their measure is that the discovered rules which have more unexpected information with respect to a user belief system are deemed as more interesting. Thus, subjective measures are both application and user dependent. In other words, a user needs to incorporate other domain specific knowledge such as user interest, utility, value, profit and action-ability (Ras and Wieczorkowska, 2000; Wang and He, 2001).

As one example, profit or utility-based mining is a special kind of constraint-based mining, taking into account of both statistical significance and profit significance (Wang, Zhou and Han, 2002). Doyle discussed the importance and usefulness of the notions of economic rationality and suggested that economic rationality can play a large role for measuring a rule (Doyle, 1992). Similarly, Barber and Hamilton proposed the notion of share measures which consider the contribution, in terms of profit, of an attribute in an attribute set (Barber and Hamilton, 2003).

Interpretations of Rules

Depending on the meanings and forms of rules, one may classify rules in many ways. For a rule in terms of $\phi \Rightarrow \psi$, the symbol $\Rightarrow$ represents a connection or a relationship between two formulas ϕ and ψ.

The meanings and interpretations of $\Rightarrow$ are varied based on user requirements or applications. Rules can be classified according to the interpretations of $\Rightarrow$ (Yao, 2001).

Some rules can be interpreted as logical implication, namely, for a rule $\phi \Rightarrow \psi$, the symbol $\Rightarrow$ is interpreted as the logical implication $\rightarrow$. A logical implication $\phi \rightarrow \psi$ can be read as *if ϕ then ψ*. Assuming that $\phi \rightarrow \psi$ is true, then the truth of ϕ is a sufficient condition for the truth of ψ, while the truth of ψ is a necessary condition for the truth of ϕ. A logical implication $\phi \rightarrow \psi$ is valid if and only if it is true on every interpretation.

Some rules deal with classifying labelled objects in a given universe. Without lose the generality, an information table can be used for classification problems by having $At = C \cup D$, where C is the set of condition attributes and D is the set of decision attributes. This kind of information tables is also called *decision tables* (Pawlak, 1991). Normally, D only contains one decision attribute, which labels the objects in the universe. A classification rule, written as $\phi \Rightarrow \psi$, indicates the inference relation from ϕ to ψ. Normally, ϕ is defined by attributes in the condition attribute set C and ψ is defined by the decision attribute. Classification rules can be either certain or probabilistic. In real data mining applications, certain rules are rare. Thus, rules are typically interpreted in terms of conditional probability. Normally, the confidence measure indicates the strength of the rule. Classification rule mining intends to discover rule with high confidence.

Some rules identify and study peculiar regulations in the given data set, and thus called peculiarity rules (Zhong, Yao and Ohshima, 2003). In mining peculiarity rules, the distribution of attribute values is taken into consideration. Attention is paid to objects whose attribute values are different from that of the other objects. After the isolation of such peculiarity data, rules with low support and high confidence, and consequently a high absolute difference, are searched. This class of association rules are thus "peculiar."

Some rules are interpreted as an association between two granules defined by ϕ and ψ. Association rules are first proposed by Agrawal *et al.* for mining rules from transaction databases, to discover implication or correlation relates co-occurring elements (Agrawal, Imielinski and Swami, 1993). It is very tempting to relate a large confidence with a strong association between two frequent itemsets. This kind of rules is called frequent itemset rules. Questions like "if a customer purchases product A, how likely is he to purchase product B?" are answered by frequent itemset rules. According to the properties of frequent itemsets and their associated association rules, this class of rule has been criticized for not providing "new" or "previously unknown" knowledge, and thus may not be profitable for real application.

Some association rules discover the disjunctive association for mutually exclusive item sets, and their disjunctive association rules (Kim, 2003). The interpretation of such disjunctive association rules can be read as: "for people who buy A, they do not buy B." Same to the frequent itemset rules, disjunctive association rules must have a high support and a high confidence to be significant. The disjunctive association rules have different practical meanings in real applications, and can be studied complementarily to the conventional association rules.

MULTIPLE STRATEGIES IN THE TECHNIQUE LAYER

In solving real world problems, we often face the choices between simple and complicated descriptions, precise and imprecise characterizations, understandability and incomprehensibility of methods, and exact and approximate solutions. In general, there is a trade-off between two opposite criteria of competing nature. Human problem solving depends crucially on a proper balance and compromise of these incompatible criteria. Different users can develop different knowledge representation frameworks and related automated learning and mining mechanisms to describe and identify abnormal situations or behaviours. Consequently, this issue must be addressed in user-centered interactive data mining.

Retaining Strategies

A retaining strategy, by its name, means to keep the quality of the rules, especially their accuracy, as high as they could be. The most commonly used accuracy measure is the confidence measure defined in the Section 2. The higher the confidence value, the more accurate the rule is. In most real situations, a rule is not always deterministic for the given universe, but rather approximate and uncertain. In other words, the confidence value of the rule is less than or equal to 100%.

Yao *et al.* advocated the use of a specific knowledge representation and data mining framework based on rules and exceptions (Yao, Wang, Wang and Zeng, 2005). In this framework, normal and abnormal situations or behaviours occur as pairs of dual entities: rule succinctly summarizes normal situations, and exceptions characterize abnormal situations. Each of these two entities provides the context of the other. Rule+exception strategies strike a practical balance between simplicity and accuracy.

Two types of exceptions can be identified, incorrect interpretations produced by the existing rules, and the interpretations that cannot be produced by the existing rules (Compton and Jansen, 1988). For simplicity, they are refereed to as incorrectly covered exceptions and uncovered exceptions, respectively. For the incorrectly covered exceptions, two potential solutions exist. A commonly used method adds an additional condition ϕ' to form a more specific condition $\phi \wedge \phi'$. The new rule $\phi \wedge \phi' \Rightarrow \psi$ should produce fewer or no exceptions. Another alternative, a rule+exception strategy treats $\phi \Rightarrow \psi$ as a general rule with probability and searches for exception rules or exception instances to the general rule. For uncovered exceptions, we could attempt to add an alternative condition to form a more general rule $\phi \vee \phi' \Rightarrow \psi'$. The extra ϕ' could cover more instance of ψ. For clarity, we can think of them as two rules $\phi \Rightarrow \psi$ and $\phi' \Rightarrow \psi$. One can view the second rule as an exception rule to handle the uncovered exceptions. In general, we can sequentially construct a set of rules to cover instances of ψ, with the new rule as an exception rule to the previous rules.

Compromising Strategies

A compromising strategy promotes the construction of more general rules containing more incorrectly covered exceptions. A compromising strategy means to compromise the accuracy to a certain level, in order to keep another important feature at a relatively high measuring level. That means that the high accuracy is often not the goal in order to preserve or improve another property, instead, a higher generality or a lower cost might be the concern.

In most cases, a compromising strategy generates shorter and simpler rules defined by a proper subset of entire feature set. By choosing $A \subseteq At$, a set of formulas Φ_A can be defined. Borrowing the concepts from rough set theory (Pawlak, 1982; Pawlak, 1991), we can define a β-positive region with respect to a target concept ψ. The β-positive region is the union of all objects satisfying the rules defined by a with the confidence greater than or equal to β, which is denoted as:

$$POS_A^\beta(\psi) = \bigcup_{\phi \in \Phi_A} \{m(\phi) \mid confidence(\phi \Rightarrow \psi) \ge \beta\}.$$

To preserve the generality, a heuristic criterion can be defined as: given a predefined β value, $POS_A^\beta(\psi) \ge POS_{At}^\beta(\psi)$. A rule set satisfies the generality preservation strategy can classify more objects in the universe than the set of rules produced by the entire set of *At*, while keeping the confidence not less than β.

A general rule may include more incorrectly covered exceptions. Suppose a set of objects in the universe can be defined by a descriptive formula ϕ. Suppose there is a learned rule, $\phi \Rightarrow \psi_1$, implies that all the objects satisfying ϕ should have the same class ψ_1. However, the rule could be too general to satisfy every object satisfying ϕ. It means that we may have an object $x \in m(\phi)$, which implies a decision value different from ψ_1, say, it satisfies a decision value ψ_2. This becomes an exception, or an error, of the learned classification rule. For a specific classification exception, denoted as (ψ_1, ψ_2), the exception count is the number of objects in the universe that possess this exception, which can be defined as:

$$errCount(\psi_1, \psi_2) = |\{x \in m(\phi) \mid \phi \Rightarrow \psi_1, \phi \Rightarrow \psi_2\}|.$$

Yao and Wong applied the Bayesian decision procedure for classification (Yao and Wong, 1992). The basic idea is that different errors may indicate different cost. A rule set satisfying the cost preservation strategy will not increase the cost.

MULTIPLE EXPLANATIONS IN THE APPLICATION LAYER

The role of explanation is to clarify, teach, and convince (Dhaliwal and Benbasat, 1996). There are many kinds of explanations. An explanation could be a definition of a term, the cause and effect of an event, or the significance of a phenomenon. Different explanations are the answers to many different kinds of questions. Explanation is both subjective and objective (Craik, 1943). It is subjective because the meaning of explanation, or the evaluation of a good explanation, is different for different people at different times. On the other hand, explanation is objective because it must win general approval as a valid explanation, or has to be withdrawn in the face of new evidence and criticism. The interpretations and explanations enhance our understanding of the phenomenon and guide us to make rational decisions.

Knowledge discovered from data should be explained and interpreted. Knowledge can be discovered by unsupervised learning methods. Unsupervised learning studies how systems can learn to represent, summarize, and organize the data in a way that reflects the internal structure (namely, a pattern) of the overall collection. This process does not explain the patterns, but describes them. The primary unsupervised techniques include clustering mining, belief networks learning, and association mining. The criteria for choosing which pattern to be explained are directly related to pattern evaluation step of data mining.

Background knowledge provides features that can possibly explain a discovered pattern. An explanation may include many branches of inquiry: physics, chemistry, human culture, logic, psychology, and the methodology of science. In data mining, explanation can be made at a shallow, syntactic level based on statistical information, or at a deep, semantic level based on domain knowledge. The required information and knowledge for explanation may not necessarily be inside the original dataset. One needs to collect additional information for explanation construction. The key question is the selection of the features that are generally explanatory to the target concept from many features that happen to be related to the current discovered pattern. Craik (1943) argued that the power of explanations involves the power of insight and anticipation. One collects certain features based on the underlying hypothesis that they may provide explanations of the discovered pattern. That something is unexplainable may simply be an expression of the inability to discover an explanation of a desired sort. The process of selecting the relevant and explanatory features may be subjective, and trial-and-error. In general, the better our background knowledge is, the more accurate the inferred explanations are likely to be.

Explanations for data mining results reason inductively, namely, drawing an inference from a set of acquired training instances, and justifying or predicting the instances one might observe in the future. Supervised learning methods can be applied for the explanation construction. The goal of supervised learning is to find a model that will correctly associate the input patterns with the classes.

In real world applications, supervised learning models are extremely useful analytic techniques. The widely used supervised learning methods include decision tree learning, rule-based learning, and decision graph learning. The learned results are represented as either a tree, or a set of if-then rules. The constructed explanations give some evidence about under what conditions (within the background knowledge) the discovered pattern is most likely to happen, or how the background knowledge is related to the pattern.

The role of explanation in data mining is positioned among proper description, relation and causality. Comprehensibility is the key factor in explanations. The accuracy of the constructed explanations relies on the amount of training examples. Explanations perform poorly with insufficient data or poor presuppositions. Different background knowledge may infer different explanations. There is no reason to believe that only one unique explanation exists. One can use statistical measures and domain knowledge to evaluate different explanations. Data mining emphasizes practicality and utility, and the results of data mining are required to be understandable and applicable. As long as these requirements are satisfied, a user can terminate the seeking. The "end of the explanation" is reached when one's actual questions have been answered. This "end" is a practical one dictated by one's interests and is not merely theoretical.

CONCLUSION

In this chapter, we focus on interactive data mining which is characterized by adding user requirement and judgement into a three-layered framework of data mining. The user-centered three-layered framework consists of the philosophy layer, the technique layer and the application layer. At the philosophy level, we discuss different decision logic languages and different measures serve for multiple views. At the technique layer, we address on multiple strategies for knowledge discovery. At the application layer, we discuss explanation-oriented data mining, which emphasizes the importance of reasoning the discovered patterns before being applied.

More effective data mining systems should support better human-machine interactivity. The concern of effectiveness and the concern of efficiency should be synchronized with user cognitive phases and requirements. Bearing user requirement in mind, the research on interactive data mining is fairly broad.

REFERENCES

Agrawal, R., Imielinski, T., & Swami, A. (1993). Mining association rules between sets of items in large databases. In *Proceedings of ACM SIGMOD International Conference on Management of Data* (pp. 207-216).

Barber, B., & Hamilton, H. (2003). Extracting share frequent itemsets with infrequent subsets. *Data Mining and Knowledge Discovery, 7*, 153–185. doi:10.1023/A:1022419032620

Brachmann, R., & Anand, T. (1996). The process of knowledge discovery in databases: a human- centered approach. *Advances in Knowledge Discovery and Data Mining* (pp. 37-57). Menlo Park, CA: AAAI Press and MIT Press.

Brin, S., Motwani, R., & Silverstein, C. (1997). Beyond market baskets: generalizing association rules to correlations. In *Proceedings of ACM SIGMOD International Conference on Management of Data* (pp. 265-276).

Compton, P., & Jansen, B. (1988). Knowledge in context: a strategy for expert system maintenance. In *Proceedings of the Second Australian Joint Conference of Artificial Intelligence* (pp. 292-306).

Craik, K. (1943). *The Nature of Explanation*. New York: Cambridge University Press.

Demri, S., & Orlowska, E. (1998). Logical analysis of indiscernibility. In E. Orlowska, (Ed.) *Incomplete Information: Rough Set Analysis* (pp. 347-380). Heidelberg: Physica-Verlag.

Dhaliwal, J. S., & Benbasat, I. (1996). The use and effects of knowledge-based system explanations: theoretical foundations and a framework for empirical evaluation. *Information Systems Research, 7*, 342–362. doi:10.1287/isre.7.3.342

Doyle, J. (1992). Rationality and its role in reasoning. *Computational Intelligence, 8*, 376–409. doi:10.1111/j.1467-8640.1992.tb00371.x

Elm, W. C., Cook, M. J., Greitzer, F. L., Hoffman, R. R., Moon, B., & Hutchins, S. G. (2004). Designing support for intelligence analysis. In *Proceedings of the Human Factors and Ergonomics Society*, pp. 20-24.

Fishburn, P. C. (1970). *Utility Theory for Decision-Making*. New York: John Wiley and Sons.

Gago, P., & Bento, C. (1998). A metric for selection of the most promising rules. In *Proceedings of PKDD* (pp. 19-27).

Han, J., Hu, X., & Cercone, N. (2003). A visualization model of interactive knowledge discovery systems and its implementations. *Information Visualization, 2*, 105–125. doi:10.1057/palgrave.ivs.9500045

Hancock, P. A., & Scallen, S. F. (1996). The future of function allocation. *Ergonomics in Design, 4*, 24–29.

Hilderman, R. J., & Hamilton, H. J. (2000). Knowledge Discovery and Measures of Interest. Boston: Kluwer Academic Publishers.

Kim, H. D. (2003). Complementary occurrence and disjunctive rules for market basket analysis in data mining. In *Proceedings of Information and Knowledge Sharing*.

Krantz, D. H., Luce, R. D., Suppes, P., & Tversky, A. (1971). *Foundations of Measurement*. New York: Academic Press.

Lee, T. T. (1987). An information-theoretic analysis of relational databases - part I: data dependencies and information metric. *IEEE Transactions on Software Engineering, 13*, 1049–1061. doi:10.1109/TSE.1987.232847

Liu, B., Hsu, W., & Chen, S. (1997). Using general impressions to analyze discovered classification rules. In *Proceedings of ACM SIGKDD International Conference on Knowledge Discovery and Data Mining* (pp. 31-36).

Pawlak, Z. (1982). Rough sets. *International Journal of Computer Information and Science, 11*(5), 341–356. doi:10.1007/BF01001956

Pawlak, Z. (1991). *Rough Sets: Theoretical Aspects of Reasoning about Data*. Dordrecht: Kluwer Academic Publishers.

Ras, Z., & Wieczorkowska, A. (2000). Action rules: how to increase profit of a company. In *Proceedings of PKDD* (pp. 587-592).

Shneiderman, B. (1998). *Designing the User Interface: Strategies for Effective Human-Computer Interaction* (3rd ed.). Addison-Wesley.

Silberschatz, A., & Tuzhilin, A. (1995). On subjective measures of interestingness in knowledge discovery. In *Proceedings of ACM SIGKDD International Conference on Knowledge Discovery and Data Mining* (pp. 275-281).

Silberschatz, A., & Tuzhilin, A. (1996). What makes patterns interesting in knowledge discovery systems? *IEEE Transactions on Knowledge and Data Engineering, 8*, 970–974. doi:10.1109/69.553165

Smyth, P., & Goodman, R. An information theoretic approach to rule induction from databases. *IEEE Transactions on Knowledge and Data Engineering, 4*, 301–316. doi:10.1109/69.149926

Tan, P. N., Kumar, V., & Srivastava, J. (2000). Selecting the right interestingness measure for association patterns. In *Proceedings of the Eighth ACM SIGKDD International Conference on Knowledge Discovery and Data Mining* (pp. 32-41).

Wang, K., & He, Y. (2001). User-defined association mining. In *Proceedings of 5th Pacific-Asia Conference on Knowledge Discovery and Data Mining* (pp. 387-399).

Wang, K., Zhou, S., & Han, J. (2002). Profit mining: from patterns to actions. In *Proceedings of International Conference on Extending Database Technology* (pp. 70-87).

Wang, Y. (2002). On cognitive informatics. In *Proceedings of the First IEEE International Conference on Cognitive Informatics* (pp. 34-42).

Wang, Y. (2004). On autonomous computing and cognitive processes. In *Proceedings of the Third IEEE International Conference on Cognitive Informatics* (pp. 3-4).

Wang, Y., & Liu, D. (2003). On information and knowledge representation in the brain. In *Proceedings of the Second IEEE International Conference on Cognitive Informatics* (pp. 26-29).

Yao, Y. Y. (2001). On modeling data mining with granular computing. In *Proceedings of COMPSAC* (pp. 638-643).

Yao, Y. Y. (2003). Information-theoretic measures for knowledge discovery and data mining. In Karmeshu (Ed.) *Entropy Measures, Maximum Entropy and Emerging Applications* (pp. 115-136). Berlin: Springer.

Yao, Y. Y. (2003). Mining high order decision rules. In M. Inuiguchi, S. Hirano & S. Tsumoto (Eds.), *Rough Set Theory and Granular Computing* (pp. 125-135). Berlin: Springer.

Yao, Y. Y. (2005). Perspectives of granular computing. In *Proceedings of 2005 IEEE International Conference on Granular Computing, 1* (pp. 85-90).

Yao, Y. Y., Chen, Y. H., & Yang, X. D. (2003). A measurement-theoretic foundation for rule interestingness evaluation. In *Proceedings of the Workshop on Foundations and New Directions in Data Mining in the 3rd IEEE International Conference on Data Mining* (pp. 221-227).

Yao, Y. Y., Wang, F. Y., Wang, J., & Zeng, D. (2005). Rule + exception strategies for security information analysis. *IEEE Intelligent Systems, 20*, 52–57. doi:10.1109/MIS.2005.93

Yao, Y. Y., & Wong, S. K. M. (1992). A decision theoretic framework for approximating concepts. *International Journal of Man-Machine Studies, 37*, 793–809. doi:10.1016/0020-7373(92)90069-W

Yao, Y. Y., Zhao, Y., & Maguire, R. B. (2003). Explanation-oriented association mining using rough set theory. In *Proceedings of Rough Sets, Fuzzy Sets and Granular Computing* (pp. 165-172).

Yao, Y. Y., & Zhong, N. (1999). An analysis of quantitative measures associated with rules. In *Proceedings of the Third Pacific-Asia Conference on Knowledge Discovery and Data Mining* (pp. 479-488).

Zhao, Y. (2007). *Interactive Data Mining*. Ph.D. Thesis, University of Regina.

Zhao, Y., & Yao, Y. Y. (2005). Interactive user-driven classification using a granule network. In *Proceedings of the Fourth IEEE International Conference on Cognitive Informatics* (pp. 250-259).

Zhong, N., Yao, Y. Y., & Ohshima, M. (2003). Peculiarity oriented multi-database mining. *IEEE Transactions on Knowledge and Data Engineering, 15*, 952–960. doi:10.1109/TKDE.2003.1209011

Zhong, N., Yao, Y. Y., Ohshima, M., & Ohsuga, S. (2001). Interestingness, peculiarity, and multi-database mining. In *Proceedings of IEEE International Conference on Data Mining* (pp. 566-573).

Chapter 8
On Concept Algebra:
A Denotational Mathematical Structure for Knowledge and Software Modeling

Yingxu Wang
University of Calgary, Canada

ABSTRACT

Concepts are the most fundamental unit of cognition that carries certain meanings in expression, thinking, reasoning, and system modeling. In denotational mathematics, a concept is formally modeled as an abstract and dynamic mathematical structure that encapsulates attributes, objects, and relations. The most important property of an abstract concept is its adaptive capability to autonomously interrelate itself to other concepts. This article presents a formal theory for abstract concepts and knowledge manipulation known as "concept algebra." The mathematical models of concepts and knowledge are developed based on the object-attribute-relation (OAR) theory. The formal methodology for manipulating knowledge as a concept network is described. Case studies demonstrate that concept algebra provides a generic and formal knowledge manipulation means, which is capable to deal with complex knowledge and software structures as well as their algebraic operations.

INTRODUCTION

In cognitive informatics, logic, linguistics, psychology, software engineering, and knowledge engineering, concepts are identified as the basic unit of both knowledge and reasoning (Anderson, 1983; Colins & Loftus, 1975; Ganter & Wille, 1999; Hampton, 1997; Hurley, 1997; Matlin, 1998; Murphy, 1993; Wang, 2006a, 2006b, 2006c, 2007a, 2007c; Wang & Wang, 2006; Wilson & Keil, 1999). The rigorous modeling and formal treatment of concepts are at the center of theories for knowledge presentation and manipulation (Smith & Medin, 1981; Wille, 1982; Murphy, 1993; Codin, Missaoui, & Alaoui, 1995;

Wilson & Keil, 1999; Yao, 2004; Chen & Yao, 2005). A *concept* in linguistics is a noun or noun-phrase that serves as the subject of a *to-be* statement (Hurley, 1997; Wang, 2002a, 2006a, 2006c, 2007d). Concepts in cognitive informatics (Wang, 2002a, 2006c, 2007b, 2007e) are an abstract structure that carries certain meaning in almost all cognitive processes such as thinking, learning, and reasoning.

Definition 1. *A concept is a cognitive unit to identify and/or model a real-world concrete entity and a perceived-world abstract subject.*

Based on concepts and their relations, meanings of real-world concrete entities may be represented and semantics of abstract subjects may be embodied. Concepts can be classified into two categories, known as the *concrete* and *abstract* concepts. The former are proper concepts that identify and model real-world entities such as the sun, a pen, and a computer. The latter are virtual concepts that identify and model abstract subjects, which cannot be directly mapped to a real-world entity, such as the mind, a set, and an idea. The abstract concepts may be further classified into *collective* concepts, such as collective nouns and complex concepts, or *attributive* concepts such as qualitative and quantitative adjectives. The concrete concepts are used to embody meanings of subjects in reasoning while the abstract concepts are used as intermediate representatives or modifiers in reasoning.

A concept can be identified by its intension and extension (Hurley, 1997; Smith & Medin, 1981; Wang, 2006c; Wille, 1982; Yao, 2004).

Definition 2. *The intension of a concept is the attributes or properties that a concept connotes.*

Definition 3. *The extension of a concept is the members or instances that the concept denotes.*

For example, the intension of the concept *pen* connotes the attributes of being a writing tool, with a nib, and with ink. The extension of the pen denotes all kinds of pens that share the common attributes as specified in the intension of the concept, such as a ballpoint pen, a fountain pen, and a quill pen.

In computing, a concept is an identifier or a name of a class. The intension of the class is a set of operational attributes of the class. The extension of the class is all its instantiations or objects and derived classes. Concept algebra provides a rigorous mathematical model and a formal semantics for object-oriented class modeling and analyses. The formal modeling of computational classes as a dynamic concept with predesigned behaviors may be referred to "system algebra" (Wang, 2006b, 2007d, 2008b, 2008d).

This article presents a formal treatment of abstract concepts and an entire set of algebraic operations on them. The mathematical model of concepts is established first. Then, the abstract mathematical structure, *concept algebra*, is developed for knowledge representation and manipulation. Based on concept algebra, a knowledge system is formally modeled as a concept network, where the methodology for knowledge manipulating is presented. Case studies demonstrate that concept algebra provides a denotational mathematical means for manipulating complicated abstract and concrete knowledge structures as well as their algebraic operations.

THE MATHEMATICAL MODEL OF ABSTRACT CONCEPTS

This section describes the formal treatment of abstract concepts and a new mathematical structure known as concept algebra in cognitive informatics and knowledge engineering. Before an abstract concept is defined, the semantic environment or context (Chen & Yao, 2005; Ganter & Wille, 1999; Hampton, 1997; Hurley, 1997; Medin & Shoben, 1988) in a given language, is introduced.

Definition 4. *Let $\mathcal{O}$ denote a finite or infinite nonempty set of objects, and $\mathcal{A}$ be a finite or infinite nonempty set of attributes, then a semantic environment or context Θ is denoted as a triple, i.e.:*

$$\Theta \triangleq (\mathcal{O}, \mathcal{A}, \mathcal{R})$$
$$= \mathcal{R} : \mathcal{O} \to \mathcal{O} \mid \mathcal{O} \to \mathcal{A} \mid \mathcal{A} \to \mathcal{O} \mid \mathcal{A} \to \mathcal{A} \qquad (1)$$

where $\mathcal{R}$ is a set of relations between $\mathcal{O}$ and $\mathcal{A}$, and | demotes alternative relations.

According to the Object-Attribute-Relation (OAR) model (Wang, 2007c, 2007d; Wang & Wang, 2006), the three essences in Θ can be defined as follows.

Definition 5. *An object o is an instantiation of a concrete entity and/or an abstract concept.*

In a narrow sense, an object is the identifier of a given instantiation of a concept.

Definition 6. *An attribute a is a subconcept that is used to characterize the properties of a given concept by more specific or precise concepts in the abstract hierarchy.*

In a narrow sense, an attribute is the identifier of a subconcept of the given concept.

Definition 7. *A relation r is an association between any pair of object-object, object-attribute, attribute-object, and/or attribute-attribute.*

On the basis of OAR and Θ, an abstract concept is a composition of the above three elements as given below.

Definition 8. *An abstract concept c on Θ is a 5-tuple, i.e.:*

$$c \triangleq (O, A, R^c, R^i, R^o) \qquad (2)$$

where

- O is a nonempty set of objects of the concept, $O = \{o_1, o_2, ..., o_m\} \subseteq \mathbb{P}\mathcal{O}$, where $\mathbb{P}\mathcal{O}$ denotes a power set of $\mathcal{O}$.
- A is a nonempty set of attributes, $A = \{a_1, a_2, ..., a_n\} \subseteq \mathbb{P}\mathcal{A}$.
- $R^c = O \times A$ is a set of internal relations.
- $R^i \subseteq C' \times C$ is a set of input relations, where C' is a set of external concepts.
- $R^o \subseteq C \times C'$ is a set of output relations.

Figure 1. The structured model of an abstract concept

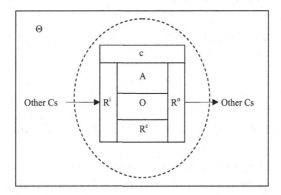

The structure of the concept model $c = (O, A, R^c, R^i, R^o)$ can be illustrated in Figure 1, where c, A, O, and R, $R = \{R^c, R^i, R^o\}$, denote the identifier of the concept, its attributes, objects, and internal/external relations, respectively.

It is interesting to compare the formal model of abstract concepts as given in Definition 8 with the notion of the concept lattice proposed by Wille (1982). Wille defined a formal concept as a pair of sets of objects and attributes, i.e.:

$$c \triangleq (O, A), O \subseteq \mathcal{O} \wedge A \subseteq \mathcal{A} \tag{3}$$

It is obvious that the abstract concept extends Wille's concept model from a pair to a triple, where the set of relations is explicitly and formally modeled in three categories known as the internal, input, and output relations. The I/O relations enable a conventional static concept to be dynamically associated to other concepts in order to represent and manipulate complicated concept operations and compositions in a concept network and knowledge hierarchy.

Theorem 1. *The dynamic and adaptive property of concepts states that an abstract concept is a dynamic mathematical structure that possesses the adaptive capability to interrelate itself to other concepts via R^i and R^o.*

Based on Definition 8, an object derived from a concept and the intension/extension of a concept can be formally defined as follows.

Definition 9. *An object of a concept o is a derived instantiation of the concept that implements an end product of the concept, $o \subset O$, i.e.:*

$$\forall c(O, A, R^c, R^i, R^o), o = c.o_i, o_i \subset O, R^o_o \equiv \varnothing$$
$$\Rightarrow o(A_o, R^c_o, R^i_o | A_o \supseteq A, R^c_o = o \times A_o, R^i_o =$$
$$\{(c, o)\})$$

$$\tag{4}$$

Equation 4 indicates that an object is a tailored end-product of a concrete concept where there is no any output-oriented relation to another concept.

Definition 10. *The intension of a concept c = (O, A, R^c, R^i, R^o), c*, is represented by its set of attributes A, i.e.:*

$$c*(O, A, R^c, R^i, R^o) \triangleq A = \bigcap_{i=1}^{\#O} A_{o_j} \subseteq \mathbb{P}A \tag{5}$$

where $\mathbb{P}A$ denotes a power set of A, and # is the cardinal operator that counts the number of elements in a given set.

Definition 10 indicates that the *narrow* sense or the exact semantics of a concept is determined by the set of common attributes shared by all of its objects. In contrary, the *broad* sense or the rough semantics of a concept is referred to the set of all attributes identified by any of its objects as defined below.

Definition 11. *The complete set of attributes of a concept c = (O, A, R^c, R^i, R^o), or the instant attributes denoted by all objects of c, is a closure of all objects' intensions, A*, i.e.:*

$$A* \triangleq \bigcup_{j=1}^{\#O} A_{o_j} \tag{6}$$

Definitions 10 and 11 specify that (a) The intension of a concept is a finite set of objectively identifiable attributes at a given level of abstraction, and (b) the intension of a concept is dynamic. When more objects for the same concept are denoted, the domain of the intension is usually shrinking in order to accommodate the new objects in the same structure of the concept.

Conventionally, the *domain* of a concept's intension is used to be perceived subjectively in literature (Hurley, 1997; Matlin, 1998). In this approach, it is deemed that a concept connotes the attributes, which occur in the minds of people who use that concept, or where something must have in order to be denoted by the concept. Both the above informal perceptions are not objectively operational in defining a complete and unambiguity domain of intensions. To solve this fundamental problem, Definition 10 provides a unique and objective determination of any given concept.

Definition 12. *The extension of a concept c = (O, A, R^c, R^i, R^o), c^+, is represented by its set of objects O, i.e.:*

$$c^+(O, A, R^c, R^i, R^o) \triangleq O = \{o_1, o_2, ..., o_m\} \subseteq \mathbb{P}O \tag{7}$$

A formal and objective definition of the domain of intension is provided below.

Definition 13. *The domain of a concept c = (O, A, R^c, R^i, R^o) is a set of attributes with a narrow sense D_{min} referring to its intension and a broad sense D_{max} referring to its closure, i.e.:*

$$D(c) \triangleq \begin{cases} D_{min}(c) = A = \bigcap_{j=1}^{\#O} A_{o_j} \\ \\ D_{max}(c) = A* = \bigcup_{j=1}^{\#O} A_{o_j} \end{cases} \tag{8}$$

It is noteworthy that in conventional literature, it is only believed that the intension of a concept determines its extension (Hurley, 1997; Matlin, 1998). However, Definition 13 reveals that the extension of a concept, particularly the common attributes elicited from the extension, determines its intension as well.

Theorem 2. *The nature of concept hierarchy states that in an abstraction hierarchy, the higher the level of a concept in abstraction, the smaller the intension of the concept; and vice versa.*

Relationships between concepts in a concept hierarchy can be illustrated in Figure 2 at three levels known as the knowledge, object, and attribute levels. The internal relations of concepts, $R^c = O \times A$ can be formally represented by concept matrixes.

Example 1. *The concept matrix of concept c_1 is given in Table 1. According to Definition 13, the intension and extension of concepts c_1 as specified in Table 1 can be objectively and uniquely determined as:* $A_{c1} = \{a_2, a_4\}$ *and* $O_{c1} = \{o_{11}, o_{12}, o_{13}\}$.

Definition 14. *The identification of a new concept $c(O, A, R^c, R^i, R^o)$ is the elicitation of its objects O, attributes A, and internal relations R^c, from the semantic environment $\Theta = (\mathcal{O}, \mathcal{A}, \mathcal{R})$, i.e.:*

Figure 2. The hierarchical relations of concepts and their internal structures

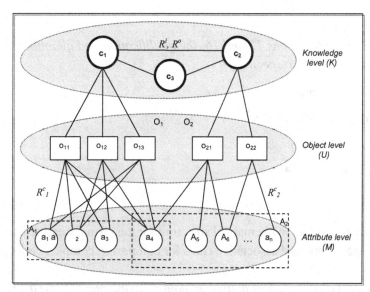

Table 1. The concept matrix of c_1

c_1	a_1	a_2	a_3	a_4
o_{11}	1	1	1	1
o_{12}		1	1	1
o_{13}	1	1		1

$$c \triangleq$$
$$(O, A, R^c, R^i, R^o \mid O \subset U \;\; A \subset M, R^c =$$
$$O \times A, R^i = \varnothing, R^c = \varnothing) \tag{9}$$

In Definition 14, $R^i = R^o = \varnothing$ denotes that the identification operation is an initialization of a newly created concept where the input and output relations may be established later.

Definition 15. *A qualification of a concept $c(O, A, R^c, R^i, R^o)$, denoted by *c, is the identification of its domain, i.e.:*

$$*c \triangleq D(c) = \begin{cases} D_{min}(c) = A = \bigcap_{j=1}^{\#O} A_{o_j} \\ D_{max}(c) = A* = \bigcup_{j=1}^{\#O} A_{o_j} \end{cases} \tag{10}$$

Definition 16. *A quantification of a concept $c(O, A, R^c, R^i, R^o)$, denoted by #c, is the cardinal evaluation of its domain in term of the number of attributes included in it, i.e.:*

$$\#c \triangleq \#D(c) = \begin{cases} \#D_{min}(c) = \#A = \#(\bigcap_{j=1}^{\#O} A_{o_j}) \\ \#D_{max}(c) = \#A* = \#(\bigcup_{j=1}^{\#O} A_{o_j}) \end{cases} \tag{11}$$

Example 2. *According to Definitions 15 and 16, the qualification and quantification of concept c_1 as given in Figure 2 are as follows, respectively:*

$$*c_1 = D(c_1) = \begin{cases} D_{min}(c_1) = A_{c_1} = \{a_2, a_4\} \\ D_{max}(c_1) = A_{c_1}* = \{a_1, a_2, a_3, a_4\} \end{cases}$$

$$\#c_1 = \#D(c_1) = \begin{cases} \#D_{min}(c_1) = \#A_{c_1} = 2 \\ \#D_{max}(c_1) = \#A_{c_1}* = 4 \end{cases}$$

Concept algebra is an abstract mathematical structure for the formal treatment of concepts and their algebraic relations, operations, and associative rules for composing complex concepts.

Definition 17. *A concept algebra CA on a given semantic environment Θ is a triple, i.e.:*

$$CA \triangleq (C, OP, \Theta) = (\{O, A, R^c, R^i, R^o\}, \{\bullet_r, \bullet_c\}, \Theta) \tag{12}$$

where $OP = \{\bullet_r, \bullet_c\}$ are the sets of relational and compositional operations on abstract concepts.

Concept algebra provides a denotational mathematical means for algebraic manipulations of abstract concepts. Concept algebra can be used to model, specify, and manipulate generic "to be" type problems, particularly system architectures, knowledge bases, and detail-level system designs in computing, software engineering, system engineering, and cognitive informatics. The relational and compositional operations on concepts will be formally described in the following sections.

RELATIONAL OPERATIONS OF CONCEPTS

The relational operations of abstract concepts are static and comparative operations that do not change the concepts involved. It is recognized that *relationships* between concepts are solely determined by the relations of both their intensions A and extensions O. The relational operations on abstract concepts in concept algebra are described below.

Lemma 1. *The relational operations $\bullet_r$ in concept algebra encompasses 8 comparative operators for manipulating the algebraic relations between concepts, i.e.:*

$$\bullet_r \triangleq \{\leftrightarrow, \nleftrightarrow, \prec, \succ, =, \cong, \sim, \triangleq\} \tag{13}$$

where the relational operators stand for *related, independent, subconcept, superconcept, equivalent, consistent, comparison,* and *definition*, respectively.

Definition 18. *The related concepts c_1 and c_2 on Θ, denoted by $\leftrightarrow$, are a pair of concepts that share some common attributes in their intensions A_1 and A_2, i.e.:*

$$c_1 \leftrightarrow c_2 \triangleq A_1 \cap A_2 \neq \varnothing \tag{14}$$

Definition 19. *The independent concepts c_1 and c_2 on Θ, denoted by $\nleftrightarrow$, are two concepts that their intensions A_1 and A_2 are disjoint, i.e.:*

$$c_1 \nleftrightarrow c_2 \triangleq A_1 \cap A_2 = \varnothing \tag{15}$$

It is obvious that related and independent concepts are mutually exclusive. That is, if $c_1 \leftrightarrow c_2$, then $\neg (c_1 \nleftrightarrow c_2)$; and vice versa.

Definition 20. *A subconcept c_1 of concept c_2 on Θ, denoted by $\prec$, is a concept that its intension A_1 is a superset of A_2, i.e.:*

$$c_1 \prec c_2 \triangleq A_1 \supset A_2 \tag{16}$$

Definition 21. *A superconcept c_2 over concept c_1 on Θ, denoted by $\succ$, is a concept that its intension A_2 is a subset of A_1, i.e.:*

$$c_2 \succ c_1 \triangleq A_2 \subset A_1 \tag{17}$$

According to Definitions 20 and 21, a subconcept and a superconcept are reflective. That is, *if* $c_1 \prec c_2$, *then* $c_2 \succ c_1$.

Definition 22. *The equivalent concepts c_1 and c_2 on Θ, denoted by =, are two concepts that their intensions (A_1, A_2), and extensions (O_1, O_2) are identical, i.e.:*

$$c_1 = c_2 \triangleq (A_1 = A_2) \wedge (O_1 = O_2) \tag{18}$$

Definition 23. *The consistent concepts c_1 and c_2 on Θ, denoted by $\cong$, are two concepts with a relation of being either a sub- or superconcept, i.e.:*

$$
\begin{aligned}
c_1 \cong c_2 &\triangleq (c_1 \succ c_1) \vee (c_1 \prec c_2) \\
&= (A_1 \subset A_1) \vee (A_1 \supset A_2)
\end{aligned}
\tag{19}
$$

Definition 24. *A comparison between two concepts c_1 and c_2 on Θ, denoted by ~, is an operation that determines the equivalency or similarity level of their intensions, i.e.:*

$$c_1 \sim c_2 \triangleq \frac{\#(A_1 \cap A_2)}{\#(A_1 \cup A_2)} * 100\% \tag{20}$$

The range of equivalency between two concepts is among 0 to 100 %, where 0% means no similarity and 100% means a full similarity. According to Definition 24, It is obvious that:

$$
c_1 \sim c_2 =
\begin{cases}
100\%, & c_1 = c_2 \\
\dfrac{\#A_2}{\#A_1} \square 100\%, & c_1 \prec c_2 \\
\dfrac{\#A_1}{\#A_2} \square 100\%, & c_1 \succ c_2
\end{cases}
\tag{21}
$$

Definition 25. *A definition of a concept c_1 by c_2 on Θ, denoted by $\triangleq$, is an association between two concepts where they are equivalent, i.e.:*

$$
\begin{aligned}
c_1(O_1, A_1, R^c_1, R^i_1, R^o_1) &\triangleq c_2(O_2, A_2, R^c_2, R^i_2, R^o_2) \\
&\triangleq c_1(O_1, A_1, R^c_1, R^i_1, R^o_1 \mid O_1 = O_2, A_1 = A_2, \\
&\quad R^c_1 = O_1 \times A_1, R^i_1 = R^i_2, R^o_1 = R^o_2)
\end{aligned}
\tag{22}
$$

COMPOSITIONAL OPERATIONS OF CONCEPTS

The compositional operations of concept algebra are dynamic and integrative operations that always change all concepts involved in parallel. Compositional operations on concepts provide a set of fundamental mathematical means to construct complex concepts on the basis of simple ones or to derive new concepts on the basis of exiting ones.

Lemma 2. *The compositional operations* $\bullet_c$ *in concept algebra encompasses nine associative operators for manipulating the algebraic compositions among concepts, i.e.:*

$$\bullet_c \triangleq \{\Rightarrow, \overset{-}{\Rightarrow}, \overset{+}{\Rightarrow}, \overset{\sim}{\Rightarrow}, \uplus, \pitchfork, \Leftarrow, \vdash, \mapsto\} \tag{23}$$

where the compositional operators stand for *inheritance, tailoring, extension, substitute, composition, decomposition, aggregation, specification,* and *instantiation,* respectively.

The compositional operations of concept algebra can be illustrated in Figure. 3. In Figure 3, $R = \{R^c, R^i, R^o\}$, and all nine compositional operations define composing rules among concepts, except instantiation that is an operation between a concept and a specific object.

Definition 26. *An inheritance of concept c_2 from concept c_1, denoted by $\Rightarrow$, is the creation of the new concept c_2 by reproducing c_1, and the establishment of new associations between them in parallel, see Box 1, where c_1 is called the parent concept, c_2 is the child concept, and $\|$ denotes that an inheritance creates new associations between c_1 and c_2 in parallel via (R^o_1, R^i_2) and (R^o_2, R^i_1).*

Definition 27. *The multiple inheritance of concept c from n parent concepts $c_1, c_2, ..., c_n$, denoted by $\Rightarrow$, is an inheritance that creates the new concept c via a set of n conjoint concepts and establishes new associations among them, see Box 2, where $\overset{\circ}{R}^{(x_i)}_{i-1}$ is known as the big-R notation (Wang, 2002b, 2008c) that denotes a repetitive behavior or recurrent structure.*

Figure 3. The compositional operations of concept algebra as concept manipulation rules

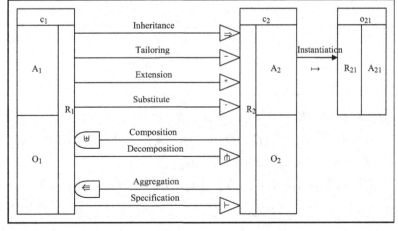

Box 1.

$$c_1(O_1, A_1, R^c_1, R^i_1, R^o_1) \Rightarrow c_2(O_2, A_2, R^c_2, R^i_2, R^o_2)$$
$$\triangleq c_2(O_2, A_2, R^c_2, R^i_2, R^o_2 \mid O_2 = O_1, A_2 = A_1, R^c_2 = O_2 \times A_2,$$
$$R^i_2 = R^i_1 \cup \{(c_1, c_2)\}, R^o_2 = R^o_1 \cup \{(c_2, c_1)\})$$
$$\mid\mid c_1(O_1, A_1, R^c_1, R^{i'}_1, R^{o'}_1 \mid R^{i'}_1 = R^i_1 \cup \{(c_2, c_1)\}, R^{o'}_1 = R^o_1 \cup \{(c_1, c_2)\})$$

$$(24)$$

Box 2.

$$\overset{n}{\underset{i=1}{R}}(c_i \Rightarrow c\ O, A, R^c, R^i, R^o)$$
$$\triangleq c(O, A, R^c, R^i, R^o \mid O = \bigcup_{i=1}^{n} O_{c_i}, A = \bigcup_{i=1}^{n} A_{c_i}, R^c = O \times A,$$
$$R^i = \bigcup_{i=1}^{n} R^i_{c_i} \cup \{\overset{n}{\underset{i=1}{R}}(c_i, c)\}, R^o = \bigcup_{i=1}^{n} R^o_{c_i} \cup \{\overset{n}{\underset{i=1}{R}}(c, c_i)\})$$
$$\mid\mid \overset{n}{\underset{i=1}{R}} c_i(O_i, A_i, R^c_i, R^{i'}_i, R^{o'}_i \mid R^{i'}_i = R^i_i \cup \{(c, c_i)\}, R^{o'}_i = R^o_i \cup \{(c_i, c)\})$$

$$(25)$$

Box 3.

$$c_1(O_1, A_1, R^c_1, R^i_1, R^o_1) \overset{\rightharpoondown}{\Rightarrow} c_2(O_2, A_2, R^c_2, R^i_2, R^o_2)$$
$$\triangleq c_2(O_2, A_2, R^c_2, R^i_2, R^o_2 \mid O_2 = O_1 \setminus O', A_2 = A_1 \setminus A', R^c_2 = O_2 \times A_2 \subset R^c_1,$$
$$R^i_2 = R^i_1 \cup \{(c_1, c_2)\}, R^o_2 = R^o_1 \cup \{(c_2, c_1)\})$$
$$\mid\mid c_1(O_1, A_1, R^c_1, R^{i'}_1, R^{o'}_1 \mid R^{i'}_1 = R^i_1 \cup \{(c_2, c_1)\}, R^{o'}_1 = R^o_1 \cup \{(c_1, c_2)\})$$

$$(26)$$

Box 4.

$$c_1(O_1, A_1, R^c_1, R^i_1, R^o_1) \overset{+}{\Rightarrow} c_2(O_2, A_2, R^c_2, R^i_2, R^o_2)$$
$$\triangleq c_2(O_2, A_2, R^c_2, R^i_2, R^o_2 \mid O_2 = O_1 \cup O', A_2 = A_1 \cup A', R^c_2 = O_2 \times A_2 \supset R^c_1,$$
$$R^i_2 = R^i_1 \cup \{(c_1, c_2)\}, R^o_2 = R^o_1 \cup \{(c_2, c_1)\})$$
$$\mid\mid c_1(O_1, A_1, R^c_1, R^{i'}_1, R^{o'}_1 \mid R^{i'}_1 = R^i_1 \cup \{(c_2, c_1)\}, R^{o'}_1 = R^o_1 \cup \{(c_1, c_2)\})$$

$$(27)$$

Box 5.

$$
\begin{aligned}
&c_1(O_1, A_1, R^c_1, R^i_1, R^o_1) \overset{\sim}{\Rightarrow} c_2(O_2, A_2, R^c_2, R^i_2, R^o_2) \\
&\triangleq c_2(O_2, A_2, R^c_2, R^i_2, R^o_2 \mid O_2 = (O_1 \setminus O'_{c_1}) \cup O'_{c_2}, A_2 = (A_1 \setminus A'_{c_1}) \cup A'_{c_2}, \\
&\qquad R^c_2 = O_2 \times A_2, R^i_2 = R^i_1 \cup \{(c_1, c_2)\}, R^o_2 = R^o_1 \cup \{(c_2, c_1)\}) \\
&\quad \| c_1(O_1, A_1, R^c_1, R^{i'}_1, R^{o'}_1 \mid R^{i'}_1 = R^i_1 \cup \{(c_2, c_1)\}, R^{o'}_1 = R^o_1 \cup \{(c_1, c_2)\})
\end{aligned}
$$

(28)

Box 6.

$$
\begin{aligned}
&c(O, A, R^c, R^i, R^o) \triangleq \biguplus_{i=1}^{n} c_i(O_i, A_i, R^c_i, R^i_i, R^o_i) \\
&= c(O, A, R^c, R^i, R^o \mid O = \bigcup_{i=1}^{n} O_{c_i}, A = \bigcup_{i=1}^{n} A_{c_i}, R^c = \bigcup_{i=1}^{n} R^c_{c_i} \cup \{(c, c_i), (c_i, c)\}, \\
&\qquad R^i = \bigcup_{i=1}^{n} R^i_{c_i} \; R^o = \bigcup_{i=1}^{n} R^o_{c_i}) \\
&\quad \| \overset{n}{\underset{i=1}{R}} c_i(O_i, A_i, R^c_i, R^{i'}_i, R^{o'}_i \mid R^{i'}_i = R^i_i \cup \{(c, c_i)\}, R^{o'}_i = R^o_i \cup \{(c_i, c)\})
\end{aligned}
$$

(29)

Definition 28. *The tailoring of concept c_2 from the parent concept c_1, denoted by $\overset{\sim}{\Rightarrow}$, is a special inheritance that creates the new concept c_2 based on c_1 with the removal of the subsets of objects O' and attributes A'; at the same time, it establishes new associations between the two concepts, see Box 3.*

Definition 29. *The extension of concept c_2 from the parent concept c_1, denoted by $\overset{+}{\Rightarrow}$, is a special inheritance that creates the new concept c_2 based c_1 with additional objects O' and/or attributes A', and establishes new associations between the two concepts, see Box 4.*

Definition 30. *The substitute of concept c_2 from the parent concept c_1, denoted by $\overset{\sim}{\Rightarrow}$, is a special inheritance that creates the new concept c_2 based on c_1 by replacing the inherited subsets of objects O'_{c1} and attributes A'_{c1} with corresponding ones O'_{c2} and A'_{c2} that share the same identifiers but possess different objects or attributes; at the same time, it establishes new associations between the two concepts, see Box 5, where $O'_{c1} \subset O_1 \wedge O'_{c2} \subset O_2 \wedge \#O'_{c1} = \#O'_{c2}$ and $A'_{c1} \subset A_1 \wedge A'_{c2} \subset A_2 \wedge \#A'_{c1} = \#A'_{c2}$.*

Binary concept tailoring, extension, and substitution can be extended to corresponding n-nary operations, similar to that of inheritance as given in Definition 27.

Definition 31. *The composition of concept c from n subconcepts $c_1, c_2, ..., c_n$, denoted by ⊎, is an integration of them that creates the new super concept c via concept conjunction; at the same time, it establishes new associations between them, see Box 6.*

It is noteworthy that, according to the calculus of incremental union ⊞ (Wang, 2006b, 2008b), the composition operation as given in Definition 31 results in the generation of new internal relations, which do not belong to any of its subconcepts. This is the most important property of concept composition.

Corollary 1. *The composition of multiple concepts is an incremental union operation, where the newly generated internal relations ΔR^c can be determined as:*

$$\Delta R^c = \bigcup_{i=1}^{n} \{(c, c_i), (c_i, c)\} \tag{30}$$

A concept decomposition is an inverse operation of concept compositions.

Definition 32. *The decomposition of concept c into n subconcepts $c_1, c_2, ..., c_n$, denoted by ⋔, is a partition of the superconcept into multiple subconcepts; at the same time, it establishes new associations between them, see Box 7.*

As specified in Definition 32, the decomposition operation results in the removal of all internal relations $\Delta R^c = \bigcup_{i=1}^{n} \{(c, c_i), (c_i, c)\}$ that are no longer belong to any of its subconcepts.

Definition 33. *The aggregation of concept c_1 from concept c_2, denoted by ⇐, is a creation of c_1 via abstraction of c_2 with a reduced intension of more generic attributes; at the same time, it establishes new associations between them, see Box 8.*

Concept aggregation is also known as concept *generalization, abstraction,* or *elicitation.* Binary aggregations can be extended to *n*-nary parallel or serial aggregations.

Definition 34. *The parallel aggregation of a concept c from a set of n concepts $c_1, c_2, ..., c_n$, denoted by ⇐, is an aggregation of c with the elicitation of all concepts in the set, see Box 9.*

Based on Definition 34, a concept may be inductively generalized by a series of aggregations with a smaller set of more abstract (super) attributes.

Definition 35. *The serial aggregation of a concept c from a set of n concepts $c_1, c_2, ..., c_n$, denoted by ⇐, is an aggregation with a total order of a series of decreasing intensions of the concepts by more abstract and generic attributes, see Box 10.*

A concept specification is an inverse operation of concept aggregations.

Definition 36. *The specification of concept c_1 by concept c_2, denoted by ⊢, is a deductive refinement of c_1 by an increasing intension with more specific and precise attributes in c_2; at the same time, it establishes new associations between them, see Box 11.*

Box 7.

$$
c(O, A, R^c, R^i, R^o) \Cap \overset{n}{\underset{i=1}{R}} c_i
$$

$$
\triangleq \overset{n}{\underset{i=1}{R}} \{ \, c_i(O_i, A_i, R^c{}_i, R^{i'}{}_i, R^{o'}{}_i \mid R^{i'}{}_i = R^i{}_i \cup \{(c, c_i)\}, R^{o'}{}_i = R^o{}_i \cup \{(c_i, c)\})
$$

$$
|| \, c(O, A, R^{c'}, R^{i'}, R^{o'} \mid R^{c'} = \overset{n}{\underset{i=1}{\bigcup}} (R^c{}_{c_i} \setminus \{(c, c_i)(c_i, c)\}),
$$

$$
\{R^{i'} = R^i \cup \overset{n}{\underset{i=1}{R}} (c_i, c)\}, R^{o'} = R^o \cup \{\overset{n}{\underset{i=1}{R}} (c, c_i)\})
$$

$$
\setminus \, c_i(O_i, A_i, R^c{}_i, R^i{}_i, R^o{}_i)
$$

$$
\}
$$

(31)

Box 8.

$$
c_1(O_1, A_1, R^c{}_1, R^i{}_1, R^o{}_1) \Lleftarrow c_2(O_2, A_2, R^c{}_2, R^i{}_2, R^o{}_2)
$$

$$
\triangleq c_1(O_1, A_1, R^c{}_1, R^i{}_1, R^o{}_1 \mid O_1 \supset O_2, A_1 \subset A_2, R^c{}_1 = (O_1 \times A_1) \cup
$$

$$
\{(c_1, c_2), (c_2, c_1)\}, R^i{}_1 = R^i{}_2 \cup \{(c_2, c_1)\}, R^o{}_1 = R^o{}_2 \cup \{(c_1, c_2)\})
$$

$$
|| \, c_2(O_2, A_2, R^c{}_2, R^{i'}{}_2, R^{o'}{}_2 \mid R^{i'}{}_2 = R^i{}_2 \cup \{(c_1, c_2)\}, R^{o'}{}_2 = R^o{}_2 \cup \{(c_2, c_1)\})
$$

(32)

Box 9.

$$
c(O, A, R^c, R^i, R^o) \Lleftarrow \overset{n}{\underset{i=1}{R}} c_i
$$

$$
\triangleq c(O, A, R^c, R^i, R^o \mid O = \overset{n}{\underset{i=1}{\bigcup}} O_i, A = \overset{n}{\underset{i=1}{\bigcap}} A_i, R^c = \overset{n}{\underset{i=1}{\bigcup}} (R^c{}_{c_i} \cup \{(c, c_i), (c_i, c)\}),
$$

$$
(R^i = \overset{n}{\underset{i=1}{\bigcup}} R^i{}_{c_i} \cup \{(c_i, c)\}), R^o = \overset{n}{\underset{i=1}{\bigcup}} (R^o{}_{c_i} \cup \{(c, c_i)\}),
$$

$$
|| \, \overset{n}{\underset{i=1}{R}} c_i(O_i, A_i, R^c{}_i, R^{i'}{}_i, R^{o'}{}_i \mid R^{i'}{}_i = R^i{}_i \cup \{(c, c_i)\}, R^{o'}{}_i = R^o{}_i \cup \{(c_i, c)\})
$$

(33)

Box 10.

$$
c(O, A, R^c, R^i, R^o) \Lleftarrow (c_1 \Lleftarrow c_2 \Lleftarrow ... \Lleftarrow c_n)
$$

$$
\triangleq c(O, A, R^c, R^i, R^o \mid O \supset O_1 \supset O_2 \supset ... \supset O_n, A \subset A_1 \subset A_2 \subset ... \subset A_n,
$$

$$
R^c = (O \times A) \cup \{(c, c_1), (c_1, c)\}, R^i = R^i{}_1 \cup \{\overset{n}{\underset{i=1}{R}} (c_i, c)\},
$$

$$
R^o = R^o{}_1 \cup \{\overset{n}{\underset{i=1}{R}} (c, c_i)\})
$$

$$
|| \, \overset{n}{\underset{i=1}{R}} c_i(O_i, A_i, R^c{}_i, R^{i'}{}_i, R^{o'}{}_i \mid R^{i'}{}_i = R^i{}_i \cup \{(c, c_i)\}, R^{o'}{}_i = R^o{}_i \cup \{(c_i, c)\})
$$

(34)

Box 11.

$$c_1(O_1, A_1, R^c{}_1, R^i{}_1, R^o{}_1) \vdash c_2(O_2, A_2, R^c{}_2, R^i{}_2, R^o{}_2)$$

$$\triangleq c_2(O_2, A_2, R^c{}_2, R^i{}_2, R^o{}_2 \mid O_2 \subset O_1, A_2 \supset A_1, R^c{}_2 = (O_2 \times A_2) \cup$$

$$\{(c_2, c_1), (c_1, c_2)\}, R^i{}_2 = R^i{}_1 \cup \{(c_1, c_2)\}, R^o{}_2 = R^o{}_1 \cup \{(c_2, c_1)\})$$

$$\| c_1(O_1, A_1, R^c{}_1, R^{i'}{}_1, R^{o'}{}_1 \mid R^{i'}{}_1 = R^i{}_1 \cup \{(c, c_1)\}, R^{o'}{}_1 = R^o{}_1 \cup \{(c_1, c)\})$$

$$(35)$$

Box 12.

$$\mathop{R}\limits_{i=1}^{n} c_i \vdash c(O, A, R^c, R^i, R^o)$$

$$\triangleq c(O, A, R^c, R^i, R^o \mid O \subset \bigcup_{i=1}^{n} O_i, A = \bigcap_{i=1}^{n} A_i, R^c = \bigcup_{i=1}^{n}(R^c{}_{c_i} \cup \{(c, c_i), (c_i, c)\}),$$

$$R^i = \bigcup_{i=1}^{n}(R^i{}_{c_i} \cup \{(c_i, c)\}), R^o = \bigcup_{i=1}^{n}(R^o{}_{c_i} \cup \{(c, c_i)\}))$$

$$\| \mathop{R}\limits_{i=1}^{n} c_i(O_i, A_i, R^c{}_i, R^{i'}{}_i, R^{o'}{}_i \mid R^{i'}{}_i = R^i{}_i \cup \{(c, c_i)\}, R^{o'}{}_i = R^o{}_i \cup \{(c_i, c)\})$$

$$(36)$$

Box 13.

$$(c_n \vdash ... \vdash c_2 \vdash c_1) \vdash c(O, A, R^c, R^i, R^o)$$

$$\triangleq c(O, A, R^c, R^i, R^o \mid O_n \supset ... \supset O_2 \supset O_1 \supset O, A_n \subset ... \subset A_2 \subset A_1 \subset A,$$

$$R^c = (O \times A) \cup \mathop{R}\limits_{i=1}^{n}\{(c, c_i), (c_i, c)\},$$

$$R^i = R^i{}_n \cup \mathop{R}\limits_{i=1}^{n}\{(c_i, c)\}), R^o = R^o{}_n \cup \mathop{R}\limits_{i=1}^{n}\{(c, c_i)\})$$

$$\| \mathop{R}\limits_{i=1}^{n} c_i(O_i, A_i, R^c{}_i, R^{i'}{}_i, R^{o'}{}_i \mid R^{i'}{}_i = R^i{}_i \cup \{(c, c_i)\}, R^{o'}{}_i = R^o{}_i \cup \{(c_i, c)\})$$

$$(37)$$

Binary specifications can be extended to *n*-nary parallel or serial aggregations.

Definition 37. *The parallel specification of concept c by a set of n concepts c_1, c_2, ..., c_n, denoted by $\vdash$, is a specification of c with the elicitation of all concepts in the set, see Box 12.*

Definition 38. *The serial specification of concept c by a set of concepts c_1, c_2, ..., c_n, denoted by $\vdash$, is a specification with a total order of a series of refinements by increasing intensions of the concepts with more specific and precise attributes, see Box 13.*

The *binary, parallel,* and *series* specifications and aggregations of concepts provide a generic means for forming a hierarchical structure of concepts in knowledge engineering.

Theorem 3. *A totally ordered series of decreasing intensions in a serial concept aggregation is reversely proportional to a totally ordered series of increasing extensions, i.e.:*

$$\forall c \Lleftarrow c_1 \Lleftarrow c_2 \Lleftarrow ... \Lleftarrow c_n,$$
$$A \subset A_1 \subset A_2 \subset ... \subset A_n \Rightarrow O \supset O_1 \supset O_2 \supset ... \supset O_n \tag{38}$$

Example 3. *The relationships between series of specifications and aggregations on the concept animal can be described as follows:*
(animal ⊢ mammal ⊢ feline ⊢ tiger) ⇒

   (animal ⇐ mammal ⇐ feline ⇐ tiger)

where, according Theorem 3, it can be obtained:

$$A_{animal} \subset A_{mammal} \subset A_{feline} \subset A_{tiger}, \text{and}$$
$$O_{animal} \supset O_{mammal} \supset O_{feline} \supset O_{tiger}$$

The compositional operations of concepts formally defined so far are those among abstract concepts. The remainder of this section describes a special compositional operation between a given concept and its objects.

Box 14.

$$c(O, A, R^c, R^i, R^o) \;\mapsto\; o(A_o, R^c_o, R^i_o)$$
$$\triangleq o(A_o, R^c_o, R^{i'}_o \mid o \subset O, A_o = A, R^c_o = o \times A_o, R^{i'}_o = R^i_o \cup \{(c,o)\})$$
$$\|\, c(O, A, R^c, R^{i'}, R^{o'} \mid R^{i'} = R^i \cup \{(o,c)\}, R^{o'} = R^o \cup \{(c,o)\}) \tag{39}$$

Box 15.

$$c(O, A, R^c, R^i, R^o) \;\mapsto\; \overset{n}{\underset{i=1}{R}}\, o_i(A_{o_i}, R^c_{o_i}, R^i_{o_i})$$
$$\triangleq \overset{n}{\underset{i=1}{R}}\, o_i(A_{o_i}, R^c_{o_i}, R^{i'}_{o_i} \mid o_i \subseteq O, A_{o_i} = A, R^c_{o_i} = o_i \times A_{o_i},$$
$$R^{i'}_{o_i} = R^i_{o_i} \cup (c, o_i)\})$$
$$\|\, c(O, A, R^c, R^{i'}, R^{o'} \mid R^{i'} = R^i \cup \{\overset{n}{\underset{i=1}{R}}(o_i, c)\}, R^{o'} = R^o \cup \{\overset{n}{\underset{i=1}{R}}(c, o_i)\}) \tag{40}$$

Definition 39. *The instantiation of a concept c, denoted by $\mapsto$, is an embodiment of its generic semantics onto a specific case or implementation known as an object o, see Box 14.*

It is noteworthy that the output relation of an object is always empty (i.e., $R^o{}_o \equiv \varnothing$), which means that the object is an end product of a concept where there is no further deduction of meanings in the hierarchy of the inheritance chain.

Definition 40. *The multiple instantiation of a concept c onto n objects, denoted by $\mapsto$, is a compound parallel instantiation that creates a set of new objects $\{o_1, o_2, ..., o_n\}$ based on c, and establishes new associations between them, see Box 15.*

CONCEPT ALGEBRA FOR KNOWLEDGE MANIPULATION

This section describes applications of concept algebra in the manipulation of abstract models of knowledge and the methodology for knowledge representation and manipulation.

The Mathematical Model of Knowledge

In cognitive informatics (Wang, 2002a, 2006a, 2007e), particularly the OAR model (Wang, 2007c; Wang & Wang, 2006) on internal knowledge representation in the brain, human *knowledge* is modeled as a concept network, where concept algebra is applied as a set of rules for knowledge composition in order to construct complex and dynamic concept networks.

Definition 41. *A generic knowledge K is an n-nary relation $\Re$ among a set of n concepts and the entire set of concepts C, i.e.:*

$$K = \Re : (\underset{i=1}{\overset{n}{\bigtimes}} C_i) \rightarrow C \tag{41}$$

where $\underset{i=1}{\overset{n}{\biguplus}} C_i = C$, and

$$\Re = \bullet_c = \{\Rightarrow, \overset{-}{\Rightarrow}, \overset{+}{\Rightarrow}, \overset{\sim}{\Rightarrow}, \uplus, \Cap, \Lleftarrow, \vdash, \mapsto\}.$$

According to Definition 41, the most simple knowledge k is a binary relation $\Re$ between two concepts in C, i.e.:

$$k = \Re : C \times C \rightarrow C. \tag{42}$$

Definition 41 indicates that the compositional operations of concept algebra, $\bullet_c$, provide a set of coherent mathematical means and rules for knowledge manipulation. Because the relations between concepts are transitive, the generic topology of knowledge is a hierarchical network as shown in Figures 2 and 3.

Theorem 4. *The generic topology of abstract knowledge systems K is a hierarchical concept network.*

Theorem 4 can be proved by the nine compositional rules in concept algebra, particularly the composition/decomposition and aggregation/specification operations, as defined in the previous section.

Corollary 2. *The property of the hierarchical knowledge architecture K in the form of concept networks is as follows:*

a.   **Dynamic:** *The knowledge network may be updated dynamically along with information acquisition and learning without destructing the existing concept nodes and relational links.*
b.   **Evolvable:** *The knowledge network may grow adaptively without changing the overall and existing structure of the hierarchical network.*

The Hierarchical Model of Concept Networks

A concept network as a generic knowledge model has been widely studied in linguistics, computing, and cognitive informatics. The notion of the *semantic network* model for knowledge representation is first proposed by Quillian in 1968 (Matlin, 1998; Quillian, 1968; Reisberg, 2001), where the semantic memory is perceived as information represented in network structures with conceptual nodes and interrelations. The meaning of a given concept depends on other concepts to which it is connected in the network. The semantic network has been extended by a number of theories such as the *hypothetical network* (Colins & Loftus, 1975), the *adaptive control of thought - star* (ADT*) model (Anderson, 1983, 1991). The latter proposes that all cognition processes in thought are controlled by unitary network models.

This subsection develops the concept network model based on concept algebra and Wang's OAR model (Wang, 2007c; Wang & Wang, 2006) for knowledge representation, which treat a concept as a basic and adaptive unit for knowledge representation and thinking.

Definition 42. *A concept network CN is a hierarchical network of concepts interlinked by the set of nine composing rules $\Re$ concept algebra, i.e.:*

$$CN = \Re : \mathop{\mathsf{X}}_{i=1}^{n} C_i \rightarrow \mathop{\mathsf{X}}_{j=1}^{n} C_j \tag{43}$$

Theorem 5. *In a concept network CN, the abstract levels of concepts ℓ_c form a partial order of a series of superconcepts, i.e.:*

$$\ell_c = (\varnothing \preccurlyeq c_1 \preccurlyeq c_2 \preccurlyeq \ldots \preccurlyeq c_n \preccurlyeq \ldots \preccurlyeq \Omega) \tag{44}$$

where $\varnothing$ is the empty concept $\varnothing = (\perp, \perp)$, and Ω the universal concept, $\Omega = (\mathcal{O}, \mathcal{A})$.

According to Theorem 5 and Definition 42, a hierarchical structure of concepts in a given semantic environment Θ can be formally described by concept algebra. The algebraic relations and compositional operations of concept algebra enable the construction of hierarchical concept networks in a dynamic process.

Box 16.

$$c_1(pen) = c_1(O_1, A_1, R^c{}_1, R^i{}_1, R^o{}_1)$$

$$\text{where } O_1 = \{o_{11}, o_{12}, o_{13}\} = \{ballpoinbt, fountain, brush\};$$

$$A_1 = \{a_1, a_2, a_3\} = \{a\_writing\_tool, using\_ink, having\_a\_nib\};$$

$$A^*{}_1 = \{a_1, a_2, a_3, a_4\} = A \cup \{with\_an\_ink\_container\};$$

$$R^c{}_1 = O_1 \times A_1 = \{(o_{11}, a_1), (o_{11}, a_2), (o_{11}, a_3)\} \cup$$

$$\{(o_{12}, a_1), (o_{12}, a_2), (o_{12}, a_3)\} \cup \{(o_{13}, a_1), (o_{13}, a_2), (o_{13}, a_3)\}$$

$$(45)$$

Example 4. *A concrete concept network, pen and printer, can be illustrated in Figure 4. The concept network may be dynamically extended along with the development of related knowledge such as to extend it to a more abstract concept network of stationery. In Figure 4, concept $c_1(pen)$ may be formally described in concept algebra, see Box 16.*

It is noteworthy that, according to Definition 10, the intension of $c_1(pen)$ does not include the attribute a_4, because it is not commonly shared by all objects of the given concept. However, A_1^* does include a_4 in the closure of attributes of the given concept *pen*.

Example 5. *An abstract concept network that is formed by the composition and aggregation of a set of related concepts c_0 through c_9, as well as objects o_1 through o_3, can be expressed in Figure 5.*

Figure 4. A concrete concept network

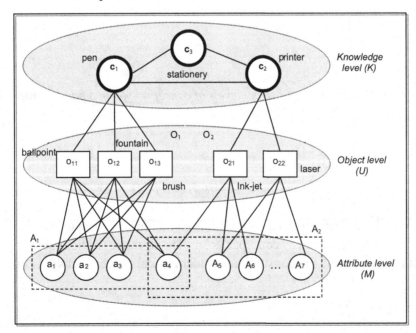

Figure 5. An abstract concept network

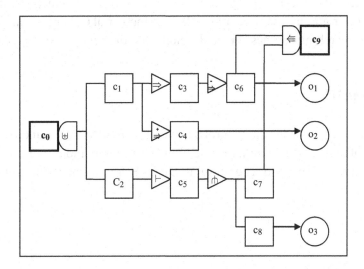

A formal description corresponding to the above concept network can be carried out using concept algebra as given below:

$$c_0 \uplus ((c_1 \Rightarrow c_3 \overset{\Rightarrow}{\Rightarrow} c_6 \mapsto o_1) \parallel (c_1 \overset{+}{\Rightarrow} c_4 \mapsto o_2))$$
$$\parallel (c_2 \vdash c_5 \pitchfork (c_7 \parallel (c_8 \mapsto o_3))$$

$$c_9 \Leftarrow (c_6 \parallel c_7) \tag{46}$$

The case studies in Examples 4 and 5 demonstrate that concept algebra and concept network are a generic and formal knowledge manipulation means that are capable to deal with complicated abstract or concrete knowledge structures and their algebraic operations. Further, detailed concept operations of concept algebra may be extended into a set of inference processes, which can be formally described by RTPA (Wang, 2002b, 2003, 2006a, 2007b, 2007d, 2008a, 2008d) as a set of behavioral processes.

CONCLUSION

A new mathematical structure, known as concept algebra, has been presented for abstract concepts and knowledge representation and manipulation. Concepts have been treated as the basic unit of cognition that carries certain meanings in almost all cognitive processes such as thinking, learning, reasoning, and system design. Abstract concepts have been formally modeled as a dynamic mathematical structure with internal attributes, objects, and their relations that possess the adaptive capability to grow in concept networks. The formal methodology for manipulating knowledge has been developed using concept algebra and concept networks. A number of case studies have been used to demonstrate the expressive power of concept algebra in knowledge representation and manipulation. A wide range of applications of concept algebra has been identified for solving common problems in cognitive informatics, logic, linguistics, psychology, knowledge engineering, data mining, software engineering, and intelligence science. One of the important applications of concept algebra is the formalization of object-oriented methodologies and the development of a rigorous semantics of UML as an industrial OO design languages. Autonomic machine learning and searching engines can be developed on the basis of concept algebra.

ACKNOWLEDGMENT

The author would like to acknowledge the Natural Science and Engineering Council of Canada (NSERC) for its partial support of this work. The author would like to thank anonymous reviewers for their valuable comments and suggestions. The author is grateful to Dr. Y. Y. Yao for many insightful discussions.

REFERENCES

Anderson, J. R. (1983). *The architecture of cognition*. Cambridge, MA: Harvard University Press.

Anderson, J. R. (1991). Is human cognition adaptive? *Behavioral and Brain Science, 14,* 71-517.

Chen, Y., & Yao, Y. Y. (2005). Formal concept analysis based on hierarchical class analysis. In *Proceedings of the Fourth IEEE International Conference on Cognitive Informatics (ICCI'05)* (pp. 285-292). Irvin, CA: IEEE CS Press.

Codin, R., Missaoui, R., & Alaoui, H. (1995). Incremental concept formation algorithms based on Galois (concept) lattices. *Computational Intelligence, 11*(2), 246-267.

Colins, A. M., & Loftus, E. F. (1975). A Spreading-activation theory of semantic memory. *Psychological Review, 82,* 407-428.

Ganter, B., & Wille, R. (1999). *Formal concept analysis.* Berlin, Germany: Springer.

Hampton, J. A. (1997). *Psychological representation of concepts of memory* (pp. 81-11). Hove, England: Psychology Press

Hurley, P. J. (1997), *A concise introduction to logic* (6th ed.). Belmony, CA: Wadsworth.

Matlin, M. W. (1998). *Cognition* (4th ed.). New York: Harcourt Brace.

Medin, D. L., & Shoben, E. J. (1988). Context and structure in conceptual combination. *Cognitive Psychology, 20,* 158-190.

Murphy, G. L. (1993). Theories and concept formation. In I. V. Mechelen et al. (Eds.), *Categories and concepts, theoretical views and inductive data analysis* (pp. 173-200). New York: Academic Press.

Quillian, M. R. (1968). Semantic memory. In M. Minsky (Ed.), *Semantic information processing*. Cambridge, MA: MIT Press.

Reisberg, D. (2001). *Cognition: Exploring the science of the mind* (2nd ed.). New York: Norton.

Smith, E. E., & Medin, D. L. (1981). *Categories and concepts.* Cambridge, MA: Harvard University Press.

Wang, Y. (2002a). Keynote lecture: On cognitive informatics. In *Proceedings of the First IEEE International Conference on Cognitive Informatics (ICCI'02)* (pp. 34-42). Calgary, Canada: IEEE CS Press.

Wang, Y. (2002b). The real-time process algebra (RTPA). *The International Journal of Annals of Software Engineering, 14,* 235-274.

Wang, Y. (2003). Using process algebra to describe human and software system behaviors. *Brain and Mind, 4*(2), 199-213.

Wang, Y. (2006a, July). Cognitive informatics and contemporary mathematics for knowledge representation and manipulation, invited plenary talk. In *Proceedings of the First International Conference on Rough Set and Knowledge Technology (RSKT'06)* (LNAI 4062, pp. 69-78). Chongqing, China: Springer.

Wang, Y. (2006b). On abstract systems and system algebra. In *Proceedinngs of the Fifth IEEE International Conference on Cognitive Informatics (ICCI'06)* (pp. 332-343). Beijing, China: IEEE CS Press.

Wang, Y. (2006c). On concept algebra and knowledge representation. In *Proceedings of the Fifth IEEE International Conference on Cognitive Informatics (ICCI'06)* (pp. 320-331), Beijing, China: IEEE CS Press.

Wang, Y. (2006d, March). On the informatics laws and deductive semantics of software. *IEEE Transactions on Systems, Man, and Cybernetics (C), 36*(2), 161-171.

Wang, Y. (2007a). The cognitive processes of formal inferences. *The International Journal of Cognitive Informatics and Natural Intelligence, 1*(4), 75-86.

Wang, Y. (2007b). Keynote speech: On theoretical foundations of software engineering and denotational mathematics. In *Proceedings of the Fifth Asian Workshop on Foundations of Software* (pp. 99-102). Xiamen, China:.

Wang, Y. (2007c). The OAR model of neural informatics for internal knowledge representation in the brain. *The International Journal of Cognitive Informatics and Natural Intelligence, 1*(3), 64-75.

Wang, Y. (2007d, July). Software engineering foundations: A software science perspective. In *CRC Series in Software Engineering: Vol. 2.* CRC Press.

Wang, Y. (2007e). The theoretical framework of cognitive informatics. *The International Journal of Cognitive Informatics and Natural Intelligence, 1*(1), 1-27.

Wang, Y. (2008a, April). Deductive semantics of RTPA. *The International Journal of Cognitive Informatics and Natural Intelligence, 2*(2), 96-121.

Wang, Y. (2008b, April). On system algebra: A denotational mathematical structure for abstract system modeling. *The International Journal of Cognitive Informatics and Natural Intelligence, 2*(2), 20-43.

Wang, Y. (2008c). On the big-R notation for describing iterative and recursive behaviors. *The International Journal of Cognitive Informatics and Natural Intelligence, 2*(1), 17-18.

Wang, Y. (2008d, April). RTPA: A denotational mathematics for manipulating intelligent and computational behaviors. *The International Journal of Cognitive Informatics and Natural Intelligence, 2*(2), 44-62.

Wang, Y., & Wang, Y. (2006, March). On cognitive informatics models of the brain. *IEEE Transactions on Systems, Man, and Cybernetics (C), 36*(2), 203-207.

Wille, R. (1982). Restructuring lattice theory: An approach based on hierarchies of concepts. In I. Rival (Ed.), *Ordered sets* (pp. 445-470). Reidel, Dordrecht

Wilson, R. A., & Keil, F. C. (Eds.). (1999). *The MIT encyclopedia of the cognitive sciences*. Cambridge, MA: The MIT Press.

Yao, Y. Y. (2004). Concept formation and learning: A cognitive informatics perspective. In *Proceedings of the Third IEEE International Conference on Cognitive Informatics (ICCI'04)* (pp. 42-51). Victoria, British Columbia, Canada: IEEE CS Press.

This work was previously published in International Journal of Cognitive Informatics and Natural Intelligence, Vol. 2, Issue 2, edited by Y. Wang, pp. 1-19, copyright 2008 by IGI Publishing (an imprint of IGI Global).

Chapter 9
On System Algebra:
A Denotational Mathematical Structure for Abstract System Modeling

Yingxu Wang
University of Calgary, Canada

ABSTRACT

Systems are the most complicated entities and phenomena in abstract, physical, information, and social worlds across all science and engineering disciplines. System algebra is an abstract mathematical structure for the formal treatment of abstract and general systems as well as their algebraic relations, operations, and associative rules for composing and manipulating complex systems. This article presents a mathematical theory of system algebra and its applications in system engineering, software engineering, and cognitive informatics. A rigorous treatment of abstract systems is described, and the algebraic relations and compositional operations of abstract systems are analyzed. System algebra provides a denotational mathematical means that can be used to model, specify, and manipulate generic "to be" and "to have" type problems, particularly system architectures and high-level system designs, in computing, software engineering, system engineering, and cognitive informatics.

INTRODUCTION

Systems are the most complicated entities and phenomena in abstract, physical, information, and social worlds across all science and engineering disciplines. Systems are needed because the physical and/ or cognitive power of an individual component or a person is not enough to carry out a work or solve a problem. System philosophy intends to treat everything as a system, and it perceives that a system always belongs to other super system(s) and contains more subsystems.

The system concept can be traced back to the 17th century, when René Descartes (1596-1650) noticed the interrelationships among scientific disciplines as a system. The general system notion was then proposed by Ludwig von Bertalanffy in the 1920s (von Bertalanffy, 1952; Ellis & Fred, 1962). The theories of system science have evolved from classic theories (Ashby, 1958, 1962; Ellis & Fred, 1962; Heylighen, 1989; G. J. Klir, 1992; R. G. Klir, 1988; Rapoport, 1962) to contemporary theories in the mid-20th century, such as I. Prigogine's dissipative structure theory (Prigogine et al., 1972), H. Haken's synergetics (Haken, 1977), and Eigen's hypercycle theory (Eigen & Schuster, 1979). Then, during the late part of the last century, there are proposals of complex systems theories (G. J. Klir, 1992; Zadeh, 1973), fuzzy theories (Zadeh, 1965, 1973), and chaos theories (Ford, 1986; Skarda & Freeman, 1987).

System algebra is an abstract mathematical structure for the formal treatment of abstract and general systems as well as their algebraic relations, operations, and associative rules for composing and manipulating complex systems. System algebra (Wang, 2005, 2006a, 2006b, 2007a, 2007c) presented in this article is the latest attempt to provide a formal and rigorous treatment of abstract systems and their properties. This article treats systems as a mathematic entity and it studies the generic rules and theories of abstract systems. A new mathematical structure of abstract systems as the most complicated mathematical entities beyond sets, functions, and processes is presented. Properties of abstract systems are modeled and analyzed. System algebra is introduced as a set of relational and compositional operations for manipulating abstract systems and their composing rules. The relational operations of system algebra are described encompassing *independent, related, overlapped, equivalent, subsystem,* and *supersystem.* The compositional operations of system algebra are explored encompassing *inheritance, tailoring, extension, substitute, difference, composition, decomposition, aggregation,* and *specification.* A wide range of applications of system algebra are identified in cognitive informatics, system science, system engineering, computing, software engineering, and intelligent systems.

THE ABSTRACT SYSTEM THEORY

This section demonstrates that systems may be treated rigorously as a new mathematical structure beyond conventional mathematical entities. Based on this view, the concept of abstract systems and their mathematical models are introduced.

Definition 1. *An abstract system is a collection of coherent and interactive entities that has stable functions and a clear boundary with the external environment.*

An abstract system forms the generic model of various real-world systems and represents the most common characteristics and properties of them.

Lemma 1. *The generality principle of system abstraction states that a system can be represented as a whole in a given level k of reasoning, $1 \leq k \leq n$, without knowing the details at levels below k.*

Definition 2. *Let C be a finite or infinite nonempty set of components, and B a finite or infinite nonempty set of behaviors, then the universal system environment U is denoted as a triple, i.e.:*

$$\mathfrak{U} \triangleq (\mathcal{C}, \mathcal{B}, \mathcal{R})$$
$$= \mathcal{R} : \mathcal{C} \to \mathcal{C} \,|\, \mathcal{C} \to \mathcal{B} \,|\, \mathcal{B} \to \mathcal{C} \,|\, \mathcal{B} \to \mathcal{B} \tag{1}$$

where $\mathcal{R}$ is a set of relations between $\mathcal{C}$ and $\mathcal{B}$, and | demotes alternative relations.

Abstract systems can be classified into two categories known as the *closed* and *open* systems. Most practical and useful systems in nature are open systems in which there are interactions between the system and its environment. However, in order to develop the theoretical framework of abstract systems, the closed systems in which there is no interaction with the external environment will be modeled first in the following subsection.

The Mathematical Model of Closed Systems

The axiom of the abstract system theory is based on the Object-Attribute-Relation (OAR) model (Wang, 2007b, 2007d; Wang & Wang, 2006c), in which the architecture of a system object O_s can be modeled by a set of attributes A and a set of binary relations R among A and O_s, i.e.:

$$O_s \triangleq (A, R) \tag{2}$$

Encompassing both architectures and behaviors of a system on the basis of Equation 2, an abstract closed system without interactions with the environment can be formally described as follows.

Definition 3. *A closed system $\hat{S}$ on $\mathfrak{U}$ is a 4-tuple, i.e.:*

$$\hat{S} \triangleq (C, R, B, \Omega) \tag{3}$$

where

- C is a nonempty set of components of the system, $C = \{c_1, c_2, ..., c_n\} \subseteq \mathbb{P}C \sqsubseteq \mathfrak{U}$.
- R is a nonempty set of relations between pairs of the components in the system, $R = \{r_1, r_2, ..., r_m\} \subseteq C \times C$.
- B is a set of behaviors (or functions), $B = \{b_1, b_2, ..., b_p\} \subseteq \mathbb{P}B \sqsubseteq \mathfrak{U}$.
- Ω is a set of constraints on the memberships of components, the conditions of relations, and the scopes of behaviors, $\Omega = \{\omega_1, \omega_2, ..., \omega_q\}$.

According to Definition 3, a closed system $\hat{S} = (C, R, B, \Omega)$ on $\mathfrak{U}$ can be illustrated in Figure 1.

It is noteworthy that system behaviors B is the most broad set of system actions implemented or embodied on the given layout of the systems, including any kind of system functions, interactions, and communications. This is the major difference that distinguishes an abstract system from other mathematical structures such as a set, lattice, group, or concept (Wang, 2008b).

Lemma 2. *A closed system $\hat{S} = (C, R, B, \Omega)$ is an asymmetric (directed) and reflective system because the relations R in it are constrained by the following rules:*

Figure 1. The abstract model of a closed system

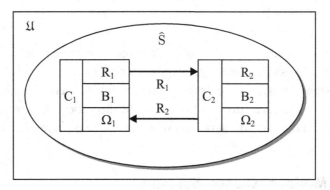

a. *Asymmetric*:
$$\forall a, b \in C \wedge a \neq b \wedge r \in R, \, r(a, b) \nRightarrow$$
$$r(b, a) \tag{4}$$

b. *Reflective*:
$$\forall c \in C, \, r(c, c) \in R \tag{5}$$

Corollary 1. *The maximum number of binary relations n_r between all pairs of the n_c components in a closed system $\widehat{S} = (C, R, B, \Omega)$ can be determined as follows:*

$$n_r = \#R = \#(C \times C) = n_c^{\,2} \tag{6}$$

if all reflective self-relations are not considered, n_r becomes the maximum number of binary relations of fully connected systems, n'_r, i.e.:

$$n'_r = n'_r - n_c = n_c(n_c - 1) \tag{7}$$

Example 1. *According to Corollary 1, the creation of relations in a closed system is solely determined by the number of components possessed in the system. This property can be illustrated in Figure 2, where $\uplus$ denotes a system composition for both closed or open systems, which will be formally explained later. The relations of the three closed systems $\widehat{S_1}$, $\widehat{S_2}$, and $\widehat{S}$ are as follows, observing that all pairwise relations are asymmetric or different:*

$$n_{r_1}(\widehat{S_1}) = n_{c_1}^{\,2} = 3^2 = 9; \; n_{r_1}(\widehat{S_2}) = 2^2 = 4;$$
$$n_r(\widehat{S}) = 5^2 = 25$$

and

$$n'_{r_1}(\widehat{S_1}) = n_{r_1} - n_{c_1} = 9 - 3 = 6;$$
$$n'_{r_2}(\widehat{S_2}) = 4 - 2 = 2; \; n'_r(\widehat{S}) = 25 - 5 = 20$$

Figure 2. Creation of relations in open and closed systems

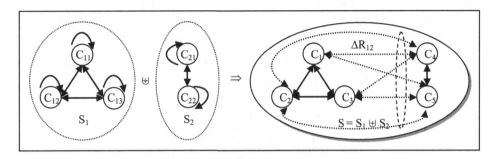

The Mathematical Model of Open Systems

Most practical systems in the real world are not closed. That is, they need to interact with external world known as the *environment* Θ in order to exchange energy, matter, and/or information. Such systems are called "open systems." Typical interactions between an open system and the environment are inputs and outputs.

Contrary to that the relations of a closed system are defined on the Cartesian product of internal components, the set of relations R of an open system needs to be extended to include both internal relations R^c and external (input/output) relations R^i and R^o, i.e.:

$$R = \{R^c \cup R^i \cup R^o\} \tag{8}$$

Definition 4. *An open system S on U is a 7-tuple, i.e.:*

$$S \triangleq (C, R, B, \Omega, \Theta), R = \{R^c, R^i, R^o\}$$
$$= (C, R^c, R^i, R^o, B, \Omega, \Theta) \tag{9}$$

where the extensions of entities beyond the closed system as given in Definition 3 are as follows:

- Θ is the environment of S with a nonempty set of components C_Θ outside C, i.e., $\Theta = C_\Theta \sqsubseteq \mathfrak{U}$.
- $R^c = C \times C$ is a set of internal relations.
- $R^i \subseteq C_\Theta \times C$ is a set of external input relations.
- $R^o \subseteq C \times C_\Theta$ is a set of external output relations.

An open system $S = (C, R^c, R^i, R^o, B, \Omega, \Theta)$ can be illustrated in Figure 3.

Lemma 3. *An open system S(C, R^c, R^i, R^o, B, Ω, Θ) on $\mathfrak{U}$ is an asymmetric and reflective system because its relations R^c, R^i, and R^o are constrained by the following rules:*

a.   *Internally asymmetric*:
     $\forall a, b \in C \land a \neq b \land r \in R^c, r(a,b)$
     $\not\Rightarrow r(b,a)$ $\tag{10}$

Figure 3. The abstract model of an open system

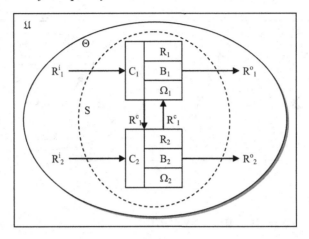

b   *Externally asymmetric*:

$$\forall a \in C \wedge \forall x \in C_\Theta \wedge r \in R^i \vee r \in R^o, r(x,a) \not\Rightarrow r(a,x) \tag{11}$$

c.   *Reflective*:

$$\forall c \in C, r(c, c) \in R^c \tag{12}$$

Corollary 2. *The maximum number of binary relations n_r and n'_r in an open system $S(C, R^c, R^i, R^o, B, \Omega, \Theta)$ is determined by the numbers of internal relations R^c as well as external relations R^i and R^o, i.e.:*
ok i

$$n_r(S) = \#R^c + \#R^i + \#R^o =$$
$$n_c^2 + 2(n_c \cdot n_{c_\Theta}) = n_c(n_c + 2n_{c_\Theta}) \tag{13}$$

$$n'_r(S) = n_r(S) - n_c = n_c \cdot (n_c + 2n_{c_\Theta}) - n_c =$$
$$n_c \cdot (n_c + 2n_{c_\Theta} - 1) \tag{14}$$

Example 2. *According to Corollary 2, the creation of relations in an open system is solely determined by the number of components possessed in the system and its environment. This property can also be illustrated in Figure 2, where S_1 is treated as the open system and S_2 as the environment Θ:*

$$n_r(S) = n_c(n_c + 2n_{c_\Theta})$$
$$= 3(3 + 2 \cdot 2) = 21$$

and

$$n'_r(S) = n_r(S) - n_c$$
$$= 21 - 3 = 18$$

According to Corollaries 1 and 2, as well as Examples 1 and 2, it is apparent that either a closed or an open system may result in a huge number of relations n_r and the exponential increases of complexity, when the number of components possessed in them is considerably large. Therefore, system algebra is introduced to formally and efficiently manipulate abstract and general systems.

Definition 5. *A system algebra SA on a given universal system environment* $\mathfrak{U}$ *is a triple, i.e.:*

$$SA \triangleq (S, OP, \Theta) =$$
$$(\{C, R^c, R^i, R^o, B, \Omega\}, \{\bullet_r, \bullet_c\}, \Theta) \tag{15}$$

where OP = {$\bullet_r$, $\bullet_c$}are the sets of relational and compositional operations on abstract systems.

System algebra provides a denotational mathematical means for algebraic manipulations of abstract systems. System algebra can be used to model, specify, and manipulate generic "to be" and "to have" type problems, particularly system architectures and high-level system designs, in computing, software engineering, system engineering, and cognitive informatics. The *relational* and *compositional* operations on abstract systems will be formally described in the following sections.

PROPERTIES OF ABSTRACT SYSTEMS

Taxonomy of Systems

Systems as the most complex entities in the physical and abstract worlds may be classified into various categories according to the key characteristics of their components (C), relations (R), behaviors (B), constraints (Ω), and/or environments (Θ). A summary of the system taxonomy is shown in Table 1, according to Definitions 3 and 4.

Table 1 shows that all types of systems fit the unified framework of system taxonomy. There are hybrid systems that may fall in two or more categories, such as a dynamic nonlinear system and a discrete fuzzy social system. The types of systems may also classified by their magnitudes as described in the following subsection.

Magnitude of Systems

Abstract and real-world systems may be very small or extremely large (Qian et al, 1990; Rosen, 1977). Therefore, a formal model of system magnitudes is needed to classify the size properties of systems and their relationship with other basic system attributes. In order to derive such a model, a set of measures on system sizes, magnitudes, and complexities is introduced next.

Definition 6. *The size of a system* S_s *is the number of components encompassed in the system, i.e.:*

$$S_s = \#C = n_c \tag{16}$$

Table 1. Taxonomy of systems

No.	System	Key Characteristics			
		Components (C)	**Relations (R)**	**Behaviors (B)**	**Environment (Θ)**
1	Concrete	Natural or real entities			
2	Abstract	Mathematical or virtual entities			
3	Physical	Natural entities			
4	Social	Humans			
5	Finite	$\#C \neq \infty$			
6	Infinite	$\#C = \infty$			
7	Closed		$R^i = \varnothing \wedge R^o = \varnothing$		
8	Open		$R^i \neq \varnothing \wedge R^o \neq \varnothing$		
9	Static			Invariable	
10	Dynamic			Variable	
11	Linear			Linear functions	
12	Nonlinear			Nonlinear functions	
13	Continuous			Continuous functions	
14	Discrete			Discrete functions	
15	Precise			Precise functions	
16	Fuzzy			Fuzzy functions	
17	Determinate			Response predictable to same stimulates	
18	Indeterminate			Response unpredictable to same stimulates	
19	White-box	Observable	Transparent	Fully observable	
20	Black-box	Unobservable	Non-transparent	Partially observable	
21	Intelligent			Autonomic	Adaptive
22	Non-intelligent			Imperative	Nonadaptive
23	Maintainable	Fixable		Recoverable	
24	Non-maintainable	Nonfixable		Nonrecoverable	

Definition 7. *The magnitude of a system M_s is the number of asymmetric binary relations among the n_c components of the system including the reflexive relations, i.e.:*

$$M_s = \#R = n_r = \#(C \times C) = n_c^2 \tag{17}$$

If all self-reflective relations are ruled out in n_r, the pure number of binary relations M'_s in the given system is determined as follows:

$$M'_s = M_s - n_c = n_c^2 - n_c = n_c(n_c - 1) \tag{18}$$

Lemma 4. *The pure number of binary relations M'_s equals to exactly two times of the number of pairwise combinations among n_c, i.e.:*

$$M'_s = n_c(n_c - 1) = 2 \bullet \frac{n_c(n_c - 1)}{2} = 2 \bullet C_{n_c}^2 \tag{19}$$

where the factor 2 represents the asymmetric binary relation r, i.e., arb ≠ bra.

The magnitude of a system determines its complexity. The complexities of systems can be classified based on if they are fully or partially connected. The former is the theoretical upper-bound complexity of systems in which all components are potentially interconnected with each other in all n-nary ways, $1 \le n \le n_c = \#C$. The latter is the more typical complexity of systems where components are only pairwisely connected.

Definition 8. *The complexity of a fully connected system C_{max} is a closure of all possible n-nary relations R^*, $1 \le n \le n_c$, among all components of the given system $n_c = \#C$, i.e.:*

$$C_{max} = R^* = 2 \sum_{k=0}^{n_r} C_{n_r}^k \approx$$
$$2 \bullet 2^{n_r} = 2^{n_r + 1} = 2^{n_c^2 + 1} = 2^{M_s + 1} \tag{20}$$

where C_{max} is also called the maximum complexity of systems.

According to Definition 8, the closure of all possible n-nary relations R^* may easily result in an extremely huge degree of complexity for a system with few components. For example, when $n_c = 10$, $C_{max} = 2^{101}$. This explains why most of the real-world systems are really too hard to be modeled and handled in conventional models and techniques.

It is noteworthy that almost all functioning systems are partially connected, because a fully connected system may not represent or provide anything meaningful. Therefore, the complexity of partially connected systems can be simplified as follows on the basis of Definition 8.

Definition 9. *The complexity of a partially connected system C_r is determined by the number of asymmetric binary relations M'_s of the system, i.e.:*

$$C_r = M'_s = 2 \bullet C_{n_c}^2 = n_c(n_c - 1) \tag{21}$$

where C_r can be referred to the relational complexity of systems.

The extent of system magnitudes (Wang, 2006d, 2007c) can be classified at seven levels known as the *empty, small, medium, large, giant, immense,* and *infinite* systems from the bottom up. A summary of the relationships between system magnitudes, sizes, internal relations, and complexities can be described in the *system magnitude model,* shown in Table 2.

Table 2. The system magnitude model

Level	Category	Size of systems $(S_s = n_c)$	Magnitude of systems $(M_s = n_r = n_c^2)$	Relational complexity of systems $(C_r = n_c(n_c - 1))$	Maximum complexity of systems $(C_{max} = 2^{n_c^2})$
1	The empty system ($\mathcal{O}$)	0	0	0	-
2	Small system	[1, 10]	$[1, 10^2]$	[0, 90]	$[2, 2^{100}]$
3	Medium system	$(10, 10^2]$	$(10^2, 10^4]$	$(90, 0.99 \bullet 10^4]$	$(2^{100}, 2^{10,000}]$
4	Large system	$(10^2, 10^3]$	$(10^4, 10^6]$	$(0.99 \bullet 10^4, 0.999 \bullet 10^6]$	∞
5	Giant system	$(10^3, 10^4]$	$(10^6, 10^8]$	$(0.999 \bullet 10^6, 0.9999 \bullet 10^8]$	∞
6	Immense system	$(10^4, 10^5]$	$(10^8, 10^{10}]$	$(0.9999 \bullet 10^8, 0.99999 \bullet 10^{10}]$	∞
7	The infinite system ($\mathfrak{U}$)	∞	∞	∞	∞

Table 2 indicates that the complexity of a small system may easily be out of control of human cognitive manageability. This leads to the following theorem.

Theorem 1. *The holism complexity of systems states that within the 7-level scale of system magnitudes, known as the empty, small, medium, large, giant, immense, and infinite systems, almost all systems are too complicated to be cognitively understood or mentally handled as a whole, except small systems or those that can be decomposed into small systems.*

According to Theorem 1, the basic principle for dealing with complicated systems is system decomposition or modularity, in which the complexity of a lower level subsystem must be small enough to be cognitively manageable. Details of system decomposition theories and the art of system architectures will be developed in the following sections.

RELATIONAL OPERATIONS ON SYSTEMS

The relational operations of abstract systems are static and comparative operations that do not change the systems involved. The relational operations on abstract systems are described below.

Lemma 5. *The relational operations $\bullet_r$ in system algebra encompasses 6 comparative operators for manipulating the algebraic relations between abstract systems, i.e.:*

$$\bullet_r \triangleq \{\leftrightsquigarrow, \leftrightarrow, \Pi, =, \sqsubseteq, \sqsupseteq\} \tag{22}$$

where the relational operators stand for independent, related, overlapped, equivalent, subsystem, and supersystem, respectively.

Algebraic Relations of Closed Systems

Relationships between two closed systems can be independent, equivalent, being subsystem, and being super system. The four relational operations of closed systems are defined as follows.

Definition 10. *Two closed systems $\widehat{S_1}$ and $\widehat{S_2}$ are independent, denoted by $\leftrightarrow$, if both their component sets and relation sets are disjoint, i.e.:*

$$\widehat{S}_1(C_1, R_1, B_1, \Omega_1) \leftrightarrow \widehat{S}_2 \ (C_2, R_2, B_2, \Omega_2)$$
$$\triangleq C_1 \cap C_2 = \varnothing \wedge R_1 \cap R_2 = \varnothing \tag{23}$$

Definition 11. *Two closed systems $\widehat{S_1}$ and $\widehat{S_2}$ are equivalent, denoted by $=$, if all sets of components, relations, behaviors, and constraints are identical, i.e.:*

$$\widehat{S}_1(C_1, R_1, B_1, \Omega_1) = \widehat{S}_2(C_2, R_2, B_2, \Omega_2)$$
$$\triangleq C_1 = C_2 \wedge R_1 = R_2 \wedge B_1 = B_2 \wedge \Omega_1 = \Omega_2 \tag{24}$$

Definition 12. *A subsystem $\widehat{S}'$ is a system that is implicated in another system $\widehat{S}$, denoted by $\sqsubseteq$, i.e.:*

$$\widehat{S}'(C, R, B, \Omega) \sqsubseteq \widehat{S}(C, R, B, \Omega)$$
$$\triangleq C' \subseteq C \wedge R' \subseteq R \wedge B' \subseteq B \wedge \Omega' \subseteq \Omega \tag{25}$$

The aforementioned definition indicates that a subsystem of a closed system is a coherent part with all integrated components, internal/input/output relations, behaviors, constraints, and the environment.

Definition 13. *A supersystem $\widehat{S}$ is a system that consists of one or more subsystems S', denoted by $\sqsupseteq$, i.e.:*

$$\widehat{S}(C, R, B, \Omega) \sqsupseteq \widehat{S}'(C', R', B', \Omega')$$
$$\triangleq C' \subseteq C \wedge R' \subseteq R \wedge B' \subseteq B \wedge \Omega' \subseteq \Omega \tag{26}$$

Algebraic Relations of OpenSystems

Relationships between two open systems can be independent, overlapped, related, equivalent, being subsystem, and being supersystem. The six compositional operations of open systems are defined as follows.

Definition 14. *Two open systems S_1 and S_2 are independent, denoted by $\leftrightarrow$, if both their component sets and external relation sets are disjoint, i.e.:*

$$S_1(C_1, R_1^c, R_1^i, R_1^o, B_1, \Omega_1, \Theta_1) \leftrightarrow$$
$$S_2(C_2, R_2^c, R_2^i, R_2^o, B_2, \Omega_2, \Theta_2)$$
$$\triangleq C_1 \cap C_2 = \emptyset \wedge R_1^i \cap R_2^i =$$
$$\emptyset \wedge R_1^o \cap R_2^o = \emptyset \tag{27}$$

Definition 15. *Two open systems S_1 and S_2 are overlapped, denoted by Π, if their component sets are joint, i.e.:*

$$S_1(C_1, R_1^c, R_1^i, R_1^o, B_1, \Omega_1, \Theta_1) \, \Pi$$
$$S_2(C_2, R_2^c, R_2^i, R_2^o, B_2, \Omega_2, \Theta_2)$$
$$\triangleq C_1 \cap C_2 \neq \emptyset \tag{28}$$

Definition 16. *Two open systems S_1 and S_2 are related, denoted by $\leftrightarrow$, if either the sets of their input relations or output relations are overlapped, i.e.:*

$$S_1(C_1, R_1^c, R_1^i, R_1^o, B_1, \Omega_1, \Theta_1) \leftrightarrow$$
$$S_2(C_2, R_2^c, R_2^i, R_2^o, B_2, \Omega_2, \Theta_2)$$
$$\triangleq R_1^i \cap (R_2^0)^{-1} \neq \emptyset \vee R_2^i \cap (R_1^0)^{-1} \neq \emptyset \tag{29}$$

where $(R_1^0)^{-1}$ or $(R_2^0)^{-1}$ denotes an inverse relation, i.e., $\forall a \in C_1 \wedge b \in C_2, r(a, b) \in R_1^0 \Rightarrow r(b, a) \in (R_2^i) = (R_1^0)^{-1}$.

It is noteworthy that, by definition, there is no closed system that is related or overlapped.

Definition 17. *Two open systems S_1 and S_2 are equivalent, denoted by =, if all sets of components, relations, behaviors, constraints, and environments are identical, i.e.:*

$$S_1(C_1, R_1^c, R_1^i, R_1^o, B_1, \Omega_1, \Theta_1) =$$
$$S_2(C_2, R_2^c, R_2^i, R_2^o, B_2, \Omega_2, \Theta_2) \triangleq$$
$$C_1 = C_2 \wedge R_1^c = R_2^c \wedge R_1^i = R_2^i \wedge R_1^o =$$
$$R_2^o \wedge B_1 = B_2 \wedge \Omega_1 = \Omega_2 \wedge \Theta_1 = \Theta_2 \tag{30}$$

Definition 18. *A subsystem S' is a system that is implicated in another system S, denoted by $\sqsubseteq$, i.e.:*

$$S'(C', R^{c'}, R^{i'}, R^{o'}, B', \Omega', \Theta') \sqsubseteq$$
$$S(C, R^c, R^i, R^o, B, \Omega, \Theta) \triangleq$$
$$C' \subseteq C \wedge R^{c'} \subseteq R^c \wedge R^{i'} \subseteq R^i \wedge R^{o'}$$
$$\subseteq R^o \wedge B' \subseteq B \wedge \Omega' \subseteq \Omega \wedge \Theta' = \Theta \tag{31}$$

The above definition indicates that a subsystem of an open system is a coherent part of it with all integrated components, internal/input/output relations, behaviors, and constraints. However, they share the same environment.

Definition 19. *A supersystem S is a system that consists of one or more subsystems S', denoted by $\sqsupseteq$, i.e.:*

$$S(C, R^c, R^i, R^o, B, \Omega, \Theta) \sqsupseteq$$
$$S'(C', R^{c'}, R^{i'}, R^{o'}, B', \Omega', \Theta')$$
$$\triangleq C' \subseteq C \wedge R^{c'} \subseteq R^c \wedge R^{i'} \subseteq R^i \wedge R^{o'}$$
$$\subseteq R^o \wedge B' \subseteq B \wedge \Omega' \subseteq \Omega \wedge \Theta' = \Theta \tag{32}$$

Relations Between Open and Closed Systems

Although, the previous subsections analyze the relations of closed and open systems separately, it is noteworthy that closed and open systems are transformable, when the environment of them is treated as a supersystem as well. This notion can be described in the following theorem and corollaries on the basis of Definitions 3 and 4.

Theorem 2. *The equivalence between open and closed systems states that an open system S is equivalent to a closed system $\widehat{S}$, or vice versa, when its environment Θ_S or $\Theta_{\widehat{S}}$ is conjoined, respectively, i.e.:*

$$\begin{cases} \widehat{S} = S \sqcup \Theta_S \\ S = \widehat{S} \sqcup \Theta_{\widehat{S}} \end{cases} \tag{33}$$

Theorem 2 can be proved by observing the embedded relation of close and open systems as illustrated in Figure 3. According to Theorem 2, the following properties of equivalence between closed and open systems can be derived.

Corollary 3. *Any subsystem $\widehat{S}_k$ of a closed system $\widehat{S}$ is an open system, i.e.:*

$$\forall \widehat{S}_k \subseteq \widehat{S} \Rightarrow R^i_k \neq \varnothing \wedge R^o_k \neq \varnothing \wedge \Theta_k = C_s \neq \varnothing \tag{34}$$

Corollary 4. *Any supersystem S of a given set of n open systems S_k conjoining with their environments Θ_k, $1 \leq k \leq n$, is a closed systems, i.e.:*

$$\forall S_k, \forall \Theta_k, \widehat{S} = \mathop{R}_{k=1}^{n}(S_k \sqcup \Theta_k) \Rightarrow$$
$$R_s^i = \varnothing \wedge R_s^o = \varnothing \wedge \Theta_S = \varnothing \tag{35}$$

where $\mathop{R}_{k=1}^{n} S_k$ is an operator known as the *big-R notation* (Wang, 2002, 2008a, 2008b, 2008c) that denotes a repetitive behavior or recurrent structure as defined in real-time process algebra (RTPA) (Wang, 2002, 2003, 2006a, 2006c, 2007a, 2007c, 2008a, 2008d).

COMPOSITIONAL OPERATIONS ON SYSTEMS

This section describes how abstract systems and their relations as modeled in previous sections may be manipulated by an algebraic system. The compositional operations of system algebra are dynamic and integrative operations that manipulate all systems involved in parallel. Compositional operations on abstract systems provide a set of fundamental mathematical means to construct complex systems on the basis of simple ones or to derive new systems on the basis of exiting ones.

Lemma 6. *The compositional operations $\bullet_c$ in system algebra encompasses 9 associative operators for manipulating the algebraic compositions among abstract systems, i.e.:*

$$\bullet_c \triangleq \{\Rightarrow, \overset{-}{\Rightarrow}, \overset{+}{\Rightarrow}, \overset{\sim}{\Rightarrow}, \boxminus, \uplus, \pitchfork, \Leftarrow, \vdash\} \tag{36}$$

where the compositional operators stand for system inheritance, tailoring, extension, substitute, difference, composition, decomposition, aggregation, and specification, respectively.

System Inheritance

Definition 20. *The inheritance of a closed system $\widehat{S_2}$ from a given system $\widehat{S_1}$, denoted by $\Rightarrow$, is the creation of the new system $\widehat{S_2}$ by reproducing $\widehat{S_1}$, i.e.:*

$$\widehat{S_1}(C_1, R_1, B_1, \Omega_1) \Rightarrow \widehat{S_2}(C_2, R_2, B_2, \Omega_2)$$
$$\triangleq \widehat{S_2}(C_2, R_2, B_2, \Omega_2 \mid C_2 = C_1, R_2 =$$
$$R_1, B_2 = B_1, \Omega_2 = \Omega_1) \tag{37}$$

where $\widehat{S_1}$ is called the parent system, $\widehat{S_2}$ the child system.

Similarly, the inheritance of open systems can be defined as follows.

Definition 21. *The inheritance of an open system S_2 from the parent system S_1, denoted by $\Rightarrow$, is the creation of the new system S_2 by reproducing S_1, and the establishment of new associations between them, see Box 1, where $\|$ denotes that an open system inheritance creates new associations between S_1 and S_2 in parallel via (R^o_1, R^i_2) and (R^o_2, R^i_1).*

Definition 22. *The multiple inheritance of an open system S from n parent systems $S_1, S_2, ..., S_n$, denoted by $\Rightarrow$, is an inheritance that creates the new system S via a set of n conjoint systems and establishes new associations among them, see Box 2.*

System Tailoring

Definition 23. *The tailoring of a closed system $\widehat{S_2}$ from the parent system $\widehat{S_1}$, denoted by $\overset{-}{\Rightarrow}$, is a special system inheritance that creates the new system $\widehat{S_2}$ based on $\widehat{S_1}$ with the removal of specific subsets of components C', behaviors B', and constraints Ω', see Box 3.*

Box 1.

$$
S_1(C_1, R_1{}^c, R_1{}^i, R_1{}^o, B_1, \Omega_1, \Theta_1) \Rightarrow S_2(C_2, R_2{}^c, R_2{}^i, R_2{}^o, B_2, \Omega_2, \Theta_2)
$$
$$
\triangleq S_2(C_2, R_2{}^c, R_2{}^i, R_2{}^o, B_2, \Omega_2, \Theta_2 \mid C_2 = C_1, R_2{}^c = R_1{}^c,
$$
$$
R^i{}_2 = R^i{}_1 \cup \{C_1 \times C_2\}, R^o{}_2 = R^o{}_1 \cup \{C_2 \times C_1\},
$$
$$
B_2 = B_1 \; \Omega_2 = \Omega_1, \Theta_2 = \Theta_1)
$$
$$
|| \; S_1(C_1, R_1{}^c, R_1{}^{i'}, R_1{}^{o'}, B_1, \Omega_1, \Theta'_1 \mid R^{i'}{}_1 = R^i{}_1 \cup \{C_2 \times C_1\},
$$
$$
R^{o'}{}_1 = R^o{}_1 \cup \{C_1 \times C_2\}, \Theta'{}_1 = \Theta_1 \cup C_2)
$$

$$\tag{38}$$

Box 2.

$$
\mathop{R}_{i=1}^{n} S_i \Rightarrow (S \; C, R^c, R^i, R^o, B, \Omega, \Theta)
$$
$$
\triangleq S(C, R^c, R^i, R^o, B, \Omega, \Theta \mid C = \bigcup_{i=1}^{n} C_i, R^c = \bigcup_{i=1}^{n} R^c{}_i, R^i = \bigcup_{i=1}^{n} R^i{}_i \cup \{\mathop{R}_{i=1}^{n}(C_i \times C)\},
$$
$$
R^o = \bigcup_{i=1}^{n} R^o{}_i \cup \{\mathop{R}_{i=1}^{n}(C \times C_i)\}, B = \bigcup_{i=1}^{n} B_i, \Omega = \bigcup_{i=1}^{n} \Omega_i, \Theta = \bigcup_{i=1}^{n} \Theta_i)
$$
$$
|| \mathop{R}_{i=1}^{n} S_i(C_i, R^c{}_i, R^i{}_i, R^o{}_i, B_i, \Omega_i, \Theta'_i \mid R^{i'}{}_i = R^i{}_i \cup \{C \times C_i\},
$$
$$
R^{o'}{}_i = R^o{}_i \cup \{C_i \times C\}, \Theta'{}_i = \Theta_i \cup C)
$$

$$\tag{39}$$

Box 3.

$$
\widehat{S_1}(C_1, R_1, B_1, \Omega_1) \overset{\rightarrow}{\Rightarrow} \widehat{S_2}(C_2, R_2, B_2, \Omega_2)
$$
$$
\triangleq \widehat{S_2}(C_2, R_2, B_2, \Omega_2 \mid C_2 = C_1 \setminus C', R_2{}^c = R_1{}^c \setminus \{C_1 \times C'\}
$$
$$
B_2 = B_1 \setminus B', \Omega_2 = \Omega_1 \setminus \Omega')
$$

$$\tag{40}$$

Similarly, the tailoring of open systems can be defined as follows.

Definition 24. *The tailoring of an open system S_2 from the parent system S_1, denoted by $\Rightarrow$, is a special system inheritance that creates the new system S_2 based on S_1 with the removal of specific subsets of components C', behaviors B', and constraints Ω'; and at the same time, it establishes new associations between them, see Box 4.*

Box 4.

$$S_1(C_1, R_1^c, R_1^i, R_1^o, B_1, \Omega_1, \Theta_1) \overset{\Rightarrow}{=} S_2(C_2, R_2^c, R_2^i, R_2^o, B_2, \Omega_2, \Theta_2)$$
$$\triangleq S_2(C_2, R_2^c, R_2^i, R_2^o, B_2, \Omega_2, \Theta_2 \mid C_2 = C_1 \setminus C', R_2^c = R_1^c \setminus \{C_1 \times C'\},$$
$$R_2^i = R_1^i \cup \{C_1 \times C_2\}, R_2^o = R_1^o \cup \{C_2 \times C_1\},$$
$$B_2 = B_1 \setminus B', \Omega_2 = \Omega_1 \setminus \Omega', \Theta_2 = \Theta_1)$$
$$\mid\mid S_1(C_1, R_1^c, R_1^{i'}, R_1^{o'}, B_1, \Omega_1, \Theta'_1 \mid R_1^{i'} = R_1^i \cup \{C_2 \times C_1\},$$
$$R_1^{o'} = R_1^o \cup \{C_1 \times C_2\}, \Theta'_1 = \Theta_1 \cup C_2)$$

$$(41)$$

Box 5.

$$\widehat{S_1}(C_1, R_1, B_1, \Omega_1) \overset{+}{\Rightarrow} \widehat{S_2}(C_2, R_2, B_2, \Omega_2)$$
$$\triangleq \widehat{S_2}(C_2, R_2, B_2, \Omega_2 \mid C_2 = C_1 \cup C', R_2^c = R_1^c \cup \{C_1 \times C'\}$$
$$B_2 = B_1 \cup B', \Omega_2 = \Omega_1 \cup \Omega')$$

$$(42)$$

Box 6.

$$S_1(C_1, R_1^c, R_1^i, R_1^o, B_1, \Omega_1, \Theta_1) \overset{+}{\Rightarrow} S_2(C_2, R_2^c, R_2^i, R_2^o, B_2, \Omega_2, \Theta_2)$$
$$\triangleq S_2(C_2, R_2^c, R_2^i, R_2^o, B_2, \Omega_2, \Theta_2 \mid C_2 = C_1 \cup C', R_2^c = R_1^c \cup \{C_1 \times C'\}$$
$$R_2^i = R_1^i \cup \{C_1 \times C_2\}, R_2^o = R_1^o \cup \{C_2 \times C_1\},$$
$$B_2 = B_1 \cup B', \Omega_2 = \Omega_1 \cup \Omega', \Theta_2 = \Theta_1)$$
$$\mid\mid S_1(C_1, R_1^c, R_1^{i'}, R_1^{o'}, B_1, \Omega_1, \Theta'_1 \mid R_1^{i'} = R_1^i \cup \{C_2 \times C_1\},$$
$$R_1^{o'} = R_1^o \cup \{C_1 \times C_2\}, \Theta'_1 = \Theta_1 \cup C_2)$$

$$(43)$$

System Extension

Definition 25. *The extension of a closed system $\widehat{S_2}$ from the parent system $\widehat{S_1}$, denoted by $\overset{+}{\Rightarrow}$, is a special system inheritance that creates the new system $\widehat{S_2}$ based $\widehat{S_1}$ with additional subsets of components C', behaviors B', and constraints Ω', see Box 5.*

Similarly, the extension of open systems can be defined as follows.

Definition 26. *The extension of an open system S_2 from the parent system S_1, denoted by $\overset{+}{\Rightarrow}$, is a special system inheritance that creates the new system S_2 based S_1 with additional subsets of components C', behaviors B', and constraints Ω'; and at the same time, it establishes new associations between the two systems, see Box 6.*

System Substitution

Definition 27. *The substitute of a closed system $\widehat{S_2}$ from the parent system $\widehat{S_1}$, denoted by $\overset{\sim}{\Rightarrow}$, is a flexible system inheritance that creates the new system $\widehat{S_2}$ based on $\widehat{S_1}$ with the new subsets of components C'_{c2}, behaviors B'_{c2}, and constraints Ω'_{c2} to replace the corresponding inherited ones C'_{c1}, B'_{c1}, and Ω'_{c2} that share the same identifiers, see Box 7. Where $C'_{S1} \subset C_1 \wedge C'_{S2} \subset C_2 \wedge \#C'_{S1} = \#C'_{S2}$; $B'_{S1} \subset B_1 \wedge B'_{S2} \subset B_2 \wedge \#B'_{S1} = \#B'_{S2}$; and $\Omega'_{S1} \subset \Omega_1 \wedge \Omega'_{S2} \subset \Omega_2 \wedge \#\Omega'_{S1} = \#\Omega'_{S2}$. Similarly, the substitute of open systems can be defined as follows.*

Definition 28. *The substitute of an open system S_2 from the parent system S_1, denoted by $\overset{\sim}{\Rightarrow}$, is a flexible system inheritance that creates the new system S_2 based on S_1 with the new subsets of components C'_{c2}, behaviors B'_{c2}, and constraints attributes Ω'_{c2} to replace the corresponding inherited ones C'_{c1}, B'_{c1}, and Ω'_{c2} that share the same identifiers; and at the same time, it establishes new associations between the two concepts, see Box 8. Where $C'_{S1} \subset C_1 \wedge C'_{S2} \subset C_2 \wedge \#C'_{S1} = \#C'_{S2}$; $B'_{S1} \subset B_1 \wedge B'_{S2} \subset B_2 \wedge \#B'_{S1} = \#B'_{S2}$; and $\Omega'_{S1} \subset \Omega_1 \wedge \Omega'_{S2} \subset \Omega_2 \wedge \#\Omega'_{S1} = \#\Omega'_{S2}$.*

Box 7.

$$
\begin{aligned}
&\widehat{S}_1(C_1, R_1, B_1, \Omega_1) \overset{\sim}{\Rightarrow} \widehat{S}_2(C_2, R_2, B_2, \Omega_2) \\
&\triangleq \widehat{S}_2(C_2, R_2, B_2, \Omega_2 \mid C_2 = (C_1 \setminus C'_{S_1}) \cup C'_{S_2}, R_2^c = (R_1^c \setminus (C_1 \times C'_{S_1})) \cup C_1 \times C'_{S_2}), \\
&\quad (B_2 = B_1 \setminus B'_{S_1}) \cup B'_{S_2}, \Omega_2 = (\Omega_1 \setminus \Omega'_{S_1}) \cup \Omega'_{S_2})
\end{aligned}
$$

$$(44)$$

Box 8.

$$
\begin{aligned}
&S_1(C_1, R_1^c, R_1^i, R_1^o, B_1, \Omega_1, \Theta_1) \overset{\sim}{\Rightarrow} S_2(C_2, R_2^c, R_2^i, R_2^o, B_2, \Omega_2, \Theta_2) \\
&\triangleq S_2(C_2, R_2^c, R_2^i, R_2^o, B_2, \Omega_2, \Theta_2 \mid C_2 = (C_1 \setminus C'_{S_1}) \cup C'_{S_2}, \\
&\quad R_2^c = (R_1^c \setminus \{C_1 \times C'_{S_1}\}) \cup \{C_1 \times C'_{S_2}\}, R_2^i = R_1^i \cup \{C_1 \times C_2\}, \\
&\quad R_2^o = R_1^o \cup \{C_2 \times C_1\}, B_2 = (B_1 \setminus B'_{S_1}) \cup B'_{S_2}, \Omega_2 = (\Omega_1 \setminus \Omega'_{S_1}) \cup \Omega'_{S_2}, \Theta_2 = \Theta_1) \\
&\| S_1(C_1, R_1^c, R_1^{i'}, R_1^{o'}, B_1, \Omega_1, \Theta'_1 \mid R_1^{i'} = R_1^i \cup \{C_2 \times C_1\}, R_1^{o'} = R_1^o \cup \{C_1 \times C_2\}, \\
&\quad \Theta'_1 = \Theta_1 \cup C_2)
\end{aligned}
$$

$$(45)$$

Binary tailoring, extension, and substitution can also be extended to corresponding *n*-nary operations, similar to that of inheritance as given in Definitions 22.

System Composition

As a preparation to describe the important property of system relations, the mathematical calculus of incremental union between sets of relations is introduced below (Wang, 2006c, 2007c).

Definition 29. *An incremental union of two sets of relations R_1 and R_2, denoted by $\boxplus$, are a union of R_1 and R_2 plus a newly generated incremental set of relations ΔR_{12}, i.e.:*

$$R_1 \boxplus R_2 \triangleq R_1 \cup R_2 \cup \Delta R_{12} \tag{46}$$

where $\Delta R_{12} \nsubseteq R_1 \wedge \Delta R_{12} \nsubseteq R_2$, but $\Delta R_{12} \subseteq R_1 \boxplus R_2$.

The number of the incremental relations ΔR_{12} generated in the incremental union can be determined as stated in the following theorem.

Theorem 3. *The maximum number of newly gained relations ΔR_{12} obtained during the incremental union of two sets of relations is a product of the numbers of elements of the two sets $\#C_1$ and $\#C_2$, i.e.:*

$$\Delta R_{12} = 2(\#C_1 \bullet \#C_2) = 2n_{c_1} n_{c_2}) \tag{47}$$

Proof: *Because ΔR_{12} is the difference between the relations of the newly generated entire system $\#R$ and those of the independent systems $\#R_1$ and $\#R_2$, according to Corollaries 1 and 2, Theorem 3 is proved by the following inference process:*

$$\begin{aligned}
\Delta R_{12} &= \#R - (\#R_1 + \#R_2) \\
&= (n_{c_1} + n_{c_2})^2 - (n_{c_1}^2 + n_{c_2}^2) \\
&= (n_{c_1}^2 + 2n_{c_1} n_{c_2} + n_{c_2}^2) - (n_{c_1}^2 + n_{c_2}^2) \\
&= 2n_{c_1} n_{c_2}
\end{aligned} \tag{48}$$

The incremental union of relations reveals an important property of systems, which indicates that the merge of two systems results in new relations, behaviors, functions, and/or constraints that are not belong to any original individual subsystems. Theorem 3 can be used to predict the maximum numbers of newly established relations, behaviors, and/or constraints in a composition of two systems. According to Theorem 3, the maximum *incremental system gain* equals to the number of by-directly interconnection between all components in both S_1 and S_2, i.e., $2(\#C_1 \bullet \#C_2)$.

Definition 29 can be extended to *n*-nary incremental unions for multiple sets of relations.

Box 9.

$$\underset{i=1}{\overset{n}{\boxplus}} R_i \triangleq \underset{i=1}{\overset{n-1}{R}} (R_i \cup R_j \cup \Delta R_{ij}), j = i+1$$

$$= (...((R_1 \cup R_2 \cup \Delta R_{12}) \cup R_3 \cup \Delta R_{2'3}) \cup ...) \cup R_n \cup \Delta R_{n-1',n}$$

$$(49)$$

Box 10.

$$\widehat{S_1}(C_1, R_1, B_1, \Omega_1) \uplus \widehat{S_2}(C_2, R_2, B_2, \Omega_2)$$

$$\triangleq \widehat{S}(C, R, B, \Omega \mid C = C_1 \cup C_2, R = R_1 \boxplus R_2, B = B_1 \boxplus B_2, \Omega = \Omega_1 \boxplus \Omega_2)$$

$$= \widehat{S}(C, R, B, \Omega \mid C = C_1 \cup C_2, R = R_1 \cup R_2 \cup \Delta R_{12},$$

$$B = B_1 \cup B_2 \cup \Delta B_{12}, \ \Omega = \Omega_1 \cup \Omega_2 \cup \Delta \Omega_{12})$$

$$(50)$$

Definition 30. *The n-nary incremental union for multiple sets of relations,*

$$\underset{i=1}{\overset{n}{\boxplus}} R_i,$$

is a series of cumulative binary incremental unions as in Box 9.

Based on the calculus of incremental union of sets of relations, system compositions can be defined as follows.

Definition 31. *The composition of two closed systems $\widehat{S_1}$ and $\widehat{S_2}$, denoted by $\uplus$, results in a super system $\widehat{S}$ that is formed by union of sets of components and environments, as well as incremental union of sets of relations, behaviors, and constraints, respectively, see Box 10.*

Theorem 4. *The system fusion principle states that new relations ΔR_{12}, new behaviors (functions) ΔB_{12}, and new constraints $\Delta \Omega_{12}$, generated in system compositions are solely a property of the new super system $\widehat{S}$, but not belong to any of the independent subsystems, i.e.:*

$$\Delta R_{12} \mathsf{E} \, \widehat{S} \wedge (\Delta R_{12} \not{\mathsf{E}} \, \widehat{S_1} \wedge \Delta R_{12} \not{\mathsf{E}} \, \widehat{S_2}) \tag{51.a}$$

$$\Delta B_{12} \mathsf{E} \, \widehat{S} \wedge (\Delta B_{12} \not{\mathsf{E}} \, \widehat{S_1} \wedge \Delta B_{12} \not{\mathsf{E}} \, \widehat{S_2}) \tag{51.b}$$

$$\Delta \Omega_{12} \mathsf{E} \, \widehat{S} \wedge (\Delta \Omega_{12} \not{\mathsf{E}} \, \widehat{S_1} \wedge \Delta \Omega_{12} \not{\mathsf{E}} \, \widehat{S_2}) \tag{51.c}$$

where E denote a membership relation of a given set in a system.

The discovery in Theorems 3 and 4 reveal that the nature of system utilities can be rigorously explained as the newly gained relations ΔR_{12}, as well as behaviors ΔB_{12} and constraints $\Delta \Omega_{12}$, during the composition of two or more systems. The empirical awareness of this key system property has been intuitively or qualitatively described in the literature of system science (Ellis & Fred, 1962; G. J. Klir, 1992). However, Theorems 3 and 4 are the first mathematical explanation of the mechanism of system gains during system compositions (Wang, 2006b, 2007c).

More generally, Definition 31 and Theorem 4 can be extended to open systems.

Definition 32. *The composition of two open systems S_1 and S_2, denoted by $\uplus$, results in a super system S that is formed by simple conjunctions both of sets of components and environments, as well as incremental unions of sets of relations, behaviors, and constraints, respectively, see Box 11.*

The operation of open system composition is illustrated in Figure 4, where the generation of the new relations ΔR^c_1 and ΔR^c_2 in S after the composition of S_1 and S_2 can be observed.

System compositions as modeled in Definitions 31 and 32 can be extended to *n*-nary compositions as follows.

Definition 33. *The composition of multiple open systems, denoted by*

$$\overset{n}{\underset{i=1}{\uplus}} S_i ,$$

is an iterative integration of a pair of systems, which cumulatively creates the new supersystem S, see Box 12.

Box 11.

$$
\begin{aligned}
&S_1(C_1, R_1^c, R_1^i, R_1^o, B_1, \Omega_1, \Theta_1) \sqcup S_2(C_2, R_2^c, R_2^i, R_2^o, B_2, \Omega_2, \Theta_2) \\
&\triangleq S(C, R^c, R^i, R^o, B, \Omega, \Theta) \mid C = C_1 \cup C_2, R^c = R_1^c \boxplus R_2^c, R^i = R_1^i \boxplus R_2^i, \\
&\quad R^o = R_1^o \boxplus R_2^o, B = B_1 \boxplus B_2, \Omega = \Omega_1 \boxplus \Omega_2, \Theta = \Theta_1 \cup \Theta_2) \\
&\parallel \overset{2}{\underset{i=1}{R}} S_i(C_i, R_i^c, R_i^{i'}, R_i^{o'}, B_i, \Omega_i, \Theta'_i \mid R_i^{i'} = R_i^i \cup \{C \times C_i\}, \\
&\quad R_i^{o'} = R_i^o \cup \{C_i \times C\}, \Theta'_i = \Theta_i \cup C) \\
&= S(C, R^c, R^i, R^o, B, \Omega\ \Theta \mid C = C_1 \cup C_2, R^c = R_1^c \cup R_2^c \cup \Delta R_{12}^c, \\
&\quad R^i = R_1^i \cup R_2^i \cup \Delta R_{12}^i, R^o = R_1^o \cup R_2^o \cup \Delta R_{12}^o, \\
&\quad B = B_1 \cup B_2 \cup \Delta B_{12}, \Omega = \Omega_1 \cup \Omega_2 \cup \Delta \Omega_{12}, \Theta = \Theta_1 \cup \Theta_2) \\
&\parallel \overset{2}{\underset{i=1}{R}} S_i(C_i, R_i^c, R_i^{i'}, R_i^{o'}, B_i, \Omega_i, \Theta'_i \mid R_i^{i'} = R_i^i \cup \{C \times C_i\}, \\
&\quad R_i^{o'} = R_i^o \cup \{C_i \times C\}, \Theta'_i = \Theta_i \cup C)
\end{aligned}
$$

$$(52)$$

Figure 4. The composition of two open systems

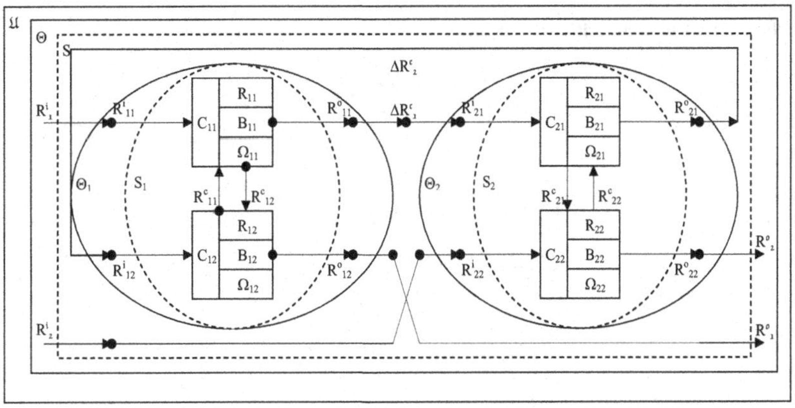

Box 12.

$$S(C, R^c, R^i, R^o, B, \Omega, \Theta) \triangleq \biguplus_{i=1}^{n} S_i(C_i, R_i^c, R_i^i, R_i^o, B_i, \Omega_i, \Theta_i)$$

$$= S(C, R^c, R^i, R^o, B, \Omega, \Theta \mid C = \bigcup_{i=1}^{n} C_i, R^c = \boxplus_{i=1}^{n} R^c_i, R^i = \boxplus_{i=1}^{n} R^i_i,$$

$$R^o = \boxplus_{i=1}^{n} R^o_i, B = \boxplus_{i=1}^{n} B_i, \ \Omega = \boxplus_{i=1}^{n} \Omega_i, \Theta = \bigcup_{i=1}^{n} \Theta_i)$$

$$\parallel \mathop{R}_{i=1}^{n} S_i(C_i, R_i^c, R_i^{i'}, R_i^{o'}, B_i, \Omega_i, \Theta'_i \mid R^{i'}_i = R^i_i \cup \{C \times C_i\},$$

$$R^{o'}_i = R^o_i \cup \{C_i \times C\}, \Theta'_i = \Theta_i \cup C)$$

$$(53)$$

The composition of multiple closed systems is similar to Definition 33, which can be tailored from Equation 53.

System composition at the top level is a complicated algebraic operation that integrates two or more systems into a supersystem with a hierarchical architecture. There are three basic types of system structural relations in system composition known as *parallel* ($\parallel$), *serial* ($\rightarrow$), and *nested* ($\rightarrowtail$) as shown in Figure 5. Complex system compositions can be represented by a combination of these three meta-architectural relations between subsystems. The syntaxes and semantics of these three system relations in system compositions can be referred to related definitions in RTPA (Wang, 2002, 2003, 2006c, 2007c, 2008a, 2008d).

According to Definition 33, a system can be integrated from the bottom up by a series of compositions, level-by-level, in a system hierarchy.

Figure 5. Basic types of system structural relations in system compositions

No.	Type of composition	Syntax	Example
1	Parallel	$S_1 \parallel S_2$	$S \triangleq S_1 \parallel S_2 \parallel \dots \parallel S_n$ 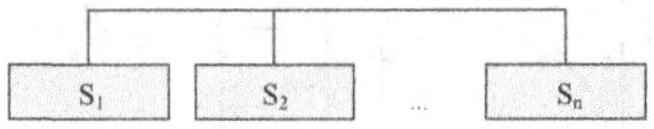
2	Serial	$S_1 \rightarrow S_2$	$S \triangleq S_1 \rightarrow S_2 \rightarrow \dots \rightarrow S_n$ 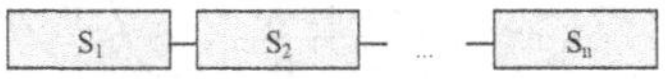
3	Nested	$S_1 \rightarrowtail S_2$	$S \triangleq S_1 \rightarrowtail S_2 \rightarrowtail \dots \rightarrowtail S_n$ 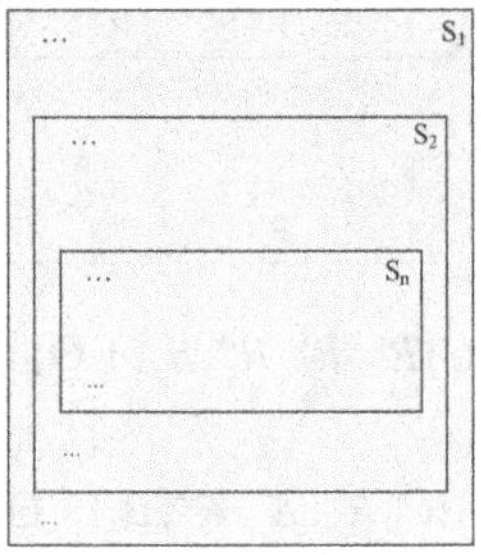

Box 13.

$$S_1(C_1, R_1, B_1, \Omega_1, \Theta_1) \triangleq S_{11} \parallel S_{12} \parallel S_{13} = (S_{111} \parallel \dots \parallel S_{11x}) \parallel S_{12} \parallel S_{13}$$

$$S_2(C_2, R_2, B_2, \Omega_2, \Theta_2) \triangleq S_{21} \rightarrow S_{22}$$

$$S_x(C_x, R_x, B_x, \Omega_x, \Theta_x) \triangleq S_{x1} \rightarrowtail S_{x11}$$

Example 3. *A composed system S(C, R, B, Ω, Θ) as given in Figure 6 can be formally described as follows:*

$$S(C, R, B, \Omega, \Theta) \triangleq S_1 \parallel S_2 \parallel \dots \parallel S_x$$

in which the subsystems of S can be refined as in Box 13.

System Difference

Definition 34. *The difference between a closed systems $\widehat{S}$ and its subsystem $\widehat{S_1}$, denoted by $\boxminus$, results in a closed subsystem $\widehat{S_2}$ that is formed by the difference of sets of components (C_1), and the differences of the*

Figure 6. The hierarchical structure of system compositions

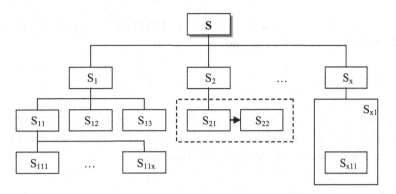

Box 14.

$$\widehat{S}(C,R,B,\Omega) \boxminus \widehat{S_1}(C_1,R_1,B_1,\Omega_1)$$
$$\triangleq \widehat{S_2}(C_2,R_2,B_2,\Omega_2 \mid C_2 = C \setminus C_1, R_2 = R \setminus (R_1 \cup \Delta R_{12}),$$
$$B_2 = B \setminus (B_1 \cup \Delta B_{12}), \Omega_2 = \Omega \setminus (\Omega_1 \cup \Delta\Omega_{12}))$$

$$(54)$$

Box 15.

$$S(C,R^c,R^i,R^o,B,\Omega,\Theta) \boxminus S_1(C_1,R_1^{\ c},R_1^{\ i},R_1^{\ o},B_1,\Omega_1,\Theta_1)$$
$$\triangleq S_2(C_2,R_2^{\ c},R_2^{\ i},R_2^{\ o},B_2,\Omega_2,\Theta_2 \mid C_2 = C \setminus C_1, R_2^{\ c} = R^c \setminus (R_1^{\ c} \cup \Delta R_{12}^{\ c}),$$
$$R_2^{\ i} = R^i \setminus R_1^{\ i}, R_2^{\ o} = R^o \setminus R_1^{\ o}, B_2 = B \setminus (B_1 \cup \Delta B_{12}),$$
$$\Omega_2 = \Omega \setminus (\Omega_1 \cup \Delta\Omega_{12}), \Theta_2 = \Theta_1)$$

$$(55)$$

internal relations, behaviors, and constraints (R_1, B_1, Ω_1) with their incremental counterparts (ΔR_{12}, ΔB_{12}, $\Delta\Omega_{12}$), see Box 14.

According to Definition 34, a difference of a subsystem from a system $\widehat{S}$, will result in the removal of not only the given subsystem but also all interrelations and incremental behaviors between the subsystem and other subsystem in it.

Similarly, the difference of open systems can be defined as follows.

Definition 35. *The difference between an open systems S and its subsystem S_1, denoted by $\boxminus$, results in an open subsystem S_2 that is formed by the difference of sets of components and I/O relations (C_1, R^i_1, R^o_1), and the differences of the internal relations, behaviors, and constraints (R^c_1, B_1, Ω_1) with their incremental coun-*

terparts (ΔR^c_{12}, ΔB_{12}, $\Delta \Omega_{12}$), see Box 15.

The operation of open system difference can also be illustrated by Figure 4, where S_1 and all related I/O relations should be removed in the operation $S_2 = S \boxminus S_1$.

System Decomposition

A system decomposition is an inverse operation of system composition that breaks up a system into two or more subsystems. System decomposition can be described based on the concept of system difference, which is an inversed operation of the incremental union of sets.

Definition 36. *The decomposition of an open systems S, denoted by ⋔, is to break up S into two or more subsystems at a given level of the system hierarchy by one of the compositional relations $R_c = \{\|, \to, \rightarrowtail\}$, see Box 16.*

As specified in Definition 36, the decomposition operation results in the removal of all internal relations $\Delta R_{ij}^c = C_i \times C_j, 1 \le i, j \le n$ that are no longer belong to any of its subsystems.

Similarly, the decomposition of a closed system into multiple subsystems can be defined as follows.

Box 16.

$$S(C, R^c, R^i, R^o, B, \Omega, \Theta) \underset{i=1}{\overset{n}{\Cap}} \mathbb{S}_i\ C_i, R_i^c, R_i^i, R_i^o, B_i, \Omega_i, \Theta_i)$$

$$\triangleq \underset{i=1}{\overset{n}{R}} \{\ S_i(C_i, R_i^c, R_i^{i'}, R_i^{o'}, B_i, \Omega_i, \Theta_i') \mid R_i^{i'} = R_i^i \cup \{C \times C_i\},$$

$$R_i^{o'} = R_i^o \cup \{C_i \times C\}, \Theta_i' = \Theta_i \cup C)$$

$$\| S(C, R^c, R^i, R^o, B, \Omega, \Theta) \boxminus S_i(C_i, R_i^c, R_i^i, R_i^o, B_i, \Omega_i, \Theta_i)$$

$$\}$$

$$(56)$$

Box 17.

$$\hat{S}(C, R, B, \Omega) \underset{i=1}{\overset{n}{\Cap}} \mathbb{S}_i(C_i, R_i, B_i, \Omega_i)$$

$$\triangleq \underset{i=1}{\overset{n}{R}} \{\ S_i(C_i, R_i^c, R_i^i, R_i^o, B_i, \Omega_i, \Theta_i \mid R_i^i = (C \times C_i), R_i^o = (C_i \times C), \Theta_i = C)$$

$$\| \hat{S}(C, R, B, \Omega) \boxminus \mathbb{S}_i(C_i, R_i, B_i, \Omega_i)$$

$$\}$$

$$(57)$$

Box 18.

$$S(C,R,B,\Omega) \;\Longleftarrow\; \overset{n}{\underset{i=1}{R}}\, S_i\,(C_i,R_i,B_i,\Omega_i)$$

$$\triangleq S(C,R,B,\Omega\,|\,C=\bigcup_{i=1}^{n}C'_i \subseteq C_i, R=C\times C,$$

$$B=\bigcup_{i=1}^{n}B_i \subseteq B_i,\ \Omega=\bigcup_{i=1}^{n}C'_i \subseteq C_i)$$

(58)

Box 19.

$$S(C,R^c,R^i,R^o,B,\Omega,\Theta) \;\Longleftarrow\; \overset{n}{\underset{i=1}{R}}\, S_i\,(C_i,R_i^c,R_i^i,R_i^o,B_i,\Omega_i,\Theta_i)$$

$$\triangleq S(C,R^c,R^i,R^o,B,\Omega,\Theta\,|\,C=\bigcup_{i=1}^{n}C'_i \subseteq C_i, R^c=\{C\times C\},$$

$$R^i=\bigcup_{i=1}^{n}(R_i^i \cup \{C_i\times C\}), R^o=\bigcup_{i=1}^{n}(R_i^o \cup \{C\times C_i\}),$$

$$B=\bigcup_{i=1}^{n}B'_i \subseteq B_i,\ \Omega=\bigcup_{i=1}^{n}C'_i \subseteq C_i,\ \Theta \subseteq C_\Theta \cup \bigcup_{i=1}^{n}\Theta_i)$$

$$\|\overset{n}{\underset{i=1}{R}}\, S_i\,(C_i,R_i^c,R_i^{i'},R_i^{o'},B_i,\Omega_i,\Theta'_i\,|\,R_i^{i'}=R_i^i \cup \{C\times C_i\},$$

$$R_i^{o'}=R_i^o \cup \{C_i\times C\}, \Theta'_i=\Theta_i \cup C)$$

(59)

Definition 37. *The decomposition of a closed system $\widehat{S}$, denoted by ⫪, is to break up $\widehat{S}$ into two or more subsystems at a given level of the system hierarchy by one of the compositional relations $R_c = \{\|, \rightarrow, \rightarrowtail\}$, see Box 17.*

Definitions 36 and 37 indicate that either an open or a closed system can be resolved from the top down by a series of decompositions, level-by-level, in the system hierarchy. It is noteworthy that both open and closed system decompositions result in a set of open subsystems.

System Aggregation

Definition 38. *The aggregation of a closed system $\widehat{S}$ from a set of n peer systems $\widehat{S}_i$, $1 \le i \le n$, denoted by $\Longleftarrow$, is an aggregation of $\widehat{S}$ with the elicitation of interested subsets of components C'_i, behaviors B'_i, and constraints Ω'_i, see Box 18. Similarly, the aggregation of open systems can be defined as follows.*

Definition 39. *The aggregation of an open system S from a set of n peer systems S_i, $1 \leq i \leq n$, denoted by $\Leftarrow$, is an aggregation of S with the elicitation of interested subsets of components C'_i, behaviors B'_i, and constraints Ω'_i; and at the same time, it establishes new associations among all aggregated systems, see Box 19. System aggregation is also known as system elicitation.*

According to Definitions 32 and 39, the difference between system composition and aggregation is that the former constructs a new system by integrating a set of entire systems as subsystems while the latter constructs a new system by eliciting interested subsets of components, behaviors, and/or constraints from a set of individual and independent systems.

System Specification

A system specification is an inverse operation of system aggregation. System specification is usually operated in a series of refinements.

Definition 40. *The specification of a closed system $\widehat{S}_0$ by a set of n refined systems $\widehat{S}_i$, $1 \leq i \leq n$, denoted by $\vdash$, is a specification of $\widehat{S}_0$ with a total order of a series of refinements by increasingly specific and detailed components C_i, behaviors B_i, and constraints Ω_i, see Box 20.*

Similarly, the specification of open systems can be defined as follows.

Definition 41. *The specification of an open system S_0 by a set of n refined systems S_i, $1 \leq i \leq n$, denoted by $\vdash$, is a specification of S_0 with a total order of a series of refinements by increasingly specific and detailed components C_i, behaviors B_i, and constraints Ω_{ij}; and at the same time, it establishes new associations among all refining systems, see Box 21.*

System specification is a refinement process where more specific and detailed components, behaviors, and constraints are developed in a consistent and coherent top-down hierarchy. The major tasks of system specifications are system architecture (component) and behavior specifications, which can be further refined by the Component Logical Models (CLMs) and processes as provided in RTPA (Wang, 2002, 2003, 2006a, 2006c, 2007c, 2008a, 2008d).

Box 20.

$$(\widehat{S}_n \vdash ... \vdash \widehat{S}_2 \vdash \widehat{S}_1) \vdash \widehat{S}_0(C_0, R_0, B_0, \Omega_0)$$

$$\triangleq \widehat{S}_0(C_0, R_0, B_0, \Omega_0 \mid C_0 = \overset{n}{\underset{i=1}{R}}(C_{i-1} \subset C_i), R_0 = (C_0 \times C_0),$$

$$B_0 = (\overset{n}{\underset{i=1}{R}} B_{i-1} \subset B_i), \Omega_0 = (\overset{n}{\underset{i=1}{R}} B_{i-1} \subset B_i))$$

$$(60)$$

Box 21.

$$(S_n \vdash ... \vdash S_2 \vdash S_1) \vdash S_0(C_0, R_0^{\,c}, R_0^{\,i}, R_0^{\,o}, B_0, \Omega_0, \Theta_0)$$

$$\triangleq S_0(C_0, R_0^{\,c}, R_0^{\,i}, R_0^{\,o}, B_0, \Omega_0, \Theta_0 \mid C_0 = \overset{n}{\underset{i=1}{R}}(C_{i-1} \subset C_i), R_0^{\,c} = \{C_0 \times C_0\},$$

$$R_0^{\,i} = \bigcup_{i=1}^{n}(R_i^{\,i} \cup \{C_i \times C_0\}), R_0^{\,o} = \bigcup_{i=1}^{n}(R_i^{\,o} \cup \{C_0 \times C_i\}),$$

$$B_0 = \overset{n}{\underset{i=1}{R}}(B_{i-1} \subset B_i), \Omega_0 = \overset{n}{\underset{i=1}{R}}(B_{i-1} \subset B_i), \Theta_0 = \Theta_1 = \Theta_2 = .. = \Theta_n)$$

$$\| \overset{n}{\underset{i=1}{R}} S_i(C_i, R_i^{\,c}, R_i^{\,i'}, R_i^{\,o'}, B_i, \Omega_i, \Theta'_i \mid R_i^{\,i'} = R_i^{\,i} \cup \{C_0 \times C_i\},$$

$$R_i^{\,o'} = R_i^{\,o} \cup \{C_i \times C_o\}, \Theta'_i = \Theta_i \cup C_0))$$

$$(61)$$

CONCLUSION

A new mathematical structure of abstract systems has been presented as the most complicated mathematical entities beyond sets, functions, concepts, and processes. A formal and rigorous treatment of abstract systems as well as their taxonomy and properties has been described. System algebra has been introduced as a set of relational and compositional operations for manipulating abstract systems and their composing rules. The former have been elicited as the algebraic operations of *independent, related, overlapped, equivalent, subsystem,* and *supersystem*. The latter have been identified as the algebraic operations of *inheritance, tailoring, extension, substitute, difference, composition, decomposition, aggregation,* and *specification*. A wide range of applications of system algebra has been recognized in cognitive informatics, system science, system engineering, computing, and software engineering. System algebra has formed a fundamental theory for denoting the rigorous semantics of conventional object-oriented design notations and methodologies such as UML in software and intelligent system engineering.

ACKNOWLEDGMENT

The author would like to acknowledge the Natural Science and Engineering Council of Canada (NSERC) for its partial support to this work. The author would like to thank anonymous reviewers for their valuable comments and suggestions.

REFERENCES

Ashby, W. R. (1958). Requisite variety and implications for control of complex systems. *Cybernetica, 1,* 83-99.

Ashby, W. R. (1962) Principles of the self-organizing system. In von H. Foerster & G. Zopf (Eds.), *Principles of self-organization* (pp. 255-278). Oxford, England: Pergamon.

Eigen, M., & Schuster, P. (1979). *The hypercycle: A principle of natural self-organization*. Berlin, Germany: Springer.

Ellis, D. O., & Fred, J. L. (1962). *Systems philosophy*. Prentice Hall.

Ford, J. (1986). Chaos: Solving the Unsolvable, predicting the unpredictable. In *Chaotic dynamics and fractals*. Academic Press.

Haken, H. (1977). *Synergetics*. New York: Springer-Verlag.

Heylighen, F. (1989). Self-organization, emergence and the architecture of complexity. In *Proceedings of the First European Conference on System Science (AFCET)* (pp. 23-32). Paris.

Klir, G. J. (1992). *Facets of systems science.* New York: Plenum Press.

Klir, R. G. (1988). Systems profile: the emergence of systems science. *Systems Research, 5*(2), 145-156.

Prigogine, I., & Nicolis, G. (1972). Thermodynamics of evolution. *Physics Today, 25,* 23-28.

Rapoport, A. (1962). Mathematical aspects of general systems theory. *General Systems Yearbook, 11,* 3-11.

Skarda, C. A., & Freeman, W. J. (1987). How brains make chaos into order. *Behavioral and Brain Sciences, 10.*

von Bertalanffy, L. (1952). *Problems of life: An evolution of modern biological and scientific thought.* London: C. A. Watts.

Wang, Y. (2002). The real-time process algebra (RTPA). *The International Journal of Annals of Software Engineering, 14,* 235-274.

Wang, Y. (2003). Using process algebra to describe human and software system behaviors. *Brain and Mind, 4*(2), 199-213.

Wang, Y. (2005). System science models of software engineering. In *Proceedings of the Eighteenth Canadian Conference on Electrical and Computer Engineering (CCECE'05)* (pp. 1802-1805). Saskatoon, Saskatchewan, Canada: IEEE CS Press.

Wang, Y. (2006a). Cognitive informatics and contemporary mathematics for knowledge representation and manipulation (Invited plenary talk). In *Proceedings of the First International Conference on Rough Set and Knowledge Technology (RSKT'06)* (LNAI 4062, pp. 69-78). Chongqing, China: Springer.

Wang, Y. (2006b). On abstract systems and system algebra. In *Proceedings of the Fifth IEEE International Conference on Cognitive Informatics (ICCI'06)* (pp. 332-343), Beijing, China: IEEE CS Press.

Wang, Y. (2006c, March). On the informatics laws and deductive semantics of software. *IEEE Transactions on Systems, Man, and Cybernetics (C), 36*(2), 161-171.

Wang, Y. (2007a). Keynote speech, on theoretical foundations of software engineering and denotational mathematics. In *Proceedings of the Fifth Asian Workshop on Foundations of Software* (pp. 99-102). Xiamen, China: BHU Press.

Wang, Y. (2007b). The OAR model of neural informatics for internal knowledge representation in the brain. *The International Journal of Cognitive Informatics and Natural Intelligence, 1*(3), 64-75.

Wang, Y. (2007c). Software engineering foundations: A software science perspective. In *CRC Series in Software Engineering: Vol. 2.* CRC Press.

Wang, Y. (2007d). The theoretical framework of cognitive informatics. *The International Journal of Cognitive Informatics and Natural Intelligence, 1*(1), 1-27.

Wang, Y. (2008a, April). Deductive semantics of RTPA. *The International Journal of Cognitive Informatics and Natural Intelligence, 2*(2), 95-121.

Wang, Y. (2008b, April). On concept algebra: A denotational mathematical structure for knowledge and software modeling. *The International Journal of Cognitive Informatics and Natural Intelligence, 2*(2), 1-19.

Wang, Y. (2008c). On the big-R notation for describing iterative and recursive behaviors. *The International Journal of Cognitive Informatics and Natural Intelligence, 2*(1), 17-28.

Wang, Y. (2008d, April). RTPA: A denotational mathematics for manipulating intelligent and computing behaviors. *The International Journal of Cognitive Informatics and Natural Intelligence (IJCINI), 2*(2), 44-62.

Wang, Y., & Wang, Y. (2006). On cognitive informatics models of the brain. *IEEE Transactions on Systems, Man, and Cybernetics (C), 36*(2), 203-207.

Zadeh, L. A. (1965). Fuzzy sets and systems. In J. Fox (Ed.), *Systems theory* (pp. 29-37). Brooklyn, NY: Polytechnic Press.

Zadeh, L. A. (1973). Outline of a new approach to analysis of complex systems. *IEEE Trans. on Sys., Man and Cyb., 1*(1), 28-44.

This work was previously published in International Journal of Cognitive Informatics and Natural Intelligence, Vol. 2, Issue 2, edited by Y. Wang, pp. 20-43, copyright 2008 by IGI Publishing (an imprint of IGI Global).

Chapter 10
RTPA:
A Denotational Mathematics for Manipulating Intelligent and Computational Behaviors

Yingxu Wang
University of Calgary, Canada

ABSTRACT

Real-time process algebra (RTPA) is a denotational mathematical structure for denoting and manipulating system behavioral processes. RTPA is designed as a coherent algebraic system for intelligent and software system modeling, specification, refinement, and implementation. RTPA encompasses 17 metaprocesses and 17 relational process operations. RTPA can be used to describe both logical and physical models of software and intelligent systems. Logic views of system architectures and their physical platforms can be described using the same set of notations. When a system architecture is formally modeled, the static and dynamic behaviors performed on the architectural model can be specified by a three-level refinement scheme at the system, class, and object levels in a top-down approach. RTPA has been successfully applied in real-world system modeling and code generation for software systems, human cognitive processes, and intelligent systems.

INTRODUCTION

The modeling and refinement of software and intelligent systems require new forms of denotational mathematics that possess enough expressive power for rigorously describing system architectures and behaviors. Real-time process algebra (RTPA) is a new denotational mathematical structure for software system modeling, specification, refinement, and implementation for both real-time and nonreal-time systems (Wang, 2002b, 2007d; Wang & King, 2000). An important finding in formal methods is that a software system can be perceived and described as the *composition* of a set of *processes*, which are constructed on the basis of algebraic operations. Theories on process algebras can be traced back to Hoare's *Communicating Sequential Processes* (CSP) (Hoare, 1978, 1985) and Milner's *Calculus of Communicating Systems* (CCS) (Milner, 1980). The *process metaphor* of software systems has evolved from concurrent processes to real-time process systems in the area of operating system research and formal methods (Boucher & Gerth, 1987; Hoare, 1978, 1985; Milner, 1980, 1989; Reed & Roscoe, 1986; Schneider, 1991).

Definition 1. *A process is an abstract model of a unit of meaningful system behaviors that represents a transition procedure of the system from one state to another by changing values of the sets of inputs, outputs, and/or internal variables.*

It is recognized that generic computing problems are 3-D problems, known as those of the behavior, space, and time dimensions, which require a denotational mathematical means for addressing the requirements in all dimensions, particularly the time dimension (Wang, 2002b, 2003b, 2007d). However, conventional process models are hybrid (Hoare, 1985), which do not distinguish the concepts of fundamental metaprocesses and process operations between them. The CSP notation models a major part of elementary software behaviors that may be used in system specification and description. However, it lacks many useful processes that are perceived essential in system modeling, such as addressing, memory manipulation, timing, and system dispatch. CSP models all input and output (I/O) as abstract channel operations that are not expressive enough to denote complex system interactions, particularly for those of real-time systems.

A number of timed extensions and variations of process algebra have been proposed (Baeten & Bergstra, 1991; Boucher & Gerth, 1987; Cerone, 2000; Corsetti, Montanari, & Ratto, 1991; Dierks, 2000; Fecher, 2001; Gerber, Gunter, & Lee, 1992; Jeffrey, 1992; Klusener, 1992; Nicollin & Sifakis, 1991; Reed & Roscoe, 1986; Schneider, 1991; Vereijken, 1995). It is found that the existing work on process algebra and their timed variations can be extended and refined to a new form of denotational mathematics, RTPA, based on a set of algebraic process operations and laws (Wang, 2002b, 2003b, 2006a, 2006c, 2007d, 2008a). RTPA can be used to formally and precisely describe and specify architectures and behaviors of software systems on the basis of algebraic process notations and rules.

Definition 2. *A process P in RTPA is a composed component of n metastatements s_i and s_j, $1 \leq i < n$, $j = i + 1$, according to certain composing relations r_{ij}, i.e.:*

$$P = (...(((s_1)\ r_{12}\ s_2)\ r_{23}\ s_3)\ ...\ r_{n-1,n}\ s_n) \tag{1}$$

where $r_{ij} \in \mathfrak{R}$, which is a set of relational process operators of RTPA that will be formally defined in Lemma 2.

Definition 2 indicates that the mathematical model of a process is a cumulative relational structure among computing operations. The simplest process is a single computational statement. Further discussion will be provided in the section on the unified mathematical model of programs.

Definition 3. *RTPA is a denotational mathematical structure for algebraically denoting and manipulating system behavioral processes and their attributes by a triple, i.e.:*

$$RTPA \triangleq (\mathfrak{T}, \mathfrak{P}, \mathfrak{R}) \tag{2}$$

where $\mathfrak{T}$ is a set of 17 primitive types for modeling system architectures and data objects, $\mathfrak{P}$ is a set of 17 metaprocesses for modeling fundamental system behaviors, and $\mathfrak{R}$ is a set of 17 relational process operations for constructing complex system behaviors.

RTPA provides a coherent notation system and a formal engineering methodology for modeling both software and intelligent systems. RTPA can be used to describe both *logical* and *physical* models of systems, where logical views of the architecture of a software system and its operational platform can be described using the same set of notations. When the system architecture is formally modeled, the static and dynamic behaviors that perform on the system architectural model can be specified by a three-level refinement scheme at the system, class, and object levels in a top-down approach.

This article presents the RTPA structure and methodology for modeling software and intelligent system behaviors. The type system, process notations, process relations, and process composing rules of RTPA are described. The type system and formal type rules of RTPA are formally described, and their usage in data object and system architectural modeling are demonstrated. The fundamental processes and their denotational functionality in modeling both human and system behaviors are presented. A set of algebraic process operations is introduced for constructing complex processes and systems. Then, applications of RTPA in computing and intelligent system modeling and manipulation are explored with case studies. A unified mathematic model of software and programs is derived based on the RTPA theories. The system specification and refinement methodology of RTPA and case studies on real-world problems are provided, which demonstrate the descriptive power of RTAP as a precise and neat algebraic system for software engineering.

THE TYPE SYSTEM OF RTPA

Computational operations of systems can be classified into the categories of *data object, behavior,* and *resource* modeling and manipulations. Based on this view, programs are perceived as the coordination of data objects and behaviors in computing. Data object modeling is a process to creatively extract and abstractly represent a real-world problem by computing objects based on the constraints of given computing resources. Using types to model the natural world can be traced back to the mathematical thought of Bertrand Russell (Russell, 1961; Schilpp, 1946) and Godel (van Heijenoort, 1997). A type is a category of variables that share a common property, such as kinds of data, domain, and allowable operations. Types are an important logical property shared by data objects in programming. Although data in their most primitive form is a string of bits, types are found expressively convenient for data representation at the logical level in computing and software engineering.

The Type System for Data Objects Modeling in RTPA

A type is a set in which all member data objects share a common logical property or attribute. The maximum range of values that a variable can assume is a type, and a type is associated with a set of predefined or allowable operations. A type can be classified as *primitive* and *derived* (complex). The former is the most elemental of types that cannot further be divided into simpler ones; the latter is a compound form of multiple primitive types based on given type rules. Most primitive types are provided by programming languages while most user-defined types are derived ones.

Definition 4. *A type system is a set of predefined templates and manipulation rules for modeling data objects and system architectures.*

RTPA types, syntaxes, and properties are given in Table 1, where the 17 primitive types in computing and human cognitive process modeling have been elicited (Cardelli & Wegner, 1985; Martin-Lof, 1975; Mitchell, 1990; Wang, 2002a, 2002b, 2003b, 2006a, 2007d, 2007e). In Table 1, the first 11 primitive types are for mathematical and logical manipulation of data objects, and the remaining 6 are for system architectural modeling.

Lemma 1. *The primary types of computational objects state that the RTPA type system $\mathfrak{T}$ encompasses 17 primitive types elicited from fundamental computing needs, i.e.:*

$$\mathfrak{T} \triangleq \{\textbf{N, Z, R, S, BL, B, H, P, TI, D, DT, RT, ST,}$$
$$@e\textbf{S}, @t\textbf{TM}, @int\textbf{⊙}, \text{⑤} s\textbf{BL}\} \tag{3}$$

RTPA adopts the *type suffix convention* in which every variable x declared in a type $\textbf{T}$, $x : \textbf{T}$, by a bold type label attached to the variable in all invocations in the form $x\textbf{T}$, where $\textbf{T}$ is any valid primitive as defined in Table 1 or a derived type based on the table. The advance of the type suffix convention is the improvement of readability. Using the type suffixes, system analysts may easily identify if all variables in a statement or expression are equivalent or compatible without referring to earlier declarations, which may be scattered in a system model across hundreds of pages in a large-scale software. The type suffix convention also greatly simplifies type checking requirements during parsing the RTPA specifications by machines (Tan, Wang, & Noglah, 2004, 2006).

An essence of type theory is that types can be classified into the domains of *mathematical* (logical) D_m, *language defined* D_l, and *user defined* D_u, as shown in Table 1 (2007d).

Theorem 1. *The domain constraints of data objects states that the following relationship between the domains of any data object in computing is always held, i.e.:*

$$D_u \subseteq D_l \subseteq D_m \tag{4}$$

It is noteworthy that although a generic computing behavior is constrained by D_m, an executable program is constrained by D_l, and, at most time, it is further restricted by the user defined domain D_u, where $D_u \subseteq D_l$. According to Theorem 1, the following corollary can be derived.

Table 1. RTPA primitive types and their domains

No.	Type	Syntax	D_m	D_l	Equivalence
1	Natural number	**N**	[0, +∞]	[0, 65535]	Arithmetic, mathematic, assignment
2	Integer	**Z**	[-∞, +∞]	[-32768, +32767]	
3	Real	**R**	[-∞, +∞]	[-2147483648, 2147483647]	
4	String	**S**	[0, +∞]	[0, 255]	String and character operations
5	Boolean	**BL**	[T, F]	[T, F]	Logical, assignment
6	Byte	**B**	[0, 256]	[0, 256]	Arithmetic, assignment, addressing
7	Hexadecimal	**H**	[0, +∞]	[0, max]	
8	Pointer	**P**	[0, +∞]	[0, max]	
9	Time	**TI = hh:mm:ss:ms**	**hh**: [0, 23] **mm**: [0, 59] **ss**: [0, 59] **ms**: [0, 999]	**hh**: [0, 23] **mm**: [0, 59] **ss**: [0, 59] **ms**: [0, 999]	Timing, duration, arithmetic (A generic abbreviation: **TI**={**TI**, **D**, **DT**})
10	Date	**D = yy:MM:dd**	**yy**: [0, 99] **MM**: [1, 12] **dd**: [1, 31}	**yy**: [0, 99] **MM**: [1, 12] **dd**: [1, 31}	
11	Date/Time	**DT = yyyy:MM:dd: hh:mm:ss:ms**	**yyyy**: [0, 9999] **MM**:[1, 12] **dd**: [1, 31] **hh**: [0, 23] **mm**: [0, 59] **ss**: [0, 59] **ms**: [0, 999]	**Yyyy**: [0, 9999] **MM**:[1, 12] **dd**: [1, 31] **hh**: [0, 23] **mm**: [0, 59] **ss**: [0, 59] **ms**: [0, 999]	
12	Run-time determinable type	**RT**	–	–	Operations suitable at run-time
13	System architectural type	**ST**	–	–	Assignment (field reference by '.')
14	Random event	**@eS**	[0, +∞]	[0, 255]	String operations
15	Time event	**@tTM**	[0**ms**, 9999 **yyyy**]	[0**ms**, 9999 **yyyy**]	Logical
16	Interrupt event	**@int◉**	[0, 1023]	[0, 1023]	Logical
17	Status	**◉sBL**	[T, F]	[T, F]	Logical

Corollary 1. *The precedence of domain determinations and type inferences in computing and software engineering is always as follows:*

$$D_u \Rightarrow D_l \Rightarrow D_m \qquad (5)$$

Advanced Types of RTPA

The most common and powerful derived type in computing is a *record*, also known as a *construct*, because its flexibility to accommodate different data fields in different primary or composed types. System architectures can be modeled on the basis of structured records. There are also a number of special advanced types introduced in RTPA, such as the *system* type, dynamic *run-time* type, and *event, interrupt,* and *status* types (Wang, 2002b, 2007d).

Definition 5. *The run-time type* **RT** *is a nondeterministic type at compile-time that can be dynamically bound during run-time with one of the predefined primitive types.*

The run-time type **RT** provides programmers a powerful means to express and handle highly flexible and nondeterministic computing objects in data modeling. Some languages such as Java and IDL (OMG, 2002) label the dynamic type **RT** as the *anytype*, for which a specific type may be bound until run time.

Definition 6. *An event is an advanced type in computing that captures the occurring of a predefined external or internal change of status, such as an action of users, an external change of environment, and an internal change of the value of a specific variable.*

The event types of RTPA can be classified into those of *operation* (@*e***S**), *time* (@*t***TM**), and *interrupt* (@*int*⊙), as shown in Table 1, where @ is the *event prefix*, and **S**, **TM**, and ⊙ the corresponding type suffixes, respectively.

A special set of complex types known as the system type **ST** is widely used for modeling system architectures in RTPA, particularly real-time, embedded, and distributed systems architectures. All the system types are nontrivial data objects in computing, rather than simple data or logical objects, which play a very important role in the whole lifecycle of complex system development including design, modeling, specification, refinement, comprehension, implementation, and maintenance of such systems.

Definition 7. *A system type* **ST** *is a system architectural type that models the architectural components of the system and their relations.*

A generic **ST** type is the *Component Logical Model* (CLM), as defined in RTPA (Wang, 2002b, 2007d). CLMs are powerful modeling means in system architectural modeling.

Definition 8. *CLMs are a record-structured abstract model of a system architectural component that represents a hardware interface, an internal logical model, and/or a common control structure of a system.*

CLMs can be used for unifying user defined complex types in system modeling. A formal treatment of CLMs will be provided in Definition 12.

It is recognized that any form of intelligence is memory based (Wang, 2002a, 2203a, 2006b, 2007c, 2007d, 2007e). All data objects, no matter language generated or user created, should be implemented as physical data objects and be bound to specific memory locations. Therefore, memory models play an important role in system modeling.

Definition 9. *The generic system memory model, MEM***ST***, can be described as a special system type* **ST** *with a finite linear space, i.e.:*

$$\text{MEM}\textbf{ST} \triangleq [addr_1\textbf{H} ... addr_2\textbf{H}]\textbf{RT} \tag{6}$$

*where addr$_1$***H** *and addr$_2$***H** *are the start and end addresses of the memory space, and* **RT** *is the type of each of the memory elements, which is usually in Byte* **B** *in computing.*

Another special system type is the I/O port type for modeling hardware architectures and their interfaces.

Definition 10. *The generic system I/O port model, PORT***ST***, can be described as a system type* **ST** *with a finite linear space, i.e.:*

$$\text{PORT}\textbf{ST} \triangleq [ptr_1\textbf{H} ... ptr_2\textbf{H}]\textbf{RT} \tag{7}$$

*where ptr$_1$***H** *and ptr$_2$***H** *are the start and end addresses of the port space, and* **RT** *is the type of each of the port I/O interfaces, which is usually in Byte* **B** *in computing.*

Formal Type Rules of RTPA

A type system specifies the data objects modeling and composing rules of a programming language as that of a grammar system which specifies the program behavior modeling and composing rules of the language. The basic *properties* of type systems are decidable, transparent, and enforceable (Cardelli & Wegner, 1985; Martin-Lof, 1975; Mitchell, 1990). Type systems should be *decidable* by a type checking system, which ensures that types of variables are both well-declared and referred. Type systems should be *transparent* that helps for diagnoses of reasons for inconsistency between variables or variables and their declarations. Type systems should be *enforceable* in order to check type inconsistence as much as possible.

A *formal type system* is a collection of all type rules for a given programming language or formal notation system. A type rule is a mathematical relation and the constraints on a given type. Type rules are defined on the basis of a type environment.

Definition 11. *The type environment* Θ_t *of RTPA is a collection of all primitive types in the formal notation system, i.e.:*

$$\begin{aligned}
\Theta_t &\triangleq \mathfrak{T} \\
&= \{\textbf{N}, \textbf{Z}, \textbf{R}, \textbf{S}, \textbf{BL}, \textbf{B}, \textbf{H}, \textbf{P}, \textbf{TI}, \textbf{D}, \textbf{DT}, \textbf{RT}, \textbf{ST}, \\
&\quad @e\textbf{S}, @t\textbf{TM}, @int\odot, \textcircled{S}s\textbf{BL}\}
\end{aligned} \tag{8}$$

where $\mathfrak{T}$ *is the set of primary types as defined in Table 1.*

Complex and derived types of RTPA can be described by composing type rules based on those of the primitive types.

Box 1.

$$\frac{\Theta_t \vdash \mathbf{ST}, \Theta_t \vdash \mathbf{T}, \Theta_t \vdash ClmID{:}\mathbf{ST}, \Theta_t \vdash ID{:}\mathbf{T}}{\Theta_t \vdash ClmID\mathbf{ST} \triangleq ClmID\mathbf{S} :: \{ \underset{i=1}{\overset{n}{R}} <ID_i{:}\mathbf{T}_i \mid \mathrm{Constraint}(ID_i\mathbf{T}_i)>;\}}$$

$$(10)$$

As given in Definition 8, a CLM is a generic system architectural type for modeling and manipulating data objects and system architectures (Wang, 2002b, 2007d).

Definition 12. *The type rule of a CLM type, CLM, is a complex system type* $\mathbf{ST}$ *in RTPA derived from* Θ_t, *i.e.:*

$$\frac{\Theta_t \vdash \mathbf{ST}}{\Theta_t \vdash CLM : \mathbf{ST}} \qquad\qquad (9)$$

The declaration of a variable, *ClmID*, with a given CLM type can be denoted by using the following type rule as given in Equation 10, where the ClmID$\mathbf{ST}$ is defined by the string type label ClmID$\mathbf{S}$ with an n-field structure, each of them specifies a metavariable ID_i in type $\mathbf{T}_i$, and its constraints denoted by Constraint($ID_i\mathbf{T}_i$), which are a set of expressions.

A *process* in RTPA is a basic behavioral unit for modeling software system operations onto the data objects. A process can be a metaprocess or a complex process composed with multiple metaprocesses by relational process operators. Because processes are so frequently used in system modeling, a derived type in RTPA known as the process type can be introduced as a special system type.

Definition 13. *The type rule of a process type, PROC, is a complex system type* $\mathbf{ST}$ *in RTPA derived from* Θ_t, *i.e.:*

$$\frac{\Theta_t \vdash \mathbf{ST}}{\Theta_t \vdash PROC : \mathbf{ST}} \qquad\qquad (11)$$

The declaration of a variable, *ProcID*, with the *PROC* type can be denoted by using the following type rule as given in Equation 11, where the ProcID$\mathbf{ST}$ is defined by the string type label ProcID$\mathbf{S}$ with a set of n inputs and a set of m outputs in a specific type, as well as a set of q I/O constructs or CLMs in a specific $\mathbf{ST}$ type.

METAPROCESSES OF RTPA

On the basis of the process metaphor, this section elicits the most general and fundamental system behaviors in computing and intelligent systems. Computational operations in conventional process algebra, such as CSP (Hoare, 1985), Timed-CSP (Boucher & Gerth, 1987; Reed & Roscoe, 1986; Schneider,

Box 2.

$$\frac{\Theta_t \vdash ProcID\textbf{:ST}}{\Theta_t \vdash ProcID\textbf{ST} \triangleq ProcID\textbf{S}}$$

$$(\text{I::}<\overset{n}{\underset{i=1}{R}} ID_i\textbf{T}_i>; \text{O::}<\overset{m}{\underset{j=1}{R}} ID_j\textbf{T}_j>; \text{CLM::}<\overset{q}{\underset{k=1}{R}} ClmID_k\textbf{ST}_k>)$$

$$(12)$$

1991), and other proposals are treated as a set of processes at the same level. This approach results in an exhaustive listing of processes. Whenever a new operation is identified or required in computing, the existing process system must be extended.

RTPA adopts the foundationalism in order to find the most primitive computational processes known as the *metaprocesses*. In this approach, complex processes are treated as derived processes from these metaprocesses, based on a set of algebraic process composition rules known as the *process relations*.

Definition 14. *A metaprocess in RTPA is a primitive computational operation that cannot be broken down to further individual actions or behaviors.*

A metaprocess is an elementary process that serves as a basic building block for modeling software behaviors. *Complex processes* can be composed from metaprocesses using *process relations*. In RTPA, a set of 17 metaprocesses has been elicited as shown in Table 2, from essential and primary computational operations commonly identified in existing formal methods and modern programming languages (Aho, Sethi, & Ullman, 1985; Higman, 1977; Hoare et al., 1987; Louden, 1993; Wilson & Clark, 1988; Woodcock & Davies, 1996). Mathematical notations and syntaxes of the metaprocesses are formally described in Table 2, while formal semantics of the metaprocesses of RTPA may be found in Wang (2006c, 2008a).

Lemma 2. *The RTPA metaprocess system $\mathfrak{P}$ encompasses 17 fundamental computational operations elicited from the most basic computing needs, i.e.:*

$$\mathfrak{P} = \{:=, \blacklozenge, \Rightarrow, \Leftarrow, \nLeftrightarrow, >, <, |>, |<, @, \triangleq, \uparrow, \downarrow, !, \otimes, \boxtimes, \S\} \qquad (13)$$

As shown in Lemma 2 and Table 2, each metaprocess is a basic operation on one or more operands such as variables, memory elements, or I/O ports. Structures of the operands and their allowable operations are constrained by their types, as described in previous sections.

It is noteworthy that not all generally important and fundamental computational operations, as shown in Table 2, had been explicitly identified in conventional formal methods (e.g., the evaluation, addressing, memory allocation/release, timing/duration, and the system processes). However, all these are found necessary and essential in modeling system architectures and behaviors (Wang, 2007d).

Table 2. RTPA Metaprocesses

No.	Meta Process	Notation	Syntax
1	Assignment	:=	$y\mathbb{T} := x\mathbb{T}$
2	Evaluation	◆	$\blacklozenge_{\mathbb{T}}exp\mathbb{T} \to \mathbb{T}$
3	Addressing	⇒	$id\mathbb{T} \Rightarrow \text{MEM}[ptr\textbf{P}]\,\mathbb{T}$
4	Memory allocation	⇐	$id\mathbb{T} \Leftarrow \text{MEM}[ptr\textbf{P}]\,\mathbb{T}$
5	Memory release	⇍	$id\mathbb{T} \nLeftarrow \text{MEM}[\perp]\mathbb{T}$
6	Read	⋗	$\text{MEM}[ptr\textbf{P}]\mathbb{T} \gg x\mathbb{T}$
7	Write	⋖	$x\mathbb{T} \ll \text{MEM}[ptr\textbf{P}]\mathbb{T}$
8	Input	|⋗	$\text{PORT}[ptr\textbf{P}]\mathbb{T} \mid\gg x\mathbb{T}$
9	Output	|⋖	$x\mathbb{T} \mid\ll \text{PORT}[ptr\textbf{P}]\mathbb{T}$
10	Timing	@	@*i***TM** $\triangleq$ §*i***TM** **TM = yy:MM:dd** **| hh:mm:ss:ms** **| yy:MM:dd:hh:mm:ss:ms**
11	Duration	≜	@t$_n$**TM** $\triangleq$ §t$_n$**TM** + Δn**TM**
12	Increase	↑	$\uparrow(n\mathbb{T})$
13	Decrease	↓	$\downarrow(n\mathbb{T})$
14	Exception detection	!	$!\,(@e\textbf{S})$
15	Skip	⊗	⊗
16	Stop	⊠	⊠
17	System	§	$\S(SysID\textbf{ST})$

ALGEBRAIC PROCESS OPERATIONS IN RTPA

The metaprocesses of RTPA developed in the preceding section identified a set of fundamental elements for modeling the most basic behaviors of computing and intelligent systems. It is interesting to realize that there is only a small set of 17 metaprocesses in system modeling. However, via the combination of a number of the metaprocesses by certain algebraic operations, any architecture and behavior of real-time or nonreal-time systems can be sufficiently described (Wang, 2002b, 2003b, 2006a, 2007d).

Definition 15. *A process relation in RTPA is an algebraic operation and a compositional rule between two or more metaprocesses in order to construct a complex process.*

A set of 17 fundamental process relational operations has been elicited from fundamental algebraic and relational operations in computing in order to build and compose complex processes in the context of real-time software systems. Syntaxes and usages of the 17 RTPA process relations are formally described in Table 3. Deductive semantics of these process relations may be found in Wang (2006c, 2008a).

Lemma 3. *The software composing rules state that the RTPA process relation system* $\Re$ *encompasses 17 fundamental algebraic and relational operations elicited from basic computing needs, i.e.:*

$$\Re = \{\rightarrow, \curvearrowright, |, |...|..., R^*, R^+, R^i, \circlearrowleft,$$
$$\rightarrowtail, \|, \text{\ff}, \|\|, », \nleftarrow, \hookrightarrow_t, \hookrightarrow_e, \hookrightarrow_i\} \tag{14}$$

As modeled in Lemma 3 and Table 3, the first seven process relations—i.e., *sequential* (#1), *jump* (#2), *branch* (#3), *switch* (#4), and *iterations* (#5 through #7)—may be identified as the Basic Control Structures (BCSs) of system behaviors (Aho et al., 1985; Hoare et al., 1987; Wilson & Clark, 1988). To represent the modern programming structural concepts, CSP (Hoare, 1985) identified the following seven

Table 3. RTPA process relations and algebraic operations

No.	Process Relation	Notation	Syntax
1	Sequence	$\rightarrow$	$P \rightarrow Q$
2	Jump	$\curvearrowright$	$P \curvearrowright Q$
3	Branch	$\|$	$\blacklozenge exp\mathbf{BL} = \mathbf{T} \rightarrow P$ $\| \blacklozenge \sim \rightarrow Q$
4	Switch	$\|$ $...$ $\|$	$\blacklozenge exp\mathbb{T} =$ $i \rightarrow P_i$ $\| \sim \rightarrow \oslash$ where $\mathbb{T} \in \{\mathbf{N}, \mathbf{Z}, \mathbf{B}, \mathbf{S}\}$
5	While-loop	R^*	$\displaystyle \mathop{R}_{exp\mathbf{BL}=\mathbf{T}}^{\mathbf{F}} P$
6	Repeat-loop	R^+	$P \rightarrow \displaystyle \mathop{R}_{exp\mathbf{BL}=\mathbf{T}}^{\mathbf{F}} P$
7	For-loop	R^i	$\displaystyle \mathop{R}_{i\mathbf{N}=1}^{n\mathbf{N}} P(i\mathbf{N})$
8	Recursion	$\circlearrowleft$	$\displaystyle \mathop{R}_{i\mathbf{N}=n\mathbf{N}}^{0} P^{\mathbf{N}} \circlearrowleft P^{\mathbf{N}-1}$
9	Function call	$\rightarrowtail$	$P \rightarrowtail F$
10	Parallel	$\|$	$P \| Q$
11	Concurrence	$\text{\ff}$	$P \text{\ff} Q$
12	Interleave	$\|\|$	$P \|\| Q$
13	Pipeline	$»$	$P » Q$
14	Interrupt	$\nleftarrow$	$P \nleftarrow Q$
15	Time-driven dispatch	$\hookrightarrow_t$	$@t_i\mathbf{TM} \hookrightarrow_t P_i$
16	Event-driven dispatch	$\hookrightarrow_e$	$@e\mathbf{S} \hookrightarrow_e P_i$
17	Interrupt-driven dispatch	$\hookrightarrow_i$	$@int_j \odot \hookrightarrow_i P_j$

additional process relations such as *recursion* (#8), *function call* (#9), *parallel* (#10), *concurrency* (#11), *interleave* (#12), *pipeline* (#13), and *interrupt* (#14). However, these process relations or operations were treated as the same of the metaprocesses in existing formal methods. That is, the conventional notation systems are not an algebraic production system rather than an exhaustive instruction system, which do not distinguish the basic computational operations and their composing rules.

RTPA (Wang, 2002b) extends the BCS's and process relations to *time-driven dispatch* (#15), *event-driven dispatch* (#16), *and interrupt-driven dispatch* (#17) in order to model the top-level system behaviors, particularly those of real-time systems. The 17 process relations (BCSs) are regarded as the foundation of programming and system behavioral design, because any complex process can be combinatory implemented by the algebraic process composing operations onto the set of the 17 metaprocesses. In Table 3, the big-R used in process relations #5 through #8 is a special calculus recently created for denoting iterative and recursive behaviors of software systems (Wang, 2008b).

Theorem 2. *The express power of algebraic modeling states that the total number of the possible computational behaviors (operations)* $\mathcal{N}$ *is a set of combinations between two arbitrary metaprocesses* $\mathbb{P}_1$, $\mathbb{P}_2 \in \mathfrak{P}$ *composed by each of the process relations* $\mathbb{R} \in \mathfrak{R}$ *in RTPA, i.e.:*

$$
\begin{aligned}
\mathcal{N} &= \#\mathfrak{R} \bullet \mathrm{C}^2_{\#\mathfrak{P}} \\
&= 17 \bullet \frac{17!}{2!(17-2)!} \\
&= 17 \bullet 136 \\
&= 2{,}312
\end{aligned}
\tag{15}
$$

Theorem 2 demonstrates the expressive power of the algebraic structure of RTPA towards computational behavior modeling and programming. It is noteworthy that an ordinary high-level programming language may introduce about 150 to 300 individual instructions. However, the expressive power of RTPA is much higher than those of programming languages and other exhaustive formal notation systems, although it just adopts a small set of 17 metaprocesses and 17 process relations.

MANIPULATION OF COMPUTATIONAL BEHAVIORS BY RTPA

As presented in previous sections, RTPA provides a neat and powerful denotational mathematics structure, which is capable to be used as a generic notation system for system architecture and behavior modeling and specifications. This section describes the usage and methodology of RTPA for software system modeling and refinement. Its applications in formally modeling intelligent systems and human cognitive processes will be presented in the next section.

The Universal Mathematical Model of Programs Based on RTPA

Program modeling is on coordination of computational behaviors with given data objects. On the basis of RTPA, a generic program model can be described by a formal treatment of statements, processes, and complex processes from the bottom up in the program hierarchy.

Definition 16. *A process P is the basic unit of an applied computational behavior that is composed by a set of statements s_i, $1 \le i \le n-1$, with left-associated cumulative relations, i.e.:*

$$P = \mathop{R}_{i=1}^{n-1} (s_i \ r_{ij} \ s_j), j = i+1$$
$$= (...(((s_1) \ r_{12} \ s_2) \ r_{23} \ s_3) \ ... \ r_{n-1,n} \ s_n) \tag{16}$$

where $s_i \in P$ and $r_{ij} \in R$.

With the formal process model as defined above, the universal mathematical model of programs can be derived below.

Definition 17. *A program $\wp$ is a composition of a finite set of m processes according to the time-, event-, and interrupt-based process dispatching rules of RTPA, i.e.:*

$$\wp = \mathop{R}_{k=1}^{m} (@ e_k \hookrightarrow P_k) \tag{17}$$

Equations 16 and 17 indicate that a program is an *embedded relational algebraic* entity, where a statement *s* in a program is an instantiation of a metainstruction of a programming language that executes a basic unit of coherent function and leads to a predictable behavior.

Theorem 3. *The Embedded Relational Model (ERM) states that a software system or a program $\wp$ is a set of complex embedded relational processes, in which all previous processes of a given process form the context of the current process, i.e.:*

$$\wp = \mathop{R}_{k=1}^{m} (@ e_k \hookrightarrow P_k)$$
$$= \mathop{R}_{k=1}^{m} [@ e_k \hookrightarrow \mathop{R}_{i=1}^{n-1} (p_i(k) \ t_{ij} \ k) \ p_j(k))], j = i+1 \tag{18}$$

The ERM model presented in Theorem 3 reveals that a program is a finite and nonempty set of embedded binary relations between a current statement and *all previous ones* that formed the *semantic context* or *environment of computing*. Theorem 3 provides a unified software model, which is a formalization of the well accepted but informal process metaphor for software systems in computing.

ADT Modeling and Specification in RTPA

Abstract data types (ADTs) are perfect software architectures at component level that will be used to explain the modeling methodology of computing architectures and behaviors in RTPA. An ADT is a logical model of complex and/or user defined data type with a set of predefined operations on it. A queue as a typical ADT is presented in this subsection to demonstrate how the RTPA notation system is used to model and specify the architecture, static behaviors, and dynamic behaviors of software systems.

There are a number of approaches to the specification of ADTs, which can be classified into the logical and algebraic approaches. The logic approach is good at specifying the static properties of ADT operations, usually in forms of preconditions and post-conditions of operations of ADTs; while the algebraic approach is good at describing dynamic and run-time behaviors of ADTs.

A queue in RTPA is modeled as an algebraic entity, which has predefined operations on a set of data objects in given types. Unlike the conventional approaches to ADT specifications that treat ADTs as static data types, ADTs in RTPA are treated as dynamic finite state machines, which have both architectures and behaviors, in order to model both structural and operational components in system design.

Architectural Modeling in RTPA

At the top level, an RTPA specification of the queue, *Queue***ST**, has three parallel facets, which are architecture, static behaviors, and dynamic behaviors, as given below.

$$
\begin{aligned}
\text{Queue}\textbf{ST} \triangleq\ &\text{Queue}\textbf{ST}.\text{Architecture} \\
&\|\ \text{Queue}\textbf{ST}.\text{StaticBehaviors} \\
&\|\ \text{Queue}\textbf{ST}.\text{DynamicBehaviors}
\end{aligned}
\tag{19}
$$

Then, Queue**ST** can be further refined by detailed specifications according to the RTPA methodology (Wang, 2007d).

The key modeling methodology for system architectures in RTPA is CLMs, as described in the subsection of advanced types. Any system architecture and data object, including their control structures, internal logic model, and hardware interface model can be rigorously described and specified by using a set of CLMs.

Example 1. *The architecture of Queue***ST** *modeled in RTPA is given in Figure 1, where both the architectural CLM and an access model are provided for the Queue.*

In Figure 1, the *access model* of Queue**ST** is a logic model for supporting external invocation of the Queue**ST** in operations, such as enqueue and service. The other parts of the model are designed for internal manipulation of the Queue**ST**, such as creation, memory allocation, and memory release.

Figure 1. The architectural model of the Queue in RTPA

```
Queue ST.Architecture ≜  CLM : ST
                      ‖ AccessModel : ST
                      ‖ Events : S
                      ‖ Status : BL

QueueST.Architecture.CLM ≜ QueueIDS :
    ( <Size : N | SizeN ≥ 0>,
      <Element : RT>,
      <CurrentPos : P | 0 ≤ CurrentPosP ≤ SizeN-1>
    )

Queue ST.Architecture.AccessModel ≜ QueueIDS(CurrentPosP)RT
```

Static Behavior Modeling in RTPA

System static behaviors in RTPA are valid operations of systems that can be determined at compile-time, which describe the configuration of processes of the component and their relations. The set of static behaviors of Queue**ST** can be modeled by a set of behavioral processes encompassing *create, release, enqueue, serve, clear, empty test,* and *full test.*

Example 2. *The detailed specification of one of the Queue's static behaviors, Queue***ST***.serve, is given in Figure 2.*

Contrasting the static behavior model of Queue**ST**.serve in RTPA as shown in Figure 2 and in conventional propositional logic (Stubbs & Webre, 1985), the advances of RTAP method and notations may be well demonstrated. Among them, the most important advantage is that an RTPA model may be seamlessly refined into code in a programming language in the succeeding phase of software engineering.

Figure 2. The static behavioral model of the Queue in RTPA

```
QueueST.Serve (<I :: QueueInstS>;
                    <O :: ⓈQueueID.ServedBL, ElementRT>)  ≜
{
  QueueIDS := QueueInstS
  → ( ◆ ⓈQueueExistBL = T ∧ CurrentPosP > 0
          → (QueueID(1))RT ≻Element RT
          → QueueID(i))RT ≻QueueID(i-1)RT
          → ↓ (QueueID.CurrentPosP)
          → ⓈQueueID.ServedBL := T
     | ◆ ~
          → ⓈQueueID.ServedBL := F
          → ! (@'QueueIDExistBL = F ∨ QueueEmptyBL = T)
     )
}
```

Figure 3. The dynamic behavioral model of the Queue in RTPA

```
QueueST.DynamicBehaviors ≜ { § →
  ( @CreateQueueS ↳ Queue.Create (<I:: QueueInstS, ElementInstRT, SizeInstN>;
                                    <O:: ⓈQueueID.AllocatedBL, ⓈQueueID.ExistBL>)
  | @ReleaseQueueS ↳ Queue.Release (<I:: QueueInstS>; <O:: ⓈQueueID.ReleasedBL>)
  | @EnqueueS     ↳ Queue.Enqueue (<I:: QueueInstS, ElementInstRT>; <O:: ⓈQueueID.EnqueuedBL>)
  | @ServeS       ↳ Queue.Serve (<I:: QueueInstS>; <O:: ⓈQueueID.ServedBL, ElementRT>)
  | @ClearS       ↳ Queue.Clear (<I:: QueueInstS>; <O:: ⓈQueueID.ClearedBL>)
  | @QueueEmptyS  ↳ Queue.EmptyTest (<I:: QueueInstS>; <O:: ⓈQueueID.FullBL>)
  | @QueueFullS   ↳ Queue.FullTest (<I:: QueueInstS>; <O:: ⓈQueueID.FullBL>)
  ) → §
}
```

Dynamic Behavior Modeling in RTPA

System dynamic behaviors in RTPA are process relations determined at run time. According to the RTPA system modeling and refinement scheme, models of system static behaviors are process models of the system. To put the component processes into a live and interacting system, the dynamic behaviors of the system in terms of process deployment and dispatch are yet to be specified.

Example 3. *The dynamic behaviors of Queue***ST** *are specified in RTPA as shown in Figure 3, where the process dispatch mechanisms of the Queue specifies detailed dynamic process relations at run time by a set of event-driven relations.*

Figures 1 through 3 model an ADT, *Queue***ST**, in a coherent system from three facets. With the RTPA specification and refinement methodology and the expressive power of the RTPA notation system, the features of ADTs as both static data types and dynamic finite machines can be specified formally and precisely.

MANIPULATION OF INTELLIGENT BEHAVIORS BY RTPA

RTPA may be used not only for modeling and description of computing behaviors but also for modeling and denoting the cognitive processes of the brain in cognitive informatics (Wang, 2002a, 2003a, 2003b, 2006a, 2006b, 2007a, 2007e, 2007f; Wang & Wang, 2006; Wang et al., 2006). A formal treatment of memorization as a cognitive process is presented in this section by a rigorous RTPA model based on the cognitive model of human memorization (Wang, 2007a).

The Cognitive Process of Memorization

Memorization as a cognitive process can be described by two phases: the *establishment* phase and the *reconstruction* phase. The former represents the target information in the form of an object-attribute-relation (OAR) model (Wang, 2007c) and creates a memory in long-term memory (LTM). The letter retrieves the memorized information and reconstructs it in the form of a concept in the short-term memory (STM). Therefore, memorization can be perceived as the transformation of information and knowledge between STM and LTM, where the forward transformation from STM to LTM is for memory establishment, and the backward transformation from LTM to STM is for memory reconstruction.

Algorithm 1. *The cognitive process of memorization can be carried out by the following steps:*

(0) Begin.
(1) Encoding: This step generates a representation of a given concept by transferring it into a sub-OAR model;
(2) Retention: This step updates the entire OAR in LTM with the sub-OAR for memorization by creating new synaptic connections between the sub-OAR and the entire OAR;
(3) Rehearsal test: This step checks if the memorization result in LTM needs to be rehearsed. If yes,

Figure 4. Formal description of the memorization process in RTPA

The Memorization Process

Memorization $(\mathbf{I}:: c(O\mathbf{S}, A\mathbf{S}, R\mathbf{S})\mathbf{ST}; \mathbf{O}:: OAR'\mathbf{ST}) \triangleq$
{I. Encoding
$c(O\mathbf{S}, A\mathbf{S}, R\mathbf{S})\mathbf{ST} \Rightarrow sOAR\mathbf{ST}$
// Concept representation

II. Retention

$\rightarrow OAR'\mathbf{ST} := OAR\mathbf{ST} \uplus sOAR\mathbf{ST}$
// Update OAR**ST** in LTM

III. Rehearsal

$\rightarrow \blacklozenge$ Rehearsal$\mathbf{BL} = \mathbf{T}$
   (IV. Retrieval
    $\rightarrowtail$ Search $(\mathbf{I}:: OAR\mathbf{ST};$
              $\mathbf{O}:: sOAR\mathbf{ST} \mid (O\mathbf{S}, A\mathbf{S}, R\mathbf{S})\mathbf{ST} \subseteq OAR\mathbf{ST}))$
      // Retrieval sOAR**ST** in LTM

    V. Decoding
    $\rightarrow (sOAR\mathbf{ST} \rightarrow c'(O\mathbf{S}, A\mathbf{S}, R\mathbf{S})\mathbf{ST})$
      // Concept reconstruction
)

VI. Repeat

$\rightarrow \blacklozenge (c'(O\mathbf{S}, A\mathbf{S}, R\mathbf{S})\mathbf{ST}) \sim c(O\mathbf{S}, A\mathbf{S}, R\mathbf{S})\mathbf{ST})$
    $\rightarrow \otimes$ // Memorization succeed
  $\mid \blacklozenge \sim$ // Retry
    $\rightarrow$ Memorization $(\mathbf{I}:: c(O\mathbf{S}, A\mathbf{S}, R\mathbf{S})\mathbf{ST}; \mathbf{O}:: OAR'\mathbf{ST})$
}

---

it continues to practice Steps (4) and (5); otherwise, it jumps to Step (7);

(4) Retrieval: This step retrieves the memorized object in the form of sub-OAR by searching the entire OAR with clues of the initial concept;

(5) Decoding: This step transfers the retrieved sub-OAR from LTM into a concept and represents it in STM;

(6) Repetitive memory test: This step tests if the memorization process was succeeded or not by comparing the recovered concept with the original concept. If need, repetitive memorization will be called.

(7) End.

It is noteworthy that the input of memorization is a structured concept formulated by learning or other cognitive processes (Wang, 2007d, 2007f; Wang et al., 2006).

Formal Description of the Memorization Process in RTPA

The cognitive process of memorization described in Algorithm 1 can be formally modeled using RTPA as given in Figure 4. According to the LRMB model (Wang et al., 2006) and the OAR model (Wang, 2007c) of internal knowledge representation in the brain, the input of the memorization process is a structured concept c(O**S**, A**S**, R**S**)**ST,** which will be transformed to update the entire OAR model of knowledge in LTM in order to create a permanent memory. Therefore, the output of memorization is the updated OAR'**ST** in LTM.

In the RTPA memorization process, as shown in Figure 4, the *encoding* subprocess is modeled as a function that maps the given concept c**ST** into a sub-OAR, sOAR**ST**. The *retention* subprocess composes the sOAR**ST** with the entire OAR**ST** in LTM that maintains the whole knowledge of an individual. In order to check the memorization quality, rehearsals are usually needed. In a rehearsal, the *retrieval* subproecss searches a related sOAR**ST** in LTM by giving clues of previously memorized objects and attributes in c**ST**. Then, the *decoding* subprocess transfers the sOAR**ST** into a recovered concept c'**ST**. In the repetitive memory test subprocess, the reconstructed c'**ST** will be compared with the original input of c**ST** in order to determine if further memorization is recursively needed.

According to the 24-hour law of memorization as stated in Wang and Wang (2006), the memorization process may be completed with a period at least 24 hours by several cycles of repetitions. Although almost all steps in the process shown in Figure 4 are conscious, the key step of *retention* is subconscious or nonintentionally controllable. Based on the LRMB model (Wang et al., 2006), the memorization process is closely related to learning (Wang, 2007f). In other words, memorization is a back-end process of learning, which retains learning results in LTM and retrieves them when rehearsals or applications are needed. The retrieve process is search-based by contents or sOAR**ST** matching.

The cognitive process of memorization formally modeled in RTPA provides a rigorous description of one of the important and complicated mental processes of the brain. This case study explains the second usage of RTPA in intelligent system modeling and human behavioral manipulation. Further models and applications of RTPA in intelligent system modeling may be referred to (Wang, 2007d; Wang & Ngolah, 2002, 2003). The applications of RTPA in modeling cognitive processes of the brain and natural intelligence may be found in Wang (2003b, 2007a, 2007f).

CONCLUSION

RTPA has been developed as a denotational mathematical means, which can be used as algebra-based, expressive, easy-to-comprehend, and language-independent notation system, and a practical specification and refinement method for software and intelligent system modeling. RTPA is capable to support top-down software system design and implementation by algebraic modeling and seamless refinement methodologies. The RTPA methodology covers the entire system lifecycle from high-level design to code generation in a coherent algebraic notation system.

This article has demonstrated that RTPA is not only useful as a generic notation and methodology for computing and software system modeling but is also good at modeling human cognitive processes and intelligent systems. A number of case studies on large-scale software system modeling and specifications have been carried out, such as the Telephone Switching System (TSS) (Wang, 2003b), the Lift Dispatching System (LDS) (Wang & Ngolah, 2002), and the Automated Teller Machine (ATM) (Wang & Zhang, 2003). The application results have encouragingly demonstrated that RTPA is a powerful and practical algebraic system for both academics and practitioners in software and intelligent system engineering.

A set of support tools for RTPA have been developed (Ngolah, Wang, & Tan, 2005b, 2006; Tan & Wang, 2006; Tan, Wang, & Ngolah, 2004a, 2004b, 2005, 2006), which encompasses the RTPA parser, type checker, and code generator in C++ and Java. The RTPA code generator enables system specifications in RTPA to be automatically translated into fully executable code. The RTPA tools will support system architects, analysts, and practitioners for developing consistent and correct specifications and architectural models of large-scale software and intelligent systems, and the automatic generation of code based on formal models and rigorous specifications in the denotational mathematical notations.

ACKNOWLEDGMENT

The author would like to acknowledge the Natural Science and Engineering Council of Canada (NSERC) for its partial support to this work. The author would like to thank anonymous reviewers for their valuable comments and suggestions.

REFERENCES

Aho, A. V., Sethi, R. & Ullman, J. D. (1985). *Compilers: Principles, techniques, and tools.* New York: Addison-Wesley.

Baeten, J. C. M., Bergstra, J. A. (1991). Real time process algebra. *Formal Aspects of Computing, 3,* 142-188.

Boucher, A., & Gerth, R. (1987). A timed model for extended communicating sequential processes. In *Proceedings of ICALP'87* (LNCS 267). Springer.

Cardelli, L., & Wegner, P. (1985). On understanding types, data abstraction and polymorphism. *ACM Computing Surveys, 17*(4), 471-522.

Cerone, A. (2000). *Process algebra versus axiomatic specification of a real-time protocol* (LNCS 1816, pp. 57-67). Berlin, Germany: Springer.

Corsetti, E., Montanari, A., & Ratto, E. (1991). Dealing with different time granularities in formal specifications of real-time systems. *The Journal of Real-Time Systems, 3*(2), 191-215.

Dierks, H. (2000). A process algebra for real-time programs (LNCS 1783, pp. 66/76). Berlin, Germany: Springer.

Fecher, H. (2001). A real-time process algebra with open intervals and maximal progress, *Nordic Journal of Computing, 8*(3), 346-360.

Gerber, R., Gunter, E. L., & Lee, I. (1992). Implementing a real-time process algebra In M. Archer,J. J. Joyce, K. N. Levitt, & P. J. Windley (Eds.), *Proceedings of the International Workshop on the Theorem Proving System and its Applications* (pp. 144-145). Los Alamitos, CA: IEEE Computer Society Press.

Higman, B. (1977). *A comparative study of programming languages* (2nd ed.). MacDonald.

Hoare, C. A. R. (1978). Communicating sequential processes. *Communications of the ACM, 21*(8), 666-677.

Hoare, C. A. R. (1985). *Communicating sequential processes*. London: Prentice Hall International.

Hoare, C. A. R., Hayes, I. J., He, J., Morgan, C. C., Roscoe, A. W., Sanders, J. W., et al. (1987). Laws of programming, *Communications of the ACM, 30*(8), 672-686.

Jeffrey, A. (1992). Translating timed process algebra into prioritized process algebra. In J. Vytopil (Ed.), *Proceedings of the Second International Symposium on Formal Techniques in Real-Time and Fault-Tolerant Systems* (LNCS 571, pp. 493-506). Nijmegen, The Netherlands: Springer-Verlag.

Klusener, A. S. (1992). Abstraction in real time process algebra. In J. W. de Bakker, C. Huizing, W. P. de Roever, & G. Rozenberg (Eds.), *Proceedings of Real-Time: Theory in Practice* (LNCS, pp. 325-352). Berlin, Germany: Springer.

Louden K. C. (1993). *Programming languages: Principles and practice*. Boston.: PWS-Kent.

Martin-Lof, P. (1975). An intuitionistic theory of types: Predicative part. In H. Rose & J. C. Shepherdson (Eds.), *Logic Colloquium 1973*. North-Holland.

Milner, R. (1980). *A calculus of communicating systems* (LNCS 92). Springer-Verlag.

Milner, R. (1989). *Communication and concurrency*. Englewood Cliffs, NJ: Prentice Hall.

Mitchell, J. C. (1990). Type systems for programming languages. In J. van Leeuwen (Ed.), *Handbook of theoretical computer science* (pp.365-458). North-Holland.

Nicollin, X., & Sifakis, J. (1991). An overview and synthesis on timed process algebras. In *Proceedings of the Third International Computer Aided Verification Conference* (pp. 376-398).

OMG. (2002, July). *IDL syntax and semantics*. 1-74.

Reed, G. M., & Roscoe, A. W. (1986). A timed model for communicating sequential processes. In *Proceedings of ICALP'86* (LNCS 226). Berlin, Germany: Springer-Verlag.

Russell, B. (1961). *Basic writings of Bertrand Russell*. London: George Allen & Unwin Ltd.

Schneider, S. A. (1991). *An operational semantics for timed CSP* (Programming Research Group Tech. Rep. TR-1-91). Oxford University.

Schilpp, P. A. (1946). The philosophy of Bertrand Russell. *American Mathematical Monthly, 53*(4), 7210.

Stubbs, D. F., & Webre, W. R. (1985). *Data structures with abstract data types and Pascal*. Monterey, CA: Brooks/Cole.

Tan, X., Wang, Y., & Ngolah, C. F. (2004). A novel type checker for software system specifications in RTPA. In *Proceedings of the 17th Canadian Conference on Electrical and Computer Engineering (CCECE'04)*. (pp. 1549-1552). Niagara Falls, Ontario, Canada: IEEE CS Press.

Tan, X., Wang, Y., & Ngolah, C. F. (2006). Design and implementation of an automatic RTPA code generator. In *Proceedings of the 19th Canadian Conference on Electrical and Computer Engineering (CCECE'06)* (pp. 1605-1608). Ottawa, Ontario, Canada: IEEE CS Press.

van Heijenoort, J. (1997). *From Frege to Godel, a source book in mathematical logic 1879-1931*. Cambridge, MA: Harvard University Press.

Vereijken, J. J. (1995). A process algebra for hybrid systems. In A. Bouajjani & O. Maler (Eds.), In *Proceedings of the Second European Workshop on Real-Time and Hybrid Systems*. Grenoble: France.

Wang, Y. (2002a). On cognitive informatics (Keynote speech). In *Proceedings of the First IEEE International Conference on Cognitive Informatics (ICCI'02)* (pp. 34-42). Calgary, Canada: IEEE CS Press.

Wang, Y. (2002b). The real-time process algebra (RTPA). *Annals of Software Engineering: An International Journal, 14,* 235-274.

Wang, Y. (2003a). On cognitive informatics. *Brain and Mind: A Transdisciplinary Journal of Neuroscience and Neurophilosophy, 4*(3), 151-167.

Wang, Y. (2003b). Using process algebra to describe human and software system behaviors. *Brain and Mind, 4*(2), 199-213.

Wang, Y. (2006a). Cognitive informatics and contemporary mathematics for knowledge representation and manipulation (Invited plenary talk). In *Proceedings of the First International Conference on Rough Set and Knowledge Technology (RSKT'06)* (LNAI 4062, pp. 69-78). Chongqing, China: Springer.

Wang, Y. (2006b). Cognitive informatics—Towards the future generation computers that think and feel (Keynote speech). In *Proceedings of the Fifth IEEE International Conference on Cognitive Informatics (ICCI'06)* (pp. 3-7). Beijing, China: IEEE CS Press.

Wang, Y. (2006c). On the informatics laws and deductive semantics of software. *IEEE Transactions on Systems, Man, and Cybernetics (C), 36*(2), 161-171.

Wang, Y. (2007a). Formal description of the cognitive process of memorization. In *Proceedings of the Sixth International Conference on Cognitive Informatics (ICCI'07)* (pp. 284-293). Lake Tahoe, CA: IEEE CS Press.

Wang, Y. (2007b). Keynote speech, on theoretical foundations of software engineering and denotational mathematics,. In *Proceedings of the Fifth Asian Workshop on Foundations of Software* (pp. 99-102). Xiamen, China.

Wang, Y. (2007c). The OAR Model of neural informatics for internal knowledge representation in the brain. *The International Journal of Cognitive Informatics and Natural Intelligence, 1*(3), 64-75.

Wang, Y. (2007d). *Software engineering foundations: A software science perspective*. In *CRC series in software engineering: Vol. 2*. CRC Press.

Wang, Y. (2007e). The theoretical framework of cognitive informatics. *The International Journal of Cognitive Informatics and Natural Intelligence, 1*(1), 1-27.

Wang, Y. (2007f). The Theoretical framework and cognitive process of learning. In *Proceedings of the Sixth International Conference on Cognitive Informatics (ICCI'07)* (pp. 470-479). Lake Tahoe, CA: IEEE CS Press.

Wang, Y. (2008a). Deductive semantics of RTPA. *The International Journal of Cognitive Informatics and Natural Intelligence, 2*(2), 95-121.

Wang, Y. (2008b). On the big-R notation for describing iterative and recursive behaviors. *The International Journal of Cognitive Informatics and Natural Intelligence, 2*(1), 17-28.

Wang, Y., & King, G. (2000). Software engineering processes: Principles and applications In *CRC Series in Software Engineering: Vol. I.*. CRC Press.

Wang, Y., & Noglah, C. F. (2002). Formal specification of a real-time lift dispatching system. In *Proceedings of the 2002 IEEE Canadian Conference on Electrical and Computer Engineering (CCECE'02)* (pp.669-674). Winnipeg, Manitoba, Canada.

Wang, Y., & Noglah, C. F. (2003). Formal description of real-time operating systems using RTPA. In *Proceedings of the 2003 Canadian Conference on Electrical and Computer Engineering (CCECE'03)* (pp.1247-1250). Montreal, Canada: IEEE CS Press

Wang, Y., & Wang, Y. (2006). Cognitive informatics models of the brain. *IEEE Transactions on Systems, Man, and Cybernetics* (C), *36*(2),203-207.

Wang, Y., Wang, Y., Patel, S., & Patel, D. (2006). A layered reference model of the brain (LRMB). *IEEE Transactions on Systems, Man, and Cybernetics* (C), *36*(2),124-133.

Wang, Y., & Zhang, Y. (2003). Formal description of an ATM system by RTPA. In *Proceedings of the 16th Canadian Conference on Electrical and Computer Engineering* (CCECE'03) (pp. 1255-1258). Montreal, Canada: IEEE CS Press.

Wilson, L. B., & Clark, R. G. (1988). *Comparative programming language.* Wokingham, England: Addison-Wesley.

Woodcock, J., & Davies, J. (1996). *Using Z: Specification, refinement, and proof.* London: Prentice Hall International.

This work was previously published in International Journal of Cognitive Informatics and Natural Intelligence, Vol. 2, Issue 2, edited by Y. Wang, pp. 44-62, copyright 2008 by IGI Publishing (an imprint of IGI Global).

Chapter 11
A Denotational Semantics of Real-Time Process Algebra (RTPA)

Yingxu Wang
University of Calgary, Canada

Xinming Tan
University of Calgary, Canada & Wuhan University of Technology, China

ABSTRACT

Real-time process algebra (RTPA) is a form of denotational mathematics for dealing with fundamental system behaviors such as timing, interrupt, concurrency, and event/time/interrupt-driven system dispatching. Because some key RTPA processes cannot be described adequately in conventional denotational semantic paradigms, a new framework for modeling time and processes is sought in order to represent RTPA in denotational semantics. Within this framework, time is modeled by the elapse of process execution. The process environment encompasses states of all variables represented as mathematical maps, which project variables to their corresponding values. Duration is introduced as a pair of time intervals and the environment to represent the changes of the process environment during a time interval. Temporal ordered durations and operations on them are used to denote process executions. On the basis of these means, a comprehensive set of denotational semantics for RTPA are systematically developed and formally expressed.

INTRODUCTION

Real-time process algebra (RTPA) is a form of denotational mathematics for the modeling, specification, and refinement of real-time and safety-critical systems (Wang, 2002, 2003, 2006a, 2006b, 2007a, 2008a-c), as well as human cognitive behaviors and processes (Wang, 2003, 2006b, 2007b). RTPA elicits a rich set of process operations including timing, interrupt, concurrency, and event/time/interrupt-driven dispatches with a rigorous algebraic structure.

The conventional forms of denotational semantics were designed to deals simple and sequential computation behaviors (Louden, 1993; McDermid, 1991; Wang, 2007a; Winskel, 1993). Efforts to represent parallel and concurrent behaviors in the denotational semantic approach focused on communications between components (Schneider, 2000). Various treatments for time and durations have been introduced (Baeten & Bergstra, 1991; Boucher & Gerth, 1987; Corsetti, Montanari, & Ratto, 1991; Dierks, 2000; Fecher, 2001; Milner, 1980; Schneider, 1995) in order to describe the real-time mechanisms in denotation semantics. Because the mathematical structure of RTPA cannot be described adequately in conventional denotational semantics paradigms (Hoare, 1978, 1985; Schneider, 2000; Wang, 2007a; Winskel, 1993), a new extension on conventional denotational semantics is introduced for modeling time and processes in RTPA, where relative time is modeled by the elapse of process execution, and a process is modeled by temporal ordered duration sequences.

The article attempts to handle the sequential, parallel, concurrent, and real-time behaviors of RTPA in a coherent system. The abstract syntax of RTPA is presented. The system environment is introduced to describe instantaneous behaviors of processes and durations. Temporal ordered duration sequences are introduced to present the semantics of RTPA meta processes and process operations. The denotational semantics for RTPA can be used as rules for correctness checking and system verification in system design and modeling using RTPA. It also facilitates the rigorous understanding of a comprehensive set of fundamental computing system behaviors as modeled in RTPA.

THE ACTIVITY DURATION CALCULUS

The activity duration calculus (ADC) is developed to describe system behaviors over time where each activity happens in a timely order and will last for a period of time or an interval. At any specific time moment, the state of the system is represented by the values of its variables at the moment (Wang, 2006a, 2008b). The time sequence of the instantaneous moments expresses the behaviors of a system. ADC uses a semantic environment, which is a map from variables to values, to record an instantaneous system state (Wang, 2006a, 2008b). It uses a duration adopted as a 2-tuple of an interval and an environment to represent a system state for a given period of time. A temporal ordered duration sequence is therefore a semantics model of system behaviors.

Variables and Values

ADC uses variables with a universal type by default. When different types of variables, such as integer, real, and Boolean, are needed, it can be considered that the various variables are in the form of set sum (Winskel, 1993), as used in the denotational semantics of RTPA.

$\mathbb{X}$ - The set of all variables.   (1)

$\mathbb{V}$ - Domain of all possible values.   (2)

When multiple variables are modeled, a subscript will be used, such as $x_1, ..., x_n, x_i \in \mathbb{X}$. So do the values $v_i \in \mathbb{V}$.

Environments

An environment, which records the current states and values of all variables of a system, is a map (RAISE, 1992) from variables to values. A map is a table structure similar to a function except in domain definition, which maps values of one type into values of another type. The domain of all environments is defined as shown in Equation 3.

$$\mathbb{EN} = \mathbb{X} \xrightarrow{m} \mathbb{V} \tag{3}$$

It is noteworthy that $\mathbb{EN}$ encompasses an inexplicit subset $\mathbb{EN}'$ known as the system's environment that is independent from the user's environment $\mathbb{EN} \setminus \mathbb{EN}'$.

For a given expression $\rho : \mathbb{X} \xrightarrow{m} \mathbb{V}$, m is a map type and ρ is a map of $\mathbb{X} \xrightarrow{m} \mathbb{V}$. An empty map is denoted by [], which is the bottom of $\mathbb{EN}$. If $x \mapsto v$ belongs to ρ, $\rho(x)$ is called the application of ρ to x, written as $\rho(x) = v$. Suppose $\rho = [x_1 \mapsto 1, x_2 \mapsto 3, x_3 \mapsto 5]$, the domain of ρ, written as *dom* ρ, is $\{x_1, x_2, x_3\}$; the range of ρ, written as *rng* ρ, is $\{1, 3, 5\}$.

The following three operations are needed for the discussion in the latter part of the article, where $\mathbb{R}^+$ is the set of non-negative real numbers.

a. The *override operation* †: It is a standard map operation (RAISE, 1992), puts mappings unique to the first argument and the whole mappings of the second argument together into the resulting environment.

$$† : \mathbb{EN} \times \mathbb{EN} \rightarrow \mathbb{EN}$$
$$\rho_1 † \rho_2 = [x \mapsto v \mid (x \in dom\ \rho_1 \wedge x \notin dom\ \rho_2 \wedge \rho_1(x) = v) \vee (x \in dom\ \rho_2 \wedge x \notin dom\ \rho_1 \wedge \rho_2(x)=v)]$$

$$\tag{4}$$

b. The *advance operation* +: It increases all the time variables in an environment by a given number r, that is:

$$+ : \mathbb{EN} \times \mathbb{R}^+ \rightarrow \mathbb{EN}$$
$$\rho + r = \rho † [t \mapsto \rho(t) + r \mid t \in dom\ \rho] \tag{5}$$

c. The *retreat operation* -: It decreases all the time variables in an environment by a given number r. If the given number is greater than the least value holding by any timing variable in the environment, the result of the operation is the same as decrease by that least value.

$$- : \mathbb{EN} \times \mathbb{R}^+ \rightarrow \mathbb{EN}$$
$$\rho - r = \rho † [t \mapsto \rho(t) - r' \mid r' \in \mathbb{R}^+ \wedge t \in dom\ \rho \wedge t_1 \in dom\ \rho \vee \forall\ t_2 \in dom\ \rho \bullet \rho(t_2) \geqslant \rho(t_1) \wedge (r < \rho(t_1)$$
$$\wedge r' = r \vee r \geqslant \rho(t_1) \wedge r' = \rho(t_1))] \tag{6}$$

Durations

An interval [a,b), where a, b $\in \mathbb{R}^+$ and b > a, denotes a period. The set of all intervals is denoted by $\mathbb{I}$ where i $\in \mathbb{I}$.

A duration is a pair of an interval and an environment, which records the activities happening during the interval.

$$\mathbb{D} = \mathbb{I} \times \mathbb{EN} \tag{7}$$

For a duration d = (i, ρ) = ([a,b), ρ) and r $\in \mathbb{R}^+$, the following operations can be defined:

Get the interval of duration:
$\quad intv(d) = i = [a,b);$
Get the beginning of duration:
$\quad begin(d) = a;$
Get the end of duration:
$\quad end(d) = b;$
Get the environment of duration:
$\quad env(d) = \rho;$
Duration advance:
$\quad advance(d, r) = d + r = (i+r, \rho+r)$
$\quad\quad\quad = ([a+r, b+r), \rho+r);$
Duration retreat:
$\quad retreat(d, r) = d - r = (i-r, \rho-r)$
$\quad\quad\quad = ([a-r, b-r), \rho-r), a \geqslant r;$
$\quad\quad\quad$ or ([0, b-a), ρ-a), a < r

$$\tag{8}$$

Temporal Ordered Duration Sequences

$\mathbb{D}^*$ is used to denote the set of finite duration sequences. An n-duration sequence consisting of durations $d_1, d_2, \ldots, d_n$ is denoted as:

$<d_1>^\wedge< d_2>^\wedge\ldots^\wedge< d_n>$
or shortly as $< d_1, d_2,\ldots, d_n >$ $\tag{9}$

$<>$ is an empty sequence.

A duration sequence c = $< d_1, d_2,\ldots, d_n >$ is in temporal order iff $end(d_k) = begin(d_{k+1})$ for all k = 1, $\ldots$, n-1. The set of all temporal ordered duration sequences is denoted as:

$$\mathbb{C} \subseteq \mathbb{D}^* \tag{10}$$

The attributes of a temporal ordered duration sequence c = $< d_1, d_2,\ldots, d_n > \in \mathbb{C}$ can be defined as follows:

$head(c) = d_1;$
$tail(c) = <d_2,\ldots, d_n>;$
$front(c) = <d_1, d_2,\ldots, d_{n-1}>;$
$back(c) = d_n;$
$first(c) = begin(d_1);$
$last(c) = end(d_n).$ (11)

When $c = <>$, all of the above operations are unspecified with the value $\bot$.

Sequence Operations

The following operations on $\mathbb{C}$ are introduced:

a. The *advance operation* +: It moves a temporal ordered duration sequence forward with a given number of time units.

$+ : \mathbb{C} \times \mathbb{R}^+ \to \mathbb{C}$
$<> + r = <>$
$<d> \,^\wedge\, c + r = <d + r> \,^\wedge\, (c + r)$ (12)

b. The *retreat operation* -: It moves a temporal ordered duration sequence backward with a given number of time units.

$- : \mathbb{C} \times \mathbb{R}^+ \to \mathbb{C}$
$<> - r = <>$
$<d> \,^\wedge\, c - r = <d - r> \,^\wedge\, (c - r)$ (13)

c. The truncate-right operation $\lhd$: It cuts off the right part of a temporal ordered duration sequence before a given time point.

$\lhd : \mathbb{C} \times \mathbb{R}^+ \to \mathbb{C}$
$<> \lhd r = <>$
$c \lhd r = <>$ $first(c) \geqslant r$
$c \lhd r = c$ $last(c) \leqslant r$
$c_1 \,^\wedge\, c_2 \lhd r = c_1$ $last(c_1) = r$ (14)

d. The truncate-left operation $\rhd$: It cuts off the left part of a temporal ordered duration sequence before a given time point.

$\rhd : \mathbb{C} \times \mathbb{R}^+ \to \mathbb{C}$
$<> \rhd r = <>$
$c \rhd r = <>$ $last(c) \leqslant r$
$c \rhd r = c$ $first(c) \geqslant r$
$c_1 \,^\wedge\, c_2 \rhd r = c_2$ $first(c_2) = r$ (15)

e.   The follow operation $\rightsquigarrow$: It puts two temporal ordered duration sequences in a temporal order.

$$\rightsquigarrow : \mathbb{C} \times \mathbb{C} \to \mathbb{C}$$
$$<> \rightsquigarrow c = c$$
$$<d> {}^\wedge c \rightsquigarrow <> = <d> {}^\wedge c$$
$$c_1 {}^\wedge <d_1> \rightsquigarrow <d_2> {}^\wedge c_2 =$$
$$\qquad c_1 {}^\wedge <d_1> {}^\wedge$$
$$\qquad (<d_2> {}^\wedge c_2 + end(d_1) - begin(d_2)) \tag{16}$$

The following sections present the denotational semantics of RTPA using ADC, which encompasses the abstract syntax of RTPA, the semantic domains of RTPA, and the semantic functions of RTPA.

THE ABSTRACT SYNTAX OF RTPA

RTPA is a denotational mathematical structure for algebraically denoting and manipulating system behavioural processes and their attributes by a triple, that is:

$$RTPA \triangleq (\mathfrak{T}, \mathfrak{P}, \mathfrak{R}) \tag{17}$$

where $\mathfrak{T}$ is a set of 17 primitive types for modeling system architectures and data objects, $\mathfrak{P}$ a set of 17 meta processes for modeling fundamental system behaviors, and $\mathfrak{R}$ a set of 17 relational process operations for constructing complex system behaviors.

Further details of $\mathfrak{T}, \mathfrak{P}$, and $\mathfrak{R}$ in RTPA may be referred to (Wang, 2002, 2007a, 2008a). The abstract syntax of RTPA adopts three syntactic categories, namely variables, expressions, and processes.

Variables of RTPA

RTPA uses identifiers with a type suffix to declare and denote a variable. In the definition of the abstract syntax of RTPA, the following conventions are adopted:

1.   When the type of a variable is not a concern, x is used to represent the variable;
2.   @e is used for event variable, ptr for pointer variable, t for time variable, and id for name (string) variable; that is:

    $$x, @e, ptr, t, id \in \mathbb{X}. \tag{18}$$

    For a pointer variable ptr, which takes value of memory addresses, an associated variable addr is attached to denote the object to which the ptr points.
3.   Integer subscripts are added when multiple variables are discussed.

Expressions of RTPA

All kinds of typical arithmetical, Boolean, and relational expressions are a part of RTPA expressions. Special expressions of RTPA are explicitly defined below:

$$e \triangleq \text{MEM}(\text{ptr}\textbf{P})\mathbb{T} \mid \text{MEM}(\perp)\mathbb{T} \mid \text{PORT}(\text{ptr}\textbf{P})\mathbb{T} \mid$$
$$\S t\textbf{TM} \mid \S t\textbf{TM} + \Delta n\textbf{N} \tag{19}$$

where $\mathbb{EXP}$ is the set of all expressions, $e \in \mathbb{EXP}$, $\mathbb{T}$ is a type suffix, MEM indicates a memory location or area, PORT indicates an I/O port, and $\S t$ stands for the system time in RTPA.

A detailed discussion on formal syntaxes of RTPA is provided in (Tan, 2006; Tan, Wang, & Ngolah, 2004; Wang, 2002, 2007a, 2008a).

Processes of RTPA

The entire process system of RTPA, $\mathbb{P}$, models 17 meta processes $\mathfrak{P}$ and 17 process relations $\mathfrak{R}$ as defined in Equtions 20 and 21, respectively (Wang, 2002, 2007a, 2008a).

$$\mathfrak{P} \triangleq \quad x\mathbb{T} := e\mathbb{T} \mid \blacklozenge e\textbf{BL} \mid id\textbf{S} \Rightarrow \text{MEM}(\text{ptr}\textbf{P})\mathbb{T} \mid$$
$$id\textbf{S} \Leftarrow \text{MEM}(\text{ptr}\textbf{P})\mathbb{T} \mid id\textbf{S} \Leftarrow \text{MEM}(\perp)\mathbb{T} \mid$$
$$\text{MEM}(\text{ptr}\textbf{P})\mathbb{T} > x\mathbb{T} \mid x\mathbb{T} < \text{MEM}(\text{ptr}\textbf{P})\mathbb{T} \mid$$
$$\text{PORT}(\text{ptr}\textbf{P})\mathbb{T} |> x\mathbb{T} \mid x\mathbb{T}| < \text{PORT}(\text{ptr}\textbf{P})\mathbb{T} \mid$$
$$@t\textbf{TM} \overset{@}{=} \S t\textbf{TM} \mid @t\textbf{TM} \triangleq \S t\textbf{TM} + \Delta n\textbf{N} \mid$$
$$(n\textbf{N}) \mid \downarrow(n\textbf{N}) \mid !(@e\textbf{S}) \mid \otimes \mid \boxtimes \mid \S(id\textbf{S}) \tag{20}$$

$$\mathfrak{R} \triangleq \quad P \rightarrow Q \mid (\blacklozenge e\textbf{BL} = \textbf{T} \rightarrow P \mid \rightarrow Q) \mid$$
$$(\blacklozenge e\textbf{N} = 1 \rightarrow P1 \mid 2 \rightarrow P2 \mid \ldots \mid \rightarrow Q) \mid$$
$$P \rightarrow Q \mid P \circlearrowright P \mid P \| Q \mid P \text{\ss} Q \mid P \| Q \mid P \gg Q \mid$$
$$@t\textbf{TM} \hookrightarrow P \mid @e\textbf{S} \hookrightarrow P \mid @i \odot \hookrightarrow P \mid P \natural Q \mid P \curvearrowright Q \mid$$
$$\underset{eBL=T}{R} (P) \mid \underset{iN=1}{R} (P(i)) \mid P \rightarrow \underset{eBL=T}{R} (P) \tag{21}$$

where $\mathbb{P}$ is the set of all RTPA processes, and $\mathfrak{P}, \mathfrak{R} \in \mathbb{P}$.

THE SEMANTIC DOMAINS OF RTPA

Apart from the three syntactic domains, five semantic domains, namely $\mathbb{V}$ - values, $\mathbb{EN}$ - environments, $\mathbb{D}$ - durations, $\mathbb{C}$ - temporal ordered duration sequences, and $\mathbb{COM}$ - prefix closure of temporal ordered duration sequences, are adopted in this section. Some other discrete domains, such as Boolean values and natural numbers, are also needed in the discussions.

The least observable interval used in defining the semantics of a process is a unit interval [a, b) such that b - a = 1 (time unit), which corresponds to the relative system clock model, $\S t\textbf{N}$, of RTPA. Therefore, the set of non-negative real numbers $\mathbb{R}^+$ used in ADC may be replaced by the natural numbers $\mathbb{N}$ when giving a denotational semantics for RTPA.

Variables and Values in RTPA

A specific value domain is needed for each type of variables, which is called the logical value domain in order to distinguish from the domain $\mathbb{V}$. Typical value domains are as follows:

$\mathbb{B}$ - Boolean values, $\mathbb{B} = \{true, false, \perp\}$.
$\mathbb{N}$ - Natural numbers with bottom $\perp$.
$\mathbb{R}$ - Real numbers with bottom $\perp$.
$\mathbb{E}$ - Values for event variables, $\mathbb{E} = \{event, reset, \perp\}$.
$\mathbb{PT}$ - Values for pointer variables.
$\mathbb{O}$ - Values for pointer associated variables.
$\mathbb{V}$ - Domain of all possible values of all variables.
$$\mathbb{V} = \mathbb{B} + \mathbb{N} + \mathbb{R} + \mathbb{E} + \mathbb{PT} + \mathbb{O} \tag{22}$$

Therefore, the domain $\mathbb{V}$ is a sum of different logical domains (Winskel, 1993). It easily can be understood from the context which value domains are in use. Therefore, we do not need to explicitly present the values in $\mathbb{V}$ in domain sum format as a pair of an index in the sum and a value of the corresponding value domains.

Process Executions in RTPA

A temporal ordered duration sequence can be considered as a denotation of one possible execution path of a process, or a specific computation. All the specified computations performed by a process describe its behaviors as the semantics of the process.

A set $\mathbb{PC} \subseteq \mathbb{C}$ is called a prefix closure if it satisfies:

1    $<> \in \mathbb{PC}$, and
2. $c_1 {}^\wedge c_2 \in \mathbb{PC} \Rightarrow c_1 \in \mathbb{PC}.$ \hfill (23)

$\mathbb{COM}$ denotes all prefix closures with set inclusion relation $\subseteq$, which has the bottom $<>$ and close at operation $\cup$.

The semantics of both expressions and processes can be described by three semantic functions, which specify what values in the domain $\mathbb{V}$ serve as the denotations for expressions and which objects in the domain $\mathbb{COM}$ serve as the denotations for processes. The semantic function for Boolean expressions is treated separately from the general expression evaluation function, because it is used quite often in the semantic definitions.

The Boolean expression evaluation function $\mathcal{B}$ evaluates logical expressions to Boolean values.

$$\mathcal{B} : \mathbb{EXP} \rightarrow \mathbb{EN} \rightarrow \mathbb{B} \tag{24}$$

The general expression evaluation function $\mathcal{E}$ evaluates all kinds of expressions to its values in $\mathbb{V}$, that is:

$\mathcal{E} : \text{EXP} \to \text{EN} \to \text{V}$

$\mathcal{E}[\![\, x\mathbb{T} \,]\!] \, (\rho) = \rho(x);$

$\mathcal{E}[\![\, e \,]\!] \, (\rho)$ follows the traditional convention if
     e is regular expression, such as arithmetic,
     Boolean, relational expression, etc;

$\mathcal{E}[\![\, \text{MEM}(\text{ptr}\mathbf{P})\mathbb{T} \,]\!] \, (\rho)$ gives an object of type $\mathbb{T}$
     located at the MEM position where a ptr
     points to;

$\mathcal{E}[\![\, \text{PORT}(\text{ptr}\mathbf{P})\mathbb{T} \,]\!] \, (\rho)$ gives an object of type $\mathbb{T}$
     located at the PORT pointed to by ptr;

$\mathcal{E}[\![\, \S t\mathbf{TM} \,]\!] \, (\rho) = \rho(\S t)$, the system time is
     determined by durations, for a given duration
     d, $\rho(\S t) = begin(d)$, which will be discussed in the following section;

$\mathcal{E}[\![\, \S T\mathbf{TM} + \Delta n\mathbf{N} \,]\!] \, (\rho) = \rho(\S t) + \rho(n).$ \hfill (25)

THE DENOTATIONAL SEMANTIC FUNCTIONS OF RTPA META PROCESSES

This section presents the denotational semantic functions of the 17 RTPA meta processes.

A process function describes what the behaviors are when a process runs under a given environment, that is:

$$\mathcal{C} : \mathbb{P} \to \text{EN} \to \text{COM} \tag{26}$$

where $\mathbb{P} \to \text{EN} \to \text{COM}$ is a function space as proposed in (Winskel, 1993). The operator $\to$ is right-associative, which means $\mathbb{P} \to \text{EN} \to \text{COM}$ is an abbreviation of $\mathbb{P} \to (\text{EN} \to \text{COM})$. Therefore, $\mathcal{C}$ is a high order function, which returns a function of type $\text{EN} \to \text{COM}$ as the result.

The semantic functions of RTPA processes are defined deductively on different process syntactic formations below:

1. **The assignment process:** The semantic function of the assignment process in RTPA is specified as follows:

$$\mathcal{C}[\![\, x\mathbb{T}\!:=\!e\mathbb{T} \,]\!] \, (\rho) \triangleq \{<(i, \rho\dagger[x \mapsto \mathcal{E}[\![\, e \,]\!] \, (\rho)])> |$$
$$\exists \, n \in \mathbb{N} \bullet i = [n, n{+}1]\} \tag{27}$$

The assignment process changes the value of the left-side variable of the assignment.

2. **The evaluation process:** The semantic function of the evaluation process in RTPA is specified as follows:

$$\mathcal{C}[\![\, \blacklozenge e\mathbf{BL} \,]\!] \, (\rho) \triangleq \{<(i, \rho\dagger[r \mapsto \mathcal{E}[\![\, e\mathbf{BL} \,]\!] \, (\rho)])> |$$
$$r \in \text{EN'} \wedge \exists \, n \in \mathbb{N} \bullet i = [n, n{+}1]\} \tag{28}$$

where $\mathbb{EN}$' is the system's environment, and the evaluation result r is set to true or false based on $\mathcal{E}[\![e\mathbf{BL}]\!](\rho)$.

3. **The addressing process:** The semantic function of the addressing process in RTPA is specified as follows.

$$
\begin{aligned}
\mathcal{C}[\![id\mathbf{S}{\rightarrow}MEM(ptr\mathbf{P})\mathbb{T}]\!](\rho) &\triangleq \\
&\{<(i, \rho\dagger[id \mapsto \mathcal{E}[\![MEM(ptr\mathbf{P})\mathbb{T}]\!](\rho)])> \mid \\
&\exists\, n \in \mathbb{N} \bullet i = [n, n{+}1)\}
\end{aligned}
\tag{29}
$$

The addressing process lets id associate to the object of type $\mathbb{T}$ located at the MEM position where ptr points to.

4. **The memory allocation process:** The semantic function of the memory allocation process in RTPA is specified as follows:

$$
\begin{aligned}
\mathcal{C}[\![id\mathbf{S}{\Leftarrow}MEM(ptr\mathbf{P})\mathbb{T}]\!](\rho) &\triangleq \{<(i, \rho_2)> \mid \\
&\exists\, n \in \mathbb{N} \bullet i = [n, n{+}1) \wedge \\
&\rho_1 = \rho\dagger[ptr \mapsto \mathcal{E}[\![MEM()\mathbb{T}]\!](\rho)] \wedge \\
&\rho_2 = \rho_1\dagger[id \mapsto \mathcal{E}[\![MEM(ptr\mathbf{P})\mathbb{T}]\!](\rho_1)]\}
\end{aligned}
\tag{30}
$$

The memory allocation process allocates memory for an object of type $\mathbb{T}$ identified by id with the address of ptr.

5. **The memory release process:** The semantic function of the memory release process in RTPA is specified as follows.

$$
\begin{aligned}
\mathcal{C}[\![id\mathbf{S}{\Leftarrow}MEM(\bot)\mathbb{T}]\!](\rho) &\triangleq \{<(i, \rho\dagger[ptr \mapsto \bot, id \mapsto \bot])> \mid \\
&\exists\, n \in \mathbb{N} \bullet i = [n, n{+}1) \}
\end{aligned}
\tag{31}
$$

The memory release process releases the memory for the object identified by id, and as a result, id points to $\bot$.

6. **The Read Process:** The semantic function of the read process in RTPA is specified as follows:

$$
\begin{aligned}
\mathcal{C}[\![MEM(ptr\mathbf{P})\mathbb{T}{\triangleright}x\mathbb{T}]\!](\rho) &\triangleq \\
&\{<(i, \rho\dagger[x \mapsto \mathcal{E}[\![MEM(ptr\mathbf{P})\mathbb{T}]\!](\rho)])> \mid \\
&\exists\, n \in \mathbb{N} \bullet i = [n, n{+}1)\}
\end{aligned}
\tag{32}
$$

The read process reads a object prescribed by $\mathcal{E}[\![MEM(ptr\mathbf{P})\mathbb{T}]\!](\rho)$ into variable x.

7. **The write process:** The semantic function of the write process in RTPA is specified as follows:

$$
\mathcal{C}[\![x\mathbb{T}{<}MEM(ptrP)\mathbb{T}]\!](\rho) \triangleq \{<(i, \rho\dagger[addr \mapsto \rho(x)])> \mid addr \in \mathbb{EN}\text{'} \wedge \exists\, n \in \mathbb{N} \bullet i = [n, n{+}1)\}
\tag{33}
$$

The write process writes the value of x into the object prescribed by addr = $\mathcal{E}[\![MEM(ptrP)\mathbb{T}]\!](\rho)$.

8. **The input process:** The semantic function of the input process in RTPA is specified as follows:

$$\mathcal{C} \llbracket \text{PORT}(\text{ptr}\mathbf{P})\mathbb{T}|\!\!>\!x\mathbb{T} \rrbracket (\rho) \triangleq$$
$$\{<(i, \rho\dagger[x \mapsto \mathcal{E} \llbracket \text{PORT}(\text{ptr}\mathbf{P})\mathbb{T} \rrbracket (\rho)])> \mid$$
$$\exists\, n \in \mathbb{N} \bullet i = [n, n+1)\} \tag{34}$$

The input process reads a object prescribed by $\mathcal{E} \llbracket \text{PORT}(\text{ptr}\mathbf{P})\mathbb{T} \rrbracket (\rho)$ into variable x.

9. **The output process:** The semantic function of the output process in RTPA is specified as follows:

$$\mathcal{C} \llbracket x\mathbb{T}|\!\!<\!\text{PORT}(\text{ptr}\mathbf{P})\mathbb{T} \rrbracket (\rho) \triangleq \{<(i, \rho\dagger[\text{addr} \mapsto \rho(x)])> \mid$$
$$\text{addr} \in \mathbb{EN}' \wedge \exists\, n \in \mathbb{N} \bullet i = [n, n+1)\} \tag{35}$$

The output process outputs the value of x to the object prescribed by $\text{addr} = \mathcal{E} \llbracket \text{PORT}(\text{ptr}\mathbf{P})\mathbb{T} \rrbracket (\rho)$.

10. **The timing process:** The semantic function of the timing process in RTPA is specified as follows:

$$\mathcal{C} \llbracket @t\mathbf{TM} \overset{@}{=} \S t\mathbf{TM} \rrbracket (\rho) \triangleq \{<(i, \rho\dagger[t \mapsto \mathcal{E} \llbracket \S t\mathbf{TM} \rrbracket (\rho)])> \mid$$
$$\exists\, n \in \mathbb{N} \bullet i = [n, n+1)\} \tag{36}$$

The timing process sets the value of variable t to the system time.

11. **The duration process:** The semantic function of the duration process in RTPA is specified as follows:

$$\mathcal{C} \llbracket @t\mathbf{TM} \triangleq \S t\mathbf{TM} + \Delta n\mathbf{N} \rrbracket (\rho) \triangleq \{<(i, \rho\dagger[t \mapsto$$
$$\mathcal{E} \llbracket \S t\mathbf{TM} + \Delta n\mathbf{N} \rrbracket (\rho)])> \mid \exists\, m \in \mathbb{N} \bullet i =$$
$$[m, m+\rho(n))\} \tag{37}$$

The system time is specified by the intervals in the temporal ordered duration sequences. The value of t is the start of the interval plus the increment. Hence, for a duration $<([a, b), \rho\dagger[t \mapsto \mathcal{E} \llbracket \S t\mathbf{TM} + \Delta n\mathbf{N} \rrbracket (\rho)])>$, the system time $\S t$ is the beginning of the interval and t will be eventually evaluated to $a + \rho(n) = begin([a, b)) + \rho(n))$.

12. **The increase process:** The semantic function of the increase process in RTPA is specified as follows:

$$\mathcal{C} \llbracket (n\mathbf{N}) \rrbracket (\rho) \triangleq \{<(i, \rho\dagger[n \mapsto \mathcal{E} \llbracket n+1 \rrbracket (\rho)])> \mid$$
$$\exists\, m \in \mathbb{N} \bullet i = [m, m+1)\} \tag{38}$$

The increase process adds one to the value of variable n.

13. **The decrease process:** The semantic function of the decrease process in RTPA is specified as follows:

$$\mathcal{C} \llbracket \uparrow(n\mathbf{N}) \rrbracket (\rho) \triangleq \{<(i, \rho\dagger[n \mapsto \mathcal{E} \llbracket n-1 \rrbracket (\rho)])> \mid$$
$$\exists\, m \in \mathbb{N} \bullet i = [m, m+1)\} \tag{39}$$

The decrease process subtracts one from the value of variable n.

14. **The exception detection process:** The semantic function of the exception detection process in RTPA is specified as follows:

$$\mathcal{C}[\![!(@e\mathbf{S})]\!](\rho) \triangleq \{<(i, \rho\dagger[addr \mapsto \rho(e)])> \mid$$
$$addr \in \mathbb{EN}' \land \exists\, n \in \mathbb{N} \bullet i = [n, n+1]\} \tag{40}$$

The exception detection process is a special output process where its contents are warning messages in string type and its port is the standard system device such as CRT or printer.

15. **The skip process:** The semantic function of the skip process in RTPA is specified as follows:

$$\mathcal{C}[\![\otimes]\!](\rho) \triangleq \{<(i, \rho\dagger[r \mapsto \mathcal{E}[\![\otimes]\!](\rho)])>$$
$$\mid r \in \mathbb{EN}' \land \exists\, n \in \mathbb{N} \bullet i = [n, n+1]\} \tag{41}$$

where the skip process results in a new executing address r, which replaces the usual system dispatching mechanism, that is, r = r+1.

16. **The stop process:** The semantic function of the stop process in RTPA is specified as follows:

$$\mathcal{C}[\![\boxtimes]\!](\rho) \triangleq \bigcup_{k=1}^{\infty} \{<(i, \rho)> \mid \exists\, n \in \mathbb{N} \bullet i = [n, n+k]\} \tag{42}$$

It indicates that no activities can be observed from the stop process, but the semantic environment keeps the same as that of the duration before the stop process.

17. **The system process:** The semantic function of the system process in RTPA is specified as follows:

$$\mathcal{C}[\![\S(id\mathbf{S})]\!](\rho) \triangleq \{<(i, \rho\dagger[id \mapsto \bot])> \mid \exists\, n \in \mathbb{N} \bullet i = [n, n+1]\} \tag{43}$$

The system process returns the control back to the host system, such as an operating system, so the application identified by an id is released.

THE DENOTATIONAL SEMANTIC FUNCTIONS OF RTPA PROCESS RELATIONS

This section presents the denotational semantic functions of the 17 RTPA process relations.

1. **The sequential process:** The semantic function of the sequential process relation in RTPA is specified as follows:

$$\mathcal{C}[\![P \rightarrow Q]\!](\rho) \triangleq \{c_1 \rightsquigarrow c_2 \mid$$
$$c_1 \in \mathcal{C}[\![P]\!](\rho) \land c_2 \in \mathcal{C}[\![Q]\!](env(back(c_1)))\} \tag{44}$$

It is noteworthy that the system time accumulates as temporal ordered duration sequences extend. By introducing the follow operator, as shown in Equation 45, the sequential process relation can be defined as shown in Equation 46.

$$; : (\mathbb{EN} \rightarrow \mathbb{COM})^2 \rightarrow \mathbb{EN} \rightarrow \mathbb{COM}$$

$$(f;g)(\rho) = \{ c_1 \rightsquigarrow c_2 \mid c_1 \in f(\rho) \wedge c_2 \in g(env(back(c_1))) \} \tag{45}$$

where $(\mathbb{EN} \rightarrow \mathbb{COM})^2$ is an abbreviation of $(\mathbb{EN} \rightarrow \mathbb{COM}) \times (\mathbb{EN} \rightarrow \mathbb{COM})$.

$$\mathcal{C} \llbracket P \rightarrow Q \rrbracket (\rho) \triangleq (\mathcal{C} \llbracket P \rrbracket ; \mathcal{C} \llbracket Q \rrbracket)(\rho) \tag{46}$$

2. **The jump process:** The semantic function of the jump process relation in RTPA is specified as follows:

$$\mathcal{C} \llbracket P \curvearrowright Q \rrbracket (\rho) \triangleq \{ c \mid \exists n \in \mathbb{N} \bullet$$
$$(c \triangleleft n) \in \mathcal{C} \llbracket P \rrbracket (\rho) \wedge (c \triangleright n) \in$$
$$\mathcal{C} \llbracket Q \rrbracket (env(back(c \triangleleft n))) \} \tag{47}$$

The definition shows that the execution control transfers from process P to process Q.

3. **The branch process:** In order to define the semantics of the branch process, the condition operator is introduced first.

cond :
$$(\mathbb{EN} \rightarrow \mathbb{B}) \times (\mathbb{EN} \rightarrow \mathbb{COM})^2 \rightarrow \mathbb{EN} \rightarrow \mathbb{COM}$$
$$cond(b, f, g)(\rho) = f(\rho), b(\rho) = true;$$
$$cond(b, f, g)(\rho) = g(\rho), \qquad b(\rho) = false;$$
$$cond(b, f, g)(\rho) = \{<>\}, b(\rho) = \bot. \tag{48}$$

The semantic function of the branch process relation in RTPA is specified as follows:

$$\mathcal{C} \llbracket \blacklozenge e\mathbf{BL=T} \rightarrow P \mid \blacklozenge \sim \rightarrow Q \rrbracket (\rho) \triangleq$$
$$cond(\mathcal{B} \llbracket e \rrbracket, \mathcal{C} \llbracket P \rrbracket, \mathcal{C} \llbracket Q \rrbracket)(\rho) \tag{49}$$

4. **The switch process:** The semantic function of the switch process relation in RTPA is specified as follows:

$$\mathcal{C} \llbracket \blacklozenge e\mathbf{N}=1 \rightarrow P_1 \mid 2 \rightarrow P_2 \mid \ldots \mid \sim \rightarrow Q \rrbracket (\rho) \triangleq$$

$$\mathcal{C} \llbracket Q \rrbracket (\rho) \cup \bigcup_{k=1}^{n} cond(\mathcal{B} \llbracket e=k \rrbracket, \mathcal{C} \llbracket P_k \rrbracket, \mathcal{C} \llbracket \varnothing \rrbracket)(\rho) \tag{50}$$

The definition shows that if expression e is evaluated to be k, process P_k will be executed; otherwise process Q will be executed as default.

5. **The while-loop process:** With the condition and follow operators, the semantic function of the while-loop process relation in RTPA can be described recursively as follows:

$$\mathcal{C} \llbracket \underset{e=T}{\overset{F}{R}}(P) \rrbracket (\rho) \triangleq cond(\mathcal{B} \llbracket e \rrbracket, \mathcal{C} \llbracket P \rrbracket ; \mathcal{C} \llbracket \underset{e=T}{\overset{F}{R}}(P) \rrbracket, \mathcal{C} \llbracket \varnothing \rrbracket)(\rho) \tag{51}$$

Since it is a recursive definition, the least fixed point operator *fix* is used to define the semantics (Winskel, 1993):

$$W : (\mathbb{EN} \to \mathbb{COM}) \to \mathbb{EN} \to \mathbb{COM}$$
$$W(\theta) = cond(\mathcal{B}\,[\![\,e\,]\!]\,, \mathcal{C}\,[\![\,P\,]\!]\,;\theta, \mathcal{C}\,[\![\,\varnothing\,]\!]\,)$$
$$\mathcal{C}\,[\![\,\underset{e=T}{\overset{F}{R}}(P)\,]\!]\,(\rho) \triangleq fix(W)(\rho) \tag{52}$$

The use of the least fixed point operator can be justified by the fact that all functions over $\mathbb{EN} \to \mathbb{COM}$ defined here are continuous functions.

6. **The repeat-loop process:** The semantic function of the repeat-loop process relation in RTPA is specified as follows:

$$\mathcal{C}\,[\![\,P \to \underset{e=T}{\overset{F}{R}}(P)\,]\!]\,(\rho) \triangleq (\mathcal{C}\,[\![\,P\,]\!]\,; \mathcal{C}\,[\![\,\underset{e=T}{\overset{F}{R}}(P)\,]\!]\,)(\rho) \tag{53}$$

It shows that the loop of process P will be carried out at least once.

7. **The for-loop process:** The semantic function of the for-loop process relation in RTPA is specified as follows:

$$\mathcal{C}\,[\![\,\overset{n}{\underset{i=1}{R}}(P)\,]\!]\,(\rho) \triangleq fix(W)(\rho)$$
$$W : (\mathbb{EN} \to \mathbb{COM}) \to \mathbb{EN} \to \mathbb{COM}$$
$$W(\theta) = cond(\mathcal{B}\,[\![\,i \leqslant n\,]\!]\,, \mathcal{C}\,[\![\,P\,]\!]\,;\theta, \mathcal{C}\,[\![\,\varnothing\,]\!]\,) \tag{54}$$

The for-loop process is similar to the while-loop process, only using a more specific condition $i \leqslant n$.

8. **The recursion process:** The semantic function of the recursion process relation in RTPA is specified as follows:

$$\mathcal{C}\,[\![\,P \circlearrowright P\,]\!]\,(\rho) \triangleq fix(W)(\rho$$
$$W : (\mathbb{EN} \to \mathbb{COM}) \to \mathbb{EN} \to \mathbb{COM}$$
$$W(\theta) = \mathcal{C}\,[\![\,P\,]\!]\,;\theta \tag{55}$$

Similarly, the technique for defining recursion is used.

9. **The function call process:** The semantic function of the function call process relation in RTPA is specified as follows:

$$\mathcal{C}\,[\![\,P \rightarrowtail Q\,]\!]\,(\rho) \triangleq \{\,c \mid \exists\, n_1, n_2 \in \mathbb{N} \bullet$$
$$n_1 < n_2 \wedge (c \triangleleft n_1) \in \mathcal{C}\,[\![\,P\,]\!]\,(\rho) \wedge$$
$$((c \triangleleft n_2) \triangleright n_1) \in \mathcal{C}\,[\![\,Q\,]\!]\,(env(back(c \triangleleft n_1))) \wedge$$
$$(c \triangleright n_2) \in \mathcal{C}\,[\![\,P\,]\!]\,(\,env(back((c \triangleleft n_2) \triangleright n_1)))\,\} \tag{56}$$

The definition shows the execution control will return to process P after process Q is completed.

10. **The parallel process:** The semantic function of the parallel process relation in RTPA is specified as follows:

$$\mathcal{C}\,[\![\,P\|Q\,]\!]\,(\rho) \triangleq \{c \mid \exists\, n \in \mathbb{N} \bullet c \lhd n \in \mathcal{C}\,[\![\,P\,]\!]\,(\rho) \wedge$$
$$c \in \mathcal{C}\,[\![\,Q\,]\!]\,(\rho) \vee c \in \mathcal{C}\,[\![\,P\,]\!]\,(\rho) \wedge c \lhd n \in \mathcal{C}\,[\![\,Q\,]\!]\,(\rho)\} \tag{57}$$

The parallel process models the single-clock multi-processor (SCMP) mechanism for the semantic environment.

11. **The concurrent process:** The semantic function of the concurrent process relation in RTPA is specified as follows:

$$\mathcal{C}\,[\![\,P\math{\ooalign{\hfil f\hfil\cr\hfil f\hfil}}Q\,]\!]\,(\rho) \triangleq \{c \mid \exists\, n \in \mathbb{N} \bullet c \lhd n \in \mathcal{C}\,[\![\,P\,]\!]\,(\rho) \wedge$$
$$c \in \mathcal{C}\,[\![\,Q\,]\!]\,(\rho) \vee c \in \mathcal{C}\,[\![\,P\,]\!]\,(\rho) \wedge c \lhd n \in \mathcal{C}\,[\![\,Q\,]\!]\,(\rho)\} \tag{58}$$

The concurrent process models the multi-clock multi-processor (MCMP) mechanism for the semantic environment.

12. **The interleave process:** The semantic function of the interleave process relation in RTPA is specified as follows:

$$\mathcal{C}\,[\![\,P\|\|Q\,]\!]\,(\rho) \triangleq \{c \mid \exists\, n \in \mathbb{N} \bullet c \lhd n \in \mathcal{C}\,[\![\,P\,]\!]\,(\rho) \wedge$$
$$c \in \mathcal{C}\,[\![\,Q\,]\!]\,(\rho) \vee c \in \mathcal{C}\,[\![\,P\,]\!]\,(\rho) \wedge c \lhd n \in \mathcal{C}\,[\![\,Q\,]\!]\,(\rho)\,\} \tag{59}$$

The parallel process models the single-clock single-processor (SCSP) mechanism for the semantic environment.

13. **The pipeline process:** The semantic function of the pipeline process relation in RTPA is specified as follows:

$$\mathcal{C}\,[\![\,P\gg Q\,]\!]\,(\rho) \triangleq \{c \mid \exists\, n \in \mathbb{N} \bullet c \lhd n \in \mathcal{C}\,[\![\,P\,]\!]\,(\rho) \wedge$$
$$c \in \mathcal{C}\,[\![\,Q\,]\!]\,(\rho) \vee c \in \mathcal{C}\,[\![\,P\,]\!]\,(\rho) \wedge c \lhd n \in \mathcal{C}\,[\![\,Q\,]\!]\,(\rho)\,\} \tag{60}$$

In the pipeline process, process P and Q run concurrently while the outputs of process P should be the inputs of process Q. However, the input/output relation can be checked statically.

14. **The interrupt process:** The semantic function of the interrupt process relation in RTPA is specified as follows.

$$\mathcal{C}\,[\![\,P\,\text{\textdownarrow}\,Q\,]\!]\,(\rho) \triangleq \{\, c \mid \exists\, n_1, n_2 \in \mathbb{N} \bullet n_1 \leq n_2 \wedge$$
$$(c \lhd n_1) \rightsquigarrow (c \rhd n_2) \in \mathcal{C}\,[\![\,P\,]\!]\,(\rho) \wedge ((c \lhd n_2) \rhd n_1) -$$
$$n_1 \in \mathcal{C}\,[\![\,Q\,]\!]\,(env(back(c \lhd n_1)))\} \tag{61}$$

The above definition shows that process P is exempted by process Q at the time point n1 and resumes execution after Q ends at the time point n2.

15. **The time-driven dispatch process:** The semantic function of the time-driven process relation in RTPA is specified as follows.

$$\mathcal{C}\,[\![\,@t\mathbf{TM}\text{\textdownarrow}P\,]\!]\,(\rho) \triangleq \{\, c_1 \rightsquigarrow c_2 \mid \exists\, n \in \mathbb{N} \bullet$$
$$c_1 \in \bigcup_{k=1}^{\rho(t)} \{<([n, n+k), \rho)>\} \wedge$$

$$c_2 \in \mathcal{C}[\![P]\!] \, (env(back(c_1)))\} \tag{62}$$

The above definition shows that the time-driven process will wait, which means keep the semantic environment unchanged, until the timeout to perform process P. Then, multi-processes wait on different timeouts becomes:

$$\mathcal{C}[\![@t_1\mathbf{TM} \hookrightarrow P_1| \, t_2\mathbf{TM} \hookrightarrow P_2|\ldots| \, t_n\mathbf{TM} \hookrightarrow P_n]\!] \, (\rho) \triangleq \\ \bigcup_{k=1} \mathcal{C}[\![@t_k\mathbf{TM} \hookrightarrow P_k]\!] \, (\rho) \tag{63}$$

16. **The event-driven dispatch process:** The semantic function of the event-driven process relation in RTPA is specified as follows:

$$\mathcal{C}[\![@e\mathbf{S} \hookrightarrow P]\!] \, (\rho) \triangleq (\mathcal{C}[\![!(@e\mathbf{S})]\!] \, ; \mathcal{C}[\![P]\!]) (\rho) \tag{64}$$

The above definition indicates that, after the occurrence of event @e captured by the system, P is executed. Then, the waiting on multiple events becomes:

$$\mathcal{C}[\![@e_1\mathbf{S} \hookrightarrow P_1| \, e_2\mathbf{S} \hookrightarrow P_2|\ldots| \, e_n\mathbf{S} \hookrightarrow P_n]\!] \, (\rho) \triangleq \\ \bigcup_{k=1}^{n} \mathcal{C}[\![@e_k\mathbf{S} \hookrightarrow P_k]\!] \, (\rho) \tag{65}$$

17. **The interrupt-driven process:** The semantic function of the interrupt-driven process relation in RTPA is specified as follows.

$$\mathcal{C}[\![@i\odot \hookrightarrow P]\!] \, (\rho) \triangleq (\mathcal{C}[\![!(@i\odot)]\!] \, ; \mathcal{C}[\![P]\!]) (\rho) \tag{66}$$

It is noteworthy that an interrupt is considered as a special kind of events in the semantics of RTPA, where the interrupt variables are defined in the system's environment $\mathbb{EN}$' and they are transparent to the environment of applications.

CONCLUSION

The denotational semantics of RTPA has been elaborated on the basis of the temporal ordered duration sequences. According to the denotational semantics of RTPA, instantaneous behaviors of processes at a given time moment have been captured by the changes of the environment. This work has provided a formal model for denoting the semantics of both concurrent and sequential processes required by RTPA in the denotational approach. An RTPA type checker and an RTPA code generator have been developed based on the formal models of deductive, denotational, and operational semantics. The denotational semantics for RTPA can be used as rules for correctness checking and system verification in system design and modeling using RTPA.

The denotational semantic framework is still not powerful enough to express some powerful features of RTPA processes. The denotational semantics of RTPA at the program level where multiple processes are composed to describe the architectures and behaviors of a given system needs to be studied further. The latest development on the *deductive semantics* of RTPA (Wang, 2006a, 2008b) and the *mathematic laws* of RTPA (Wang, 2008d) has addressed the above problems with more rigorous treatment. A comparative analysis of a set of comprehensive formal semantics for RTPA has been carried out (Wang, 2007a). The deductive semantics of RTPA is presented in (Wang, 2008b). The operational semantics of RTPA is reported in (Wang & Ngolah, 2008). RTPA has been used not only in software system specifications, but also in human and intelligent system modeling (Wang, 2007b, 2007c). The formal semantics of RTPA has helped to the comprehension and understanding of the RTPA syntactical and semantic rules as well as its expressive power in software engineering, cognitive informatics, and computational intelligence.

ACKNOWLEDGMENT

The authors would like to acknowledge the Natural Science and Engineering Council of Canada (NSERC) for its partial support to this work. We would like to thank the anonymous reviewers for their valuable comments and suggestions.

REFERENCES

Baeten, J.C.M. & Bergstra, J.A. (1991). Real time process algebra. *Formal Aspects of Computing, 3,* 142-188.

Boucher, A. & Gerth, R. (1987). A timed model for extended communicating sequential processes. *Proceedings of ICALP'87*, Springer LNCS 267.

Corsetti E., Montanari, A., & Ratto, E. (1991). Dealing with different time granularities in formal specifications of real-time systems. *The Journal of Real-Time Systems, 3*(2), 191-215.

Dierks, H. (2000). A process algebra for real-time programs. *LNCS #1783*, Springer, Berlin, pp. 66-76.

Fecher, H. (2001). A real-time process algebra with open intervals and maximal progress. *Nordic Journal of Computing, 8*(3), 346-360.

Hoare, C.A.R. (1978). Communicating sequential processes. *Communications of the ACM, 21*(8), 666-677.

Hoare, C.A.R. (1985). *Communicating sequential processes.* London: Prentice-Hall International.

Louden K.C. (1993). *Programming languages: Principles and practice.* Boston: PWS-Kent Publishing Co.

McDermid, J. (Ed.) (1991). *Software engineer's reference book.* Oxford, UK: Butterworth Heinemann Ltd.

Milner, R. (1980). *A calculus of communicating systems.* LNCS #92, Springer-Verlag.

RAISE (1992). *The RAISE specification language.* London: Prentice Hall.

Schneider, S. (1995). An operational semantics for timed CSP. *Information and Computation, 116*(2), 193-213.

Schneider, S. (2000). *Concurrent and real-time systems: The CSP approach*. Wiley.

Tan, X. (2006). Toward automatic code generation based on real-time process algebra (RTPA). PhD Thesis, University of Calgary, Canada.

Tan, X., Wang, Y. & Ngolah, C.F. (2004). Specification of the RTPA grammar and its recognition. *Proceedings of the 2004 IEEE International Conference on Cognitive Informatics (ICCI'04)*, IEEE CS Press, Victoria, Canada, August, pp. 54-63.

Wang, Y. (2002). The real-time process algebra (RTPA). *Annals of Software Engineering: A International Journal, 14*, 235-274.

Wang, Y. (2003). Using process algebra to describe human and software system behaviors. *Brain and Mind, 4*(2), 199–213.

Wang, Y. (2006a). On the informatics laws and deductive semantics of software. *IEEE Transactions on Systems, Man, and Cybernetics (C), 36*(2), 161-171.

Wang, Y. (2006b). Cognitive informatics and contemporary mathematics for knowledge representation and manipulation, invited plenary talk. *Proceedings of the 1st International Conference on Rough Set and Knowledge Technology* (RSKT'06), LNAI #4062, Springer, Chongqing, China, July, pp. 69-78.

Wang, Y. (2007a). *Software engineering foundations: A software science perspective*. New York: Auerbach Publications.

Wang, Y. (2007b). The theoretical framework of cognitive informatics. *International Journal of Cognitive Informatics and Natural Intelligence* (IJCINI), *1*(1), 1-27.

Wang, Y. (2007c). On theoretical foundations of software engineering and denotational mathematics, keynote speech. *Proceedings of the 5th Asian Workshop on Foundations of Software*, BHU Press, Xiamen, China, pp. 99-102.

Wang, Y. (2008a). RTPA: A denotational mathematics for manipulating intelligent and computational behaviors. *International Journal of Cognitive Informatics and Natural Intelligence* (IJCINI), *2*(2), 44-62.

Wang, Y. (2008b). Deductive semantics of RTPA. *International Journal of Cognitive Informatics and Natural Intelligence* (IJCINI), *2*(2), 95-121.

Wang, Y. (2008c). On the Big-R notation for describing iterative and recursive behaviors. *International Journal of Cognitive Informatics and Natural Intelligence* (IJCINI), *2*(1), 17-28.

Wang, Y. (2008d). Mathematical laws of software. *Transactions of Computational Science, 2*(2).

Wang, Y. & Ngolah, C.F. (2008). An operational semantics of real-time process algebra (RTPA). *International Journal of Cognitive Informatics and Natural Intelligence* (IJCINI), *2*(3), July.

Winskel, G. (1993). *The formal semantics of programming languages*. MIT Press.

This work was previously published in International Journal of Cognitive Informatics and Natural Intelligence, Vol. 2, Issue 3, edited by Y. Wang, pp. 57-70, copyright 2008 by IGI Publishing (an imprint of IGI Global).

Chapter 12
An Operational Semantics of Real-Time Process Algebra (RTPA)

Yingxu Wang
University of Calgary, Canada

Cyprian F. Ngolah
University of Calgary, Canada &
University of Buea, Republic of Cameroon

ABSTRACT

The need for new forms of mathematics to express software engineering concepts and entities has been widely recognized. Real-time process algebra (RTPA) is a denotational mathematical structure and a system modeling methodology for describing the architectures and behaviors of real-time and nonreal-time software systems. This article presents an operational semantics of RTPA, which explains how syntactic constructs in RTPA can be reduced to values on an abstract reduction machine. The operational semantics of RTPA provides a comprehensive paradigm of formal semantics that establishes an entire set of operational semantic rules of software. RTPA has been successfully applied in real-world system modeling and code generation for software systems, human cognitive processes, and intelligent systems.

INTRODUCTION

Real-time process algebra (RTPA) is a denotational mathematical structure and a system modeling methodology for describing the architectures and behaviors of real-time and nonreal-time software systems (Wang, 2002, 2003, 2006a, 2006b, 2007a, 2008a-c). RTPA provides a coherent notation system and a rigorous mathematical structure for modeling software and intelligent systems. RTPA can be used to describe both *logical* and *physical* models of systems, where logic views of the architecture of a software system and its operational platform can be described using the same set of notations. When the system architecture is formally modelled, the static and dynamic behaviors that perform on the system architectural model, can be specified by a three-level refinement scheme at the system, class, and object levels in a top-down approach. Although CSP (Hoare, 1978, 1985), the timed CSP (Boucher & Gerth, 1987; Fecher, 2001; Nicollin & Sifakis, 1991), and other process algebra (Baeten & Bergstra, 1991; Milner, 1980, 1989) treated a computational operation as a process, RTPA distinguishes the concepts of meta processes from complex and derived processes by algebraic process operations.

Definition 1: *Operational semantics of a programming language or a formal notation system is the semantics perceived on a given virtual machine, known as the abstract reduction machine, that denotes the semantics of programs or formal system models by its equivalent behaviors implemented on the reduction machine.*

One way to define an operational semantics for a language or formal notation system is to provide a state transition system for the language, which allows a formal analysis of the language and permits the study of relations between programs (Jones, 2003; Plotkin, 1981; Schneider, 1995). An alternative way is to describe the operations of the language on an abstract deductive machine whose operations are precisely defined (Sloneger & Barry, 1995; Winskel, 1993). In operational semantics, the reduction machine is a virtual machine that is adopted for reducing a given program to values of identifiers modeled in the machine by a finite set of permissible operations (Louden, 1993; McDermid, 1995).

This article presents a comprehensive operational semantics for RTPA on the basis of an abstract reduction machine, which defines inference rules for repetitively reducing a system model in RTPA into the computational values of identifiers and data objects. The abstract syntaxes of RTPA are introduced, and the reduction machine of RTPA is elaborated. Based on these, the operational semantics of 17 RTPA meta processes and 17 RTPA process relations are systematically developed. A comparative analysis of a set of comprehensive formal semantics for RTPA may be referred to (Wang, 2007a). The *deductive semantics* of RTPA is presented in Wang (2006a, 2008b). The *denotational semantics* of RTPA is reported in Tan and Wang (2008).

THE ABSTRACT SYNTAX OF RTPA

On the basis of the process metaphor of software systems, abstract processes can be rigorously treated as a mathematical entity beyond sets, relations, functions, and abstract concepts. RTPA is a denotational mathematical structure for denoting and manipulating system behavioral processes (Wang, 2002, 2003, 2006a, 2006b, 2008a-c). RTPA is designed as a coherent algebraic system for software and intelligent system modeling, specification, refinement, and implementation. RTPA encompasses 17 meta processes and 17 relational process operations.

Definition 2: *RTPA is a denotational mathematical structure for algebraically denoting and manipulating system behavioural processes and their attributes by a triple, that is:*

Table 1. The meta processes of RTPA

No.	Meta Process	Notation	Syntax
1	Assignment	:=	$y\mathbb{T} := exp\mathbb{T}$
2	Evaluation	◆	$◆_\pi exp\mathbb{T} \to \mathbb{T}$
3	Addressing	⇒	$id\mathbb{T} \Rightarrow \mathrm{MEM}[ptr\mathbf{P}]\ \mathbb{T}$
4	Memory allocation	⇐	$id\mathbb{T} \Leftarrow \mathrm{MEM}[ptr\mathbf{P}]\ \mathbb{T}$
5	Memory release	⇍	$id\mathbb{T} \not\Leftarrow \mathrm{MEM}[\bot]\mathbb{T}$
6	Read	⋗	$\mathrm{MEM}[ptr\mathbf{P}]\mathbb{T} > x\mathbb{T}$
7	Write	⋖	$x\mathbb{T} < \mathrm{MEM}[ptr\mathbf{P}]\mathbb{T}$
8	Input	|⋗	$\mathrm{PORT}[ptr\mathbf{P}]\mathbb{T}\ |> x\mathbb{T}$
9	Output	|⋖	$x\mathbb{T}\ |< \mathrm{PORT}[ptr\mathbf{P}]\mathbb{T}$
10	Timing	@	$@i\mathbf{TM}\ @\S i\mathbf{TM}$ $\mathbf{TM} = \underline{\underline{\mathbf{yy:MM:dd}}}$ $\|\ \mathbf{hh:mm:ss:ms}$ $\|\ \mathbf{yy:MM:dd:hh:mm:ss:ms}$
11	Duration	≜	$@t_n\mathbf{TM} \triangleq \S t_n\mathbf{TM} + \Delta n\mathbf{TM}$
12	Increase	↑	$\uparrow(n\mathbb{T})$
13	Decrease	↓	$\downarrow(n\mathbb{T})$
14	Exception detection	!	$!\,(@e\mathbf{S})$
15	Skip	⊗	$⊗$
16	Stop	⊠	$⊠$
17	System	§	$\S(SysID\mathbf{ST})$

$$RTPA \triangleq (\mathfrak{T}, \mathfrak{P}, \mathfrak{R}) \tag{1}$$

where

- $\mathfrak{T}$ is a set of 17 primitive types for modeling system architectures and data objects;
- $\mathfrak{P}$ a set of 17 meta processes for modeling fundamental system behaviors;
- $\mathfrak{R}$ a set of 17 relational process operations for constructing complex system behaviors.

Detailed descriptions of $\mathfrak{T}$, $\mathfrak{P}$, and $\mathfrak{R}$ in RTPA will be extended in the following subsections (Wang, 2007a).

The Meta Processes of Software Behaviors in RTPA

RTPA adopts the foundationalism in order to elicit the most primitive computational processes known as the *meta processes*. In this approach, complex processes are treated as derived processes from these meta processes based on a set of algebraic process composition rules known as the *process relations*.

Definition 3: *A meta process in RTPA is a primitive computational operation that cannot be broken down to further individual actions or behaviors.*

A meta process is an elementary process that serves as a basic building block for modeling software behaviors. *Complex processes* can be composed from meta processes using *process relations*. In RTPA, a set of 17 meta processes has been elicited from essential and primary computational operations commonly identified in existing formal methods and modern programming languages (Aho, Sethi, & Ullman, 1985; Higman, 1977; Hoare et al., 1986; Louden, 1993; Wilson & Clark, 1988; Woodcock & Davies, 1996). Mathematical notations and syntaxes of the meta processes are formally described in Table 1.

Lemma 1: *The essential computing behaviours state that the RTPA meta process system $\mathfrak{P}$ encompasses 17 fundamental computational operations elicited from the most basic computing, that is:*

$$\mathfrak{P} = \{:=, \blacklozenge, \Rightarrow, \Leftarrow, \nLeftarrow, >, <, |>, |<, @, \triangleq, \uparrow, \downarrow, !, \otimes, \boxtimes, \S\} \tag{2}$$

As shown in Lemma 1 and Table 1, each meta process is a basic operation on one or more operands such as variables, memory elements, or I/O ports. Structures of the operands and their allowable operations are constrained by their types as described in previous sections. It is noteworthy that not all generally important and fundamental computational operations, as shown in Table 1, had been explicitly identified in conventional formal methods. For instances, the evaluation, addressing, memory allocation/release, timing/duration, and the system processes. However, all these are found necessary and essential in modeling system architectures and behaviors.

Process Operations of RTPA

Definition 4: *A process relation in RTPA is an algebraic operation and a compositional rule between two or more meta processes in order to construct a complex process.*

A set of 17 fundamental process relations has been elicited from fundamental algebraic and relational operations in computing in order to build and compose complex processes in the context of real-time software systems. Syntaxes and usages of the 17 RTPA process relations are formally described in Table 2. Deductive semantics of these process relations may be referred to (Wang, 2006a, 2007a, 2008a).

Lemma 2: *The software composing rules state that the RTPA process relation system $\mathfrak{R}$ encompasses 17 fundamental algebraic and relational operations elicited from basic computing needs, that is:*

$$\mathfrak{R} = \{\rightarrow, \curvearrowright, |, |...|..., R^{*}, R^{+}, R^{i}, \circlearrowright, \rightarrowtail, \|, \oiint, \|\|, », \nleftrightarrow, \hookrightarrow_{t}, \hookrightarrow_{e}, \hookrightarrow_{i}\} \tag{3}$$

The Type System of RTPA

A type is a set in which all member data objects share a common logical property or attribute. The maximum range of values that a variable can assume is a type, which is associated with a set of predefined or allowable operations. A type can be classified as *primitive* and *derived* (complex) types. The former is the most elemental types that cannot further divided into simpler ones; the latter is a compound form of multiple primitive types based on given type rules. Most primitive types are provided by programming languages; while most user defined types are derived ones.

Definition 5: *A type system specifies data object modeling and manipulation rules in computing.*

The 17 RTPA primitive types in computing and human cognitive process modeling have been elicited from works in (Cardelli & Wegner, 1985; Martin-Lof, 1975; Mitchell, 1990; Stubbs & Webre, 1985; Wang, 2002, 2003, 2007a), which is summarized in the following lemma.

Table 2. The process relations and algebraic operations of RTPA

No.	Process Relation	Nota-tion	Syntax
1	Sequence	$\rightarrow$	$P \rightarrow Q$
2	Jump	$\curvearrowright$	$P \curvearrowright Q$
3	Branch	$\mid$	$\blacklozenge exp\mathbf{BL} = \mathbf{T} \rightarrow P$ $\mid \blacklozenge \sim \rightarrow Q$
4	Switch	$\mid$ $...$ $\mid$	$\blacklozenge exp\mathbb{T} =$ $i \rightarrow P_i$ $\mid \sim \rightarrow \oslash$ where $\mathbb{T} \in \{\mathbf{N, Z, B, S}\}$
5	While-loop	R^*	$\overset{\mathbf{F}}{\underset{exp\mathbf{BL}=\mathbf{T}}{R}} P$
6	Repeat-loop	R^+	$P \rightarrow \overset{\mathbf{F}}{\underset{exp\mathbf{BL}=\mathbf{T}}{R}} P$
7	For-loop	R^i	$\overset{n\mathbf{N}}{\underset{i\mathbf{N}=1}{R}} P(i\mathbf{N})$
8	Recursion	$\circlearrowleft$	$\overset{0}{\underset{i\mathbf{N}=n\mathbf{N}}{R}} P^{i\mathbf{N}} \circlearrowleft P^{i\mathbf{N}-1}$
9	Function call	$\rightarrowtail$	$P \rightarrowtail F$
10	Parallel	$\parallel$	$P \parallel Q$
11	Concurrence	$\oiint$	$P \oiint Q$
12	Interleave	$\mid\mid\mid$	$P \mid\mid\mid Q$
13	Pipeline	$\gg$	$P \gg Q$
14	Interrupt	$\rotatebox{90}{$\lightning$}$	$P \rotatebox{90}{$\lightning$} Q$
15	Time-driven dispatch	$\overset{}{\underset{t}{\hookrightarrow}}$	$@t_i\mathbf{TM} \overset{}{\underset{t}{\hookrightarrow}} P_i$
16	Event-driven dispatch	$\overset{}{\underset{e}{\hookrightarrow}}$	$@e_i\mathbf{S} \overset{}{\underset{e}{\hookrightarrow}} P_i$
17	Interrupt-driven dispatch	$\overset{}{\underset{i}{\hookrightarrow}}$	$@int_j\odot \overset{}{\underset{i}{\hookrightarrow}} P_j$

Lemma 3: *The primary types of computational objects state that the RTPA type system* $\mathfrak{T}$ *encompasses 17 primitive types elicited from fundamental computing needs, that is:*

$$\mathfrak{T} \triangleq \{\mathbf{N}, \mathbf{Z}, \mathbf{R}, \mathbf{S}, \mathbf{BL}, \mathbf{B}, \mathbf{H}, \mathbf{P}, \mathbf{TI}, \mathbf{D}, \mathbf{DT}, \mathbf{RT}, \mathbf{ST}, @e\mathbf{S}, @t\mathbf{TM}, @int\odot, ⓢs\mathbf{BL}\} \quad (4)$$

where the primitive types stand for natural number, integer, real, string, Boolean, byte, hexadecimal, pointer, time, date, date/Time, run-time determinable type, system architectural type, random event, time event, interrupt event, and status.

In Lemma 3, the first 11 primitive types are for mathematical and logical manipulation of data objects in computing, and the remaining six are for system architectural modeling. More rigorous description of RTPA type rules may be referred to (Wang, 2007a).

THE REDUCTION MACHINE OF RTPA

A reduction machine is an abstract machine that defines inference rules for repetitively reducing language constructs until a solid value or behavior is obtained. Reduction machines model the operational semantics of a given language or formal notation system in three components: *specification*, *control*, and *store*. In other words, an operational semantics describes how the *control* of the machine reduces a given *specification* to values of variables and how the *memory (store)* is changed during the execution of the specification.

In the operational semantics approach, the underlying target machine that operates and implements the semantic rules is modeled by an abstract reduction machine. A program and its behavior space or the semantic environment are realized by the target computer. An abstract model of a generic reduction machine as the system platform for embodying software semantics can be modeled below.

Figure 1. The abstract model of the RTPA deduction machine

$$
\begin{array}{ll}
\S = \text{SysID}\mathbf{S} :: & \\
\quad \{ < \mathop{R}\limits_{i\mathbf{N}=0}^{n_{proc}\mathbf{N}-1} \text{P}_i\mathbf{ST}> & // \text{ Processes} \\
\quad \| < \mathop{R}\limits_{addr\mathbf{P}=0}^{n_{Mem}\mathbf{N}-1} \text{MEM}[\text{ptr}\mathbf{P}]\mathbf{RT}> & // \text{ Memory} \\
\quad \| < \mathop{R}\limits_{ptr\mathbf{P}=0}^{n_{Port}\mathbf{N}-1} \text{PORT}[\text{ptr}\mathbf{P}]\mathbf{RT}> & // \text{ Ports} \\
\quad \| <\S t\mathbf{TM}> & // \text{ The system clock} \\
\quad \| < \mathop{R}\limits_{k\mathbf{N}=0}^{n_e\mathbf{N}-1} @\text{e}_i\mathbf{S} \hookrightarrow \text{P}_k> & // \text{ Event-driven dispatch} \\
\quad \| < \mathop{R}\limits_{k\mathbf{N}=0}^{n_t\mathbf{N}-1} @\text{t}_k\mathbf{TM} \hookrightarrow \text{P}_k> & // \text{ Time-driven dispatch} \\
\quad \| < \mathop{R}\limits_{k\mathbf{N}=0}^{n_{int}\mathbf{N}-1} \S\text{int}_k\odot \hookrightarrow \text{P}_k > & // \text{ Interrupt-driven dispatch} \\
\quad \| < \mathop{R}\limits_{i\mathbf{N}=0}^{n_V\mathbf{N}-1} ⓢ\text{V}_i\mathbf{BL}> & // \text{ System variables} \\
\quad \| < \mathop{R}\limits_{i\mathbf{N}=0}^{n_S\mathbf{N}-1} ⓢ\text{S}_i\mathbf{BL}> & // \text{ System states} \\
\quad \} &
\end{array}
$$

Definition 6: *The reduction machine, §, is an abstract logical model of the executing platform of a target machine denoted by a set of parallel or concurrent computing resources as shown in Figure 1.*

As shown in Figure 1, the reduction machine § for operational semantics is the executing platform that controls all the computing resources of an abstract target machine. The system is logically abstracted as a set of processes and underlying resources, such as the memory, ports, variables, statuses, and the system clock. A process is dispatched and controlled by the system §, which is triggered by various external, system timing, or interrupt events. The reduction machine of RTPA is not only the platform of the computing resources such as processes, memory, ports, and system clocks, but also the implementation of the computing mechanisms such as system dispatches, timing, interrupt handling, and system event captures.

Definition 7. *The semantic environment of the deduction machine, Θ, is the entire set of identifiers and their combinations declared and constrained in the abstract reduction machine, that is:*

$$
\begin{aligned}
\Theta \quad &\triangleq (I, T, V, A) \\
&= I \times T \times V \times A
\end{aligned}
\tag{5}
$$

where I is a nonempty set of identifies, T is a set of types corresponding to each identifier in I, V is a set of values corresponding to each identifier in I, and A is a set of addresses corresponding to each identifier in I.

The semantic environment Θ can be divided into three subcategories known as the *operational environment* Θ_{op}, *system environment* Θ_{sys}, and *interrupt environment* Θ_{int}, that is:

$$
\Theta \triangleq \Theta_{op} \cup \Theta_{sys} \cup \Theta_{int}
\tag{6}
$$

where only the operational environment Θ_{op} is controllable by users and applications.

Definition 8. *An inference rule in operational semantics, R_{os}, is a formal structure in which a propositional conclusion C is derived based on a set of given true premises P, that is:*

$$
R_{OS} \triangleq \frac{\text{Premise(s)}}{\text{Conclusion}} = P \vdash C
\tag{7}
$$

where P and C are usually Boolean propositions. However, C can be a sequence of behavioral processes.

The semantic environment Θ forms the context of inference rules in operational semantics. Therefore, the following convention is adopted in all notations of inference rules:

$$
< P \parallel \Theta > \Rightarrow < \varnothing \parallel \Theta' >
\tag{8}
$$

where $\parallel$ denotes a parallel relationship between a *process* or an *expression P* and its underlying semantic environment Θ, $\Rightarrow$ denotes a transition between a pair of semantic items, $\varnothing$ denotes an empty operation

Box 1.

$$\frac{exp\textbf{RT}, y\textbf{RT} \in \Theta, \mathrm{T}(exp\textbf{RT} \parallel \Theta) = \mathrm{T}(y\textbf{RT} \parallel \Theta)}{<(y\textbf{RT} := exp\textbf{RT}) \parallel \Theta> \;\Rightarrow\; (< \; \mathrm{V}(y\textbf{RT}) = \mathrm{V}(exp\textbf{RT})) \parallel \Theta' >}$$

(Rule 1)

Box 2.

$$\frac{exp\textbf{BL}, \textbf{T}, \textbf{F} \in \Theta, <\blacklozenge exp\textbf{BL} \parallel \Theta > \;\Rightarrow\; \mathrm{V}(exp\textbf{BL}) = \textbf{T} \parallel \Theta'_{sys} >}{<(\blacklozenge exp\textbf{BL} \rightarrow \textbf{BL}) \parallel \Theta > | \Rightarrow\; < exp\textbf{BL} = \textbf{T} \mid \Theta' >}$$

$$\frac{exp\textbf{BL}, \textbf{T}, \textbf{F} \in \Theta, <\blacklozenge exp\textbf{BL} \parallel \Theta > \;\Rightarrow\; \mathrm{V}(exp\textbf{BL}) = \textbf{F} \parallel \Theta'_{sys} >}{<(\blacklozenge exp\textbf{BL} \rightarrow \textbf{BL}) \parallel \Theta > | \Rightarrow\; < exp\textbf{BL} = \textbf{F} \mid \Theta' >}$$

(Rule 2.a)

and/or the completion of a preceding process, and Θ' denotes an updated semantic environment as a result of the operation or effect of a process.

Definition 9. *The evaluations of an identifier id on its type t, value v, and address addr in Θ can be denoted as follows:*

$$t_{id} \triangleq T(id \parallel \Theta)$$
$$v_{id} \triangleq V(id \parallel \Theta)$$
$$addr_{id} \triangleq A(id \parallel \Theta)$$

(9.a-c)

where $id \in I \sqsubseteq \Theta$, or simply denoted $id \in \Theta$ when there is no confusion.

OPERATIONAL SEMANTICS OF RTPA META-PROCESSES

Using the reduction machine as defined in preceding section, the operational semantics for the 17 meta processes of RTPA can be described as follows.

Definition 10. *The reduction rule for the assignment process of RTPA, $y\textbf{RT} := exp\textbf{RT}$, in operational semantics is shown in Box 1. The assignment rule indicates that an assignment transfers the value of $exp\textbf{RT}$ into $y\textbf{RT}$ whenever both variables' types are identical or equivalent.*

Definition 11. *The reduction rule for the Boolean evaluation process of RTPA, $\blacklozenge exp\textbf{BL} \rightarrow \textbf{BL}$, in operational semantics is shown in Box 2, where | denotes a pair of alternative rules.*

The above rule for Boolean evaluation can be extended to more general cases where numerical evaluations are needed. The reduction rule for the *numerical evaluation process*, $\blacklozenge exp\mathbb{T} \to \mathbb{T}$, in operational semantics is shown in Box 3,where $\mathbb{T}$ is a numerical type, i.e., $\mathbb{T} = \{\mathbf{N}, \mathbf{Z}, \mathbf{R}, \mathbf{B}\} \subset T \sqsubseteq \Theta$.

It is noteworthy that, although the evaluation process does not affect Θ_{op}, but it changes Θ_{sys}.

Definition 12. *The reduction rule for the addressing process of RTPA, $id\mathbf{S} \Rightarrow ptr\mathbf{P}$, in operational semantics is shown in Box 4.*

Definition 13. *The reduction rule for the memory allocations process of RTPA, $id\mathbf{S} \Leftarrow \mathrm{MEM}[ptr\mathbf{P}]\mathbf{RT}$, in operational semantics is shown in Box 5, where size(RT) is the length of a certain type of variable, RT, in bytes, which is implementation specific.*

Definition 14. *The reduction rule for the memory release process of RTPA, $id\mathbf{S} \nLeftarrow \mathrm{MEM}[\perp]\mathbf{RT}$, in operational semantics is shown in Box 6, where $\perp$ denotes an empty or unassigned value.*

Definition 15. *The reduction rule for the read process of RTPA, $\mathrm{MEM}[ptr\mathbf{P}]\mathbf{RT} > x\mathbf{RT}$, in operational semantics isshown in Box 7.*

Definition 16. *The reduction rule for the write process of RTPA, $\mathrm{MEM}[ptr\mathbf{P}]\mathbf{RT} < x\mathbf{RT}$, in operational semantics is shown in Box 8.*

Definition 17. *The reduction rule for the input process of RTPA, $\mathrm{PORT}[ptr\mathbf{P}]\mathbf{RT}|> x\mathbf{RT}$, in operational semantics is shown in Box 9.*

Box 3.

$$
\begin{array}{c}
exp\mathbb{T}, n\mathbb{T} \in \Theta, \mathbb{T} = \{\mathbf{N}, \mathbf{Z}, \mathbf{R}, \mathbf{B}\} \subset \Theta, < (\blacklozenge exp\mathbb{T} \to \mathbb{T}) \parallel \Theta > \;\Rightarrow \\
< \mathrm{V}(exp\mathbb{T}) = n\mathbb{T} \parallel \Theta'_{sys} > \\
\hline
<(\blacklozenge exp\mathbb{T} \to \mathbb{T}) \parallel \Theta' > \;\Rightarrow\; < exp\mathbb{T} = n\mathbb{T} \parallel \Theta' >
\end{array}
\quad \text{(Rule 2.b)}
$$

Box 4.

$$
\begin{array}{c}
id\mathbf{S}, ptr\mathbf{P} \in \Theta, < (id\mathbf{S} \Rightarrow ptr\mathbf{P}) \parallel \Theta > \;\Rightarrow\; < \varnothing \parallel \Theta' > \\
\hline
<(id\mathbf{S} \Rightarrow ptr\mathbf{P}) \parallel \Theta > \mathrm{A} \Rightarrow\; < (id\mathbf{S}) = ptr\mathbf{P} \parallel \Theta' >
\end{array}
$$

(Rule 3)

Box 5.

$$
\begin{array}{c}
id\mathbf{S}, ptr\mathbf{P}, n\mathbf{N} \in \Theta, < id\mathbf{S} \Leftarrow \mathrm{MEM}[ptr\mathbf{P}]\mathbf{RT} > \;\Rightarrow \\
< \varnothing \parallel \Theta' > \\
\hline
<(id\mathbf{S} \Leftarrow \mathrm{MEM}[ptr\mathbf{P}]\mathbf{RT}) \parallel \Theta> \;\Rightarrow \\
< \mathrm{A}(id\mathbf{S}) = [ptr\mathbf{P}, ptr + \mathrm{size}(\mathbf{RT})\text{-}1] \parallel \Theta' >
\end{array}
$$

(Rule 4)

Box 6.

$$\frac{id\mathbf{S}, ptr\mathbf{P} \in \Theta, < id\mathbf{S} \not\Leftarrow \mathrm{MEM}[\perp]\mathbf{RT} > \Rightarrow}{< \varnothing \parallel \Theta' >}$$
$$<(id\mathbf{S} \not\Leftarrow \mathrm{MEM}[\perp]\mathbf{RT}) \parallel \Theta> \Rightarrow \{< \mathrm{MEM}_{\mathrm{free}} \cup \mathrm{MEM}[\mathrm{A}(id\mathbf{S}),$$
$$\mathrm{A}(id\mathbf{S})+\mathrm{size}(\mathbf{RT})\text{-}1] \parallel \Theta' > \rightarrow <(\mathrm{A}(id\mathbf{S})=\perp) \parallel \Theta'' >\}$$

(Rule 5)

Box 7.

$$\frac{x\mathbf{RT}, ptr\mathbf{P}, \mathrm{MEM}\mathbf{RT} \in \Theta, <(\mathrm{MEM}[ptr\mathbf{P}]\mathbf{RT} > x\mathbf{RT}) \parallel \Theta> \Rightarrow <\varnothing \parallel \Theta' >}{<(\mathrm{MEM}[ptr\mathbf{P}]\mathbf{RT} > x\mathbf{RT}) \parallel \Theta> \Rightarrow \{<(x\mathbf{RT} = \mathrm{MEM}[ptr\mathbf{P}]\mathbf{RT}) \parallel \Theta' >}$$

(Rule 6)

Box 8.

$$\frac{x\mathbf{RT}, ptr\mathbf{P}, \mathrm{MEM}\mathbf{RT} \in \Theta, <(\mathrm{MEM}[ptr\mathbf{P}]\mathbf{RT} < x\mathbf{RT}) \parallel \Theta> \Rightarrow <\varnothing \parallel \Theta' >}{<(\mathrm{MEM}[ptr\mathbf{P}]\mathbf{RT} < x\mathbf{RT}) \parallel \Theta> \Rightarrow \{<(\mathrm{MEM}[ptr\mathbf{P}]\mathbf{RT} = x\mathbf{RT} > \parallel \Theta' >}$$

(Rule 7)

Definition 18. *The reduction rule for the output process of RTPA,* $x\mathbf{RT} \mathbin{|} < \mathrm{PORT}[ptr\mathbf{P}]\mathbf{RT}$, *in operational semantics is shown in Box 10.*

Definition 19. *The reduction rule for the timing process of RTPA,* $@t\mathbf{TM} \underline{@} \S t\mathbf{TM}$, *in operational semantics is shown in Box 11.*

Definition 20. *The reduction rule for the duration process of RTPA,* $@t\mathbf{TM} \underline{\triangleq} \S t\mathbf{TM} + \Delta d\mathbf{Z}$, *in operational semantics is shown in Box 12.*

Definition 21. *The reduction rule for the increase process of RTPA,* $\uparrow(x\mathbf{RT})$, *in operational semantics is shown in Box 13.*

Definition 22. *The reduction rule for the decrease process of RTPA,* $\downarrow(x\mathbf{RT})$, *in operational semantics is shown in Box 14.*

Definition 23. *The reduction rule for the exceptional detection process of RTPA,* $!(@e\mathbf{S})$, *in operational semantics is shown in Box 15, where CRT*$\mathbf{ST}$ *is the standard output device of the reduction machine for displaying system information in the type of strings.*

Definition 24. *The reduction rule for the skip process of RTPA,* $\otimes$, *in operational semantics is shown is:*

$$< \otimes \parallel \Theta > \Rightarrow < \varnothing \parallel \Theta'_{\mathrm{sys}} >$$

(Rule 15)

Box 9.

$$\frac{x\mathbf{RT}, ptr\mathbf{P}, \text{PORT}\mathbf{RT} \in \Theta, <(\text{PORT}[ptr\mathbf{P}]\mathbf{RT} \rhd x\mathbf{RT}) \parallel \Theta> \Rightarrow <\varnothing \parallel \Theta'>}{<(\text{PORT}[ptr\mathbf{P}]\mathbf{RT} \rhd x\mathbf{RT}) \parallel \Theta> \Rightarrow \{<(x\mathbf{RT} = \text{PORT}[ptr\mathbf{P}]\mathbf{RT}) \parallel \Theta'>}$$

(Rule 8)

Box 10.

$$\frac{x\mathbf{RT}, ptr\mathbf{P}, \text{PORT}\mathbf{RT} \in \Theta, <(\text{PORT}[ptr\mathbf{P}]\mathbf{RT} \mid< x\mathbf{RT}) \parallel \Theta> \Rightarrow <\varnothing \parallel \Theta'>}{<(\text{PORT}[ptr\mathbf{P}]\mathbf{RT} \mid< x\mathbf{RT}) \parallel \Theta> \Rightarrow \{<(\text{PORT}[ptr\mathbf{P}]\mathbf{RT} = x\mathbf{RT} > \parallel \Theta'>}$$

(Rule 9)

Box 11.

$$\frac{\begin{array}{c} t\mathbf{TM}, \S t\mathbf{TM}, \Delta d\mathbf{Z} \in \Theta, <(@ t\mathbf{TM} = \S t\mathbf{TM}) \parallel \Theta'>, \\ <(@ t\mathbf{TM} \underline{\underline{@}} \S t\mathbf{TM}) \parallel \Theta> \Rightarrow <\varnothing \parallel \Theta'>, <P \parallel \Theta> \Rightarrow <\varnothing \parallel \Theta'> \end{array}}{\begin{array}{c} <(@ t\mathbf{TM} \underline{\underline{@}} \S t\mathbf{TM}) \parallel \Theta> \Rightarrow \{<(@ t\mathbf{TM} = \S t\mathbf{TM}) \parallel \Theta'> \rightarrow \\ <@ t\mathbf{TM} \hookrightarrow P \parallel \Theta''>\} \end{array}}$$

(Rule 10)

Box 12.

$$\frac{\begin{array}{c} t\mathbf{TM}, \S t\mathbf{TM}, \Delta d\mathbf{Z} \in \Theta, <(t\mathbf{TM} = \S t\mathbf{TM}+\Delta d\mathbf{Z}) \parallel \Theta'>, \\ <(@ t\mathbf{TM} \underline{\underline{\Delta}} \S t\mathbf{TM}+\Delta d\mathbf{Z}) \parallel \Theta> \Rightarrow <\varnothing \parallel \Theta'>, <P \parallel \Theta> \Rightarrow <\varnothing \parallel \Theta'> \end{array}}{\begin{array}{c} <(@ t\mathbf{TM} \underline{\underline{\Delta}} \S t\mathbf{TM}+\Delta d\mathbf{Z}) \parallel \Theta> \Rightarrow \{<(@ t\mathbf{TM}=\S t\mathbf{TM}+\Delta d\mathbf{Z}) \parallel \Theta'> \rightarrow \\ <@ t\mathbf{TM} \hookrightarrow P \parallel \Theta''>\} \end{array}}$$

(Rule 11)

As defined above, the rule for the skip process of RTPA is an axiom, which does nothing functionally from users' point of view, but jumps to a new point of process by changing the control variables of program execution sequence in Θ'_{sys}.

Definition 25. *The reduction rule for the stop process of RTPA, $\boxtimes$, in operational semantics is as follows:*

$$<\boxtimes \parallel \Theta> \Rightarrow <\varnothing \parallel \Theta' = \varnothing>$$

(Rule 16)

The rule for the stop process in RTPA is an axiom, which terminates the current system and releases all existing identifiers and their values in the environment.

Definition 26. *The reduction rule for the system process of RTPA, $\S(SysID\mathbf{S})$, in operational semantics is shown in Box 16.*

Box 13.

$$x\mathbf{RT} \in \Theta, \mathbf{RT} \in \{\mathbf{N, B, H, Z, P, TM}\} \subset \Theta, <(\uparrow(x\mathbf{RT})) \parallel \Theta> \Rightarrow <\varnothing \parallel \Theta'>$$
$$<(\uparrow(x\mathbf{RT})) \parallel \Theta> \Rightarrow \{<(x\mathbf{RT} = x\mathbf{RT}+1) \parallel \Theta'>$$

(Rule 12)

Box 14.

$$x\mathbf{RT} \in \Theta, \mathbf{RT} \in \{\mathbf{N, B, H, Z, P, TM}\} \subset \Theta, <(\downarrow(x\mathbf{RT})) \parallel \Theta> \Rightarrow <\varnothing \parallel \Theta'>$$
$$<(\downarrow(x\mathbf{RT})) \parallel \Theta> \Rightarrow \{<(x\mathbf{RT} = x\mathbf{RT}-1) \parallel \Theta'>$$

(Rule 13)

Box 15.

$$e\mathbf{S}, ptr\mathbf{P}, \mathrm{CRT}\mathbf{P} \in \Theta, < ptr\mathbf{P} = \mathrm{A}(\mathrm{CRT}\mathbf{ST}) \parallel \Theta'>,$$
$$<(!(@e\mathbf{S})) \parallel \Theta> \Rightarrow <\varnothing \parallel \Theta'>$$
$$<(!(@e\mathbf{S})) \parallel \Theta> \Rightarrow \{<(\mathrm{PORT}[ptr\mathbf{P}]\mathbf{S} = @e\mathbf{S}) \parallel \Theta'>$$

(Rule 14)

Box 16.

$$<\S(SysID\mathbf{S}) \parallel \Theta> \Rightarrow <\varnothing \parallel \Theta' = (I \cup \{SysID\}),$$
$$t(SysID) = \mathbf{S}, v(SysID) = \S = (\bot, \bot, \bot, \bot),$$
$$a(SysID) = A(SysID)>$$

(Rule 17)

The rule for the system process in RTPA is an axiom, which does nothing functionally from users' point of view, but it creates the system identifier and allocates necessary resources to the newly created system.

OPERATIONAL SEMANTICS OF PROCESS RELATIONS

RTPA process relations are rules of algebraic operations of processes, which describe how the meta processes can be combined to form complex processes. The operational semantics of the 17 process relations of RTPA is elaborated in this section on the platform of the reduction machine.

Definition 27. *The reduction rule for the sequential process of RTPA, $P \rightarrow Q$, in operational semantics is shown in Box 17.*

Definition 28. *The reduction rule for the jump process of RTPA, $P \curvearrowright Q$, in operational semantics is shown in Box 18.*

Definition 29. *The reduction rule for the branch process of RTPA, $\blacklozenge exp\mathbf{RT} \rightarrow P | \blacklozenge \rightsquigarrow Q$, in operational semantics is shown in Box 19, where | denotes a pair of alternative sub-rules dependent on given conditions.*

Box 17.

$$\frac{<P \parallel \Theta> \Rightarrow <\varnothing \parallel \Theta'>, <Q \parallel \Theta> \Rightarrow <\varnothing \parallel \Theta'>}{<(P \rightarrow Q) \parallel \Theta> \Rightarrow \{<P \parallel \Theta'> \rightarrow <Q \parallel \Theta''>\}}$$

(Rule 18)

Box 18.

$$\frac{<P \parallel \Theta> \Rightarrow <\varnothing \parallel \Theta'>, <Q \parallel \Theta> \Rightarrow <\varnothing \parallel \Theta'>}{<(P \curvearrowright Q) \parallel \Theta> \Rightarrow \{<P \parallel \Theta'> \rightarrow <\varnothing \parallel \Theta' \cup \Theta'_{sys}> \rightarrow}$$
$$<Q \parallel \Theta'' \cup \Theta'_{sys}>\}$$

(Rule 19)

Box 19.

$$\frac{exp\mathbf{BL} \in \Theta, <exp\mathbf{BL} \parallel \Theta> \Rightarrow exp\mathbf{BL} =\mathbf{T}, <P \parallel \Theta> \Rightarrow <\varnothing \parallel \Theta'>}{<\blacklozenge exp\mathbf{RT} \rightarrow P \mid \blacklozenge \sim \rightarrow Q> \Rightarrow <P \parallel \Theta'>}$$

$$\frac{exp\mathbf{BL} \in \Theta, <exp\mathbf{BL} \parallel \Theta> \Rightarrow exp\mathbf{BL} =\mathbf{F}, <Q \parallel \Theta> \Rightarrow <\varnothing \parallel \Theta'>}{<\blacklozenge exp\mathbf{RT} \rightarrow P \mid \blacklozenge \sim \rightarrow Q> \Rightarrow <Q \parallel \Theta'>}$$

(Rule 20)

Definition 30. *The reduction rule for the switch process of RTPA,* $\blacklozenge exp_i\mathbf{RT} \rightarrow P_i \mid \blacklozenge \sim \rightarrow \otimes$, *in operational semantics is shown in Box 20, where*

$$\mathop{R}_{i\mathbf{N}=1}^{n\mathbf{N}}$$

denotes a set of recurrent structures.

The operational semantics of iterations are presented in the following definitions. It is noteworthy that iterations were diversely interpreted in literature (Louden, 1993; McDermid, 1991). Although the decision point may be denoted by branch constructs, most existing operational semantic rules failed to express the key semantics of "while" and the rewinding action of loops. Further, the semantics for more complicated types of iterations, such as the repeat-loop and for-loop, are rarely found in the literature.

Definition 31. *The reduction rule for the while-loop process of RTPA,*

$$\mathop{R}_{exp\mathbf{BL}=\mathbf{T}}^{\mathbf{F}} P,$$

in operational semantics is shown in Box 21, where the while-loop is defined recursively on Θ.

The above rule indicates that, when a Boolean expression $exp\mathbf{BL}$ in the environment Θ is true, the execution of the loop body P as a process for an iteration under Θ can be reduced to the same loop under an updated environment Θ', which is resulted by the last execution of P; When $exp\mathbf{BL} = \mathbf{F}$ in Θ, the loop is reduced to a termination or exit $\otimes$.

Box 20.

$$i\mathbf{N}, n\mathbf{N} \in \Theta, <exp\mathbf{RT} \| \Theta> \Rightarrow exp\mathbf{RT} = i\mathbf{N}, 1 \leq i\mathbf{N} \leq n\mathbf{N},$$

$$< \underset{i\mathbf{N}=1}{\overset{n\mathbf{N}}{R}} P \| \Theta> \Rightarrow <P_i \| \Theta'>$$

$$<\blacklozenge exp_i \mathbf{RT} \to P_i \mid \blacklozenge \sim \to \otimes> \Rightarrow <P_i \| \Theta'>$$

$$i\mathbf{N}, n\mathbf{N} \in \Theta, <exp\mathbf{RT} \| \Theta> \Rightarrow exp\mathbf{RT} = i\mathbf{N}, i\mathbf{N} \notin [1, n\mathbf{N}],$$

$$< \underset{i\mathbf{N}=1}{\overset{n\mathbf{N}}{R}} P \| \Theta> \Rightarrow <\otimes \| \Theta>$$

$$\mid \quad \frac{}{<\blacklozenge exp_i \mathbf{RT} \to P_i \mid \blacklozenge \sim \to \otimes> \Rightarrow <\otimes \| \Theta'_{sys}>}$$

(Rule 21)

Box 21.

$$exp\mathbf{BL} \in \Theta, <exp\mathbf{BL} \| \Theta> \Rightarrow exp\mathbf{BL} = \mathbf{T}, <P \| \Theta> \Rightarrow <\varnothing \| \Theta'>$$

$$\frac{}{< \underset{exp\mathbf{BL}=\mathbf{T}}{\overset{\mathbf{F}}{R}} P \| \Theta> \Rightarrow \{<P \| \Theta'> \to < \underset{exp\mathbf{BL}=\mathbf{T}}{\overset{\mathbf{F}}{R}} P \| \Theta'>\}}$$

$$exp\mathbf{BL} \in \Theta, <exp\mathbf{BL} \| \Theta> \Rightarrow exp\mathbf{BL} = \mathbf{F}, <\otimes \| \Theta'_{sys}>$$

$$\mid \quad \frac{}{< \underset{exp\mathbf{BL}=\mathbf{T}}{\overset{\mathbf{F}}{R}} P \| \Theta> \Rightarrow <\otimes \| \Theta'_{sys}>}$$

(Rule 22)

Box 22.

$$exp\mathbf{BL} \in \Theta, <P \| \Theta> \Rightarrow <\varnothing \| \Theta>$$

$$<P \to \underset{exp\mathbf{BL}=\mathbf{T}}{\overset{\mathbf{F}}{R}} P \| \Theta> \Rightarrow \{<P \| \Theta'> \to$$

$$\left(\frac{<exp\mathbf{BL} \| \Theta'> \Rightarrow exp\mathbf{BL} = \mathbf{T}, <P \| \Theta'> \Rightarrow <\varnothing \| \Theta''>}{< \underset{exp\mathbf{BL}=\mathbf{T}}{\overset{\mathbf{F}}{R}} P \| \Theta'> \Rightarrow \{<P \| \Theta''> \to < \underset{exp\mathbf{BL}=\mathbf{T}}{\overset{\mathbf{F}}{R}} P \| \Theta''>\}} \right.$$

$$\left. \mid \frac{<exp\mathbf{BL} \| \Theta'> \Rightarrow exp\mathbf{BL} = \mathbf{F}, <\otimes \| \Theta'_{sys}>}{< \underset{exp\mathbf{BL}=\mathbf{T}}{\overset{\mathbf{F}}{R}} P \| \Theta'> \Rightarrow <\otimes \| \Theta'_{sys}>} \right)$$

$$\}$$

(Rule 23)

Definition 32. *The reduction rule for the repeat-loop process of RTPA,*

$$P \to \underset{exp\mathbf{BL}=\mathbf{T}}{\overset{\mathbf{F}}{R}} P,$$

in operational semantics is shown in Box 22.

The above rule indicates that the semantics of a repeat-loop process is semantically equivalent to the sequential composition of *P* and a while-loop.

Box 23.

$$\frac{i\mathbf{N}, n\mathbf{N} \in \Theta, 1 \le i\mathbf{N} \le n\mathbf{N}, <P_i \| \Theta> \Rightarrow <\varnothing \| \Theta'>}{< \underset{i\mathbf{N}=1}{\overset{n}{R}} P(i\mathbf{N}) \| \Theta > \Rightarrow \{<P(i\mathbf{N}=1) \| \Theta'> \to \\ <P(i\mathbf{N}=2) \| \Theta"> \to \dots \to \\ <P(i\mathbf{N}=n\mathbf{N}) \| \Theta^{n}>\}}$$

(Rule 24)

Box 24.

$$\frac{<\blacklozenge(1 \le i\mathbf{N} \le n)\mathbf{BL} \| \Theta> \Rightarrow \mathbf{T}, <P_i \| \Theta> \Rightarrow <\varnothing \| \Theta'>}{< \underset{i\mathbf{N}=1}{\overset{n}{R}} P \| \Theta > \Rightarrow \{<P_i \| \Theta'> \to \ <i\mathbf{N}=i\mathbf{N}+1> \ \to < \underset{i\mathbf{N}=1}{\overset{n}{R}} P \| \Theta'>\}}$$

$$\frac{<\blacklozenge(1 \le i\mathbf{N} \le n)\mathbf{BL} \| \Theta> \Rightarrow \mathbf{F}, <\otimes \| \Theta'_{sys}>}{< \underset{i\mathbf{N}=1}{\overset{n}{R}} P \| \Theta > \Rightarrow < \otimes \| \Theta'_{sys}>}$$

(Rule 25)

Box 25.

$$\frac{<P \| \Theta> \Rightarrow \{<P' \| \Theta'> \to <P" \| \Theta">\}, <F \| \Theta> \Rightarrow <\varnothing \| \Theta'>}{<P \rightarrowtail F \| \Theta> \Rightarrow \{<P' \| \Theta'> \to <F \| \Theta"> \to <P" \| \Theta'">\}}$$

(Rule 26)

Box 26.

$$\frac{<P \| \Theta> \Rightarrow \{<P' \| \Theta'> \to <P" \| \Theta">\}, <P \| \Theta> \Rightarrow <\varnothing \| \Theta'>}{<P \circlearrowright P \| \Theta> \Leftrightarrow <P' \| \Theta'> \to <P \circlearrowright P \| \Theta"> \to <P" \| \Theta'">\}}$$

(Rule 27)

Definition 33. *The reduction rule for the for-loop process of RTPA,*

$\underset{i\mathbf{N}=1}{\overset{n}{R}} P(i\mathbf{N}),$

in operational semantics is shown in Box 23.

The above rule indicates that the semantics of a for-loop process is semantically equivalent to a sequence of *n* serial processes. The semantic rule of for-loop processes may also be defined recursively as that of the while-loop rule as shown in Box 24.

Definition 34. *The reduction rule for the function call process of RTPA, $P \rightarrowtail F$, in operational semantics is shown in Box 25.*

232

Box 27.

$$\frac{i\mathbf{N}, n\mathbf{N} \in \Theta, 1 \leq i\mathbf{N} \leq n\mathbf{N}, <P^{i\mathbf{N}} \parallel \Theta> \Rightarrow <P^{i\mathbf{N}-1} \parallel \Theta'>, P^0 = const\mathbf{N}}{<P \circlearrowleft P \parallel \Theta> (\Rightarrow \mathop{R}\limits_{i\mathbf{N}=n\mathbf{N}}^{1} < P^{i\mathbf{N}} \rightarrow P^{i\mathbf{N}-1}) \parallel \Theta^{i} >}$$

(Rule 28)

Box 28.

$$\frac{\begin{array}{c}<P \parallel \Theta> \Rightarrow <\varnothing \parallel \Theta'>, <Q \parallel \Theta> \Rightarrow <\varnothing \parallel \Theta'>, <S_1 \parallel \Theta> \Rightarrow \\ <\varnothing \parallel \Theta>, <S_2 \parallel \Theta> \Rightarrow <\varnothing \parallel \Theta>\end{array}}{\begin{array}{c}<(P \parallel Q) \parallel \Theta> \Rightarrow \{<S_1 \parallel \Theta_{sys}> \rightarrow \left\langle \begin{array}{c}\rightarrow <P \parallel \Theta'> \rightarrow \\ \rightarrow <Q \parallel \Theta''> \rightarrow\end{array}\right\rangle \rightarrow \\ <S_2 \parallel \Theta' \cup \Theta'' \cup \Theta'_{sys}>\}\end{array}}$$

(Rule 29)

Box 29.

$$\frac{\begin{array}{c}<P \parallel \Theta_P> \Rightarrow <\varnothing \parallel \Theta'_P>, <Q \parallel \Theta_Q> \Rightarrow <\varnothing \parallel \Theta'_Q>, \\ <C_1 \parallel \{\Theta_P \parallel \Theta_Q\}> \Rightarrow <\varnothing \parallel \{\Theta_P \parallel \Theta_Q\}>, \\ <C_2 \parallel \{\Theta_P \parallel \Theta_Q\}> \Rightarrow <\varnothing \parallel \{\Theta_P \parallel \Theta_Q\}>\end{array}}{\begin{array}{c}<(P \iint Q) \parallel \{\Theta_P \parallel \Theta_Q\}> \Rightarrow \{<C_1 \parallel \{\Theta_P \parallel \Theta_Q\}> \\ \rightarrow \left\langle \begin{array}{c}\rightarrow <P \parallel \Theta'_P> \rightarrow \\ \rightarrow <Q \parallel \Theta'_Q> \rightarrow\end{array}\right\rangle \rightarrow <C_2 \parallel \{\Theta'_P \parallel \Theta'_Q\}>\}\end{array}}$$

(Rule 30)

Definition 35. *The reduction rule for the recursion process of RTPA, $P \circlearrowleft P$, in operational semantics is shown in Box 26.*

The semantic rule of recursion processes may also be defined iteratively as that of the for-loop rule as shown in Box 27, where the base process P^0 should be able to be reduced to a constant.

Definition 36. *The reduction rule for the parallel process of RTPA, $P \parallel Q$, in operational semantics is shown in Box 28, where S_1 and S_2 are two additional synchronization processes introduced by the system.*

The parallel process rule models the process relation with the single-clock multi-processor (SCMP) structure. In other words, it behaves in a synchronized system or a common environment.

Definition 37. *The reduction rule for the concurrent process of RTPA, $P \iint Q$, in operational semantics is shown in Box 29, where C_1 and C_2 are two additional communication processes introduced in two separated system environments Θ_P and Θ_Q.*

Box 30.

$$iN, nN \in \Theta, 1 \le iN \le nN, <P \parallel \Theta> \Rightarrow \mathop{R}_{iN=1}^{nN} <P_i \parallel \Theta_i>,$$

$$<Q \parallel \Theta> \Rightarrow \mathop{R}_{iN=1}^{nN} <Q_{i.} \parallel \Theta_i>$$

$$<(P \parallel\parallel Q) \parallel \Theta> \Rightarrow \mathop{R}_{iN=1}^{nN} (<P_i \parallel \Theta_i> \to <Q_i \parallel \Theta'_i>)$$

(Rule 31)

Box 31.

$$O_P, I_Q, iN, nN \in \Theta, \mathop{R}_{iN=1}^{nN} o_P = i_Q, o_P \in O_P, i_Q \in I_Q, \#O_P = \#I_Q,$$

$$<P \parallel \Theta> \Rightarrow <\varnothing \parallel \Theta'>\}, <Q \parallel \Theta> \Rightarrow <\varnothing \parallel \Theta'>$$

$$<P \gg Q \parallel \Theta> \Rightarrow \{<P \parallel \Theta'> \to <Q \parallel \Theta''>\}$$

(Rule 32)

Box 32.

$$<P \parallel \Theta> \Rightarrow \{<P' \parallel \Theta'> \to <P'' \parallel \Theta''>\},$$

$$<Q \parallel \Theta_{int} \subset \Theta> \Rightarrow <\varnothing \parallel \Theta'_{int}>$$

$$<(P \between Q) \parallel \Theta> \Rightarrow \{<P' \parallel \Theta'> \to$$

$$<Q \parallel \Theta'_{int}> \to$$

$$<P'' \parallel \Theta'' \cup \Theta'_{int}>\}$$

(Rule 33)

The concurrent processes model the process relation with the multi-clock multi-processor (MCMP) structure. In other words, it behaves in an asynchronized system or a separated environments linked by the communication means.

Definition 38. *The reduction rule for the interleave process of RTPA, $P \parallel\parallel Q$, in operational semantics is shown in Box 30.*

The rule of interleave processes models the process relation with the single-clock single-processor (SCSP) structure in a synchronized environment.

Definition 39. *The reduction rule for the pipeline process of RTPA, $P \gg Q$, in operational semantics is shown in Box 31.*

The rule of pipeline processes shows that from the functional point view, a pipeline process relation is equivalent to a sequential relation as long as the corresponding outputs O_P and inputs I_Q are one-to-one coupled between the two processes.

Box 33.

$$kN,\ nN,t_k\mathbf{TM} \in \Theta, 1 \le kN \le nN,$$

$$<P \parallel \Theta> \Rightarrow \overset{nN}{\underset{kN=1}{R}} <P_k \parallel \Theta'>,<\S \parallel \Theta> \Rightarrow <\S \parallel \Theta'>$$

$$\overline{<(@t_k\mathbf{TM} \hookrightarrow P_k) \parallel \Theta > \Rightarrow \{<\S \parallel \Theta> \to <P_k \parallel \Theta'> \to <\S \parallel \Theta''>\}}$$

(Rule 34)

Box 34.

$$kN,\ nN,e_k\mathbf{S} \in \Theta, 1 \le kN \le nN,$$

$$<P \parallel \Theta> \Rightarrow \overset{nN}{\underset{kN=1}{R}} <P_k \parallel \Theta'>,<\S \parallel \Theta> \Rightarrow <\S \parallel \Theta'>$$

$$\overline{<(@e_k\mathbf{S} \hookrightarrow P_k) \parallel \Theta> \Rightarrow \{<\S \parallel \Theta> \to <P_k \parallel \Theta > \to <\S \parallel \Theta''>\}}$$

(Rule 35)

Box 35.

$$kN,\ nN,int_k\odot \in \Theta, 1 \le kN \le nN,$$

$$<P \parallel \Theta_{int}> \Rightarrow \overset{nN}{\underset{kN=1}{R}} <P_k \parallel \Theta'_{int} >,<\S \parallel \Theta> \Rightarrow <\S \parallel \Theta'>$$

$$\overline{<(@int_k\odot \hookrightarrow P_k) \parallel \Theta> \Rightarrow \{<\S \parallel \Theta > \to <P_k \parallel \Theta'_{int} > \to <\S \parallel \Theta \cup \Theta'_{int} >\}}$$

(Rule 36)

Definition 40. *The reduction rule for the interrupt process of RTPA, $P \not\lightning Q$, in operational semantics is shown in Box 32, where the interrupt semantic environment Θ_{int} is a subset of Θ as defined in Equation 6.*

The rule of interrupt processes shows that the main environment Θ is protected when an interrupt occurs. However, the interrupt subroutine Q may affect Θ via global or shared variables and data structures after its completion.

Definition 41. *The reduction rule for the time-driven process of RTPA, $@t_k\mathbf{TM} \hookrightarrow P_k$, in operational semantics is shown in Box 33.*

The rule of time-driven processes models a top level system dispatching behavior where the system transfers control to a process P_k after capturing a corresponding timing event $@t_k\mathbf{TM}$; upon its completion, it returns the control of system resources and the environment to the system.

Definition 42. *The reduction rule for the event-driven process of RTPA, $@e_k\mathbf{TM} \hookrightarrow P_k$, in operational semantics is shown in Box 34.*

The rule of event-driven processes models the second type of top level system dispatching behaviors, where the system transfers control to a process P_k after capturing a corresponding event $@e_k\mathbf{S}$; upon its completion, it returns the control of system resources and the environment to the system.

Definition 43. *The reduction rule for the interrupt-driven process of RTPA, $@int_k \odot \hookrightarrow P_k$, in operational semantics is shown in Box 35.*

The rule of interrupt-driven processes models the third type of top level system dispatching behaviors, where the system transfers the control to an interrupt subroutine P_k after capturing a corresponding interrupt event $@int_k \odot$; upon its completion, it returns the control of system resources and the environment to the system.

CONCLUSION

The operational semantics of Real-Time Process Algebra (RTPA) has been developed in this article, which explains how syntactic constructs in RTPA can be reduced to values on an abstract reduction machine. The operational semantics of RTPA has provided a comprehensive paradigm of formal semantics, which extends the conventional express power of operational semantics to an entire set of semantic rules for complicated RTPA process structures and their algebraic operations. Especially, the operational semantics of the parallel, concurrent, and system dispatches have been formally and systematically elaborated.

RTPA has been presented as both a denotational mathematical structure and a system modeling methodology for describing the architectures and behaviors of real-time and nonreal-time software systems. The formal semantics of RTPA has helped to the comprehension and understanding of the RTPA syntactical and semantic rules as well as its expressive power in software engineering, cognitive informatics, and computational intelligence. RTPA has been used not only in software system specifications, but also in human and intelligent system modeling.

ACKNOWLEDGMENT

The authors would like to acknowledge the Natural Science and Engineering Council of Canada (NSERC) for its partial support to this work. We would like to thank the anonymous reviewers for their valuable comments and suggestions.

REFERENCES

Aho, A.V., Sethi, R., & Ullman, J.D. (1985). *Compilers: Principles, techniques, and tools.* New York: Addison-Wesley Publication Co.

Baeten, J.C.M. & Bergstra, J.A. (1991). Real time process algebra. *Formal Aspects of Computing, 3,* 142-188.

Boucher, A. & Gerth, R. (1987). A timed model for extended communicating sequential processes. *Proceedings of ICALP'87*, Springer LNCS, 267.

Cardelli, L. & Wegner, P. (1985). On understanding types, data abstraction and polymorphism. *ACM Computing Surveys, 17*(4), 471-522.

Fecher, H. (2001). A real-time process algebra with open intervals and maximal progress. *Nordic Journal of Computing, 8*(3), 346-360.

Higman, B. (1977). *A comparative study of programming languages*, 2nd ed. MacDonald.

Hoare, C.A.R. (1978). Communicating sequential processes. *Communications of the ACM, 21*(8), 666-677.

Hoare, C.A.R. (1985). *Communicating sequential processes*. London: Prentice-Hall International.

Jones, C. B. (2003). Operational semantics: Concepts and their expression. *Information Processing Letters, 88*(1-2), 27 – 32.

Louden K.C. (1993). *Programming languages: Principles and practice*. Boston: PWS-Kent Publishing Co.

Martin-Lof, P. (1975). *An intuitionistic theory of types: Predicative part*. In H. Rose & J. C. Shepherdson (Eds.), Logic Colloquium 1973, NorthHolland.

McDermid, J. (Ed.) (1991). *Software engineer's reference book*. Oxford, UK: Butterworth Heinemann Ltd.

Milner, R. (1980). *A calculus of communicating systems*, LNCS #92. Springer-Verlag.

Milner, R. (1989). *Communication and concurrency*. Englewood Cliffs, NJ: Prentice-Hall

Mitchell, J.C. (1990). Type systems for programming languages. In J. van Leeuwen (Ed.), *Handbook of theoretical computer science* (pp. 365-458). North Holland.

Nicollin, X. & Sifakis, J. (1991). An overview and synthesis on timed process algebras. *Proceedings of the 3rd International Computer Aided Verification Conference*, pp. 376-398.

Plotkin, G. (1981). A structural approach to operational semantics. *Technical Report DAIMI FN-19*, Aarhus University, Denmark.

Schneider, S. (1995). An operational semantics for timed CSP. *Information and Computation, 116*(2), 193-213.

Slonneger, K., & Barry, L.K. (1995). *Formal syntax and semantics of programming languages: A laboratory based approach,* (Chapter 8), Reading, MA: Addison-Wesley Publishing Company.

Stubbs, D.F. & Webre, N.W. (1985). *Data structures with abstract data types and Pascal*. Monterey, CA: Brooks/Cole Publishing Co.

Tan, X. & Wang, Y. (2008). A denotational semantics of real-time process algebra (RTPA). *The International Journal of Cognitive Informatics and Natural Intelligence (IJCINI), 2*(3).

Tan, X., Wang, Y., & Ngolah, C.F. (2006). Design and implementation of an automatic RTPA code generator. *Proceedings of the 19th Canadian Conference on Electrical and Computer Engineering (CCECE'06)*, Ottawa, ON, Canada, May, pp. 1605-1608.

Wang, Y. (2002). The real-time process algebra (RTPA). *Annals of Software Engineering: An International Journal, 14*, 235-274.

Wang, Y. (2003). Using process algebra to describe human and software system behaviors. *Brain and Mind, 4*(2), 199–213.

Wang, Y. (2006a). On the informatics laws and deductive semantics of software. *IEEE Transactions on Systems, Man, and Cybernetics (C), 36*(2), 161-171.

Wang, Y. (2006b). Cognitive informatics and contemporary mathematics for knowledge representation and manipulation, invited plenary talk. *Proceedings of the 1st International Conference on Rough Set and Knowledge Technology* (RSKT'06), LNAI #4062, Springer, Chongqing, China, July, pp. 69-78.

Wang, Y. (2007a). *Software engineering foundations: A software science perspective.* New York: Auerbach Publications.

Wang, Y. (2007b). The theoretical framework of cognitive informatics. *International Journal of Cognitive Informatics and Natural Intelligence* (IJCINI), *1*(1), 1-27.

Wang, Y. (2007c). On theoretical foundations of software engineering and denotational mathematics, keynote speech. *Proceedings of the 5th Asian Workshop on Foundations of Software*, BHU Press, Xiamen, China, pp. 99-102.

Wang, Y. (2008a). RTPA: A denotational mathematics for manipulating intelligent and computational behaviors. *International Journal of Cognitive Informatics and Natural Intelligence (IJCINI), 2*(2), 44-62.

Wang, Y. (2008b). Deductive semantics of RTPA. *International Journal of Cognitive Informatics and Natural Intelligence* (IJCINI), *2*(2), 95-121.

Wang, Y. (2008c). On the Big-R notation for describing iterative and recursive behaviors. *International Journal of Cognitive Informatics and Natural Intelligence* (IJCINI), *2*(1), 17-28.

Wang, Y. & King, G. (2000). Software engineering processes: Principles and applications, CRC series in software engineering, Vol. I. CRC Press.

Wilson, L.B. & Clark, R.G. (1988). *Comparative programming language.* Wokingham, UK: Addison-Wesley Publishing Co.

Winskel, G. (1993). *The formal semantics of programming languages.* MIT Press.

Woodcock, J. & Davies, J. (1996). *Using Z: Specification, refinement, and proof.* London: Prentice Hall International.

This work was previously published in International Journal of Cognitive Informatics and Natural Intelligence, Vol. 2, Issue 3, pp. 71-89 copyright 2008 by IGI Publishing (an imprint of IGI Global).

Chapter 13
Formal Modeling and Specification of Design Patterns Using RTPA

Yingxu Wang
University of Calgary, Canada

Jian Huang
University of Calgary, Canada

ABSTRACT

Software patterns are recognized as an ideal documentation of expert knowledge in software design and development. However, its formal model and semantics have not been generalized and matured. The traditional UML specifications and related formalization efforts cannot capture the essence of generic patterns precisely, understandably, and essentially. A generic mathematical model of patterns is presented in this article using real-time process algebra (RTPA). The formal model of patterns are more readable and highly generic, which can be used as the meta model to denote any design patterns deductively, and can be translated into code in programming languages by supporting tools. This work reveals that a pattern is a highly complicated and dynamic structure for software design encapsulation, because of its complex and flexible internal associations between multiple abstract classes and instantiations. The generic model of patterns is not only applicable to existing patterns' description and comprehension, but also useful for future patterns' identification and formalization.

INTRODUCTION

Design patterns are a powerful tool for capturing software design notions and best practices, which provide common solutions to core problems in software development. Design patterns are a promising technique that extends reusability of software from code to design notions. A representative work of design patterns is initiated by Gamma and his colleagues in *Design Patterns: Elements of Reusable Object-Oriented Software* in 1994 (Gamma, Helm, Johnson, & Vlissides, 1995). Design patterns may speed up the development process by providing tested and proven development paradigms. Reusing design patterns helps to prevent subtle issues in large-scale software development and improves code readability for architects and programmers. Design patterns can contribute to the definition, design, and documentation of class libraries and frameworks, offering elegant and reusable solutions to design problems, and consequently increasing productivity and development quality (Gamma et al., 1995; Wang, 2007a). Each design pattern lets some aspects of the system structure vary independently of other aspects, thereby making the system more robust to a particular kind of change.

Design patterns are used to be modeled and specified in natural language narratives, object-oriented programming languages, and UML diagrams. The traditional means are either inherently ambiguous or inadequate (Lano, Goldsack, & Bicarregui, 1996; Vu & Wang, 2004; Wang & Huang, 2005). The major problems in current methodologies for pattern specification are identified as follows:

- **The lack of a unified and generic architecture of patterns as a multilayered complex entity with a set of abstract and concrete classes and their interrelations:** Patterns have been classified in three categories known as the *creational*, *structural*, and *behavioral* patterns (Gamma et al., 1995). However, the theories for the nature of patterns and their generic architecture are yet to be sought.
- **The lack of abstraction:** Almost all patterns are described as a specific and concrete case in natural language, UML diagrams, or some formal notations. However, no generic mathematical model of patterns is rigorously established, which may form a deductive basis for deriving concrete and application-specific patterns.
- **The lack of uniqueness:** In the conventional pattern framework, there are different patterns that may be implemented by similar code; Reversely, the same pattern may be implemented in various ways.
- **The use of unstructured semantic means to denote highly complicated design knowledge in patterns:** The informal descriptions of patterns puzzle users and cause substantial confusions. Even the creators of patterns demonstrate inconsistent over the semantics of certain patterns.

The authors perceive that the above fundamental problems can be alleviated by introducing formal semantics for design patterns and their generic mathematical models (Wang, 2002, 2003, 2006a-c, 2007a-c). This approach allows for unambiguous specifications, enables reasoning about the relationships between abstract and concrete patterns, and promotes a coherent framework for the rapidly growing body of software patterns in software engineering (Beck, Coplien, Crocker, & Dominick, 1996; Bosch, 1996; Wang, 2002, 2006a, 2007a). This article presents a generic model of design patterns and a formal specification method for design patterns using Real-Time Process Algebra (RTPA) (Wang, 2002, 2003, 2007a). The approach proposed in this article aimed at the following objectives:

- **It is generic:** The same pattern model can be adopted to specify any existing and future pattern, particularly user defined patterns. To some extent, the general pattern model is the pattern of patterns.
- **It is formalized:** The mathematical semantics and formal notation system are based on RTPA (Wang, 2002, 2003, 2007a).
- **It is expressive:** Only 34 notations are used to denote class association relationship and specify patterns from three facets known as the architecture, static behaviors, and dynamic behaviors of patterns.

- **It is structured:** Patterns are described from high-level to detailed-level via stepwise refinement using a coherent set of notations.

In this article, existing pattern specification techniques are reviewed in the following section. The RTPA methodology for pattern specification is introduced. A generic model of design patterns is rigorously modeled. Based on the mathematical semantics and general model, case studies on deriving specific pattern specifications are presented using three well known patterns such as the State, Strategy, and the MasterSlave patterns.

APPROACHES TO SOFTWARE PATTERN DESCRIPTION

A number of pattern modeling methodologies have been proposed, such as the layout object model (Bosch, 1996), the constraint diagrams (Lauder & Kent, 1998), the *language for pattern uniform specification* (Eden, Gil, Hirshfield & Yehudai, 2005), *meta-models* (Pagel & Winter, 1996; Sunye, Guennee, & Jezequel, 2000), *object calculus* (Lano et al., 1996), *pattern visualization techniques* (Lauder et al., 1998), and the *design pattern modeling language* (Mapelsden, Hosking, & Grundy et al., 1992). This section briefly reviews three major pattern specification methods and comparatively analyzes their strengths and weaknesses.

The Layout Object Model

The layout object model (LayOM) (Bosch, 1996) is an extension of object-oriented languages containing components that are not supported by the conventional object models such as layers, categories, and states. It supports the representation of design patterns in object-oriented programming languages.

In LayOM, layers are used to encapsulate objects and intercept messages that are sent to and by the objects. The layers are organized into classes and each layered class represents a concept, such as a relation with another object or a design pattern. A *state* in LayOM is a dimension of the abstract object state that is an externally visible abstraction of the internal, concrete state of objects. A *category* is defined as a client category that describes the discriminating characteristics of a subset of possible clients. *Relations* in LayOM are denoted by structural, behavioral, and application-domain relations.

For example, the *adapter* design pattern can be described in LayOM, as shown in Figure 1, which converts the interface of a class into another interface that is expected by its clients. The adapter layer can be used to class adaptation by defining a new adapter class consisting only of two layers.

Figure 1. The adapter pattern described in LayOM (Bosch, 1996)

```
              class Adapter
                 layers
    adapt: Adapter (accept mess1 as newMessA,
        accept mess2 and mess3 as newMessB);
               inh: Inherit (Adaptee);
                   end;
```

Figure 2. The constrain diagram of an abstract factory pattern (Lauder & Kent, 1998)

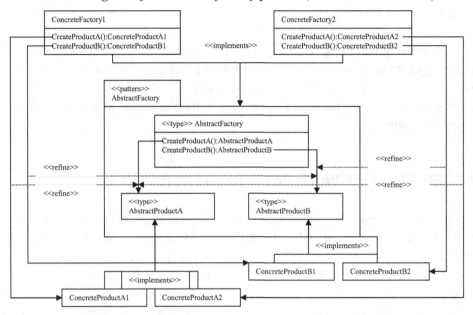

In LayOM, a one-to-one mapping between the design and implementation of a pattern is provided. Another advantage of it is that there is no requirement for defining a method for every method that needs to be adapted. However, a disadvantage of the adapter technique is that the arguments of the message will be passed as is, which is not flexible to cover semantic analyses. Another drawback is the implementation overhead, because messages sent to or from an object need to pass all the defined layers.

The Constraint Diagrams

The *constraint diagram* (CD) (Lauder & Kent, 1998) denotes a pattern by three separate models known as the role, type, and class. A *role* model in CD is the most abstract and depicts layer that describes the essential spirit of a pattern without specific details. A *type* model in CD refines to the role model with abstract states and operation interfaces forming a domain-specific refinement of the pattern. A *class* in CD model implements the type model, thus deploying the underlying pattern in terms of concrete classes.

An *abstract factory pattern* deployed as a constraint model is shown in Figure 2. The core of the pattern is represented as a role mode, further refined by a type model, and implemented by a class model. However, a graphical model is not enough for a precise and unambiguous specification. There is still a need to describe additional constraints about the objects in the model. Otherwise, ambiguities cannot be avoided in the model (OMG, 1997).

Figure 3. The LePUS Specification of the strategy pattern (Eden et al., 2005)

$$\exists context, client \in C$$
$$operations \in F$$
$$Algorithm, Configure - Contexts \in 2^{F}.$$
$$Strategies \in H$$
$$clan(operation, context) \wedge$$
$$clan(Algorithm, Strategies) \wedge$$
$$tribe(Configure - Context, client) \wedge$$
$$Invocation^{->}(operation, Configure - Context) \wedge$$
$$Invocation^{<->}(Algorithm, context) \wedge$$
$$Argument - 1^{->}(Algorithm, context) \wedge$$
$$Creation^{->H}(Configure - Context, Strategies) \wedge$$
$$Assigment^{->H}(Context, Configure - Context, Strategies) \wedge$$
$$Reference - to - Single^{<->}(context, Strategies)$$

LePUS: Language for Patterns Uniform Specification

Language for patterns uniform specification (LePUS) is a declarative language based on logic intro-duced in 1997 (Eden et al., 2005). It models class relationships and semantics, and facilitates reasoning with higher order sets. LePUS permits concise description of complex software artifacts. In LePUS, a program is represented primarily as a set of ground entities and relationships among them. Various interactions and associations that occur between participants of design patterns are abstracted classes and functions. A uniform set of classes of a dimension d is denoted by the class of dimension $d+1$. Total relations are functions that describe the relations between two sets of entities. Bijective and regular correlations between sets of functions, classes, and hierarchies may also be modeled. A specification of the *strategy* pattern in LePUS is shown in Figure 3.

The advantage of LePUS is its higher order logic means. However, it is difficult to directly map a LePUS specification of patterns into executable programs. In addition, patterns specified in LePUS are application specific rather than generic.

Other Approaches

Meta-models for design pattern instantiations and validations are proposed in Pagel and Winter (1996) and Sunye et al. (2000) without supporting for code generation. In Florijn, Meijers, and Wionsen (1997), the *fragment-based technique* allows the representation and composition of design patterns. A design pattern proof techniques is proposed in Lano et al. (1996) using the *object calculus* as a semantic frame-work. The *design pattern modeling language* (DPML) is proposed in Mapelsden et al. (1992) as a visual language for modeling patterns and their instances.

A common weakness of the methods proposed so far is that they concentrate only on specific pattern descriptions. The essence of pattern structures and the generic pattern theory are overlooked. Therefore, there is still a need to seek a more powerful means and methodology that help users to utilize pattern theories and models freely in pattern-based system design.

Figure 4. Abstract class specification in RTPA

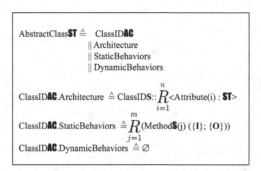

THE RTPA METHODOLOGY FOR PATTERN MODELING AND SPECIFICATION

In the preceding section, it can be seen that existing methods for pattern specifications were inadequate and inefficient in generic pattern specifications. This section adopts RTPA to formally specify design patterns, which is a set of new mathematical notations for formally describing system architectures, static and dynamic behaviors (Wang, 2002, 2006b).

RTPA is a mathematic-based software engineering notation system and a formal method for addressing problems in software system specification, refinement, and implementation. RTPA provides an expressive means for the formal and explicit description of software patterns in order to enhance the readability of pattern architecture, semantics, and behaviors. In RTPA, a software system is perceived and described mathematically as a set of coherent processes. RTPA encompasses 17 meta processes and 17 algebraic process combination rules known as the process relations. Detailed description of RTPA may be referred to Wang (2002, 2003, 2007a).

The Generic Model of Classes in RTPA

A unified notion of classes can be formally described by RTPA as given in "Wang (2007a)." The fundamental types of classes are the Abstract Classes (ACs) and the Concrete Classes (CCs). The former is

Figure 5. Concrete class specification in RTPA

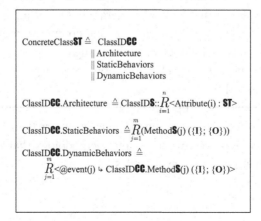

Figure 6. The generic mathematical model of design patterns (Wang, 2007a)

$$Pattern\mathbf{ST} \triangleq$$
$$\{$$
$$\quad Architecture : \mathbf{ST}$$
$$\| StaticBehaviors : \mathbf{ST}$$
$$\| DynamicBehaviors: \mathbf{ST}$$
$$\}$$

$$Pattern\mathbf{ST}.Architecture\mathbf{ST} \triangleq$$
$$\{$$
$$\quad <Interfaces>$$
$$\| <Implementations>$$
$$\| <Instantiations>$$
$$\| <Associations>$$
$$\}$$

$$Pattern\mathbf{ST}.Architecture\mathbf{ST}.Interfaces\mathbf{ST} \triangleq$$
$$PatternID\mathbf{ST}::$$
$$\{$$
$$\quad \overset{n}{\underset{i=1}{R}}<Attributes(i) : \mathbf{RT}>$$
$$\| \overset{m}{\underset{j=1}{R}}<AbstractClass(j) : \mathbf{AC}>$$
$$\}$$

$$Pattern\mathbf{ST}.Architecture\mathbf{ST}.Implementation\mathbf{ST} \triangleq$$
$$\{ \overset{q}{\underset{k=1}{R}}<ConcreteClass(k) : \mathbf{CC}> \}$$

$$Pattern\mathbf{ST}.Architecture\mathbf{ST}.Instantiations\mathbf{ST} \triangleq$$
$$\{ \overset{r}{\underset{v=1}{R}}<Instatiatin(v) : \mathbf{CC}> \}$$

$$Pattern\mathbf{ST}.Architecture\mathbf{ST}.Association\mathbf{ST} \triangleq$$
$$\{$$
$$\quad \overset{m}{\underset{j=1}{R}}(Interface(j)\mathbf{AC} : \mathbf{SC} \ // \mathbf{SC} \text{ is a system class}$$
$$\quad | \overset{q}{\underset{m=1}{R}}<Interface(j) \mathbf{AC}.M_m : Interface(j')\mathbf{AC})$$
$$\| \overset{}{\underset{k=1}{R}}<Implementation(k)\mathbf{CC} : \mathbf{AC}(j)>$$
$$\| \overset{r}{\underset{v=1}{R}} <Instantiation(v)\mathbf{CC} : \mathbf{CC}(k)>$$
$$\}$$

a class that serves as a general and conceptual model to be inherited but not be instantiated. The latter is an ordinary class derived from an AC that can be instantiated.

A generic AC specified in RTPA is shown in Figure 4. The architecture part is used to specify the architectural attributes of the abstract class, which include internal variables shared by the hierarchy of classes. The static behavior part of an AC is used to define the method signatures of the AC class, where detailed implementation will be left to be done in derived concrete classes. It is noteworthy that an AC has no dynamic behavior in the specification because ACs cannot be instantiated.

Similarly, a generic CC can be formally specified in RTPA, as shown in Figure 5. The CC implements the dynamic behaviors that can be instantiated and executed in a derived object. Possible events that drive a method in a **CC** can be classified into message, time, and interrupt. More formal treatment of classes and their relational operations may be referred to RTPA (Wang, 2002, 2003, 2007a) and concept algebra (Wang, 2006a, 2007c).

The Generic Model of Patterns in RTPA

A pattern is a highly reusable and coherent set of complex classes that are encapsulated to provide certain functions. According to "Gamma et al. (1995)," patterns can be classified into the *creational, structural,* and *behavioral* ones. Using RTPA notations and methodology, a pattern is denoted by three parallel components known as the *architecture, static,* and *dynamic* behaviors, as shown in Figure 6. The architecture of a pattern specifies how many classes and components are used to compose the pattern and what relationships are among those components. The static behaviors of a pattern define what kinds of components are used to compose this pattern and what rules all components should abide. The dynamic behaviors of a pattern describe how those components interact and collaborate to realize functionality at run-time.

In Figure 6, the *architecture* of the generic pattern can be refined by a set of component logic models (CLMs), which describes the structures of a class, particularly its attributes (Wang, 2002). The *static behaviors* of the generic pattern are refined by a set of processes that are corresponding to each of the methods within the class. The process behaviors are denoted by RTPA meta-processes and their combinations using process relations for manipulating internal attributes or interacting with external components of the generic pattern. The *dynamic behaviors* of the generic pattern are refined by event-driven processes deployed by the system.

The generic pattern model may be treated as a super metapattern in object-oriented system design and programming, which models any specific software pattern at four levels known as the *interface, implementation, instantiations,* and *associations.* According to the generic model of patterns, the features of patterns lie in the hierarchical architectures as described by Pattern**ST**.Architecture**ST**, as shown in Figure 6. It is noteworthy that a class is usually modeled as a two-level structure with only the class *interface* and *implementations* in literature (Taibi, & Ngo, 2003; Vu & Wang, 2004). However, the four-level hierarchical model introduced here reveals the nature of how classes may be used to form complex patterns via *instantiations* and *associations.*

The *interface* of a pattern, Pattern**ST**.Architecture**ST**.Interface**ST**, isolates users of the pattern from its internal implementation. Users may only access the pattern via its interface. This mechanism enables the implementation of the pattern independent of its users. Whenever the internal implementation needs to be changed, it is transparent to the users of the pattern as long as the interface keeps the same (Wang & Huang, 2005). The interface of a pattern specifies the communication protocol among pattern components. Although instances could extend their behaviors beside those interface defined in this part their communication should abide those definition. The interface is the only access point of a component inside a pattern.

Because a pattern is a highly reusable construct of a software entity, the *implementation* of a pattern, Pattern**ST**.Architecture**ST**.Implementation**ST**, is kept at a generic abstract class until the pattern is invoked by a specific application or instantiation. In other words, because a pattern is a generic model of reusable functions, specific behaviors in an execution instance are dependent on run-time information provided by users of the pattern.

The forth component in the generic pattern hierarchy is the internal *associations,* which is used to model the interrelationships among other three-level abstractions of classes and interfaces within the pattern.

Figure 7. The UML structure of the State pattern

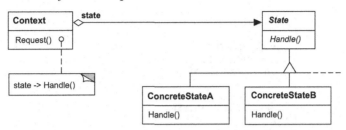

The *associations* of the pattern define relationships among all components in the pattern. Component collaborations are the soul of patterns that capture component collaborations. The flexibility, reusability, and differences of patterns are embodied by the associations (Wang & Huang, 2005). A comprehensive set of pattern association rules may be referred to Concept Algebra (Wang, 2006b, 2007c).

The generic model of patterns or the meta pattern model describes software patterns in a coherent, concise, and unambiguous way. External relationship among patterns could be deduced by this formula as well, when a super pattern is considered beyond all the component patterns. The method developed in this section helps readers avoid the drawbacks of conventional patterns, in order to develop more efficient, reusable, flexible, and predicable software systems.

CASE STUDIES ON FORMAL SPECIFICATIONS OF PATTERNS IN RTPA

This section applies the RTPA pattern specification methodology in three case studies. The *State* and *Strategy* patterns are used to demonstrate that differences between these two patterns can be clearly distinguished by RTPA specifications, while other methods rendering vague message to users. The *MasterSlave* pattern (Buschmann, 1995) is used to demonstrate the expressive power of RTPA specifications. All cases studies show that not only conventional design patterns, but also newly discovered patterns can be precisely specified by RTPA.

Formal Specification of the State Pattern

The *State* pattern allows an object to alter its behavior when its internal state changes. The structure of this pattern proposed in Gamma et al. (1995) is shown in Figure 7.

A formal model of the state pattern can be derived on the basis of the generic pattern model developed in Figure 6. Corresponding to Figure 7, the RTPA specification of the *State* pattern is given in Figure 8.

Formal Specification of the Strategy Pattern

The *Strategy* pattern defines a family of algorithms, encapsulates them in a coherent structure, and makes them interchangeable (Gamma et al., 1995). This pattern lets the algorithm vary independently from clients that use it. The structure of the Strategy pattern is shown in Figure 9.

Figure 8. The RTPA specification of the State pattern

StatePattern**ST** $\triangleq$
{
    Architecture: **ST**
  || StaticBehaviors: **ST**
  || DynamicBehaviors: **ST**
}

StatePattern**ST**.Architecture**ST** $\triangleq$
{
    \<Interfaces\>
  || \<Implementations\>
  || \<Instantiations\>
  || \<Associations\>
}

StatePattern**ST**.Architecture**ST**.Interfaces**ST** $\triangleq$ State**ST**::
{ $\displaystyle\mathop{R}_{i=1}^{n}$ \<Attributes(i) : **RT**\>

  || \<AbstractState : **AC**\>
}

StatePattern**ST**.Architecture**ST**.Implementations**ST** $\triangleq$
{
    ConcreteContext**CC** : **CC**
  || $\displaystyle\mathop{R}_{j=1}^{m}$ \<ConcreteState(j)**CC** : AbstractState**AC**\>
}

StatePattern**ST**.Architecture**ST**.Instantiations**ST** $\triangleq$
{
    Context**CC** : **CC**
  || $\displaystyle\mathop{R}_{k=1}^{q}$ \<State(k)**CC** : ConcreteState(k)**CC**\>
}

StatePattern**ST**.Architecture**ST**.Associations**ST** $\triangleq$
{
  // Inheritance
  $\displaystyle\mathop{R}_{i=1}^{n}$ ConcreteState(i)**CC** : AbstractState**AC**
  // Composition
  || $\displaystyle\mathop{R}_{v=1}^{r}$ (ConcreteContext**CC**.M$_v$: ConcreteState**CC**(v) |
            ConcreteContext**CC**(v)
              || ConcreteState**CC**(v))
  // Delegation
  || $\displaystyle\mathop{R}_{i=1}^{n}$ (ConcreteContext**CC**(i) ↳ ConcreteState**CC**(i))
}

A formal model of the Strategy pattern can be derived on the basis of the generic pattern model developed in Figure 6. Corresponding to Figure 9, the RTPA specification of the strategy pattern is shown in Figure 10.

Contrasting the State and Strategy patterns in UML, it is noteworthy that both patterns share almost identical structures. In other words, UML class diagrams, as shown in Figures 7 and 9, may not be able to discriminate the differences between these two patterns. This results in the main confusions, ambiguities, and difficulties in pattern comprehension and applications using UML-based methodologies.

Figure 9. The UML structure of the Strategy pattern

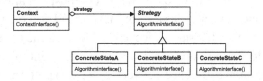

Figure 10. The RTPA specification of the Strategy pattern

StrategyPattern**ST** ≜
{
   Architecture: **ST**
|| StaticBehaviors: **ST**
|| DynamicBehaviors: **ST**
}

StrategyPattern**ST**.Architecture**ST** ≜
{
   <Interfaces>
|| <Implementations>
|| <Instantiations>
|| <Associations>
}

StrategyPattern**ST**.Architecture**ST**.Interfaces**ST** ≜ Strategy**ST**
::
{
  $\overset{n}{\underset{i=1}{R}}$<Attributes(i) : **RT**>

  || <AbstractStrategy : **AC**>
}

StrategyPattern**ST**.Architecture**ST**.Implementations**ST** ≜
{
  ConcreteContext**CC** : **CC**
  $||\overset{m}{\underset{j=1}{R}}$(ConcreteStrategy(j)**CC** : AbstractStrategy**AC**)
}

StrategyPattern**ST**.Architecture**ST**.Instantiations**ST** ≜
{
  Context**CC** : **CC**
  $||\overset{q}{\underset{k=1}{R}}$<Strategy(k)**CC** : ConcreteStrategy(k)**CC**>
}

StrategyPattern**ST**.Architecture**ST**.Associations**ST** ≜
{
// Inheritance
$\overset{n}{\underset{i=1}{R}}$ConcreteStrategy(i)**CC** : AbstractStrategy**AC**

// Composition
|| (ConcreteContext**CC**.M : ConcreteStrategy**CC** |
         ConcreteContext**CC**
         || ConcreteStrategy**CC**)
// Delegation
|| ConcreteContext**CC** ↳ ConcreteStrategy**CC**
}

However, the specifications in RTPA, as shown in Figures 8 and 10, can clearly capture the differences in the sections of class associations by different composition approaches. The RTPA models show that in the former, all concrete state classes are instantiated by concrete classes simultaneously, where the concrete state objects have the same lifecycle as those of the concrete context objects; while in the latter, only one concrete strategy object alive within any point of time in the concrete context object lifecycle. This is the essential difference between those two patterns, which cannot be expressed explicitly by UML syntaxes and semantics.

Formal Specification of the MasterSlave Pattern

It is observed that traditional methods for pattern modeling are focused on existing and specific patterns proposed in "Gamma et al. (1995)." However, most practical patterns in software engineering are user-defined rather than pre-specified. Therefore, a generic pattern model is needed to support users to deductively model new patterns in practice.

A system pattern, *MasterSlave* (Buschmann, 1995) as shown in Figure 11, is presented in this subsection in order to demonstrate the application of the generic pattern model and the expressive power of RTPA for modeling patterns. The *MasterSlave* pattern handles the computation of replicated services of a software system to achieve fault tolerance and robustness. Replication of services and the delegation of the same task to several independent slave servers is a common strategy to handle fault-tolerant requirements in safety-critical software systems.

The *MasterSlave* pattern consists of two kinds of components: the master and the slaves. Clients of the pattern interact with the master component directly. However, the master component does not implement services by itself. It delegates the services to a number of slave components, where at least two identical slave components exist in the system with the same set of functionality. The slave components are completely independent of each other, and they may use different strategies for providing the designated service. The master component delegates a requested service to all slave components and chooses one of the most suitable responses as the result for the client.

A formal model of the MasterSlave pattern can be derived on the basis of the generic pattern model developed in Figure 6. Corresponding to Figure 11, the RTPA specification of the MasterSlave pattern is given in Figure 12. The derived pattern precisely describes the architecture and associations between member classes of the *MasterSlave* pattern. Several strategies may be available for the master component to select results provided by the slaves, such as the result first returned, the majority result returned by all slaves, or the average result of all slaves.

CONCLUSION

This article has reviewed existing pattern specification methods and problems yet to be solved. A generic mathematical model of patterns has been presented using Real-Time Process Algebra (RTPA). Based on it any design patterns, either system-specified or user-defined, can be derived. With the RTPA support tool, a pattern specified in RTPA can be automatically translated into code in programming languages (Tan, Wang, & Ngolah, 2006).

This work has revealed that a software pattern is a highly reusable design encapsulation that encompasses complex and flexible internal associations between a coherent set of abstract classes and

Figure 11. The UML structure of the MasterSlave pattern

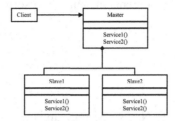

Figure 12. The RTPA specification of the MasterSlave pattern

MasterSlavePattern**ST** ≜
{
  Architecture : **ST**
|| StaticBehaviors : **ST**
|| DynamicBehaviors : **ST**
}

MasterSlavePattern**ST**.Architecture**ST** ≜
{
  <Interfaces>
|| <Implementations>
|| <Instantiations>
|| <Associations>
}

MasterSlavePatternST.ArchitectureST.Interfaces**ST** ≜
Master**ST** ::
{
  $\underset{i=1}{\overset{n}{R}}$<Attributes(i) : **RT**>

|| <AbstractMasterComponent : **AC**>
}

MasterSlavePattern**ST**.Architecture**ST**.Implementations**ST** ≜
{
  <ConcreteMasterComponent**CC** : **CC**>
|| $\overset{m}{R}$<ConcreteSlaveComponent(j)**CC** : **CC**>
} $j=1$

MasterSlavePattern**ST**.Architecture**ST**.Instantiations**ST** ≜
{
ConcreteMasterInstance**CC**: AbstractMasterComponent**AC**
|| $\underset{k=1}{\overset{q}{R}}$<ConcreteSlaveInstance(k)**CC** :
    ConcreteSlaveComponent(j**N**)**CC**>
}

MasterSlavePattern**ST**.Architecture**ST**.Associations**ST** ≜
{
  // Inheritance
ConcreteMasterComponent**CC** :
        AbstractMasterComponent**AC**
  // Delegation
|| (ConcreteMasterComponent**CC** ↳
       $\underset{j=1}{\overset{m}{R}}$ConcreteSlaveComponent(j)**CC**)
  // Aggregation
|| ($\underset{k=1}{\overset{q}{R}}$ConcreteMasterComponent**CC**.M :
  ConcreteSlaveComponent**CC** (k) |
        ConcreteMasterComponent**CC**
        ⨕ ConcreteSlaveComponent**CC**)
}

instantiations. The generic model of patterns has provided a pattern of patterns. It is not only applicable to existing patterns' modeling and comprehension, but also useful for future patterns' identification and formalization.

ACKNOWLEDGMENT

The authors would like to acknowledge the Natural Science and Engineering Council of Canada (NSERC) for its partial support to this work. We would like to thank the anonymous reviewers for their valuable comments and suggestions.

REFERENCES

Beck, K., Coplien, J. O., Crocker, R., & Dominick, L. (1996, March). Industrial experience with design patterns. In *Proceedings of the 19th Intel. Conf. on Software Engineering*, (pp. 103-114). Berlin: IEEE CS Press.

Bosch, J. (1996). Relations as object model components. *Journal of Programming Languages*, *4*(1), 39-61.

Buschmann, F. (1995). *The MasterSlave Pattern, pattern languages of program design*. Addison-Wesley.

Eden, A. H., Gil, J., Hirshfeld, Y., & Yehudai, A. (2005). *Towards a mathematical foundation for design patterns (*Tech. Rep.). Dept. of Computer Science, Concordia University, Montreal, Canada.

Florijn, G., Meijers, M., & Wionsen, P. V. (1997). Tool support for object-oriented patterns. In *Proceedings of the 11th European Conference on Object-Oriented Programming* (ECOOP'97)(pp. 472-495), Jyvaskyla, Finland.

Gamma, E., Helm, R., Johnson, R., & Vlissides, J. (1995). *Design patterns: Elements of reusable object oriented software*. Reading, MA: Addison-Wesley.

Lano, K., Goldsack, S., & Bicarregui, J. (1996). Formalizing design patterns. In *Proceedings of the 1st BCS-FACS Northern Formal Methods Workshop* (p. 1).

Lauder, A., & Kent, S. (1998). Precise visual specification of design patterns. In *Proceedings of the 12th European Conference on Object-Oriented Programming* (ECOOP'98), (LNCS, 1445, pp. 114-134). Springer-Verlag.

Mapelsden, D., Hosking, J., & Grundy, J. (1992). *Design pattern modeling and instantiation using DPML*, (Tech. Rep.). Department of Computer Science, University of Auckland.

OMG. (1997). *Object Constraint Language Specification 1.1.*

Pagel, B. U., & Winter, M. (1996). Towards pattern-based tools. In *Proceedings of the EuropLop'96*, (pp. 3.1-3.11).

Sunye, G., Guennec, A. L., & Jezequel, J. M. (2000). Design patterns application in UML. In *Proceedings of the 14th European Conference on Object-Oriented Programming* (ECOOP'00)(pp. 44-62), Sophia Antipolis, France.

Taibi, T., & Ngo, D. C. L. (2003). Formal specification of design patterns–a balanced approach. *Journal of Object Technology*, *2*(4), 127-140.

Tan, X., Wang, Y., & Ngolah, C. F. (2006, May). Design and implementation of an automatic RTPA code generator. In *Proceedings of the 2006 Canadian Conference on Electrical and Computer Engineering (CCECE'06)*, (pp. 1605-1608). Ottawa, Canada: IEEE CS Press.

Vu, N. C., & Wang, Y. (2004, May). Specification of design patterns using real-time process algebra (RTPA). In *Proceedings of the 2004 Canadian Conference on Electrical and Computer Engineering* (CCECE'04), (pp. 1545-1548). Niagara, Falls, Ontario: IEEE CS Press.

Wang, Y. (2002, October). The real-time process algebra (RTPA). *Annals of Software Engineering: An International Journal*, *14*, 235-274.

Wang, Y. (2003). Using process algebra to describe human and software behaviors. *Brain and Mind: A Transdisciplinary Journal of Neuroscience and Neurophilosophy, 4*(2), 199-213.

Wang, Y. (2006a, July). On concept algebra and knowledge representation. In *Proceedings of the 5th IEEE International Conference on Cognitive Informatics (ICCI'06)*, (pp. 320-331). Beijing, China: IEEE CS Press.

Wang, Y. (2006b). On the informatics laws and deductive semantics of software. *IEEE Transactions on Systems, Man, and Cybernetics (C), 36*(2), 167-171.

Wang, Y. (2006c, July). Cognitive informatics and contemporary mathematics for knowledge representation and manipulation, Invited Plenary Talk. In *Proceedings of the 1st International Conference on Rough Set and Knowledge Technology* (RSKT'06), (pp. 69-78). Lecture Notes in Artificial Intelligence, LNAI 4062. Chongqing, China: Springer-Verlag.

Wang, Y. (2007a, July). *Software engineering foundations: A software science perspective.* CRC Book Series in Software Engineering (Vol. II). USA: CRC Press.

Wang, Y. (2007b, January). The theoretical framework of cognitive informatics. *The International Journal of Cognitive Informatics and Natural Intelligence (IJCiNi), 1*(1), 1-27. Hershey, PA: IGI Publishing.

Wang, Y. (2007c). Keynote speech, on theoretical foundations of software engineering and denotational mathematics. In *Proceedings of the 5th Asian Workshop on Foundations of Software*, Xiamen, China, (pp. 99-102).

Wang, Y., & Huang, J. (2005, May). Formal models of object-oriented patterns using RTPA. In *Proceedings of the 2005 Canadian Conference on Electrical and Computer Engineering* (CCECE'05), Saskatoon, Canada, (pp. 1822-1825). IEEE CS Press.

This work was previously published in International Journal of Cognitive Informatics and Natural Intelligence, Vol. 2, Issue 1, pp. 100-111 copyright 2008 by IGI Publishing (an imprint of IGI Global).

Chapter 14
Deductive Semantics of RTPA

Yingxu Wang
University of Calgary, Canada

ABSTRACT

Deductive semantics is a novel software semantic theory that deduces the semantics of a program in a given programming language from a unique abstract semantic function to the concrete semantics embodied by the changes of status of a finite set of variables constituting the semantic environment of the program. There is a lack of a generic semantic function and its unified mathematical model in conventional semantics, which may be used to explain a comprehensive set of programming statements and computing behaviors. This article presents a complete paradigm of formal semantics that explains how deductive semantics is applied to specify the semantics of real-time process algebra (RTPA) and how RTPA challenges conventional formal semantic theories. Deductive semantics can be applied to define abstract and concrete semantics of programming languages, formal notation systems, and large-scale software systems, to facilitate software comprehension and recognition, to support tool development, to enable semantics-based software testing and verification, and to explore the semantic complexity of software systems. Deductive semantics may greatly simplify the description and analysis of the semantics of complicated software systems specified in formal notations and implemented in programming languages.

INTRODUCTION

Semantics in linguistics is a domain that studies the interpretation of words and sentences, and analysis of their meanings. Semantics deals with how the meaning of a sentence in a language is obtained, hence the sentence is comprehended. Studies on semantics explore mechanisms in the understanding of languages and their meanings on the basis of syntactic structures (Chomsky, 1956, 1957, 1959, 1962, 1965, 1982; Tarski, 1944).

Software semantics in computing and computational linguistics have been recognized as one of the key areas in the development of fundamental theories for computer science and software engineering (Bjoner, 2000; Gries, 1981; Hoare, 1969; McDermid, 1991; Slonneg & Kurts, 1995; Wang, 2006b, 2007c). The semantics of a programming language is the behavioral meaning that constitute what a syntactically correct instructional statement in the language is supposed to do during run time. The development of formal semantic theories of programming is one of the pinnacles of computing and software engineering (Gunter, 1992; Meyer, 1990; Louden, 1993; Bjoner, 2000; Pagan, 1981).

Definition 1. *The semantics of a program in a given programming language is the logical consequences of an execution of the program that results in the changes of values of a finite set of variables and/or the embodiment of computing behaviors in the underpinning computing environment.*

A number of formal semantics, such as the *operational* (Marcotty & Ledgard, 1986; Ollongren, 1974; Wegner, 1972; Wikstrom, 1987), *denotational* (Bjorner and Jones, 1982; Jones, 1980; Schmidt, 1988, 1994, 1996; Scott, 1982; Scott & Strachey, 1971), *axiomatic* (Dijktra, 1975, 1976; Gries, 1981; Hoare, 1969), and *algebraic* (Goguen, Thatcher, Wagner, & Wright, 1977; Gougen & Malcolm, 1996; Guttag & Horning, 1978), have been proposed in the last three decades for defining and interpreting the meanings of programs and programming languages. The classic software semantics are oriented on a certain set of software behaviors that are limited at the level of language statements rather than that of programs and software systems. There is a lack of a generic semantic function and its unified mathematical model in conventional semantics, which may be used to explain a comprehensive set of programming statements and computing behaviors. The mathematical models of the target machines and the semantic environments in conventional semantics seem to be inadequate to deal with the semantics of complex programming requirements, and to express some important instructions, complex control structures, and the real-time environments at run time. For supporting systematical and machine enabled semantic analysis and code generation in software engineering, the *deductive semantics* is developed that provides a systematic semantic analysis methodology.

Deduction is a reasoning process that discovers new knowledge or derives a specific conclusion based on generic premises such as abstract rules or principles (Wang, 2006b, 2007a, 2007c). The nature of semantics of a given programming language is its computational meanings or embodied behaviors expressed by an instruction in the language. Because the carriers of software semantics are a finite set of variables declared in a given program, program semantics can be reduced onto the changes of values of these variables over time. In order to provide a rigorous mathematical treatment of both the abstract and concrete semantics of software, a new type of formal semantics known as the deductive semantics is presented.

Definition 2. *Deductive semantics is a formal semantics that deduces the semantics of a program in a given programming language from a generic abstract semantic function to the concrete semantics, which are embodied onto the changes of status of a finite set of variables constituting the semantic environment of computing.*

This article presents a comprehensive theory of deductive semantics of software systems. The mathematical models of deductive semantics and the fundamental properties are described. The deductive models of semantics, semantic function, and semantic environment at various composing levels of programs are introduced. Properties of software semantics and relationships between the software behavioral space and the semantic environment are studied. New methods such as the semantic differential and semantic matrix are developed to facilitate deductive semantic analyses from a generic semantic function to a specific semantic matrix, and from semantics of statements to those of processes and programs. The establishment of the deductive semantic rules of RTPA (Wang, 2002, 2003, 2006a, 2006b, 2007a, 2007b, 2008a, 2008b) is described, where the semantics of a comprehensive set of processes is systematically modeled.

THE THEORY OF DEDUCTIVE SEMANTICS

This section presents the theory of deductive semantics (Wang, 2006b, 2007c). A generic mathematical model of deductive semantics of software is developed, and the concepts of semantic environment and semantic function are rigorously defined. Based on them, deductive semantics of programs at different composition levels are rigorously modeled. Then, common properties of software semantics are analyzed.

The Semantic Environment and Semantic Function

Definition 3. *A semantic environment Θ of a programming language is a logical model of a set of identifiers I and their values V bound in pairs, i.e.:*

$$
\begin{aligned}
\Theta &\triangleq f : I \to V, V \subseteq \mathbb{R} \\
&= \{ \underset{k=1}{\overset{\#I}{R}} (i_k, v_k) \} \\
&= \{ (i_1, v_1), (i_2, v_2), \dots, (i_{\#I}, v_{\#I}) \}
\end{aligned}
\tag{1}
$$

where $\mathbb{R}$ is the set of real numbers, $i_k \in I$, $v_k \in V \subseteq \mathbb{R}$, and $\#I$ the number of elements in I.

Note the big-R notation is adopted to denote a set of recurring structures or repetitive behaviors (Wang, 2002, 2007c, 2008a). The semantic environment constituting the behaviors of software is inherently a three dimensional structure known as those of operations, memory space, and time.

Definition 4. *The behavioral space Ω of a program executed on a certain machine is a finite set of variables operated in a 3-D state space determined by a triple, i.e.:*

$$
\Omega \triangleq (OP, T, S)
\tag{2}
$$

where *OP* is a finite set of *operations*, *T* is a finite set of discrete *time* points of program execution, and *S* is a finite set of *memory locations* or their logical representations by *identifiers* of variables.

According to Definitions 3 and 4, the set of *variables* of a program, *S*, plays an important role in semantic modeling and analysis, because they are the objects of software behavioral operations and the carriers of program semantics. Variables can be classified as *free* and *system* variables. The former are user defined and the latter are language provided. From a functional point of view, variables can be classified into *object representatives, control variables, result containers,* and *address locaters*. The life spans or scopes of variables can be categorized as *persistent, global, local,* and *temporal.* The persistent variables are those that their lifespan are longer than the program that generates them, such as data in a database or files in a distributed network.

A new calculus introduced in deductive semantics is the *partial differential of sets* (Wang, 2006b, 2007c), which is used to facilitate the instantiation of abstract semantics by concrete ones, as described below.

Definition 5. *Given two sets X and U, $X \subseteq \text{Þ}U$, a partial differential of X on U with elements x, $x \in X$, denoted by $\partial U / \partial x$, is an elicitation of interested elements from U as specified in X, i.e.:*

$$\frac{\partial U}{\partial x} \triangleq X \cap U, \ x \in X$$
$$= X, \ X \subseteq \text{Þ}U \tag{3}$$

where ÞU denotes a power set of U.

The partial differential of sets can be easily extended to double, triple, or more generally, multiple partial differentials as defined below.

Definition 6. *A multiple partial differential of X_1, X_2, ..., and X_n on ÞU with elements $x_1 \in X_1$, $x_2 \in X_2$, ..., and $x_n \in X_n$, denoted by*

$$\frac{\partial^n}{\partial x_1 \, \partial x_2 \, ... \, \partial x_n} U,$$

is a Cartesian product of all partial differentials that select interested elements from U as specified in X_1, X_2, ..., and X_n, respectively, i.e.:

$$\frac{\partial^n}{\partial x_1 \, \partial x_2 \, ... \, \partial x_n} U \triangleq X_1 \times X_2 \times ... \times X_n \tag{4}$$

where X_1, X_2,..., $X_n \subseteq \text{Þ}U$ and $\forall i \neq j$, $1 \leq i, j \leq n$, $X_i \cap X_j = \emptyset$.

For example,

$$\frac{\partial^2}{\partial x \, \partial y} U = X \times Y, \ x \in X, y \in Y, and \ X, Y \subseteq \text{Þ}U$$

and

$$\frac{\partial^3}{\partial x \, \partial y \, \partial z} U = X \times Y \times Z, x \in X, y \in Y, x \in X, \text{and } X, Y, Z \subseteq \text{Þ}U.$$

On the basis of the definitions of software behavioral space and partial differential of sets, the semantic environment of software can be formally described.

Definition 7. *The semantic environment Θ of a program on a certain target machine is its run-time behavioral space Ω projected onto the Cartesian plane determined by T and S, i.e.:*

$$\Theta = \frac{\partial^2 \Omega}{\partial t \, \partial s}, \; t \in T \wedge s \in S$$
$$= \frac{\partial^2 \Omega}{\partial t \, \partial s}(OP, T, S) \tag{5}$$
$$= T \times S$$

As indicated in Definition 7, the semantic environment of a program is a dynamic space over time, because following each execution of a statement in the program, the semantic environment Θ, particularly the sets of variables S and their values V, may be changed.

In semantic analysis, the changed part of the semantic environment Θ is particularly interested, which is the embodiment of software semantics. A generic semantic function is developed below, which can be used to derive a specific and concrete semantic function for a given statement, process, or program by mathematical deduction.

Definition 8. *A semantic function of a program $\wp$, $f_\theta(\wp)$, is a function that maps the semantic environment Θ into a finite set of values V determining by a Cartesian product on a finite set of executing steps T and a finite set of variables S, i.e.:*

$$f_\theta(\wp) \triangleq f : T \times S \to V =$$

$$\begin{pmatrix} & s_1 & s_2 & \cdots & s_m \\ t_0 & \perp & \perp & \cdots & \perp \\ t_1 & v_{11} & v_{12} & & v_{1m} \\ \vdots & \vdots & \vdots & \ddots & \vdots \\ t_n & v_{n1} & v_{n1} & \cdots & v_{nm} \end{pmatrix} \tag{6}$$

where $T = \{t_0, t_1, ..., t_n\}$, $S = \{s_1, s_2, ..., s_m\}$, and V is a finite set of values $v(t_i, s_j)$, $0 \le i \le n$, and $1 \le j \le m$.

In Equation 6, all values of $v(t_i, s_j)$ at t_0 is undefined for a program as denoted by the bottom symbol $\perp$, i.e. $v(0, s_j) = \perp$, $1 \le j \le m$. However, for a statement or a process, it is usually true that $v(0, s_j) \ne \perp$ dependent on the context of previous statement(s) or the initialization of the system.

According to Definitions 7 and 8, the semantic environment and the domain of a semantic function can be illustrated by a semantic diagram as described below (Wang, 2006b, 2007c).

Definition 9. *A semantic diagram is a sub Cartesian-plane in the semantic environment Θ that forms the domain of the semantic function for a given process P with $f_\theta(P) = f : T_P \times S_P \to V_P$*

For example, the semantic diagram of an abstract process P, $f_\theta(P)$, as defined in Definition 9 can be illustrated in Figure 1, where V_P is the domain of dynamic variable values of process P over time, i.e., $V_P = T_P \times S_P$. The semantic diagram of two sequential processes, $P \to Q$, can be referred to Figure 3.

The semantic diagram can be used to analyze complex semantic relations, and to demonstrate semantic functions and their semantic environments. Observing Figures 1 and 3, the flowing properties of process relations can be derived.

Lemma 1. *The variables of two arbitrary processes P and Q, S_P and S_Q, in the semantic environment Θ possess the following properties:*

a. *The entire set of variables:*
$$S = S_P \cup S_Q \tag{7}$$

b. *Global variables:*
$$S_G \subseteq S_P \cap S_Q \tag{8}$$

c. *Local variables:*
$$S_L = S - S_G, \; S_L \subseteq S_P \oplus S_Q,$$

where $S_{Lp} = S_L \setminus S_Q$ and $S_{Lq} = S_L \setminus S_P$ $\tag{9}$

Deductive Semantics of Programs at Different Levels of Compositions

According to the generic model and the hierarchical architecture of programs, the semantics of a program in a given programming language can be described and analyzed at various composition levels, such as those of *statement*, *process*, and *system* from the bottom-up (Wang, 2007c, 2008b).

Definition 10. *The semantics of a statement p, $\theta(p)$, on a given semantic environment Θ is a double partial differential of the semantic function $f_\theta(p)$ on executing steps T and the set of variables S, i.e.:*

Figure 1. The semantic diagram of a process

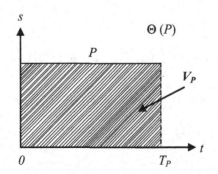

$$\theta(P) \triangleq \frac{\partial^2}{\partial t \, \partial s} f_\theta(p)$$

$$= \mathop{R}_{i=0}^{\#T(p)} \left(\mathop{R}_{j=1}^{\#S(p)} v_p \ t_i, s_j \right)$$

$$= \mathop{R}_{i=0}^{1} \left(\mathop{R}_{j=1}^{\#\{s_1, \, s_2, \, \ldots, \, s_m\}} v_p \ t_i, s_j \right)$$

$$= \begin{pmatrix} & s_1 & s_2 & \cdots & s_m \\ t_0 & v_{01} & v_{02} & \cdots & v_{0m} \\ (t_0, t_1] & v_{11} & v_{12} & \cdots & v_{1m} \end{pmatrix} \tag{10}$$

where t denotes the discrete time immediately before and after the execution of p during (t_0, t_1), and # is the cardinal calculus that counts the number of elements in a given set, i.e. $n = \#T(p)$ and $m = \#S(p)$.

In Definition 10, the first partial differential selects all related variable $S(p)$ of the statement p from Θ. The second partial differential selects a set of discrete steps of p's execution $T(p)$ from Θ. According to Definition 10, the semantics of a statement can be reduced onto a semantic function that results in a 2-D matrix with the changes of values of all variables over time of program execution.

On the basis of Definitions 8 and 10, semantics of individual statements can be analyzed using Equation 10 in a deductive process.

Example 1. *Analyze the semantics of Statement 3, $\theta(p_3)$, in the following program entitled sum:*

Box 1.

$$\theta^*(p) = \mathop{R}_{j=1}^{\#S(p)} \left(v_p(t_i, s_j) \oplus v_p(t_{i+1}, s_j) \right)$$

$$= \mathop{R}_{j=1}^{\#S(p)} < v_p(t_i, s_j) \to v_p(t_{i+1}, s_j) \mid v_p(t_i, s_j) \neq v_p(t_{i+1}, s_j) > \tag{12}$$

Box 2.

$$\theta^*(p_3) = \mathop{R}_{j=1}^{\#S(p_3)} < v_{p_3}(t_2, s_j) \to v_{p_3}(t_3, s_j) \mid v_{p_3}(t_2, s_j) \neq v_{p_3}(t_3, s_j) >$$

$$= \mathop{R}_{j=1}^{\#(x,y,z)} < v_{p_3}(t_2, s_j) \to v_{p_3}(t_3, s_j) \mid v_{p_3}(t_2, s_j) \neq v_{p_3}(t_3, s_j) >$$

$$= \{ < v_{p_3}(t_2, z) = \perp \ \to v_{p_3}(t_3, z) = 10 > \}$$

```
void sum;
{
  (0) int x, y, z;
  (1) x = 8;
  (2) y = 2;
  (3) z := x + y;
}
```

According to Definition 10, the semantics of Statement p_3 is as follows:

$$
\begin{aligned}
\theta(p_3) &= \frac{\partial^2}{\partial t\,\partial s} f_\theta(p_3) \\
&= \mathop{R}_{i=2}^{3}\,(\mathop{R}_{j=1}^{\#S(p_3)} v_{p_3}\, t_i, s_j) \\
&= \mathop{R}_{i=2}^{3}\,(\mathop{R}_{j=1}^{\#\{x,y,z\}} v_{p_3}\, t_i, s_j) \\
&= \begin{pmatrix}
 & \mathbf{x} & \mathbf{y} & \mathbf{z} \\
\mathbf{t_2} & 8 & 2 & \perp \\
\mathbf{(t_2,t_3]} & 8 & 2 & 10
\end{pmatrix}
\end{aligned}
\tag{11}
$$

This example shows how the concrete semantics of a statement can be derived on the basis of the generic and abstract semantic function as given in Definition 10.

Definition 11. *The semantic effect of a statement p, $\theta^*(p)$, is the resulted changes of values of variables by its semantic function $\theta(p)$ during the time interval immediately before and after the execution of p, $\Delta t = (t_i, t_{i+1})$, see Box 1, where $\rightarrow$ denotes a transition of values for a given variable.*

Example 2. *For the same statement p_3 as given in Example 1, determine its semantic effect $\theta^*(p_3)$.*

Box 3.

$$
\begin{aligned}
\theta(P) &= \frac{\partial^2}{\partial t\,\partial s} f_\theta(P) \\
&= \mathop{R}_{k=1}^{n-1}\,\{[\frac{\partial^2}{\partial t\,\partial s} f_\theta(P_k)]\, r_{kl}\, [\frac{\partial^2}{\partial t\,\partial s} f_\theta(P_l)]\}, l = k+1 \\
&= \mathop{R}_{k=1}^{n-1}\,\{[\mathop{R}_{i=0}^{\#T(P_k)} \mathop{R}_{j=1}^{\#S(P_k)} v_{P_k}(t_i, s_j)]\, r_{kl}\, [\mathop{R}_{i=0}^{\#T(P_l)} \mathop{R}_{j=1}^{\#S(P_l)} v_{P_l}(t_i, s_j)]\} \\
&= \begin{pmatrix}
\mathbf{V_{p_1}} & & & \mathbf{V_G} \\
 & \mathbf{V_{p_2}} & & \mathbf{V_G} \\
 & & \ddots & \vdots \\
 & & & \mathbf{V_{p_{n-1}}} & \mathbf{V_G}
\end{pmatrix}
\end{aligned}
\tag{13}
$$

According to Equation 12, the semantic effect $\theta^*(p_3)$ is seen in Box 2.

It is noteworthy in Examples 1 and 2 that deductive semantics can be used not only to describe the *abstract* and *concrete* semantics of programs, but also to elicit and highlight their semantic effects.

Considering that a program or a process is composed by individual statements with given rules of compositions, the definition and mathematical model of deductive semantics at the statement level can be extended onto the higher levels of program hierarchy.

Definition 12. *The semantics of a process P, $\theta(P)$, on a given semantic environment Θ is a double partial differential of the semantic function $f_\theta(\boldsymbol{P})$ on the sets of variables S and executing steps T, see Box 3, where V_{p_k}, $1 \leq k \leq n-1$, is a set of values of local variables that belongs to processes P_k, and V_G is a finite set of values of global variables.*

On the basis of Definition 12, the semantics of a program at the top-level composition can be deduced to the combination of the semantics of a set of processes, each of which can be further deduced to the composition of all statements' semantics as described below.

Definition 13. *The semantics of a program $\wp$, $\theta(\wp)$, on a given semantic environment Θ, is a combination of the semantic functions of all processes $\theta(P_k)$, $1 \leq k \leq n$, i.e.:*

$$
\begin{aligned}
\theta(\wp) &= \mathop{R}_{k=1}^{\#K(\wp)} \frac{\partial^2}{\partial t \, \partial s} f_\theta(\wp) \\
&= \mathop{R}_{k=1}^{\#K(\wp)} \theta\, P_k) \\
&= \mathop{R}_{k=1}^{\#K(\wp)} [\mathop{R}_{i=0}^{\#T(P_k)} (\mathop{R}_{j=1}^{\#S(P_k)} v_{P_k}\, t_i, s_j)]
\end{aligned}
\tag{14}
$$

where $\#K(\wp)$ is the number of processes or components encompassed in the program.

It is noteworthy that Equation 14 will usually result in a very large matrix of semantic space, which can be quantitatively predicated as follows.

Definition 14. *The semantic space of a program $S_\Theta(\wp)$ is a product of $\#S(\wp)$ variables and $\#T(\wp)$ executing steps, i.e.:*

$$
\begin{aligned}
S_\Theta(\wp) &= \#S(\wp) \bullet \#T(\wp) \\
&= \sum_{k=1}^{\#K(\wp)} \#S(\wp_k) \bullet \sum_{k=1}^{\#K(\wp)} \#T(\wp_k)
\end{aligned}
\tag{15}
$$

The semantic space of programs provides a useful measure of software complexity. Due to the tremendous size of the semantic space, both program composition and comprehension are innately a hard problem in terms of complexity and cognitive difficulty.

Properties of Software Semantics

Observing the formal definitions and mathematical models of deductive semantics developed in previous subsections, a number of common properties of software semantics may be elicited, which are useful for explaining the fundamental characteristics of software semantics.

Figure 2. Relationship between software behavior space and the semantic environment

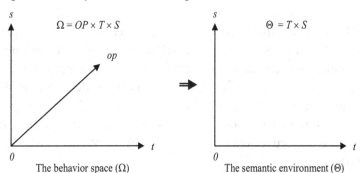

One of the most interesting characteristics of program semantics is its invariance against different executing speeds as described in the following theorem.

Theorem 1. *The asynchronicity of program semantics states that the semantics of a relatively timed program is invariant with the changes of executing speed, as long as any absolute time constraint is met.*

Theorem 1 asserts that, for most non real-time or relatively timed programs, different executing speeds or simulation paces will not alter the semantics of the software system. This explains why a programmer may simulate the run-time behaviors of a given program executing at a speed of up to 10^9 times faster than that of human beings. It also explains why computers with different system clock frequencies may correctly run the same program and obtain the same behavior.

Definition 15. *The behavior of a computational statement is a set of observable actions or changes of status of objects operated by the statement.*

According to Definition 4, the behavioral space of software, Ω, is three dimensional, while as given in Definition 7, the semantic environment Θ is two dimensional. Therefore, to a certain extent, semantic analysis is a projection of the 3-D software behaviors into the 2-D semantic environment Θ as shown in Figure 2.

The theory of deductive semantics can be systematically applied to formally and rigorously model and describe the semantics of the RTPA *metaprocesses* and the *process relations* (operations). On the basis of the mathematical models and properties of deductive semantics, the following sections formally describe a comprehensive set of RTPA semantics, particularly the 17 metaprocesses and the 17 process relations (Wang, 2002, 2003, 2007c, 2008a, 2008b). This work extends the coverage of semantic rules of programming languages to a complete set of features that encompasses both basic computing operations and their algebraic composition rules. Because RTPA is a denotational mathematical structure based on process algebra that covers a comprehensive set of computing and programming requirements, any formal semantics that is capable to process RTPA is powerful enough to express the semantics of any programming language.

DEDUCTIVE SEMANTICS OF RTPA METAPROCESSES

Metaprocesses of RTPA are elicited from basic computational requirements. Complex processes can be composed with multiple metaprocesses. RTPA identified 17 metaprocesses, $\mathfrak{P}$, on fundamental computing operations such as assignment, system control, event/time handling, memory and I/O manipulation, i.e., $\mathfrak{P} = \{:=, \blacklozenge, \Rightarrow, \Leftarrow, \nleftrightarrow, >, <, |>, |<, @, \triangleq, \uparrow, \downarrow, !, \otimes, \boxtimes, \S\}$. Detailed descriptions of the metaprocesses of RTPA and their syntaxes may be referred to (Wang, 2002, 2007c, 2008b), where each metaprocess is a basic operation on one or more operands such as variables, memory elements, or I/O ports. Based on Definitions 8 and 12, the deductive semantics of the set of RTPA metaprocesses can be defined in the following subsections.

The Assignment Process

Definition 16. *The semantics of the assignment process on a given semantic environment* Θ, $\theta(y\mathbf{RT} := x\mathbf{RT})$, *is a double partial differential of the semantic function* $f_\theta(y\mathbf{RT} := x\mathbf{RT})$ *on the sets of variables S and executing steps T, i.e.:*

$$
\theta(y\mathbf{RT} := x\mathbf{RT}) \triangleq \frac{\partial^2}{\partial t\,\partial s} f_\theta(y\mathbf{RT} := x\mathbf{RT})
$$

$$
= \mathop{R}_{i=0}^{\#T(y\mathbf{RT}\,:=\,x\mathbf{RT})} \left(\mathop{R}_{j=1}^{\#S(y\mathbf{RT}\,:=\,x\mathbf{RT})} v\, t_i, s_j \right) \tag{16}
$$

$$
= \mathop{R}_{i=0}^{1} \mathop{R}_{j=1}^{2} v(t_i, s_j)
$$

$$
= \begin{pmatrix} & x\mathbf{RT} & y\mathbf{RT} \\ t_0 & x\mathbf{RT} & \perp \\ (t_0, t_1] & x\mathbf{RT} & x\mathbf{RT} \end{pmatrix}
$$

where the size of the matrix is $\#T \bullet \#S$.

The Evaluation Process

Definition 17. *The semantics of the evaluation process on* Θ, $\theta(\blacklozenge exp\mathbb{T} \to \mathbb{T})$, *is a double partial differential of the semantic function* $f_\theta(\theta(\blacklozenge exp\mathbb{T} \to \mathbb{T})$ *on the sets of variables S and executing steps T in the following two forms, i.e.:*

$$
\theta(\blacklozenge(exp\mathbf{BL}) \to \mathbf{BL}) \triangleq \frac{\partial^2}{\partial t\,\partial s} f_\theta(\blacklozenge(exp\mathbf{BL}) \to \mathbf{BL}) \tag{17a}
$$

$$
= \mathop{R}_{i=0}^{\#T(\blacklozenge exp\mathbf{BL}\to\mathbf{BL})} \mathop{R}_{j=1}^{\#S(\blacklozenge exp\mathbf{BL}\mathbf{B} \blacktriangleright \mathbf{L})} v(t_i, s_j)
$$

$$
= \mathop{R}_{i=0}^{1} \mathop{R}_{j=1}^{2} v(t_i, s_j)
$$

$$
= \begin{pmatrix} & exp(17b) & \blacklozenge(exp\mathbf{BL})\mathbf{BL} \\ (t_0, t_1] & \delta(exp\mathbf{BL})\mathbf{BL} & \perp \\ (t_1, t_2] & \mathsf{T} & \mathsf{T} \\ (t_1, t_2] & \mathsf{F} & \mathsf{F} \end{pmatrix}
$$

or

Box 4.

$$\theta\,(\mathrm{id}\mathbf{S} \Leftarrow \mathrm{MEM}[\mathrm{ptr}\mathbf{P}]\mathbf{RT}) \triangleq \frac{\partial^2}{\partial t \,\partial s}\, f_\theta\,(\mathrm{id}\mathbf{S} \Leftarrow \mathrm{MEM}[\mathrm{ptr}\mathbf{P}]\mathbf{RT})$$

$$= \mathop{R}_{i=0}^{\#T(\mathrm{id}\mathbf{S}\Leftarrow\mathrm{MEM}[\mathrm{ptr}\mathbf{P}]\mathbf{RT})} \Big(\mathop{R}_{j=1}^{\#S(\mathrm{id}\mathbf{S}\Leftarrow\mathrm{MEM}[\mathrm{ptr}\mathbf{P}]\mathbf{RT})} v\; t_i, s_j \Big)$$

$$= \mathop{R}_{i=0}^{1} \mathop{R}_{j=1}^{3} v(t_i, s_j)$$

$$= \begin{pmatrix} & \mathbf{id S} & \mathbf{ptr P} & \mathbf{MEM RT} \\ \mathbf{t_0} & id\mathbf{S} & \perp & \perp \\ (\mathbf{t_0},\mathbf{t_1}] & id\mathbf{S} & \pi(id\mathbf{S})\mathbf{H} & \mathrm{MEM}[ptr\mathbf{P}]\mathbf{RT} \end{pmatrix}$$

$$\tag{19}$$

$$\theta\,(\blacklozenge exp\mathbb{T} \to \mathbb{T}) \triangleq \frac{\partial^2}{\partial t \,\partial s}\, f_\theta\,(\blacklozenge exp\mathbb{T} \to \mathbb{T})$$

$$= \mathop{R}_{i=0}^{\#T(\blacklozenge exp\mathbb{T}\to\mathbb{T})} \Big(\mathop{R}_{j=1}^{\#S(\blacklozenge exp\mathbb{T}\to\mathbb{T})} v\; t_i, s_j \Big)$$

$$= \mathop{R}_{i=0}^{1} \mathop{R}_{j=1}^{2} v(t_i, s_j)$$

$$= \begin{pmatrix} & exp\mathbb{T} & \blacklozenge(exp\mathbb{T})\mathbb{T} \\ (\mathbf{t_0},\mathbf{t_1}] & \delta(exp\mathbb{T})\mathbb{T} & \perp \\ (\mathbf{t_1},\mathbf{t_2}] & n\mathbb{T} & n\mathbb{T} \end{pmatrix}$$

*where ◆(exp**BL**) is the Boolean evaluation function on expBL that results in **T** or **F**. ◆(exp𝕋) is a more general cardinal or numerical evaluation function on exp𝕋 that results in 𝕋 = {**N, Z, R, B**}, i.e., in types of nature number, integer, real number, and byte, respectively (Wang, 2002).*

The Addressing Process

Definition 18. *The semantics of the addressing process on Θ, θ(id**S** ⇒ ptr**P**), is a double partial differential of the semantic function $f_\theta(id\mathbf{S} \Rightarrow ptr\mathbf{P})$ on the sets of variables S and executing steps T, i.e.:*

$$\theta\,(id\mathbf{S} \Rightarrow ptr\mathbf{P}) \triangleq \frac{\partial^2}{\partial t \,\partial s}\, f_\theta\,(id\mathbf{S} \Rightarrow ptr\mathbf{P})$$

$$\tag{18}$$

$$= \mathop{R}_{i=0}^{\#T(\mathrm{id}\mathbf{S}\,\mathrm{p}\Rightarrow\,\mathrm{tr}\mathbf{P})} \Big(\mathop{R}_{j=1}^{\#S(\mathrm{id}\mathbf{S}\Rightarrow\mathrm{ptr}\mathbf{P})} v\; t_i, s_j \Big)$$

$$= \mathop{R}_{i=0}^{1} \mathop{R}_{j=1}^{2} v(t_i, s_j)$$

$$= \begin{pmatrix} & \mathbf{id S} & \mathbf{ptr P} \\ \mathbf{t_0} & id\mathbf{S} & \perp \\ (\mathbf{t_0},\mathbf{t_1}] & id\mathbf{S} & \pi(id\mathbf{S})\mathbf{H} \end{pmatrix}$$

Box 5.

$$\theta\,(\mathrm{MEM[ptr\textbf{P}]\textbf{RT}} > x\textbf{RT})$$

$$\triangleq \frac{\partial^2}{\partial t\,\partial s} f_\theta\,(\mathrm{MEM[ptr\textbf{P}]\textbf{RT}} > x\textbf{RT})$$

$$= \overset{\#T(\mathrm{MEM[ptr\textbf{P}]\textbf{RT}}>x\textbf{RT})}{\underset{i=0}{R}} \left(\overset{\#S(\mathrm{MEM[ptr\textbf{P}]\textbf{RT}}>x\textbf{RT})}{\underset{j=1}{R}} v\ t_i,s_j \right)$$

$$= \overset{1}{\underset{i=0}{R}}\ \overset{3}{\underset{j=1}{R}}\ v(t_i,s_j)$$

$$= \begin{pmatrix} & \textbf{ptrP} & \textbf{MEM(ptrP)RT} & \textbf{xRT} \\ t_0 & ptr\textbf{P} & \bot & \bot \\ (t_0,t_1] & ptr\textbf{P} & \mathrm{MEM}[ptr\textbf{P}]\textbf{RT} & \mathrm{MEM}[ptr\textbf{P}]\textbf{RT} \end{pmatrix}$$

$$(21)$$

where $\pi(id\textbf{S})\textbf{H}$ is a function that associates a declared identifier $id\textbf{S}$ to its hexadecimal memory address located by the pointed $ptr\textbf{P}$.

The Memory Allocation Process

Definition 19. *The semantics of the memory allocation process on Θ, $\theta(id\textbf{S} \Leftarrow MEM(ptr\textbf{P})\textbf{RT})$, is a double partial differential of the semantic function $f_\theta(id\textbf{S} \Leftarrow MEM(ptr\textbf{P})\textbf{RT})$ on the sets of variables S and executing steps T, see Box 4. Where $\pi(id\textbf{S})\textbf{H}$ is a mapping function that associates an identifier $id\textbf{S}$ to a memory block starting at a hexadecimal address located by the pointed $ptr\textbf{P}$. The ending address of the allocated memory block, $ptr\textbf{P}+size(\textbf{RT})-1$, is dependent on a machine implementation of the size of a given variable in type* **RT**.

The Memory Release Process

Definition 20. *The semantics of the memory release process on Θ, $\theta(id\textbf{S} \nLeftarrow MEM(\bot)\textbf{RT})$, is a double partial differential of the semantic function $f_\theta(id\textbf{S} \nLeftarrow MEM(\bot)\textbf{RT})$ on the sets of variables S and executing steps T, i.e.:*

$$\theta\,(id\textbf{S} \nLeftarrow \mathrm{MEM[}\bot\mathrm{]}\textbf{RT}) \triangleq \frac{\partial^2}{\partial t\,\partial s} f_\theta\,(id\textbf{S} \nLeftarrow \mathrm{MEM[}\bot\mathrm{]}\textbf{RT})$$

$$= \overset{\#T(id\textbf{S}\nLeftarrow\mathrm{MEM[}\bot\mathrm{]}\textbf{RT})}{\underset{i=0}{R}} \left(\overset{\#S(id\textbf{S}\nLeftarrow\mathrm{MEM[}\bot\mathrm{]}\textbf{RT})}{\underset{j=1}{R}} v\ t_i,s_j \right) \tag{20}$$

$$= \overset{1}{\underset{i=0}{R}}\ \overset{3}{\underset{j=1}{R}}\ v(t_i,s_j)$$

$$= \begin{pmatrix} & \textbf{idRT} & \textbf{ptrP} & \textbf{MEMRT} \\ t_0 & (id\textbf{S}) & \pi(id\textbf{S})\textbf{H} & \mathrm{MEM}(ptr\textbf{P})\textbf{RT} \\ (t_0,t_1] & \bot & \bot & \bot \end{pmatrix}$$

The Read Process

Definition 21. *The semantics of the read process on* Θ, *θ(MEM(ptr***P***)***RT***>x***RT***), is a double partial differential of the semantic function* f_θ*(MEM(ptr***P***)***RT***>x***RT***) on the sets of variables S and executing steps T, see Box 5.*

The Write Process

Definition 22. *The semantics of the write process on* Θ, *θ(MEM(ptr***P***)***RT***<x***RT***), is a double partial differential of the semantic function* f_θ*(MEM(ptr***P***)***RT***<x***RT***) on the sets of variables S and executing steps T, i.e.:*

$\theta(\text{MEM[ptr}\mathbf{P}]\mathbf{RT} < x\mathbf{RT})$

$$\triangleq \frac{\partial^2}{\partial t\,\partial s} f_\theta(\text{MEM[ptr}\mathbf{P}]\mathbf{RT} < x\mathbf{RT}) \tag{22}$$

$$= \mathop{R}_{i=0}^{\#T(\text{MEM[ptr}\mathbf{P}]\mathbf{RT}<x\mathbf{RT})} \left(\mathop{R}_{j=1}^{\#S(\text{MEM[ptr}\mathbf{P}]\mathbf{RT}\ x\mathbf{RT})} v\ t_i, s_j \right)$$

$$= \mathop{R}_{i=0}^{1} \mathop{R}_{j=1}^{3} v(t_i, s_j)$$

$$= \begin{pmatrix} & x\mathbf{RT} & \text{ptr}\mathbf{P} & \text{MEM[ptr}\mathbf{P}]\mathbf{RT} \\ t_0 & x\mathbf{RT} & \bot & \bot \\ (t_0, t_1] & x\mathbf{RT} & ptr\mathbf{P} & x\mathbf{RT} \end{pmatrix}$$

The Input Process

Definition 23. *The semantics of the input process on* Θ, *θ(PORT(ptr***P***)***RT***|>x***RT***), is a double partial differential of the semantic function* f_θ*((PORT(ptr***P***)***RT***|>x***RT***) on the sets of variables S and executing steps T, i.e.:*

$\theta(\text{PORT[ptr}\mathbf{P}]\mathbf{RT}|> x\mathbf{RT}) \tag{23}$

$$\triangleq \frac{\partial^2}{\partial t\,\partial s} f_\theta(\text{PORT[ptr}\mathbf{P}]\mathbf{RT}|> x\mathbf{RT})$$

$$= \mathop{R}_{i=0}^{\#T(\text{PORT[ptr}\mathbf{P}]\mathbf{RT}|>x\mathbf{RT})} \left(\mathop{R}_{j=1}^{\#S(\text{PORT[ptr}\mathbf{P}]\mathbf{RT}|\ x\mathbf{RT})} v\ t_i, s_j \right)$$

$$= \mathop{R}_{i=0}^{1} \mathop{R}_{j=1}^{3} v(t_i, s_j)$$

$$= \begin{pmatrix} & \text{ptr}\mathbf{P} & \text{PORT[ptr}\mathbf{P}]\mathbf{RT} & x\mathbf{RT} \\ t_0 & ptr\mathbf{P} & \bot & \bot \\ (t_0, t_1] & ptr\mathbf{P} & \text{PORT[}ptr\mathbf{P}]\mathbf{RT} & \text{PORT[}ptr\mathbf{P}]\mathbf{RT} \end{pmatrix}$$

The Output Process

Definition 24. *The semantics of the output process on* Θ, $\theta(x\textbf{RT} \mid \ll PORT(ptr\textbf{P})\textbf{RT})$, *is a double partial differential of the semantic function* $f_\theta(x\textbf{RT} \mid \ll PORT(ptr\textbf{P})\textbf{RT})$ *on the sets of variables S and executing steps T, i.e.:*

$$\theta(x\textbf{RT} \mid \ll \text{PORT}[ptr\textbf{P}]\textbf{RT})$$

$$\triangleq \frac{\partial^2}{\partial t\,\partial s} f_\theta(x\textbf{RT} \mid \ll \text{PORT}[ptr\textbf{P}]\textbf{RT}) \tag{24}$$

$$= \mathop{R}_{i=0}^{\#T(x\textbf{RT}\mid\ll\text{PORT}[ptr\textbf{P}]\textbf{RT})} \left(\mathop{R}_{j=1}^{\#S(x\textbf{RT}\mid\ll\text{PORT}[ptr\textbf{P}]\textbf{RT})} v\, t_i, s_j \right)$$

$$= \mathop{R}_{i=0}^{1} \mathop{R}_{j=1}^{3} v(t_i, s_j)$$

$$= \begin{pmatrix} & x\textbf{RT} & ptr\textbf{P} & \text{PORT}[ptr\textbf{P}]\textbf{RT} \\ t_0 & x\textbf{RT} & \bot & \bot \\ (t_0, t_1] & x\textbf{RT} & ptr\textbf{P} & x\textbf{RT} \end{pmatrix}$$

The Timing Process

Definition 25. *The semantics of the timing process on* Θ, $\theta(@t\textbf{TM} \triangleq \S t\textbf{TM})$, *is a double partial differential of the semantic function* $f_\theta(@t\textbf{TM} \triangleq \S t\textbf{TM})$ *on the sets of variables S and executing steps T, i.e.:*

$$\theta(@ t\textbf{TM}@\S t\textbf{TM}) \triangleq \frac{\partial^2}{\partial t\,\partial s} f_\theta(@ t\textbf{TM}@\S t\textbf{TM})$$

$$= \mathop{R}_{i=0}^{\#T(@ t\textbf{TM}@\S t\textbf{TM})} \left(\mathop{R}_{j=1}^{\#S(@ t\textbf{TM}@\S t\textbf{TM})} v\, t_i, s_j \right) \tag{25}$$

$$= \mathop{R}_{i=0}^{1} \mathop{R}_{j=1}^{2} v(t_i, s_j)$$

$$= \begin{pmatrix} & \S t\textbf{TM} & @t\textbf{TM} \\ t_0 & \S t\textbf{TM} & \bot \\ (t_0, t_1] & \S t\textbf{TM} & \S t\textbf{TM} \end{pmatrix}$$

where **TM** *represents the three timing types, i.e.,* **TM** = *{***yy:MM:dd, hh:mm:ss:ms, yy:MM:dd:hh:mm:ss:ms***}.*

The Duration Process

Definition 26. *The semantics of the duration process on* Θ, $\theta(@t\textbf{TM} \triangleq \S t\textbf{TM}+\Delta d\textbf{Z})$, *is a double partial differential of the semantic function* $f_\theta(@t\textbf{TM} \triangleq \S t\textbf{TM}+\Delta d\textbf{N})$ *on the sets of variables S and executing steps T, i.e.:*

$$\theta\ (@\ t\mathbf{TM}\underline{\mathbb{A}}\S t\ \mathbf{M}+\Delta d\mathbf{Z})$$

$$\triangleq \frac{\partial^2}{\partial t\ \partial s}\ f_\theta\ ((@\ t\mathbf{TM}\underline{\mathbb{A}}\S t\ \mathbf{M}+\Delta d\mathbf{Z})$$

$$=\ \underset{i=0}{\overset{\#T(@\ t\mathbf{TM}\underline{\mathbb{A}}\S t\ \mathbf{M})}{R}}\ (\ \underset{j=1}{\overset{\#S(@\ t\mathbf{TM}\underline{\mathbb{A}}\S t\mathbf{TM})}{R}}\ v\ t_i,s_j)$$

$$=\underset{i=0}{\overset{1}{R}}\ \underset{j=1}{\overset{3}{R}}\ v(t_i,s_j)$$

$$=\begin{pmatrix} & \S t\mathbf{TM} & \Delta d\mathbf{N} & @t\mathbf{TM} \\ t_0 & \S t\mathbf{TM} & \Delta d\mathbf{N} & \perp \\ (t_0,t_1] & \S t\mathbf{TM} & \Delta d\mathbf{N} & \S t\mathbf{TM}+\Delta d\mathbf{N} \end{pmatrix}$$

$$(26)$$

where $\mathbf{TM}$ = *{*yy:MM:dd, hh:mm:ss:ms, yy:MM:dd:hh:mm:ss:ms*}*.

The Increase Process

Definition 27. *The semantics of the increase process on* Θ, $\theta(\uparrow(x\mathbf{RT}))$, *is a double partial differential of the semantic function* $f_\theta(\uparrow(x\mathbf{RT}))$ *on the sets of variables S and executing steps T, i.e.:*

$$\theta(\uparrow(x\mathbf{RT}))\triangleq\frac{\partial^2}{\partial t\ \partial s}\ f_\theta(\uparrow(x\mathbf{RT}))$$

$$=\ \underset{i=0}{\overset{\#T(\uparrow(x\mathbf{RT}))}{R}}\ \underset{j=1}{\overset{\#S(\uparrow(x\mathbf{RT}))}{R}}\ v(t_i,s_j)$$

$$=\underset{i=0}{\overset{1}{R}}\ \underset{j=1}{\overset{1}{R}}\ (t_i,s_j)$$

$$=\begin{pmatrix} & x\mathbf{RT} \\ t_0 & x\mathbf{RT} \\ (t_0,t_1] & x\mathbf{RT}+1 \end{pmatrix}$$

$$(27)$$

where the run-time type $\mathbf{RT}$ = *{*N, Z, B, H, P, TM*}*

The Decrease Process

Definition 28. *The semantics of the decrease process on* Θ, $\theta(\downarrow(x\mathbf{RT}))$, *is a double partial differential of the semantic function* $f_\theta(\downarrow(x\mathbf{RT}))$ *on the sets of variables S and executing steps T, i.e.:*

$$\theta(\downarrow(x\mathbf{RT}))\triangleq\frac{\partial^2}{\partial t\ \partial s}\ f_\theta(\downarrow(x\mathbf{RT}))$$

$$=\ \underset{i=0}{\overset{\#T(\downarrow(x\mathbf{RT}))}{R}}\ \underset{j=1}{\overset{\#S(\downarrow(x\mathbf{RT}))}{R}}\ v(t_i,s_j)$$

$$=\underset{i=0}{\overset{1}{R}}\ \underset{j=1}{\overset{1}{R}}\ (t_i,s_j)$$

$$=\begin{pmatrix} & x\mathbf{RT} \\ t_0 & x\mathbf{RT} \\ (t_0,t_1] & x\mathbf{RT}-1 \end{pmatrix}$$

$$(28)$$

where the run-time type **RT** = {**N, Z, B, H, P, TM**}

The Exception Detection Process

Definition 29. *The semantics of the exception detection process on* Θ, $\theta(!(@)e\mathbf{S})$, *is a double partial differential of the semantic function* $f_\theta(!(@)e\mathbf{S}))$ *on the sets of variables S and executing steps T, i.e.:*

$$
\theta(!(@e\mathbf{S}) \triangleq \frac{\partial^2}{\partial t\, \partial s} f_\theta(!(@e\mathbf{S}))
$$

$$
= \mathop{R}_{i=0}^{\#T(!(@e\mathbf{S}))} (\mathop{R}_{j=1}^{\#S(!(@e\mathbf{S}))} v\, t_i, s_j)
$$

$$
= \mathop{R}_{i=0}^{1} \mathop{R}_{j=1}^{3} v(t_i, s_j)
$$

$$
= \begin{pmatrix} & @e\mathbf{S} & ptr\mathbf{P} & PORT(ptr\mathbf{P})\mathbf{S} \\ t_0 & @e\mathbf{S} & \bot & \bot \\ (t_0, t_1] & @e\mathbf{S} & ptr\mathbf{P} & @e\mathbf{S} \end{pmatrix}
$$

(29)

Equation 29 indicates that the semantics of exception detection is the output of a string $@e\mathbf{S}$ to a designated port PORT[$ptr\mathbf{P}$]$\mathbf{S}$, where the pointer $ptr\mathbf{P}$ points to a CRT or a printer. Therefore, the semantics of exception detection can be described based on the semantics of the output process as defined in Equation 24, i.e.:

$$
\theta((!(@e\mathbf{S})) = \theta(@e\mathbf{S} \,|\!< PORT[ptr\mathbf{P}]\mathbf{S})
$$

(30)

The Skip Process

Definition 30. *The semantics of the skip process on* Θ, $\theta(\otimes)$, *is a double partial differential of the semantic function* $f_\theta(\otimes)$ *on the sets of variables S and executing steps T, i.e.:*

$$
\theta(\otimes) \triangleq \theta(P^k \curvearrowright P^{k-1})
$$

$$
= \frac{\partial^2}{\partial t\, \partial s} f_\theta(P^k \curvearrowright P^{k-1})
$$

$$
= \mathop{R}_{i=0}^{\#T(P^k \curvearrowright P^{k-1})} (\mathop{R}_{j=1}^{\#S(P^k \curvearrowright P^{k-1})} v\, t_i, s_j)
$$

$$
= \mathop{R}_{i=0}^{1} \mathop{R}_{j=1}^{2} v(t_i, s_j)
$$

$$
= \begin{pmatrix} & S_{p^{k-1}} & S_{p^k} \\ t_0 & S_{p^{k-1}} & S_{p^k} \\ (t_0, t_1] & S_{p^{k-1}} \setminus S_{p^k} & \bot \end{pmatrix}
$$

(31)

where P^k is a process P at a given embedded layer k in a program with P^0 at the uttermost layer, and $\curvearrowright$ denotes the jump process relation where its semantics will be formally defined in the next section.

According to Definition 30, the skip process $\otimes$ has no semantic effect on the current process P^k at the given embedded layer k in a program, such as a branch, loop, or function. However, it redirects the system to jump to execute an upper-layer process P^{k-1} in the embedded hierarchy. Therefore, skip is also known as *exit* or *break* in programming languages.

The Stop Process

Definition 31. *The semantics of the stop process on* Θ, θ *(⨎), is a double partial differential of the semantic function* $f_\theta(\boxtimes)$ *on the sets of variables S and executing steps T, i.e.:*

$$\theta(\boxtimes) \triangleq \theta(P \curvearrowright \S)$$

$$= \frac{\partial^2}{\partial t\ \partial s} f_\theta(P \curvearrowright \S) \tag{32}$$

$$= \mathop{R}_{i=0}^{\#T(P \curvearrowright \S)} (\mathop{R}_{j=1}^{\#S(P \curvearrowright \S)} v\ t_i, s_j)$$

$$= \mathop{R}_{i=0}^{1} \mathop{R}_{j=1}^{2} v(t_i, s_j)$$

$$= \begin{pmatrix} & \mathbf{S_\S} & \mathbf{S_P} \\ \mathbf{t_0} & S_\S & S_P \\ \mathbf{(t_0, t_1]} & S_\S \setminus S_P & \bot \end{pmatrix}$$

where the stop process $\boxtimes$ *does nothing but returns the control of execution to the system.*

Box 6.

$$\theta(P_0 \to P_1 \to ... \to P_5) = \frac{\partial^2}{\partial t\ \partial s} f_\theta(P_0 \to P_1 \to ... \to P_5)$$

$$= \frac{\partial^2}{\partial t\ \partial s} f_\theta(P_0) \to \frac{\partial^2}{\partial t\ \partial s} f_\theta(P_1) \to ... \to \frac{\partial^2}{\partial t\ \partial s} f_\theta(P_5)$$

$$= \mathop{R}_{i=0}^{\#T(P_0)} (\mathop{R}_{j=1}^{\#S(P_0)} v_{P_0}\ t_i, s_j) \to \mathop{R}_{i=0}^{\#T(P_1)} (\mathop{R}_{j=1}^{\#S(P_1)} v_{P_1}\ t_i, s_j) \to ... \to \mathop{R}_{i=0}^{\#T(P_5)} \mathop{R}_{j=1}^{\#S(P_5)} v_{P_5}(t_i, s_j)$$

$$= \mathop{R}_{i=0}^{\#T(P_0\ P_1\ ...\ P_5)} (\mathop{R}_{j=1}^{\#S(P_0 \cup P_1 \cup ... \cup P_5)} v\ t_i, s_j)$$

$$= \mathop{R}_{i=0}^{5} \mathop{R}_{j=1}^{4} v(t_i, s_j)$$

$$= \begin{pmatrix} & \mathbf{x} & \mathbf{y} & \mathbf{z} & \mathbf{PORT[CRTP]N} \\ \mathbf{t_0} & \bot & \bot & \bot & \bot \\ \mathbf{(t_0, t_1]} & 2 & \bot & \bot & \bot \\ \mathbf{(t_1, t_2]} & 2 & 8 & \bot & \bot \\ \mathbf{(t_2, t_3]} & 2 & 8 & 10 & \bot \\ \mathbf{(t_3, t_4]} & 2 & 8 & 20 & \bot \\ \mathbf{(t_4, t_5]} & 2 & 8 & 20 & 20 \end{pmatrix}$$

$$\tag{34}$$

DEDUCTIVE SEMANTICS OF RTPA PROCESS RELATIONS

The preceding section provides formal definitions of metaprocesses of RTPA for software system modeling. Via the composition of multiple metaprocesses by the 17 process relations, $R = \{\rightarrow, \curvearrowright, |, |...|..., R^*, R^+, R^i, \circlearrowleft, \rightarrowtail, \|, \text{\ss}, \|\|, », \lightning, \hookrightarrow_t, \hookrightarrow_e, \hookrightarrow_i\}$, complex architectures and behaviors of software systems, in the most complicated case, a real-time system, can be sufficiently described (Wang, 2002, 2006a, 2007c, 2008b). On the basis of Definitions 8 and 12, the semantics of the RTPA process relations can be formally defined and analyzed as follows.

The Sequential Process Relation

Definition 32. *The semantics of the sequential relation of processes on Θ, $\theta(P \rightarrow Q)$, is a double partial differential of the semantic function $f_\theta(P \rightarrow Q)$ on the sets of variables S and executing steps T, i.e.:*

$$
\begin{aligned}
\theta(P \rightarrow Q) &\triangleq \frac{\partial^2}{\partial t\, \partial s} f_\theta(P \rightarrow Q) \\[6pt]
&= \frac{\partial^2}{\partial t\, \partial s} f_\theta(P) \rightarrow \frac{\partial^2}{\partial t\, \partial s} f_\theta(Q) \\[6pt]
&= \mathop{R}_{i=0}^{\#T(P)} (\mathop{R}_{j=1}^{\#S(P)} v_P\ t_i, s_j) \rightarrow \mathop{R}_{i=0}^{\#T(Q)} (\mathop{R}_{j=1}^{\#S(Q)} v_Q\ t_i, s_j) \\[6pt]
&= \mathop{R}_{i=0}^{\#T(P\frown Q)} (\mathop{R}_{j=1}^{\#S(P\cup Q)} v\ t_i, s_j) \\[6pt]
&= \begin{pmatrix} & s_P & s_Q & s_{PQ} \\ t_0 & \perp & \perp & \perp \\ (t_0, t_1] & V_{1P} & - & V_{1PQ} \\ (t_1, t_2] & - & V_{2Q} & V_{2PQ} \end{pmatrix} \\[6pt]
&= \begin{pmatrix} V_P & & V_{PQ} \\ & V_Q & V_{PQ} \end{pmatrix}
\end{aligned}
$$

(33)

where $P \frown Q$ indicates a concatenation of these two processes over time, and in the simplified notation of the matrix, $V_P = v(t_P, s_P)$, $0 \le t_P \le n_P$, $1 \le s_P \le m_P$; $V_Q = v(t_Q, s_Q)$, $0 \le t_Q \le n_Q$, $1 \le s_Q \le m_Q$; and $V_{PQ} = v(t_{PQ}, s_{PQ})$, $0 \le t_{PQ} \le n_{PQ}$, $1 \le s_{PQ} \le m_{PQ}$.

In Equation 33, the first partial differential selects a set of related variables in the sequential processes P and Q, $S(P \cup Q)$. The second partial differential selects a set of time moments $T(P \frown Q)$. The semantic diagram of the sequential process relation as defined in Equation 33 is illustrated in Figure 3 on Θ.

The following example shows the physical meaning of Equation 33 and how the abstract syntaxes and their implied meanings are embodied onto the objects (variables) and their dynamic values in order to obtain the concrete semantics in deductive semantics.

Example 3. *Analyze the semantics of the sequential processes P_0 through P_5 in the following program:*

Box 7.

$$\theta\left(\blacklozenge expRT \to P \mid \blacklozenge\sim \to Q\right) \triangleq \frac{\partial^2}{\partial t\,\partial s}\,f_\theta\left(\blacklozenge expRT \to P \mid \blacklozenge\sim \to Q\right)$$

$$= \quad \blacklozenge expBL \to \frac{\partial^2}{\partial t\,\partial s}\,f_\theta(P)$$

$$\mid \quad \blacklozenge \quad \to \frac{\partial^2}{\partial t\,\partial s}\,f_\theta(Q)$$

$$= \quad \blacklozenge expBL \to \mathop{R}_{i=0}^{\#T(P)}\left(\mathop{R}_{j=1}^{\#S(P)} v_P\ t_i, s_j\right)$$

$$\mid \quad \blacklozenge \quad \to \mathop{R}_{i=0}^{\#T(Q)}\left(\mathop{R}_{j=1}^{\#S(Q)} v_Q\ t_i, s_j\right)$$

$$= \begin{pmatrix} & \mathbf{expBL} & \mathbf{S_P} & \mathbf{S_Q} & \mathbf{S_{PQ}} \\ (t_0, t_1] & \delta(expBL) & \perp & \perp & \perp \\ (t_1, t_2] & \mathbf{T} & V_{2P} & - & V_{2PQ} \\ (t_1, t_{2'}] & \mathbf{F} & - & V_{3Q} & V_{3PQ} \end{pmatrix}$$

$$(36)$$

Figure 3. The semantic diagram of the sequential process relation

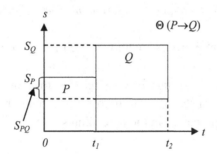

```
void sequential_sum;
  {
        int x, y, z;              // P₀
      x = 2;           // P₁
      y = 8;           // P₂
      z := x + y; // P₃
      z := x + y + z;   // P₄
      print z;          // P₅
  }
```

According to Definition 32, the semantics of the above program can be analyzed as seen in Box 6. Where PORT[*CRT***P**]**N** denotes a system monitor of type **N** located by the pointer *CRT***P**.

The Jump Process Relation

Definition 33. *The semantics of the jump relations of processes on* Θ, $\theta(P \curvearrowright Q)$, *is a double partial differential of the semantic function* $f_\theta(P \curvearrowright Q)$ *on the sets of variables S and executing steps T, i.e.:*

$$
\begin{aligned}
\theta(P \curvearrowright Q) &\triangleq \frac{\partial^2}{\partial t\,\partial s} f_\theta(P \curvearrowright Q) \\
&= \frac{\partial^2}{\partial t\,\partial s} f_\theta(P) \left(\curvearrowright \frac{\partial^2}{\partial t\,\partial s} f_\theta\, Q \right) \\
&= \overset{\#T(P)}{\underset{i=0}{R}} \left(\overset{\#S(P)}{\underset{j=1}{R}} v_P\, t_i, s_j \right) \curvearrowright \overset{\#T(Q)}{\underset{i=0}{R}} \left(\overset{\#S(Q)}{\underset{j=1}{R}} v_Q\, t_i, s_j \right) \\
&= \overset{\#T(\bar{P}Q)}{\underset{i=0}{R}} \left(\overset{\#S(P\cup Q)}{\underset{j=1}{R}} v\, t_i, s_j \right) \\
&= \begin{pmatrix}
 & S_P & S_Q & S_{PQ} & \text{addr}\mathbf{H} \\
[t_0, t_1] & V_{IP} & \perp & V_{IPQ} & \perp \\
(t_1, t_2] & - & - & - & \pi(Q\mathbf{S})\mathbf{H} \\
(t_2, t_3] & - & V_{3Q} & V_{3PQ} &
\end{pmatrix}
\end{aligned}
$$

(35)

where $\pi(Q\mathbf{S})\mathbf{H}$ *is a system addressing function of the system that directs the program control flow to execute the new process Q, which physically located in a different memory address at addr$\mathbf{H}$ = $\pi(Q\mathbf{S})\mathbf{H}$.*

The semantic diagram of the jump process relation as defined in Equation 35 is illustrated in Figure 4 on $\Theta(P \curvearrowright Q)$.

The jump process relation is an important process relation that forms a fundamental part of many other processes and constructs. For instances, the jump process relation has been applied in expressing the semantics of the *skip* and *stop* processes in the preceding section.

The Branch Process Relation

Definition 34. *The semantics of the branch relation of processes on* Θ, $\theta(\blacklozenge exp\mathbf{BL} = \mathbf{T} \to P \mid \blacklozenge{\sim} \to Q)$, *abbreviated by* $\theta(P|Q)$, *is a double partial differential of the semantic function* $f_\theta(P|Q)$ *on the sets of variables S and executing steps T, see Box 7, where* $\delta(exp\mathbf{BL})$ *is the evaluation function on the value of exp$\mathbf{BL}$,* $\delta(exp\mathbf{BL}) \in \{\mathbf{T}, \mathbf{F}\}$.

The semantic diagram of the branch process relation as defined in Equation 34 is illustrated in Figure 5 on $\Theta(exp\mathbf{BL} \to P \mid \neg\, exp\mathbf{BL} \to Q)$.

The Switch Process Relation

Definition 35. *The semantics of the switch relations of processes on* Θ, $\theta(\blacklozenge exp_i\mathbf{RT} \to P_i \mid \blacklozenge{\sim} \to \varnothing)$, *abbreviated by* $\theta(P_i \mid \varnothing)$, *is a double partial differential of the semantic function* $f_\theta(P_i \mid \varnothing)$ *on the sets of variables S and executing steps T, i.e.:*

Figure 4. The semantic diagram of the jump process relation

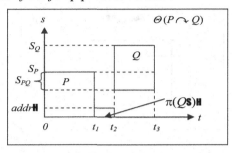

Figure 5. The semantic diagram of the branch process relation

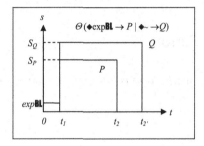

$$\theta\,(\blacklozenge exp_i \mathbf{RT} \rightarrow P_i \mid \blacklozenge \quad \rightarrow \otimes)$$

$$\triangleq \frac{\partial^2}{\partial t\,\partial s}\,f_\theta\,(\blacklozenge exp_i \mathbf{RT} \rightarrow P_i \mid \blacklozenge \quad \rightarrow \otimes) \tag{37}$$

$$= \blacklozenge exp\mathbf{RT} = 0 \rightarrow \frac{\partial^2}{\partial t\,\partial s}\,f_\theta\,(P_0)$$

$$\mid \dots$$

$$\mid \blacklozenge exp\mathbf{RT} = n-1 \rightarrow \frac{\partial^2}{\partial t\,\partial s}\,f_\theta\,(P_{n-1})$$

$$\mid \blacklozenge exp\mathbf{RT} = n \rightarrow \frac{\partial^2}{\partial t\,\partial s}\,f_\theta\,(\otimes)$$

$$= \blacklozenge exp\mathbf{RT} = 0 \rightarrow \mathop{R}_{i=0}^{\#T(P_0)} \mathop{R}_{j=1}^{\#S(P_0)} v_{P_0}(t_i, s_j)$$

$$\mid \dots$$

$$\mid \blacklozenge exp\mathbf{RT} = n-1 \rightarrow \mathop{R}_{i=0}^{\#T(P_{n-1})} \mathop{R}_{j=1}^{\#S(P_{n-1})} v_{P_{n-1}}(t_i, s_j)$$

$$\mid \blacklozenge exp\mathbf{RT} = n \rightarrow \varnothing$$

$$= \begin{pmatrix} & \mathbf{expRT} & \mathbf{S}_{P_0} & \cdots & \mathbf{S}_{P_{n-1}} & \mathbf{S_G} \\ [t_0, t_1] & \delta\,(exp\mathbf{RT}) & \bot & \cdots & \bot & \bot \\ (t_1, t_{2_0}] & 0 & V_{2_0 P} & \cdots & - & V_G \\ \vdots & \vdots & \vdots & \ddots & \vdots & \vdots \\ (t_1, t_{2_{n-1}}] & n-1 & - & \cdots & V_{2_{n-1} P} & V_G \\ (t_1, t_{2_n}] & n & - & \cdots & - & V_G \end{pmatrix}$$

where V_G is a set of global variables shared by P_0, P_1, and P_{n-1}.

Figure 6. The semantic diagram of the switch process relation

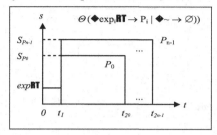

The semantic diagram of the switch process relation as defined in Equation 37 is illustrated in Figure 6 on $\Theta(\blacklozenge exp_i \mathbf{RT} \to P_i \mid \blacklozenge \sim \to \varnothing)$.

The While-Loop Process Relation

Definition 36. *The semantics of the while-loop relations of processes on Θ,*

$$\theta(\mathop{R}_{exp\mathbf{BL}=\mathbf{T}}^{\mathsf{F}*}(P)),$$

is a double partial differential of the semantic function

$$f_\theta(\mathop{R}_{exp\mathbf{BL}=\mathbf{T}}^{\mathsf{F}*}(P))$$

on the sets of variables S and executing steps T, i.e.:

$$\theta(\mathop{R}_{exp\mathbf{BL}=\mathbf{T}}^{\mathsf{F}*}(P)) \triangleq \frac{\partial^2}{\partial t \, \partial s} f_\theta(\mathop{R}_{exp\mathbf{BL}=\mathbf{T}}^{\mathsf{F}*}(P))$$

$$= \mathop{R}_{exp\mathbf{BL}=\mathbf{T}}^{\mathsf{F}*}(\frac{\partial^2}{\partial t \, \partial s} f_\theta(P))$$

$$= \mathop{R}_{exp\mathbf{BL}=\mathbf{T}}^{\mathsf{F}*}(\mathop{R}_{i=0}^{\#T(P)} \mathop{R}_{j=1}^{\#S(P)} v_P(t_i, s_j))$$

$$= \begin{pmatrix} & exp\mathbf{BL} & S_P \\ [t_0, t_1] & \delta(exp\mathbf{BL}) & \perp \\ (t_1, t_2] & \mathbf{T} & V_P \\ (t_1, t_{2'}] & \mathbf{F} & \otimes \\ \vdots & \vdots & \vdots \\ (t_3, t_4] & \delta(exp\mathbf{BL}) & - \\ (t_4, t_5] & \mathbf{T} & V_P \\ (t_4, t_{5'}] & \mathbf{F} & \otimes \end{pmatrix}$$

(38)

where $\varnothing$ denotes exit, and $\delta(exp\mathbf{BL})$ is the evaluation function on the Boolean expression, $\delta(exp\mathbf{BL}) \in \{\mathbf{T}, \mathbf{F}\}$.

Figure 7. The semantic diagram of the while-loop process relation

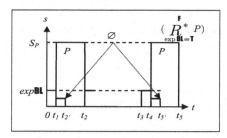

The semantic diagram of the while-loop process relation as defined in Equation 38 is illustrated in Figure 7 on Θ.

The Repeat-Loop Process Relation

Definition 37. *The semantics of the repeat-loop relations of processes on* Θ,

$$\theta\left(\underset{expBL=T}{\overset{F}{R}}^{+}(P)\right),$$

is a double partial differential of the semantic function

$$f_{\theta}\left(\underset{expBL=T}{\overset{F}{R}}^{+}(P)\right)$$

on the sets of variables S and executing steps T, i.e.:

$$\theta\left(\underset{expBL=T}{\overset{F}{R}}^{+}(P)\right) \triangleq \frac{\partial^2}{\partial t\,\partial s} f_{\theta}\left(\underset{expBL=T}{\overset{F}{R}}^{+}(P)\right)$$

$$= \underset{expBL=T}{\overset{F}{R}}^{+}\left(\frac{\partial^2}{\partial t\,\partial s} f_{\theta}(P)\right) \qquad (39)$$

$$= P \to \underset{expBL=T}{\overset{F}{R}}^{*}\left(\underset{i=0}{\overset{\#T(P)}{R}} \underset{j=1}{\overset{\#S(P)}{R}} v_P(t_i, s_j)\right)$$

$$= \begin{pmatrix} & \mathbf{expBL} & \mathbf{S_P} \\ [t_0, t_1] & \bot & V_P \\ (t_1, t_2] & \delta(\mathbf{expBL}) & - \\ (t_2, t_3] & \mathbf{T} & V_P \\ (t_2, t_{3'}] & \mathbf{F} & \otimes \\ \vdots & \vdots & \vdots \\ (t_4, t_5] & \delta(\mathbf{expBL}) & - \\ (t_5, t_6] & \mathbf{T} & V_P \\ (t_5, t_{6'}] & \mathbf{F} & \otimes \end{pmatrix}$$

The semantic diagram of the repeat-loop process relation as defined in Equation 39 is illustrated in Figure 8 on Θ.

The For-Loop Process Relation

Definition 38. *The semantics of the for-loop relations of processes on* Θ,

$$\theta(\mathop{R}\limits_{i\mathbb{N}=1}^{n} P(i)),$$

is a double partial differential of the semantic function

$$f_\theta(\mathop{R}\limits_{i\mathbb{N}=1}^{n} P(i))$$

on the sets of variables S and executing steps T, i.e.:

$$
\begin{aligned}
\theta(\mathop{R}\limits_{i\mathbb{N}=1}^{n} P(i)) &\triangleq \frac{\partial^2}{\partial t\,\partial s}\, f_\theta\,(\mathop{R}\limits_{i\mathbb{N}=1}^{n} P(i)) \\[4pt]
&= \mathop{R}\limits_{k\mathbb{N}=1}^{n}\left(\frac{\partial^2}{\partial t\,\partial s}\, f_\theta\,(P_i)\right) \\[4pt]
&= \mathop{R}\limits_{k\mathbb{N}=1}^{n}\left(\mathop{R}\limits_{i=0}^{\#T(P_k)} \mathop{R}\limits_{j=1}^{\#S(P_k)} v_{P_k}(t_i, s_j)\right) \\[4pt]
&=\begin{pmatrix}
 & k\mathbb{N} & S_P \\
[t_0, t_1] & 1 & \bot \\
(t_1, t_2] & 1 & V_P \\
\vdots & \vdots & \vdots \\
(t_{n-2}, t_{n-1}] & n & - \\
(t_{n-1}, t_n] & n & V_P
\end{pmatrix}
\end{aligned}
$$

(40)

The semantic diagram of the for-loop process relation as defined in Equation 40 is illustrated in Figure 9 on Θ.

Figure 8. The semantic diagram of the repeat-loop process relation

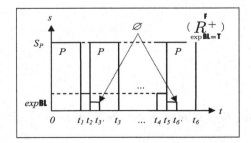

Figure 9. The semantic diagram of the for-loop process relation

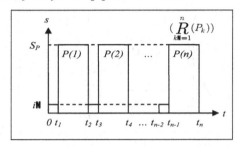

The Function Call Process Relation

Definition 39. *The semantics of the function call relations of processes on* Θ, $\theta(P \rightarrowtail Q)$, *is a double partial differential of the semantic function* $f_\theta(P \rightarrowtail Q)$ *on the sets of variables S and executing steps T, i.e.:*

$$
\begin{aligned}
\theta(P \rightarrowtail Q) &\triangleq \frac{\partial^2}{\partial t \, \partial s} f_\theta(P \rightarrowtail Q) \\[4pt]
&= \frac{\partial^2}{\partial t \, \partial s} f_\theta(P) \rightarrowtail \frac{\partial^2}{\partial t \, \partial s} f_\theta(Q) \\[4pt]
&= \mathop{R}_{i=0}^{\#T(P)} \left(\mathop{R}_{j=1}^{\#S(P)} v_P \, t_i, s_j \right) \rightarrowtail \mathop{R}_{i=0}^{\#T(Q)} \left(\mathop{R}_{j=1}^{\#S(Q)} v_Q \, t_i, s_j \right) \\[4pt]
&= \mathop{R}_{i=0}^{\#T([t_0,t_1] (t_1,t_2] (t_2,t_3])} \left(\mathop{R}_{j=1}^{\#S(P \cup Q)} v \, t_i, s_j \right)
\end{aligned}
\tag{41}
$$

$$
= \begin{pmatrix}
 & \mathbf{S_P} & \mathbf{S_Q} & \mathbf{S_{PQ}} \\
\mathbf{t_0} & \bot & \bot & \bot \\
\mathbf{(t_0, t_1]} & V_{1P} & - & V_{1PQ} \\
\mathbf{(t_1, t_2]} & - & v_{2Q} & V_{2PQ} \\
\mathbf{(t_2, t_3]} & V_{3P} & - & V_{3PQ}
\end{pmatrix}
$$

The semantic diagram of the procedure call process relation as defined in Equation 41 is illustrated in Figure 10 on $\Theta(P \rightarrowtail Q)$.

The Recursive Process Relation

Definition 40. *The semantics of the recursive relations of processes on* Θ, $\theta(P \circlearrowleft P)$, *is a double partial differential of the semantic function* $f_\theta(P \circlearrowleft P)$ *on the sets of variables S and executing steps T, i.e.:*

Figure 10. The semantic diagram of the function call process relation

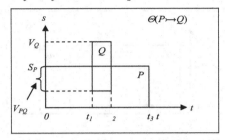

Figure 11. The semantic diagram of the recursive process relation

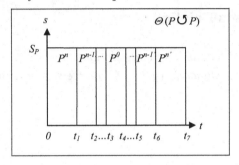

$$
\begin{aligned}
\theta(P \circlearrowleft P) &\triangleq \frac{\partial^2}{\partial t\, \partial s} f_\theta (P \circlearrowleft P) \\
&= \frac{\partial^2}{\partial t\, \partial s} f_\theta (P) \circlearrowleft \frac{\partial^2}{\partial t\, \partial s} f_\theta (P) \\
&= \mathop{R}_{i=0}^{\#T(P)} \mathop{R}_{j=1}^{\#S(P)} (R\, v\, t_i, s_j) \circlearrowleft \mathop{R}_{i=0}^{\#T(P)} \mathop{R}_{j=1}^{\#S(P)} (R\, v\, t_i, s_j) \\
&= \mathop{R}_{i=0}^{\#T(P)} \mathop{R}_{j=1}^{\#S(P)} (R\, v\, t_i, s_j) \\
&= \begin{pmatrix}
 & \mathbf{S_P} \\
[t_0, t_1] & V_{P^n} \\
(t_1, t_2] & V_{P^{n-1}} \\
\vdots & \vdots \\
(t_3, t_4] & V_{P^0} \\
\vdots & \vdots \\
(t_5, t_6] & V_{P'^{n-1}} \\
(t_6, t_7] & V_{P'^n}
\end{pmatrix}
\end{aligned}
$$

(42)

The semantic diagram of the recursive process relation as defined in Equation 42 is illustrated in Figure 11 on $\Theta(P \circlearrowleft P)$.

The Parallel Process Relation

Definition 41. *The semantics of the parallel relations of processes on Θ, $\theta(P\|Q)$, is a double partial differential of the semantic function $f_\theta(P\|Q)$ on the sets of variables S and executing steps T, i.e.:*

Figure 12. The semantic diagram of the parallel process relation

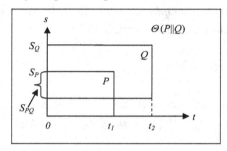

Figure 13. The semantic diagram of the concurrent process relation

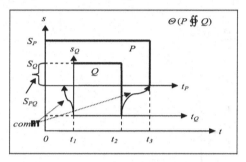

$$\theta(P \parallel Q) \triangleq \frac{\partial^2}{\partial t \, \partial s} f_\theta(P \parallel Q)$$

$$= \frac{\partial^2}{\partial t \, \partial s} f_\theta(P) \parallel \frac{\partial^2}{\partial t \, \partial s} f_\theta(Q)$$

$$= \mathop{R}_{i=0}^{\#T(P)} \left(\mathop{R}_{j=1}^{\#S(P)} v_P \ t_i, s_j \right) \parallel \mathop{R}_{i=0}^{\#T(Q)} \left(\mathop{R}_{j=1}^{\#S(Q)} v_Q \ t_i, s_j \right)$$

$$= \mathop{R}_{i=0}^{\max(\#T(P), \#T(Q))} \left(\mathop{R}_{j=1}^{\#S(P \cup Q)} v \ t, s \right)$$

$$= \begin{pmatrix} & \mathbf{S_P} & \mathbf{S_Q} & \mathbf{S_{PQ}} \\ \mathbf{t_0} & V_{0P} & V_{0Q} & V_{0PQ} \\ \mathbf{(t_0, t_1]} & V_{1P} & V_{1Q} & V_{1PQ} \\ \mathbf{(t_1, t_2]} & - & V_{2Q} & V_{2PQ} \end{pmatrix}$$

(43)

where $t_2 = max(\#T(P), (\#T(Q))$ is the synchronization point between two parallel processes.

The semantic diagram of the parallel process relation as defined in Equation 43 is illustrated in Figure 12 on $\Theta(P \parallel Q)$.

It is noteworthy that parallel processes P and Q are interlocked. That is, they should start and end at the same time. In case $t_1 \neq t_2$, the process completed earlier, should wait for the completion of the other. The second condition between parallel processes is that the shared resources, in particular variables, memory space, ports, and devices should be protected. That is, when a process operates on a shared resource, it is locked to the other process until the operation is completed. A variety of interlocking and synchronization techniques, such as *semaphores, mutual exclusions,* and *critical regions,* have been proposed in real-time system techniques (McDermid, 1991).

The Concurrent Process Relation

Definition 42. *The semantics of the concurrent relations of processes on* Θ, $\theta(P \text{ ⫴⫴ } Q)$, *is a double partial differential of the semantic function* $f_\theta(P \text{ ⫴⫴ } Q)$ *on the sets of variables S and executing steps T, i.e.:*

$$
\begin{aligned}
\theta(P \text{ ⫴⫴ } Q) &\triangleq \frac{\partial^2}{\partial t\, \partial s} f_\theta (P \text{ ⫴⫴ } Q) \\
&= \frac{\partial^2}{\partial t\, \partial s} f_\theta(P) \text{ ⫴⫴ } \frac{\partial^2}{\partial t\, \partial s} f_\theta\, Q) \\
&= \mathop{R}_{i=0}^{\#T(P)} (\mathop{R}_{j=1}^{\#S(P)} v_P\ t_i, s_j) \text{ ⫴⫴ } \mathop{R}_{i=0}^{\#T(Q)} \mathop{R}_{j=1}^{\#S(Q)} v_Q(t_i, s_j) \\
&= \mathop{R}_{i=0}^{\max(\#T(P), \#T(Q))} (\mathop{R}_{j=1}^{\#S(P \cup Q)} v\ t_i, s_j)
\end{aligned}
\tag{44}
$$

$$
= \begin{pmatrix}
 & \mathbf{S_P} & \mathbf{S_Q} & \mathbf{S_{PQ}} & \mathbf{comRT} \\
\mathbf{t_0} & V_{0P} & V_{0P} & V_{0P} & V_{0com} \\
\mathbf{(t_0, t_1]} & V_{1P} & - & V_{1PQ} & V_{1com} \\
\mathbf{(t_1, t_2]} & V_{2P} & V_{2Q} & V_{2PQ} & V_{2com} \\
\mathbf{(t_2, t_3]} & V_{3P} & - & V_{3PQ} & V_{3com}
\end{pmatrix}
$$

where comRT is a set of interprocess communication variables that are used to synchronize P and Q executing on different machines based on independent system clocks.

The semantic diagram of the concurrent process relation as defined in Equation 44 is illustrated in Figure 13 on $\Theta(P \text{ ⫴⫴ } Q)$.

The Interleave Process Relation

Definition 43. *The semantics of the interleave relations of processes on* Θ, $\theta(P \,|||\, Q)$, *is a double partial differential of the semantic function* $f_\theta(P \,|||\, Q)$ *on the sets of variables S and executing steps T, i.e.:*

Figure 14. The semantic diagram of the interleave process relation

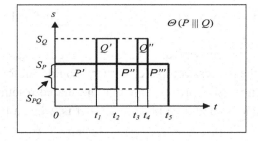

$$\theta(P \parallel\mid Q) \triangleq \frac{\partial^2}{\partial t\,\partial s} f_\theta(P \parallel\mid Q)$$

$$= \frac{\partial^2}{\partial t\,\partial s} f_\theta(P) \parallel\mid \frac{\partial^2}{\partial t\,\partial s} f_\theta(Q)$$

$$= \mathop{R}_{i=0}^{\#T(P)} (\mathop{R}_{j=1}^{\#S(P)} v_P\ t_i, s_j) \parallel\mid \mathop{R}_{i=0}^{\#T(Q)} \mathop{R}_{j=1}^{\#S(Q)} v_Q(t_i, s_j)$$

$$= \mathop{R}_{i=0}^{\#T([t_0,t_1]\ (t_1,t_2]\ (t_2,t_3]\ (t_3,t_4]\ (t_4,t_5])} (\mathop{R}_{j=1}^{\#S(P \cup Q)} v\ t_i, s_j)$$

$$=
\begin{pmatrix}
 & S_P & S_Q & S_{PQ} \\
t_0 & V_{0P} & V_{0Q} & V_{0PQ} \\
(t_0, t_1] & V_{1P'} & - & V_{1PQ} \\
(t_1, t_2] & - & V_{2Q'} & V_{2PQ} \\
(t_2, t_3] & V_{3P''} & - & V_{3PQ} \\
(t_3, t_4] & - & V_{4Q''} & V_{4PQ} \\
(t_4, t_5] & V_{5P'''} & - & V_{5PQ}
\end{pmatrix}
\tag{45}$$

The semantic diagram of the interleave process relation as defined in Equation 45 is illustrated in Figure 14 on $\Theta(P \parallel\mid Q)$.

Figure 15. The semantic diagram of the pipeline process relation

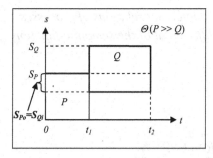

Figure 16. The semantic diagram of the interrupt process relation

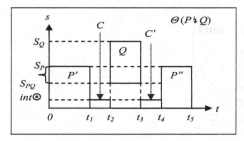

The Pipeline Process Relation

Definition 44. *The semantics of the pipeline relations of processes on* Θ, $\theta(P \gg Q)$, *is a double partial differential of the semantic function* $f_\theta(P \gg Q)$ *on the sets of variables S and executing steps T, i.e.:*

$$
\begin{aligned}
\theta(P \gg Q) &\triangleq \frac{\partial^2}{\partial t\, \partial s} f_\theta(P \gg Q) \\
&= \frac{\partial^2}{\partial t\, \partial s} f_\theta(P) \gg \frac{\partial^2}{\partial t\, \partial s} f_\theta(Q) \\
&= \underset{i=0}{\overset{\#T(P)}{R}}\ \underset{j=1}{\overset{\#S(P)}{R}}\ v_P(t_i,s_j) \gg \underset{i=0}{\overset{\#T(Q)}{R}}\ \underset{j=1}{\overset{\#S(Q)}{R}}\ v_Q(t_i,s_j) \\
&= \underset{i=0}{\overset{\#T(\widehat{PQ})}{R}}\ (\underset{j=1}{\overset{\#S(P\cup Q)}{R}}\ v\, t_i,s_j) \\
&= \begin{pmatrix} & S_P & S_{Po}=S_{Qi} & S_Q \\ t_0 & V_{0P} & V_{0PQ} & V_{0Q} \\ (t_0,t_1] & V_{1P} & V_{1PQ} & - \\ (t_1,t_2] & - & V_{2PQ} & V_{2Q} \end{pmatrix}
\end{aligned}
$$

(46)

where S_{P_o} *and* S_{Q_i} *denote a set of n one-to-one connections between the outputs of P and inputs of Q, respectively, as follows:*

$$
\underset{k=0}{\overset{n-1}{R}}\ (P_o(i) = Q_i(i))
$$

(47)

The semantic diagram of the pipeline process relation as defined in Equation 46 is illustrated in Figure 15 on $\Theta(P \gg Q)$.

The Interrupt Process Relation

Definition 45. *The semantics of the interrupt relations of processes,* $\theta(P \nleftarrow Q)$, *on a given semantic environment* Θ *is a double partial differential of the semantic function* $f_\theta(P \nleftarrow Q)$ *on the sets of variables S and executing steps T, i.e.:*

$$
\begin{aligned}
\theta(P \nleftarrow Q) &\triangleq \frac{\partial^2}{\partial t\, \partial s} f_\theta(P \nleftarrow Q) \\
&= \frac{\partial^2}{\partial t\, \partial s} f_\theta(P) \nleftarrow \frac{\partial^2}{\partial t\, \partial s} f_\theta(Q) \\
&= \underset{i=0}{\overset{\#T(P)}{R}}\ (\underset{j=1}{\overset{\#S(P)}{R}} v_P\, t_i,s_j) \nleftarrow \underset{i=0}{\overset{\#T(Q)}{R}}\ (\underset{j=1}{\overset{\#S(Q)}{R}} v_Q\, t_i,s_j) \\
&= \underset{i=0}{\overset{\#T(P\smallfrown Q\smallfrown P'')}{R}}\ (\underset{j=1}{\overset{\#S(P\cup Q)}{R}} v\, t_i,s_j) \\
&= \begin{pmatrix} & S_P & S_Q & S_{PQ} & int\odot \\ [t_0,t_1] & V_{1P'} & \bot & V_{1PQ} & \bot \\ (t_1,t_2] & - & - & V_{2PQ} & V_{2int\odot} \\ (t_2,t_3] & - & V_{3Q} & V_{3PQ} & - \\ (t_3,t_4] & - & - & V_{4PQ} & V_{4int'\odot} \\ (t_4,t_5] & V_{5P'} & - & V_{5PQ} & - \end{pmatrix}
\end{aligned}
$$

(48)

The semantic diagram of the interrupt process relation as defined in Equation 48 is illustrated in Figure 16 on $\Theta(\,P \nrightarrow Q)$, where $C(\text{int}'\odot)$ and $C'(\text{int}'\odot)$ are the interrupt and interrupt-return points, respectively.

The deductive semantics of the three system dispatch process relations will be presented in the next section.

DEDUCTIVE SEMANTICS OF SYSTEM-LEVEL PROCESSES OF RTPA

The deductive semantics of systems at the top level of programs can be reduced onto a dispatch mechanism of a finite set of processes based on the mechanisms known as time, event, and interrupt. This section first describes the deductive semantics of the system process. Then, the three system dispatching processes will be formally modeled.

The System Process

Definition 46. *The semantics of the system process § on Θ, $\theta(\S)$, is an abstract logical model of the executing platform with a set of parallel dispatched processes based on internal system clock, external events, and system interrupts, i.e.:*

$$
\begin{aligned}
\theta(\S) &\triangleq \frac{\partial^2}{\partial t\ \partial s} f_\theta(\S) \\
&= \frac{\partial^2}{\partial t\ \partial s} f_\theta\{\ \underset{i\mathbb{N}=0}{\overset{n_e\mathbb{N}-1}{R}}(@e_i\mathbf{s}\hookmapsto P_i) \\
&\qquad \|\ (\underset{j\mathbb{N}=0}{\overset{n_t\mathbb{N}-1}{R}}@t_j\mathbf{TM}\hookmapsto P_j) \\
&\qquad \|\ (\underset{k\mathbb{N}=0}{\overset{n_{\text{int}}\mathbb{N}-1}{R}}@int_k\mathbf{s}\hookmapsto P_k) \\
&\qquad \} \\
&= \underset{SysShuntDown\mathbf{BL}=\mathbf{F}}{\overset{\mathbf{T}}{R}}\{\ (\underset{i\mathbb{N}=0}{\overset{n_e\mathbb{N}-1}{R}}@e_i\mathbf{s}\hookmapsto P_i) \\
&\qquad \|\ (\underset{j\mathbb{N}=0}{\overset{n_t\mathbb{N}-1}{R}}@t_j\mathbf{TM}\hookmapsto P_j) \\
&\qquad \|\ (\underset{k\mathbb{N}=0}{\overset{n_{\text{int}}\mathbb{N}-1}{R}}@int_k\mathbf{s}\hookmapsto P_k) \\
&\qquad \}
\end{aligned}
\tag{49}
$$

where the semantics of the parallel relations has been given in Definition 41, and those of the system dispatch processes will be described in the following subsections.

Figure 17. The semantic diagram of time-driven dispatch relation

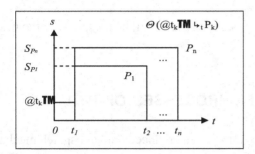

Figure 18. The semantic diagram of the event-driven dispatch relation

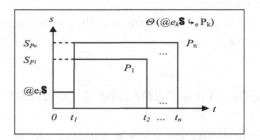

Figure 19. The semantic diagram of the interrupt-driven dispatch relation

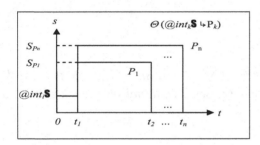

The Time-Driven Dispatching Process Relation

Definition 47. *The semantics of the time-driven dispatching relations of processes on* Θ, $\theta(@t_k\textbf{TM} \hookrightarrow_t P_k)$, *is a double partial differential of the semantic function* $f_\theta(@t_k\textbf{TM} \hookrightarrow_t P_k)$ *on the sets of variables S and executing steps T, i.e.:*

$$
\begin{aligned}
\theta(@t_k\textbf{TM} \hookrightarrow_k P_k) &\triangleq \frac{\partial^2}{\partial t\, \partial s} f_\theta(@t_k\textbf{TM} \hookrightarrow_k P_k) \\
&= \mathop{R}_{k=1}^{n} (@t_k\textbf{TM} \to \frac{\partial^2}{\partial t\, \partial s} f_\theta(P_k)) \\
&= \mathop{R}_{k=1}^{n} (@t_k\textbf{TM} \to \mathop{R}_{i=0}^{\#T(P_k)} \mathop{R}_{j=1}^{\#S(P_k)} v_{P_k}(t_i,s_j)) \\
&= \blacklozenge @t_1\textbf{TM} \to \mathop{R}_{i=0}^{\#T(P_1)} (\mathop{R}_{j=1}^{\#S(P_1)} v_{P_1}\, t_i,s_j) \\
&\quad | \, ... \\
&\quad | \, \blacklozenge @t_n\textbf{TM} \to \mathop{R}_{i=0}^{\#T(P_n)} \mathop{R}_{j=1}^{\#S(P_n)} v_{P_n}(t_i,s_j) \\
&= \begin{pmatrix}
 & @t_k\textbf{TM} & \textbf{S}_{P_1} & ... & \textbf{S}_{P_n} \\
[t_0,t_1] & \delta(@t_k\textbf{TM}) & \bot & \cdots & \bot \\
(t_1,t_2] & @t_1 & V_{P_1} & \cdots & - \\
\vdots & \vdots & \vdots & \ddots & \vdots \\
(t_1,t_n] & @t_n & - & \cdots & V_{P_n}
\end{pmatrix}
\end{aligned}
$$

(50)

where $\blacklozenge(@t_k\mathbf{TM}) = \blacklozenge(@t_k\mathbf{N})$ *is the evaluation function as defined in Equation 17b.*

The semantic diagram of the time-driven dispatching process relation as defined in Equation 50 is illustrated in Figure 17 on Θ.

The Event-Driven Dispatching Process Relation

Definition 48. *The semantics of the event-driven dispatching relations of processes on* Θ, $\theta(@e_k\mathbf{S} \hookrightarrow_e P_k)$, *is a double partial differential of the semantic function* $f_\theta(@e_k\mathbf{S} \hookrightarrow_e P_k)$ *on the sets of variables S and executing steps T, i.e.:*

$$
\begin{aligned}
\theta(@e_k\mathbf{S} \hookrightarrow_e P_k) &\triangleq \frac{\partial^2}{\partial t\,\partial s} f_\theta(@e_k\mathbf{S} \hookrightarrow_e P_k) \\
&= \mathop{R}_{k=1}^{n}(@e_k\mathbf{S} \to \frac{\partial^2}{\partial t(P_k)\partial s(P_k)} f_\theta(P_k)) \\
&= \mathop{R}_{k=1}^{n}(@e_k\mathbf{S} \to \mathop{R}_{i=0}^{\#T(P_k)} \mathop{R}_{j=1}^{\#S(P_k)} v_{P_k}(t_i,s_j)) \\
&= \blacklozenge @e_1\mathbf{S} \to \mathop{R}_{i=0}^{\#T(P_1)} \mathop{R}_{j=1}^{\#S(P_1)} v_{P_1}(t_i,s_j) \\
&\quad | \dots \\
&\quad | \blacklozenge @e_n\mathbf{S} \to \mathop{R}_{i=0}^{\#T(P_n)} \mathop{R}_{j=1}^{\#S(P_n)} v_{P_n}(t_i,s_j) \\
&= \begin{pmatrix}
 & @e_k\mathbf{S} & \mathbf{S}_{P_1} & \dots & \mathbf{S}_{P_n} \\
[t_0,t_1] & \delta(@e_k\mathbf{S}) & \bot & \cdots & \bot \\
(t_1,t_2] & @e_l & V_{P_l} & \cdots & - \\
\vdots & \vdots & \vdots & \ddots & \vdots \\
(t_1,t_n] & @e_n & - & \cdots & V_{P_n}
\end{pmatrix}
\end{aligned}
\tag{51}
$$

The semantic diagram of the event-driven process relation as defined in Equation 51 is illustrated in Figure 18 on Θ.

The Interrupt-Driven Dispatching Process Relation

Definition 49. *The semantics of the interrupt-driven dispatching relations of processes on* Θ, $\theta(@int_k\mathbf{S} \hookrightarrow_i P_j)$, *is a double partial differential of the semantic function* $f_\theta(@int_k\mathbf{S} \hookrightarrow_i P_j)$ *on the sets of variables S and executing steps T, i.e.:*

287

$$\theta(@int_k \mathbf{S} \, \mathbf{P}^\cdot_{i\ k}) \triangleq \frac{\partial^2}{\partial t\, \partial s} f_\theta(@int_k \mathbf{S} \hookrightarrow_i P_k)$$

$$= \mathop{R}_{k=1}^{n}(@int_k \mathbf{S} \rightarrow \frac{\partial^2}{\partial t(P_k)\partial s(P_k)} f_\theta(P_k))$$

(52)

$$= \mathop{R}_{k=1}^{n}(@int_k \mathbf{S} \rightarrow \mathop{R}_{i=0}^{\#T(P_k)} \mathop{R}_{j=1}^{\#S(P_k)} v_{P_k}(t_i, s_j))$$

$$= @int_1 \mathbf{S} \rightarrow \mathop{R}_{i=0}^{\#T(P_1)} (\mathop{R}_{j=1}^{\#S(P_1)} v_{P_1}\ t_i, s_j)$$

$$|\ \ldots$$

$$|\ @int_n \mathbf{S} \rightarrow \mathop{R}_{i=0}^{\#T(P_n)} \mathop{R}_{j=1}^{\#S(P_n)} v_{P_n}(t_i, s_j)$$

$$= \begin{pmatrix} & @int_k\mathbf{S} & S_{P_1} & \ldots & S_{P_n} \\ [t_0, t_1] & \delta(@int_k\mathbf{S}) & \bot & \cdots & \bot \\ (t_1, t_2] & @e_1 & V_{P_1} & \cdots & - \\ \vdots & \vdots & \vdots & \ddots & \vdots \\ (t_1, t_n] & @e_n & - & \cdots & V_{P_n} \end{pmatrix}$$

The semantic diagram of the interrupt-driven process relation as defined in Equation 52 is illustrated in Figure 19 on Θ.

CONCLUSION

Semantics plays an important role in cognitive informatics, computational linguistics, computing, and software engineering theories. Deductive semantics is a formal software semantics that deduces the semantics of a program in a given programming language from a generic abstract semantic function to the concrete semantics, which are embodied by the changes of statuses of a finite set of variables constituting the semantic environment of computing. Based on the mathematical models and architectural properties of programs at different composing levels, deductive models of software semantics, semantic environment, and semantic matrix have been formally defined. Properties of software semantics and relations between the software behavioral space and semantic environment have been discussed. Case studies on the deductive semantic rules of RTPA have been presented, which serve not only as a comprehensive paradigm, but also the verification of the expressive and analytic capacity of deductive semantics.

A rigorous treatment of deductive semantics of RTPA has been presented in this article, which enables a new approach towards deductive reasoning of software semantics at all composing levels of the program hierarchy (i.e., statements, processes, and programs) from the bottom up. Deductive semantics has greatly simplified the description and analysis of the semantics of complicated software systems implemented in programming languages or specified in formal notations. Deductive semantics can be used to define both abstract and concrete semantics of large-scale software systems, facilitate software comprehension and recognition, support tool development, enable semantics-based software testing and verification, and explore the semantic complexity of software systems.

ACKNOWLEDGMENT

The author would like to acknowledge the Natural Science and Engineering Council of Canada (NSERC) for its partial support to this work. The author would like to thank anonymous reviewers for their valuable comments and suggestions.

REFERENCES

Bjorner, D. (2000, November). Pinnacles of software engineering: 25 years of formal methods. In Y. Wang & D. Patel (Eds.), *Annals of software engineering: An international journal,10,* 11-66.

Bjorner, D., & Jones, C. B. (1982). *Formal specification and software development.* Englewood Cliffs, NJ: Prentice Hall.

Chomsky, N. (1956). Three models for the description of languages. *I.R.E. Transactions on Information Theory, 2*(3), 113-124.

Chomsky, N. (1957). *Syntactic structures.* The Hague, The Netherlands: Mouton.

Chomsky, N. (1982). *Some concepts and consequences of the theory of government and binding.* Cambridge, MA: MIT Press

Dijkstra, E. W. (1975). Guarded commands, nondeterminacy, and the formal derivation of programs. *Communications of the ACM, 18*(8), 453-457.

Dijkstra, E. W. (1976). *A discipline of programming.* Englewood Cliffs, NJ: Prentice Hall.

Goguen, J. A., & Malcolm, G. (1996). *Algebraic semantics of imperative programming.* Cambridge, MA: MIT Press.

Goguen, J.A., Thatcher, J. W., Wagner, E. G., & Wright, J. B. (1977). Initial algebra semantics and continuous algebras. *Journal of the ACM, 24*(1), 68-59.

Gries, D. (1981). *The science of programming.* Berlin, Germany: Spinger Verlag

Gunter, C. A. (1992). Semantics of programming languages: Structures and techniques. In M. Garey & A. Meyer (Eds.), *Foundations of computing.* Cambridge, MA: MIT Press.

Guttag, J. V., & Horning, J. J. (1978). The algebraic specification of abstract data types. *Acta Informatica, 10,* 27-52.

Hoare, C. A. R. (1969). An axiomatic basis for computer programming. *Communications of the ACM, 12*(10), 576-580.

Jones, C. B. (1980). *Software development: A rigorous approach.* London: Prentice Hall International.

Louden, K. C. (1993). *Programming languages: Principles and practice.* Boston: PWS-Kent.

Marcotty, M., & Ledgard. H. (1986). *Programming language landscape* (2nd ed.). Chicago: SRA.

McDermid, J. A. (Ed.). (1991). *Software engineer's reference book*. Oxford, England: Butterworth-Heinemann.

Meyer, B. (1990). *Introduction to the theory of programming languages*. Englewood Cliffs, NJ: Prentice Hall

Ollongren, A. (1974). *Definition of programming languages by interpreting automata*. New York: Academic Press.

Pagan, F. G. (1981). *Semantics of programming languages: A panoramic primer*. Englewood Cliffs, NJ: Prentice Hall.

Schmidt, D. (1988). *Denotational semantics: A methodology for language development*. Dubuque, IA: Brown.

Schmidt, D. (1996, March). Programming language semantics. *ACM Computing Surveys, 28*(1).

Schmidt, D. A. (1994). *The structure of typed programming languages*. Cambridge, MA: MIT Press.

Scott, D. (1982). Domains for denotational semantics. In *Automata, languages and programming IX* (pp. 577-613). Berlin, Germany: Springer Verlag.

Scott, D. S., & Strachey, C. (1971). *Towards a mathematical semantics for computer languages*. (Programming Research Group Tech. Rep. PRG-1-6). Oxford University.

Slonneg, K., & Kurts, B. (1995). *Formal syntax and semantics of programming languages*. Addison-Wesley.

Tarski, A. (1944). The semantic conception of truth. *Philosophic Phenomenological Research, 4*, 13-47.

Wang, Y. (2002). The real-time process algebra (RTPA). *Annals of Software Engineering: A International Journal, 14*, 235-274.

Wang, Y. (2003). Using Process algebra to describe human and software system behaviors. *Brain and Mind, 4*(2), 199-213.

Wang, Y. (2006a). Cognitive informatics and contemporary mathematics for knowledge representation and manipulation (Invited plenary talk). In *Proceedings of the First International Conference on Rough Set and Knowledge Technology (RSKT'06)* (LNAI 4062, pp. 69-78). Chongqing, China: Springer.

Wang, Y. (2006b). On the informatics laws and deductive semantics of software, *IEEE Transactions on Systems, Man, and Cybernetics (C), 36*(2), 161-171.

Wang, Y. (2007a). The Cognitive Processes of Formal Inferences. *The International Journal of Cognitive Informatics and Natural Intelligence, 1*(4), 75-86.

Wang, Y. (2007b). Keynote speech on theoretical foundations of software engineering and denotational mathematics. In *Proceedings of the Fifth Asian Workshop on Foundations of Software* (pp. 99-102). Xiamen, China:

Wang, Y. (2007c). *Software engineering foundations:A software science perspective.* Auerbach Publications, NY., July.

Wang, Y. (2008a). On the big-R notation for describing iterative and recursive behaviors. *The International Journal of Cognitive Informatics and Natural Intelligence, 2*(1),17-28.

Wang, Y. (2008b, April). RTPA: A denotational mathematics for manipulating intelligent and computational behaviors. *The International Journal of Cognitive Informatics and Natural Intelligence*, 2(2), 44-62.

Wegner, P. (1972). The Vienna definition language. *ACM Computing Surveys, 4*(1), 5-63.

Wikstrom, A. (1987). *Functional programming using standard ML.* Englewood Cliffs, NJ: Prentice Hall.

This work was previously published in International Journal of Cognitive Informatics and Natural Intelligence, Vol. 2, Issue 2, pp. 95-121, copyright 2008 by IGI Publishing (an imprint of IGI Global).

Chapter 15
On the Big–R Notation for Describing Iterative and Recursive Behaviors

Yingxu Wang
University of Calgary, Canada

ABSTRACT

Iterative and recursive control structures are the most fundamental mechanisms of computing that make programming more effective and expressive. However, these constructs are perhaps the most diverse and confusable instructions in programming languages at both syntactic and semantic levels. This article introduces the big-R notation that provides a unifying mathematical treatment of iterations and recursions in computing. Mathematical models of iterations and recursions are developed using logical inductions. Based on the mathematical model of the big-R notation, fundamental properties of iterative and recursive behaviors of software are comparatively analyzed. The big-R notation has been adopted and implemented in Real-Time Process Algebra (RTPA) and its supporting tools. Case studies demonstrate that a convenient notation may dramatically reduce the difficulty and complexity in expressing a frequently used and highly recurring concept and notion in computing and software engineering.

INTRODUCTION

A repetitive and efficient treatment of recurrent behaviors and architectures is one of the most premier needs in computing. Iterative and recursive constructs and behaviors are most fundamental to computing because they enable programming to be more effective and expressive. However, unlike the high commonality in branch structures among programming languages, the syntaxes of loops are far more than unified. There is even a lack of common semantics of all forms of loops in modern programming languages (Louden, 1993; Wang, 2006a; Wilson and Clark, 1988).

When analyzing the syntactic and semantic problems inherited in iterations in programming languages, B. L. Meek concluded that: "There are some who argue that this demonstrates that the procedural approach to programming languages must be inadequate and fatally flawed, and that coping with something so fundamental as looping must therefore entail looking at computation in a different way rather than trying to devise better procedural syntax. There are others who would argue that the possible applications of looping so it cannot simply be removed or obviated. As ever it is probably this last argument that will hold sway until (or unless) someone proves them wrong, whether with a brilliant stroke of procedural syntactic genius, or an effective and comprehensive new approach to the whole area" (Meek, 1991).

This article introduces the big-R notation that provides a unifying mathematical treatment of iterations and recursions in computing. It summarizes the basic control structures of computing, and introduces the big-R notation on the basis of mathematical inductions. The unified mathematical models of iterations and recursions are derived using the big-R notation. Basic properties of iterative and recursive behaviors and architectures in computing are comparatively analyzed. The big-R notation has been adopted and implemented in Real-Time Process Algebra (RTPA) and its supporting tools (Wang, 2002, 2003; Tan, Wang, & Ngolah, 2004). Application examples of the big-R notation in the context of RTPA will be provided throughout this article.

THE BIG-R NOTATION

Although modern high-level programming languages provide a variety of iterative constructs, the mechanisms of iteration may be expressed by the use of conditional or unconditional jumps with a body of linear code. The proliferation of various loop constructs in programming indicates a fundamental need for expressing the notion of repetitive, cyclic, recursive behaviors, and architectures in computing.

In the development of RTPA (Wang, 2002, 2003, 2006a, 2007a, 2007b), it is recognized that all iterative and recursive operations in programming can be unified on the basis of a big-R notation (Wang, 2006b). This section introduces the big-R notation and its mathematical foundation. It can be seen that a convenient notation may dramatically reduce the difficulty and complexity in expressing a frequently used and highly recurring concept and notion in programming.

The Basic Control Structures of Computing

Before the big-R notation is introduced, a survey of essential basic control structures in computing is summarized and reviewed below.

Definition 1. *Basic control structures (BCS's) are a set of essential flow control mechanisms that are used for modeling logical architectures of software.*

The most commonly identified BCS's in computing are known as the *sequential, branch, case (switch), iterations (three types), procedure call, recursion, parallel,* and *interrupt* structures (Backhouse, 1968; Dijkstra, 1976; Wirth, 1976; Backus, 1978; de Bakker, 1980; Jones, 1980; Cries, 1981; Hehner, 1984; Hoare, 1985, Hoare et al., 1987; Wilson & Clark, 1988; Louden, 1993; Wang, 2002; Horstmann & Budd,

2004). The 10 BCS's as formally modeled in RTPA (Wang, 2002) are shown in Table 1. These BCS's provide essential compositional rules for programming. Based on them, complex computing functions and processes can be composed.

As shown in Table 1, the iterative and recursive BCS's play a very important role in programming. The following theorem explains why iteration and recursion are inherently vital in determining the basic expressive power of computing.

Table 1. BCS's and their mathematical models

Category	BCS	Structural model	RTPA model
Sequence	Sequence (SEQ)		$P \to Q$
Branch	If-then-[else] (ITE)		$(\blacklozenge\exp\mathbf{BL} = \mathbf{T}) \to P$ $\mid (\blacklozenge\sim) \to Q$
Branch	Case (CASE)		$\blacklozenge\exp\mathbf{RT} =$ $0 \to P_0$ $\mid 1 \to P_1$ $\mid \dots$ $\mid n\text{-}1 \to P_{n-1}$ $\mid \text{else} \to \varnothing$
Iteration	While-do (R^*)		$\overset{F}{\underset{\exp\mathbf{BL}=\mathbf{T}}{R}}(P)$
Iteration	Repeat-until (R^+)		$P \to \overset{F}{\underset{\exp\mathbf{BL}=\mathbf{T}}{R}}(P)$
Iteration	For-do (R^i)		$\overset{n}{\underset{i=1}{R}}P(i)$
Embedded component	Procedure call (PC)		$P \looparrowright Q$
Embedded component	Recursion ($R^\circlearrowleft$)		$P \circlearrowleft P$
Concurrence	Parallel (PAR)		$P \parallel Q$
Concurrence	Interrupt (INT)		$P \between Q$

Theorem 1. *The need for software is necessarily and sufficiently determined by the following three conditions:*

a.   The *repeatability:* Software is required when one needs to do something for more than once.
b.   The *flexibility* or *programmability:* Software is required when one needs to repeatedly do something not exactly the same.
c.   The *run-time determinability:* Software is required when one needs to flexibly do something by a series of choices on the basis of varying sequences of events determinable only at run-time.

Theorem 1 indicates that the above three situations, namely repeatability, flexibility, and run-time determinability, form the necessary and sufficient conditions that warrant the requirement for a software solution in computing (Wang, 2006a).

The Big-R Notation for Denoting Iterations and Recursions

The big-R notation is introduced first in RTPA (Wang, 2002) intending to provide a unified and expressive mathematical treatment of iterations and recursions in computing. In order to develop a general mathematical model for unifying the syntaxes and semantics of iterations, the inductive nature of iterations needs to be recognized.

Definition 2. *An iteration of a process P is a series of n+1 repetitions, R_i, $1 \leq i \leq n+1$, of P by mathematical induction, that is:*

$$R_0 = \varnothing,$$
$$R_1 = P \rightarrow R_0,$$
$$\dots$$
$$R_{n+1} = P \rightarrow R_n, n \geq 0 \tag{1}$$

where $\varnothing$ denotes a skip, or doing nothing but exit.

Based on Definitions 2, the big-R notation can be introduced below.

Definition 3. *The big-R notation is a mathematical operator that is used to denote: (a) a finite set of repetitive behaviors, or (b) a finite set of recurring architectural constructs in computing, in the following forms:*

(a) $\displaystyle \mathop{R}_{exp\mathbf{BL}=\mathbf{T}}^{\mathbf{F}} P \tag{2.1}$

(b) $\displaystyle \mathop{R}_{i\mathbf{N}=1}^{n} P(i) \tag{2.2}$

where **BL** and **N** are the type suffixes of Boolean and natural numbers, respectively, as defined in RTPA. Other useful type suffixes that will appear in this article are integer (**Z**), string (**S**), pointer (**S**), hexadecimal (**H**), time (**TM**), interrupt (⊙), run-time type (**RT**), system type (**I**), and the Boolean constants

(**T**) and (**F**) (Wang, 2002, 2007a).

The mechanism of the big-R notation can be in analogy with the mathematical notations Σ and Π, or programming notations of while-loop and for-loop as shown in the following examples.

Example 1. *The big-Σ notation $\sum_{i=1}^{n}$ is a widely used calculus for denoting repetitive additions. Assumming that the operation of addition is represented by sum(x), the mechanism of the big-Σ can be expressed more generally by the big-R notation, that is:*

$$\sum_{i=1}^{n} x_i = \mathop{R}_{i=1}^{n} sum(x_i) \tag{3}$$

According to Definition 3, the big-R notation can be used to denote not only repetitive operational behaviors in computing, but also recurring constructs of architectures and data objects, as shown below.

Example 2. *The architecture of a two-dimensional array with n $\times$ m integer elements, A_{nm}, can be denoted by the big-R notation as follows:*

$$A_{nm} = \mathop{R}_{i=0}^{n-1} \mathop{R}_{j=0}^{m-1} A[i, j]\mathbf{N} \tag{4}$$

Because the big-R notation provides a powerful and expressive means for denoting iterative and recursive behaviors and architectures of systems or human beings, it is a general mathematical operator for system modeling in terms of repetitive "*to do*" and recurrent "*to be,*" respectively (Wang, 2002, 2003, 2006a, 2006b, 2006c, 2007a, 2007b). From this point of view, Σ and Π are only special cases of the big-R for repetitively doing additions and multiplications, respectively.

Definition 4. *An infinitive iteration can be denoted by the big-R notation as:*

$$\mathop{R}P \triangleq \gamma \bullet P \curvearrowright \gamma \tag{5}$$

where $\curvearrowright$ denotes a jump, and γ is a label that denotes the rewinding point of a loop known as the fixpoint mathematically (Tarski, 1955).

The infinitive iteration may be used to formally describe any everlasting behavior of systems.

Example 3. *A simple everlasting clock (Hoare, 1985), CLOCK, which does nothing but tick, that is:*

$$CLOCK \triangleq tick \rightarrow tick \rightarrow tick \rightarrow \ldots \tag{6}$$

can be efficiently denoted by the big-R notation as simply as follows:

$$CLOCK \triangleq \mathop{R} tick \tag{7}$$

A more generic and useful iterative construct is the conditional iteration.

Definition 5. *A conditional iteration can be denoted by the big-R notation as:*

$$
\overset{\mathsf{F}}{\underset{exp\mathsf{BL}=\mathsf{T}}{\mathsf{R}}} \; P \triangleq \gamma \bullet (\; \blacklozenge \; exp\mathsf{BL} = \mathsf{T}
$$
$$
\rightarrow P
$$
$$
\curvearrowright \gamma
$$
$$
| \; \blacklozenge \sim
$$
$$
\rightarrow \varnothing
$$
$$
)
\tag{8}
$$

where $\varnothing$ denotes a skip.

The conditional iteration is frequently used to formally describe repetitive behaviors on given conditions. Equation 8 expresses that the iterative execution of P will go on while the evaluation of the conditional expression is true ($exp\mathsf{BL} = \mathsf{T}$), until $exp\mathsf{BL} = \mathsf{F}$ abbreviated by '$\sim$'.

MODELING ITERATIONS USING THE BIG-R NOTATION

The importance of iterations in computing is rooted in the basic need for effectively describing recurrent and repetitive software behaviors and system architectures. This section reviews the diversity of iterations provided in programming languages and develops a unifying mathematical model for iterations based on the big-R notation.

Existing Semantic Models of Iterations

Since the wide diversity of iterations in programming, semantics of iterations have been described in various approaches, such as those of the *operational, denotational, axiomatic,* and *algebraic* semantics. For example, the while-loop may be interpreted in different semantics as follows.

a. An *operational semantic description* of the while-loop (Louden, 1993) can be expressed in two parts. When an expression E in the environment Θ is true, the execution of the loop body P for an iteration under Θ can be reduced to the same loop under a new environment Θ', which is resulted by the last execution of P, that is:

$$
\frac{<E \parallel \Theta> \Rightarrow E = T, <P \parallel \Theta> \Rightarrow \Theta'}{<\text{'while'} \; E \; \text{'do'} \; P \; ';' \parallel \Theta> \Rightarrow <\text{'while'} \; E \; \text{'do'} \; P \; ';' \parallel \Theta>}
\tag{9}
$$

where the while-loop is defined recursively, and $\parallel$ denotes a parallel relation between an identifier/statement and the semantic environment Θ.

When $E = F$ in Θ, the loop is reduced to a termination or exit, that is:

$$
\frac{<E \parallel \Theta> \Rightarrow E = \mathsf{F}, <P \parallel \Theta>}{<\text{while} \; E \; \text{do} \; P \; ; \parallel \Theta> \Rightarrow \Theta}
\tag{10}
$$

b.   An *axiomatic semantic description* of the while-loop is given below (McDermid, 1991):

$$\frac{\vdash \{\Theta \land E\}\, P\, \{Q\}}{\vdash \{\Theta\}\, \text{while } E \text{ do } P\, \{\Theta \land \neg E\}} \tag{11}$$

where the symbol $\vdash$ is called the syntactic turnstile.

c.   A *denotational semantic description* of the while-loop by recursive if-then-else structures in the literature is described below (Louden, 1993; Wirth, 1976):

$$\begin{aligned}
\boldsymbol{S}\,[\,&'while'\,E\,'do'\,P\,';'\,] \parallel \Theta = \\
&\boldsymbol{S}\,[\,\text{if } \boldsymbol{E}[\![E]\!] \parallel \Theta = \boldsymbol{\mathsf{T}} \\
&\quad\quad \text{then } \boldsymbol{P}\,[\![P]\!] \parallel \Theta \\
&\quad\quad\quad \text{else } \Theta \\
&\,]\parallel \Theta
\end{aligned} \tag{12}$$

where P is a statement or a list of statements, $\boldsymbol{S}$ and $\boldsymbol{P}$ are semantic functions of statements, and $\boldsymbol{E}$ is a semantic function of expressions.

Observing the above classical examples, it is noteworthy that the semantics of a simple while-loop could be very difficultly and diversely interpreted. Although the examples interpreted the decision point very well by using different branch constructs, they failed to denote the key semantics of "while" and the rewinding action of loops. Further, the semantics for more complicated types of iterations, such as the repeat-loop and for-loop, are rarely found in the literature.

A Unified Mathematical Model of Iterations

Based on the inductive property of iterations, the big-R notation as defined in Equation 8 is found to be a convenient means to describe all types of iterations including the while-, repeat-, and for-loops.

Definition 6. *The while-loop R^* is an iterative construct in which a process P is executed repeatedly as long as the conditional expression expBL is true, that is:*

$$\begin{aligned}
R^* P \triangleq\ &\overset{\text{expBL}=\mathsf{T}}{\overset{f}{R}}\, P \\
=\ &\gamma \bullet (\ \ \blacklozenge\ \exp\boldsymbol{\mathsf{BL}} = \boldsymbol{\mathsf{T}} \\
&\quad\quad\quad \to \boldsymbol{\mathsf{P}} \\
&\quad\quad\quad \curvearrowright \gamma \\
&\quad | \ \blacklozenge \sim \\
&\quad\quad\quad \to \varnothing \\
&\ )
\end{aligned} \tag{13}$$

*where * denotes an iteration for 0 to n times, $n \geq 0$. That is, P may not be iterated in the while-loop at run-time if exp$\boldsymbol{\mathsf{BL}} \neq \boldsymbol{\mathsf{T}}$ at the very beginning.*

According to Equation 13, the semantics of the while-loop is deduced to a series of repetitive conditional operations, where the branch "? $\sim\ \to\ \varnothing$" denotes an exit of the loop when exp$\boldsymbol{\mathsf{BL}} \neq \boldsymbol{\mathsf{T}}$. Note that the update of the control expression exp$\textbf{BL}$ is not necessarily to be explicitly specified inside the body of the loop. In other words, the termination of the while-loop, or the change of exp$\textbf{BL}$, can either be a result of internal effect of P or that of other external events.

Definition 7. *The repeat-loop* R^+ *is an iterative construct in which a process P is executed repetitively for at least once until the conditional expression exp$\textbf{BL}$ is no longer true, that is:*

$$
\begin{aligned}
R^+P \triangleq{}& P \to_r R^*P \\
={}& P \to \overset{expBL=T}{\underset{r}{R}} P \\
={}& P \to \gamma \bullet (\quad \blacklozenge exp\textbf{BL} = \textbf{T} \\
&\qquad\qquad\quad \to \textbf{P} \\
&\qquad\qquad\quad \curvearrowright \gamma \\
&\qquad\quad | \blacklozenge \sim \\
&\qquad\qquad\quad \to \varnothing \\
&\qquad)
\end{aligned}
$$

$$(14)$$

where $^+$ *denotes an iteration for 1 to n times, $n \geq 1$. That is, P will be executed at least once in the repeat loop until exp$\textbf{BL}$ $\neq$ $\textbf{T}$.*

According to Equation 14, the semantics of the repeat-loop is deduced to a single sequential operation of P succeeded by a series of repetitive conditional operations whenever expBL=T. Or simply, the semantics of the repeat-loop is equivalent to a single sequential operation of P plus a while-loop of P.

In Equations 13 and 14, the loop control variable exp$\textbf{BL}$ is in the type Boolean. When the loop control variable i is numeric, say in type $\textbf{N}$ with known lower bound $n_1\textbf{N}$ and upper bounds $n_2\textbf{N}$, then a special variation of iteration, the *for* loop, can be derived below.

Definition 8. *The for-loop* R^i *is an iterative construct in which a process P indexed by an identification variable i$\textbf{N}$, P(i$\textbf{N}$), is executed repeatedly in the scope $n_1\textbf{N} \leq i\textbf{N} \leq n_2\textbf{N}$, that is:*

$$
\begin{aligned}
R^iP(i\textbf{N}) \triangleq{}& \overset{n_2\textbf{N}}{\underset{i\textbf{N}:=n_1\textbf{N}}{R}} P(i\textbf{N}) \\
={}& i\textbf{N} := n_1\textbf{N} \\
&\to \gamma \bullet (\quad \blacklozenge\ i\textbf{N} \leq n_2\textbf{N} \\
&\qquad\qquad\quad \to P\,(i\textbf{N}) \\
&\qquad\qquad\quad \to \uparrow (i\textbf{N}) \\
&\qquad\qquad\quad \curvearrowright \gamma \\
&\qquad\quad | \blacklozenge \sim \\
&\qquad\qquad\quad \to \varnothing \\
&\qquad) \\
={}& i\textbf{N} := n_1\textbf{N} \\
&\to exp\textbf{BL} \underset{r}{=} (i\textbf{N} \leq n_2\textbf{N}) \\
&\qquad \to \underset{expBL=T}{R} (\ P(i\textbf{Z}) \\
&\qquad\qquad \to \uparrow\ (i\textbf{N}) \\
&\qquad)
\end{aligned}
$$

$$(15)$$

where i denotes the loop control variable, and $\uparrow(i\mathbf{N})$ increases iN by one.

According to Equation 15, the semantics of the for-loop is a special case of while-loop where the loop control expression is $\exp\mathbf{BL} = i\mathbf{N} \leq n_2\mathbf{N}$, and the update of the control variable iN must be explicitly specified inside the body of the loop. In other words, the termination of the for-loop is internally controlled.

Based on Definition 8, the most simple for-loop that iteratively executes $P(i\mathbf{N})$ for k times, $1 \leq i \leq k$, can be derived as follows:

$$R^i P(i\mathbf{N}) \triangleq \mathop{R}_{i\mathbf{N}=1}^{k} P(i\mathbf{N}) \tag{16}$$

It is noteworthy that a general assumption in Equations 15 and 16 is that i is a natural number and the iteration step $\Delta i\mathbf{N} = +1$. In a more generic situation, i may be an arbitrary integer $\mathbf{Z}$ or in other numerical types, and $\Delta i\mathbf{Z} \neq +1$. In this case, the lower bound of a for-loop can be described as an expression, or the incremental step $\Delta i\mathbf{Z}$ can be explicitly expressed inside the body of the loop, for example:

$$R^i P(i\mathbf{Z}) \triangleq \mathop{R}_{i\mathbf{Z}=0}^{-10} (P(i\mathbf{Z}) \\ \rightarrow i\mathbf{Z} := i\mathbf{Z} - \Delta i\mathbf{Z} \\ ) \tag{17}$$

where $\Delta i\mathbf{Z} \geq 1$.

MODELING RECURSIONS USING THE BIG-R NOTATION

Recursion is a powerful tool in mathematics for a neat treatment of complex problems following a fundamental *deduction-then-induction* approach. Godel, Herbrand, and Kleene developed the theory of recursive functions using an equational calculus in the 1930s (Kleene, 1952; McDermid, 1991). More recent work on recursions in programming may be found in Mendelson (1964); Peter (1967); Hermes (1969); Hoare (1985); Rayward-Smith (1986); Louden (1993); and Wang (2006a, 2007a). The idea is to construct a class of effectively computable functions from a collection of base functions using fundamental techniques such as function composition and inductive referencing.

Properties of Recursions

Recursion is an operation that a process or function invokes or refers to itself.

Definition 9. *A recursion of process P can be defined by mathematical induction, that is:*

$F^0(P) = P,$
$F^1(P) = F(F^0(P)) = F(P),$
...
$F^{n+1}(P) = F(F^n(P)), n \geq 0 \tag{18}$

A recursive process should be terminable or noncircular, that is, the depth of recursive d_r must be finite. The following theorem guarantees that $d_r < \infty$ for a given recursive process or function.

Theorem 2. *A recursive function is noncircular, that is, $d_r < \infty$, iff:*

a. A *base value* exists for certain arguments for which the function does not refer to itself;

b. In each recursion, the argument of the function must be closer to the base value.

Example 4. *The factorial function can be recursively defined, as shown in Equation 19.*

$$(n\mathbf{N})! \triangleq \{ \; \blacklozenge \; n\mathbf{N} = 0$$
$$\rightarrow (n\mathbf{N})! := 1$$
$$| \; \blacklozenge \sim$$
$$\rightarrow (n\mathbf{N})! := n\mathbf{N} \bullet (n\mathbf{N}-1)!$$
$$\}$$
$$(19)$$

Example 5. *A C++ implementation of the factorial algorithm, as given in Example 4, is provided below.*

```
int factorial (int n)
{
  int factor;
  if (n==0)
     factor = 1;
     else factor = n * factorial(n-1);
 return factor;
}                                                    (20)
```

In addition to the usage of recursion for efficiently modeling repetitive behaviors of systems as above, it has also been found useful in modeling many fundamental language properties.

Example 6. *Assume the following letters are used to represent their corresponding syntactic entities in the angle brackets:*

P <program>,
L <statement list>,
S <statement>,
E <expression>,
I <identifier>,
A <letter>,
N <number>, and
D <digit>

The abstract syntax of grammar rules for a simple programming language may be recursively specified in BNF as follows.

E ::= E '+' E
    | E '-' E

$$| \text{E '*' E}$$
$$\quad | \text{'(' E ')'}$$
$$\quad | \text{I}$$
$$\quad | \text{N}$$
$$\text{I} ::= \text{I A} \mid \text{A}$$
$$\text{A} ::= \text{'a'} \mid \text{'b'} \mid \dots \mid \text{'z'}$$
$$\text{N} ::= \text{N D} \mid \text{D}$$
$$\text{D} ::= \text{'0'} \mid \text{'1'} \mid \dots \mid \text{'9'} \tag{21}$$

It can be seen in Equation 21 that expression E is recursively defined by operations on E itself, an identifier I, or a number N. Further, I is recursively defined by itself or letter A; and N is recursively defined as itself or digit D. Because any form of E as specified above can be eventually deduced on terminal letters ('a', 'b', ..., 'z'), digits ('0', '1', ..., '9'), or predefined operations ('+', '-', '*', '(', ')'), the BNF specification of E as shown in Equation 21 is well-defined (Louden, 1993).

The Mathematical Model of Recursions

Definition 10. *Recursion is an embedded process relation in which a process P calls itself. The recursive process relation can be denoted as follows:*

$$P \circlearrowright P \tag{22}$$

The mechanism of recursion is a series of *embedding* (deductive, denoted by $\circlearrowright$) and *de-embedding* (inductive, denoted by $\circlearrowleft$) processes. In the first phase of embedding, a given layer of nested process is deduced to a lower layer until it is embodied to a known value. In the second phase of de-embedding, the value of a higher layer process is induced by the lower layer starting from the base layer, where its value has already been known at the end of the embedding phase.

Recursion processes are frequently used in programming to simplify system structures and to specify neat and provable system functions. It is particularly useful when an infinite or run-time determinable specification has to be clearly expressed.

Instead of using self-calling in recursions, a more generic form of embedded construct that enables interprocess calls is known as the procedural call.

Definition 11. *A procedural call is a process relation in which a process P calls another process Q as a predefined subprocess. A procedure-call process relation can be defined as follows:*

$$P \hookrightarrow Q \tag{23}$$

In Equation 23, the called process Q can be regarded as an embedded part of process P (Wang, 2002).

Using the big-R notation, a recursion can be defined formally as follows.

Definition 12. *Recursion* $R^\circ P^i$ *is a multilayered, embedded process relation in which a process P at layer i of embedment, P^i, calls itself at an inner layer i-1, P^{i-1}, $0 \leq i \leq n$. The termination of P^i depends on the termination of P^{i-1} during its execution, that is:*

$$R^\circ P^i \triangleq \mathop{R}_{i\mathbf{N}=n\mathbf{N}}^{0} (\quad \blacklozenge \ i\mathbf{N} > 0$$
$$\rightarrow P^{i\mathbf{N}} := P^{i\mathbf{N}-1}$$
$$| \ \blacklozenge \ \sim$$
$$\rightarrow P^0$$
$$)$$

(24)

where *n* is the *depth of recursion* or embedment that is determined by an explicitly specified conditional expression $exp\mathbf{BL} = \mathbf{T}$ inside the body of *P*.

Example 7. *Using the big-R notation, the recursive description of the algorithm provided in Example 4 can be given as follows:*

$$(n\mathbf{N})! \triangleq \mathop{R}_{0}^{\circ} (n\mathbf{N}) \, !$$
$$= \mathop{R}_{i\mathbf{N}=n\mathbf{N}} (\quad \blacklozenge \ i\mathbf{N} > 0$$
$$\rightarrow (i\mathbf{N})! := i\mathbf{N} \bullet (i\mathbf{N}-1)!$$
$$| \ \blacklozenge \ \sim$$
$$\rightarrow (i\mathbf{N})! := 1$$
$$)$$

(25)

COMPARATIVE ANALYSIS OF ITERATIONS AND RECURSIONS

In the literature, iterations were often treated as the same as recursions, or iterations were perceived as a special type of recursions. Although, both iteration $R^i P(i)$ and recursion $R^\circ P^i$ are repetitive and cyclic constructs, the fundamental differences between their traces of execution at run-time are that the former is a linear structure, that is:

$$R^i P(i) = P_1 \rightarrow P_2 \rightarrow ... \rightarrow P_n$$

(26)

However, the latter is an embedded structure, that is:

$$R^\circ P^i = P^n \circlearrowleft P^{n-1} \circlearrowleft ... \circlearrowleft P^1 \circlearrowleft P^0 \circlearrowleft P^1$$
$$\circlearrowleft ... \circlearrowleft P^{n-1} \circlearrowleft P^n$$

(27)

The generic forms of iterative and recursive constructs in computing can be contrasted as illustrated in Figures 1 and 2 as follows.

It is noteworthy that there is always a pair of counterpart solutions for a given repetitive and cyclic problem with either the recursive or iteration approach. For instance, the corresponding iterative version of Example 7 can be described below.

Figure 1. The linear architecture of iterations

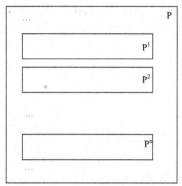

Figure 2. The nested architecture of recursions

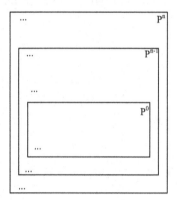

Example 8. *Applying the big-R notation, the iterative description of the algorithm as provided in Example 7 is shown below.*

$$(n\mathbf{N})! \triangleq \{$$
$$\text{factorial}\mathbf{N} := 1$$
$$\rightarrow \mathop{R}_{i\mathbf{N}=1}^{n\mathbf{N}}(\text{factorial}\mathbf{N} := i\mathbf{N} \bullet \text{factorial}\mathbf{N})$$
$$\rightarrow (n\mathbf{N})! := \text{factorial}\mathbf{N}$$
$$\}$$

$$(28)$$

It is interesting to compare both formal algorithms of factorial with recursion and iteration as shown in Equations 25 and 28.

Example 9. *On the basis of Example 8, an iterative implementation of Example 5 in C++ can be developed as follows.*

```
int factorial (int n)
{
    int factor = 1;
    for (int i = 1; i <= n ; i++)
        factor = i * factor;
    return factor;
}
```
                                                                                    (29)

The above examples show the difference between the recursive and iterative techniques for implementing the same algorithm for repetitive and cyclic computation. Contrasting Examples 4 and 8, or Examples 5 and 9, it can be seen that the recursive solution for a given problem is usually more expressive, but less efficient in implementation in terms of time and space complexity than its iterative counterpart. As Peter Deutsch, the creator of the GhostScript interpreter, put it: "To iterate is human, to recurse divine."

CONCLUSION

The efficient treatment of repetitive and recurrent behaviors and architectures has been recognized as one of the most premier needs in computing. However, surprisingly, there have been such a variety of iterative and recursive constructs in modern programming languages and there was still no settled consensus on some of the fundamental issues in their syntaxes and semantics.

This article has introduced the big-R notation that provides a unifying mathematical treatment of iterative and recursive behaviors and architectures in computing. Unified mathematical models of iterations and recursions have been derived using the big-R notation. Based on the big-R notation, the fundamental properties of iterative and recursive behaviors in computing have been comparatively analyzed. This article has demonstrated that a convenient notation may dramatically reduce the difficulty and complexity in expressing a frequently used and highly recurring concept and notion in computing. A wide range of applications of the big-R notation have been identified for effectively and rigorously modeling iterations and recursions in computing, software engineering, and intelligent systems.

ACKNOWLEDGMENT

The author would like to acknowledge the Natural Science and Engineering Council of Canada (NSERC) for its partial support to this work. The author would like to thank the anonymous reviewers for their valuable comments and suggestions.

REFERENCES

Backhouse, R. C. (1968). *Program construction and verification*. London: Prentice Hall International.

Backus, J. (1978). Can programming be liberated from the van Neumann Style? *Communications of the ACM, 21*(8), 613-641.

Cries, D. (1981). *The science of programming.* New York: Springer-Verlag.

de Bakker, J. W. (1980). *Mathematical theory of program correctness.* London: Prentice Hall International.

Dijkstra, E. W. (1976). *A discipline of programming.* Englewood Cliffs, NJ: Prentice Hall.

Hehner, E. C. R. (1984). Predicative programming, parts I and II. *Communications of the ACM, 27*(2), 134-151.

Hermes, H. (1969). *Enumerability, decidability, computability.* New York: Springer-Verlag.

Hoare, C. A. R. (1985). *Communicating sequential processes.* London: Prentice Hall International.

Hoare, C. A. R., Hayes, I. J., He, J., Morgan, C. C., Roscoe, A. W., Sanders, J. W., et al. (1987, August). Laws of programming. *Communications of the ACM, 30*(8), 672-686.

Horstmann, C., & Budd, T. (2004). *Big C++.* Danvers, MA: John Wiley & Sons.

Jones, C. B. (1980). *Software development: A rigorous approach.* London: Prentice Hall International.

Kleene, S. C. (1952). *Introduction to meta-mathematics.* North Holland, Amsterdam.

Louden, K. C. (1993). *Programming languages: Principles and practice.* Boston: PWS-Kent Publishing.

McDermid, J. (Ed.). (1991). *Software engineer's reference book.* Oxford: Butterworth Heinemann.

Meek, B. L. (1991). Early high-level languages (Chapter 43). In J. McDermid (Ed.), *Software engineer's reference book.* Oxford: Butterworth Heinemann.

Mendelson, E. (1964). *Introduction to mathematical logic.* New York: Van Nostrand Reinhold.

Peter, R. (1967). *Recursive functions.* New York: Academic Press.

Rayward-Smith, V. J. (1986). *A first course in computability.* Oxford: Blackwell Scientific.

Tan, X., Wang, Y., & Ngolah, C. (2004, August). Specification of the RTPA grammar and its recognition. In *Proceedings of the 3rd IEEE International Conference on Cognitive Informatics (ICCI'04),* Victoria, Canada, (pp. 54-63). IEEE CS Press.

Tarski, A. (1955). A lattice-theoretic fixed point theorem and its applications. *Pacific Journal of Mathematics, 5,* 285-309.

Wang, Y. (2002, October). The real-time process algebra (RTPA). *Annals of Software Engineering: An International Journal, 14,* 235-274. Kluwer Academic Publishers.

Wang, Y. (2003). Using process algebra to describe human and software system behaviors. *Brain and Mind: A Transdisciplinary Journal of Neuroscience and Neurophilosophy, 4*(2), 199-213.

Wang, Y. (2006a, March). On the informatics laws and deductive semantics of software. *IEEE Transactions on Systems, Man, and Cybernetics (Part C), 36*(2), 161-171.

Wang, Y. (2006b, May 8-10). A unified mathematical model of programs. In *Proceedings of the 19th Canadian Conference on Electrical and Computer Engineering* (CCECE'06), Ottawa, ON, Canada, (pp. 2346-2349).

Wang, Y. (2006c, July). Cognitive informatics and contemporary mathematics for knowledge representation and manipulation, invited plenary talk. In *Proceedings of the 1st International Conference on Rough Set and Knowledge Technology* (RSKT'06), Chongqing, China, (pp. 69-78). Lecture Notes in Artificial Intelligence, LNAI 4062: Springer-Verlag.

Wang, Y. (2007a). Software engineering foundations: A software science perspective. *CRC book series on software engineering* (Vol. II). Boca Raton, FL: CRC Press.

Wang, Y. (2007b). Keynote speech: On theoretical foundations of software engineering and denotational mathematics. In *Proceedings of the 5th Asian Workshop on Foundations of Software*, Xiamen, China, (pp. 99-102).

Wilson, L. B., & Clark, R. G. (1988). *Comparative programming language*. Wokingham, UK: Addison-Wesley Publishing.

Wirth, N. (1976). *Algorithms + data structures = programs*. Englewood Cliffs, NJ: Prentice Hall.

This work was previously published in International Journal of Cognitive Informatics and Natural Intelligence, Vol. 2, Issue 1, pp. 17-28, copyright 2008 by IGI Publishing (an imprint of IGI Global).

Chapter 16
Formal RTPA Models for a Set of Meta–Cognitive Processes of the Brain

Yingxu Wang
University of Calgary, Canada

ABSTRACT

The cognitive processes modeled at the metacognitive level of the layered reference mode of the brain (LRMB) encompass those of object identification, abstraction, concept establishment, search, categorization, comparison, memorization, qualification, quantification, and selection. It is recognized that all higher layer cognitive processes of the brain rely on the metacognitive processes. Each of this set of fundamental cognitive processes is formally described by a mathematical model and a process model. Real-time process algebra (RTPA) is adopted as a denotational mathematical means for rigorous modeling and describing the metacognitive processes. All cognitive models and processes are explained on the basis of the object-attribute-relation (OAR) model for internal information and knowledge representation and manipulation.

INTRODUCTION

A layered reference model of the brain (LRMB) is developed in order to investigate the fundamental mechanisms of the brain as well as natural and computational intelligence (Wang, 2007e; Wang, Wang, Patel, & Patel, 2006). LRMB reveals that the brain is functioning with 39 fundamental cognitive processes in seven layers known as the sensation, memory, perception, action, metacognition, meta-inference, and higher cognition layers from the bottom up. The metacognitive-process layer as modeled in LRMB is one of the crucial layers of the brain because almost all higher layer cognitive processes rely on it

(Gray, 1994; Matlin, 1998; Pinel, 1997; Reisberg, 2001; Smith, 1993; Wang, 2007e; Wang et al.; Westen, 1999; Wilson & Keil, 2001).

Definition 1. *A meta-cognitive function of the brain is a fundamental and elementary life function of the brain that is commonly used to support the higher layer cognitive life functions.*

The metacognitive functions at Layer 5 of LRMB encompass the basic cognitive life functions of object identification, abstraction, concept establishment, search, categorization, comparison, memorization, qualification, quantification, and selection, as described in Figure 1.

The modeling of LRMB is a part of the development of the theoretical framework of cognitive informatics (Wang, 2002a, 2003a, 2006a, 2007e; Wang et al., 2006). The methodologies and denotational mathematics (Wang, 2007d, in press) adopted in this article are concept algebra (Wang, 2008c) and real-time process algebra (RTPA; Wang, 2002b, 2003b, 2007d, 2008d). The former is used to denote the mathematical model and algebraic operations of concept as the basic unit of thinking and inferences. The latter is adopted as the mathematical means for rigorously modeling and describing cognitive processes as a series of dynamic actions and behaviors.

This article presents a set of formal descriptions of the eight metacognitive processes at Layer 5 as shown in Figure 1. Two of the ten metacognition processes, that is, the cognitive processes of abstraction and memorization, have been presented in Wang (2007a) and Wang (2007b), respectively. In the following sections, the mathematical model of each metaprocess will be created, and its cognitive process will be rigorously described in RTPA. All cognitive models and processes are explained on the basis of the object-attribute-relation (OAR) model (Wang, 2007c; Wang, Liu, & Wang, 2003; Wang & Wang, 2006) for internal information and knowledge representation.

Figure 1. Cognitive processes at the metacognition layer of LRMB

LRMB Layer 5: The Meta-Cognitive Processes

Meta-Cognitive Processes $\triangleq$
(MCP5.1_Object_Identification
|| MCP5.2_Abstarction

|| MCP5.3_Concept_Establishment
|| MCP5.4_Search
|| MCP5.5_Categirization
|| MCP5.6_Comparison
|| MCP5.7_Memorization
|| MCP5.8_Qualification
|| MCP5.9_Quantification
|| MCP5.10_Selection
)

THE COGNITIVE PROCESS OF OBJECT IDENTIFICATION

According to LRMB, object identification is a cognitive process of the brain at the metacognition layer that identifies an object by relating it to a concept or comprehends a concept by known meanings. An object and its attributes as well as relations can be defined as follows.

Definition 2. *An object o is a representation of an entity in the real world and/or a concept in the abstract world.*

Definition 3. *An attribute a is a subconcept that is used to characterize the properties of a given concept by more specific or precise concepts in the abstract hierarchy.*

Definition 4. *A relation r is an association or interrelationship between any pair of objects, an object and an attribute, an attribute and an object, and/or attributes.*

To rigorously explain the forms of internal knowledge representation in the brain, a logical model known as the OAR model is described below on the basis of neural informatics (Wang, 2007c).

Theorem 1. *The OAR model states that long-term memory can be described as a triple, that is,*

$$OAR \triangleq (O, A, R), \tag{1}$$

where O is a finite set of objects identified by unique symbolic names, that is,

$$O = \{o_1, o_2, ..., o_i, ..., o_n\}. \tag{2}$$

For each given $o_i \in O$, $1 \leq i \leq n$, A_i is a finite set of attributes for characterizing the object:

$$A_i = \{A_{i1}, A_{i2}, ..., A_{ij}, ..., A_{im}\}, \tag{3}$$

where each $o_i \in O$ or $A_{ij} \in A_i$, $1 \leq i \leq n$, $1 \leq j \leq m$ is physiologically corresponding to a neuron in the brain (Sternberg, 1998; Wang, 2007c).

For each given $o_i \in O$, $1 \leq i \leq n$, R_i is a set of relations between o_i and other objects or attributes of other objects, that is,

$$R_i = \{R_{i1}, R_{i2}, ..., R_{ik}, ..., R_{iq}\}, \tag{4}$$

where R_{ik} is a relation between two objects, o_i and $o_{i'}$, and their attributes A_{ij} and $A_{i'j}$, $1 \leq i \leq n$, $1 \leq j \leq m$:

$$
\begin{aligned}
R_{ik} = \ & r(o_i, o_{i'}) \\
& |\ r(o_i, A_{ij}) \\
& |\ r(A_{ij}, o_{i'}) \\
& |\ r(A_{ij}, A_{i'j}),\ 1 \leq k \leq q,
\end{aligned}
\tag{5}
$$

in which more complex *n*-nary relations may be formed on the basis of the four types of binary relations.

To a certain extent, the entire knowledge in the brain can be modeled as a global and dynamic OAR model.

Definition 5. *Object identification (OI is a cognitive process to identify the related sets of attributes A and relations R for a given object oS in order to form a sub-OAR model:*

$$OI \triangleq f_{OI}:oS \rightarrow sOAR\text{ST}$$
$$= sOAR(o, A, R)\text{ST}.$$

(6)

Object identification is a typical abstract object-recognition process related to knowledge representation, learning, perception, and memorization. It is noteworthy that human visual object and visual pattern recognition are represented and processed in a semantic or abstract approach (Wang, 2008b), which allows recognition to occur relatively independent of size, contrast, spatial frequency, position on the retina, angle of view, and so forth.

Based on the mathematical model of object identification as described in Equation 6, a formal description of the cognitive process of object identification in RTPA is presented in Figure 2. The object identification process is divided into three steps involving search, sub-OAR formation, and memorization. In this process, two other metaprocesses, search and memorization, are invoked as predefined lower layer supporting processes.

The object identification process calls the search process (see Figure 4) to search the internal memory and external resources in parallel in order to find out all $A\text{ST}/A_{ext}\text{ST}$ and $R\text{ST}/R_{ext}\text{ST}$. The detailed process of cognitive search will be elaborated in Definition 11. The findings related to oS will then be represented by a target concept $c\text{ST}$ in the form of a sub-OARST. The memorization step may be skipped when the object identification process is composed of or called by other processes. That is, there is only one final

Figure 2. The cognitive process of object identification in RTPA

```
            The Object Identification Process

ObjectIdentification (I:: oS; O:: cST, OAR'ST)ST ≜
{ I. Search
 ( ↣ Search (I:: oS, OARST; O:: ASET, RSET) ST
        // Internal search
 || ↣ Search (I:: oS, ExtDatabaseST; O:: A_ext SET, R_ext SET)ST
        // External search
 )

  II. Form a sub-OAR
  → A'SET := ASET ∪ A_ext SET
  → R'SET := RSET ∪ R_ext SET
  → sOARST := c(OS, A'SET, R'SET)ST

  III. Memorization
  → OAR'ST := OARST ⊎ sOARST
  ↣ Memorization (OAR'ST )ST
}
```

memorization step in long-term memory establishment everyday, usually during sleep, when multiple processes are composed, sharing intermediate information in the short-term memory according to the memorization mechanisms and process, particularly the 24-hour law (Wang, 2007b; Wang & Wang, 2006).

THE COGNITIVE PROCESS OF CONCEPT ESTABLISHMENT

According to LRMB, concept establishment is a cognitive process of the brain at the metacognition layer that constructs a *to-be* relation between an object, attributes, and other existing objects or attributes.

Definition 6. *Let U denote a finite nonempty set of objects, and M be a finite nonempty set of attributes. A semantic environment or context* Θ *is denoted as a triple, that is,*

$$\Theta = (U, M, R)$$
$$= R: U \to U \mid U \to M \mid M \to U \mid M \to M, \tag{7}$$

where R is a set of relations between U and M.

On the basis of OAR and Θ, an abstract concept is a composition of the above three elements as given below.

Definition 7. *An abstract concept c is a five-tuple:*

$$c \triangleq (O, A, R^c, R^i, R^o), \tag{8}$$

where

- O is a nonempty set of objects of the concept $O = \{o_1, o_2, ..., o_m\} \subseteq \Thorn U$, where $\Thorn U$ denotes a power set of U,
- A is a nonempty set of attributes $A = \{a_1, a_2, ..., a_n\} \subseteq \Thorn M$,
- $R^c \subseteq O \times A$ is a set of internal relations,
- $R^i \subseteq A' \times A$, $A' \sqsubseteq C' \wedge A \sqsubseteq c$ is a set of input relations, where C' is a set of external concepts $C' \subseteq \Theta$ (for convenience, $R^i = A' \times A$ may be simply denoted as $R^i = C' \times c$), and
- $R^o \subseteq c \times C'$ is a set of output relations.

Definition 8. *The intension of a concept c = (O, A, R^c, R^i, R^o), c*, is determined by its set of attributes A:*

$$c^* (O, A, R^c, R^i, R^o) = A$$
$$= \{a_1, a_2, ..., a_n\}, A \subset \Thorn M, \tag{9}$$

where $\Thorn M$ *denotes a power set of M.*

Definition 9. *The extension of a concept c = (O, A, R^c, R^i, R^o), c$^+$, is represented by the set of objects O denoted by c, that is,*

$$c^+(O, A, R^c, R^i, R^o) = O$$
$$= \{a_1, a_2, ..., a_n\}, O \subset ÞU. \tag{10}$$

Concepts are used to construct propositional reasoning, to interpret our current experience by classifying it as being of a particular kind of relation to prior knowledge, and to be a means of understanding the world. Concept establishment is a fundamental cognitive process in developing knowledge representation systems. According to Definition 9 and the OAR model, concept establishment can be described below. More rigorous treatment of abstract concepts may be referred to concept algebra (Wang, 2008c).

Definition 10. *Concept establishment CE is a cognitive process that forms a concept c(O, A, R^c, R^i, R^o) by identifying its objects O, attributes A, and internal relations R^c from the semantic environment Θ = (U, M, R) or the entire OAR model in memory:*

$$CE \triangleq f_{CE}\!:o\mathbf{S} \to c\mathbf{ST}$$
$$= c(O, A, R^c, R^i, R^o|\ O \subset U, A \subset M,$$
$$R^c \subset O \times A, R^i = \varnothing, R^0 = \varnothing)\mathbf{ST}. \tag{11}$$

In Definition 10, $R^i = R^o = \varnothing$ denotes that the identification operation is an initialization of a newly created concept where the input and output relations will be established later.

Based on the mathematical model of concept establishment as described in Equation 11, a formal description of the cognitive process of concept establishment in RTPA is presented in Figure 3. The concept establishment process is divided into three steps: (a) search for related attributes and relations, (b) form a concept, and (c) memorize. In this process, two other predefined metaprocesses, search and

Figure 3. The cognitive process of concept establishment in RTPA

The Concept Establishment Process

ConceptEstablishment (I:: o**S**; O:: c**ST**, OAR'**ST**)**ST** ≜
{I. Search related attributes and relations
    ↣ Search (I:: o**S**, OAR**ST**; O:: A**SET**, R**SET**)**ST**
      // Internal search
   || ↣ Search (I:: o**S**, ExtDatabase**ST**; O:: A$_{ext}$**SET**, R$_{ext}$**SET**)**ST**
      // External search
)

   II. Form a concept
   → A'**SET** := A**SET** ∪ A$_{ext}$**SET**
   → R'**SET** := R**SET** ∪ R$_{ext}$**SET**
   → sOAR**ST** := c(O**S**, A'**SET**, R'**SET**)**ST**

   III. Memorization
   → OAR'**ST** := OAR**ST** ⊎ sOAR**ST**
   ↣ Memorization (OAR'**ST**)**ST**
}

memorization, are invoked. The former will be elaborated in Definition 11, while the latter has been formally described in Wang (2007b). The memorization step may be skipped when the concept establishment process is composed of or called by other processes.

THE COGNITIVE PROCESS OF SEARCH

According to LRMB, search is a cognitive process of the brain at the metacognition layer that is based on trial-and-error explorations to find a set of correlated objects, attributes, or relations for a given object or concept or to find useful solutions for a given problem. The cognitive process of search is a basic subconscious content-sensitive search, as defined in concept algebra (Wang, 2007e), where no conscious-level search strategy or heuristics are explicitly involved. However, advanced search in thinking as a higher level cognitive life function may be implemented based on the fundamental search.

Definition 11. *Search $\mathcal{SE}$ is a cognitive process to allocate and retrieve a piece of knowledge in the memory by a given concept c**ST**, in which an equivalent or similar concept c_i**ST** may be found:*

$$\mathcal{SE} \triangleq \mathop{R}_{i\mathbf{N}=1}^{n\mathbf{N}} \blacklozenge (c\mathbf{ST} = c_i\mathbf{ST} \vee c\mathbf{ST} \cong c_i\mathbf{ST})$$
$$\rightarrow c'\mathbf{ST} = c\mathbf{ST} \uplus c_i\mathbf{ST}, \tag{12}$$

where $n\mathbf{N}$ is the maximum number of elements in the designated searching space in long-term memory, and $c\mathbf{ST} = c_i\mathbf{ST}$ and $c\mathbf{ST} \cong c_i\mathbf{ST}$ denote an equivalent concept and similar concept, respectively.

A search process may be systematic or nonsystematic. The former takes a global search strategy that guarantees finding an optimal solution if one exists. The latter is based on stochastic approaches that do not guarantee finding a solution. Search may be carried out inside the long-term memory of the brain or in external resources such as libraries, databases, and the Internet.

Based on the mathematical model of search as described in Equation 12, a formal description of the cognitive process of search in RTPA is presented in Figure 4. The search process is divided into two

Figure 4. The cognitive process of search in RTPA

The Search Process
Search (I:: c$\mathbf{ST}$; O:: c'$\mathbf{ST}$, OAR'$\mathbf{ST}$)$\mathbf{ST}$ $\triangleq$ { I. Retrieve equivalent concept $\rightarrow \mathop{R}\limits_{i\mathbf{N}=1}^{n\mathbf{N}} \blacklozenge (c\mathbf{ST} = c_i\mathbf{ST} \vee c\mathbf{ST} \cong c_i\mathbf{ST})$ $\rightarrow$ // Form new concept $c'\mathbf{ST} = c\mathbf{ST} \uplus c_i\mathbf{ST}$ II. Memorization $\rightarrow$ sOAR$\mathbf{ST}$:= c' $\mathbf{ST}$ $\rightarrow$ OAR'$\mathbf{ST}$:= OAR$\mathbf{ST} \uplus$ sOAR$\mathbf{ST}$ $\rightarrowtail$ Memorization (OAR'$\mathbf{ST}$)$\mathbf{ST}$ }

steps: retrieving an equivalent concept and memorization. In this process, an existing metaprocess, memorization, is called, which may be skipped when the search process is composed of or called by other processes.

The above search process explains the fundamental mechanism of systematic exhaustive search, also known as brute-force search. More flexible search may be adopted in real life for improving efficiency. Typical nonexhaustive searches are hill climbing and heuristic searches (Bender, 2001; Payne & Wenger, 1998). The former uses a series of tests on each present state in order to find an optimal next move toward the goal. The latter adopts a general principle or rule of thumb as the guidance in the selection of the next move from a given present state toward the goal. Both nonexhaustive searches may be treated as iterative applications of the fundamental exhaustive search according to certain empirical strategies.

It is noteworthy that many higher layer cognitive processes are based on the search process such as the processes of comprehension, learning, problem solving, decision making, and formal inferences (Wang, 2007e). In other words, natural intelligence is not only functioning based on algorithmic or procedural mechanisms, but also dependent on searching mechanisms intensively. More generally, human behaviors and actions highly rely on search-based memory manipulations because any intelligence is memory based.

It is recognized that the creation of knowledge is a conservative process that establishes a novel relation between two or more objects or concepts by searching and evaluating a vast space of possibilities in order to explain a set of natural phenomena or abstract problems. Since the relational memory capacity of a human can be as high as $10^{8,432}$ bits as estimated in Wang et al. (2003), the complexity in the search for new knowledge is necessarily infinite if a shortcut should not be discovered by chance during extensive and persistent thoughts (Wang, 2008a). However, the acquisition of knowledge is to simply add a known relation in the long-term memory of an existing knowledge structure. This is why the effort for acquiring existing knowledge is quite less than that of knowledge creation.

Theorem 2. *For specific new knowledge K, the effort spent in its creation $E_c(K)$ is far greater than that of its acquisition $E_a(K)$:*

$$E_c(K) \gg E_a(K). \tag{13}$$

The mechanisms of information retrieval from the memory of the brain are via attribute-sensitive search, which can be manipulated by concept algebra. According to concept algebra, information retrieval is fundamentally different from that of machine memory where address-specific reading is applied. However, if human memory and knowledge may be stored and sought in the form of indexed knowledge bases in an external memory, then the costly internal search process may be reduced to a key-based reading or address-sensitive retrieval.

THE COGNITIVE PROCESS OF CATEGORIZATION

According to LRMB, categorization, or classification, is a cognitive process of the brain at the meta-cognition layer that identifies common and equivalent attributes or properties shared among a group of entities or objects. These common attributes or properties are used to identify a group of entities.

In *A Study of Thinking*, Bruner, Goodnow, and Austin (1956) explain why categorization is needed in thinking by listing the following five advantages: (a) to reduce the complexity of thinking, (b) to identify objects more efficiently, (c) to establish powerful superconcepts with limited samples, (d) to predicate the behavior of an unknown instance of things in a known category, and (e) to study higher level relations among categories of objects and events. Similar observations on the importance of categorization have been formally stated in mathematics that resulted in the principle of abstraction in set theory (Lipschutz, 1964, Wang, 2007a), category theory (Rydeheard & Burstall, 1988), otology (Wilson & Keil, 2001), and description logics (Baader, Calvanese, McGuinness, Nardi, & Patel-Schneider, 2003).

Definition 12. *Categorization* CG *is a cognitive process to determine the particular class or superconcept* C *of a given concept x, that is,*

$$CG \triangleq f_{CG}{:}x \to C$$
$$= x \prec C \mid A_x \subset A_C, \tag{14}$$

where $\prec$ *denotes a superconcept relation in concept algebra, and* A_x *and* A_C *are sets of attributes of concepts x and C, respectively.*

According to concept algebra (Wang, 2008c), categorization is equivalent to the operation to find the holonym or superconcept C for a given concept x. It may also be treated as the determination of a membership of x in a certain set C where $x \in C$. Although categorization may be carried out subjectively and in multiple ways, basic strategies for categorization are the identification of similar and coherent attributes between the given concept and a superconcept.

Categorization is one of the most fundamental and pervasive cognitive processes because it enables reasoning to be carried out at a higher abstract level and permits predictions to be derived on the basis of common properties of a category of entities or phenomena. Categorization is an incredibly powerful ability of human beings to discriminate among objects (Bruner et al., 1956; Payne & Wenger, 1998).

Based on the mathematical model of categorization as described in Equation 14, a formal description of the cognitive process of categorization in RTPA is presented in Figure 5. The categorization process is divided into two steps: finding the superconcept and memorization. In this process, two other metaprocesses, search and memorization, are invoked as predefined supporting processes. The memorization step may be skipped when the categorization process is composed of or called by other processes.

Categorization has a close relationship with abstraction. The differences between them are that the former is aimed at determining the membership of a concept to a category in terms of a set while the latter is aimed at finding common properties of a set of concepts (Wang, 2007a).

THE COGNITIVE PROCESS OF COMPARISON

According to LRMB, comparison is a cognitive process of the brain at the metacognition layer that contrasts the intensions of two concepts and finds out the similarity between them.

Figure 5. The cognitive process of categorization in RTPA

```
                The Categorization Process

Categorization (I:: xST; O:: CST, OAR'ST)ST ≜
{ I. Find super concept
    ↣ Search (I:: xS;  O:: CST, sOARST)ST

  → ( ◆ Aₓ ⊂ A_C
          → R'ₓSET := RSET ∪ (xST ≺ CST)

    | ◆~
          → R'ₓSET := RSET ∪ (xST ↮ CST)
    )

  II. Memorization
  → sOARST := x(oₓ, Aₓ, Rₓ ∪ R'ₓ)ST
  → OAR'ST := OARST ⊎ sOARST
  ↣ Memorization (OAR'ST )ST
}
```

Definition 13. *Comparison CP is a cognitive process to evaluate the similarity of two arbitrary concepts x and y, and determine the extent of overlaps of their intensions represented by both sets of attributes A_x and A_y:*

$$CP \triangleq f_{OP} : x \to y \wedge y \to x$$
$$= x \underset{\sim}{~} y$$
$$= \frac{\#(A_x \cap A_y)}{\#(A_x \cup A_y)} \cdot 100\%, \tag{15}$$

where ~ denotes a concept equivalence operation in concept algebra.

The result of the comparison process is the extent of similarity between the given concepts in terms of a percentage of equivalence ($x \cong y$) or overlaps in their intensions. The higher the value of *CP*, the greater the equivalence between the given pair of concepts (Wang, 2008c); when *CP* = 100%, both concepts are exactly identical (i.e., $x = y$).

Based on the mathematical model of comparison as described in Equation 15, a formal description of the cognitive process of comparison in RTPA is presented in Figure 6. The comparison process is divided into two steps: determining the level of equivalence and memorization. In this process, an existing metaprocess, memorization, is called, which may be skipped when the comparison process is composed of or called by other processes.

THE COGNITIVE PROCESS OF QUALIFICATION

According to LRMB, qualification is a cognitive process of the brain at the metacognition layer that maps a numerical or abstract variable into a category or determines the membership of a given variable.

Definition 14. *Qualification QL is a cognitive process to determine if a concept x is a member of a given category of superconcept C, that is,*

Figure 6. The cognitive process of comparison in RTPA

The Comparison Process

Comparison (I:: x**ST**, y**ST**; O:: CP(x~y)**N**, OAR'**ST**)**ST** ≙
{ I. Determine level of equivalence

$$\rightarrow \text{CP}\mathbf{N} := \frac{\#(A_x \cap A_y)}{\#(A_x \cup A_y)} \cdot 100\%$$

→ R' := R ∪ (CP(x~y)**N**)

II. Memorization
→ OAR'**ST** := OAR**ST** ⊎ (R ∪ R')**SET**
↪ Memorization (OAR'**ST**)**ST**
}

Figure 7. The cognitive process of qualification in RTPA

The Qualification Process

Qualification (I:: x**ST**, C**ST**, ρ%**N**; O:: QL(x~C)**BL**, OAR'**ST**)**ST** ≙
{ I. Find the super concept/category
↪ Comparison (x**ST**, C**ST**)**ST**
→ (◆ CP(x~C)**N** ≥ ρ%**N**
        → QL(x~C)**BL** := **T**
  | ◆~
        → QL(x~C)**BL** := **F**
)
→ R'$_x$**SET** := R**SET** ∪ QL(x~C)**BL**

II. Memorization
→ OAR'**ST** := OAR**ST** ⊎ (R$_x$ ∪ R'$_x$)**SET**
↪ Memorization (OAR'**ST**)**ST**
}

$$\mathcal{QL} \triangleq f_{QL} : x \rightarrow C$$
$$= \begin{cases} \mathbf{T}, x \prec C \vee CP(x \sim C) \geq \rho \\ \mathbf{F}, x \not\leftrightarrow C \vee CP(x \sim C) < \rho, \end{cases} \tag{16}$$

where ρ is a subjective threshold for an acceptable confidence level of the membership, and CP(x ~ C) is a concept comparison as given in Definition 13.

Based on the mathematical model of qualification as described in Equation 16, a formal description of the cognitive process of qualification in RTPA is presented in Figure 7. The qualification process is divided into two steps: finding the superconcept or category, and memorization. In this process, two other metaprocesses, comparison and memorization, are invoked as predefined supporting processes.

The memorization step may be skipped when the qualification process is composed of or called by other processes.

THE COGNITIVE PROCESS OF QUANTIFICATION

According to LRMB, quantification is a cognitive process of the brain at the metacognition layer that measures and specifies the quantity of an object or attribute by using a quantifier such as *all*, *some*, *most*, and *none*, or by using a more exact rational measurement scale.

Definition 15. *Quantification QT is a cognitive process to determine or measure a quantity or an attribute of an object x in a predefined numerical scale S_B on a base B:*

$$
\begin{aligned}
QT &\triangleq f_{QT}{:}x \to S_B \\
&= f_{QT_{BL}}{:}x \to S_{BL} \\
&\mid f_{QT_N}{:}x \to S_N \\
&\mid f_{QT_R}{:}x \to S_R,
\end{aligned}
\tag{17}
$$

*where B = {**BL**, **N**, **R**}, which represents a scale in the type Boolean, integer, and real number, respectively.*

In RTPA (Wang, 2002b, 2003b, 2006b, 2007d, 2008d), a quantification is defined as an evaluation function $\delta(exp\mathbb{T}) \to \mathbb{T}$, where $\mathbb{T} = \{\mathbf{N}, \mathbf{R}, \mathbf{BL}\}$. When $\mathbb{T} = \mathbf{BL}$, $\delta(exp\mathbf{BL}) \to \mathbf{BL}$ is a special case of Boolean evaluation on $exp\mathbf{BL}$ that results in **T** or **F**. In concept algebra, the quantification of a concept is defined as a cardinal evaluation of its intension in terms of the number of attributes included in it (Wang, 2008c).

Quantifications QT between x and S_B can be classified into universal quantification ($\forall$) or existential quantification ($\exists$). The former indicates a quantification or numerical evaluation QT is established for an entire domain of x while the latter denotes a unique or instantiation qualification for a specific object x.

The base of the qualification or measurement scale B may be transformed into any other base B' determined by the following equation:

$$
B = B' \bullet q + r, \ 0 \le r \le q,
\tag{18}
$$

where B', q, and r are the new base (the divisor), quotient, and remainder, respectively.

A typical quantification or digitalization base is usually $B' = 2$ representing binary digits, which transfer a given quantity into a series of bits. For example, $5_{10} = 2_2 \bullet 2 + 1 = 101_2$, where subscripts 10 and 2 denote the bases of digits in the transformation.

Based on the mathematical model of quantification as described in Equation 17, a formal description of the cognitive process of quantification in RTPA is presented in Figure 8. The quantification process is divided into two steps: quantification and memorization. In this process, memorization is called, which may be skipped when the quantification process is composed of or called by other processes.

Figure 8. The cognitive process of quantification in RTPA

```
                    The Quantification Process

Quantification (I:: xBL | xN | xR;
                O:: QTBL | QTN | QTR, OAR'ST)ST ≜
{ I. Quantification
  → ( δ (xBL)BL = T
          → QTBL := T
    | δ (xBL)BL = F
          → QTBL := F
    | δ (xN) → SN
          → QTN := SN - (SN - xN)
    | δ (xR) → SR
          → QTR := SR - (SR - xR)
    )
  II. Memorization
  → sOARST := (x, A ∪ QTBL | QTN | QTR,
                R ∪ (QTBL | QTN | QTR = xBL | xN | xR)ST
  → OAR'ST := OARST ⊎ sOARST
  ↪ Memorization (OAR'ST )ST
}
```

THE COGNITIVE PROCESS OF SELECTION

According to LRMB, selection is a cognitive process of the brain at the metacognition layer that distinguishes the attributes of a given concept in (a) Boolean categories such as large or small, long or short, high or low, or heavy or light, or (b) numeric categories such as a set or a scope.

The axiom of selection (Lipschutz, 1964) states that there exists a selection function for any nonempty collection of nonempty disjoint sets of alternatives.

Definition 16. *Let $\{A_i \mid i \in I\}$ be a collection of disjoint sets $A_i \subseteq U$ and $A_i \neq \varnothing$. Then, a function*

$$c: \{A_i\} \rightarrow A_i, \ i \in I \tag{19}$$

is a selection function if $f_s(A_i) = a_i$, $a_i \in A_i$. Alternatively, an element $a_i \in A_i$ may be chosen by f_s, where A_i is called the set of alternatives, U the universal set, and I a set of natural numbers.

Definition 17. *Selection $\mathcal{SL}$ is a cognitive process to determine a choice of states or an action P or Q on the basis of given conditions or criteria:*

$$\begin{aligned}
\mathcal{SL} \ &\triangleq f_{SL} : x \rightarrow P|Q \\
&= \blacklozenge \, x\mathbf{BL} = \mathbf{T} \rightarrow P \\
&\quad | \ \blacklozenge \sim \ \rightarrow Q,
\end{aligned} \tag{20}$$

where $\blacklozenge$ denotes the evaluation function as defined in RTPA.

Figure 9. The cognitive process of selection in RTPA

```
The Selection Process

Selection (I:: xBL, PST, QST;  O:: SLST, OAR'ST)ST ≙
{ I. Selection
  → ( ◆ xBL = T
         → SLST := PST

     | ◆~
         → SLST := QST
    )

  II. Memorization
  → sOARST := (O, A, R ∪ SLST)ST
  → OAR'ST :=  OARST ⊎ sOARST
  ↣ Memorization (OARST)ST
}
```

Based on the mathematical model of selection as described in Equation 20, a formal description of the cognitive process of selection in RTPA is presented in Figure 9. The selection process is divided into two steps: selection and memorization. In this process, memorization is called, which may be skipped when the selection process is composed of or called by other processes.

On the basis of the choice function and the axiom of selection, a decision can be rigorously defined as follows (Wang & Ruhe, 2007).

Definition 18. *A decision d is a selected alternative* $a \in \mathcal{A}$ *from a nonempty set of alternatives* $\mathcal{A}$, $\mathcal{A} \subseteq U$, *based on a given set of criteria C; that is,*

$$\begin{aligned} d &= f(\mathcal{A}, C) \\ &= f\colon \mathcal{A} \times C \rightarrow \mathcal{A},\ \ \mathcal{A} \subseteq U,\ \mathcal{A} \neq \varnothing, \end{aligned} \tag{21}$$

where $\times$ *represents a Cartesian product.*

Based on Definition 18, decision making can be perceived as a process of decision selection from available alternatives against the chosen criteria for a given decision goal, where the number of possible decisions n can be determined by the sizes of $\mathcal{A}$ and C:

$$n = \#\mathcal{A} \bullet \#C, \tag{22}$$

where # is the cardinal calculus on sets and $\mathcal{A} \cap C = \varnothing$.

The selection theories and cognitive process provide a fundamental mathematical model for decision making, which reveals that the factors determining a decision are the alternatives $\mathcal{A}$ and criteria C for a given decision-making goal. A unified theory on fundamental cognitive decision making has been developed in Wang and Ruhe (2007).

CONCLUSION

A set of the fundamental cognitive processes of the brain has been formally modeled in this article, which addresses the cognitive processes of object identification, concept establishment, categorization, comparison, qualification, quantification, selection, and search at the metacognition level of LRMB. Two denotational mathematics, RTPA and concept algebra, have been adopted to rigorously model and specify the metacognitive processes. All cognitive models and processes are explained on the basis of the OAR model for internal information and knowledge representation. Theorems 1 and 2 have explained the mechanisms and complexities of internal information and knowledge processing. It has been found that the mechanisms of information retrieval from the memory of the brain are via attribute-sensitive search, which can be manipulated by concept algebra.

ACKNOWLEDGMENT

The author would like to acknowledge the Natural Science and Engineering Council of Canada (NSERC) for its partial support to this work. The author would like to thank Professor Du Zhang and anonymous reviewers for their valuable comments and suggestions to this work.

REFERENCES

Baader, F., Calvanese, D., McGuinness, D. L., Nardi, D., & Patel-Schneider, P. F. (2003). *The description logic handbook: Theory, implementation, applications.* Cambridge, UK: Cambridge University Press.

Bender, E. A. (1996). *Mathematical methods in artificial intelligence.* Los Alamitos, CA: IEEE CS Press.

Bruner, J. S., Goodnow, J. J., & Austin, G. A. (1956). *A study of thinking.* New York: Wiley.

Gray, P. (1994). *Psychology* (2nd ed.). New York: Worth Publishers, Inc.

Lipschutz, S. (1964). *Schaum's outline of theories and problems of set theory and related topics.* New York: McGraw-Hill Inc.

Matlin, M. W. (1998). *Cognition* (4th ed.). Orlando, FL: Harcourt Brace College Publishers.

Payne, D. G., & Wenger, M. J. (1998). *Cognitive psychology.* Boston: Houghton Mifflin Co.

Pinel, J. P. J. (1997). *Biopsychology* (3rd ed.). Needham Heights, MA: Allyn and Bacon.

Reisberg, D. (2001). *Cognition: Exploring the science of the mind* (2nd ed.). W. W. Norton & Company, Inc.

Rydeheard, D., & Burstall, R. (1988). *Computational category theory.* Prentice Hall.

Smith, R. E. (1993). *Psychology.* St. Paul, MN: West Publishing Co.

Sternberg, R. J. (1998). *In search of the human mind* (2nd ed.). New York: Harcourt Brace & Co.

Wang, Y. (2002a, August). On cognitive informatics (keynote speech). In *Proceedings of the First IEEE International Conference on Cognitive Informatics (ICCI'02)*, Calgary, Canada (pp. 34-42). IEEE CS Press.

Wang, Y. (2002b). The real-time process algebra (RTPA). *Annals of Software Engineering: An International Journal, 14*, 235-274.

Wang, Y. (2003a). On cognitive informatics. *Brain and Mind: A Transdisciplinary Journal of Neuroscience and Neurophilosophy, 4*(3), 151-167.

Wang, Y. (2003b). Using process algebra to describe human and software behaviors. *Brain and Mind: A Transdisciplinary Journal of Neuroscience and Neurophilosophy, 4*(2), 199-213.

Wang, Y. (2006a, July). Cognitive informatics: Towards the future generation computers that think and feel (keynote speech). In *Proceedings of the Fifth IEEE International Conference on Cognitive Informatics (ICCI'06)*, Beijing, China (pp. 3-7). IEEE CS Press.

Wang, Y. (2006b). On the informatics laws and deductive semantics of software. *IEEE Transactions on Systems, Man, and Cybernetics (C), 36*(2), 161-171.

Wang, Y. (2007a). The cognitive process of formal inferences. *International Journal of Cognitive Informatics and Natural Intelligence, 1*(4).

Wang, Y. (2007b, August). Formal description of the cognitive process of memorization. In *Proceedings of the Sixth International Conference on Cognitive Informatics (ICCI'07)*. CA: IEEE CS Press.

Wang, Y. (2007c). The OAR model of neural informatics for internal knowledge representation in the brain. *International Journal of Cognitive Informatics and Natural Intelligence, 1*(3), 64-75.

Wang, Y. (2007d). *Software engineering foundations: A software science perspective* (CRC Book Series in Software Engineering, Vol. 2). New York: Auerbach Publications.

Wang, Y. (2007e). The theoretical framework of cognitive informatics. *International Journal of Cognitive Informatics and Natural Intelligence, 1*(1), 1-27.

Wang, Y. (2008a, August). On cognitive foundations of creativity and the cognitive process of creation. In *Proceedings of the Seventh International Conference on Cognitive Informatics (ICCI'08)*, Stanford, CA.

Wang, Y. (2008b, August). A cognitive informatics theory for visual information processing. In *Proceedings of the Seventh International Conference on Cognitive Informatics (ICCI'08)*, Stanford, CA.

Wang, Y. (2008c). On concept algebra: A denotational mathematical structure for knowledge and software modeling. *International Journal of Cognitive Informatics and Natural Intelligence, 2*(2), 1-19.

Wang, Y. (2008d). RTPA: A denotational mathematics for manipulating intelligent and computational behaviors. *International Journal of Cognitive Informatics and Natural Intelligence, 2*(2), 44-62.

Wang, Y. (2008e, June). On contemporary denotational mathematics for computational intelligence. *Transactions on Computational Science, 2*(3), 6-29.

Wang, Y., Liu, D., & Wang, Y. (2003). Discovering the capacity of human memory. *Brain and Mind: A Transdisciplinary Journal of Neuroscience and Neurophilosophy, 4*(2), 189-198.

Wang, Y., & Ruhe, G. (2007). The cognitive process of decision making. *International Journal of Cognitive Informatics and Natural Intelligence, 1*(2), 73-85.

Wang, Y., & Wang, Y. (2006). Cognitive informatics models of the brain. *IEEE Transactions on Systems, Man, and Cybernetics (C), 36*(2), 203-207.

Wang, Y., Wang, Y., Patel, S., & Patel, D. (2006). A layered reference model of the brain (LRMB). *IEEE Transactions on Systems, Man, and Cybernetics (C), 36*(2), 124-133.

Westen, D. (1999). *Psychology: Mind, brain, and culture* (2nd ed.). New York: John Wiley & Sons, Inc.

Wilson, R. A., & Keil, F. C. (2001). *The MIT encyclopaedia of the cognitive sciences.* MIT Press.

This work was previously published in International Journal of Cognitive Informatics and Natural Intelligence, Vol. 2, Issue 4, edited by Y. Wang, pp. 15-28, copyright 2008 by IGI Publishing (an imprint of IGI Global).

Chapter 17
Unifying Rough Set Analysis and Formal Concept Analysis Based on a Logic Approach to Granular Computing

Bing Zhou
University of Regina, Canada

Yiyu Yao
University of Regina, Canada

ABSTRACT

Granular computing is an emerging field of research that attempts to formalize and explore methods and heuristics for human problem solving with multiple levels of granularity and abstraction. A fundamental issue of granular computing is the construction, representation and utilization of granules and granular structures. Basic granules represent the basic pieces of knowledge. A granular structure reflects the connections between different pieces of knowledge. The main objective of this book chapter is to examine a logic approach to granular computing for combining rough set analysis and formal concept analysis. Following the classical interpretation of concepts that a concept consists of a pair of an extension and an intension, the authors interpret a granule as a pair containing a set of objects and a logic formula describing the granule. The building blocks of granular structures are basic granules representing elementary concepts or pieces of knowledge. They are treated as atomic formulas of a logic language. Different types of granular structures can be constructed by using logic connectives. Within this logic framework, this chapter shows that rough set analysis and formal concept analysis can be interpreted uniformly by using the proposed logic language. The two theories share high-level similarities, but differ in their choices of definable granules and granular structures. Algorithms and evaluation measures can be designed uniformly for both theories.

DOI: 10.4018/978-1-60566-902-1.ch017

INTRODUCTION

Cognitive science (Simon & Kaplan, 1989) and cognitive informatics (Wang, 2003a, 2003b) study information and knowledge processing in the abstract, in the brain, and in machines. Some of the salient features of human intelligence and problem solving are the conceptualization of a problem at multiple levels of abstraction, the representation of information and knowledge with different-sized granules, the choice of a suitable level of granularity, and the switching of views and granularity in response to changes in environments. An emerging field of study known as granular computing aims at formalizing and exploring these features (Bargiela & Pedrycz, 2002; Yao, 2004c, 2006b, 2007a; Zadeh, 1997). The results from granular computing may shed new light on the study of cognitive informatics (Wang, 2003a, 2003b, 2007a, 2007b; Yao, 2006a).

A central notion of granular computing is multilevel granular structures consisting of a family of interrelated and interacting granules. Granular computing can be considered as an umbrella term covering topics that concern granularity and has been studied either implicitly or explicitly in many fields. It focuses on problem solving by describing and representing a problem and its solution in various levels of granularity so that one can focus on things that serve a specific interest and ignore unimportant and irrelevant details. Granular computing makes use of knowledge structures and hence has a significant impact on the study of human intelligence and the design of intelligent systems.

Granular computing can be studied based on a triarchic model consisting of the philosophy of structured thinking, the methodology of structured problem solving, and the computation of structured information processing (Yao, 2001b, 2004d, 2006b, 2007a). Many concrete models of granular computing have been proposed and studied. The main objective of the book chapter is to make further contribution along this line by investigating a logic approach to granular computing.

We introduce a logic language L to study granular computing in a logic setting. The language is an extension of the decision logic language used in rough set theory (Pawlak, 1991). Instead of expressing atomic formulas by a particular concrete type of conditions, we treat them as abstract notions to be interpreted in different applications. This flexibility enables us to describe granules in different applications. The language is interpreted in the Tarski's style through the notion of a model and satisfiability (Demri & Orlowska, 1997; Pawlak, 1991; Pawlak & Skowron, 2007; Yao, 2001b; Yao & Liau, 2002). The model is defined as a pair consisting of a domain and knowledge about the domain. The meaning of a formula is given by a set of objects satisfying the formula. Like the representation of a concept by a pair of intension and extension, a granule is interpreted as a pair of a set of objects of the domain and a formula of the language L. Thus, we can study granular structures in both a set-theoretic setting and a logic setting. The basic granules are represented by atomic formulas. An object satisfies a formula if the object has the properties as specified by the formula.

Rough set analysis and formal concept analysis are two concrete models of granular computing for knowledge representation and data analysis (Nguyen, Skowron & Stepaniuk, 2001; Pawlak, 1991; Pawlak & Skowron, 2007; Wille, 1982, 1992; Yao, 2004a). Rough set analysis studies the object-attribute relationships in an information table and formal concept analysis studies these relationships in single-valued and many-valued formal contexts. With the introduced language, the two theories can be interpreted in a unified way. On one hand, the two theories share high-level similarities in their treatments of granular structures. On the other hand, they use different atomic formulas, definable granules and granular structures formed by definable granules. The unified study of the two theories not only demonstrates the potential of the logic approach to granular computing, but also brings more insights into data analysis using the two theories.

The rest of the book chapter is organized as follows. The Overview of Granular Computing section introduces granular structures and the triarchic model of granular computing. The Logic Language section introduces the formulation of the language L, as well as the interpretation of granules, granular structures, and rules. In the Language L in Rough Set Analysis and the Language L in Formal Concept Analysis section, we consider the interpretations of the language L in both rough set analysis and formal concept analysis, respectively. The last section gives concluding remarks.

OVERVIEW OF GRANULAR COMPUTING

Granular computing is a new area of research. Its main purpose is to model, state, and solve real-world problems at multiple levels of granularity (Bargiela & Pedrycz, 2002; Lin, Yao & Zadeh, 2002; Yao, 2007a). The fundamental issues, principles and methodologies of granular computing can be studied based on granular structures from different perspectives (Yao, 2001a, 2004a, 2004d, 2006b, 2007a).

Granular Structures

A granular structure provides structured description of a system or an application under consideration.

Basic granules are the building blocks to form a granular structure. They represent the basic human observations of a problem in the real world. The connections of different granules form different levels of a granular structure reflect structured knowledge. A granular structure at least contains three basic components (Yao, 2004c, 2006b, 2007a):

- Internal structure of a granule;
- Collective structure of a family of granules;
- Hierarchical structure of a web of granules.

The internal structure of a granule represents the characterization of the granule. Analyzing the internal structure of a granule helps us to understand why objects are drawn together. Granules in the same level are formed with respect to a certain level of abstraction and collectively show a certain structure. The collective structures are related to granules in other levels.

Granules in different levels are linked by order relations, interpreted as "more general than" or "more specific than." Granules can be ordered based on their generalities or sizes. For example, in the set-theoretic setting, the size of a granule can be defined by its cardinality. One can define operations on granules so that a set of smaller granules can be formed into larger granules and larger granules can be decomposed into a set of smaller granules. Granules in a higher level can be decomposed into many smaller granules with more details shown at a lower level, and conversely, granules in a lower level can form more abstract larger granules in a higher level. The connections of different levels form a multi-level hierarchical structure. The graph representation of a granular structure is a lattice-like line diagram.

In summary, granular structures are the results of a structured understanding, interpretation, and representation of a real-world problem. Each granular structure represents a particular point-of-view of the problem with multiple levels of granularity. A complete understanding of the problem requires a series of granular structures which should reflect multiple views with multiple levels (Chen & Yao, 2007; Yao, 2007a).

The Triarchic Model of Granular Computing

There are three different perspectives of granular computing, namely, the philosophy, the methodology and the computation perspectives. These three perspectives together form a triarchic model of granular computing (Yao, 2001b, 2004d, 2006b, 2007a, 2007c).

From the philosophy perspective, granular computing is a way of structured thinking that focuses on modeling human perception of the reality and cognitive process. It unifies two complementary philosophical views about the complexity of real-world problems, namely, the reductionist thinking and the systems thinking. Granular computing stresses the importance of conscious effects in thinking in terms of hierarchical structures.

The methodology perspective focuses on methods and strategies for finding structured solutions. As an effective method of structured problem solving, granular computing promotes systematic approaches and practical strategies that have been used effectively by humans for solving real-world problems. An important issue is the exploration of granular structures. This involves three basic tasks: constructing granular structures, working within a particular level of the structure, and switching between levels. The methodology of granular computing is inspired by human problem solving.

The computation perspective focuses on the implementation of computer based systems. As a paradigm of structured information processing (Bargiela & Pedrycz, 2002), two related notions, namely, representations and processes (Marr, 1982), need to be discussed. A representation is a formal description and specification of entities in information systems. A process can be interpreted as the computational actions occurred in information processing. For example, information granulation and computation with granules are two basic processes of granular computing.

THE LOGIC LANGUAGE L

In this section, we introduce a logic language L to facilitate our studies of the properties of the various models of granular computing. Similar to any existing formal languages (Harrison, 1978), the language L consists of two aspects: syntax and semantics. The syntax of L is defined based on a 0-order, propositional logic consisting of atomic formulas and compound formulas. The semantics of L are given in Tarski's style (Demri & Orlowska, 1997; Pawlak & Skowron, 2007; Tarski, 1956; Yao, 2001b; Yao & Liau, 2002), namely, a set-theoretic, two-valued semantics. In such semantics, every formula of L is assigned an extension, such that each object is either in that extension or not in that extension. Given any formula and any object, the formulas of L are not vague; it either applies or fails to apply to that object. Tarski's style semantics allow us to study granular computing in both a set-theoretic setting and a logic setting, and are more appropriate for us to precisely define granules, granular structures and rules than many-valued semantics (Bziau, 2006).

Syntax and Semantics

The syntax of the language L can be formally defined based on the standard propositional language. In general, one may also consider a first-order language. For the discussion of this book chapter, a propositional language is sufficient. Atomic formulas are the building blocks of the language L, denoted by:

$$A = \{p, q...\}.$$

Each atomic formula may be interpreted as representing one piece of basic knowledge. We assume that they are the elementary units that one uses to represent and understand a real-world problem. The physical meaning of atomic formulas becomes clearer in a particular application. In general, an atomic formula corresponds to one particular property of an object under discussion. The construction of atomic formulas is an essential step of knowledge representation. The set of atomic formulas provides a basis on which more complex knowledge can be represented. Compound formulas can be built recursively from atomic formulas by using logic connectives. If φ and ψ are formulas, then so are $(\neg\varphi)$, $(\varphi \wedge \psi)$, $(\varphi \vee \psi)$, $(\varphi \rightarrow \psi)$, and $(\varphi \leftrightarrow \psi)$.

The semantics of the language L is given in the Tarski's style by using the notions of a model and satisfiability. The model is defined as a pair $M = (D, K)$, where D is a nonempty set of objects called the domain of L, denoted by $D = \{x, y...\}$, and K is available knowledge about objects of D. For example, in the decision logic used in rough set theory, the knowledge K is a set of finite attributes used to describe the set of objects of D. The satisfiability of an atomic formula by objects of D is viewed as the basic knowledge describable by the language L. In general, an object satisfies a formula if the object has the properties as specified by the formula. For an atomic formula p, we assume that the available knowledge K enables us to decide that an object $x \in D$ either satisfies p, written as $x \models p$, or does not satisfy p, written as $x - p$. Let φ and ψ be two formulas, the satisfiability of compound formulas is defined as follows:

(1). $x \models \neg\varphi$ iff $x - \varphi$,
(2). $x \models \varphi \wedge \psi$ iff $x \models \varphi$ and $x \models \psi$,
(3). $x \models \varphi \vee \psi$ iff $x \models \varphi$ or $x \models \psi$,
(4). $x \models \varphi \rightarrow \psi$ iff $x \models \neg\varphi \vee \psi$,
(5). $x \models \varphi \leftrightarrow \psi$ iff $x \models \varphi \rightarrow \psi$ and $x \models \psi \rightarrow \varphi$.

To emphasize the roles played by the set of objects D and the set of atomic formulas A, we also rewrite the language as L as $L(A, D, \{\neg, \wedge, \vee, \rightarrow, \leftrightarrow\})$.

The model M describes the meaning of formulas in D. If formulas are interpreted in the model, then each formula becomes meaningful and describes properties of some objects (Pawlak, 1991). The meaning of the formula is the set of all objects having the properties described by the formula. If φ is a formula of L, the meaning of φ in the model M is the set of objects defined by:

$$m(\varphi) = \{x \in D \mid x \models \varphi\}. \tag{1}$$

That is, $m(\varphi)$ is the set of objects satisfying the formula φ. This establishes a correspondence between logic connectives and set-theoretic operators. The following properties hold (Pawlak, 1991):

(C1). $m(\neg\varphi) = -m(\varphi)$,

(C2). $m(\varphi \wedge \psi) = m(\varphi) \cap m(\psi)$,

(C3). $m(\varphi \vee \psi) = m(\varphi) \cup m(\psi)$,

(C4). $m(\varphi \rightarrow \psi) = -m(\varphi) \cup m(\psi)$,

(C5). $m(\varphi \leftrightarrow \psi) = (m(\varphi) \cap m(\psi)) \cup (-m(\varphi) \cap -m(\psi))$,

where $-m(\varphi) = D - m(\varphi)$ denotes the set complement of $m(\varphi)$.

Differences between L and Other Decision Logic Languages

A fundamental difference between the language L and other decision logic languages is the treatment of the set of atomic formulas. In early works, atomic formulas are defined using specific forms. For example, atomic formulas can be defined in an information table based on the values of attributes (Pawlak, 1991; Yao & Liau, 2002). In this study, we treat atomic formulas as abstract notions that need to be made concrete in different applications. Many concrete examples of the language can be obtained by various definitions of atomic formulas. The construction of the set of atomic formulas and the model M depends on a particular application. For modeling different problems, we may choose different sets of atomic formulas and models. When a model is switched from one to another, the structures of language L remain the same. The flexibility in semantics interpretations enables us to describe a variety of problems.

Two Sub-Languages of L

The language L provides a formal method for describing and interpreting rules in data mining and machine learning (Yao & Zhou, 2007; Yao, Zhou & Chen, 2007). In many situations, one is only interested in certain types of rules. For example, rules contain only the logical connective $\wedge$. This requires us to consider a restriction of the language L to certain logical connectives. In this study, we consider two sub-languages of L. One uses only the conjunctive connective $\wedge$, written as $L\wedge(A, D, \wedge)$, and the other uses only the disjunctive connective $\vee$, written as $L\vee(A, D, \vee)$.

Interpretation of Granules

In the study of concepts (Van et al., 1993; Smith, 1989; Sowa, 1984), many interpretations have been proposed and examined. The classical view regards a concept as a unit of thoughts consisting of two parts, namely, the intension and extension of the concept (Demri & Orlowska, 1997; Van et al., 1993; Wille, 1992; Yao, 2004b). By using the language L, we obtain a simple and precise representation of a concept in terms of its intension and extension. That is, a concept is defined by a pair $(m(\varphi), \varphi)$. The formula φ is the description of properties shared by objects in $m(\varphi)$, and $m(\varphi)$ is the set of objects satisfying φ. A concept is thus described jointly by its intension and extension. This formulation enables us to study concepts in a logic setting in terms of intensions and in a set-theoretic setting in terms of extensions.

Following the classical view of concept, we also treat a granule as a pair $(m(\varphi), \varphi)$ of a set of objects $m(\varphi) \subseteq D$ and a logic formula φ. Thus, we obtain both a set-theoretic description and a logic description of granules. In subsequent discussion, we use the two descriptions interchangeably. However, it should be noted that for the same set of objects $X \subseteq D$, one may find more than one formula in the language such that $m(\varphi) = X$.

We can classify granules by the number of atomic formulas in their intensions. In the sub-language $L\wedge(A, D, \wedge)$, a granule involving k atomic formulas is called a k-conjunction. A k-conjunction granule is more general than its $(k + 1)$-conjunctions, and more specific than its $(k - 1)$-conjunctions. In the sub-language $L\vee(A, D, \vee)$, a granule involving k atomic formulas is called a k-disjunction. In this case, a k-disjunction granule is more general than its $(k - 1)$-disjunctions, and more specific than its $(k + 1)$-disjunctions.

Interpretation of Granular Structures

The introduction of the language L also enables us to study granular structures in logic terms. There are at least two ways to construct a granular structure based on the order relations between granules. As examples, we briefly discuss two granular structures called $\cap$-closure and $\cup$-closure (Yao & Zhou, 2007).

Let $GS_{\cap}(L\wedge)$ denote the $\cap$-closure granular structure. We can formally define it by the sub-language $L\wedge(A, D, \wedge)$, written as:

$$GS_{\cap}(L\wedge) = (Def(L\wedge(A, D, \wedge)), \cap),$$

where $Def(L\wedge(A, D, \wedge))$ is the family of granules defined by the sub-language $L\wedge(A, D, \wedge)$.

The process of constructing an $\cap$-closure granular structure is a top-down process, which involves dividing a larger granule into smaller and lower level granules. Each granule is labeled by the formulas of the language $L\wedge(A, D, \wedge)$. At the top level, the most general granule is labeled by the formula T, which is satisfied by every object, that is, $m(T) = D$. The next level is the elementary granules labeled by atomic formulas. The intersections of two elementary granules produce the next level of granules labeled by the conjunction of the two atomic formulas, and so on. Finally, at the bottom level, we close the structure by the most specific granule labeled by the formula $\bot$, which is not satisfied by any object of the formal context, that is, $m(\bot) = \varnothing$. In the set-theoretic setting, the $\cap$-closure granular structure is in fact a closure system that contains D and is closed under set intersections.

Let $GS_{\cup}(L\vee)$ denote the $\cup$-closure granular structure. We can formally define it by the sub-language $L\vee(A, D, \vee)$, written as:

$$GS_{\cup}(L\vee) = (Def(L\vee(A, D, \vee)), \cup),$$

where $Def(L\vee(A, D, \vee))$ is the family of granules defined by the sub-language $L\vee(A, D, \vee)$.

The process of constructing a $\cup$-closure granular structure is a bottom-up process, which involves the process of forming a larger and higher level granule with smaller and lower level granules. At the bottom level, the most specific granule is labeled by the formula $\bot$, which is not satisfied by any object. The upper level is the elementary granule labeled by atomic formulas. The unions of two elementary granules produce the upper level of granules labeled by the disjunction of the two atomic formulas, and so on. Finally, at the top level, we close the structure by the most general granule labeled by the formula T.

In the set-theoretic settings, all possible granules form a structure known as the power set of the domain D, written as 2^D. For a concrete granular computing model, one is only interested in a subset of 2^D which is considered "meaningful" in that model, called a subsystem $G \subseteq 2^D$. The choice of G relies on the domain knowledge. For example, in rough set analysis (Pawlak, 1991; Pawlak & Skowron, 2007), the granules of G are granules that are definable by a set of attributes, and they are the unions of some equivalence classes. In formal concept analysis (Ganter & Wille, 1999; Wille, 1982), granules of *G* are the extensions of formal concepts. In knowledge spaces theory (Falmagne, Koppen, Villano, Doignon & Johannesen, 1990), granules of *G* are the feasible knowledge statements. With respect to the language L, a granule is definable if we can find a formula whose meaning set is that granule (Yao, 2007b).

Interpretation of Rules

By identifying the basic pieces of knowledge in different granular computing models as basic granules, the differences and high-level similarities of these models can be abstracted and serve as foundations for further data analysis. Rules, as a commonly used form for representing knowledge, can be studied uniformly for different granular computing models. The conditions in rules can be interpreted as granules while entire rules as the relationships between granules. Different types of granules may generate different kinds of rules. Rule learning algorithms can be designed based on granular structures. Different rule applications, such as decision-making, prediction, classification, and pattern recognition, can be systematically analyzed under this scheme.

THE LANGUAGE L IN ROUGH SET ANALYSIS

Rough set analysis (Pawlak, 1991; Pawlak & Skowron, 2007) studies relationships between objects and their attribute values in an information table. We use rough set analysis as a concrete granular computing model to show the usefulness and the flexibility of the language L.

Information Tables

An information table provides a convenient way to describe a finite set of objects by a finite set of attributes. Formally, an information table can be expressed as:

$$S = (U, At, \{V_a \mid a \in At\}, \{\{R_a\} \mid a \in At\}, \{I_a \mid a \in At\}),$$

where

> U is a finite nonempty set of objects,
> At is a finite nonempty set of attributes,
> V_a is a nonempty set of values for $a \in At$,
> $\{R_a\}$ is a family of binary relations on V_a,
> $I_a: U \to V_a$ is an information function.

Each information function I_a maps an object in U to a value of V_a for an attribute $a \in At$.

The above definition of an information table considers more knowledge and information about relationships between values of attributes. Each relation R_a can represent similarity, dissimilarity, or ordering of values in V_a (Demri & Orlowska, 1997). The equality relation = is only a special case of R_a. The standard rough set theory uses the trivial equality relation on attribute values (Pawlak, 1991). Pawlak and Skowron (Pawlak & Skowron, 2007) consider a more generalized notion of an information table.

For each attribute $a \in At$, a relational structure R_a over V_a is introduced. A language can be defined based on the relational structures. A binary relation is a special case of relational structures.

Granules in Rough Set Analysis

The indiscernibility relation is a fundamental notion in rough set theory. It indicates why objects are drawn together to form granules. By using the language L, we can formally define an indiscernibility relation in an information table. For a subset $A_0 \subseteq A$, two objects $x, y \in U$ are indistinguishable if no formula in A_0 can distinguish them, so they can be put into the same granule. Let us define a mapping from U to A as follows:

$$m'(x) = \{p \in A \mid x \models p\}.$$

That is, $m'(x)$ is the set of atomic formulas satisfied by x. For a subset $A_0 \subseteq A$, the indiscernibility relation can be defined by:

$$x \sim_{A0} y \text{ iff } m'(x) \cap A_0 = m'(y) \cap A_0$$

The definition of indiscernibility relation is slightly different from the conventional definition (Pawlak, 1991). One can easily show that the conventional definition is a special case with a properly chosen A_0.

Based on the indiscernibility relation, we can construct the language L by using an information table as the model M. There are at least two types of granules that can be formally defined. They represent two different types of knowledge that one can derive from an information table (Yao, Zhou & Chen, 2007).

First, we consider objects of the domain D as objects in the universe U. The set of atomic formulas are constructed from attribute-value pairs. With respect to an attribute $a \in At$ and an attribute value $v \in V_a$, an atomic formula of the language L is denoted by (a, R_a, v). An object $x \in U$ satisfies an atomic formula by (a, R_a, v) if the value of x on attribute a is R_a-related to the value v, written as $I_a(x) R_a v$:

$$x \models (a, R_a, v) \text{ iff } I_a(x) R_a v.$$

We rewrite the language as L $(\{(a, R_a, v)\}, U, \{\neg, \wedge, \vee, \rightarrow, \leftrightarrow\})$. The granule corresponding to the atomic formula (a, R_a, v), namely, its meaning set, is defined as:

$$m(a, R_a, v) = \{x \in U \mid I_a(x) R_a v \}.$$

Granules corresponding to the atomic formulas are elementary granules in an information table. Granules corresponding to the compound formulas can be formally defined according to Equation (1).

A subset or a granule $X \subseteq U$ is definable in an information table if and only if there exits a formula φ in the language L$(\{(a, R_a, v)\}, U, \{\neg, \wedge, \vee, \rightarrow, \leftrightarrow\})$ such that, $X = m(\varphi)$. Otherwise, it is undefinable. Accordingly, the family of granules is defined as:

$$Def(\text{L}(\{(a, R_a, v)\}, U, \{\neg, \wedge, \vee, \rightarrow, \leftrightarrow\})) = \{ m(\varphi) \mid \varphi \in \text{L}(\{(a, R_a, v)\}, U, \{\neg, \wedge, \vee, \rightarrow, \leftrightarrow\})\}.$$

In this way, the language L only enables us to define certain subsets of U. For an arbitrary subset of U, we may not be able to construct a formula for it. In other words, depending on the set of atomic formulas, the language L can only describe a restricted family of subsets of U.

Second, we consider objects of the domain D as object pairs in $U \times U$. With respect to an attribute $a \in$ At, an atomic formula of the language L is denoted by (a, R_a). A pair of objects $(x, y) \in U \times U$ satisfies an atomic formula (a, R_a) if the value of x is R_a-related to the value of y on the attribute a, that is, $I_a(x) R_a I_a(y)$. We show this with the following:

$$(x,y) \models (a, R_a) \text{ iff } I_a(x) R_a I_a(y).$$

We rewrite the language as L $(\{(a, R_a)\}, U \times U, \{\neg, \wedge, \vee, \rightarrow, \leftrightarrow\})$. The granule corresponding to the atomic formula (a, R_a), i.e., the meaning set, is defined as:

$$m(a, R_a) = \{(x,y) \in U \mid I_a(x) R_a I_a(y)\}.$$

Accordingly, the granules corresponding to the compound formulas of the language L $(\{(a, R_a)\},$ $U \times U, \{\neg, \wedge, \vee, \rightarrow, \leftrightarrow\})$ can be defined by Equation (1), and the family of all definable sets or granules is defined as:

$$Def(\text{L}(\{(a, R_a)\}, U \times U, \{\neg, \wedge, \vee, \rightarrow, \leftrightarrow\})) = \{ m(\varphi) \mid \varphi \in \text{L}(\{(a, R_a)\}, U \times U, \{\neg, \wedge, \vee, \rightarrow, \leftrightarrow\})\}.$$

For granules that are undefinable, it is impossible to construct a formula with the set as its meaning set. In order to characterize an undefinable set, one may approximate it from below and above by two definable sets, called lower and upper approximations in rough set theory.

Interpretation of Low and High Order Rules

Rules are a commonly used form for representing knowledge. The language L provides a formal method for describing and interpreting conditions in rules as granules and rules as relationships between granules. In last section, two types of granules are constructed in an information table. One consists of a set of objects that s attribute value. The other consists of object pairs that cannot be distinguished based on the values of attributes. Two types of rules, called low and high order rules, can be defined to describe relationships between these two types of granules accordingly (Yao, Zhou & Chen, 2007).

A low order rule expresses connections between attribute values of the same object. Classification rules are a typical example of low order rules. For example, a classification rule may state that "if the Hair color is blond and Eye color is blue, then the Class is +." A high order rule expresses connections of different objects in terms of their attribute values. Functional dependencies are a typical example of high order rules. For example, a functional dependency rule may state that "if two persons have the same Hair color, then they will have the same Eye color." In general, a high order rule summarizes the results of a family of low order rules. We express rules in the form $\varphi \Rightarrow \psi$ by using formulas of the language L.

A low order rule can be derived according to the relationships between the first types of granules. For easy understanding, we express the formula (a, R_a, v) in another form based on the definition of satisfiability of the atomic formulas. An example of a low order rule is given as:

$$\bigwedge_{i=1}^{n}(I_{a_i}(x)R_{a_i}v_{a_i}) \Rightarrow \bigwedge_{j=1}^{m}(I_{d_j}(x)R_{d_j}v_{d_j}),$$

where $x \in U, v_{a_i} \in V_{a_i}, v_{d_j} \in V_{d_j}, a_i \in At$, and $d_j \in At$. For simplicity, we only consider the set conjunction $\wedge$ in the rule.

A high order rule can be derived according to the relationships between the second type of granules. Similarly, we express the formula (a, R_a) in the form based on the definition of satisfiability of the atomic formulas. An example of a high order rule is given as:

$$\bigwedge_{i=1}^{n}(I_{a_i}(x)R_{a_i}I_{a_i}(y)) \Rightarrow \bigwedge_{j=1}^{m}(I_{d_j}(x)R_{d_j}I_{d_j}(y)),$$

where $(x, y) \in U \times U, a_i \in At, d_j \in At$.

The meanings and interpretations of a rule $\varphi \Rightarrow \psi$ can be further clarified by using the extensions $m(\varphi)$ and $m(\psi)$ of the two concepts. More specifically, we can define quantitative measures indicating the strength of a rule. A systematic analysis of probabilistic quantitative measures can be found in (Yao & Zhong, 1999). Two examples of probabilistic quantitative measures are (Tsumoto, 1999):

$$accuracy(\phi \Rightarrow \varphi) = \frac{|m(\phi \wedge \varphi)|}{|m(\phi)|}, \text{ and}$$

$$coverage(\phi \Rightarrow \varphi) = \frac{|m(\phi \wedge \varphi)|}{|m(\varphi)|},$$

where $|\cdot|$ denotes the cardinality of a set. The two measures are applicable to both low and high order rules. This demonstrates the flexibility and power of the language L.

While the accuracy reflects the correctness of the rule, the coverage reflects the applicability of the rule. If $accuracy(\varphi \Rightarrow \psi) = 1$, we have a strong association between φ and ψ. A smaller value of accuracy indicates a weaker association. A higher coverage suggests that the relationships of more objects can be derived from the rule. The accuracy and coverage are not independent of each other; one may observe a trade-off between accuracy and coverage. A rule with higher coverage may have a lower accuracy, while a rule with higher accuracy may have a lower coverage.

Granular Structures in Rough Set Analysis

The indiscernibility relation used in the standard rough set analysis is an equivalence relation on the set of objects (Pawlak, 1991; Pawlak & Skowron, 2007; Nguyen, Skowron & Stepaniuk, 2001). Let E denote an equivalence relation that partitions the universe into disjoint subsets known as equivalence classes and is denoted by U/E. Equivalence classes are basic granules of the universe which can be interpreted using atomic formulas of the language L with the equality relation =. That is, we consider a language L $(\{(a, =, v)\}, U, \{\neg, \wedge, \vee, \rightarrow, \leftrightarrow\})$ with atomic formulas of the form of $(a, =, v)$.

An object $x \in U$ satisfies an atomic formula $(a, =, v)$ if the value of x on attribute a is v, that is, $I_a(x) = v$. We write:

$x \models (a, =, v)$ iff $I_a(x) = v$.

The granule corresponding to the atomic formula $(a, =, v)$ is:

$m(a, =, v) = \{x \in U \mid I_a(x) = v\}$.

The granule $m(a, =, v)$ is also referred to as the block defined by the attribute-value pair (a, v) (Grzymala-Busse, 2005). The granules corresponding to the compound formulas of the L ($\{(a, =, v)\}$, U, $\{\neg, \wedge, \vee, \rightarrow, \leftrightarrow\}$) can be defined by Equation (1). Equivalence classes construct a subsystem of 2^U by taking set intersections, unions and complements of equivalence classes. This subsystem is in fact an σ-algebra of subsets of the universe, written as $\sigma(U/E)$. That is, it contains the empty set $\varnothing$, the entire set U, equivalence classes and is closed under set intersection, union and complement. The partition U/E is a base of $\sigma(U/E)$. he σ-algebra $\sigma(U/E)$ (Yao, 2007b). That is:

$Def(\mathrm{L}(\{(a, =, v)\}, U, \{\neg, \wedge, \vee, \rightarrow, \leftrightarrow\})) = \sigma(U/E)$.

For a set that is undefinable in the universe U, one can approximate it by the lower and upper approximations. For a subset of objects $X \subseteq U$, we define a pair of lower and upper approximation as (Yao, 2007b):

$\underline{apr}(X) = \cup\{Y \mid Y \in Def(\mathrm{L}(\{(a, =, v)\}, U, \{\neg, \wedge, \vee, \rightarrow, \leftrightarrow\})), Y \subseteq X\}$,

$\overline{apr}(X) = \cap\{Y \mid Y \in Def(\mathrm{L}(\{(a, =, v)\}, U, \{\neg, \wedge, \vee, \rightarrow, \leftrightarrow\})), X \subseteq Y\}$.

This is, $\underline{apr}(X)$ is the largest definable set contained in X, and $\overline{apr}(X)$ is the smallest definable set containing X.

We can construct the $\cap$-closure and $\cup$-closure granular structures in an information table by using granules in $\sigma(U/E)$. Formally, we can rewrite the $\cap$-closure granular structure as:

$GS_\cap(\mathrm{L}\wedge) = (Def(\mathrm{L}\wedge((a, =, v), U, \{\wedge\})), \cap)$,

Similarly, we can rewrite the $\cup$-closure granular structure as:

$GS_\cup(\mathrm{L}\vee) = (Def(\mathrm{L}\vee((a, =, v), U, \{\vee\})), \cup)$.

Example 1. Table 1 is an information table taken from (Quinlan, 1983). Each object is described by four attributes. The column labeled by "Class" denotes an expert's classification of the objects. The possible values for three attributes {Height, Hair, Eyes} are:

$V_{\text{Height}} = \{\text{short, tall}\}$,

$V_{\text{Hair}} = \{\text{blond, dark, red}\}$,

V_{Eyes} = {blue, brown}.

If the attribute "Height" is chosen, we can partition the universe into the following equivalence classes or elementary granules:

$\{O_1, O_2, O_8\}, \{O_3, O_4, O_5, O_6, O_7\},$

corresponding to atomic formulas (Height, =, short) and (Height, =, tall), respectively. Similarly, the use of attribute "Hair" produces the following equivalence classes or elementary granules:

$\{O_1, O_2, O_6, O_8\}, \{O_3\}, \{O_4, O_5, O_7\},$

corresponding to atomic formulas (Hair, =, blond), (Hair, =, red), and (Hair, =, dark), respectively. For the attribute "Eyes", we have:

$\{O_1, O_3, O_4, O_5, O_6\}, \{O_2, O_7, O_8\},$

corresponding to atomic formulas (Eyes, =, blue) and (Eyes, =, brown), respectively.

Smaller granules are set intersections of elementary granules. For example, sets

$\{O_1, O_2, O_8\} \cap \{O_1, O_2, O_6, O_8\} = \{O_1, O_2, O_8\}$

$\{O_3, O_4, O_5, O_6, O_7\} \cap \{O_4, O_5, O_7\} \cap \{O_2, O_7, O_8\} = \{O_7\},$

are smaller granules with the corresponding compound formulas (Height, =, short) $\wedge$ (Hair, =, blond) and (Height, =, tall) $\wedge$ (Hair, =, dark) $\wedge$ (Eyes, =, brown), respectively.

Figure 1 draws part of the $\cap$-closure granular structure for Table 1. In the figure, we assume that an attribute appears at most once in each formula of $GS_\cap(L\wedge)$. An atomic formula is simply represented by the attribute value. For example, the atomic formula (Height, =, short) is simply written as short.

Larger granules are set unions of elementary granules. For example, sets

Table 1. An information table

Object	Height	Hair	Eyes	Class
O_1	short	blond	blue	+
O_2	short	blond	brown	-
O_3	tall	red	blue	+
O_4	tall	dark	blue	-
O_5	tall	dark	blue	-
O_6	tall	blond	blue	+
O_7	tall	dark	brown	-
O_8	short	blond	brown	-

Figure 1. An example of $\cap$-closure granular structure

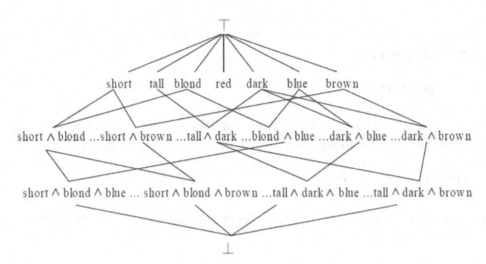

$$\{O_1, O_2, O_8\} \cup \{O_4, O_5, O_7\} = \{O_1, O_2, O_4, O_5, O_7, O_8\},$$

$$\{O_3, O_4, O_5, O_6, O_7\} \cup \{O_3\} \cup \{O_2, O_7, O_8\} = \{O_2, O_3, O_4, O_5, O_6, O_7, O_8\},$$

are larger granules for the corresponding compound formulas (Height, =, short) $\vee$ (Hair, =, dark) and (Height, =, tall) $\vee$ (Hair, =, red) $\vee$ (Eyes, =, brown), respectively.

Figure 2 draws part of the $\cup$-closure granular structure for Table 1.

THE LANGUAGE L IN FORMAL CONCEPT ANALYSIS

Formal concept analysis (Ganter & Wille, 1999) studies relationships between objects and their attributes in a formal context. In this section, we use formal concept analysis as another concrete granular computing model to further demonstrate the usefulness and flexibility of the language L.

Formal Contexts

A formal context is a triple (O, A, R) consisting of two sets O and A and a binary relation $R \subseteq O \times A$ between O and A. The elements of O are called the objects, and the elements of A are called the attributes that the objects might have. If $(x, a) \in R$, we say that the object x has the attribute a; we also write it as xRa.

In many situations, attributes are not just properties which objects may or may not have. Attributes such as "Size", "Prize", and "Weight" have values. A formal context with many-valued attributes can be defined as a many-valued context (O, A, V, R) consisting of sets O, A, V and a ternary relation $R \subseteq O \times A \times V$. The elements of A are many-valued attributes and the elements of V are their possible attribute values. A many-valued formal context satisfies the following condition:

Figure 2. An example of ∪-closure granular structure

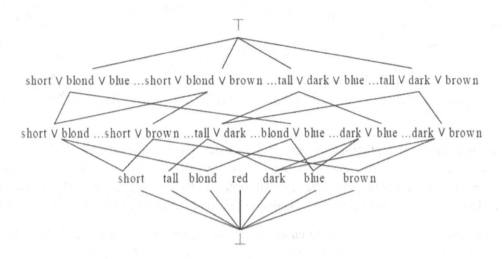

$(x, a, v_1) \in R \land (x, a, v_2) \in R \Rightarrow (v_1 = v_2).$

In the language of rough set analysis, one can define a partial map from O to V with respect to an attribute a of a many-valued context (O, A, V, R). If $(x, a, v) \in R$, we write $I_a(x) = v$.

A many-valued context can be represented by an information table, the rows of the table are the objects and columns are attributes. The entry in row x and column a represents the attribute value $I_a(x)$. If the attribute a does not have a value for object x, then there is no entry. A many-valued formal context can be translated into a single-valued context through a process called conceptual scaling which contains two essential steps.

In the first step, each attribute of a many-valued context is interpreted into a scale. A scale for the attribute a of a many-valued context can be defined as a single-valued context $S_a = (O_a, A_a, R_a)$. The objects of a scale are called scale values, and attributes are called scale attributes. The binary relation can be interpreted differently according to different types of scales (Ganter & Wille, 1999). For better understanding, we explain three elementary scales in a simple example.

Example 2. Table 2 is an example of a many-valued context for some televisions. The scale contexts of three attributes, "Type", "Clarity", and "Price" are given in Table 3.

The first type of scale is called nominal scale. It is used to scale attributes with the values that mutually exclude each other. The attribute "Type" with the values {CRT, LCD, Plasma} in Table 3 uses this kind of scale.

The second type of scale is called ordinal scale. It is used to scale attributes with the values that are ordered and each value implies the weak ones. The attribute "Clarity" with the values {clear, very clear, extremely clear} in Table 3 uses this kind of scale.

The third type of scale is called interordinal scale. It is used to scale attributes with the values that have bipolar orderings. The attribute "Price" with the values {\$0 ≤ Price < \$1000, \$1000 ≤ Price < \$3000, \$3000 ≤ Price < \$4000} in Table 3 uses this kind of scale.

Table 2. An example of a many-valued formal context

Object	Type	Clarity	Price
tv_1	CRT	clear	$1000
tv_2	LCD	very clear	$2500
tv_3	Plasma	extremely clear	$3500
tv_4	LCD	very clear	$3900

The second step of conceptual scaling is to join the scales together to make a single-valued context. In the case of plain scaling, the object set O of the many-valued context remains unchanged, every many-valued attribute a is replaced by the scale attributes of the scale (O_a, A_a, R_a). That is, the attribute set of the derived single-valued context is the disjoint union of scale attribute sets. We can rewrite the scale attribute set A_a to $\dot{A}_a = \{a\} \times A_a$ to ensure that those scale attribute sets are disjoint. Therefore, the derived single-valued formal context from many-valued context (O, A, V, R) with respect to plain scaling can be defined as (O, B, R') with:

$$B = \bigcup_{a \in A} \dot{A}_a$$

and

$$x R'(a,b) \leftrightarrow I_a(x) = v \wedge v R_a b.$$

That is, an object $x \in O$ has the attribute value $b \in B$ with respect to the attribute $a \in A$ in the context (O, B, R') if and only if x has the attribute value v with respect to attribute a in the many-valued context (O, A, V, R), and v is R_a related to b in the scale context S_a. Table 4 shows the derived single-valued context by combining the many-valued context of Table 2 and the scale contexts of Table 3.

Table 3. Examples of scale contexts

S_{Type}	CRT	LCD	Plasma
CRT	×		
LCD		×	
Plasma			×
$S_{Clarity}$	≤ clear	≤ very clear	≤ extremely clear
clear	×	×	×
very clear		×	×
extremely clear			×
S_{Price}	cheap	mid-range	expensive
$0 ≤ Price < $1000	×		
$1000 ≤ Price < $3000		×	
$3000 ≤ Price < $4000			×

Granules in Formal Concept Analysis

The processes of defining granules and granular structures are different in rough set analysis and formal concept analysis. They build granules and granular structures based on two different interpretations of the notion of definability. In rough set analysis, a definable granule is the union of some equivalence classes. In formal concept analysis, one is interested in granules of objects that are extensions of formal concepts. A concept derived from a formal context is a pair of a set of objects and a set of attributes, called the extension and intension of the concept. Furthermore, the extension and intension are mutually definable, that is, the intension of the extension is the extension of the intension and vice versa.

For a many-valued formal context (O, A, V, R), one first needs to transfer this many-valued context into a single-valued context (O, B, R'). The formal concepts constructed from this derived single-valued context are then interpreted as the formal concepts of the many-valued context.

Since a many-valued formal context (O, A, V, R) can be translated into a single-valued context (O, B, R'), it is sufficient to consider the construction process of formal concepts in (O, B, R'). We can construct the language L by using a single-valued formal context as the model M, O as the domain D, and the set of atomic formulas is given by $A = \{b \mid b \in B\}$. That is, atomic formula is denoted as the attribute value (b) or simply b. An object $x \in O$ satisfies an atomic formula b if the object has the attribute b:

$x \models b$ iff $x R' b$.

We rewrite the language as $L(\{b\}, O, \{\neg, \wedge, \vee, \rightarrow, \leftrightarrow\})$. In Table 2, examples of atomic formulas are (Type, CRT) and (Clarity, ≤very clear). For simplicity, we also write them as "CRT" and "≤very clear", respectively.

By using the language L, we can formally define a formal concept in a formal context. For a set $X \subseteq O$ of objects, we define a mapping $O \rightarrow A$ as:

$m'(X) = \{b \in A \mid x \models b \text{ for all } x \in X\}$,

that is, the set of atomic formulas satisfied by all the objects in X. Correspondingly, for a set $P \subseteq A$ of atomic formulas, we define a mapping $A \rightarrow O$ as:

$m(P) = \{x \in O \mid x \models b \text{ for all } b \in P\} = \{x \in O \mid x \models \bigwedge_{b \in P} b\}$,

Table 4. Derived single-valued context

	Type			Clarity			Price		
	a	b	c	d	e	f	g	h	i
tv_1	×			×			×		
tv_2		×		×	×			×	
tv_3			×	×	×	×			×
tv_4		×		×	×				×

a: CRT; b: LCD; c: Plasma; d: ≤clear; e: ≤very clear;
f: ≤extremely clear; g: cheap; h: mid-range; i: expensive.

Figure 3. Concept Lattice of Table 4

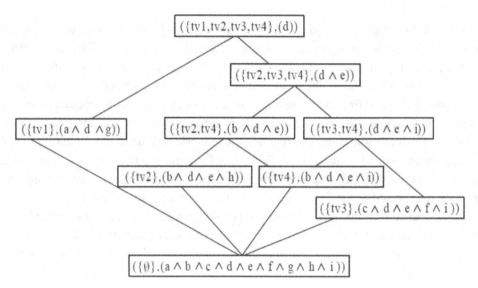

that is, the set of objects satisfies all the atomic formulas in P. With these two mappings being defined, a formal concepts can be defined as a pair satisfying the condition:

$$(X, P) = \{X \subseteq O, P \subseteq A \mid X = m(P), P = m'(X) \}.$$

The set of objects $X = extent(X, P)$ is the extension and the set of atomic formulas $P = intent(X, P)$ is the intension of the formal concept. By using logic formulas, we can rewrite a formal concept as $(X, \bigwedge_{b \in P} b)$.

For an atomic formula $b \in A$, we can derive a formal concept $(m(\{b\}), m'(m(\{b\})))$. A subset or a granule $X \subseteq O$ is definable in a formal context if and only if there exits a subset of atomic formulas $P \in A$ in the language $L(\{b\}, O, \{\neg, \wedge, \vee, \rightarrow, \leftrightarrow\})$ such that (X, P) is a formal concept, that is, $X = m(P)$ and $P = m'(X)$. Otherwise, it is undefinable. Let $\mathbf{B}(O, B, R')$ or simply $\mathbf{B}$ denote the set of all formal concepts of the context, the family of definable granules is given by:

$$Def(L(\{b\}, O, \{\neg, \wedge, \vee, \rightarrow, \leftrightarrow\})) = \{extent(X, P) \mid (X, P) \in \mathbf{B}\}.$$

If a formal context (O, B, R') is treated as a binary information table, one can easily observe a close relationship between rough set analysis and formal concept analysis. A definable set of objects in formal concept analysis is a definable set in rough set analysis, but the reverse in not true.

Granular Structures in Formal Concept Analysis

The family of all formal concepts forms a complete lattice called a concept lattice through which the relationships between formal concepts can be visualized (Ganter & Wille, 1999). The meet and join of the lattice are defined based on the set-theoretic operators of intersection ($\cap$), union ($\cup$) and the mappings between object set O and atomic formula set A, written as:

$(X1, P1) \wedge (X2, P2) = (X1 \cap X2, m'(m(P1 \cup P2)))$,

$(X1, P1) \vee (X2, P2) = (m(m'(X1 \cup X2)), P1 \cap P2)$.

The order relation of the concept lattice can be defined as follows. For two formal concepts $(X1, P1)$ and $(X2, P2)$, if $X1 \subseteq X2$ (which is equivalent to $P2 \subseteq P1$), then $(X2, P2)$ is a superconcept of $(X1, P1)$ and $(X1, P1)$ is a subconcept of $(X2, P2)$, written as $(X1, P1) \leq (X2, P2)$.

From the viewpoint of granular computing, the extensions of superconcepts are larger granules that may be decomposed into smaller granules as extensions of subconcepts. We consider a concept lattice as an $\cap$-closure granular structure which only includes granules that are extensions of formal concepts. Each granule in a concept lattice can be labeled by formulas of the language $L\wedge$.

Example 3. The process of forming a concept lattice from Table 4 can be illustrated as follows. If attribute "≤clear" is chosen, objects satisfied this attribute construct the most general granule which includes all the objects of this context, the corresponding formal concept is $(\{tv_1, tv_2, tv_3, tv_4\},$ ≤clear), where "≤clear" is an atomic formula. The second level are the granules whose intensions only include the conjunction of two atomic formulas, the corresponding formal concept is $(\{tv_2, tv_3, tv_4\},$ ≤clear $\wedge$ ≤very clear). The third level are the granules whose intensions only include the conjunction of three atomic formulas, the corresponding formal concept is $(\{tv_1\},$ CRT $\wedge$ ≤clear $\wedge$ cheap), $(\{tv_2, tv_4\},$ LCD $\wedge$ ≤clear $\wedge$ ≤very clear) and $(\{tv_3, tv_4\},$ ≤clear $\wedge$ ≤very clear $\wedge$ expensive). The intersections of granules produce the smaller granules in the fourth level and so on. For example, the set,

$\{tv_2, tv_4\} \cap \{tv_3, tv_4\} = \{tv_4\}$, is a smaller granule corresponding to the formal concept $(\{tv_4\},$ LCD $\wedge$ ≤clear $\wedge$ ≤very clear $\wedge$ expensive). Finally, the most specific granule is the empty set $\varnothing$ corresponding to the conjunction of all atomic formulas as its intension.

The line diagram in Figure 3 represents the concept lattice of Table 4 that includes 9 formal concepts. The intensions of each formal concept are labeled by formulas of the language $L\wedge$.

Implications and Dependencies in Formal Concept Analysis

Relationships between attributes of a formal context can be automatically generated from a concept lattice. There are two types of these relationships, called implications and dependencies (Ganter & Wille, 1999). An implication expresses relationships between attribute values of objects in a formal context, which is a typical example of low order rules. An example of the implications in Figure 3 is, "every object that has attribute expensive also has attribute ≤clear, so expensive implies ≤clear." A dependency expresses relationships between object pairs with regards to certain attributes in a formal concept, which is a typical example of high order rules. An example of dependencies in Figure 3 is, "if two objects have the same Type, then they must have the same Clarity, so Clarity depends on Type." In general, dependencies can be seen as an abstraction of implications. Identifying these relationships from large databases is a well-known problem in the field of knowledge discovery. The introduction of formal concept analysis provides an important mathematical methodology for addressing this problem. We express implications and dependencies by using formulas of the language L.

An implication can be written as $P \Rightarrow C$ for a formal context (O, B, R'), where P and C are subsets of attribute set B. The set P is called the premise and C is called the conclusion of this implication. The implication $P \Rightarrow C$ holds in the context (O, B, R') if objects having attributes in P also have attributes in C. An example of an implication is given based on the previous defined satisfiability of atomic formulas:

$$\bigwedge_{i=1}^{n}(xR'p_i) \Rightarrow \bigwedge_{j=1}^{m}(xR'c_j),$$

where $p_i \in P$ and $c_j \in C$. Note that an arbitrary attribute set $P \subseteq B$ or $C \subseteq B$ is not necessarily the intensions of some formal concepts.

A dependency between attributes can be written as $H \Rightarrow K$ for a many-valued context (O, A, V, R), where H and K are subsets of an attribute set A. The dependency $H \Rightarrow K$ holds in the context (O, A, V, R), if two objects have the same attribute values with respect to all attributes in H. The same must also be true for the attributes in K. An example of a dependency is given by following the way of interpreting high order rules of an information table:

$$\bigwedge_{i=1}^{n}(I_{a_i}(x)R_{a_i}I_{a_i}(y)) \Rightarrow \bigwedge_{j=1}^{m}(I_{d_j}(x)R_{d_j}I_{d_j}(y)),$$

where $(x,y) \in O \times O, a_i \in H, d_j \in K$.

Implications and dependencies are simple forms of regularities that can be used for the reasoning about knowledge. In a practical case, there may be too many irrelevant implications or dependencies existing in a context since they will be held even if there is only one object that satisfies the rule. To alleviate this problem, quantitative measures can be used to evaluate the statistical significance of the rules that hold. One may choose a threshold value and only select those rules whose measures are above the threshold value. The quantitative measures of mining association rules can be used to measure the strength of implications and dependencies (Agrawal, Imielinsky & Swami, 1993).

There are two types of quantitative measures based on a threshold value, called the support and confidence measures. By using the language L, the meanings and interpretations of an implication or dependency $\varphi \Rightarrow \psi$ can be further clarified by using the extensions $m(\varphi)$ and $m(\psi)$ of the two concepts. We can formally interpret these two measures in formal concept analysis as:

$$support(\phi \Rightarrow \varphi) = \frac{|m(\phi \wedge \varphi)|}{|O|},$$

$$confidence(\phi \Rightarrow \varphi) = \frac{|m(\phi \wedge \varphi)|}{|m(\phi)|},$$

where $|\cdot|$ denotes the cardinality of a set and $|O|$ denotes the number of objects in a context. The two measures are applicable to both implications and dependencies. The implication or dependency holds in a context if the value of support or confidence is above the threshold $minsupp \in [0,1]$ or $minconf \in [0,1]$. This demonstrates the flexibility and power of the language L.

CONCLUSION

Granular computing models human problem solving with different-sized grains of knowledge. Fundamental notions of granular computing are basic granules, granular structures and rules. Basic granules are the elementary units of granular computing and represent the basic pieces of knowledge. A granular structure provides a structured description of a system or an application under discussion. Rules, as a commonly used form for representing knowledge, can be thought of as relationships between granules. A fundamental issue of granular computing is the representation, construction and utilization of these basic notions. In this book chapter, we address this issue by proposing a logic approach to precisely describe the definability of basic granules and to construct the granular structures and rules. The tasks of granular computing are formalized during this process. Different granular computing models can be analyzed within this logic framework.

We introduce a logic language L. Atomic formulas correspond to basic granules. Other formulas of the language are recursively constructed from a set of atomic formulas. The meaning of a formula is defined in Tarski's style semantics by using the model $M = (D, K)$. Based on the knowledge K of the model, it is assumed that an object in the domain D either satisfies a formula or does not satisfy a formula. A granule is jointly described by a pair $(m(\phi), \phi)$ consisting of a subset $m(\phi)$ of the domain D and a formula ϕ of the language L. The main difference between L and other existing decision logic languages is the treatment of atomic formulas. Instead of defining an atomic formula specifically as an (attribute, value) pair (Pawlak, 1991) or an (attribute, relation, value) triplet (Yao & Liau, 2002), we postpone the definition of atomic formulas to particular applications. That is, we build the language based on a set of atomic formulas without giving them a concrete physical meaning. This flexibility enables us to interpret granules and granular structures in different applications. Furthermore, the notions of indiscernibility and definability are formally defined. Two sub-languages of L are introduced, each of them using only one logic connective. They lead to the introduction of two types of granular structures, namely, ∩-closure and ∪-closure granular structures. Different types of rules can be generated from different types of granules, and rule learning algorithms can be designed based on granular structures.

Depending on the particular application, we can interpret the language by using different types of atomic formulas and the associated models. The flexibility of the language L is demonstrated by considering two concrete granular computing models, namely, rough set analysis and formal concept analysis. These two theories study object-attribute relationships in a data table. They share high-level similarities and can be interpreted uniformly by L. The main differences between them are their choices of definable granules and granular structures. The unified study of these two theories demonstrates the potential of L for granular computing. Table 5 shows the unified interpretation of rough set analysis and formal concept analysis. We suggest that one may study data analysis and rule mining in a much wider class of granular computing models. Algorithms and evaluation measures can be designed uniformly for these models.

ACKNOWLEDGMENT

This study is partially supported by an NSERC Canada Discovery grant. The authors thank Professor Yingxu Wang for encouragement and anonymous reviewers for their constructive comments.

Table 5. The unified interpretation of RSA and FCA

Rough Set Analysis		Formal Concept Analysis	
Basic notions	Interpretations	Basic notions	Interpretations
Information tables	$M = (D, K)$	Formal contexts	$M = (O, K)$
Indiscernibility relation	$x \sim_{A0} y$ iff $m'(x) \cap A_0 = m'(y) \cap A_0$	Conceptual Scaling	$B = \bigcup_{a \in A} \overset{\bullet}{A_a}$ and $x R'(a,b) \Leftrightarrow I_a(x) = v \wedge v R_a b$
Basic granules	(a, R_a, v) (a, R_a)	Basic granules	(b)
Definable granules	$X = m(\varphi)$	Definable granules	$X = m(P)$ and $P = m'(X)$
Granular strictures	$GS_\cap(L \wedge)$ $GS_\cup(L \vee)$	Concept lattice	$GS_\cap(L \wedge)$
Low-order rules	$\bigwedge_{i=1}^{n}(I_{a_i}(x)R_{a_i}v_{a_i}) \Rightarrow \bigwedge_{j=1}^{m}(I_{d_j}(x)R_{d_j}v_{d_j})$	Implications	$\bigwedge_{i=1}^{n}(xR'p_i) \Rightarrow \bigwedge_{j=1}^{m}(xR'c_j)$
High-order rules	$\bigwedge_{i=1}^{n}(I_{a_i}(x)R_{a_i}I_{a_i}(y)) \Rightarrow \bigwedge_{j=1}^{m}(I_{d_j}(x)R_{d_j}I_{d_j}(y))$	Dependencies	$\bigwedge_{i=1}^{n}(I_{a_i}(x)R_{a_i}I_{a_i}(y)) \Rightarrow \bigwedge_{j=1}^{m}(I_{d_j}(x)R_{d_j}I_{d_j}(y))$

REFERENCES

Agrawal, R., Imielinsky, T., & Swami, A. (1993). Mining association rules between sets of items in large databases. In *Proceedings of the 1993 International Conference on Management of Data (SIGMOD 93)* (pp. 207-216).

Bziau, J. Y. (2006). Many-valued and Kripke Semantics. In J. van Benthem (Ed.), *The Age of Alternative Logics* (pp. 89-101). Dordrecht: Springer.

Chen, Y. H., & Yao, Y. Y. (2007). A multiview approach for intelligent data analysis based on data operators. *Information Sciences*, *178*(1), 1–20. doi:10.1016/j.ins.2007.08.011

Demri, S., & Orlowska, E. (1997). Logical analysis of indiscernibility. In E. Orlowska (Ed.), *Incomplete Information: Rough Set Analysis* (pp. 347-380). Heidelberg: Physica Verlag.

Falmagne, J.-C., Koppen, M., Villano, M., Doignon, J.-P., & Johannesen, L. (1990). Introduction to knowledge spaces: how to build, test and search them. *Psychological Review*, 201–224. doi:10.1037/0033-295X.97.2.201

Ganter, B., & Wille, R. (1999). *Formal Concept Analysis, Mathematical Foundations*. Berlin: Springer.

Grzymala-Busse, J. W. (2005). Incomplete data and generalization of indiscernibility relation, definability, and approximations. *Rough Sets, Fuzzy Sets, Data Mining, and Granular Computing. Proceedings of 10th International Conference* (LNAI 3641, pp. 244-253).

Harrison, M. A. (1978). *Introduction to Formal Language Theory*. Addison-Wesley.

Lin, T. Y., Yao, Y. Y., & Zadeh, L. A. (Eds.). (2002). *Data Mining, Rough Sets and Granular Computing*. Heidelberg: Physica-Verlag.

Marr, D. (1982). *Vision, A Computational Investigation into Human Representation and Processing of Visual Informatio*. San Francisco: W.H. Freeman and Company.

Nguyen, H. S., Skowron, A., & Stepaniuk, J. (2001). Granular computing: a rough set approach. *Computational Intelligence, 17*, 514–544. doi:10.1111/0824-7935.00161

Pawlak, Z. (1991). *Rough Sets - Theoretical Aspects of Reasoning about Data*. Boston: Kluwer Publishers.

Pawlak, Z., & Skowron, A. (2007). Rough sets: some extensions. *Information Science, 177*, 28–40. doi:10.1016/j.ins.2006.06.006

Quinlan, J. R. (1983). Learning efficient classification procedures and their application to chess endgames. In J.S. Michalski et al.(Eds.), *Machine Learning: An Artificial Intelligence Approach* (pp. 463-482). Morgan Kaufmann.

Simon, H. A., & Kaplan, C. A. (1989). Foundations of cognitive science. In M. I. Posner (Ed.), *Foundations of Cognitive Science* (pp. 1-47). Cambridge, MA: MIT Press.

Smith, E. E. (1989). Concepts and induction. In M. I. Posner (Ed.), *Foundations of Cognitive Science* (pp. 501-526). Cambridge, MA: MIT Press.

Sowa, J. F. (1984). *Conceptual Structures, Information Processing in Mind and Machine*. Reading, MA: Addison-Wesley

Tarski, A. (1956). *Logic, Semantics, Metamathematics: Papers from 1923 to 1938*. Oxford: Clarendon Press.

Tsumoto, S. (1999). Automated discovery of plausible rules based on rough sets and rough inclusion. In *Proceedings of PAKDD'99* (LNAI 1574, pp. 210-219).

Van, M. I., Hampton, J., Michalski, R.S., & Theuns, P. (Eds.) (1993). *Categories and Concepts, Theoretical Views and Inductive Data Analysis*. New York: Academic Press.

Wang, Y. (2003a). Cognitive informatics: a new transdisciplinary research field. *Brain and Mind: A Transdisciplinary Journal of Neuroscience and Neurophilosophy, 4*, 115-127.

Wang, Y. (2003b). On cognitive informatics. *Brain and Mind: A Transdisciplinary Journal of Neuroscience and Neurophilosophy, 4*, 151-167.

Wang, Y. (2007a). Cognitive informatics: Exploring theoretical foundations for natural intelligence, neural informatics, autonomic computing, and agent systems. *International Journal of Cognitive Informatics and Natural Intelligence, 1*(1), 1–10.

Wang, Y. (2007b). The theoretical framework of cognitive informatics. *International Journal of Cognitive Informatics and Natural Intelligence, 1*, 1–27.

Wille, R. (1982). Restructuring lattice theory: an approach based on hierarchies of concepts. In I.Rival (Ed.), *Ordered Sets* (pp. 445-470). Boston/Dordrecht: Reidel.

Wille, R. (1992). Concept lattices and conceptual knowledge systems. *Computers & Mathematics with Applications (Oxford, England), 23*, 493–515. doi:10.1016/0898-1221(92)90120-7

Yao, J. T. (2007). A ten-year review of granular computing. In *Proceedings of the 3ʳᵈ IEEE International Conference on Granular Computing* (pp. 299-302).

Yao, Y. Y. (2001a). Information granulation and rough set approximation. *International Journal of Intelligent Systems, 16*, 87–104. doi:10.1002/1098-111X(200101)16:1<87::AID-INT7>3.0.CO;2-S

Yao, Y. Y. (2001b). Modeling data mining with granular computing. In *Proceedings of the 25th Annual International Computer Software and Applications Conference* (pp. 638-643).

Yao, Y. Y. (2004a). A comparative study of formal concept analysis and rough set theory in data analysis. In *International Conference on Rough Sets and Current Trends in Computing (RSCTC'2004),* pp. 59-68.

Yao, Y. Y. (2004b). Concept formation and learning: A cognitive informatics perspective. In *Proceedings of the Third IEEE International Conference on Cognitive Informatics.*

Yao, Y. Y. (2004c). Granular computing. In *Proceedings of the Fourth Chinese National Conference on Rough Sets and Soft Computing* (pp. 1-5).

Yao, Y. Y. (2004d). A partition model of granular computing. *LNCS transactions on rough sets (. LNCS, 3100*, 232–253.

Yao, Y. Y. (2006a). Granular computing and cognitive informatics. In *Proceedings of the Fifth IEEE International Conference on Cognitive Informatics* (pp. 17-18).

Yao, Y. Y. (2006b). Three perspectives of granular computing. In *Proceedings, International Forum on Theory of GrC from Rough Set Perspective, Journal of Nanchang Institute of Technology* (pp. 16-21).

Yao, Y. Y. (2007a). The art of granular computing. In *Proceeding of the International Conference on Rough Sets and Emerging Intelligent Systems Paradigms* (LNAI 4585, pp. 101-112).

Yao, Y.Y. (2007b). A note on definability and approximations. *Transactions on Rough Sets*, 274-282.

Yao, Y. Y. (2007c). Granular computing for web intelligence and brain informatics. *The 2007 IEEE/WIC/ACM International Conference on Web Intelligence* (pp.1-20).

Yao, Y. Y., & Liau, C.-J. (2002). A generalized decision logic language for granular computing. *FUZZ-IEEE'02 in The 2002 IEEE World Congress on Computational Intelligence* (pp. 1092-1097).

Yao, Y. Y., & Zhong, N. (1999). An analysis of quantitative measures associated with rules. In . *Proceedings of PAKDD*, *99*, 479–488.

Yao, Y. Y., & Zhou, B. (2007). A logic language of granular computing. In *Proceedings of the 6th IEEE International Conference on Cognitive Informatics* (pp. 178-185).

Yao, Y. Y., Zhou, B., & Chen, Y. H. (2007). Interpreting low and high order rules: a granular computing approach. In *Proceedings of International Conference on Rough Sets and Emerging Intelligent System Paradigms (RSEISP'07), Lecture Notes in Artificial Intelligence* (LNAI 4585, pp. 371-380).

Zadeh, L. A. (1997). Towards a theory of fuzzy information granulation and its centrality in human reasoning and fuzzy logic. *Fuzzy Sets and Systems*, *19*, 111–127. doi:10.1016/S0165-0114(97)00077-8

Chapter 18
On Foundations and Applications of the Paradigm of Granular Rough Computing

Lech Polkowski
Polish-Japanese Institute of Information Technology, Poland

Maria Semeniuk-Polkowska
Warsaw University, Poland

ABSTRACT

Granular computing, initiated by Lotfi A. Zadeh, has acquired wide popularity as a tool for approximate reasoning, fusion of knowledge, cognitive computing. The need for formal methods of granulation, and means for computing with granules, has been addressed in this work by applying methods of rough mereology. Rough mereology is an extension of mereology taking as the primitive notion the notion of a part to a degree. Granules are formed as classes of objects which are a part to a given degree of a given object. In addition to an exposition of this mechanism of granulation, we point also to some applications like granular logics for approximate reasoning and classifiers built from granulated data sets.

NOTIONS CENTRAL TO GRANULATION OF KNOWLEDGE

Granulation of knowledge is one of important aspects of the way in which the human brain works (see, e.g., Pal, 2004). A vast literature on emulating such aspects of the brain workings as granulation, fusion of knowledge, classification by means of neural networks, fuzzy logics, and so on, does witness the role the computer science society attaches to them. These aspects are studied with at least a twofold purpose. First, to get an insight into the processes of perception, concept formation, and reasoning in the brain; second, to transfer this knowledge into the realm of applications.

The emergence of ample paradigms like cognitive informatics and natural intelligence (see, e.g., Chan, Kisner, Wang. & Miller, 2004; Kinsner, Zang, Wang, & Tsai, 2005; Patel, Patel, & Wang, 2003; Wang, 2007, Wang, Johnston, & Smith, 2002; Yao, Shi, Wang, & Kinsner, 2006) is due in large part to these studies and emulations of vital aspects of the brain mechanism. This emergence is welcomed as it provides a forum for an intradisciplinary study of mechanisms of perception, cognition, and reasoning.

Our work is devoted to the aspect of granulation of knowledge with applications to synthesis (fusion) of knowledge from various sources, reasoning in uncertain situations by means of approximate logics and data classification: all these aspects vital for human intelligence.

In this section, we describe basic tools applied in our analysis of granulation. First, we discuss basic principles of rough set theory (Pawlak, 1982, 1991) in particular, the notion of an information system. Next, we give space to an introduction to mereology (Leśniewski, 1916) whose techniques are important in our development of granular computing. Then, similarity is discussed briefly as a bridge to the final part of this section devoted to rough mereology (Polkowski, 2005, 2006; Polkowski & Skowron, 1997).

Rough Set Analysis of Knowledge

This approach consists in understanding knowledge as an ability to classify objects in a given universe into classes of objects identical with respect to a given collection of features (attributes). The formal framework for defining knowledge is an *information system* which is a pair $I = (U, A)$, where U is a set of objects and A is a set of *attributes*, each $a \in A$ being a mapping $a{:}U \to V_a$ from U into the *value set* V_a.

The collection of *a-indiscernibility relations* $IND(I) = \{ind(a){:}a \in A\}$, where $ind(a) = \{(u, v){:} u, v \in U, a(u) = a(v)\}$ describes indiscernibility of objects induced by the attribute a, in the spirit of *Leibniz's identity of indiscernibles principle*.

For any subset $B \subseteq A$, the relation $ind(B) = \bigcap_{a \in B} ind(a)$ is the relation of *B-indiscernibility*. Its classes $[u]_B = \{v \in U{:}(u, v) \in ind(B)\}$ form *B-elementary granules of knowledge*. Unions of granules of the form $[u]_B$ are *B-granules of knowledge*. Indiscernibility relations submit a set-theoretical tool for defining granules; from the logical point if view, indiscernibility classes can be regarded as meanings of certain formulas of a description logic.

Elementary formulas of description logic are *descriptors* (see, e.g., Pawlak, 1991), of the form $(a = v)$, with the meaning defined as the set $[(a = v)] = \{u \in U{:} a(u) = v\}$. The meaning is extended to the set of formulas obtained from descriptors by means of connectives $\lor, \land, \neg, \Rightarrow$ of propositional calculus, with recursively extended semantics:

1. $[\alpha \lor \beta] = [\alpha] \cup [\beta]$
2. $[\alpha \land \beta] = [\alpha] \cap [\beta]$
3. $[\neg \alpha] = U \setminus [\alpha]$
4. $[\alpha \Rightarrow \beta] = [\neg \alpha \lor \beta]$ (1)

For an indiscernibility class $[u]_B$, the following equality holds,

$$[u]_B = [\bigwedge_{\alpha \in \beta}(a = a(u))]$$ (2)

i.e., the meaning of the formula $\varphi_B(u): \wedge_{a \in B}(a = a(u))$ is equal to the class $[u]_B$. Thus, indiscernibility classes, hence granules, are *definable* in description logic. For this reason, they are also called *exact sets* (see Pawlak, 1991). Other sets of objects, which are not exact, are called *rough*. The notion of a granule and an exact set are thus interchangeable in case granules are defined in attribute-value based languages.

A particular case of an information system is a *decision system*; that is, a triple (U, A, d) in which d is a singled out attribute called the *decision*. Decision is an attribute whose value is set by an expert in its own language. In order to relate the *conditional* knowledge $(U, IND(I))$ to the *world knowledge* $(U, ind(d))$, *decision rules* are in use. A decision rule is an implication, in description logic:

$$\underset{\alpha \in \beta}{\wedge} (a = v_a) \Rightarrow (d = w) \tag{3}$$

The decision rule is *true*, or *certain*, in case $[\wedge_{a \in A} (a = v_a)] \subseteq [(d = w)]$; otherwise, the decision rule is *partially true*, or *possible*. A *classifier* is a set of decision rules. We return to this notion in the last Section of this article. We close this section with an example of a decision system.

Example 1. *In Table 1, a random sample of 20 objects with all nine attribute values (where the last attribute is the decision) from Pima Indians Diabetes data set (UCI repository) is given.*

Table 1. A sample of 20 objects from Pima Indians diabetes

obj	a1	a2	a3	a4	a5	a6	a7	a8	d
o1	11	143	94	33	146	36.6	0.254	51	1
o2	4	144	58	28	140	29.5	0.287	37	0
o3	5	124	74	0	0	34	0.22	38	1
o4	8	109	76	39	114	27.9	0.64	31	1
o5	4	122	68	0	0	35	0.394	29	0
o6	0	165	90	33	680	52.3	0.427	23	0
o7	9	152	78	34	171	34.2	0.893	33	1
o8	4	146	78	0	0	38.5	0.52	67	1
o9	1	119	88	41	170	45.3	0.507	26	0
o10	0	95	80	45	92	36.5	0.33	26	0
o11	1	71	62	0	0	21.8	0.416	26	0
o12	6	99	60	19	54	26.9	0.497	32	0
o13	2	108	64	0	0	30.8	0.158	21	0
o14	11	136	84	35	130	28.3	0.26	42	1
o15	2	120	54	0	0	26.8	0.455	27	0
o16	1	106	70	28	135	34.2	0.142	22	0
o17	0	99	0	0	0	25	0.253	22	0
o18	6	125	78	31	0	27.6	0.565	49	1
o19	5	117	86	30	105	39.1	0.251	42	0
o20	2	122	70	27	0	36.8	0.34	27	0

Mereology

Mereology is a theory of concepts based on a binary *relation of being a part*, proposed first by Stanislas Leśniewski (Leśniewski, 1916). It serves us as a theoretical framework in which we define granules formally and establish their properties.

A relation π of a *part*, on a given universe U of objects, satisfies the conditions,

$$1. \neg (x \, \pi \, x). \quad 2. \ x \, \pi \, y \wedge y \, \pi \, z \Rightarrow x \, \pi \, z \tag{4}$$

Thus, *part* renders the intuition of a *proper part*. The notion of an *improper part*, associated with the part relation π, is expressed with the help of the notion of an *ingredient*, ing_π,

$$xing_\pi y \Leftrightarrow x \, \pi \, y \vee x = y. \tag{5}$$

Then, the *element* relation *el* holds if for each z, from $zing_\pi x$ it follows that $zing_\pi y$. The association with the notion of a subset is evident, and actually, in mereology the notions of an ingredient, an element and a subset are equivalent (see Leśniewski, 1916).

The reader will check easily, for instance, that the relation $\subset$ of proper containment in naive set theory is a part relation with the relation of improper containment $\subseteq$ as the associated ingredient relation.

Mereology is a theory of individual objects, and passing to it from ontology, the theory of distributive concepts, is realized by means of the *class operator*. The definition of the class operator is the following. For any nonempty collection F of objects; that is, an ontological concept F, the individual representing F is given as the *class of F*, *ClsF*, subject to the following conditions,

$$1. u \in F \Rightarrow uing_\pi ClsF.$$
$$2. \ uing_\pi ClsF \Rightarrow \exists v, \ w.ving_\pi u \wedge ving_\pi w \wedge w \in F \tag{6}$$

In the sequel, the subscript π will be mostly omitted. In plain words, *ClsF* consists of those objects whose each part has a part in common with an object in F.

The reader will easily recognize that the union $\bigcup F$ of a family F of sets is the class of F with respect to the part relation $\subset$. This example shows the most important property of mereology: it dispels with families of concepts replacing them automatically with concepts. In mereological theories there is no need or any place for hierarchies of concepts.

The most important tool in mereological reasoning is the *Leśniewski Inference Rule*, (see Leśniewski, 1916).

The Inference Rule. *If for each v, $ving_\pi u$ implies $ving_\pi t$ for some t such that $ting_\pi w$ then $uing_\pi w$.*

Using this rule, the reader may prove for themselves all statements about granules given in this work.

Rough Mereology and Rough Inclusions

Rough mereology is a theory which combines ideas of mereology and rough set theory in order to introduce the notion of a *part to a degree* (see, e.g., Polkowski, 2004, 2005, 2006; Polkowski & Skowron, 1997).

The notion of a part to a degree is formally rendered as a relation $\mu(u, v, r) \subseteq U \times U \times [0, 1]$ (reading "the object u is a part of the object v to a degree of r"). The relation μ is called a *rough inclusion*.

To introduce rough inclusions, and to give some motivation for their properties, we go back to Henri Poincare' (1905). Poincare' considered a relation $\tau(x, y)$ which holds if and only if $d(x,y) < r$ for some fixed r and a metric d. The relation τ is a *tolerance relation*, i.e., it is reflexive and symmetric.

We generalize this idea. We let $\mu_d(x, y, r)$ if and only if $d(x,y) \leq 1 - r$. Then, the predicate μ_d does satisfy a number of conditions which follow from properties of a metric:

1. $\mu_d(x, y, 1)$ if and only if $x=y$.
2. If $\mu_d(x, y, 1)$ and $\mu_d(z, x, r)$ then $\mu_d(z, y, r)$.
3. If $\mu_d(x, y, r)$ and $s < r$ then $\mu_d(x, y, s)$.
4. If $\mu_d(x, y, r)$ and $\mu_d(y, z, s)$ then $\mu_d(x, z, L(r, s))$,

where $L(r, s) = \max\{0, r + s - 1\}$ is the well-known Łukasiewicz functor of many-valued logics, see, e.g., (Ha'jek, 1998; Polkowski, 2002).

Properties 1-3 are singled out by us as characteristic for *rough inclusions*; property 4, which does reflect the triangle inequality for the metric d, is the *transitivity property* of rough inclusions of the form μ_d. These properties will be established as well for rough inclusions defined in the sequel.

An abstract definition of a rough inclusion will refer to properties 1-3 with an additional important factor, viz., property 1 will be in general referred to an ingredient relation of mereology.

A *rough inclusion* $\mu_d(x, y, r)$, where x, y are individual objects in the universe $U, r \in [0, 1]$, and π part relation of a chosen mereological description of concepts, does satisfy the following requirements:

1. $\mu_\pi(x, y, 1) \Rightarrow xing_\pi y$.
2. $\mu_\pi(x, y, 1)$ and $\mu_\pi(z, x, r)$ imply $\mu_\pi(z, y, r)$.
3. $\mu_\pi(x, y, r)$ and $s < r$ imply $\mu_\pi(x, y, s)$. $\hspace{2cm}$ (7)

These requirements seem to be intuitively clear. (1) demands that the predicate μ_π is an extension to the relation ing_π of the underlying system of mereology; (2) does express monotonicity of μ_π, and (3) assures the reading: "to degree at least r."

Condition 1 states that on U an exact decomposition into parts π is given and that μ_π extends this exact scheme into an approximate one. The exact scheme is a skeleton along which approximate reasoning is carried out. This interpretation opens up a venue for various applications, some of which will be discussed in the sequel. We now include a section on rough inclusions with methods for their definitions in information/decision systems as our principal aim.

Rough Inclusions in Information Systems

The idea of defining a rough inclusion by means of a metric, can be implemented with metrics on the universe U of an information/decision system $I = (U,A)$. Such metrics are defined on objects in U by means of object representations.

For each object $u \in U$, the *information set* of u is defined as $Inf(u) = \{(a, a(u)): a \in A\}$. Most commonly applied metrics (see, e.g., Wojna, 2005), include the reduced Hamming metric, the Euclidean metric, the Manhattan (city) metric, l^p metrics of Minkowski. Each of them induces a rough inclusion according to the previous discussion. We show here the rough inclusion induced by the reduced Hamming metric due to its importance in our granulation scheme.

The Rough Inclusion from the Hamming Metric

The reduced Hamming metric on U is defined as

$$h(u,v) = \frac{|\operatorname{Inf}(u) \cap \operatorname{Inf}(v)|}{|A|}$$

where $|X|$ denotes the number of elements in the set X. Thus, $h(u,v)$ is the fraction of attributes which do not discern between u and v. The induced by h rough inclusion μ_h is thus defined as follows,

$$\mu_h(u,v,r) \text{ iff } \frac{ind(u,v)}{|A|} \geq r, \tag{8}$$

where $ind(u,v)$ is $|\{a \in A: a(u)=a(v)\}|$.

Other tool for inducing rough inclusions is offered by *t-norms* (for this notion, see, e.g., Ha'jek, 1998; Polkowski, 2002). We here recall only that a t-norm $t:[0,1] \times [0,1] \to [0,1]$ is a mapping satisfying 1. $t(x,0)=0$. 2. $t(x,1)=x$. 3. t is increasing in each coordinate. 4. t is symmetric: $t(x,y)=t(y,x)$. 5. t is associative: $t(x,(t(y,z))=t(t(x,y),z)$.

Rough Inclusions from T-Norms

First, we refer to *Archimedean t-norms*, i.e. t-norms t with the property that $t(x,x) < x$ for each $x \in (0,1)$.

These t-norms are known to admit a representation $t(x,y)=g_t(f_t(x)+f_t(y))$, where the function $f_t:[0,1] \to [0,1]$ is continuous decreasing with $f_t(1)=0$, and g_t is the pseudo-inverse to f_t (see, e.g., Polkowski, 2002).

The induced by an Archimedean t-norm t rough inclusion μ_t is defined as follows:

$$\mu_t(u,v,r) \text{ iff } g_t(\frac{dis(u,v)}{|A|}) \geq r, \tag{9}$$

where $dis(u,v)=|\{a \in A: a(u) \neq a(v)\}|$. Clearly, $dis(u,v)=1- ind(u,v)$.

Taking, as exemplary Archimedean t-norm, the *Łukasiewicz t-norm*,

$$L(x,y)=\max\{0, x+y-1\} \tag{10}$$

for which $g_L(x)=1-x$, we obtain the rough inclusion μ_L as,

$$\mu_L(u,v,r) \text{ iff } \frac{ind(u,v)}{|A|} \geq r. \tag{11}$$

The formula (11) defines similarity of objects to degree at least r whenever the probability is r that a randomly chosen attribute takes the same value on u and v. In this case reasoning based on the rough inclusion is a probabilistic one. We observe that μ_L is the same as μ_h induced in (8) by the reduced Hamming distance.

It is well-known (see, e.g., Ha'jek, 1998) that up to an isomorphism, there are only two Archimedean t-norms. Except for the Łukasiewicz t-norm, there is the *product t-norm P(x,y)= x·y*. This fact restricts the number of induced rough inclusions to two. However, it is also known (see, e.g., Ha'jek, 1998) that each *continuous t-norm t* can be expressed as a combination of the two Archimedean t-norms, viz., as the set $I_t=\{x[0,1]:t(x,)=x\}$ is closed, its complement is the union of countably many disjoint open intervals (a_i, b_i) for $i=1, 2, \dots$. Setting on each interval (a_i, b_i) either L or P, would produce a rough inclusion.

We mention a recently studied by us family of rough inclusions induced by continuous t-norms by means of their residua. For a continuous t-norm $t(x,y)$, the *residuum* (see, e.g., Ha'jek, 1998), $x \Rightarrow_t y$ is defined as max$\{z: t(x,z) \leq y\}$.

Thus, the equivalence takes place: $t(x,z) \leq y$ if and only if $x \Rightarrow_t y \geq z$.

One can check easily that $\mu_{\Rightarrow_t}(x,y,r)$ if and only if $x \Rightarrow_t y \geq r$ is a rough inclusion on the interval [0,1]. It remains now to transfer this rough inclusion to the given information system $I=(U,A)$ with respect to a given part relation π on U.

Assume that a mapping $f:U \rightarrow [0,1]$ is given and that f has the property $uing_\pi v$ if and only if $f(u) \leq f(v)$. Thus, is a morphism from the relational system (U, ing_π) to the relational system $([0,1], \leq)$.

The rough inclusion μ_f on U is defined as follows:

$$\mu_f(u,v,r) \text{ iff } f(u) \Rightarrow_t f(v) \geq r. \tag{12}$$

It remains to indicate some plausible forms for f. One is related to *templates*, i.e., objects in a sense standard (e.g. classified with certainty). Choosing a template s, we define $f_s(u)$ as, e.g., *dis(s,u)* or *ind(s,u)* and we obtain a rough inclusion on U.

It can be proved (Polkowski, 2004), that rough inclusions induced by means of either Archimedean t-norms or from residua of continuous t-norms satisfy the *transitivity property*.

Transitivity Property: *From $\mu_t(u,v,r)$ and $\mu_t(v,w,s)$ it follows that $\mu_t(u,w,t(r,s))$.*

We have completed our survey of basic notions and we pass to the topic of granulation.

GRANULATION OF KNOWLEDGE

The issue of granulation of knowledge as a problem on its own, has been posed by Zadeh (1979, 2005). The issue of granulation has been a subject of intensive studies within rough set community, as witnessed by a number of papers (e.g., Lin, 1997, 2005; Polkowski, 1999a, 1999b; Polkowski & Skowron, 1997; Qing, 2006; Skowron, 2001, 2004; Yao, 2000, 2004, 2005).

Rough set context offers a natural venue for granulation, and indiscernibility classes were recognized as *elementary granules* whereas their unions serve as *granules of knowledge*; these granules and their direct generalizations to various similarity classes induced by general binary relations were subject to a research (see, e.g., Lin, 1997, 2005; Yao, 2000, 2004, 2005).

Granulation of knowledge by means of rough inclusions was studied in Polkowski and Skowron (1997, 1999a, 1999b) and in Polkowski (2003, 2004, 2005, 2006). Granulation is a strong tool in data mining and computational approach to perceptions—tasks performed very efficiently by a human brain (see Pal, 2004).

Granules from Rough Inclusions

The general scheme for inducing granules on the basis of a rough inclusion is as follows.

For an information system $I=(U,A)$ and a rough inclusion μ on U, for each object u and each real number r, we define the *granule* $g_{\mu}(u,r)$ *about u of the radius r, relative to* μ:

$$g_{\mu}(u,r) \text{ is } ClsF(u,r), \tag{13}$$

where the property $F(u,r)$ is satisfied with an object v if and only if $\mu(v,u,r)$ holds and Cls is the class operator of Mereology defined in (6).

It was shown in Polkowski (2004; Thm. 4), that in case of a transitive μ,

$$ving\ g_{\mu}(u,r)\ iff\ \mu(v,u,r) \tag{14}$$

Property (14) allows for representing the granule $g_{\mu}(u,r)$ as the list or a set of those objects v for which $\mu(v,u,r)$ holds.

For a given granulation radius r, and a rough inclusion μ, we form the collection $U_{r,\mu}^{G}$ of all granules of the radius r relative to μ.

We include an example of finding a granule. The information system for this example is given in Example 1 as Table 1.

Example 2. *For the granulation radius of* $r = 0.25$, *and the object o13, the granule* $g_{\mu_L}(o13,0.25)$ *about the object o13 of the radius* $r = 0.25$ *with respect to the rough inclusion* μ_L *defined in (11), consists of objects o13, o3, o5, o8, o11, o15, o17, o20, collected in Table 2.*

Table 2. Objects composing the granule g(o13,0.25)

obj	a1	a2	a3	a4	a5	a6	a7	a8	d
o3	5	124	74	0	0	34	0.22	38	1
o5	4	122	68	0	0	35	0.394	29	0
o8	4	146	78	0	0	38.5	0.52	67	1
o11	1	71	62	0	0	21.8	0.416	26	0
o13	2	108	64	0	0	30.8	0.158	21	0
o15	2	120	54	0	0	26.8	0.455	27	0
o17	0	99	0	0	0	25	0.253	22	0
o20	2	122	70	27	0	36.8	0.34	27	0

Granules defined from rough inclusions have some regular properties:

5.   If $ving_\pi u$ then $ving_\pi g_\mu(u,r)$.
6.   If $ving_\pi g_\mu(u,r)$ and $wing_\pi v$ then $wing_\pi g_\mu(u,r)$.
7.   If $\mu(v,u,r)$ then $ving_\pi g_\mu(u,r)$.

Properties 1-3 follow from properties in sect. 2.2 and the fact that ing_π is a partial order, in particular it is transitive.

Regarding granules as objects, calls for a procedure for evaluating rough inclusion degrees among granules. First, we have to define the notion of an ingredient among granules. We let, for granules g, h,

$$ging_\pi h \ iff \ zing_\pi g \ implies \ there \ is \ t \ such \ that$$
$$zing_\pi t, \ ting_\pi h \tag{15}$$

and, more generally, for granules g, h, and a rough inclusion μ,

$$\mu(g,h,r) \ \ iff \ for \ each \ wing_\pi g \ there \ is \ v$$
$$such \ that \ \mu_t(w,v,r), \ ving_\pi h \tag{16}$$

Then: μ *is a rough inclusion on granules*. This procedure may be iterated to granules of granules, and so on. Let us note that due to our use of class operator (being, for our set theoretical representation of granules, the union of sets operator), we always remain on the level of collections of objects despite forming higher level granules.

This concludes our discussion of granulation on the theoretical level and we proceed with some applications. These applications are essentially related to the following topics of interest in the realm of natural intelligence.

8.   Reasoning about uncertain cases
9.   Synthesis of knowledge from distributed sources (fusion of knowledge)
10.   Classification on the basis of perceived features

In the following sections, we address these topics.

Granular RM-Logics

Granular rm (rough mereological)-logics are constructed as many-valued intensional logics (Polkowski, 2005). The symbol *In* denotes the intension of a formula; that is, speaking informally the mapping induced by this formula from possible worlds into the set of logical values. In our approach, possible worlds are granules of knowledge.

Given a granule g, we denote with the symbol $In_g^\vee(\phi)$ the extension of *In* at the granule g valued at a formula ϕ, i.e., $In_g^\vee(\phi) = In(g,\phi)$.

We adopt the following interpretation of logical connectives N of negation and C of implication, where $[[.]]$ is the meaning of a formula, defined as the set of objects satisfying the formula:

$$[[Np]]=U-[[p]]$$ (17)

and,

$$[[Cpq]] = (U - [[p]]) \cup [[q]]$$ (18)

This interpretation conforms with the interpretation of formulae of description logic (1).

Rough Inclusions on Sets

We should define specimens of regular rough inclusions μ on $(2^U)^2 \times [0,1]$, where 2^U is the powerset of U. Following our discussion for the case of information systems, we define the value of μ_t where t is an Archimedean t-norm, and X, Y are sets of objects in U, the universe of an information system $I = (U,A)$, as:

$$\mu_t(X,Y,r) \; iff \; g_t(\frac{|X-Y|}{|A|}) \ge r.$$ (19)

In particular, with the Łukasiewicz t-norm, (19) becomes

$$\mu_L(X,Y,r) \; iff \; 1-(\frac{|X-Y|}{|A|}) \ge r,$$ (20)

which may be rewritten in a well-known form:

$$\mu_L(X,Y,r) \; iff \; (\frac{|X \cap Y|}{|A|}) \ge r$$ (21)

We now define the value $In_g^{\vee}(\phi)$ of the extension of In relative to μ_t at g, ϕ as follows,

$$In_g^{\vee}(\phi) \ge r \; iff \; \mu_t(g, [[\phi]], r)$$ (22)

where $[[\phi]]$ is the meaning of ϕ. The value $In_g^{\vee}(\phi)$ can be interpreted as the degree of truth of the statement ϕ with respect to the granule g relative to the chosen rough inclusion.

As a plausible application of rm-logics, we present an abstract form of networked granular computing. An application presented here concerns a case of *fusion of knowledge* which is yet another important aspect of natural intelligence, witnessed, for example, in intelligent robotics, where sensor fusion is a basic issue.

Networks of Granular Agents

Synthesis of knowledge from various sources is one of the main tasks of natural intelligence and it is performed automatically by the human brain (see, e.g., Shastri & Wendelken, 1999). We address this issue from rm-logical point od view.

A granular agent *ag* in its simplest form is a tuple:

$$ag^* = (U_{ag}, A_{ag}, \mu_{ag}, Pred_{ag}, UncProp_{ag}, GSynt_{ag}, LSynt_{ag}),$$

where $(U_{ag}, A_{ag}) = I_{ag}$ is an information system of the agent *ag*. μ_{ag} is a rough inclusion induced from I_{ag} and $Pred_{ag}$ is a set of first-order predicates interpreted in U_{ag}.

$UncProp_{ag}$ is the function that describes how uncertainty measured by rough inclusions at agents connected to *ag* propagates to *ag*. The operator $GSynt_{ag}$, the *granular synthesizer* at *ag*, takes granules sent to the agent from agents connected to it, and makes those granules into a granule at *ag*.

Similarly, $LSynt_{ag}$, the *logical synthesizer* at *ag*, takes formulas sent to the agent *ag* by its connecting neighbors. it makes these formulas into a formula describing objects at *ag*.

A *network of granular agents* is a directed acyclic graph $N=(Ag,C)$, where *Ag* is its set of vertices (i.e., granular agents). *C* is the set of edges (i.e., connections among agents), along with subsets *In, Out* $\subset Ag$ of, respectively, input and output agents. A discussion of such a network on a less abstract level may be found in Polkowski (2004) and in Pal (2004).

Example 3. *This example shows workings of an elementary network of agents. We consider an agent* $ag \in Ag$ *and—for simplicity reasons—we assume that ag has two incoming connections from agents* ag_1, ag_2. *The number of outgoing connections is of no importance as ag sends along each of them the same information.*

We assume that each agent is applying the rough inclusion μ_L induced by the Łukasiewicz t-norm *L*, see (11), in its granulation procedure. Each agent is applying the rough inclusion on sets of the form (21) in evaluations related to extensions of formulae intensions.

Clearly, there exists a fusion operator $\circ_{ag}$ which assembles from objects $x \in U_{ag_1}$, U_{ag_2} the object $\circ_{ag}(x, y) \in U_{ag}$.

We assume that $\circ_{ag} = id_{ag_1} \times id_{ag_2}$, i.e., $\circ_{ag}(x, y) = (x, y)$.

Similarly, we assume that the set of attributes at *ag* is given as $A_{ag} = A_{ag_1} \times A_{ag_2}$, i.e., attributes in A_{ag} are pairs (a_1, a_2) with $a_i \in A_{ag_i}$ $(i=1, 2)$. The value of this attribute is defined as $(a_1, a_2)(x, y)= (a_1(x), a_2(y))$.

It follows that the condition holds

$$\circ_{ag}(x, y)ind(A_{ag}) \circ_{ag}(x', y') \text{ iff } x ind(A_{ag_1})x' \text{ and } y ind(A_{ag_2})y'.$$

Concerning the function $Uncprop_{ag}$, we consider objects x, x', y, y'. Clearly, for the set

$$DIS_{ag}(u,v) = \{a \in A_{ag} : a(u) \neq a(v)\}$$

we have,

$$DIS_{ag}(\circ_{ag}(x, y), \circ_{ag}(x', y')) \subseteq DIS_{ag_1}(x, x') \times A_{ag_2} \cup A_{ag_1} \times DIS_{ag_1}(y, y'), \tag{23}$$

and hence

$$|DIS_{ag}(\circ_{ag}(x, y), \circ_{ag}(x', y'))| \leq |DIS_{ag_1}(x, x') \times A_{ag_2}| + |A_{ag_1} \times DIS_{ag_1}(y, y')|. \tag{24}$$

By (24),

$$\mu_{ag}(\circ_{ag}(x,y), \circ_{ag}(x',y'), r) \ iff$$

$$1 - \frac{|DIS_{ag}(\circ_{ag}(x,y), \circ_{ag}(x',y'))|}{|A_{ag_1}| \cdot |A_{ag2}|} \ge r,$$

$$1 - \frac{|DIS_{ag_1}(x,x') \cdot |A_{ag_2}| + |A_{ag_1}| \cdot |DIS_{ag_2}(y,y')|}{|A_{ag_1}| \cdot |A_{ag_2}|} =$$

$$1 - \frac{DIS_{ag_1}(x,x')}{|A_{ag_1}|} + 1 - \frac{DIS_{ag_2}(y,y')}{|A_{ag_2}|} - 1 \ge r.$$

It follows that: if $\mu_{ag_1}(x,x',r)$, $\mu_{ag_2}(y,y',s)$ then $\mu_{ag}(\circ_{ag}(x,y), \circ_{ag}(x',y'), L(r,s))$.

Hence $UncProp_{ag} = L$, the Łukasiewicz t-norm. In consequence, the granule synthesizer $GSynt_{ag}$ can be defined in our example as follows.

$$GSynt_{ag}(g_{ag_1}(x,r), g_{ag_2}(y,s)) = g_{ag}(\circ_{ag}(x,y), L(r,s)). \tag{25}$$

The definition of logic synthesizer follows directly from our assumptions:

$$LSynt_{ag}(\phi_1, \phi_2) = \phi_1 \wedge \phi_2. \tag{26}$$

Finally, we consider extensions of our logical operators of intensional logic. We have for the extension

$$In^{\vee}_{GSynt(g1,g_2)} LSynt_{ag}(\phi_1, \phi_2) :$$

$$In^{\vee}_{GSynt(g1,g_2)} LSynt_{ag}(\phi_1, \phi_2) = In^{\vee}_{g_1}(\phi_1) \cdot In^{\vee}_{g_2}(\phi_2), \tag{27}$$

which follows directly from (22), (25), (26). Thus, in our case, each agent works according to regular t-norms: the Łukasiewicz t-norm L on the level of rough inclusions and uncertainty propagation and the product t-norm P on the level of extensions of logical intensions.

This simple example can be applied in more complex cases with obviously a more complicated analysis.

A Granular Approach to Data Classification

The idea of a granular decision system was posed in (Polkowski, 2005). For a given information system $I=(U,A)$, a rough inclusion μ and $r \in [0,1]$, the new universe $U^G_{r,\mu}$ is given of all μ-induced granules of the radius r. We apply a strategy G to choose a covering $Cov^G_{r,\mu}$ of the universe U by granules from $U^G_{r,\mu}$.

We apply a strategy S in order to assign the value $a^*(g)$ of each attribute $a \in A$ to each granule $g \in Cov^G_{r,\mu}$: $a^*(g) = S(\{a(u):u \in g\})$. The granular counterpart to the information system I is the quadruple $I^G_{r,\mu} = U^G_{r,\mu}, S, G, \{a^*:a \in A\})$.

Analogously, we define granular counterparts to decision systems by adding the factored decision d^*.

The heuristic principle that *objects, similar with respect to conditional attributes in the set A, should also reveal similar (i.e., close) decision values, and therefore, granular counterparts to decision systems should lead to classifiers satisfactorily close in quality to those induced from original decision systems*, was stated in Polkowski (2005) and borne out by simple hand examples. This hypothesis has been tested currently with real data sets. We include some results that bear out our hypothesis. More results are given in Polkowski and Artiemjew (2007).

Classification of cases is also one of the main tasks of Natural Intelligence and the human brain, see, e.g. (Poldrack et al., 2001). We address it here with our granulation mechanism in view.

For a decision system *D=(U,A,d)*, classifiers are sets of rules (3). Induction of rules was a subject of research in rough set theory since its beginning. In most general terms, building a classifier consists in searching in the pool of descriptors for their conjuncts that describe sufficiently well decision classes. As distinguished in (Stefanowski, 1998), there are three main kinds of classifiers searched for: *minimal*, i.e., consisting of minimum possible number of rules describing decision classes in the universe, *exhaustive* (i.e., consisting of all possible rules), *satisfactory* (i.e., containing rules tailored to a specific use). In our exemplary classification task, the algorithm applied is the exhaustive algorithm supplied with the system RSES (Skowron et al., 1994).

Classifiers are evaluated globally with respect to their ability to properly classify objects, usually by *error* which is the ratio of the number of correctly classified objects to the number of test objects, *total accuracy* being the ratio of the number of correctly classified cases to the number of recognized cases, and *total coverage* (i.e, the ratio of the number of recognized test cases to the number of test cases).

An important class of methods for classifier induction are those based on similarity or analogy reasoning; most generally, this method of reasoning assigns to an object *u* the value of an attribute *a* from the knowledge of values of *a* on a set *N(u)* of objects whose elements are selected on the basis of a similarity relation, usually but not always based on an appropriate metric.

A study of algorithms based on similarity relations is (Nguyen, 2000). The main tool in inducing similarity relations are *generalized templates* (i.e., propositional formulas built from *generalized descriptors* of the form $(a \in W_a)$ where W_a is a subset of the value set V_a of *a*). In establishing similarity metrics like the Manhattan, Hamming, Euclidean, are also used.

A realization of analogy-based reasoning idea is the *k-nearest neighbors* (k-nn) method in which for a fixed number *k*, values of *a* at *k* nearest to *u* objects in the training set are the basis for finding the value of *a* at *u*. Finding nearest objects is based on some similarity measure among objects that in practice is a metric. Metrics to this end are built on the two basic metrics: the Manhattan metric for numerical values and the Hamming metric for nominal values (see, e.g., Wojna, 2005).

Our approach based on granulation can be also placed in similarity based reasoning as rough inclusions are measures of similarity degree among objects. We assume a given decision system *D=(U,A,d)*.

For each $u \in U$, we select a set *N(u)* of objects and assign a value of decision *d(u)* on the basis of values of *d(v)* for $v \in N(u)$. Our sets *N(u)* are formed as granules of the form $g_\mu(u, r)$ with μ, *r* fixed. For each such granule *g*, and each attribute $u \in A \cup \{d\}$, the factored value $a^*(g)$ is defined as *S*.

Contrary to the practice of using a metric that combines values of all attributes, in our approach, attributes are involved independently; similarity is driven by the rough inclusion μ. As a result, each granule g does produce a new object g^*, with attribute values $a(g^*) = a^*(g)$ for each a. The object g^* is possibly not in the data set universe U.

From the set $U^G_{r,\mu}$ of all granules of the form $g_\mu(u, r)$, by means of a strategy G, we choose a covering $Cov^G_{r,\mu}$ of the universe U.

Thus, a decision system $D^* = (\{g^*:g \in Cov^G_{r,\mu}\}, A^*, d^*)$ is formed, called the *granular counterpart relative to strategies S,G* to the decision system *(U,A)*. This new system is substantially smaller in size for intermediate values of r, hence, classifiers induced from it have correspondingly smaller number of rules. Clearly, in case *r=1.0*, the granular system does coincide with the original system, as granules are in this case indiscernibility classes.

Example 4. *We produce a representation of an object representing the granule $g_{\mu_L}(o13, 0.25)$ shown in Table 2 of Example 2. The majority voting strategy S returns the decision value 0 for the new object $g_{\mu_L}(o13, 0.25)^*$. Values of other attributes are determined by this strategy in the same way. The new object representing the granule $g_{\mu_L}(o13, 0.25)^*$ may be, for example, that in Table 3.*

We report here experiments with the data set *Credit card application approval data set (Australian credit)* (UCI repository).

In rough set literature there are results of tests with other algorithms on Australian credit data set. We recall best of them in Table 4 and we give also best granular cases obtained in our research.

Table 3. New object determined by majority voting which represents the granule g(o13,0.25)

new.obj.	a1	a2	a3	a4	a5	a6	a7	a8	d
$g(o13,0.25)^*$	2	122	64	0	0	26.8	0.22	27	0

Table 4. Best results for Australian credit by some rough set based algorithms

work	method	accuracy	coverage
(Bazan, 1998)	SNAPM(0.9)	0.87	-
(Nguyen S.H.,2000)	Simple templates	0.929	0.623
(Nguyen S.H., 2000)	General templates	0.886	0.905
(Nguyen S.H.,2000)	Closest simple templates	0.821	1.0
(Nguyen S.H., 2000)	Closest general templates	0.855	1.0
(Nguyen S.H., 2000)	Tolerance simple templates	0.842	1.0
(Nguyen S.H.,2000)	Tolerance general templates	0.875	1.0
(Wroblewski, 2000)	Adaptive classifier	0.863	-
(Polkowski&Artiemjew, 2007)	Granular,r=0.64	0.867	1.0
(Polkowski&Artiemjew, 2007)	Granular,r=0.71	0.875	1.0
(Polkowski&Artiemjew, 2007)	Granular,concept dependent,r=0.78	0.997	0.9995

Table 4 does witness that granulation of knowledge applied in Polkowski and Artiemjew (2007) as a new idea in data classification can lead to better results than the analysis based on individual objects. This confirms the validity of granular approach and reflects the fact that granularity is so important in Natural Reasoning.

Granules in this example have been computed with respect to the rough inclusion μ_L. For any granule g and any attribute a, the reduced attribute value $a^*(g)$ at the granule g has been estimated by means of the majority voting strategy and ties have been resolved at random.

A *concept* in the narrow sense is a decision/classification class. Granulation in this sense consists in computing granules for objects in the universe U and for all distinct granulation radii as previously, with the only restriction that given any object $u \in U$ and $r \in [0,1]$, the new concept dependent granule $g^{cd}(u,r)$ is computed with taking into account only objects $v \in U$ with $d(v)=d(u)$, i.e., $g^{cd}(u,r)= g(u,r) \cap \{v \in U : d(v)= d(u)\}$. This method increases the number of granules in coverings but it is also expected to increase quality of classification, as expressed by accuracy and coverage. Our results in Table 4 bear out this anticipation.

SUMMARY AND CONCLUSION

We have presented the approach to granulation of knowledge based on ideas of rough mereology. Granules obtained in this way are exact sets in the sense of rough set theory so they are described with certainty with respect to knowledge encoded in data set. On the basis of granules, granular computing has been developed: granular logics and their applications to reasoning in many agent and distributed systems. The application of granulation to the task of classification has also been addressed: granular data sets have been introduced and classification of data on the basis of granulated data has been discussed. Results included in this work witness high efficiency of this approach.

ACKNOWLEDGMENT

The authors would like to thank the reviewers of this article for their careful work and many suggestions which improved the exposition. This research was supported by a grant from the Ministry of Higher Education of the Republic of Poland obtained through the Polish-Japanese Institute of Information Technology.

REFERENCES

Bazan, J. G. (1998). A comparison of dynamic and non-dynamic rough set methods for extracting laws from decision tables. In L. Polkowski & A. Skowron (Eds.), *Rough sets in knowledge discovery 1* (pp. 321-365). Heidelberg, Germany: Physica-Verlag.

Bazan, J. G., Nguyen, H. S., Nguyen, S. H., Synak, P., & Wróblewski, J.(2000). Rough set algorithms in classification problems. In L. Polkowski, S. Tsumoto, & T. Y. Lin (Eds.), *Rough set methods and applications* (pp. 49-88). Heidelberg, Germany: Physica-Verlag.

Chan, C., Kinsner, W., Wang, Y., & Miller, M. (Eds.). (2004, August). *Proceedings of the Third IEEE International Conference on Cognitive Informatics (ICCI'04)*. Los Alamitos, CA: IEEE Computer Society Press.

Ha'jek, P. (1998). *Metamathematics of fuzzy logic*. Dordrecht, Germany: Kluwer.

Kinsner, W., Zhang, D., Wang, Y., & Tsai, J. (Eds.). (2005, August). *Proceedings of the Fourth IEEE International Conference on Cognitive Informatics (ICCI'05)*. Los Alamitos, CA: IEEE Computer Society Press.

Kloesgen, W., & Żytkow, J. (Eds.). (2002). *Handbook of data mining and knowledge discovery*. Oxford, England: Oxford University Press.

Leśniewski, S. (1916). *Podstawy ogólnej teoryi mnogosci* [On the foundations of set theory]. Moscow: The Polish Scientific Circle.

Lin, T. Y. (1997). From rough sets and neighborhood systems to information granulation and computing with words. In *Proceedings of the European Congress on Intelligent Techniques and Soft Computing* (pp. 1602-1606).

Lin, T .Y. (2005). Granular computing: Examples, intuitions, and modeling. In *Proceedings of IEEE 2006 Conference on Granular Computing GrC06* (pp. 40-44).

Nguyen, S. H. (2000). Regularity analysis and its applications in data mining. In L. Polkowski, S. Tsumoto, & T. Y. Lin (Eds.), *Rough set methods and applications* (pp. 289-378). Heidelberg, Germany: Physica-Verlag.

Pal, S. K. (2004). Soft data mining, computational theory of perception and rough-fuzzy approach. *Information Sciences, 163*(1/3), 5-12.

Pal, S. K., Polkowski, L., & Skowron, A. (Eds.). (2004). *Rough-neural computing: Techniques for computing with words*. Berlin, Germany: Springer Verlag.

Patel, D., Patel, S., & Wang, Y. (Eds.). (2003, August). In *Proceedings of the Second IEEE International Conference on Cognitive Informatics (ICCI'03*. Los Alamitos, CA: IEEE Computer Society Press.

Pawlak, Z. (1982). Rough sets. *International Journal of Computer and Information Sciences, 11*, 341-356.

Pawlak, Z. (1991). *Rough sets: Theoretical aspects of reasoning about data*. Dordrecht, Germany: Kluwer.

Pawlak, Z., & Skowron, A. (1994). Rough membership functions. In R. R. Yager, M. Fedrizzi, & J. Kasprzyk (Eds.), *Advances in the Dempster-Shafer theory of evidence* (pp. 251-271). New York: Wiley.

Poldrack, R. A., et al. (2001, November 29). Interactive memory systems in the human brain. *Nature*, 546-50.

Polkowski, L. (2002). *Rough sets. Mathematical foundations*. Heidelberg, Germany: Physica-Verlag.

Polkowski, L. (2003). A rough set paradigm for unifying rough set theory and fuzzy set theory (a plenary talk). In *Proceedings RSFDGrC03*, Chongqing, China (LNAI 2639, pp. 70-78).

Polkowski, L. (2004a). A note on 3-valued rough logic accepting decision rules. *Fundamenta Informaticae, 61,* 37-45.

Polkowski, L. (2004b). A rough-neural computation model based on rough mereology. In Pal et al. (Eds.), (pp. 85-108).

Polkowski, L. (2004c). Toward rough set foundations. Mereological approach (a plenary talk). In *Proceedings of RSCTC04,* Uppsala, Sweden (LNAI 3066, pp. 8-25). Berlin, Germany: Springer Verlag.

Polkowski, L. (2005a). Formal granular calculi based on rough inclusions (a feature talk). In *Proceedings of the IEEE 2005 Conference on Granular Computing (GrC05)* (pp. 57-62).

Polkowski, L. (2005b). Rough-fuzzy-neurocomputing based on rough mereological calculus of granules. *International Journal of Hybrid Intelligent Systems, 2,* 91-108.

Polkowski, L. (2006). A model of granular computing with applications (a feature talk). In *Proceedings of IEEE 2006 Conference on Granular Computing (GrC06)* (pp. 9-16).

Polkowski, L. (2007). Granulation of knowledge in decision systems: The approach based on rough inclusions. The method and its applications (a plenary talk). In *Proceedings of RSEISP 07,* Warsaw, Poland (LNAI 4585). Berlin, Germany: Springer Verlag.

Polkowski, L., & Artiemjew, P. (2007a). On granular rough computing: Factoring classifiers through granulated structures. In *Proceedings of RSEISP07* (LNAI 4585, pp. 280-289). Berlin, Germany: Springer Verlag.

Polkowski, L., & Artiemjew, P. (2007b). On granular rough computing with missing values. In *Proceedings of RSEISP07* (LNAI 4585, pp. 271-279). Berlin, Germany: Springer Verlag.

Polkowski, L., & Semeniuk-Polkowska, M. (2005). On rough set logics based on similarity relations. *Fundamenta Informaticae, 64,* 379-390.

Polkowski, L., & Skowron, A. (1997). Rough mereology: A new paradigm for approximate reasoning. *International Journal of Approximate Reasoning, 15*(4), 333-365.

Polkowski, L., & Skowron, A. (2001). Rough mereological calculi of granules: A rough set approach to computation. *Computational Intelligence: An International Journal, 17*(3), 472-492.

Polkowski, L., & Skowron, A. (1999a). Grammar systems for distributed synthesis of approximate solutions extracted from experience. In Gh. Paun & A. Salomaa (Eds.), *Grammatical models of multi-agent systems* (pp. , 316-333). Amsterdam: Gordon & Breach.

Polkowski, L., & Skowron, A. (1999b). Towards an adaptive calculus of granules. In L. A. Zadeh & J. Kacprzyk (Eds.), *Computing with words in information/intelligent systems,1,* (pp. 201-228). Heidelberg, Germany: Physica-Verlag.

Qing, L., & Hui, S. (2006). Theoretical study of granular computing. In *Proceedings of the RSKT06,* Chongqing, China (LNAI 4062, pp. 92-102). Berlin, Germany: Springer Verlag.

Shastri, L., & Wendelken, C. (1999). Knowledge fusion in the large—Taking cues from the brain. In *Proceedings of FUSION'99.*

Skowron, A., et al. (1994). RSES: A system for data analysis. Retrieved from www.logic.mimuw.edu. pl/ rses/

Skowron, A., & Stepaniuk, J. (2001). Information granules: Towards foundations of granular computing. *International Journal of Intelligent Systems, 16,* 57-85.

Skowron, A., & Stepaniuk, J. (2004). Information granules and rough-neural computing. In S. K. Pal et al. (Eds.), (pp. 43-84).

Stefanowski, J. (1998). On rough set based approaches to induction of decision rules. In L. Polkowski & A. Skowron (Eds.), *Rough sets in knowledge discovery 1,* (pp. 500-529). Heidelberg, Germany: Physica-Verlag.

Wang, Y. (2007, January-March). The theoretical framework of cognitive informatics. *International Journal of Cognitive Informatics and Natural Intelligence, 1*(1), 1-27.

Wang Y., Johnston, R. H., & Smith, M. R. (Eds.). (2002, August). *Proceedings of the First IEEE International Conference on Cognitive Informatics (ICCI'02),* Calgary, Canada. Los Alamitos, CA: IEEE Computer Society Press.

Wojna, A. (2005). Analogy-based reasoning in classifier construction. *Transactions on Rough Sets IV* (LNCS 3700, pp. 277-374). Berlin, Germany: Springer Verlag.

Wroblewski, J. (2000). Adaptive aspects of combining approximation space. In S. K. Pal et al. (Eds.), (2004) (pp. 139-156).

Yao, Y. Y. (2000). Granular computing: Basic issues and possible solutions. In *Proceedings of the Fifth Joint Conference Information Sciences I,* (pp. 186-189). Atlantic, NJ: Assoc. Intell. Machinery.

Yao, Y. Y. (2004). Information granulation and approximation in a decision-theoretic model of rough sets. In S. K. Pal et al. (Eds.), (2004), (pp. 491-516).

Yao, Y. Y. (2005). Perspectives of granular computing. In *Proceedings of the IEEE 2005 Conference on Granular Computing (GrC05)* (pp. 85-90).

Yao, Y. Y., Shi, Z., Wang, Y., & Kinsner, W. (Eds.). (2006, July). *Proceedings of the Fifth IEEE International Conference on Cognitive Informatics (ICCI'06),* Beijing, China. Los Alamitos CA: IEEE Computer Society Press.

Zadeh, L. A. (1979). Fuzzy sets and information granularity. In M. Gupta, R. Ragade, & R. Yager (Eds.), *Advances in fuzzy set theory and applications* (pp. 3-18). Amsterdam: NorthHolland.

Zadeh, L. A. (2005). Graduation and granulation are keys to computation with information described in natural language. In *Proceedings of the IEEE 2005 Conference on Granular Computing (GrC05)* (p. 30).

This work was previously published in the International Journal of Cognitive Informatics and Natural Intelligence, Vol. 2, Issue 2, edited by Y. Wang, pp. 80-94, copyright 2008 by IGI Publishing (an imprint of IGI Global).

Chapter 19
Robust Independent Component Analysis for Cognitive Informatics

N. Gadhok
University of Manitoba, Canada

W. Kinsner
University of Manitoba, Canada

ABSTRACT

This article evaluates the outlier sensitivity of five independent component analysis (ICA) algorithms (FastICA, Extended Infomax, JADE, Radical, and β-divergence) using (a) the Amari separation performance index, (b) the optimum angle of rotation error, and (c) the contrast function difference in an outlier-contaminated mixture simulation. The Amari separation performance index has revealed a strong sensitivity of JADE and FastICA (using third- and fourth-order nonlinearities) to outliers. However, the two contrast measures demonstrated conclusively that β-divergence is the least outlier-sensitive algorithm, followed by Radical, FastICA (exponential and hyperbolic-tangent nonlinearities), Extended Infomax, JADE, and FastICA (third- and fourth-order nonlinearities) in an outlier-contaminated mixture of two uniformly distributed signals. The novelty of this article is the development of an unbiased optimization-landscape environment for assessing outlier sensitivity, as well as the optimum angle of rotation error and the contrast function difference as promising new measures for assessing the outlier sensitivity of ICA algorithms.

INTRODUCTION

Functional magnetic resonance imaging (fMRI) and electroencephalogram (EEG) signals are two standard tools for investigating brain activity and, in turn, human cognition, as studied in cognitive informatics

(Zhang, Wang, & Kinsner, 2007) and other disciplines. Of particular interest are the location of various activities within the brain and the dynamics of those functional regions as observed through the EEG signal. While fMRI shows the location of the active brain regions reasonably well, the recorded temporal EEG signal may not be a good indicator of the dynamics because it does not originate from the brain alone, but is a mixture of the EEG itself with the electrocardiogram (ECG) representing heart activity and the electromyogram (EMG) caused by the activity of the muscular system. In addition, the EEG and EMG signals have non-Gaussian probability distribution functions (pdfs) and broadband coloured noise-like frequency spectra. Consequently, to reduce the impact of such unwanted signals, demixing of the recorded EEG signal should be used. A technique called independent component analysis (ICA) can demix the recordings in order to analyze them as close to their pure forms as possible (Gadhok, 2006; Hyvärinen, Karhunen, & Oja, 2001; Makeig et al., 2002; McKeown et al., 1998).

However, various ICA algorithm implementations are sensitive to outliers (i.e., the extreme values that do not comply with the pdf of the signal) because the implementations are based on high-order statistics that include moments higher than two. In fact, contamination of biomedical recordings by outliers is an unavoidable aspect of signal processing. For example, Hampel, Ronchetti, Rousseeuw, and Stahel (1986) provided a real-world situation related to EEG data obtained by a fully automatic recorder. The recorder equipment was working properly and the histogram was adequate except for some seemingly unimportant jitter of the plotter in the tails in the pdf. Yet, the third and fourth moments were far too large. A search revealed that there was a spike of about two dozen out of a quarter million data points when the equipment was turned on, and these few points caused the high moments and the jitter in the plot. Thus, the impact of outliers on the signal separation performance of an ICA algorithm is an important characteristic in assessing the algorithm's utility for cognitive informatics.

Blind source separation (BSS) is defined as the problem of demixing an additive combination of statistically independent signals based on observations of those mixtures only. ICA is a statistical method for extracting sources from their mixtures without the knowledge of the sources themselves. It uses the information contained in the higher order statistics of the observed mixtures, under the assumption of non-Gaussian distributed sources, to separate the signals into their original sources up to an arbitrary scale and permutation (Hyvärinen et al., 2001).

The objective of this article is to study the outlier sensitivity of ICA algorithms in an unbiased optimization-landscape environment by measuring their separation performance and changes to their respective contrast functions (ICA estimators) in an outlier-contaminated simulation. This is a novel approach as most ICA outlier robustness research has been concerned with either the boundedness of the influence function (IF) of an ICA estimator, or the separation performance in a biased optimization-landscape environment with outlier-contaminated simulations (Hampel et al., 1986; Hyvärinen et al., 2001; Minami & Eguchi, 2003).

Unfortunately, the boundedness of the IF does not give a direct answer to the question of how sensitive the separation performance is to outliers, and in simulations the potential suboptimal searches of the ICA optimization landscape (by techniques such as a quasi-Newton method, or rotation or exhaustive search, depending on the algorithm, along with unfair simulation conditions) lead to inconsistent results for the comparison of ICA estimators. The aim of this article is to go halfway between the theoretical and empirical measurements by evaluating the outlier sensitivity through (a) the Amari separation performance index (API), (b) the optimum angle of rotation error, and (c) the contrast function difference in an outlier-contaminated simulation with fair optimization conditions for the algorithms. Computational demands are not considered because they do not impact the rotation sensitivity analysis.

The data set studied is a mixture of two uniform distributions due to its ability to reveal outlier sensitivities. Outliers are selected based on the number of standard deviations, σ, from the mean of the distribution. Thus, when an outlier distributional model is applied, the risks can be assessed. Finally, the article studies the FastICA (fast fixed-point ICA), Extended Infomax, JADE (joint approximate diagonalization of eigenmatrices), Radical (robust, accurate, direct, independent component analysis algorithm), and β-divergence ICA algorithms' contrast functions due to their popularity in research and their claimed outlier robustness in literature (Cardoso, 1999; Hyvärinen et al., 2001; Learned-Miller & Fisher, 2003; Lee, Girolami, & Sejnowski, 1999; Mihoko & Eguchi, 2002).

INDEPENDENT COMPONENT ANALYSIS

ICA is a statistical method for estimating a set of unknown sources only from the observations of their mixtures. Figure 1 shows a linear ICA model with n unknown linearly mixed sources $\mathbf{s}$, and n output observations $\mathbf{x}$. These observations are used to estimate adaptively the demixing matrix $\mathbf{W}$ such that the estimates $\mathbf{y}$ are statistically independent.

Let $\mathbf{s}$ be a random vector of n unknown, mutually independent non-Gaussian source signals, and $\mathbf{A}$ be an unknown nonsingular mixing matrix of size n. We observe a random vector $\mathbf{x}$ of size n mixed signals, expressed as

$$\mathbf{x} = \mathbf{As} \tag{1}$$

The ICA algorithm attempts to find the demixing matrix $\mathbf{W}$ such that $\mathbf{y} = \mathbf{Wx}$. Under ideal circumstances,

$$\mathbf{y} = \mathbf{Wx} = \mathbf{\Lambda\Pi s} \tag{2}$$

where $\mathbf{\Lambda}$ is a diagonal scaling matrix and $\mathbf{\Pi}$ is a permutation matrix (Hyvärinen et al., 2001). In this article, the linear ICA model is employed. It assumes that (a) the number of sources equals the number of sensors, (b) mixing is linear, and (c) at most, one source, s_i, has a Gaussian distribution.

The demixing matrix $\mathbf{W}$ is estimated by means of a contrast function (e.g., based on the source separation principle of minimizing the mutual information between the joint density of the source estimate and the product of its marginals by a Kullback-Leibler divergence) and an optimization technique (e.g., gradient descent). To determine $\mathbf{W}$, a contrast function $C(\mathbf{y}, \mathbf{W})$ is selected such that the components

Figure 1. Linear ICA model

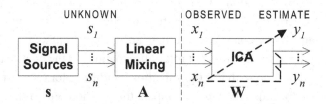

of **y** become statistically independent at the minimization or maximization of its expectation. Thus, of interest is the sensitivity to outliers of these contrast functions as arising from the FastICA, Extended Infomax, JADE, Radical, and β-divergence algorithms. In order to understand the differences between these techniques, a brief review of the theory, implementation, and outlier robustness of each is provided next.

FastICA

Fast fixed-point ICA, originally developed by Hyvärinen to make the neural network optimization of a kurtosis-based ICA contrast faster, uses a quasi-Newton method to maximize an approximation of negentropy (a non-Gaussianity measure) in order to estimate independent sources (Hyvärinen et al., 2001; Hyvärinen & Oja, 1997). The weight vector **w** (i.e., a row of **W**) is selected by a quasi-Newton method such that the negentropy of $\mathbf{w}^T\mathbf{x}$ is maximized (under the constraint that the $L2$-norm of **w**, $\|\mathbf{w}\|_2$ = 1, and the rows of **W** are orthogonal). This follows from the additive central limit theorem stating that an additive mixture of non-Gaussian distributions moves closer to Gaussian; thus, the **w** that creates the least-Gaussian distribution must produce an independent source. For tractability, Hyvärinen devised an approximation to negentropy based on nonpolynomial moments. Consequently, this approximation requires the selection of an appropriate nonpolynomial function (Hyvärinen et al.).

Extended Infomax

The Extended Infomax algorithm uses a natural gradient to maximize log likelihood between the source density estimate and the hypothesized source density to estimate the independent sources. The extended nature of this algorithm is due in part to the selection of the hypothesized source density based on an estimate of the super- and sub-Gaussianity of the source in order to separate super- and sub-Gaussian sources, as opposed to only super-Gaussian sources in the original Infomax algorithm (Bell & Sejnowski, 1995). The source separation principle arose from the field of neural networks and the goal of maximizing the information transmission (Infomax) between the inputs and outputs of a neural network. Infomax is achieved by maximizing the output Shannon entropy of a nonlinear transformation of the inputs, and occurs when the nonlinear transfer is equal to the cumulative density function of the input. The by-product is the minimization of the redundancy between the output units of the neural network, thus creating independent sources. Infomax has been proven to be equivalent to maximum-likelihood contrast, which is currently employed by the Extended Infomax algorithm (Lee et al., 1999).

JADE

Joint approximate diagonalization of eigenmatrices uses the algebraic structure of the fourth-order cumulant tensor of whitened observations (the separation principle being that the columns of **A** are the eigenvectors of transformed cumulant matrices) to devise a contrast that requires the minimization of the off-diagonal components of a maximal set of cumulant matrices by orthogonal transformations to estimate the demixing matrix. The minimization is achieved by a joint approximate diagonalization (Jacobi optimization), which (in the case of two sources) optimizes by a plane rotation. However, the optimization becomes unwieldy as the number of sources increases (Cardoso, 1999).

Radical

The robust, accurate, direct, independent component analysis algorithm uses an altered *m*-spacings estimate of entropy by Vasicek and an exhaustive rotation search in order to solve the BSS problem. Its objective is to minimize the mutual information between the joint density of the source estimate and the product of its marginals. Whitening reduces the task to minimizing the Vasicek entropy of the source estimates by searching exhaustively for the appropriate rotation matrix (Learned-Miller & Fisher, 2003).

Beta-Divergence

Beta-divergence for BSS uses a quasi-Newton Broyden-Fletcher-Goldfarb-Shanno (BFGS) optimization to minimize the β-divergence between the density of the source estimates and the product of its hypothesized marginal densities (Mihoko & Eguchi, 2002). This is the same source separation concept as the minimization of the mutual information between the source estimates using a Kullback-Leibler divergence, except the β-divergence is used. The β-divergence ($0 \leq \beta \leq 1$) is a continuum between the Kullback-Leibler divergence ($\beta = 0$) and a mean squared error divergence ($\beta = 1$) that gives smaller weights to possible outliers so that their influence on the estimate is weakened. This is an important algorithm to be studied as it has been proven to be B-robust (the influence of an outlier on the estimator is finite) in contrast to most other ICA estimators that have been proven to be non-B-robust (Mihoko & Eguchi).

Whitening

Preprocessing the observed samples by whitening is a common requirement of the given ICA algorithms, except β-divergence, as it reduces the search to optimize its contrast function to the rotation matrix (Hyvärinen et al., 2001). However, with smaller sample sizes, standard whitening techniques (Hyvärinen et al.) estimate the true source mean and variance incorrectly, and lead to ICA algorithms (depending on the optimization technique) incapable of estimating the optimum demixing matrix. Improper whitening introduces additional rotation and nonrotational mixing to the data set.

MEASURES OF OUTLIER ROBUSTNESS

Three nonblind robustness measures are selected to evaluate the sensitivity of an ICA algorithm to outliers (Gadhok, 2006). API evaluates the sensitivity to outliers of the overall ICA algorithm (implemented contrast function and its optimization). The optimum rotation-angle error evaluates the sensitivity of the rotation angle that the contrast function identifies for separation. Finally, the contrast function difference evaluates the shape changes in the contrast function based on a rotation due to an outlier. In terms of robustness analysis, the optimum rotation-angle error is more important than the contrast function difference since it is related directly to the separation performance of an ICA algorithm. Furthermore, since the rotation angle is based inherently on higher order statistics, so is the pseudomeasurement of the sensitivity of those statistics to outliers.

Amari Separation Performance Index

API is a nonnegative measure of the matrix $\mathbf{P} = \mathbf{AW}$, taking into account the scale and permutation invariance of ICA, to gauge the accuracy of the demixing matrix (Potter, Gadhok, & Kinsner, 2002). In a perfect simulation $\mathbf{P} = \mathbf{\Lambda\Pi}$, API equals zero. The maximum of the API is dependent on the size of the demixing matrix, but in this article it is normalized to one.

Optimum Rotation-Angle Error

Rotation matrices between 0 and 90 degrees (solutions repeat every 90 degrees), along with the known mixing and whitening matrices in a simulation, are used to determine the angle at which API is lowest. For example, if the sources were mixed with a rotation matrix, an API of 0 could be reached. However, improper whitening does alter the mixing such that a perfect separation by a rotation matrix cannot be achieved. In any event, this step identifies the optimum angle of rotation that minimizes API. Next, given a contrast function and the observed samples (outlier contaminated or not), the set of rotation matrices is used to find the angle of rotation given by the minimum or maximum of the contrast function. The difference between the optimum angle and the extracted angle (absolute maximum error of 45 degrees) at the optimum of the contrast is defined as the optimum rotation-angle error.

Contrast Function Difference

Rotation matrices between 0 and 90 degrees are used to solve a given contrast function and a set of observed samples (that have been whitened robustly). Next, an outlier is introduced into the observed data set, and the process is repeated. The results are normalized and aligned at the optima, and the difference is taken. This shape difference is known as the contrast function difference.

DESIGN OF EXPERIMENTS

The single simulation that would be the most revealing in terms of outlier sensitivity is a mixture of two independent, identically distributed (iid) signals that are uniform with unit norm and variance contaminated by outliers. Although outlier identification is potentially the simplest in this case, the interest is in the sensitivity of the algorithms. Just as well, the symmetric nature of the distribution allows a focus on the fourth-order statistics, and the knowledge that those ICA algorithms that use fourth-order statistics, specifically JADE, should perform well.

To produce the outlier-contaminated observations, sources s_1 and s_2 are first mixed by a rotation matrix, $\mathbf{A}$, of either 0 or 45 degrees, as shown in Figure 2. Then the mixtures, s_{1m} and s_{2m}, are numerically whitened (via eigenvalue decomposition) to produce s_{1w} and s_{2w}. Finally, outlier pairs are appended to the stream to produce the outlier-contaminated observations x_1 and x_2.

The rotation mixing matrices are selected to ensure that those ICA algorithms that optimize by a rotation only should perform similarity to those that have fewer optimization restrictions, that is, an unbiased optimization landscape. Again, the interest is in the rotation sensitivity of the algorithms to outliers and not the ability or inability of the ICA algorithm to separate the mixture. Now, the sources

Figure 2. Experiment setup

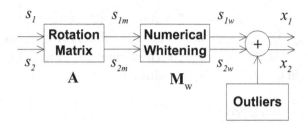

are still theoretically white after only a rotation, but the numerical whitening adds realism to the simulation. It does defeat (slightly) the purpose of an unbiased optimization landscape, but it adds a standard error occurring in most situations.

To create a plausible outlier-contaminated situation, an outlier is allowed to occur only at one of the sensors. Thus, s_{1w} is appended with an outlier at 0, 1, 3, 5, or 7 standard deviations (σ) from the mean of the distribution, and the corresponding sample point in s_{2w} is at location 0, the mean of s_2 (Gadhok & Kinsner, n.d.).

To help highlight the sensitivities of the contrast functions, source sample sizes are either 100 or 200 sample pairs. These sample sizes refer to practical ICA processing when dealing with signals that are stationary only over small periods of time, but nonstationary over a long period of time. For example, in voice processing, since speech can be considered stationary within 10 to 50 ms, then 44,100 samples per second (sps) produce a few hundred samples. In biomedical signal processing (e.g., the electrocardiogram), 300 sps are common. In EEGs, 600 samples per event-related potential is common (Lee et al., 1999).

Finally, after generating the observations, the samples are processed by a Matlab implementation of the ICA algorithms (Cardoso, n.d.; Gävert, Hurri, Särelä, & Hyvärinen, 2005; Learned-Miller, n.d.; Makeig et al., n.d.) and their respective contrast functions. Based on the available literature, the authors have implemented the β-divergence algorithm in Matlab (Gadhok & Kinsner, n.d.).

Contrast Function Setup

The ICA contrast functions have been implemented in Matlab by the authors based on the following literature.

a. FastICA: Equation 8.25 in Hyvärinen et al. (2001), with the nonlinearities G1 from "tanh," G2 from "gauss," G3 from "pow3," and G4 from "skew" (see Gävert et al., n.d.)
b. Extended Infomax: Equations 2.7, 2.12, and 2.18 in Lee et al. (1999)
c. JADE: Equation 3.11 in Cardoso (1999)
d. Radical: Equation 8 in Learned-Miller and Fisher (2003); note that the Radical algorithm (Learned-Miller, n.d.) does not include the normalizing terms N+1/m and 1/N-m
e. β-divergence: Equation 3.3 in Mihoko and Eguchi (2002) and density $\sqrt{2}\Gamma\left(0.25\right)^{-1}\exp\left(-0.25z^4\right)$

Note that the FastICA and β-divergence contrast functions are multiplied by a negative sign in experiments. This modification uniforms the objective to a minimization of each contrast function.

Parameters Used in Software

Since the individual ICA algorithms were optimized for this simulation, they were set up to produce the best possible results. The stopping criteria and rotation precisions were selected such that they had a numerically insignificant effect on API. FastICA, Extended Infomax, and β-divergence stop when the norm of the change in the demixing matrix is less than 1×10^{-6}. However, this does not ensure that this criterion was met as each algorithm also has a maximum number of iterations allowed before halting. JADE natively has a stopping criterion that has a numerically insignificant effect on API. Finally, Radical rotation search precision was increased from 150 to 300 divisions between 0 and 90 degrees. FastICA is orthogonalized symmetrically to reduce the chance of errors carrying through the estimation. A range of βs (0, 0.05, 0.1, 0.2, and 0.3) are selected because the automatic selection of β described in (Minami & Eguchi, 2003) is not implemented in this article due to time constraints. Thus, $\beta = 0$ is selected because it makes the algorithm become equivalent to a Kullback-Leibler divergence and is important for the comparison of algorithms. The other βs were selected to see their effects on the results of sensitivity evaluation. Although larger βs tend to create a more outlier-robust estimator, βs past 0.3 are not selected as they might result in a large variance of the divergence estimate (Minami & Eguchi). The density selected for β-divergence was sub-Gaussian. For Extended Infomax, the number of sub-Gaussian sources is specified as two. Finally, the demixing matrices were initialized by random positive definite matrices to ensure unbiased optimization and to not violate the Hessian of the contrasts being concave.

Reporting of Results

Ten simulations were performed per experiment. Experiments were permuted based on sample size (100 or 200 pairs), mixing (0 or 45 degrees), and outlier location (none, 0, 1, 3, 5, or 7 standard deviations σ). The median value of API over the 10 simulations is reported. Unfortunately, this does not capture results where the algorithm completely fails at determining the demixing matrix. The first norm (sum of the absolute values) of the optimum rotation-angle error is reported over 10 simulations, but does capture major failures. The maximum possible value is 450 over 10 trials. Finally, the first norm of the mean contrast error is reported over 10 simulations. The maximum possible value is 10 over 10 trials. For each algorithm, the same data set is used. Samples are not regenerated, except when repeating the entire experiment. Thus, 2,000 sample pairs are generated and were segmented to 100 and 200 sample pairs to use in the 10 simulations per experiment. These metrics are selected as they are the most revealing of the sensitivities that could be condensed and displayed for this article.

RESULTS AND DISCUSSION

This section describes only some of the simulation results, using 100 samples and a mixing matrix of 0 degrees. In the other simulations (100 samples with a 45-degree rotation, and 200 samples with 0- and 45-degree rotations), the relative results remained the same. A detailed analysis of random samples from each run of the experiment was not done, but a histogram of the entire data set confirmed the uniformity of the sources. In addition, a power spectrum analysis of all the 2,000 sample pairs showed a flat spectrum to ensure the whiteness and broadband nature of the random samples.

Amari Separation Performance

Figure 3a shows that JADE (denoted by ■) became sensitive to an outlier past 3 standard deviations (σ) and FastICA G3 (×) past 1σ; FastICA G4 (+) performed poorly in the simulation. JADE became sensitive to outliers as it uses fourth-order estimates of the cumulants, which are very sensitive to outliers. FastICA G3 and G4 are calculating expectations of third- and fourth-order polynomials and are sensitive as well. FastICA G4 performs poorly even without any outliers as it expects a skewed distribution to separate. Thus, it weighs the samples incorrectly, destroying the demixing matrix estimate. Beta-divergence (▲, ▶, ▼, ◀, ♦), Radical (★), FastICA G1 (•) and G2 (●), and Extended Infomax (*) have similar APIs, but do not overtly show sensitivity to outliers (Figure 3b). In the experiment without outliers, β-divergence had the lowest API because it is not restricted when optimizing the contrast function. Although the mixing was a rotation, whitening pushes it slightly off a rotation, and the other algorithms are unable to optimize as well as β-divergence.

The entire simulation was repeated without numerical whitening, and the effects of outliers on the API of FastICA (G1 and G2) and Extended Infomax were more pronounced. Thus, a simulation with a rotation as a mixing, with symmetric distributions, and with no numerical whitening can best show the sensitivities to outliers via API.

Optimum Angle of Rotation Error

Figure 4a shows the sensitivity of the rotation angle given by the contrasts to outliers. Beta-divergence, Radical, and FastICA G4 were relativity insensitive to outliers affecting their rotation angle. Radical was insensitive because the outlier adds a bias term to the entropy estimate and does not impact the

Figure 3. (a) Normalized Amari separation performance of the experiment focused on JADE (denoted by ■*), FastICA G3 (×), and FastICA G4 (+); (b) normalized API zoomed on the performance of β-divergence* (▲, ▶, ▼, ◀, ♦), *Radical (★), FastICA G1 (•) and G2 (●), and Extended Infomax (*)*

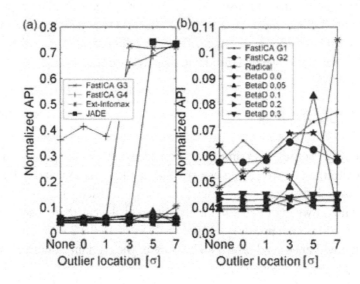

Figure 4. (a) First norm of the error in estimation of optimum angle of rotation over 10 experiments; (b) first norm of the mean of the difference in the contrast functions with and without outliers over 10 experiments

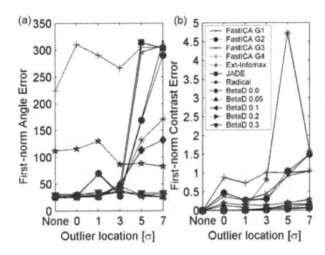

location of the minimum in the contrast. Clearly, this novel measure reveals the sensitivity of the ICA algorithms to outliers.

Contrast Function Difference

Figure 4b shows that Extended Infomax followed by FastICA G2, G4, G1, and then G3 have contrasts that deviate in shape. Beta-divergence, Radical, and JADE have contrasts that do not change in shape.

Figure 5 shows an example of how the sinusoidal shape of the JADE contrast function is insensitive to outliers. The minimum of the contrast function without outliers estimates that a rotation of 40 degrees would separate the mixtures. However, the JADE contrast function with outliers shows that a rotation of 87 degrees is required. This gives an optimum rotation-angle error of 43. Yet, the contrast function difference measure is small. This suggests that JADE could have an improved API if an outlier-robust fourth-order cumulant estimate were used (such as Hogg's measure of the tail weight or the ratio of two interfractile ranges; Ruppert, 1987).

The most important result is that β-divergence is unaffected. Since in β-divergence smaller weights are given to samples far from the mean of the distribution, the influence of these outliers on the estimate is negligible. Thus, together, the two contrast measures reveal that β-divergence is the least outlier-sensitive algorithm followed by Radical, FastICA G2 and G1, Extended Infomax, JADE, and FastICA G3 and G4 in an outlier-contaminated mixture of two uniformly distributed signals. Notice that a higher weighting to the rotation sensitivity was given in this ranking.

Furthermore, it seems that there might be a relationship between the contrast function difference and the influence function. The IF is a directional derivative of the contrast function between an outlier-contaminated density and an outlier-free density (Hampel et al., 1986). The contrast function difference appears to be a numerical derivative, but with the rotation error removed. A proof of this relationship would be required in order to link the IF and separation performance on an ICA algorithm.

Figure 5. A plot of the JADE contrast function without outliers (solid line), with an outlier at 5σ (dotted line), and the contrast function difference (dashed-dotted line) from a test run

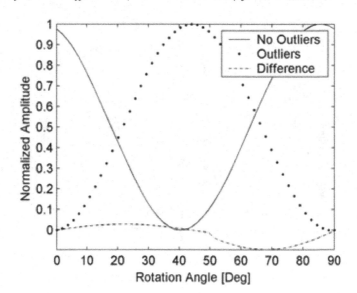

Other Considerations

Although the outlier sensitivity of ICA algorithms and their contrast functions were demonstrated in this article, two important considerations must be kept in mind. First, the ICA algorithms were designed to perform optimally for the cases considered and may not be optimal for other cases. The APIs presented should be considered as a lower bound on the effects of outliers in ICA separation performance. Second, the computational complexity of the different algorithms studied varies considerably; for example, the implementation of β-divergence for BSS requires four times the processing time than the other ICA algorithms. The interplay between the allowable optimization landscape, computational processing, and the sensitivity to outliers should be investigated further to improve the evaluation of the outlier robustness of ICA algorithms.

CONCLUSION

API is a good outlier sensitivity measure when an unbiased optimization landscape is presented. In experiments, it revealed a strong sensitivity of JADE and FastICA (G3 and G4 nonlinearities) to outliers. However, the contrast measures demonstrated conclusively the outlier sensitivity of various ICA contrast functions. Specifically, the optimum angle of rotation error and the contrast difference revealed the resilience of the β-divergence algorithm to outliers. Thus, when using ICA for cognitive informatics, the β-divergence algorithm is the most robust to outliers.

ACKNOWLEDGMENT

The authors would like to thank Delta Group, in particular, Michael Potter, for their helpful discussions related to this topic. This work is supported by the Natural Sciences and Engineering Research Council (NSERC) of Canada.

REFERENCES

Bell, A., & Sejnowski, T. (1995). An information-maximization approach to blind separation and blind deconvolution. *Neural Computation, 7*, 1129-1159.

Cardoso, J. F. (1999). Higher-order contrasts for independent component analysis. *Neural Computation, 11*, 157-192.

Cardoso, J. F. (n.d.). JADE for Matlab (Version 1.5) [Computer software]. Retrieved February 2, 2005, from http://www.tsi.enst.fr/~cardoso/Algo/Jade/jadeR.m

Gadhok, N. (2006). *A study of outliers for robust independent component analysis.* Unpublished master's thesis, Department of Electrical and Computer Engineering, University of Manitoba, Winnipeg, Canada.

Gadhok, N., & Kinsner, W. (n.d.). ICA by Beta Divergence for Matlab (Version 1.0) [Computer software]. Retrieved October 16, 2006, from http://www.ee.umanitoba.ca/~kinsner/projects

Gävert, H., Hurri, J., Särelä, J., & Hyvärinen A. (n.d.). FastICA for Matlab (Version 2.3) [Computer software]. Retrieved February 2, 2005, from http://www.cis.hut.fi/projects/ica/fastica

Hampel, F. R., Ronchetti, E. M., Rousseeuw, P. J., & Stahel, W. A. (1986). *Robust statistics: The approach based on influence functions.* New York: John Wiley & Sons.

Hyvärinen, A., Karhunen, J., & Oja, E. (2001). *Independent component analysis.* New York: John Wiley & Sons.

Hyvärinen, A., & Oja, E. (1997). A fast fixed-point algorithm for independent component analysis. *Neural Computation, 9*(7), 1483-1492.

Learned-Miller, E. (n.d.). RADICAL for Matlab (Version 1.1) [Computer software]. Retrieved February 2, 2005, from http://www.cs.umass.edu/~elm/ICA

Learned-Miller, E., & Fisher, J., III. (2003). ICA using spacing estimates of entropy. *Journal of Machine Learning Research, 4*, 1271-1295.

Lee, T., Girolami, M., & Sejnowski, T. (1999). Independent component analysis using an extended infomax algorithm for mixed subgaussian and supergaussian sources. *Neural Computation, 11*, 417-441.

Makeig, S., et al. (n.d.). EEGLAB: ICA toolbox for psychophysiological research (Version 4.5) [Computer software]. Retrieved February 2, 2005, from http://sccn.ucsd.edu/eeglab

Makeig, S., Westerfield, M., Jung, T., Enghoff, S., Townsend, J., Courchesene, E., et al. (2002). Dynamic brain sources of visual evoked responses. *Science, 295*(5555), 690-694.

McKeown, M., Jung, T., Makeig, S., Brown, G., Kindermann, S., Lee, T., et al. (1998). Spatially independent activity patterns in functional MRI data during the Stroop color-naming task. In *Proceedings of the National Academy of Science U.S.A.* (Vol. 95, pp. 803-810).

Mihoko, M., & Eguchi, S. (2002). Robust blind source separation by beta divergence. *Neural Computation, 14*, 1859-1886.

Minami, M., & Eguchi, S. (2003). Adaptive selection for minimum β-divergence method. In *Fourth International Symposium on Independent Component Analysis and Blind Signal Separation (ICA 2003)* (pp. 475-480).

Potter, M., Gadhok, N., & Kinsner, W. (2002). Separation performance of ICA on simulated EEG and ECG signals contaminated by noise. *Canadian Journal of Electrical and Computer Engineering, 27*(3), 123-127.

Ruppert, D. (1987). What is kurtosis? An influence function approach. *American Statistician, 41*(1), 1-5.

Zhang, D., Wang, Y., & Kinsner, W. (Eds.). (2007). *Proceedings of the Sixth IEEE International Conference on Cognitive Informatics.*

This work was previously published in the International Journal of Cognitive Informatics and Natural Intelligence, Vol. 2, Issue 4, edited by Y. Wang, pp. 44-54, copyright 2008 by IGI Publishing (an imprint of IGI Global).

Chapter 20
A Relative Fractal Dimension Spectrum for a Perceptual Complexity Measure

W. Kinsner
University of Manitoba, Canada

R. Dansereau
University of Manitoba, Canada

ABSTRACT

This article presents a derivation of a new relative fractal dimension spectrum, DRq, to measure the dis-similarity between two finite probability distributions originating from various signals. This measure is an extension of the Kullback-Leibler (KL) distance and the Rényi fractal dimension spectrum, Dq. Like the KL distance, DRq determines the dissimilarity between two probability distibutions X and Y of the same size, but does it at different scales, while the scalar KL distance is a single-scale measure. Like the Rényi fractal dimension spectrum, the DRq is also a bounded vectorial measure obtained at different scales and for different moment orders, q. However, unlike the Dq, all the elements of the new DRq become zero when X and Y are the same. Experimental results show that this objective measure is consistent with the subjective mean-opinion-score (MOS) when evaluating the perceptual quality of images reconstructed after their compression. Thus, it could also be used in other areas of cognitive informatics.

INTRODUCTION

This article is related to measuring the quality of various multimedia materials used in perception, cognition and evolutionary learning processes. The multimedia materials may include temporal signals such as sound, speech, music, biomedical and telemetry signals, as well as spatial signals such as still images, and spatio-temporal signals such as animation and video. A comprehensive review of the scope of multimedia storage and transmission, as well as quality metrics is presented (Kinsner, 2002). Most of multimedia original materials are altered (compressed, or enhanced, or watermarked) either to fit the available storage or bandwidth during their transmission, or to enhance perception of the materials, or to protect the original material from alterations and copying. Since the signals may also be contaminated by noise during different stages of their processing and transmission, various denoising techniques must be used to minimize the noise, without affecting the signal itself (Kinsner, 2002). Different classes of coloured and fractal noise are described (Kinsner, 1994, June 15). A review of approaches to distinguish broadband signals and noise from chaos was provided (Kinsner, 2003). Very often, multimedia compression is lossy in that the signals are altered with respect not only to their redundancy, but also to their perceptual and cognitive relevancy. Since the signals are presented to humans (rather than machines), cognitive processes must be considered in the development of suitable quality metrics. Energy-based metrics are not suitable for such cognitive processes (Kinsner, 2004). A very fundamental class of metrics based on entropy was described (Kinsner, 2004), with a discussion on its usefulness and limitations in the area of cognitive informatics (CI) (Wang, 2002) and autonomic computing (Kinsner, 2005a). An extension from the single-scale entropy-based metrics to multiscale metrics through a unified approach to fractal dimensions was presented in (Kinsner, 2005b). The main realization presented in that article was that not all fractal dimensions are the same, and that the morphological (projective) dimensions are just a subset of the entropy-based dimensions. That article also stressed the importance of moving away from scalar to vectorial, multiscale, and bounded measures in CI, which is a requirement satisfied by the Rényi fractal dimension spectrum.

This article presents a fundamental extension in the form of a new *relative fractal dimension spectrum* that is not only multiscale, vectorial and bounded, but also produces a zero vector if the distributions of the source X and its reconstruction Y are the same. Experimental results obtained by the authors indicate that this quality measure is the best perceptual quality metrics devised so far (Dansereau, 2001; Dansereau & Kinsner, 2001; Kinsner & Dansereau, 2006).

Other practical applications of the new relative measure include its use in: (i) the fine tuning of algorithms to compress or enhance signals, and (ii) the improved feature extraction for characterization and classification by neural networks.

BACKGROUND ON FRACTAL MEASURES

Single Fractal Dimension Measures

In one form or another, all fractal dimension measures determine the critical exponent that stabilizes a power-law relation of the following form:

$$N_{s_k} : s_k^{D_H} \quad \text{for } s_k \to 0, \ k \to \infty \tag{1}$$

where N_{s_k} is a measure of the complexity of the object or data set (e.g., a simple count of a covering (Kinsner, 2005b), or a functional measure on the covering) at the kth *scale* of the measurements, s_k. This scale s_k is related to the *reduction factor* r_k of a volume element (*vel* for short) at each kth covering through $s_k = (1/r_k)$ (Kinsner, 2005b). For example, if the reduction factor is 1/3, the scale is 3. The sign ~

in (1) reads "is proportional to." The critical exponent D_H that makes this power-law relationship constant is called the *fractal dimension* of the object in the context of the measurement used to calculate N_s.

When the logarithm of both sides of this power-law relation is taken, and then solved for the critical exponent, the following expression for the fractal dimension D_H is obtained as $s_k \to 0$.

$$D_H = \lim_{s_k \to 0} \frac{\log(N_s)}{\log(s_k)} \tag{2}$$

The subscript k is introduced to signify the importance of multiscale measurements; a single-scale measurement produces just a single point on the log-log plot, and at least three measurements must be done to calculate the slope of the fitted line. The subscript H in D_H is introduced here to recognize Hausdorff's contributions to this multiscale analysis. Notice that this class of Hausdorff fractal dimensions, D_H, has noninteger values in general, although it may also be integer for either simple objects (such as a line, or a surface), or very complex objects such as "fat" fractals.

There are many possible measurement approaches for N_s. When it is a simple count of *volume elements* (vels for short) in the covering, the fractal dimension, D_H, must be morphological (projective) which is sufficient for *monofractals* (i.e., fractals with a single dimension). However, if the object is a *multifractal* (i.e., a mixture of monofractals), then D_H can reveal the largest dimension in the mixture only.

Multifractal Dimension Measures

We have just established that the single D_H is sufficient to characterize a signal (an object), if the measured signal has homogeneous complexity features. What happens in the case of a signal with inhomogeneous complexity features, such as audio, or an electroencephalogram (EEG) that changes characteristics over time, or an image where spatial variations contribute to inhomogeneous complexity? These inhomogeneous complexity features can result from multiple underlying processes, growth characteristics, or other driving phenomena forming the signal.

Thus, if the probability distribution of the fractal covering is nonuniform, entropy-based measures must be used. Let us define the probability p_{jk} in terms of the relative frequency:

$$p_{jk} \triangleq \lim_{k \to \infty} \left(\frac{n_{jk}}{N_{Tk}} \right) \tag{3}$$

where the symbol $\triangleq$ reads "is defined as," n_{jk} is a measure of the object's intersection with the jth vel in a covering at the kth scale, and N_{Tk} is the total measure of all the N_k vels in the kth-scale covering given by

$$N_{Tk} \triangleq \sum_{j=1}^{N_k} n_{jk} \tag{4}$$

This constitutes a finite-size probability vector at the kth scale denoted by $P_k = [p_{1k}, p_{2k}, ..., p_{Nk}]$. This vector provides a basis for the corresponding finite-size *probability mass function* (distribution).

For each probability, Shannon defined *self information* as (Shannon, 1948):

$$I_{jk} \triangleq \log \frac{1}{p_{jk}} \tag{5}$$

with its value increasing to ∞ for $p_{jk} \to 0$, and decreasing to 0 for $p_{jk} \to 1$. The average self information H_{1k} is the weighted sum of I_{jk} as given by:

$$H_{1k} @ \sum_{k=1}^{N_k} p_{jk} I_{jk} = \left(-\sum_{k=1}^{N_k} p_{jk} \log p_{jk} \right) \tag{6}$$

where the subscript 1 denotes the first-order Shannon entropy, and k denotes the kth scale.

Let us consider the following power-law relation on a finite probability distribution P_k at a kth scale of s.

$$c^{H_{1k}} @ s_k^{D_I} \quad \text{for } s_k \to 0, k \to \infty \tag{7}$$

In solving for the fractal information dimension D_I in Equation 7, the following expression is obtained:

$$D_I = \lim_{s_k \to 0} \frac{H_{1k}}{\log(s_k)}. \tag{8}$$

Notice that $D_I = D_H$ if and only if the distribution is uniform because $H_{1k} = N_{1k}$; otherwise, $D_I < D_H$.

Other entropy-based fractal dimensions also exist, and are distinct from D_H and D_I for multifractals, as discussed in (Kinsner, 2005b).

Rényi Fractal Dimension Spectrum

An extension of the information dimension can be made by considering the generalized approach to probability distributions given by Rényi (1955, 1959). Of particular importance is the following generalization of Shannon entropy introduced by Rényi (1960):

$$H_q(P_k) = \frac{1}{1-q} \log \frac{\sum_{j=1}^{N_k} p_{jk}^q}{\sum_{j=1}^{N_k} p_{jk}}, \quad 0 \le q \le \infty \tag{9}$$

where the distribution mass function can be complete or incomplete. This generalization is commonly referred to as the *Rényi generalized entropy*, or Rényi entropy, or Rényi exponent. A number of interesting features exist for H_q. The most prominent feature is the inclusion of the continuous parameter q, also known as the moment order. Using different values of q, different entropy characteristics are revealed from each finite probability distribution P_k. A second important feature of H_q is that the equation is normalized by $\sum p_{jk}$. This allows for incomplete probability distributions to be used where $0 < \sum p_{jk} \le 1$. One important observation about H_q is that when $q \to 1$, it can be shown that H_q reduces to the H_1 in Equation 6. Therefore, H_q is considered a generalization of the first-order Shannon entropy.

Using this generalized form of entropy H_q, Hentschel and Procaccia (1983) introduced a generalized form of the information dimension D_1. This new dimension measure can be generalized further by initially forming the following power-law relation:

$$\left(\frac{\sum_{j=1}^{N_k} p_{jk}^q}{\sum_{j=1}^{N_k} p_{jk}}\right)^{\frac{1}{1-q}} : s_k^{D_q}, \quad s_k \to 0, k \to \infty$$

(10)

where q is used as the moment order for the finite probability distribution P_k. Solving for the critical exponent D_q gives

$$D_q = \lim_{s_k \to 0} \frac{1}{1-q} \frac{\log \dfrac{\sum_{j=1}^{N_k} p_{jk}^q}{\sum_{j=1}^{N_k} p_{jk}}}{\log(s_k)} = \lim_{s_k \to 0} \frac{H_{qk}}{\log(s_k)}$$

(11)

which is called the Rényi fractal dimension for a given q. Because the range of q is normally extended from the nonnegative interval to $\infty \le q \le \infty$, D_q actually forms an infinite number of dimensions and, hence, D_q can also be referred to as the *Rényi dimension spectrum* over all values of q.

Given the Rényi dimension spectrum, one can derive the *Mandelbrot singularity spectrum* (Kinsner, 1994, May), by taking either a Legendre transform of D_q, as described by Halsey, Jenson, Kadanoff, Procaccia, and Shraiman (1986), or a new direct calculation approach (Potter & Kinsner, 2007). An alternative route to the Mandelbrot spectrum is through the wavelet transform.

Notice that there are many other generalizations of entropy, and the corresponding fractal dimension spectra.

MEASURING CLOSENESS OF PROBABILITY MODELS

One of the goals in this research is to use complexity measures, such as fractal and multifractal measures, to compare different signals for perceptual evaluation purposes. For instance, this comparison can be in the form of comparing a signal and an approximation to that signal. Since the fractal and multifractal measures under consideration are based on calculations over finite probability distributions, a method is desired for comparing the multifractal complexity between two probability distributions, say X and Y. Notice that we have moved away from the symbol P to avoid indexing the distinct probabilities.

It is generally agreed that energy comparison of singular (fractal) objects does not produce good results (Kinsner, 2004). A better approach would be to use the Rényi generalized entropy of the two distributions, as shown in Figure 1. Since $H_q(Y)$ has a larger span than $H_q(X)$, the complexity of Y has been increased due to a transformation from X to Y. A better approach uses the Rényi dimension spectrum which exhibit similar difference as in Figure 1, but with a different range between the limiting dimensions $D_{-\infty}$ and D_∞.

The approach taken in this article for the probability model comparison is based on that given by Lanterman, O'Sullivan, & Miller (1999). The *Kullback-Leibler (KL) distance* (Kullback & Leibler, 1951) (or *relative entropy* (Cover & Thomas, 1991, p. 18)) is given by:

Figure 1. Comparing Rényi entropy spectra for a source X and its reconstruction Y

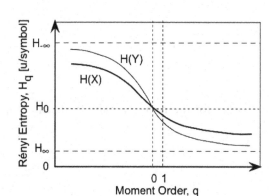

$$H(X \| Y) = \sum_{j=1}^{N} x_j \log \frac{x_j}{y_j} \tag{12}$$

where X is the complete probability mass distribution of the true signal, and Y is the probability mass distribution of an approximation (reconstruction) to the signal, x_j and y_j are the one-to-one elements of the probability distributions, respectively, and N is the size of the finite probability distributions, $N = |X| = |Y|$. The KL distance has the following property

$$0 = H(X \| X) \leq H(X \| Y) \tag{13}$$

which means that the KL distance is zero for the same distribution, but is greater than zero for two distinct distributions. "Lanterman et al. (1999)" also show that the KL distance can be used to compare the relative closeness of two probability model approximations, $Y1$ and $Y2$, to a true probability distribution X. That is, if

$$H(X \| Y1) \leq H(X \| Y2) \tag{14}$$

then $Y1$ is considered a better approximation compared to $Y2$ because the KL distance of $Y1$ to the true distribution X is smaller. These fundamental ideas are used in the development of the relative multifractal measure, as discussed next.

RELATIVE MULTIFRACTAL DIMENSION MEASURES

Derivation

What is proposed in this article is that the form of relative comparison in Equations 13 and 14 can be extended from the KL distance to the Rényi generalized entropy. It turns out that such a *Rényi relative entropy*, H_{R_q}, is given by Dansereau (2001, p. 202):

$$H_{Rq}(X \| Y) = \frac{1}{q-1} \log \frac{\sum\limits_{j=1}^{N} y_j \left(\frac{x_j}{y_j}\right)^q}{\sum\limits_{j=1}^{N} x_j}, \quad -\infty \le q \le \infty$$

(15)

This expression has many of the desired characteristics. First, it provides a relative comparison between two finite probability distributions, X and Y. Second, since the moment order of q is included, a spectrum of the relative measures is possible. Third, when $q \to 1$ then H_{Rq} reduces to the KL distance. This formulation also allows for negative values.

What is proposed as a new multifractal measure is to replace $H_q(X)$ in Equation 9 with $H_{Rq}(X\|Y)$ to form the following definition.

Definition 1: *Let X_k and Y_k be finite probability distributions at a kth scale of s. The relative Rényi fractal dimension spectrum, D_{Rq}, is defined as*

$$D_{Rq}(X_k \| Y_k) = \lim_{s_k \to 0} \frac{H_{Rq}(X_k \| Y_k)}{\log(s_k)}$$

(16)

where H_{Rq} is the Rényi relative entropy, as given by 15. Some notes should be made about D_{Rq}. The first comes from the following theorem.

Lemma 1: The relative Rényi dimension spectrum D_{Rq} is a monotonic nonincreasing function in q.

Proof: Let $z_j \equiv z_{j_k} = x_{j_k}/y_{j_k}$. Begin by considering the first derivative of H_{Rq} with respect to q.

$$\frac{dH_{Rq}}{dq} = \frac{\sum\limits_{j=1}^{N} z_j^q \log \sum\limits_{j=1}^{N} y_j z_j^q - (q-1) \sum\limits_{j=1}^{N} z_j^q \log z_j}{(q-1)^2 \sum\limits_{j=1}^{N} z_j^q}$$

(17)

We must show that Equation 17 is negative everywhere with only a finite number of zeros for the strictly decreasing case. It is easy to show that the denominator is always greater than zero because z_j is always positive for the probability distributions X_k and Y_k.

The numerator of Equation 17 can be shown to be negative everywhere using Jensen's inequality (Cover & Thomas, 1991) for the convex function $f(u) = u \log u$ with $u = z_j^{q-1}$ as follows

$$E\left[z_j^{q-1}\right] \ge E\left[z_j^{q-1}\right] \log \left\{E\left[z_j^{q-1}\right]\right\}$$

(18)

where $E[\cdot]$ denotes expectation. Expanding the expectations in the inequality results in

$$\sum\limits_{j=1}^{N} z_j^q \log z_j^{q-1} \ge \sum\limits_{j=1}^{N} z_j^q \log \sum\limits_{j=1}^{N} z_j^q.$$

(19)

Rearranging this inequality gives

$$\sum_{j=1}^{N} z_j^q \log \sum_{j=1}^{N} z_j^q - (q-1) \sum_{j=1}^{N} z_j^q \log z_j \le 0 \tag{20}$$

This final inequality is almost the numerator of Equation 17 with the exception of the y_j factors. Since $0 \le y_j \le 1$, the following holds

$$\sum_{j=1}^{N} z_j^q \log \sum_{j=1}^{N} y_j z_j^q \le \sum_{j=1}^{N} z_j^q \log \sum_{j=1}^{N} z_j^q \tag{21}$$

This results in the numerator of Equation 17 being less than or equal to zero. Therefore, H_{Rq} is a monotonic nonincreasing function with respect to q.

Another interesting property of H_{Rq} can be stated as follows.

Lemma 2: *Let X_k and Y_k be finite probability distributions, either complete or incomplete, such that*

$$0 \le \sum_{j=1}^{N} y_j = \sum_{j=1}^{N} x_j \le 1 \tag{22}$$

Then, the relative Rényi dimension spectrum D_{Rq} as a function of q has a zero crossing at $q = 0$ such that:

$$D_{Rq}(X_k \parallel Y_k) = 0 \tag{23}$$

Proof: This is easy to check since for q = 0, H_{Rq} reduces to:

$$D_{Rq}(X_k \parallel Y_k) = \lim_{s_k \to 0} \left(\log \frac{\sum_{j=1}^{N} x_j}{\sum_{j=1}^{N} y_j} / \log(s_k) \right) \tag{24}$$

and is clearly zero for the equality assumed in 22. Therefore, $D_{Rq} = 0$.

The Rényi relative entropy of Equation 15 reduces to the KL distance when q → 1. Therefore, the following can be stated (with a trivial proof).

Lemma 3: *For q → 1, the relative Rényi dimension spectrum D_{Rq} becomes*

$$D_{Rq \to 1}(X_k \parallel Y_k) = \lim_{q \to 1} \lim_{s_k \to 0} \frac{H_{Rq}(X_k \parallel Y_k)}{\log(s_k)} = \lim_{s_k \to 0} \frac{H_1(X_k \parallel Y_k)}{\log(s_k)} \tag{25}$$

Other interesting points for D_{Rq} as a function of q is to consider what happens when $q \to \infty$ or $q \to -\infty$. This is addressed in the following lemmata.

Lemma 4: *For $q \rightarrow \infty$, we have*

$$D_{Rq \rightarrow \infty}(X_k \| Y_k) = \lim_{s_k \rightarrow 0} \frac{\log \sup \left(\dfrac{x_j}{y_j} \right)}{\log(s_k)} \tag{26}$$

Proof: As $q \rightarrow \infty$, the summation in Equation 15 is dominated by $\sup[y_j(x_j/y_j)^q]$, where the $\sup(\cdot)$ is the supremum function. Therefore,

$$H_{Rq \rightarrow \infty} = \lim_{q \rightarrow \infty} \frac{1}{q-1} \log \sup \left[y_j \left(\frac{x_j}{y_j} \right)^q \right] \tag{27}$$

$$= \lim_{q \rightarrow \infty} \frac{1}{q-1} \sup \left[\log y_j + \log x_j^q - \log y_j^q \right] \tag{28}$$

$$= \lim_{q \rightarrow \infty} \frac{q}{q-1} \sup \left[\frac{\log y_j}{q} + \log x_j - \log y_j \right] \tag{29}$$

$$= \sup \left[\log x_j - \log y_j \right] \tag{30}$$

$$= \log \sup \left(\frac{x_j}{y_j} \right) \tag{31}$$

Replacing this result in Equation 15 gives Equation 26.

It can similarly be shown that for $q \rightarrow -\infty$, the following lemma holds.

Lemma 5: *For $q \rightarrow -\infty$, we have*

$$D_{Rq \rightarrow -\infty}(X_k \| Y_k) = \lim_{s_k \rightarrow 0} \frac{\log \inf \left(\dfrac{x_j}{y_j} \right)}{\log(s_k)} \tag{32}$$

where the $\inf(\cdot)$ is the infimum function.

Using these lemmata, the general behaviour for D_{R_q} as a function of q can be determined. What is important for signal complexity comparison in this article is how the D_{R_q} vs q function converges toward the ordinate. As given in Lemma 2, D_{R_q} as a function of q passes through the ordinate. Lemma 4 and Lemma 5 in conjunction with monotonicity shown in Lemma 1 indicate that this curve is bounded around the ordinate. Not only is D_{R_q} as a function of q bounded around the ordinate, but it converges toward the ordinate as the two probability distributions X and Y converge. This behaviour is suggested by Lemma 4 and Lemma 5 since $\log \sup(x_j/y_j)$ and $\log \inf(x_j/y_j)$ approach the ordinate as the probability distributions X and Y are closer in one-to-one correspondence. This behaviour corresponds to what is desired, and is similar in function to Equations 13 and 14 that use the KL distance.

Notice that after we have completed the development of the relative Rényi fractal dimension spectrum, we had come across a article describing a similar concept (Riedi & Scheuring, 1997).

Image Quality Metric, IQM

Although the D_{R_q} relationship is good for automatic quality tuning of the compression algorithms and feature extraction, it is still too complex to use for comparison with a scalar measure such as the mean-opinion score, MOS. We propose the following translation from a vector to a scalar *image quality metric:*

$$\text{IQM}(X_k \parallel Y_k) = \sum_{\forall q} D_{Rq}(X_k \parallel Y_k)$$

(33)

where the range of q is taken from the computed values, usually [-20 , 20].

Since the human visual system is highly nonlinear, the computational mean-opinion score (cMOS) could be expressed as

$$\text{cMOS} = 1 / \log(\text{IQM}).$$

(34)

If both measures are compatible, a graph of cMOS vs. MOS should be linear. This would be remarkable, as such a perceptual measure has not been reported in literature before.

COMPUTATIONAL CONSIDERATIONS

While the theory behind fractal dimension measures is elegant, implementation of fractal dimension calculations is quite error prone. One of the key problems with performing fractal dimension measure calculations is in determining the value of the critical exponent D_H in Equation 1 and all the other fractals dimensions discussed in this article. Numerous techniques for estimating D_H have been proposed (Kinsner, 2005b). These techniques include coverings such as the Hausdorff box-counting, the differential box counting, the infimum overlapping, the supremum nonoverlapping (Kinsner, 1994, May), and the most general Hausdorff-Besicovitch cover (Kinsner, 1994, June 20). These techniques differ in their selection of the covering schemes, and have other properties that make them sensitive to different classes of complexities in the fractal objects. For the sake of reproducibility, we will take some time to describe our approach for estimating D_H from real signals and, in particular, from greyscale images.

Choice of Probabilities

When dealing with the Rényi dimension spectrum and our newly developed relative Rényi dimension spectrum, one of the key factors to meaningful fractal dimension calculations is the careful selection of probability distributions for the data. This article focuses on the complexity of greyscale images. For these greyscale images, let $g(u,v)$ be the value of the greyscale pixel at coordinates (u,v) in the image. Since, as discussed in Sec. 6, all the images used are 8-bit greyscale, the value of $g(u,v)$ has the range $0 \leq g(u,v) \leq 2^8 - 1 = 255$.

To form the probability distributions X_k and Y_k at the kth scale s, the respective original and reconstructed images are partitioned into adjacent identical square volume elements (vels) to form a non-overlapping covering. The jth vel in such a partitioning at the kth scale s is denoted by b_{jk}, and the set of all the vels is a union denoted by $B_k = b_{1k} \cup b_{2k} \cup \ldots \cup b_{Nk}$. The finite probability distribution X_k (or Y_k) is then obtained from

$$x_{jk} = \frac{\sum\limits_{\forall (u,v) \in b_{jk}} \left(g(u,v) + 1 \right)}{\sum\limits_{\forall (u,v) \in B_{jk}} \left(g(u,v) + 1 \right)} \tag{35}$$

where x_{jk} is the probability of vel b_{jk}. The numerator denotes the sum of all the pixel values within the jth vel at the kth covering, while the denominator denotes all the pixel values in the kth covering.

This choice of probability calculation forms a probability distribution based on the greyscale intensities within a section of the image vs. those of the entire image. While other probability choices are possible, as we will see this choice of probability will provide some interesting results in terms of signal complexity.

Avoidance of Zero Probabilities

A special note should be made about the selection of the probabilities in Equation 35. Each of the terms in the summation include the addition of 1. These extra terms are included to avoid having any vel with a probability of zero, down to a scale s of a single pixel. Effectively, this is done to avoid "holes" in the object being measured.

While in some applications we want to consider the "holes" in an object (where the probability is zero), for this article we wish to consider the images to produce a continuous probability density function surface. If a probability of zero is allowed then the problem of these "holes" appearing in our curve or surface must be considered. If the probability calculation is made so that no $x_{jk} = 0$, then it is assured that $D_{q=0}(X_k)$ is the morphological dimension of the support for the measure (i.e., 1 for a time series, and 2 for an image). This may seem to be self evident, but many approaches to fractal dimension calculation ignore any volume elements where the probability is zero. In these cases, $D_{q=0}(X_k)$ could be less than the morphological dimension of the support for the measure. It is also important to ensure no $y_{jk} = 0$ for the relative measures in $D_{R_q}(X_k \| Y_k)$ since, otherwise, a divide by zero is possible.

Avoiding the possibility of x_{jk} or y_{jk} being zero makes the comparison between two different signals less error prone. Although the fractal dimension itself is bounded, probabilities of zero can cause the results to be shifted slightly, depending on the rest of the approach for the calculation.

Sufficiency of the Number of Data Points

Another important part in the estimation of a fractal dimension is to determine what happens in the limit case when the scale s approaches 0. Unfortunately, this is not an easy task, primarily because real data sets are always finite. The fractal dimension equations indicate that the critical exponent must be determined in the limiting case as $s \to 0$, but this is obviously impossible with a sampled and recorded signal.

The only hope for accurate calculation is to ensure that (i) the data set is obtained from a sufficiently-sampled acquisition process (i.e., satisfying the Nyquist theorem), and (ii) and that the object has a sufficiently large number of points (pixels for images). If the first condition is violated, the undersampled signal produces aliases that were never in the original signal, and any estimation of fractal dimensions produces meaningless results.

On the other hand, if the number of samples is too small, the estimate may also be meaningless. We found that most strange attractors can produce good results with 5,000 points, although attractors of higher complexity (e.g., the Ikeda strange attractor) may require 50,000 or more samples.

Robust Slope Estimation

From the power-law relation, it is evident that the critical exponent is simply the slope of a log-log plot of the number of M_k measurements vs. the scale s. This is the approach generally taken for estimating the fractal dimension, and it works well if some care is taken in determining the slope of the plot. A usual approach is to form the log-log plot, fit a line to the data points, and estimate the slope of the line.

A few problems exist with determining the slope of the log-log plot when using real data sets. The first problem is that real data sets often plateau, either on one end of the plot, or both. While not observed with all data sets, when a plateau does exist in the log-log plot, care must be taken in the slope estimation so that these points are not used. These plateau regions generally occur at the larger scales of s where the measurement is very coarse, and occur less frequently at the finer scales of s. By including the saturation levels at the ends of the scattered plot, the slope is always underestimated. In these cases, our experiments have found that line-fitting techniques (such as the least-squares line fitting) react adversely to these plateaus and any occasional outliers. Robust line fitting techniques must be used instead to remove these plateau and outlier difficulties.

Another important misstep often taken when calculating the log-log plot is to change the scale s only in a *dyadic* (i.e., doubling or halving of s) manner. Many of the other implementations we have studied have used this approach of changing the scale in dyadic increments, and all of these techniques have produced less than optimal results, particularly on a small number of points in the strange attractor. With the small size of most data sets, a dyadic decrement in scale s produces very few points in the log-log plot. Having few points makes the job of even a robust line-fitting algorithm very difficult. Including a wider range of nondyadic scale decrements affords a line-fitting algorithm with more points to consider and, hence, improves the estimation of the fractal dimension.

EXPERIMENTAL RESULTS

We have conducted many experiments with images such as the standard **lena**, **baboon**, and **peppers**, as well with aerial ortho images such as **urban** and **farm**. Because the latter images are quite large (5,000x5,000 pixels), and they must be delivered to the destination quickly, we have developed new progressive (streaming) image transmission techniques to achieve this objective (e.g., (Dansereau & Kinsner, 1998, 1999, 2000). Within a fraction of a percent of the original image, the essential features of the image are delivered very quickly, while more details are delivered progressively during the study of the image. If the image is of no interest, another image is transmitted.

For example, the urban image shown in Figure 2a requires 0.924% of the original image shown in Figure 2b. Even at 0.139%, the main features are fully recognizable.

One of the practical applications of the fractal dimensions described in this article is to fine tune all the intricacies of image compression using wavelets (e.g., Daubechies, 1990; Mallat, 1989), wavelet

Figure 2. Progressive transmission of **urban**

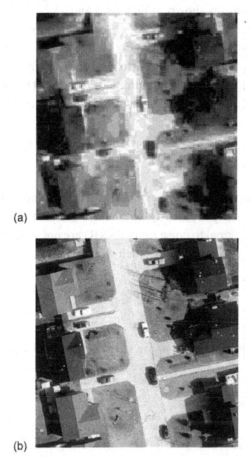

(a)

(b)

(a) 0.924% of the original, (b) Original 100%

packets, and affine transformations (Peitgen, Jurgens, & Saupe, 1992), so that the reconstruction is the highest perceptual quality possible. Because the space in this article does not allow us to discuss the tuning details, we shall show examples of the major metrics for eight progressive image snapshots.

Figure 3 shows the Rényi generalized entropy spectrum, H_q, for eight progressive images of **urban**. It is seen that although there is a difference in the curves for each image, their spread is small. This prompted a study of residuals between the original and the reconstruction, resulting in larger differences.

Figure 4 shows the Rényi multifractal dimension spectrum, D_q, for eight progressive reconstruction images of **urban**. The curves are similar to H_q, but with a different range of values. The main difference is that the dimensions are now multiscale measures. These calculations were also done for residuals.

Figure 5 shows the relative Rényi multifractal dimension spectrum, D_{Rq}, for eight progressive re-constructions of **lena**, using the Daubechies 4 discrete wavelet transform with a quad-tree coding and hard thresholding of 2^n, for $n = 0$ to 10. As expected, the curves pass through the origin for $q=0$. It is seen that when the quality of the images improves, the curves converge to the abscissa. If the scale of the plot is changed to smaller values, one can see the intricacies of the convergence better. Notice that we have switched to a different image (from **urban** to **lena**) because the subjective testing of a familiar image produces consistent results (as shown in Figures 6 and 7).

The image quality measure, IQM, defined by 33 is shown in Figure 6. The relationship is exponential, with small values for good images, and large for poor images.

Finally, Figure 7 shows how well this IQM correlates with the mean-opinion score (MOS) experimental results. We have used a well-established protocol for MOS (Dansereau, 2001). The correlation is excellent, although more experimental work must be done on more difficult and unfamiliar images.

CONCLUSION

This article has provided a theoretical development of the new relative Rényi multifractal dimension spectrum, D_{Rq}, and an image quality metric, IQM. We have confirmed experimentally that the energy-based metrics (such as the peak signal to noise ratio, PSNR) are not suitable for subjective image quality assessment. Instead, the energy-based metrics (such as the Rényi generalized entropy spectrum, H_q),

Figure 3. Rényi generalized entropy spectrum for **urban**

Figure 4. Rényi multifractal dimension spectrum for **urban**

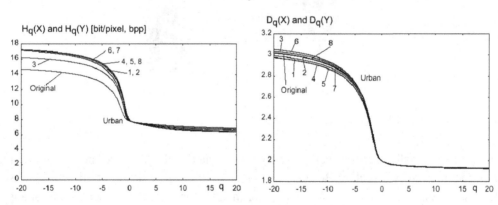

Figure 5. Relative Rényi multifractal dimension spectrum for **lena**

Figure 6. Image quality metric, IQM, for **lena**

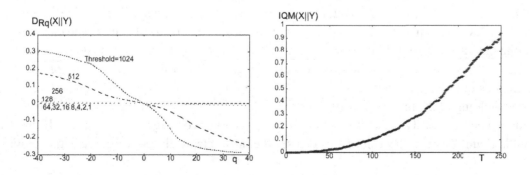

can evaluate the *complexity* of an object, and can be used for fine-tuning of compression algorithms, or in feature extraction for characterization or classification.

A better approach is to use multiscale entropy-based metrics such as the Rényi multifractal dimension spectrum, D_q. Still a better approach is to use the relative Rényi multifractal dimension spectrum, D_{Rq}, which provides convergence to zero for high-quality images. We have shown experimentally that this cMOS measure is closely related to the subjective mean-opinion score, MOS. Clearly, although this measure is not the last development in the quest to find better metrics for cognitive informatics, it appears to be the best so far.

ACKNOWLEDGMENT

This research was supported in part through a research scholarship and grant from the Natural Sciences and Engineering Research Council (NSERC) of Canada. Also, this work was funded in part by Telecommunications Research Laboratories (TRLabs).

REFERENCES

Cover, T. M., & Thomas, J. A. (1991). *Elements of information theory.* New York: Wiley.

Dansereau, R. (2001, May). *Progressive image transmission using fractal and wavelet complexity measures.* Doctoral Thesis, Department of Electrical & Computer Engineering, University of Manitoba, Winnipeg.

Dansereau, R., & Kinsner, W. (1998, May). Progressive transmission of images using wavelets: Evaluation using the Rényi generalized entropy. In *Proceedings of the IEEE Canadian Conference on Elec. and Comp. Eng. (CCECE98),* (pp. 273-276).

Dansereau, R., & Kinsner, W. (1999, May). Rényi generalized entropy analysis of images from a progressive wavelet image transmission. In *Proceedings of the IEEE Canadian Conf. on Elec. and Comp. Eng. (CCECE99).*

Dansereau, R., & Kinsner, W. (2000, May). Progressive image transmission using wavelet packets guided by metrics. In *Proceedings of the Mathematical Modelling and Scientific Computing.*

Dansereau, R., & Kinsner, W. (2001, May) New relative multifractal dimension measures. In *Proceedings of the IEEE International Conference Acoustics, Speech and Signal Processing, ICASSP2001,* (Vol. 3, pp. 1741-1744).

Daubechies, I. (1990, September). Orthonormal bases of compactly supported wavelets. *IEEE Trans. Inform. Theory, 36*(5), 961-1005.

Halsey, T. C., Jensen, M. H., Kadanoff, L. P., Procaccia, I., & Shraiman, B. I. (1986, February). Fractal measures and their singularities: The characterization of strange sets. *Phys. Rev.,* A33, 1141-1151. (See also Halsey, T. C., Jensen, M. H., Kadanoff, L. P., Procaccia, I., & Shraiman, B. I. (1986, August). Erratum: Fractal measures and their singularities: The characterization of strange sets. *Phys. Rev.,* A34, 1601).

Hentschel, H. G. E., & Procaccia, I. (1983, July). The infinite number of generalized dimensions of fractals and strange attractors. *Physica D: Nonlinear Phenomena, D8*(3), 435-444.

Kinsner, W. (1994, May). *Fractal dimensions: Morphological, entropy, spectral and variance classes* (Tech. Rep. DEL94-4). Winnipeg, MB: University of Manitoba.

Kinsner, W. (1994, June 20). *The Hausdorff-Besicovitch Dimension Formulation for Fractals and Multifractals* (Tech. Rep. *DEL94-7)*. Winnipeg, MB: University of Manitoba.

Kinsner, W. (1994, June 15). *Batch and real-time computation of a fractal dimension based on variance of a time series* (Tech. Rep. *DEL94-6)*. Winnipeg, MB: University of Manitoba.

Kinsner, W. (2002, August). Compression and its metrics for multimedia. In *Proceedings f the IEEE 2002 International Conference on Cognitive Informatics (ICCI02),* (pp. 107-121).

Kinsner, W. (2003, August). Characterizing chaos through Lyapunov metrics. In *Proceedings of the IEEE 2003 International Conference On Cognitive Informatics (ICCI03),* (pp. 189-201).

Kinsner, W. (2004, August). Is entropy suitable to characterize data and signals for cognitive informatics? In *Proceedings of the IEEE 2004 International Conference on Cognitive Informatics (ICCI04),* (pp. 6-21).

Kinsner, W. (2005a). Signal processing for autonomic computing. In *Record Can. Applied & Industrial Mathematical Sciences (CAIMS05).*

Kinsner, W. (2005b). A unified approach to fractal dimensions. In *Proceedings of the IEEE 2005 International Conference on Cognitive Informatics (ICCI05),* (pp. 58-72).

Kinsner, W., & Dansereau, R. (2006, August). A relative fractal dimension spectrum as a complexity measure. In *Proceedings of the IEEE 2006 International Conference on Cognitive Informatics (ICCI06)* (pp. 200-208).

Kullback, S., & Leibler, R. A. (1951). On information and sufficiency. *Annals of Math. Stats., 22*(1), 79-86.

Lanterman, A. D., O'Sullivan, J. A., & Miller, M. I. (1999, December). Kullback-Leibler distances for quantifying clutter and models. *Optical Engineering, 38*(12), 2134-2146.

Mallat, S. G. (1989, July). A theory for multiresolution signal decomposition: The wavelet representation. *IEEE Trans. Pattern Anal. Machine Intell., 11*(7), 674-693.

Peitgen, H.-O., Jürgens, H., & Saupe, D. (1992). *Chaos and fractals: New frontiers of science.* New York: Springer-Verlag.

Potter, M., & Kinsner, W. (2007, August). Direct calculation of the fractal singularity spectrum. In *Proceedings of the IEEE 2007 International Conference on Cognitive Informatics (ICCI07),* (pp. 7).

Rényi, A. A. (1955). On a new axiomatic theory of probability. *Acta Mathematica Hungarica, 6,* 285-335.

Rényi, A. A. (1959). On the dimension and entropy of probability distributions. *Acta Mathematica Hungarica, 10,* 193-236.

Rényi, A. A. (1960). On measures of entropy and information. In *Proceedings of the Fourth Berkeley Symposium on Math. Statist. Probab.*, (Vol. 1, pp. 547-561).

Riedi, R.H., & Scheuring, I. (1997). Conditional and relative multifractal spectra. *Fractals*, 5(1), 153-168.

Shannon, C. E. (1948, July & October). A mathematical theory of communications. *Bell Syst. Tech. J.*, 27, 379-423 & 623-656.

Wang, Y. (2002, August). On cognitive informatics. In *Proceedings of the 1st IEEE International Conference on Cognitive Informatics (ICCI02)*, (pp. 34-42).

This work was previously published in the International Journal of Cognitive Informatics and Natural Intelligence, Vol. 2, Issue 1, edited by Y. Wang, pp. 73-86, copyright 2008 by IGI Publishing (an imprint of IGI Global).

Chapter 21
3D Object Classification Based on Volumetric Parts

Weiwei Xing
Beijing Jiaotong University, China

Weibin Liu
Beijing Jiaotong University, China

Baozong Yuan
Beijing Jiaotong University, China

ABSTRACT

This article proposes a 3D object classification approach based on volumetric parts, where Superquadric-based Geon (SBG) description is implemented for representing the volumetric constituents of 3D object. In the approach, 3D object classification is decomposed into the constrained search on interpretation tree and the similarity measure computation. First, a set of integrated features and corresponding constraints are presented, which are used for defining efficient interpretation tree search rules and evaluating the model similarity. Then a similarity measure computation algorithm is developed to evaluate the shape similarity of unknown object data and the stored models. By this classification approach, both whole and partial matching results with model shape similarity ranks can be obtained; especially, focus match can be achieved, in which different key parts can be labeled and all the matched models with corresponding key parts can be obtained. Some experiments are carried out to demonstrate the validity and efficiency of the approach for 3D object classification.

Cognitive informatics studies intelligent behavior from a computational point of view. It is the interdisciplinary study of cognitive and information sciences that investigates into the internal information processing mechanisms and processes of the natural intelligence in human brains and minds, such as reasoning, understanding, visual and auditory perception, and so forth (Wang, 2003, 2007; Wang & Kinsner, 2006). The work in this article mainly focuses on 3D object classification by intelligent computation, which is one of the basic research topics of visual information representation and interpretation.

Specifically, the problem considered in this article is how to classify 3D object into one of the known object classes based on volumetric parts and obtain the 3D models in the library with shape similarity measures. It is well known that complete and precise description of 3D objects and elaborate matching are essential to the 3D object classification. Volumetric representation has been used popularly in 3D object recognition (Krivic & Solina, 2004; Medioni & François, 2000; Pentland, 1987) because it is viewpoint independent, insensitive to local variations, and supported by extensive psychological evidence, most notably "Biederman (1987)."

Superquadric-based geon (SBG) description is implemented in this article for representing volumetric parts of 3D objects, which combines superquadric quantitative parametric information and geon's qualitative geometrical attributes. There has been much research work focused on object recognition with superquadrics or geons (Borges & Fisher, 1997; Dickinson, 1997; Krivic & Solina, 2004; Pentland, 1987; Raja & Jain, 1992). Especially, in "Borges and Fisher (1997)," superquadrics and geons were used for volumetric representation, and interpretation tree (Grimson, 1990) was implemented for 3D recognition. The models were arranged by the qualitative shape information (geon types) of model's parts. The indexing stage selects a subset of the model library to be fully searched based on the geon type. However, only the obtained geon types are not precise to determine the search space of 3D models due to the possible classification error and the ambiguity of geon type comparison of two corresponding parts of models, which may lead to miss the correct recognition results. As well, "Csákány and Wallace (2003)" studied the 3D meshed object classification, in which the bounding surface of objects was segmented into patches that can be described by some shape properties. Learning by some examples and class generation are two key components of the system.

In this article, we present a volumetric part based 3D object classification approach, in which the classification problem is looked upon as two subproblems, the constrained search on interpretation tree and the shape similarity measure computation. The article mainly makes the following contributions:

1. A set of integrated shape features of 3D object are proposed based on the SBG description. These features not only reflect the individual parts' geometrical shape, but the models' topological information among volumetric parts, which have powerful representative and discriminative capability;
2. A shape similarity measure computation algorithm is developed to evaluate the similarity measure between the unknown object data and 3D models in the library;
3. Both whole and partial matches can be accomplished with model shape similarity ranks by the proposed classification approach. Particularly, focus match can be achieved, in which different key parts of interest are labeled and all the matched models including the corresponding parts are obtained with similarity measures. This is very significant for some application areas, such as the retrieval and assembly of industrial CAD parts.

PROBLEM DESCRIPTION

The specific problem we consider in this article is to classify 3D object into one of the known object classes and obtain models with shape similarity measures. We do not discuss how 3D data is segmented and fitted by superquadrics, which have performed well in much research work (Gupta & Bajcsy, 1993; Jaklic, Leonardis, & Solina, 2000; Liu & Yuan, 2001).

We are given a set of object data parts represented by SBGs, and the prestored models with object class labels. The classification of 3D objects can be regarded as the match between 3D object data and models, which is structured as an Interpretation Tree (Grimson, 1990). In Figure 1, let $\{m_1, m_2, ..., m_i, ..., m_p\}$ be a set of model parts and $\{d_1, d_2, ..., d_j, ..., d_q\}$, be the object data parts, starting at a root node, we construct a tree in a depth-first fashion, assigning one model part to different data parts at each level of the tree.

In order to deal with the possible nonexistence of a feasible match between the current model part and the data parts, the "wild card" (*) is introduced to match a null data part with a model part in the tree for improving the robustness. A path through this tree represents a set of feasible correspondences or matching pairs, that is, a consistent interpretation.

Volumetric Representation: Superquadric-Based Geon (SBG)

RBC Theory and Geons

Biederman's RBC theory (Biederman, 1987) provides a promising computational framework for the object recognition and postulates a finite set of distinct volumetric shapes called "geons" as the basis for representation of objects. RBC theory maintains that the set of geons apparently have sufficient representational power to express humans' capacity for basic visual recognition, and the visual system readily decomposes the objects into such components and represents them in terms of their geons and the invariant relationships among them. Geons are classified due to four qualitative geometrical properties: axis shape, cross-section edge shape, cross-section size sweeping function, and cross-section symmetry.

These attributes provide distinct shape characteristics useful for symbolic object recognition (Bergevin & Levine, 1993). Psychological experimentation has provided supports for the descriptive power of geon-based description (Biederman & Gerhardstein, 1993) and geon models have been proposed as a basis for numbers of object recognition systems (Bergevin & Levine, 1993; Dickinson, 1997).

Figure 1. Complete interpretation tree structure

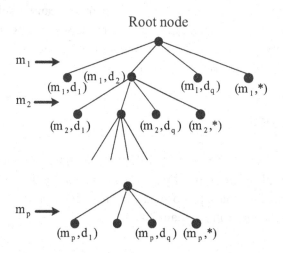

Superquadric Models

Superquadrics as a family of parametric shapes can describe a wide variety of relatively complex and realistic 3D primitive shapes effectively with compact parameters (Barr, 1981). A basic superquadric surface may be defined by an implicit equation:

$$f(x,y,z) = \left(\left(\tfrac{x}{a_x}\right)^{2/\varepsilon_2} + \left(\tfrac{y}{a_y}\right)^{2/\varepsilon_2} \right)^{\varepsilon_2/\varepsilon_1} + \left(\tfrac{z}{a_z}\right)^{2/\varepsilon_1} - 1 = 0 \tag{1}$$

where a_x, a_y, a_z are defined for the size along X, Y, Z axis, ε_1, ε_2 are square parameters and control the shape of superquadric model.

The modeling power of superquadrics is augmented by applying various deformation operations which include bending, tapering, and so forth (Barr, 1981; Solina & Bajcsy, 1990) to the basic superquadrics.

Superquadric-Based Geons

Because the information offered by geons is only qualitative in nature (Dickinson, 1997), using geon-based description for 3D object recognition directly would not be very efficient in usual cases. In the article, superquadrics as a unified quantitative parametric shape models are implemented for representing geons because of superquadric powerful modeling capability and extensive implementation in computer vision, which brings a compositive volumetric representation called Superquadric-based Geons (SBG) in this article.

Geons are classified by a labeling A-B-C, where A∈{s=straight, b=bent}, axis shape; B∈{s=straight, c=curved}, cross-section edge shape; C∈{co=constant, id=increasing-and-decreasing, t=tapered}, cross-section size sweeping function.

Obviously, SBG combines superquadric quantitative parametric description and the geon's qualitative geometrical attributes, which have powerful representative and discriminative capability. In this article, we use 12 geon types, shown in Figure 2.

SBG Extraction

In order to implement SBGs for representing the volumetric parts of 3D object, the superquadric parameters and geon type of each part have to be obtained by the following three steps:

1. Superquadric fitting to 3D part data with real-coded genetic algorithm (RCGA) is performed for reconstructing the parametric description of volumetric parts, and the superquadric quantitative information is obtained.
2. A set of discriminative features are derived from the superquadric parameters for the next SVM-based geon classification.
3. Geon classification is implemented utilizing SVM-based multiclass classifier that is trained by fast SMO (sequential minimal optimization) algorithm and the qualitative attribute, geon type is achieved.

Figure 2. The set of twelve SBGs

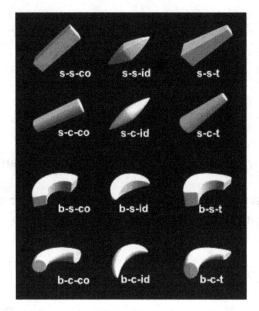

Thus, SBG description of volumetric part is extracted including the superquadric parameters and the geon type that the part belongs to.

3D Models

All the models used in this article were created manually using a modeler called AVRMODEL that we developed. First, individual parts of 3D model represented by SBGs are created and edited, including superquadric shape, size, and geon type; Next, the created parts are assembled together to construct a complete 3D model, including positions, rotations, and connection attributes of these parts.

FEATURES, CONSTRAINTS, AND TREE SEARCH

The efficacy of interpretation tree method as a matching algorithm is the use of some constraints to prune the branches of the tree which lead to inconsistent interpretations. In this work, we present a set of integrated part features with powerful discriminative capability, based on which of the corresponding constraints and the tree search rules are defined to fast find possible consistent interpretations.

Features and Corresponding Constraints

Unary Features and Constraints

All the following unary constraints forced by the corresponding features are applied to the newest pair (m_i, d_{j_i}) in an interpretation tree.

- Part connection number FU_{Pnum}: It is the number of parts connecting with the current part. For example, in Figure 3, as for the desk part m_1, it connects with the parts m_2, m_3, m_4 and m_5, and hence FU_{Pnum} of m_1 is 4.
Considering $FU_{Pnum}^{m_i}$ of model part m_i and $FU_{Pnum}^{d_{ji}}$ of object data part d_{ji}, we define the constraint for FU_{Pnum} as:

$$FU_{Pnum}\_constraint(i, j_i) = True \text{ iff } FU_{Pnum}^{m_i} = FU_{Pnum}^{d_{ji}}$$

- Volume rate FU_{Vrate}: It is defined as the ratio of current part volume to the whole model volume, which reflects the part's spatial occupancy. The constraint forced by FU_{Vrate} is:

$$FU_{Vrate}constraint(i, j_i) = True \text{ iff } \left| FU_{Vrate}^{m_i} - FU_{Vrate}^{d_{ji}} \right| \le \varepsilon_v$$

This constraint says that the volume rate FU_{Vrate} of m_i must differ from that of d_{ji} by no more than a bounded measurement tolerance.

- 3D spherical harmonic descriptor FU_{sph}: This feature is a 3D rotation invariant describing volumetric part shape. The FU_{sph} extraction of volumetric part represented by SBG is decomposed into three steps: first, sample regularly on superquadric surface along the longitude and latitude directions; second, construct spherical function describing superquadric surface based on the obtained samples; finally, implement fast spherical harmonic transform on the spherical function and obtain the 3D spherical harmonic descriptor (Xing, Liu, & Yuan, 2005). Since FU_{sph} is a vector, we let

$$FU_{sph}\_constraint(i, j_i) = True \text{ iff } \| FU_{sph}^{m_i} - FU_{sph}^{d_{ji}} \| \le \varepsilon_s$$

- Geon type FU_{geon}: This is the qualitative attribute of volumetric parts. The related constraint is defined as:

$$FU_{geon}\_constraint(i, j_i) = True \text{ iff } FU_{geon}^{m_i} = FU_{geon}^{d_{ji}}$$

Figure 3. A sample model of desk

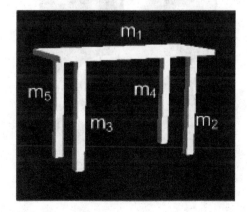

- Elongation FU_{elong}: It consists of two elements $FU_{elong1} = \frac{a_{\max}}{a_{med}}$ and $FU_{elong2} = \frac{a_{med}}{a_{\min}}$, in which $a_{\max}$, a_{med}, $a_{\min}$ are the maximal, medium, and minimal superquadric size parameters of volumetric part along X, Y, Z axis respectively. Here, we let:

$$FU_{elong\_}\text{constraint}(i, j_i) = True \text{ iff } \left\| FU_{elong}^{m_i} - FU_{elong}^{d_{j_i}} \right\| \leq \varepsilon_e$$

That is to say, the distance between FU_{elong}s of m_i and d_{j_i} must not beyond a predefined tolerance ε_e.

Binary Features and Constraints

Suppose current matching pairs are $\{(m_i, d_{j_i})\}$, $i = 1, ..., k$, and given a new pair $(m_{k+1}, d_{j_{k+1}})$, the used binary features and corresponding constraints on $(m_{k+1}, d_{j_{k+1}}; m_i, d_{j_i})$ are as follows:

- Connections $FB_{connect}$: This feature represents the connecting relationship of one part with other parts of 3D model and the related constraint can be written as:

$$FB_{connect\_}\text{contraint}(k + 1, j_{k+1}; i, j_i) = True \text{ iff } FB_{connect}^{m_{k+1}, m_i} = FB_{connect}^{d_{j_{k+1}}, d_{j_i}}$$

- Connection type $FB_{contype}$: It reflects the number of intersections between two parts. For instance, in Figure 4, there are two intersections marked with A and B between part m_1 and part m_3, but one intersection between m_1 and m_2, which leads to the different connection type of (m_1, m_3) and (m_1, m_2). Similar to $FB_{connect\_}$contraint, the $FB_{contype\_}$contraint is defined by:

$$FB_{contype\_}\text{contraint}(k + 1, j_{k+1}; i, j_i) = True \text{ iff } FB_{contype}^{m_{k+1}, m_i} = FB_{contype}^{d_{j_{k+1}}, d_{j_i}}$$

Figure 4. A sample model for illustrating the feature of connection type

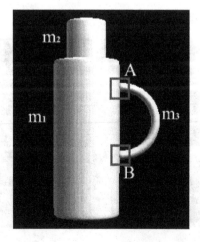

- Volume ratio FB_{Bratio}: The feature is defined as the ratio of one part volume to another part volume. The related constraint is that the difference of $\frac{V_{m_{k+1}}}{V_{m_i}}$ and $\frac{V_{d_{j_{k+1}}}}{V_{d_{j_i}}}$ must be restricted within a bounded measurement tolerance for $i = 1, ..., k$, which is formulated as:

$$FB_{vratio}\_contraint(k + 1, j_{k+1}; i, j_i) = True \text{ iff } \left| FB_{vratio}^{m_{k+1}, m_i} - FB_{vratio}^{d_{j_{k+1}}, d_{j_i}} \right| \leq \varepsilon_{vr}$$

The above tolerances $\varepsilon_v, \varepsilon_s, \varepsilon_e$, and ε_{vr} are predefined empirically.

The unary features and constraints represent the volumetric part shape, while the binary feature constraints mainly reflect the topological structure of 3D model, which are efficient for the interpretation tree search.

Constrained Tree Search

Given these feature constraints, the constrained tree search process consists of a depth first search. Suppose the search process is currently at some node at level k in the interpretation tree and with a consistent partial interpretation given by

$$I_k = \{(m_1, d_{j_1}), (m_2, d_{j_2}), ..., (m_k, d_{j_k})\}.$$

We now consider the next model part m_{k+1}, and its possible assignment to object data part $d_{j_{k+1}}$, where j_{k+1} varies from 1 to $q + 1$, and q is the number of object data parts. This leads to a potential new interpretation:

$$I_{k+1} = \{(m_1, d_{j_1}), ..., (m_k, d_{j_k}), (m_{k+1}, d_{j_{k+1}})\}$$

Due to implementing the volumetric parts instead of the surface patches, the computational complexity is decreased greatly, which allows defining the looser pruning in the tree search rules so that more possible consistent interpretations and matching results are obtained.

The following rules are defined and applied in the constrained tree search.

- If $(m_{k+1}, d_{j_{k+1}})$ is a wild card match, then the new interpretation I_{k+1} is consistent and we continue the tree search downward.
- If m_{k+1} and $d_{j_{k+1}}$ are both real parts, we must verify that the unary constraints hold for the pair $(m_{k+1}, d_{j_{k+1}})$ and binary constraints hold for the pairs $(m_{k+1}, d_{j_{k+1}}; m_i, d_{j_i})$, for $i = 1, ..., k$.
- If N_1 unary constraints and N_2 binary constraints are true, where N_1 and N_2 are predefined as the threshold according to the required matching precision, then the new interpretation I_{k+1} is a consistent interpretation, and we continue the depth first search; otherwise, I_{k+1} is an inconsistent interpretation. In this case, we increment the object data part index j_{k+1} by 1 and try again with a new I_{k+1}, until $j_{k+1} = q + 1$.
- If the number of wild card matches along one branch is beyond a predefined threshold, then this branch is considered as an inconsistent interpretation.

However, if the search process is currently at some node at level k in the interpretation tree, and has an inconsistent partial interpretation given by:

$$I_k = \{(m_1, d_{j_1}), (m_2, d_{j_2}), ..., (m_k, d_{j_k})\}$$

then it is in the process of backtracking.

Once the search process reaches a leaf of the interpretation tree, a consistent interpretation is achieved, which represents a feasible match between the model and the object data. Finally, one or more consistent interpretations are obtained as the feasible part matches between the model and the object data. We may get the best match according to the similarity measure computation, which is described in the following the third section.

SIMILARITY MEASURE COMPUTATION

Based on the obtained consistent interpretations and the presented features, a shape similarity measure computation algorithm is developed to achieve matching results with model similarity ranks. The algorithm mainly consists of the following: (1) Part similarity measure; (2) Whole and partial match; (3) Focus match on the key parts; (4) Classification.

Definitions: *Let one certain object class include r models M_l, l, ... , r, and the unknown object data D and model M_l be represented as a set of parts*

$$\begin{cases} M_l = \{m_{l,1}, m_{l,2}, \cdots, m_{l,i}, \cdots, m_{l,p}\} \\ D = \{d_1, d_2, \cdots, d_{j_i}, \cdots, d_q\} \end{cases}$$

The nodes of interpretation tree denote the part matching pairs $(m_{l,i}, d_{j_i})$ of M_l and D, for $i = 1, 2, ..., p$ and $j_i = 1, 2, ..., q$. Each part $m_{l,i}$ or d_{j_i} can be formulated as a vector *fm* or *fd* in Equation 2, where u_k or v_k may be a scalar or a vector corresponding to the features described in the second section.

$$fm = [u_1, u_2, \cdots, u_k, \cdots, u_n]$$
$$fd = [v_1, v_2, \cdots, v_k, \cdots, v_n] \tag{2}$$

Part Similarity Measure - $Psim(m_{l,i}, d_{j_i})$

Part similarity is computed on one matching pair $(m_{l,i}, d_{j_i})$ of the model part and object data part. Due to the different effect of features on shape similarity measure, it is natural to assign different weights $\{w_1, w_2, ..., w_k, ..., w_n\}$. The weight values are determined empirically, and reflect the experience by some tests on the importance of each feature. The part similarity measure consists of two components $Psim_U$ and $Psim_B$, corresponding to the unary and binary features, respectively.

First, for two corresponding features u_k and v_k, the feature similarity $Fsim_U(u_k, v_k)$ can be calculated by Equations 3 or 4. For FU_{Pnum}, FU_{geon} and $FB_{connect}$, FB_{contye}, Equation 3 is implemented,

$$Fsim_U(u_k, v_k) = \begin{cases} 1, & if \quad u_k = v_k \\ 0, & if \quad u_k \neq v_k \end{cases} \tag{3}$$

And for the other features, Equation 4 is implemented,

$$Fsim_U(u_k, v_k) = \left\| 1 - \frac{\|u_k - v_k\|}{\max(\|u_k\|, \|v_k\|)} \right\|, 1 \leq k \leq n \tag{4}$$

Then the part similarity measure $Psim(m_{l,i}, d_{j_i})$ of $m_{l,i}$ and d_{j_i} will be calculated by,

$$Psim(m_{l,i}, d_{j_i}) = w_{un} \cdot \sum_{k=1}^{s} w_k \cdot Fsim(u_k, v_k)$$
$$+ w_{bi} \cdot \sum_{k=s+1}^{s+t} w_k \cdot Fsim(u_k, v_k) \tag{5}$$

where s and t are the number of unary and binary features respectively, $s = 6$ and $t = 3$ here. In Equation 5, the part similarity measure $Psim$ is the sum of two terms, the former $Psim_U$ and the latter $Psim_B$, where w_{un} and w_{bi} are the related normalized weights. In particular, for the nodes at first level, $Psim_B$ is always assigned to 1; and the wild card matches have no contribution to the part similarity computation, and thus are assigned to 0.

Whole and Partial Similarity Measure - $Msim_l^W$ and $Msim_l^P$

Model shape similarity measure $Msim_l$ of model M_l and object data D corresponds to an obtained feasible consistent interpretation. We define two kinds of matches for the model similarity measure, whole match and partial match. The whole match focuses on the global shape similarity of M_l and D; however, when the part number q of object data D is less than that p of model M_l, that is, the object is superimposed on the 3D model, there also exists partial match that emphasizes the local accurate correspondence.

Let the part similarity of the pair $(m_{l,i}, d_{j_i})$ in a consistent interpretation be $Psim_i$, the whole similarity measure $Msim_l^W$ of M_l and D can be calculated by:

$$Msim_l^W = \frac{\sum_{i=1}^{\max(p,q)} Psim(m_{l,i}, d_{j_i})}{\max(p,q)} \tag{6}$$

where p and q are the part number of model and object data, respectively. The similarity measure $Msim_l^P$ of partial match is evaluated by:

$$Msim_l^P = \frac{\sum_{i=1}^{q} Psim(m_{l,i}, d_{j_i})}{q} \tag{7}$$

where q is less than p.

Focus Similarity Measure - FOsim

Generally, the parts concerned for matching of same object data are different according to different tasks or aims, which is just the motivation of the focus match presented here. In focus match, the different key parts of object data may be labeled and all the models containing the corresponding key parts can be matched. Let the labeled key parts number of object data be N_{Dkey}, two supplementary constraints will be added in the tree search especially for the focus match. First, only the model with part number p that is not less than N_{Dkey} may be passed to the interpretation tree search process; second, the allowed number of the wild card matching pairs along a path must not be more than $p - N_{Dkey}$, otherwise the branch will be pruned. These two constraints ensure all the key parts of object data will have a real match. The focus matching similarity is achieved by

$$FOsim = \frac{\sum_{i=1}^{N_{Dkey}} Psim(m_{l,i}, d_{j_i})}{N_{Dkey}} \tag{8}$$

Classification

The following rules are applied in classification.

1. Select all the models with similarity measure more than a predefined threshold; for each object class, evaluate the object class similarity measure by averaging the model similarity measure values of the selected models belonging to the current object class.
2. The unknown object data will be classified into the object class that has the highest class similarity measure obtained in (1).

EXPERIMENTAL RESULTS AND EVALUATION

For evaluating the performance of the proposed classification approach, experiments have been carried out. We match the query object selected randomly from the 3D library with all the models in the library and analyze how well the result ranks correspond to human's similarity classification of the models. We construct a number of models for each object class according to the actual diversity of the class, which greatly improves the 3D model library's completeness and realities of representing object categories. Twenty four object classes are built on AVRMODEL and used in the experiments. The domain of the objects explored is that of some man-made commodities.

In each Table, the leftmost column shows the query object, the middle columns show the first several closest models in the library which are ranked from left to right according to the shape similarity measures, and the rightmost column is the obtained object class which the query object belongs to.

Whole Match

Table 1 shows three experiments on the whole match. In each result, the query object to be classified is the first of the similarity ranks and the corresponding similarity measure value is 1. It is obvious that the ranked models according to the obtained similarity measures are consistent with human visual perception on object shape similarity.

Whole Match and Partial Match

As described in the third section, whole match emphasizes the global shape similarity of all the parts between the query object and the models in 3D library; while partial match is suitable to the case that the query object has less parts than that of the model in similarity match, that is to say, the query object is superimposed on the model.

Table 2 shows two experiments on the objects of cup class and bed class, respectively, and the results demonstrate the difference between whole match and partial match clearly. In the first experiment, the query object is a cup with only one part of the body. In the case of whole match, the matched models with higher similarity measures are the cups that consist of only one part because they have the higher global shape similarity to the query cup, such as the second and third models (cup10 and cup9) in the shaded cells. As for the partial match, it is obvious that cup6 and cup5 contain the more similar part, cup body, to the query and have better local shape similarity, and thus achieve higher similarity measures. In the second experiment on the bed object, although both the third models matched are bed8 in the whole match and partial match cases, the value of similarity measure in the partial match is higher than that in the whole match. The experimental results clearly show the different focuses of whole match and partial match.

Focus Match on Key Parts

Table 3 shows some experimental results of focus match. As for the same query chair and query bed, respectively, the labeled key parts are different, as illustrated in the left "key parts" column, and hence

Table 1. Whole match of the objects belonging to the lamp, phone handle and bed class

Query	Model Similarity Rank					Class Label
Query 1	lamp1	lamp4	lamp2	lamp5	lamp3	Lamp
	1.0000	0.9564	0.9123	0.8768	0.7266	
Query 2	phone1	phone2	phone3	phone7	phone4	Phone
	1.0000	0.8706	0.7924	0.7351	0.6125	
Query 3	bed11	bed12	bed18	bed17	bed19	Bed
	1.0000	0.9143	0.9087	0.8902	0.8706	

the different matching results are achieved. In the comparison experiments on the chair, the five key parts, 1 seat and 4 legs, are labeled for the first experiment, and the six parts with an extra crossbar between two legs are labeled for the second experiment. In the results of both experiments, the models with the corresponding key parts are matched. Because there are only three chair models with the six corresponding key parts in the 3D library, the fourth match is a desk that contains six parts similar to the labeled key parts, while its similarity measure is very low due to the great shape difference.

CONCLUSION AND FURTHER DIRECTIONS

In this article, we have proposed a volumetric part based approach to solve 3D object classification problem, which mainly consists of the constrained interpretation tree search and the shape similarity measure computation algorithm. In the approach, a set of integrated features and related constraints are presented, which reflect both individual parts' shape features and 3D model's global topological information. These feature constraints are very efficient for the constrained tree search and have powerful discriminative capability for the classification. By this approach, both whole match and partial match with model shape similarity measures can be accomplished. In particular, the focus matching computation can be completed on different labeled key parts, which is suitable for different specific tasks.

We have shown the performance of the proposed classification approach on a set of 3D objects built from synthetic 3D data. The future research directs toward the further improvement of feature constraints, the build-up of large scale 3D model library, and tests on the laser-scanned 3D data.

Table 2. Comparison experiments of whole match and partial match

Table 3. Focus match of the objects belonging to the chair class and bed class

Query	Model Similarity Rank				Class Label
					Chair
Key parts	chair2 1.0000	chair3 0.9450	chair6 0.9420	chair5 0.9082	
Query1					Chair
Key parts	chair2 1.0000	chair6 0.9496	chair5 0.9156	table5 0.8344	
					Bed
Key parts	bed12 1.0000	bed11 0.9995	bed13 0.9987	bed5 0.9984	
Query2					Bed
Key parts	bed12 1.0000	bed11 0.9995	bed18 0.9650	bed19 0.9500	

ACKNOWLEDGMENT

This work is supported by the National Grand Fundamental Research 973 Program under Grant 2006CB303105, the University Research Foundation No.K06J0170 and No.JS2005J0503, and the National Natural Science Foundation of China under Grant 60441002.

REFERENCES

Barr, A. (1981). Superquadrics and angle-preserving transformations. *IEEE Transactions on Computer Graphics and Applications, 1*(1), 11-23.

Bergevin, R., & Levine, M. (1993). Generic object recognition: Building and matching coarse descriptions from line drawings. *IEEE Transactions on Pattern Analysis and Machine Intelligence, 15*(1), 19-36.

Biederman, I. (1987). Recognition-by-components: A theory of human image understanding. *Psychological Review, 94*, 115-147.

Biederma, I., & Gerhardstein, P. (1993). Recognizing depth-rotated objects: Evidence for 3D viewpoint invariance. *Journal of Experimental Psychology: Human Perception and Performance, 19*, 1162-1182.

Borges, D. L., & Fisher, R. B. (1997). Class-based recognition of 3D objects represented by volumetric primitives. *Image and Vision Computing, 15*(8), 655-664.

Csákány, P., & Wallace A. M. (2003). Representation and Classification of 3-D Objects. *IEEE Transactions on Systems, Man, and Cybernetics - Part B: Cybernetics, 33*(4), 638-647.

Dickinson S.J., Bergevin R., Biederman I., Eklundh J. O., Munck-Fairwood R., Jain A.K., Pentland A. (1997). Panel report: The potential of geons for generic 3-D object recognition. *Image and Vision Computing, 15*(4), 277-292.

Grimson, W. E. L. (1990). *Object recognition by computer: The role of geometric constraints.* USA: MIT Press.

Gupta, A., & Bajcsy R. (1993). Volumetric segmentation of range images of 3-D objects using superquadric models. *Computer Vision, Graphics, and Image Processing, 58*(3), 302-326.

Jaklic, A., Leonardis, A., & Solina F. (2000). *Segmentation and recovery of superquadrics.* The Netherlands: Kluwer Academic Publishers.

Krivic, J., & Solina, F. (2004). Part-level object recognition using superquadrics. *Computer Vision and Image Understanding, 95*(1), 105-126.

Liu, W. B., & Yuan, B. Z. (2001). Superquadric based hierarchical reconstruction for virtualizing free form objects from 3D data. *Chinese Journal of Electronics, 10*(1), 100-105.

Medioni, G., & François, A. (2000). 3-D structures for generic object recognition. In *Proceedings of the 15th International Conference on Pattern Recognition (ICPR'00)*, Barcelona, Spain, (pp. 1030-1037).

Pentland, A. (1987). Recognition by parts, In *Proceedings of the First International Conference on Computer Vision (ICCV'87)*, London, England, (pp. 612-620).

Raja, N., & Jain, A. (1992). Recognizing geons from superquadrics fitted to range data. *Image and Vision Computing, 10*(3), 179-190.

Solina, F., & Bajcsy, R. (1990). Recovery of parametric models from range images: The case for superquadrics with global deformations. *IEEE Transactions on Pattern Analysis and Machine Intelligence, 12*(2), 131-147.

Xing, W. W., Liu, W. B., & Yuan, B. Z. (2005). Superquadric similarity measure with spherical harmonics in 3D object recognition. *Chinese Journal of Electronics, 14*(3), 529-534.

Wang, Y. (2003). On cognitive informatics. *Brain and Mind: A Transdisciplinary Journal of Neuroscience and Neurophilosophy, 4*(2), 151-167.

Wang, Y. (2007, January). The theoretical framework of cognitive informatics. *The International Journal of Cognitive Informatics and Natural Intelligence (IJCiNi), 1*(1), 1-27. IGI Publishing, USA.

Wang, Y., & Kinsner, W. (2006, March). Recent advances in cognitive informatics. *IEEE Transactions on Systems, Man, and Cybernetics (C), 36*(2), 121-123.

This work was previously published in the International Journal of Cognitive Informatics and Natural Intelligence, Vol. 2, Issue 1, edited by Y. Wang, pp. 87-99, copyright 2008 by IGI Publishing (an imprint of IGI Global).

Chapter 22
Modeling Underwater Structures

Michael Jenkin
York University, Canada

Andrew Hogue
York University, Canada

Andrew German
University of Ontario Institute of Technology, Canada

Sunbir Gill
York University, Canada

Anna Topol
York University, Canada

Stephanie Wilson
York University, Canada

ABSTRACT

Deliberate exploitation of natural resources and excessive use of environmentally abhorrent materials have resulted in environmental disruptions threatening the life support systems. A human centric approach of development has already damaged nature to a large extent. This has attracted the attention of environmental specialists and policy makers. It has also led to discussions at various national and international conventions. The objective of protecting natural resources cannot be achieved without the involvement of professionals from multidisciplinary areas. This chapter recommends a model for the creation of knowledge-based systems for natural resources management. Further, it describes making use of unique capabilities of remote sensing satellites for conserving natural resources and managing natural disasters. It is exclusively for the people who are not familiar with the technology and who are given the task of framing policies.

INTRODUCTION

Intelligent machines must interact with their world. Such machines must be able to construct internal representations of their environment, reason about these representations, and then move purposefully within their environment using these representations. Building internal representations of the external world and reasoning about them is also a key goal of the field of cognitive informatics (Wang, 2003). However, in spite of decades of advances in mobility and sensing and reasoning algorithms, building fully autonomous machines remain an elusive goal. Achieving full autonomy requires systems that are sufficiently robust such that they can deal with the vagaries of complex environments and external effects that are difficult or impossible to model, and have the ability to reason with representations of complex structures and events. Although there have been many advances in terms of autonomous systems, much of the ongoing research concentrates on the development of robots that operate in "clean" research labs that do not present the full complexity of the outside world. Research that has addressed robots in the field typically assumes that the problem is constrained to a plane or that there is a preferred orientation with respect to gravity. Here we explore what is perhaps the most difficult external environment: underwater. The underwater environment presents numerous challenges for the design of visually guided robots, yet it is these constraints and challenges that make this environment almost ideal for the development and evaluation of robotic sensing technologies. The underwater medium limits robot-human communication to low-bandwidth mechanisms such as an acoustic modem or visual markers (e.g., Dudek et al., 2007; Sattar, Bourque, Giguere, & Dudek, 2007) and thus underwater robots must present a higher degree of autonomy than that required in the terrestrial domain. Failures that are minor for terrestrial vehicles can be catastrophic for vehicles operating underwater. These devices must cope with the realities of six-degrees-of-freedom (6DOF) motion in highly unstructured environments. In addition, unknown external forces such as currents act upon the vehicle, and sensing is complicated by fish and suspended particulate matter (aquatic snow).

Because of these complexities, the underwater environment provides a vast range of applications for which the reconstruction of complex 3-D structures is desired. For example, a sensor capable of autonomously reconstructing a 3-D model of a ship's hull would enable the inspection and analysis of its structural integrity and the search for malicious payloads (Negahdaripour & Firoozfam, 2006). Similarly, a 3-D model of a ship wreck could aid in determining the cause of the event. In addition to man-made structures there is a significant need for the analysis of natural structures, such as coral reefs. Coral reefs are important for the global underwater ecosystem. They provide both shelter and nutrition for many species of aquatic life. Reefs are composed of extremely fragile organisms that can be destroyed by slight changes in water temperature, salinity, and pollution. One metric for establishing the health of the reef is to monitor its size with respect to time. Manually measuring reef size is an error-prone and time-consuming effort. Divers swim along the transect and use video to record the reef. Random samplings are then made of these videos to estimate various reef populations (Aronson, Edmunds, Precht, Swanson, & Levitan, 1994). Although it is well known that such analysis introduces systematic biases into the recorded data due to perspective distortions and other factors (Porter & Meier, 1992), this approach remains the basis of current reef monitoring techniques. More sophisticated image processing techniques (e.g., Gintert et al., 2007) typically concentrate on 2-D image mosaics rather than investigating 3-D object recovery. Automatic 3-D reconstructions could be used to analyze the health of the reef by measuring changes to both the true size of the reef and the population density of the coral itself.

Given the importance of the underwater environment in terms of applications it is thus not surprising that there has been considerable interest in the development of autonomous and semiautonomous underwater systems. For example, Eustice, Singh, Leonard, Walter, and Ballard (2005) describe a tethered system that was used to map parts of the RMS Titanic, and Ribes and Borrelly (1997) describe a visually guided underwater pipe inspection robot.

In addition to addressing a wealth of application-specific needs, visual sensing is an enabling technology for autonomous underwater vehicles (AUVs). A critical requirement for many AUVs is the need to maintain an ongoing representation of its position with respect to some environmental representation (a map), and to construct the map while maintaining the vehicle's position with respect to the map itself. There is a long history of research in the problem of simultaneous localization and mapping (SLAM) for robotic vehicles (e.g., Montemerlo, Thrun, Koller, & Wegbreit, 2003; Nettleton, Gibbens, & Durrant-Whyte, 2000; Smith & Cheeseman, 1987; Smith, Self, & Cheeseman, 1990). Terrestrial SLAM algorithms often assume a predictable vehicle odometry model in order to assist in the probabilistic association of sensor information with salient visual features. The underwater domain necessitates solutions to the SLAM problem that are more dependent upon sensor information than is traditional in the terrestrial domain. This has prompted recent research in robotic vehicle design, sensing, localization, and mapping for underwater vehicles (e.g. Eustice, 2005; Eustice et al., 2005; Pizarro, Eustice, & Singh, 2004; Williams & Mahon, 2004). SLAM is important in order to be able to create intelligent vehicles that operate fully autonomously. If the map-making process can be performed in real time, then the vehicle can use the recovered representation to reason about its environment. This promotes the creation of vehicles capable of determining how to traverse an underwater area safely and return to base while monitoring other more immediate constraints such as battery life and vehicle safety.

Although being able to construct a map autonomously is a complex technical problem, the environmental representations obtained by SLAM algorithms are not necessarily the most suitable representations for later processing. It can be extremely useful to decompose such maps into semantic objects. For example, when mapping a ship's hull to look for suspicious attachments, it would be useful to be able to segment out those portions of the hull that correspond to normal hull features from those that are not. Similarly, when constructing a model of a coral reef, the availability of tools to autonomously or semiautonomously segment the coral reef from the background is highly desirable.

The segmentation of 2-D and 3-D structures is a highly studied problem (see Southall, Buxton, Marchant, & Hague, 2000, for a recent survey of 2-D techniques, and Wirjaid, 2007, for a recent survey of 3-D segmentation techniques). Although there have been considerable advances in the development of automatic tools for 2-D and 3-D segmentation, recent work in the development of semiautomatic tools for image segmentation has demonstrated considerable success in 2-D images (e.g., Li, Sun, Tang, & Shum, 2004). An extremely effective 2-D segmentation algorithm results from the combination of a human observer's ability to provide basic cues to segmentation along with a machine's ability to integrate and apply cues over a wide range of pixel combinations. A 3-D version of this type of system could be applied to the results of a 6DOF SLAM algorithm to obtain segmented 3-D models of complex 6DOF underwater scenes.

In order to address the problem of constructing segmented 3-D models of complex scenes, we have developed a novel sensor and associated SLAM and map segmentation software. A stereo vision-inertial sensor known as the AQUASensor (Hogue, German, Zacher, & Jenkin, 2006) is used to construct 3-D models of complex surfaces (such as those encountered in the underwater domain). The AQUASensor solves the SLAM problem in the underwater domain and in the process estimates the motion of the sensor and constructs a sensor-reading-based model of the structure of the environment. The raw data obtained from the SLAM process can be described as a 3-D point cloud that represents the results of stereo-imagery samples of opaque surface structure integrated over the sensor motion. This point cloud is then segmented using a 3-D version of "lazy snapping" (Li et al., 2004) and converted to a textured polygon mesh in order to produce a segmented polygon-based scene description.

We begin by describing the amphibious vehicle upon which this work is based and the sensor that has been developed. Details of the process of obtaining dense 3-D environmental maps are discussed. We then describe the process of converting portions of the map into textured polygon-based semantic structures that represent salient features in the environment. We conclude the article with a short summary of the results and a description of ongoing work with the robot, its sensor, and the sensing algorithms.

AQUA AND THE AQUASENSOR

Traditional aquatic robots and teleoperated devices utilize thrusters and controller surfaces for mobility. In contrast, the AQUA robot (see Figure 1; Dudek et al., 2007) is a hexapod capable of amphibious operation. Developed through a collaboration between researchers at Dalhousie University, McGill University, and York University, the AQUA vehicle is visually guided. On land, its legs provide foot-ground contact that propels the vehicle. Underwater these same legs act as flippers or fins to drive the vehicle both along the surface of the water and at depths of up to 30m. The vehicle relies on internal power and computation and can be tethered via an optical fiber tether in order to communicate with operators on the surface. The sensing needs of the AQUA robot are met through a series of visual-inertial sensors (Hogue et al., 2006). A sonar-based sensor would not be appropriate as the robot operates both in and out of the water and thus AQUA relies on vision to sense its external environment. The primary goal of the visual-inertial sensors is to collect high-frame-rate multicamera video imagery coupled with synchronized time-stamped inertial information. The data is later processed to obtain 6DOF egomotion

Figure 1. The AQUA robot shown with a diver for scale. The robot is powered by six fins that give it direct access to five degrees of freedom of motion. The robot can operate completely autonomously, although it is shown here tethered via an optical cable.

and 3-D models of the environment. At present the sensing hardware is deployed in a stand-alone sensor package and the near-term goal is to incorporate the algorithms within the vehicle itself.

In order to permit the sensor package to be operated independently of the robot, an independent sensor package known as the AQUASensor (Figure 2) has been developed. The AQUASensor provides a compact, fully contained unit that is sufficiently portable to be used by a single diver and whose components, suitably repackaged, can be integrated within the AQUA robot itself. The AQUASensor combines range information extracted from stereo imagery with 3DOF orientation from an inertial measurement unit (IMU) within a SLAM algorithm to accurately estimate dense 3-D models of the environment and the trajectory of the sensor. It is important to note that although the AQUASensor does not process the collected data in real time, the algorithms used to analyze the data were developed with real-time performance in mind.

The AQUASensor is sealed within a custom underwater housing that enables operation of the device to a depth of 30m. The sensor is operated either via an IEEE 802.11g wireless link for surface operation, or via waterproof switches mounted on the exterior of the sensor. The wireless interface on board the sensor provides status information and sample imagery to off-board devices. LEDs mounted on the exterior of the sensor provide status information to the operator. The LEDs and waterproof switches are the only communication possible with the device when submerged.

Although designed primarily to be integrated within the AQUA housing, the AQUASensor was also designed to be deployed independently of the AQUA vehicle. It is bulky when handled in the terrestrial domain, however, is easily operated by a single diver underwater (Figure 2b).

OBTAINING LOCAL SURFACE MODELS

Upon return to the surface the data from the AQUASensor is off-loaded to higher performance computers and a larger disk array for processing. The process of estimating egomotion and environmental structure (SLAM) is accomplished by integrating stereo image surface recovery over time via visual feature tracking integrated with changes in vehicle orientation as monitored by the onboard IMU. Complete details of

Figure 2. AQUASensor 3.0

(a) front view of the sensor with its underwater housing *(b) the sensor deployed to scan an underwater barge*

this process can be found in Dudek et al. (2007) and Hogue, German, and Jenkin (2007). The basic steps are summarized below.

Recovering accurate depth from stereo imagery is performed by leveraging the optimized sum-of-squared-differences algorithm implemented in the Point Grey Triclops library (Point Grey Research, 2003). This provides a dense set of 3-D points per acquired image frame. To estimate the motion of the camera, the 3-D point sets from different times are combined into a common reference frame. The change in the 6DOF position and orientation of the sensor between frames is estimated by tracking interesting features temporally using features that correspond to estimated 3-D locations in both frames. Given these 3-D correspondences the sensor position and orientation over multiple frames is estimated using a least-squares algorithm. The change in pose associated with each frame is integrated over time, meaning that any error in the estimate also accumulates over time. Also, since the intrinsic calibration parameters for the cameras are not known perfectly, any pose error caused by miscalibration also accumulates, which can cause the trajectory to diverge. To reduce this error, a 3DOF IMU is used to provide complimentary information about the orientation of the device.

VISUAL EGOMOTION ESTIMATION

First, "good" features are extracted from the reference camera at time t using the Kanade-Lucas-Tomasi feature-tracking algorithm (Shi & Tomasi, 1994) and are tracked into the subsequent image at time $t+1$. Using the disparity map previously extracted for both time steps, tracked points that do not have a corresponding disparity at both time t and $t+1$ are eliminated. Surviving points are subsequently triangulated to determine the metric 3-D points associated with each disparity.

In underwater scenes, many objects and points are visually similar and thus many of the feature tracks will be incorrect. Dynamic illumination effects, aquatic snow, and moving objects (e.g., fish) increase the number of spurious points that may be tracked from frame to frame. To overcome these problems, robust statistical estimation techniques are employed to label the feature tracks as belonging to either a static or nonstatic world model. This is achieved by estimating a rotation and translation model under the assumption that the scene is stationary, and rejecting matches that violate this assumption. The resulting 3-D temporal correspondences associated with stable scene points form the basis of later processing.

The camera orientation is represented as a quaternion, and the least-squares best-fit rotation and translation are computed for the sequence in a two-stage process. First, using RANSAC (Fischler & Bolles, 1981), the best linear least-squares transformation using Horn's (1987) absolute orientation method is estimated. The rotation and scale are estimated using a linear least-squares approach (detailed in Horn). After estimating the rotation, the translation is estimated by transforming the centroids into a common frame and subtracting.

The final step is to refine the rotation and translation using a nonlinear Levenberg-Marquardt minimization over six parameters (Press, Teukolsky Vetterling, & Flannery, 2002). For this stage, the rotation is parameterized as a Rodrigues vector, and the rotation and translation parameters are estimated by minimizing the transformation error in an iterative fashion. In practice, the minimization takes a few iterations to minimize the error to acceptable levels and as such does not preclude real-time operation. This approach to pose estimation differs from the traditional bundle-adjustment approach (e.g., Triggs, McLauchlan, Hartley, & Fitzgibbon, 2000) in the structure-from-motion literature in that it does not refine the 3-D locations of the features as well as the trajectory. We chose not to refine the 3-D structure to limit the number of unknowns in our minimization and thus provide a solution to our system more quickly.

IMU INTEGRATION

Egomotion estimation via visual motion introduces at least two sources of error in the estimate of 6DOF pose. First, the point-cloud registration computed from feature tracks can never be perfect. There is always a small residual error in the registration per frame and this error accumulates over time. Second, the intrinsic camera parameters are not known perfectly and any error in these parameters introduces an error in each 3-D point. In particular, the radial distortion estimate of the lens is prone to error and as a result, the per-point error is nonuniform over the visual field. This can introduce an artificial surface curvature in the 3-D point clouds, which is subtle but noticeable when many frames are registered. To help counteract this effect, we utilize a 3DOF IMU to provide more information about the orientation of the device. The IMU provides us with a quaternion representing absolute orientation in 3-D space. Rather than using the absolute orientation obtained from the IMU, which is subject to drift, we utilize the change in absolute orientation instead. We enforce the fact that the change in orientation as computed from the vision system must be consistent with the change in the absolute orientation of the device as measured by the IMU.

SEGMENTING LOCAL MODELS

Although the raw data obtained with the sensor are useful for a number of applications including SLAM, there exists a range of applications where the raw data must be segmented into semantically important structures for later processing. Consider the task of investigating the cause of a sinking. For this application the surface that belongs to the wreck may be of interest while for other applications, such as monitoring ecosystem health, the surface that belongs to the coral will be more salient. For these and similar applications, automatic and semiautomatic tools are required to segment the data set into appropriate components.

Lazy snapping (Li et al., 2004) has proven to be an effective technique for assisted segmentation of 2-D data sets. Here we extend this technique to 3-D surfaces. As in the 2-D version of lazy snapping, the user provides cues to the object to be segmented by identifying sample foreground and background elements of the image. The system then selects those surfaces it considers to be part of the object and rejects those it considers to be part of the background. The user can then either augment the set of foreground and background structures and allow the system to recompute the selection, or manually adjust regions that have been misclassified. Because most of the classification is performed automatically the demand on the user is greatly reduced as compared to manual segmentation.

3-D LAZY SNAPPING

As in the 2-D case, the problem of segmenting a 3-D data set can be expressed as a graph-cut problem. In the 2-D case, pixels in the image correspond to nodes in the graph, with adjacent pixels connected by edges. Edge weights are established based on the similarity between adjacent nodes and seed foreground and background pixels. Source and sink seed nodes are created, and a min-cut/max-flow algorithm is used to segment the image into foreground and background regions. In the 3-D case nonempty voxels in the recovered 3-D data set are used to form nodes in the graph. Adjacent nonempty voxels are considered to be connected nodes. Sink and source nodes are connected to the graph and, similar to the 2-D algorithm, edge weights are established based on the similarity between connected nodes and seed foreground and background voxels. Again a graph-cut algorithm is used to segment the graph into foreground and background voxels. The basic steps in the process of snapping a 3-D data set are summarized below.

Starting with a 3-D polygon mesh or point cloud, a voxel representation is constructed from the input representation. For a given voxel resolution, the colour of a voxel is set to the mean colour of all 3-D scene points that intersect that voxel. Once the voxel representation of the point cloud has been created, the next task is to allow the user to specify seed voxels. Seed voxels are nonempty voxels tagged by the user as being either *foreground* or *background*. The user swipes a cursor through the 3-D voxel scene, and voxels that map to the 2-D display surface are marked as being either *foreground* or *background*. An arbitrary number of voxels may be marked by the user and the view of the 3-D scene can be translated and rotated to allow the user to mark voxels that may be hidden in some views. Based on this marking stage, each nonempty voxel is assigned a state attribute: one of coloured, foreground, or background.

The task of marking voxels as either *foreground* or *background* is an instance of the common problem of 3-D ray picking. When a user wishes to mark a voxel, the 2-D window coordinate of the mouse position is converted into a 3-D ray directed into the 3-D voxel grid. Each voxel intersected along the ray into the grid is tested. The first nonempty voxel encountered is tagged.

A graph is then constructed in which a node exists in the graph for each nonempty voxel, and edges are constructed between nodes that represent adjacent cells in the voxel grid. Given the 3x3x3 voxel

Figure 3. A 3-D model of a section of coral bed with the camera trajectory overlaid. The insert in the lower left shows a snapshot of the rectified stereo video and the instantaneous structure with egomotion vectors overlaid.

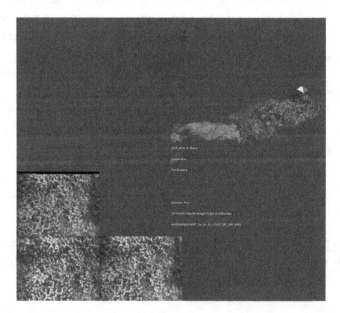

structure, a single node in the graph may have up to 26 edges to other voxel nodes if its corresponding voxel is completely surrounded by nonempty voxels.

The voxel grid is converted into a graph as follows. First, a source and sink node are created. These nodes are not associated with any image voxels; rather, they represent the foreground (source) and background (sink). Then a graph node is created for each nonempty voxel. Edges are constructed between the nodes that correspond to adjacent voxels, and an edge is created from each voxel node to both the source and sink terminal nodes. Each edge is then assigned a nonnegative weight.

If the user has tagged a node as *foreground*, then the edge from the source terminal to the node is assigned an infinite weight. If the node is tagged as *background*, then the edge from this node to the sink terminal is given an infinite weight. All other edges in the graph are given finite, non-negative weights as described below and summarized in Table 1.

Graph edges that correspond to edges between connected voxels have weights so that edges connecting similar voxels have a high weight while edges connecting dissimilar voxels have a low weight. This has the effect of causing similar adjacent nodes to be less likely to be on different sides of the segmentation boundary. Similar to the method used by Li et al. (2004), the colours in the foreground and background seeds are clustered using the *k*-means method (Duda, Hart, & Stork, 2000). For each node in the graph the minimum distance from its colour to the foreground and background colours is computed. The likelihood of a node being identified as *foreground* or *background* is represented as the weight between the node and the source and sink nodes. This weight is applied to the node-source and node-sink edges. This has the effect of making nodes with similar colours to the foreground being more likely to be marked as *foreground*, and similarly for *background*.

Table 1 summarizes the graph edge weights. Let F_n be the *n* mean colours of the foreground voxels marked by the user, and let B_m represent the *m* mean colour of the background voxels marked by the user. Then, $dF_n=\min_n|C-F_n|$ represents the minimum distance from colour C to one of the mean colours in the foreground and $B_n=\min_m|C-B_m|$ represents the minimum distance from colour C to one of the mean colours in the background. Edges between voxels have a weight given by $g(C_1,C_2)$ where $g(a,b)=1/(1+(C_1-C_2)^2)$. The source (foreground) node is connected to all voxel nodes with an edge weight given as infinity for voxels marked as being *foreground* by the user, 0 for voxels marked as being *background* by the user, and $dF_1/(dF_1+dB_1)$ for all other voxel nodes. The sink (background) node is connected to all voxel nodes with an edge weight given as 0 for voxels marked as being *foreground* by the user, infinity for voxels marked as being *background* by the user, and $dB_1/(dF_1+dB_1)$ for all other nodes.

Table 1. Edge weight calculations for the voxel graph

From Node	To Node	Weight
Foreground (Source)	Foreground Voxel	Infinity
Foreground (Source)	Background Voxel	0
Background (Sink)	Foreground Voxel	0
Background (Sink)	Background Voxel	Infinity
Foreground (Source)	Nonseed Voxel	$dF_1/(dF_1+dB_1)$
Background (Sink)	Nonseed Voxel	$dB_1/(dF_1+dB_1)$
Voxel	Adjacent Voxel	$g(C_1,C_2)$

The graph is segmented using a standard min-cut/max-flow algorithm (Boykov & Kolmogorov, 2004). After the cut operation, all nodes that are connected to the source are labeled as foreground nodes and all nodes that are connected to the sink are labeled as background nodes. The data set is now fully labeled and can be redisplayed using this semantic information.

Once the nodes in the graph have been marked, surface reconstruction can be performed. Points contained within voxels with corresponding graph nodes marked as *foreground* are identified as foreground points. The remaining points are background points. A variation of the marching-cubes algorithm (Lorenson & Cline, 1987) is applied to the foreground points to generate a 3-D texture-mapped triangle mesh representation of the foreground object.

EXAMPLE SEGMENTATION

Figure 4 shows the results of segmenting a coral growth from the 3-D mesh recovered from a wreck in the Folkstone Marine Reserve, Barbados. The coral growth seen in Figure 4a was segmented from the background through the 3-D lazy-snapping process. Figure 4b shows the voxel scene representation of the raw point-cloud data. The user marks portions of the scene as being *foreground* or *background* (Figure 4c). Given this assignment, a weighted graph representation was constructed using the identified foreground and background voxels. The 3-D lazy-snapping algorithm was then used to identify regions as being *foreground* (here, the coral growth) or *background* (everything else; Figure 4d). The resulting segmentation is shown in Figure 4e and 4f as both a textured polygon surface as well as a wire-frame representation. Note that the user does not have to provide a particularly accurate or complete set of features to describe the foreground and background voxels.

Discussion and Future Work

The lack of high-bandwidth communications underwater requires that untethered underwater robot systems exhibit a high level of autonomy. This autonomy requires effective sensing and reasoning. Traditional underwater sensing devices have relied on active sensors (sonar in particular) to recover three-dimensional environmental structure. Advances in stereo sensing and data-fusion technologies demonstrate that passive stereo is a sufficiently robust technology to be applied in the aquatic domain. Although this domain presents unique challenges to traditional vision algorithms, robust noise-suppression mechanisms can be used to overcome many of these difficulties. Results from land-based experiments demonstrate the accuracy of our reconstruction system (see Hogue & Jenkin, 2006, for terrestrial performance evaluation), and futher experiments to assess the accuracy underwater are on going. Results from underwater field trials also functionally demonstrate the system's ability to reconstruct qualitatively correct 3-D models of the aquatic environment. The entire reconstruction system operates at four frames per second (seven frames per second via a GPU implementation) and produces approximately 8 million 3-D points per minute of data.

The ability to obtain 3-D surface models of terrestrial and aquatic structures makes this an enabling technology. The models can be used for specific applications and can also be used as the basis of simultaneous localization and mapping, a critical ability in the development of fully autonomous systems. By combining binocular imagery with inertial sensors it is possible to construct reasonably large local surface models, and when placed within a SLAM formalism, it is possible to use the sensor to con-

Figure 4. The 3-D lazy-snapping process

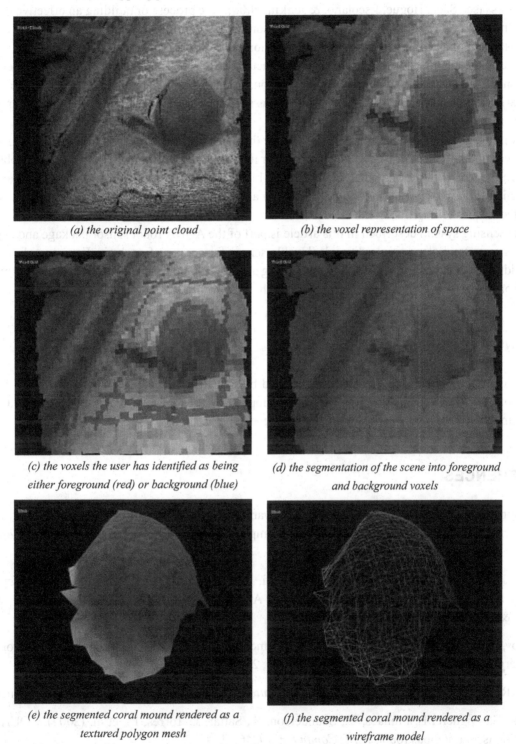

(a) the original point cloud

(b) the voxel representation of space

(c) the voxels the user has identified as being either foreground (red) or background (blue)

(d) the segmentation of the scene into foreground and background voxels

(e) the segmented coral mound rendered as a textured polygon mesh

(f) the segmented coral mound rendered as a wireframe model

struct surface models of extended areas and maintain an ongoing estimate of the pose of the sensor in the process (see Saez, Hogue, Escolano, & Jenkin, 2006). The process of building an effective internal representation of the external world and then reasoning and acting based on this model is an explicit demonstration of a cognitive informatics information-matter-energy model (Wang, 2003).

Once an environmental model has been constructed, various techniques can be applied to the model to segment salient features from the representation. The 3-D lazy-snapping algorithm is an assisted alternative to manual feature segmentation that has shown promise in segmenting both terrestrial and aquatic models.

Future plans in the underwater domain include the construction of realistic models of a large-scale shipwreck and larger coral structures. Of particular interest here is to compare the 3-D models obtained using the sensor with models obtained by marine biologists using traditional techniques. We are also examining the use of the sensor and segmentation algorithm in a range of terrestrial applications and GPU techniques to improve frame rates.

The sensing system described in this article is part of the AQUA robot sensor package and can also be used as a stand-alone single-diver-deployable sensor for coral reef analysis. Future work includes embedding the technology within the robot housing and developing a more robust SLAM algorithm that incorporates large loop closing to further reduce the pose error over long distances.

ACKNOWLEDGMENT

We graciously acknowledge the funding provided by NSERC and IRIS NCE for the AQUA project. We also would like to thank the AQUA team for support and the McGill Bellairs Research Institute for providing a positive atmosphere during the field research trials.

REFERENCES

Aronson, R. B., Edmunds, P. J., Precht, W. F., Swanson, D. W., & Levitan, D. R. (1994). Large-scale, long-term monitoring of Caribbean coral reefs: Simple, quick, inexpensive techniques. *Atoll Research Bulletin, 421*, 1-19.

Battle, J., Ridao, P., Garcia, R., Carreras, M., Cufi, X., El-Fakdi, A., et al. (2004). *URIS: Underwater robotic intelligent system.* In Automar, Instiuto de Automatica Industrial, CSIC, J. Aranda, M. A. Armada, & J. M. de la Cruz (Eds.) pp 177-203.

Boykov, Y., & Kolmogorov, V. (2004). An experimental comparison of min-cut/max-flow algorithms for energy minimization in vision. In IEEE PAMI, 26, 1124-1137.

Duda, R. O., Hart, P. E., & Stork, D. G. (2000). *Pattern classification* (2nd ed.). Wiley-Interscience.

Dudek, G., Giguere, P., Prahacs, C., Saunderson, S., Sattar, J., Torres, L., et al. (2007). AQUA: An amphibious autonomous robot. *IEEE Computer, 40*, 46-53.

Dudek, G., Sattar, J., & Xu, A. (2007). A visual language for robot control and programming: A human-interface study. In *Proceedings of IEEE ICRA*, Rome (pp. 2507-2513).

Eustice, R. (2005). *Large-area visually augmented navigation for autonomous underwater vehicles.* Unpublished doctoral dissertation, Woods Hole Oceanographic Institute, Massachusetts Institute of Technology, Cambridge.

Eustice, R., Singh, H., Leonard, J., Walter, M., & Ballard, R. (2005). Visually navigating the RMS Titanic with SLAM information filters. *In Proceedings of Robotics: Science and Systems (RSS),* Cambridge, MA. (pp 57-64).

Fischler, M., & Bolles, R. (1981). Random sample consensus: A paradigm for model fitting with application to image analysis and automated cartography. *Communications of the ACM, 24,* 381-385.

Gintert, B. E., Madijdi, H., Reid, R. P., Boynton, G. C., Negahdaripour, S., Miller, M., et al. (2007). Documenting hurricane impacts on coral reefs using two-dimensional video-mosaic technology. *Marine Ecology, 28,* 254-258.

Hogue, A., German, A., & Jenkin, M. (2007). Underwater environment reconstruction using stereo and inertial data. In *Proceedings of IEEE SMC*, Montreal, Canada.

Hogue, A., German, A., Zacher, J., & Jenkin, M. (2006). Underwater 3D mapping: Experiences and lessons learned. In *Proceedings of the Third Canadian Conference on Computer and Robot Vision (CRV).* Quebec City, Canada.

Hogue, A., & Jenkin, M. (2006). *Development of an underwater vision sensor for 3D reef mapping.* Paper presented at IEEE/RSJ IROS, Beijing, China.

Horn, B. (1987). Closed-form solution of absolute orientation using unit quaternions. *AI Magazine, A,* 629.

Johnson, E. A., Jr. (2002). *Unmanned undersea vehicles and guided missile submarines: Technological and operational synergies* (Occasional Paper No. 27). AL: Center for Strategy and Technology, Air War College, Air University.

Li, Y., Sun, J., Tang, C., & Shum, N. (2004). Lazy snapping. *ACM Transactions on Graphics, 23,* 303-308.

Lorenson, W. E., & Cline, H. E. (1987). Marching cubes: A high resolution 3D surface construction algorithm. In *Proceedings of the 14th Annual Conference on Computer Graphics and Interactive Techniques* (pp. 163-169).

Montemerlo, M., Thrun, S., Koller, D., & Wegbreit, B. (2003). FastSLAM 2.0: An improved particle filtering algorithm for simultaneous localization and mapping that provably converges. In *Proceedings of the 18th International Joint Conference on Artificial Intelligence (IJCAI).*

Negahdaripour, S., & Firoozfam, P. (2006). An ROV stereovision system for ship-hull inspection. *IEEE Journal of Oceanic Engineering, 31*, 551-564.

Nettleton, E., Gibbens, P., & Durrant-Whyte, H. (2000). Closed form solutions to the multiple platform simultaneous localisation and map building SLAM problem. In B. Dasarathy (Ed.), *Sensor fusion: Architectures, algorithms, and applications IV* (pp. 428-437).

Pizarro, O., Eustice, R., & Singh, H. (2004). Large area 3D reconstructions from underwater surveys. In *Proceedings of the MTS/IEEE OCEANS Conference and Exhibition*, Kobe, Japan (pp. 678-687).

Point Grey Research. (2003). *TRICLOPS: Software Development KIT (SDK) version 3.1 user's guide and command reference.*

Porter, J. W., & Meier, O. W. (1992). Quantification of loss and change in Floridian reef coral populations. *American Zoologist, 32*, 625-640.

Press, W., Teukolsky, S., Vetterling, W., & Flannery, B. (2002). *Numerical recipes in C.* Cambridge University Press.

Ribes, P., & Borrelly, J.-J. (1997). Underwater pipe inspection task using visual serving techniques. In *Proceedings of IEEE/RSJ IROS* (pp. 63-68).

Saez, J., Hogue, A., Escolano, F., & Jenkin, M. (2006). Underwater 3D SLAM through entropy minimization. In *Proceedings of the IEEE International Conference on Robotics and Automation (ICRA)* (pp. 3562-3567).

Sattar, J., Bourque, E., Giguere, P., & Dudek, G. (2007). Fourier tags: Smoothly degradable fiducial markers for use in human-robot interaction. In *Proceedings of the Canadian Conference on Computer and Robot Vision (CRV)*, (pp 165-174) Montreal, Canada.

Shi, J., & Tomasi, C. (1994). Good features to track. In *Proceedings of the IEEE Conference on Computer Vision and Pattern Recognition (CVPR)* (pp. 593-600).

Smith, R., & Cheeseman, P. (1987). On the representation and estimation of spatial uncertainty. *International Journal of Robotics Research, 5*, 56-68.

Smith, R., Self, M., & Cheeseman, P. (1990). Estimating uncertain spatial relationships in robotics. In I. Cox, and G. Wilfong (Eds) *Autonomous Robot Vehicles*, 167-193.

Southall, B., Buxton, B., Marchant, J., & Hague, T. (2000). On the performance characterisation of image segmentation algorithms: A case study. In *Proceedings of ECCV 2000*, Dublin, Ireland (Vol. 2, pp. 351-365).

Triggs, B., McLauchlan, P., Hartley, R., & Fitzgibbon, A. (2000). Bundle adjustment: A modern synthesis. In *Lecture notes in computer science* (pp. 278-375). Springer-Verlag.

Wang, Y. (2003). On cognitive informatics. *Brain and Mind, 4*, 151-167.

Williams, S., & Mahon, I. (2004). Simultaneous localisation and mapping on the Great Barrier Reef. In *Proceedings of the IEEE International Conference on Robotics and Automation (ICRA)*(pp. 1771-1776).

Wirjadi, O. (2007). *Survey of 3D image segmentation methods* (Tvech. Rep. No. 123). Fraunhofer Institut, Techno- und Wirtschaftsmathematik.

This work was previously published in the International Journal of Cognitive Informatics and Natural Intelligence, Vol. 2, Issue 4, edited by Y. Wang, pp. 1-14, copyright 2008 by IGI Publishing (an imprint of IGI Global).

Chapter 23
A Novel Plausible Model for Visual Perception

Zhiwei Shi
Chinese Academy of Science, China

Zhongzhi Shi
Chinese Academy of Science, China

Hong Hu
Chinese Academy of Science, China

ABSTRACT

Traditionally, how to bridge the gap between low-level visual features and high-level semantic concepts has been a tough task for researchers. In this article, we propose a novel plausible model, namely cellular Bayesian networks (CBNs), to model the process of visual perception. The new model takes advantage of both the low-level visual features, such as colors, textures, and shapes, of target objects and the inter-relationship between the known objects, and integrates them into a Bayesian framework, which possesses both firm theoretical foundation and wide practical applications. The novel model successfully overcomes some weakness of traditional Bayesian Network (BN), which prohibits BN being applied to large-scale cognitive problem. The experimental simulation also demonstrates that the CBNs model outperforms purely Bottom-up strategy 6% or more in the task of shape recognition. Finally, although the CBNs model is designed for visual perception, it has great potential to be applied to other areas as well.

INTRODUCTION

Cognitive informatics (CI) is a transdisciplinary enquiry of cognitive and information sciences that investigates the internal information processing mechanisms and processes of the brain and natural intelligence (Wang, 2007). It covers a wide range of research fields, including the information-matter-energy (IME) model (Wang, 2003b), the layered reference model of the brain (LRMB) (Wang, Wang, Patel & Patel, 2006), the object-attribute-relation (OAR) model of information representation in the brain (Wang, 2006d; Wang & Wang, 2006), the cognitive informatics model of the brain (Wang, Liu, & Wang, 2003; Wang & Wang, 2006), natural intelligence (NI) (Wang, 2003b), autonomic computing (AC) (Wang, 2004), neural informatics (NeI) (Wang, 2002, 2003b, 2006a), CI laws of software (Wang, 2006b), the mechanisms of human perception processes (Wang, 2005a), the cognitive processes of formal inferences (Wang, 2005b), and the formal knowledge system (Wang, 2006c). Of all these branches, perception, as an interesting research field of CI, mainly focuses on how human beings perceive external world. Researchers have proposed an excellent model, the motivation/attitude-driven behavioral (MADB) model (Wang & Wang, 2006), to formally and quantitatively describe the relationship between the internal emotion, motivation, attitude, and the embodied external behaviors. In this article, we limit our work to visual perception, and propose a connectivity-based model to formally mimic the perceptual function of human beings.

The primary task of visual perceptual is to organize the visual features of an image into some already known objects. Yet, how to bridge the gap between low-level visual features and high-level semantic concept has long been a tough problem, which puzzles researchers all along. Until now, most of the proposed algorithms just focus on some particular objects, such as human faces, cars, people, and so forth (see e.g., Papageorgiou & Poggio, 2000; Schneiderman & Kanade, 2000; Tamminen a& Lampinen, 2003). Researchers utilize various schemes (see e.g., Broek et. al., 2005; Lai, Chang, Chang, Cheng, & Crandell, 2002; Tamminen & Lampinen, 2003]) to integrate the low-level visual features, including colors, textures and shapes into the profiles of target objects. Although some people (Murphy, Torralba, & Freeman, 2004) exploit background, or scene, information to improve the recognition, they do not take advantage of interrelationships between objects to help the identification process.

As a matter of fact, interrelationships between objects are of great importance to perceptual organization. Researchers (Geisler & Murray, 2002) have shown that there might exist some visual patterns in human brains, which enable human beings to recognize some simple objects, for example, English letters, as soon as they see them. Besides, they also point out that the speed of processing visual information is very limited in human brains. Consequently, it is highly plausible that human beings utilize interrelationships between objects, or concepts, to facilitate the recognition of complex, unfamiliar objects based on the recognition of some simple, familiar objects. Obviously, the interrelationships will largely reduce the information required for recognition, and improve the effectiveness and efficiency as well. Furthermore, the lateral connections, which widely exist in the cortex of human brains (Choe 2001), also provide the biological support of the usage of interrelationships between objects.

Meanwhile, due to large amount of uncertainty in the process of perceptual organization, Bayesian methods are widely used in the modeling of perceptual organization or object identification (see e.g., (Geisler & Diehl, 2003; Jacobs, 2002; Lee & Mumford, 2003). Typically, uncertainties can rise in a large amount of cases. For example, a target object is too small in some visual scene, or only part of the target object is visible due to some obstructions, or the visual scene is vague in some bad weather. As a result, Bayesian method, which can deal with uncertainties and make use of uncertainties, is obviously a favorite option for many researchers.

In this article, we propose a variation of traditional Bayesian network, a cellular Bayesian network (CBNs), which makes use of both low-level visual features and interrelationships between high-level objects under a Bayesian framework to model visual perception.

The rest of this article is organized as follows: in the second section, we will briefly review the related works, mainly the Bayesian network, and analyze the weakness of traditional Bayesian network in the task of visual perception; next, in the third section, we propose our novel model, the Cellular Bayesian Networks (CBNs), including definitions, learning methods and inference in CBNs; after that, a small simulation is presented in the fourth section, where we demonstrate how to perform visual perception via a CBNs and make an experimental comparison between the CBNs and a purely Bottom-up strategy; then, in the fifth section, we discuss the merits and demerits of CBNs for the task of visual perception; finally, we conclude our article with a short review of our work in this article and possible directions in the future in the last section.

RELATED WORK

Bayesian Network

Bayesian network, as a probabilistic graphical model, is an increasingly popular tool for encoding uncertain knowledge in complex domains, and, in the last decade, it gains wide applications in many areas, such as decision support systems, information retrieval, discovery of gene regulatory pathways, natural language processing (see e.g., (Beinlich, Suermondt, Chavez, & Cooper, 1989; Friedman, Linial, Nachman, & Peer, 2000; Lam, Low, & Ho, 1997), and especially object detection (see e.g., (Jorge, Marques, & Abrantes, 2002; Kang & Cho, 2004; Schneiderman, 2004). Mathematically, a Bayesian network can be defined as follows:

A Bayesian network is a pair (G, P), where $G = (V, E)$ is a directed acyclic graph (DAG). Here V is the node set, where each node represents the variables in the problem domain, and E is the edge set, where each edge denotes the direct dependent relationship between nodes. Another component of a Bayesian network, P, is the set of conditional probabilistic distribution (CPD) of child nodes, given their parent nodes. Additionally, G and P must satisfy the Markov condition: every variable, $X \in V$, is independent of any subset of its nondescendant variables conditioned on the set of its parents (Pearl, 1988). In many cases, a directed edge from one node to another can be interpreted as a causal relationship although the absence of the edge does not mean the independence between the two nodes. So, in some cases, a Bayesian network is also called a causal network.

Let $pa(X)$ denote the set of parents of X, then the conditional independence property can be represented as follows:

$$P(X \mid V \setminus X) = P(X \mid pa(X))\tag{1}$$

This property largely relaxes the strict memory and computing power requirements by simplifying the computation in a Bayesian network. For example, the joint distribution of the set of all the variables in V can be expressed as a product of conditional probabilities as follows:

$$P(V) = \prod_{X \in V} P(X \mid pa(X)\tag{2}$$

The Weakness of Bayesian Network

Although Bayesian network has many attractive properties, such as firm theoretical foundation, simple representation and the capability of encoding interrelationships between objects (variables), it cannot be employed as the model of perceptual organization directly without any modification. Here are some reasons.

The most important reason is about incomplete data. As we all know, each piece of our observation contains only a tiny part of the real world, as well as its reflection in our mind. It is absolutely impossible to have a completed sample of all the objects that we know within just one observation. This means that the task of learning a Bayesian network will inevitably depend on the techniques of learning with incomplete data. Although, in the last decade, with the rapid progress in the research on Bayesian network, numerous algorithms (Friedman, 1997; Ramoni & Sebastiani, 2001; Wu, Wun, & Chou, 2004) have been developed to deal with the incomplete data problem in learning of Bayesian network, the proportion of missing data in their researches is relative small. Typically, their missing rate is less than 50%. Therefore, in the cases that only several objects are observed with millions of objects missing, their methods will definitely become powerless.

The second problem is that, in a Bayesian network, the edges between nodes are one-way directed. Yet, the interrelationships between the objects, which exist in the real world and can be reflected in human brains, sometimes are bidirectional. In these cases, the traditional Bayesian network is incapable for the task of perceptual organization due to its inherent limitation.

The last point comes from the feasibility. The problem of learning an exact Bayesian network from data under certain broad conditions has been proven worst-case NP-hard (Chickering, Meek, & Heckerman, 2003). Although researchers have proposed heuristic polynomial learning algorithms (Brown, Tsamardinos, & Aliferis, 2005) to alleviate the work, it is, computationally, still intractable for dealing with the problem with millions of variables in the domain. Additionally, researches have shown that making inference on such a large-scale network is also infeasible (Dagum & Luby, 1993).

Based on the analyses above, we get that it is not wise to exploit a huge global Bayesian network to construct a perceptual model. This might be the reason why Bayesian network is merely applied to single object detection. Consequently, we modify the original Bayesian network according to the observations of the order of nature, and propose a novel perceptual model, Cellular Bayesian Networks (CBNs), in accordance. In the following section, we will discuss the model in detail.

CELLULAR BAYESIAN NETWORKS (CBNS)

Motivation

Before we depict our model, we will examine some nature principles, which inspire us to construct our model.

Basically, our model comes out from the following observation of the order of nature, by which everything in the world exists and functions.

Firstly, everything in the world is unique. Everything has its distinctive features that make it different from others. Many object identification algorithms (see e.g., Broek et. al., 2005; Lai et. al., 2002; Tamminen & Lampinen, 2003) are developed based on this principle. Secondly, the appearance of each object has variety. One object will present various different appearances due to different illumination, or different visual angles of the observer, or some other factors. That is why many researchers intend to exploit Bayesian method to deal with the uncertainty in the observation. Thirdly, everything exists in some particular local circumstances, or scenes, and has more or less relationships with its neighbors. It is a pity that researchers (Murphy et. al., 2004) take the circumstance information into account, while leave the relationships between objects alone.

The rules above describe the way in which physical world exists. According to the isomorphism[1] of Gestalt Theory, the brain field of human beings should have the similar structure with that of the external circumstances, which is reflected by the inside perceptual model. Accordingly, it is highly reasonable to make a perceptual model that takes advantage of both the unique visual features of individual objects and the interrelationships between objects.

Model Description

As we have seen, a global Bayesian network is incapable to model the perceptual organization. So, in our model, we interconnect numerous overlapped local Bayesian network into a whole to avoid the problems listed in the previous section.

Definition 3.1 *In a directed acyclic graph $G = (V, E)$, a node $C \in V$ is called a* **center node** *if and only if for any node $X \in V \backslash \{C\}$, condition $<X, C> \in E$ is satisfied[2]. For example, in Figure 1, the node n_2 in the graph G_1 and the node n_3 in G_2 are all center nodes in their graphs respectively.*

Definition 3.2 *A directed acyclic graph is a* **centered graph** *if and only if it has only one center node, and there is no edges ending at noncenter nodes. For example, the graph G_1 is a centered graph, and the graph G_2 is not due to extra edges between noncenter nodes. The center node of a centered graph is specified shortly to $C(G)$. So, in Figure 1, we have $C(G_1) = n_2$.*

Definition 3.3 *A* **cellular Bayesian network** *(CBN) is a pair (G, P), where $G = (V, E)$ is a centered graph, and P is a set of conditional probabilistic distribution (CPD) of the center node of G given its parents. For convenience, we also call the center of G, $C(G)$, the center of the CBN, shortly for $C(CBN)$.*

Definition 3.4 *For any two given cellular Bayesian networks $B_1 = (G_1, P_1)$ and $B_2 = (G_2, P_2)$, if $C(B_1) \neq C(B_2)$, the* **union** *$B = B_1 \cup B_2$ of the CBN B_1 and CBN B_2 is a pair (G, P), where G is the union of G_1 and G_2, and P is the union of P_1 and P_2.*

Figure 1. The sample graphs

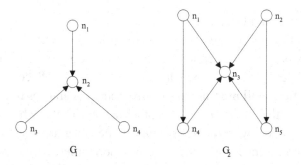

Figure 2 illustrates a sample union of two CBN. From the figure, we can see that, in the left oval is one CBN B_1, whose edge is solid arrowed lines, and in the right oval is the other CBN B_2, whose edge is dot arrowed line. The union of B_1 and B_2 is also a labeled graph model, whose graph structure is just the union of the graphs of the two CBN, and its notation P is the union of the notations of B_1 and B_2. Obviously, the union of two CBN is not a CBN any more, because the center node is not guaranteed, and more CPD are included.

Definition 3.5 *A Cellular Bayesian Networks (CBNs) is a union, **CBNs** = $B_1 \cup B_2 \cup ... \cup B_n$, where B_i (i = 1, ..., n) is cellular Bayesian network, and they are subject to the following constraints:*

$$C(B_i) \neq C(B_j) \quad 1 \leq i < j \leq n \tag{3}$$

and

$$C(B_i) \in \left(\bigcup_{j \neq i} V_j \right) \quad i = 1, ..., n \tag{4}$$

where V_j is the node set of B_j.

The first constraint makes every component network unique. In the later section, we will find that each center node of a CBN represents a complicated object to be recognized. The second constraint makes all the component networks connected in terms of center nodes. If a center node corresponds to a complicated object, the second constraint just encodes the interrelationships between these objects and indicates that no complicated object is isolated from other complicated ones.

Any common Bayesian network can be viewed as CBNs, if we regard each family of a child node, including the child node and its parent nodes, as a CBN. Yet we cannot transfer some CBNs into a common Bayesian network, if there exists a directed loop in the CBNs.

Learning a CBNs

Since a CBNs consists of many interconnected but overlapped component Bayesian networks, the learning task of the model can be divided into many independent parallelizable tiny learning task. Each task

Figure 2. The union of two CBN

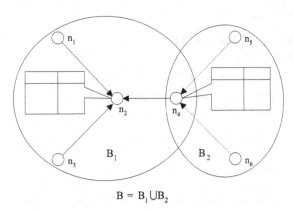

$$B = B_1 \cup B_2$$

just focuses on one component network. Compared with common Bayesian network, a cellular Bayesian network is much simpler, because, for a given problem domain, or a set of variables, and a center node, the network structure can be fixed (all edges pointing to the center node from the noncenter nodes), and only the CPD of the center node needs to be learned. As a result, only the parameter learning technique of Bayesian network is needed, and the learning process can be much more efficient than traditional Bayesian network due to the simplicity of CBN.

Inference on a CBNs

The inference on the model is a little complicated. As we presented above, a CBNs is composed of numerous overlapped CBN. It is highly possible that there exist directed circles among the nodes, though the graph model of each CBN is acyclic. In these cases, traditional inference algorithms will not work, because the inference process among the nodes will be recursive. One feasible solution is to update the state, or value, of the center node of each CBN recursively, until there is no state changing or the number of recursion is beyond the fixed threshold. Here, the recursion number actually reflects the time limitation for reasoning. The detailed algorithm is listed in Figure 3.

In this algorithm, Ev denotes the set of initial evidences; $NewEv$ specifies the new set of evidences after each iteration; V_i is the node set of the ith CBN (CBN_i); and $C(CBN_i)$ is the center node of CBN_i. In the boldfaced line, any practical method can be used to determine the state of the center node. As a matter of fact, this operation includes two steps: Firstly, the posterior distribution of a center node is updated according to the evidences. Any feasible inference algorithm for common Bayesian network will be competent for this simple task. Then we can sample a state for the center node based on its posterior distribution via some predefined process, for example, Monte Carlo method or some other similar method.

Figure 3. The algorithm for inference on the CBNs

```
num = 1
while(Ev != Φ or num < Threshold ) {
num++;
NewEv = Φ;
For each CBN_i {
    Ev_i = Ev∩(V_i\{C(CBN_i)} )
    If (Ev_i != Φ) {
        Update the state of C(CBN_i) according to Ev_i;
        If (the state of C(CBN_i) changed)
            NewEv = NewEv∪C(CBN_i);
    }
}
Ev = NewEv;
}
```

Model Visual Perception with CBNs

In this subsection, we will exploit CBNs to model visual perception.

The fundamental issue is to map the objects of problem domain to the variables, or nodes, in CBNs. Typically, the objects, or variables, in a perceptual system refer to the perceptible stuffs in the real world. Note that the identification of any target object involves both basic visual features, such as colors, textures, and shapes, and other related objects, which have more or less relationship with the target object. So, to make the model uniform, we regard basic visual features, including colors, textures and shapes, as objects in CBNs as well. Thus, the entire set of objects can be divided into two categories. One is for the basic objects, which can be detected by the model directly without any inference. This category will include, but not be limited to, the basic visual features. The other is for the high-level objects, which is detected based on the identification of other objects and some necessary inference. The variables representing the objects in the first category, namely **elementary objects**, will correspond to the noncenter nodes in a CBNs. In contrast, the variables representing the objects in the second category, namely **complicated objects**, will become the center nodes in a CBNs.

Another key issue of constructing CBNs is how to decide the node set of each component network CBN_i, $i = 1, \ldots, n$. As we mentioned previously, everything in the world exists in some particular circumstances and often co-occur with some other objects. It is nature to use the frequency of the co-occurrence in a same visual scene of the two objects to quantify the relationship between them. Because each CBN corresponds to a complicated object, we can figure out that the node set of a CBN will include all the elementary features of its center object, and all the complicated objects that have ever co-occurred with the center object in a same scene.

After the CBNs for visual perception is defined. The learning method mentioned in section 3.3 can be used to learn the parameters of the CBNs. Then, the inference algorithm, described in section 3.4, will be utilized to recognize objects according to some visual input.

SIMULATION

In this section, we present a simple simulation, in which we apply CBNs to recognize shapes in visual scenes.

Dataset

The dataset we use here is a subset of shapes from the Kimia silhouette database[3]. This subset contains 216 shape images, which belong to 18 semantic concepts. For each concept, there are 12 different shape images. Table 1 lists all these semantic concepts and their representative shape images. As we mentioned previously, everything in the world exists in some particular circumstances and often co-occur with some other objects. Consequently, to mimic this situation, we artificially create some visual scenes and perform shape recognition in these visual scenes. To recognize shape in visual scenes, a scene generator program is utilized to generate a set of visual scenes. The scene generator firstly divides 18 concepts into 3 categories, which is listed in Table 2. Then it random selects shape images to form three-shape visual scenes, so that each visual scene contains three shapes from different concepts. A sample visual scene

Table 1. 18 semantic concepts and their representative shapes in the database

Table 2. Categories of 18 concepts

Category ID	Concepts
C1	Bird, Bone, Brick, Camel, Car, Children
C2	Classic, Elephant, Face, Fork, Fountain, Glass
C3	Hammer, Heart, Key, Misk, Ray, Turtle

is illustrated in Figure 4. In this step, all the concepts in the same scene must come from same category listed in Table 2 to mimic local appearance. After 10,000 random scenes are created for learning CBNs, another 500 random scenes are generated to test its shape recognition capability.

Contrast Detector

From section 3.4 we get that CBNs relies much on belief propagation than Bottom-up information during perception, although it utilizes the Bottom-up information as its initial input. Hence, to make a comparison, we employ a purely Bottom-up shape detector, which makes use of only low-level visual features. The Bottom-up shape recognizing strategy is described as follows.

Firstly, each shape image is represented as a closure contour. Then, on each contour, a 48-component Gabor feature vector is constructed based on Manjunathi and Ma's work (Manjunath & Ma, 1996). Here, we favor the Gabor features mainly because it has similar property to that of the visual cells in human retina (Ringach, 2002). For simplicity, we do not exploit any other low-level visual features. Next, 18 centroid feature vectors are generated as profiles of 18 concepts. Finally, for any test shape, we

Figure 4. A sample visual scene composed of a bird, a bone and a camel

compare its Gabor feature vector with 18 concept profiles. The most similar concept profile indicates what concept the test shape belongs to.

Constructing CBNs

Here, we depict how to build a CBNs according to the dataset and how to use it to recognize shapes in visual scenes.

- **Model Design:** Firstly, each shape image acts as an elementary object in this simulation. So it corresponds to a noncenter node in the CBNs. In contrast, each concept listed in Table 2 corresponds to a complex object or a center node in CBNs. Next, each CBN is composed of a center concept node, several related concept nodes and all the noncenter nodes, because any shape has certain probability to be recognized as a known concept. Each node takes two states: 1 for active and 0 for inactive. The probability of state "1" states the active strength of a node. Besides, to indicate different positions in a three-shape visual scene, we also introduce three position nodes into the model. They will be either complete active or complete inactive, and never be active at the same time. All the concept nodes activated simultaneously with a position node will compete to be the final perceptual result. The competitive relationship results in that the active strengths of nodes in the same position are normalized to 1.
- **Learning Process:** In the learning process, all the training scenes are sequentially processed one pass. After the reading of each scene, related concepts are recorded as new nodes if they are not in the model yet; the neighbor relationships between the concepts are interpreted as bidirectional links; and related statistics in the model is either created or updated. For example, after processing the sample scene in Figure 4, three new nodes, corresponding to "bird," "bone," and "camel," respectively, and three bidirectional links "bird ←→ bone," "bone ←→ camel," and "bird ←→ camel," are added to the model. The co-occurrence number of "bird" and "bone" and other concept pairs are created and set to "1." With more samples leant, more nodes, links, and statistics are added to the model, and the statistics will continuously updated.
- **Shape Recognition:** When a shape in a test scene is read into the CBNs, the initial active strengths of all the concept nodes are determined by the Bottom-up strategy. Then the inference process is performed according to subsection 3.4. After a period of belief propagation, the final champion nodes at three different positions form the perceptual result.

Performance Evaluation

Table 3 lists the recognition performance of CBNs and Bottom-up detector over 1,500 shapes in 500 random visual scenes. From the result we can see that CBNs gains 6% precision improvement over the Bottom-up strategy. To further examine the property of CBNs, we perform a series of shape recogni-

Table 3. Recognizing precision of CBNs and bottom-up strategy

	CBNs	Bottom-up
Recognition Precision	96.67%	91.20%

Figure 5. The recognition precision of CBNs and bottom-up strategy under different size of Gabor features

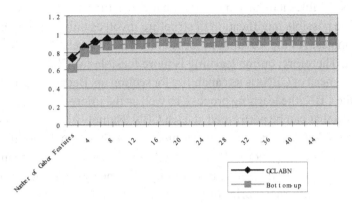

tion tasks on the same test scenes but with different size of visual features. Figure 5 demonstrates the recognition precision of CBNs and Bottom-up detector with different size of visual features, which are composed of from 2-component to 48-compoment Gabor features. In general, CBNs outperforms Bottom-up detector about 6-7% according to the figure. Yet, the less the visual features used, the more CBNs outperforms Bottom-up strategy (more than 16% improvement in the 2-component feature case). Meanwhile, we also find that in this shape recognition task, 8-10 Gabor features are enough, and more visual features do not bring much higher precision.

Besides, during the simulation, we find that the time consumption of belief propagation in CBNs is much less than we expected. In fact, the number of iteration in belief propagation (in the algorithm depicted in Figure 3) never exceeds 10 in this shape recognition task.

DISCUSSION

In this section, we will examine the merits and demerits of the CBNs for the task of visual perception. As we show in the previous section, CBNs employs Bayesian network as its component, so it gains all the merits of Bayesian network, such as the theoretical foundation and the simple representation. Besides, the CBNs also possesses the merits that the traditional Bayesian network does not have.

The most distinctive merit of CBNs is that its structure fully represents the order of nature about how things in the physical world exist. For it encodes both the distinctive visual features of perceptual objects and the interrelationship between them. Furthermore, it exploits the Bayesian framework to deal with the uncertainty in perceptual process. The model is greatly consistent with the nature of the physical world.

Another significant merit of CBNs is that it has predefined network structure (all noncenter nodes pointing to the center node), which encodes more prior knowledge than the common Bayesian network does. The prior knowledge not only makes the model more reasonable, but also largely reduces the time consumed in the learning process.

In addition, the CBNs supports both batch learning and online learning. As we all know, it is hard to perform online learning for common Bayesian networks, because the fresh incoming data will modify both the parameters and the structure of the Bayesian network. And the searching of proper structure is extremely time consuming (Chickering et. al., 2003). On the contrary, the property of predefined network structure in CBNs enables it to have more stationary structure. In most cases, only the parameters need to be updated. The possible modification of structure involves only putting on new edges between the objects in new samples. As the learning process is limited to a relative small area, the learning is actually very efficient. Therefore, online learning is more feasible for CBNs.

The last but not least merit of CBNs is its capability for scaling up. Because the CBNs is an aggregation of numerous autonomic CBN, the learning process, as well as the inference process, can be decomposed into many isolated tasks that can be performed at each CBN. Namely, the CBNs is a distributed system. Any fresh CBN can be added into the model at any moment, without much modification to the existing model. Actually, only several neighbor CBN need slight modification. That means the system can be easily scaled up. Furthermore, with more CBN coming into the system, the system will accumulate more knowledge about the external world. In this sense, the CBNs is a real learning system that can make accumulation of knowledge.

Certainly, CBNs does have its weaknesses, especially the inference process. Due to its high possibility to have directed circles in the model, the inference will, theoretically, be more time consuming than the common Bayesian network. So, more mechanisms should be added to the model in the future to speed up the inference process. In addition, there also needs to be some limitation on the number of the connections from the neighbor center nodes to prevent too much complicated network structure.

CONCLUSION

How to integrate various visual features from scenes to form known objects has traditionally been a tough task for researchers. In this article, we propose a novel model, namely cellular Bayesian networks (CBNs), to deal with the visual perception task. The proposed model takes both the distinctive visual features of target objects and the interrelationship between them into account. Meanwhile, the Bayesian framework is employed to handle the uncertainty during perceptual process. From the meticulous analysis we can gain that the CBNs is much more suitable for perception task than the traditional Bayesian network due to its prominent features. Furthermore, experimental result also indicates that it can improve the recognition precision over the Bottom-up method. Additionally, although the CBNs is designed for visual perception, it also has great potential to be applied to other areas.

ACKNOWLEDGMENT

The research work in this article is supported by the National Science Foundation of China (No. 60173017, 60435010), the Nature Science Foundation of Beijing (No. 4052025), the 863 Project (No.2003AA115220), and National Basic Research Priorities Programme (No. 2003CB317004).

REFERENCES

Beinlich, I., Suermondt, G., Chavez, R., & Cooper, G. (1989). The ALARM monitoring system: A case study with two probabilistic inference techniques for belief networks. In *Proceedings of the 2nd European Conference on AI and Medicine*, (Vol. 38, pp. 247-256). Berlin: Springer-Verlag.

Broek, E. L., van den, Rikxoort, E. M. van, & Schouten, Th.E. (2005). Human-centered object-based image retrieval. *Lecture Notes in Computer Science* (Advances in Pattern Recognition), (Vol. 3687, pp. 492-501).

Brown, L. E., Tsamardinos, I., & Aliferis, C. F. (2005). A comparison of novel and state-of-the-art polynomial bayesian network learning algorithms. *AAAI* 2005, 739-745.

Chickering, D., Meek, C., & Heckerman, D. (2003). Large-sample learning of bayesian networks is np-hard. In *Proceedings of the 19th Annual Conference on Uncertainty in Artificial Intelligence* (UAI-03), (pp. 124–133).

Choe, Y. (2001). *Perceptual grouping in a self-organizing map of spiking neurons.* Doctoral dissertation thesis, Department of Computer Sciences, The University of Texas at Austin.

Dagum, P., & Luby, M. (1993). Approximating probabilistic inference in bayesian belief networks is np-hard. *Artificial Intelligence, 60*, 141-153.

Friedman, N. (1997). Learning belief networks in the presence of missing values and hidden variables. In *Proceedings of the Fourteenth International Conference on Machine Learning*, San Francisco, CA, USA, (pp.125-133).

Friedman, N., Linial,M., Nachman, I., & Pe'er, D. (2000). Using bayesian networks to analyze expression data. *Computational Biology, 7*, 601-620.

Geisler, W., & Diehl, R. L. (2003). A Bayesian approach to the evolution of perceptual and cognitive systems. *Cognitive Science, 27*, 379-402.

Geisler, W., & Murray, R. (2003). Practice doesn't make perfect. *Nature, 423*, 696-697.

Jacobs, R.A. (2002 August). What determines visual cue reliability? *TRENDS in Cognitive Sciences, 6*(8), 345-350.

Jorge, P. M., Marques, J. S., & Abrantes, A. J. (2004). Estimation of the bayesian network architecture for object tracking in video sequences. In *Proceedings of the 17th International Conference on Pattern Recognition* (ICPR'04), (Vol. 2, pp. 732-735).

Kang, H.-B., & Cho, S.-H. (2004). Adaptive object tracking using bayesian network and memory. In *Proceedings of the ACM 2nd International Workshop on Video Surveillance & Sensor Networks*, New York (pp. 104-113).

Lai, W.-C., Chang, C., Chang, E., Cheng, K.-T., & Crandell, M. (2002). Pbir-mm: Multimodal image retrieval and annotation. In *Proceedings of the Tenth ACM International Conference on Multimedia*, (pp. 421-422).

Lam, W., Low, K. F., & Ho, C. Y. (1997). Using a Bayesian network induction approach for text categorization. In *Proceedings of IJCAI97, 15th International Joint Conference on Artificial Intelligence*, Nagoya, Japan, (pp. 745-750).

Lee, T. S., & Mumford, D. (2003). Hierarchical bayesian inference in the visual cortex. *Journal of the Optical Society of America. A, Optics, Image Science, and Vision*, *20*(7), 1434-48.

Luchins, A. S., & Luchins, E. H. (1999). Isomorphism in Gestalt Theory: Comparison of Wertheimer's and Köhler's concepts. *GESTALT THEORY, 21*(3), 208-234.

Manjunath B. S., & Ma, W. Y. (1996). Texture features for browsing and retrieval of image data. *IEEE Transactions on Pattern Analysis and Machine Intelligence, 18*(8), 837-842.

Murphy, K., Torralba, A., & Freeman, W. T. (2004). Using the forest to see the trees: A graphical model relating features, objects, and scenes. *Advances in neural information processing systems* 16 (NIPS). Vancouver, British Columbia: MIT Press.

Papageorgiou, C., & Poggio, T. (2000). A trainable system for object detection. *International Journal of Computer Vision, 38*(1), 15-33.

Pearl, J. (1988). *Probabilistic reasoning in intelligent systems*. San Mateo, CA: Morgan Kaufmannn.

Ramoni, M., & Sebastiani, P. (2001). Robust learning with missing data. *Machine Learning, 45*(2), 147-170.

Ringach, D. (2002). Spatial structure and symmetry of simple-cell receptive fields in macaque primary visual cortex, *Journal of Neurophysiology, 88*, 455-463.

Schneiderman, H. (2004). Learning a restricted bayesian network for object detection. In *Proceedings of the IEEE Computer Society Conference on Computer Vision and Pattern Recognition* (CVPR'04) (Vol. 2, pp. 639-646).

Schneiderman, H., & Kanade, T. (2000). A statistical model for 3d object detection applied to faces and cars. In *Proceedings of the IEEE Conference on Computer Vision and Pattern Recognition*.

Tamminen, T., & Lampinen, J. (2003). Bayesian object matching with hierarchical priors and Markov chain Monte Carlo. *Bayesian statistics 7*. Oxford University Press.

Viola, P., & Jones, M. (2004). Robust real-time object detection. *International Journal of Computer Vision, 57*(2), 137-154.

Wang, Y. (2002, August). On cognitive informatics (Keynote Speech). In *Proceedings of the 1st IEEE International Conference on Cognitive Informatics* (ICCI'02) (pp. 34-42). Calgary, Canada: IEEE CS Press.

Wang, Y. (2003, August). Cognitive informatics models of software agent systems and autonomic computing (Keynote Speech). In *Proceedings of the International Conference on Agent-Based Technologies and Systems* (ATS'03) (p. 25). Calgary Canada: University of Calgary Press.

Wang, Y. (2004, August). On autonomic computing and cognitive processes (Keynote Speech). In *Proceedings of the 3rd IEEE International Conference on Cognitive Informatics* (ICCI'04) (pp. 3-4). Victoria: Canada. IEEE CS Press.

Wang, Y. (2005, August). On the cognitive processes of human perceptions. In *Proceedings of the 4th IEEE International Conference on Cognitive Informatics* (ICCI'05) (pp. 203-211). Irvin, CA: IEEE CS Press.

Wang, Y. (2005, August). The cognitive processes of abstraction and formal inferences. In *Proceedings of the 4th IEEE International Conference on Cognitive Informatics* (ICCI'05), (pp. 18-26), Irvin, CA: IEEE CS Press.

Wang, Y. (2006, July). Cognitive informatics towards the future generation computers that think and feel. In *Proceedings of the 5th IEEE International Conference on Cognitive Informatics* (ICCI'06) (pp. 3-7). Beijing, China: IEEE CS Press.

Wang, Y. (2006). On the informatics laws and deductive semantics of software. *IEEE Transactions on Systems, Man, and Cybernetics (Part C), 36(*2), 161-171.

Wang, Y. (2006). *Software engineering foundations: A transdisciplinary and rigorous perspective* (CRC Book Series in Software Engineering 2). Boca Raton, FL: CRC Press.

Wang, Y. (2006, May). The OAR model for knowledge representation. In *Proceedings of the 19th IEEE Canadian Conference on Electrical and Computer Engineering* (CCECE'06). Ottawa, Canada, (pp. 1696-1699).

Wang, Y. (2007, January). The theoretical framework of cognitive informatics. *The International Journal of Cognitive Informatics and Natural Intelligence* (IJCiNi), IGP, USA, (Vol. 1, No. 1, pp.1-27).

Wang, Y., Liu, D., & Wang, Y. (2003). Discovering the capacity of human memory. *Brain and Mind: A Transdisciplinary Journal of Neuroscience and Neurophilosophy, 4*(2), 189-198.

Wang, Y., & Wang, Y. (2006, March). On cognitive informatics models of the brain. *IEEE Transactions on* Wang, Y., Wang, Y., Patel, S., & Patel, D. (2006, March). A layered reference model of the brain (LRMB). *IEEE Transactions on Systems, Man, and Cybernetics* (Part C), *36*(2), 124-133.

Wu, C.-H., Wun, C.-H., & Chou, H.-J. (2004). Using association rules for completing missing data. In *Proceedings of the Fourth International Conference on Hybrid Intelligent Systems* (HIS'04), (pp. 236-241).

ENDNOTES

[1]   In mathematics an isomorphism between two systems requires a one-to-one correspondence between their elements (that is, each element of one system corresponds to one and only one element of the other system, and vice versa), which also preserves structures. In Gestalt psychology, the one-to-one correspondence between elements is not required; similarity of structures is required. (Luchins & Luchins, 1999)

[2]   Here X is the start point of the edge.

[3]   Available at http://www.lems.brown.edu/vision/software/216shapes.tar.gz

This work was previously published in the International Journal of Cognitive Informatics and Natural Intelligence, Vol. 2, Issue 1, edited by Y. Wang, pp. 44-57, copyright 2008 by IGI Publishing (an imprint of IGI Global).

Chapter 24
An Efficient and Automatic Iris Recognition System Using ICM Neural Network

Guangzhu Xu
China Three Gorges University, P.R. China

Yide Ma
Lanzhou University, P.R. China

Zaifeng Zhang
Lanzhou University, P.R. China

ABSTRACT

Iris recognition has been shown to be very accurate for human identification. In this chapter, an efficient and automatic iris recognition system using Intersecting Cortical Model (ICM) neural network is presented which includes two parts mainly. The first part is image preprocessing which has three steps. First, iris location is implemented based on local areas. Then the localized iris area is normalized into a rectangular region with a fixed size. At last the iris image enhancement is implemented. In the second part, the ICM neural network is used to generate iris codes and the Hamming Distance between two iris codes is calculated to measure the dissimilarity. In order to evaluate the performance of the proposed algorithm, CASIA v1.0 iris image database is used and the recognition results show that the system has good performance.

INTRODUCTION

Today, biometrics is a common and reliable way to authenticate the identity of a living person based on physiological or behavioral characteristics. A physiological characteristic is relatively stable physical characteristics, such as fingerprint, iris pattern, facial feature, etc. (Jain, Bolle, & Pankanti, 1999; Wayman, 2001). The human iris is an annular part between pupil and sclera and its complex pattern contains many distinctive features such as arching ligaments, furrows, ridges, crypts, and a zigzag collarette. Iris

DOI: 10.4018/978-1-60566-902-1.ch024

structure patterns are different for different persons even if they are twins or multiple births. At the same time the iris is protected from the external environment behind the cornea and the eyelid. No subject to deleterious effects of aging, the small-scale radial features of the iris remain stable and fixed from about one year of age throughout one's life. All these advantages let the iris recognition be a promising topic of biometrics and get more and more attentions (Boles, 1998; Daugman, 1993; Liam, 2002; Lim, 2001; Ma, 2002; Tisse, 2002; Wilds, 1997).

In Daugman's (1993) system an Integro-differential operator was used to locate the iris. And 2D Gabor filters and phase coding were used to obtain 2048 binary feature code for the iris representation. In order to measure the dissimilarity between two irises, the Hamming Distance is computed between the pair of iris codes.

Different from Daugman, Wildes (1997) exploited the gradient-based Hough transform for localizing the iris area, and made use of Laplacian pyramid constructed with four different resolution levels to generate iris code. The degree of similarity is evaluated with the normalized correlation between the acquired and database representations.

Boles (1998) used the knowledge-based edge detector for iris localization, and implemented the system operating the set of 1-D signals composed of normalized iris signatures at a few intermediate resolution levels and obtaining the iris representation of these signals via the zero-crossing of the dyadic wavelet transform. It made use of two dissimilarity functions to compare a new pattern and the reference patterns.

Lim (2001) exploited 2D Haar wavelet transform to extract high frequency information of iris to form an 87-bit code and implemented the classification using a modified competitive learning neural network. A bank of Gabor filters was used to capture both local and global iris characteristics in Ma's (2002) algorithm. And the iris matching is based on the weighted Euclidean distance between the two corresponding iris vectors.

Monro (2007) uses the discrete cosine transform for feature extraction. They apply the DCT to overlapping rectangular image patches rotated 45 degree from the radial axis. "The differences between the DCT coefficients of adjacent patch vectors are then calculated and a binary code is generated from their zero crossings." (Monro, 2007 pp.590).

In our research, a method based on local areas of pupil and iris is used to complete iris location quickly at first. Then the located iris region is normalized into Polar coordinates from Cartesian. In order to extract iris features such as furrows, ridges, crypts, freckles and so on, the Intersecting Cortical Model (ICM) neural network is used. In our system, the normalized iris is put into ICM neural network after enhancement processing. And the output pulse image produced by ICM neural network is chosen as the iris code. At last the Hamming Distance is computed to measure the dissimilarity of two iris images.

IRIS IMAGE PREPROCESSING

The iris image preprocessing part includes three steps: iris location (pupil location and iris outer boundary location), normalization and iris enhancement.

Pupil Location

Because the pupil is similar to a dark circular disk, pupil location is equal to find the black circular region in an eye image. We contrive a simple and fast solution to this problem. In order to get a binary image that contains pupil but no more other parts of the eye, an appropriate threshold is necessary. We divide the original image into 224 rectangle blocks and find out the first one with the minimum average intensity. Then use this value as a threshold to get a binary image (in case of the non-uniform brightness in the pupil area, we raise the threshold a little by adding eight to it). At last, eliminate the lighting spots in pupil and some small black spots caused by eyelashes and iris complex textures using mathematical morphological operators. (Figure 1a, b, c illustrate this process). The aim of pupil location is to find the circle fitting the pupil's outer boundary best. In our algorithm the rectangle block found at the beginning is extended to the boundaries of pupil automatically in the binary image as follows to complete pupil location (Figure 1d-f illustrate this process.)

Figure 1. The process of for pupil location (a) Divided origin image (b) The rectangular block which has the smallest average intensity. (c) The binary image after processing of morphological operator (d) Extending result (e) Pupil boundaries coordinates (f) Pupil location result

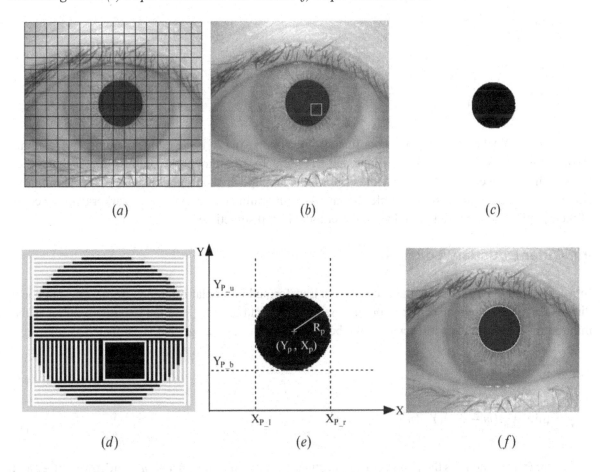

(a) (b) (c)

(d) (e) (f)

1. Extend the rectangle block towards left and right to search for left and right boundaries of pupil. And when the number of white points on the left and right sides of the rectangle block equals the length of both sides, the temporary left and right boundaries of pupil are found. Renew the size of the rectangle block.
2. Continue the last step, but different from the first step, the extending direction is towards top and bottom. The boundaries found are considered as real top and bottom boundaries of the pupil. Renew the size of the rectangle block again.
3. Extend the rectangle resized by step two towards left and right again to find the left and right boundaries of pupil and take them as the real left and right boundaries of pupil.

After these three steps the left, right, top and bottom boundaries of the pupil are found out. Given that the coordinates of four boundaries are X_{p_l}, X_{p_r}, Y_{p_u} and Y_{p_d}, and the circle center coordinates and radius of pupil can be estimated as follows:

$$X_p = \frac{(X_{p\_l} + X_{p\_r})}{2} \tag{1}$$

$$Y_p = \frac{(Y_{p\_t} + Y_{p\_b})}{2} \tag{2}$$

$$R_p = \frac{|X_{p\_r} - X_{p\_l}| + |Y_{p\_t} - Y_{p\_b}|}{4} \tag{3}$$

Where (Y_p, X_p) denotes the center coordinates of the pupil. And R_p is the radius of pupil. The relationship among X_{p_l}, X_{p_r}, Y_{p_t} and Y_{p_b} is illustrated in Figure 1e. Commonly the pupil is darker than other parts of the eye, even with there are some bright lights in pupil area our method has good performance. But when the skin color of some people (Indian, African or miner) is as dark as or darker than the color of their pupils, the proposed pupil location method will fail sometimes.

Iris Outer Boundary Location

In iris outer boundary location, the eye image is transformed into polar reference from Cartesian coordinates firstly based on the center of pupil. The minimum radius is r_{min} and the maximum radius is the minimum value from the pupil center to the boundaries of the eye image that is estimated as follows:

$$r_{min} = R_p + 5 \tag{4}$$

$$r_{max} = \min(X_p, (m - X_p), Y_p, (n - Y_p)) \tag{5}$$

Where (x_p, y_p) and R_p is the pupil center coordinates and pupil radius, n and m is the row number and the column number of an eye image separately (as shown in Figure 2a). From the Figure 2 (a) we can

Figure 2. Iris outer boundary location (a) Unwrapping processing of origin image areas (b) iris outer boundary detection (c) Iris location samples

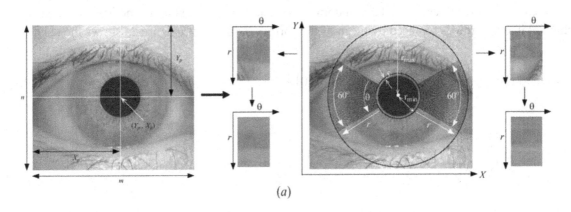

(a)

(b)

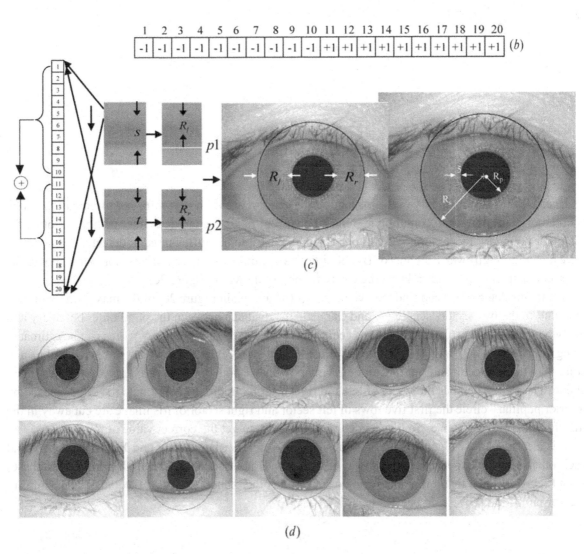

(c)

(d)

find that some parts of the iris region are occluded by upper and lower eyelids and eyelashes, so only two opposing 60° cones centered on the horizontal meridian are selected (as shown in Figure 2a). In order to eliminate the effects caused by random noises and complex texture of the iris, the intensity of each pixel in every row is replaced by mean of the corresponding row. (Figure 2a shows the results.)

$$R_l = \arg\max_x \left\{ \sum_{x=10}^{s-10} \left[\left(\sum_{i=1}^{10} I_l(x+i) - I_l(x+i-10) \right) \right] \right\} \tag{6}$$

$$R_r = \arg\max_x \left\{ \sum_{x=10}^{t-10} \left[\left(\sum_{i=1}^{10} I_r(x+i) - I_r(x+i-10) \right) \right] \right\} \tag{7}$$

$$R_s = 5 + \frac{(R_r + R_l)}{2} + R_p \tag{8}$$

$$Y_s = Y_p \tag{9}$$

$$X_s = X_p + \frac{(R_r - R_l)}{2} \tag{10}$$

Because the outer boundary of the iris tends to be extremely soft in near infra-red illumination which is commonly used in iris recognition systems, the current reliable edge detection method is not fit for iris outer boundary location directly. In our research a simple but efficient edge detector template (as shown in Figure 2b) was introduced. By moving this template on the two iris region parts above, the outer boundaries of left and right can be easily found (as shown in Figure 2c).

Using this detector we can find the two positions (*p1* and *p2* in Figure 2c) of the maximum 'summed gradient' in the two sectors separately and calculate the distance between the pupil outer boundary and the two position using (6) and (7).The iris center coordinate and outer boundary radius can be estimated using equation (8), (9) and (10). (Figure 2c illustrates this process). I_l and I_r can be considered as any column of the left sector and right sector of iris image because both of them are averaged in row as stated above. The *s* and *t* denotes the width of left and right sectors. In order to eliminate the effect caused by inferior pupillary circle the first five rows of left sector and right sector of iris image are cut away in the transforming process above. So it is needed to add 5 in (8) to get the correct value of R_s.

It is clear the above algorithm doesn't consider the difference between Y_p and Y_s, just let them equal each other. But the experimental results in CASIA (v1.0) iris database (CASIA Iris Image Database) from Figure 2d show that it is available to do so. On the other hand, assuming Y_p equals Y_s can simplify the normalization processing below.

Normalization

Commonly, irises captured from different people have different size, and even for the same person, the size may change because of the variation of the illumination and other factors. At the same time pupil and iris are non-concentric. In order to compensate the stretching of the iris texture and break the non-concentricity of the iris and the pupil, the normalization of the iris image is implemented. This transformation will project the iris disk to a rectangular region with a fixed size. And the center of the pupil is considered as the reference point and the following remapping formulas are used to convert the points on the Cartesian scale to the polar scale. Figure 3a illustrates this process.

Figure 3. Iris normalization process (a) Normalization sketch map (b) Normalization geometric relationship (c) Normalized iris image

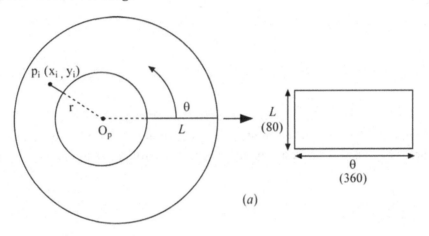

(a)

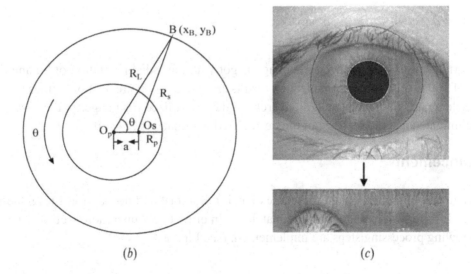

(b)   *(c)*

$$\theta \in [0, 2\pi] \quad r \in [R_p, R_L(\theta)]$$

$$x_i = x_p + r \times \cos\theta \tag{11}$$

$$y_i = y_p + r \times \sin\theta \tag{12}$$

Where (x_i, y_i) is the coordinate of the point p_i which is a point between the pupillary and limbic boundaries in the direction θ. (x_p, y_p) and R_p are respectively the center coordinates and radius of the pupil. $R_L(\theta)$ is the distance between O_p and the point of limbic boundary which is the function of θ. Given B is a point on the limbic boundary (as shown in Figure 3b) and its coordinate (x_B, y_B) can be calculated as follows:

$$x_B = x_p + R_L(\theta) \times \cos\theta \tag{13}$$

$$y_B = y_p + R_L(\theta) \times \sin\theta \tag{14}$$

As shown in Figure 3b, $R_L(\theta)$ can be calculated using equation (17) based on equations (13), (14), (15) and (16). Where (x_s, y_s) and R_s are respectively the center coordinates and radius of the iris.

$$a = x_s - x_p = \frac{(R_r - R_l)}{2} \tag{15}$$

$$(x_s - x_B)^2 + (y_s - y_B)^2 = |O_s B| = R_s^2 \tag{16}$$

$$R_L = |O_p B| = a \times \cos\theta + \sqrt{R_s^2 - a^2 \sin\theta^2} \tag{17}$$

After normalization a normalized iris image is got with the radial resolution of 80 and the angular resolution of 360 pixels. Some normalization results are shown in Figure 3c. Sometimes there are some pupil and sclera parts in the top and bottom areas of the normalized iris image, so the first and last four rows are eliminated and the real size of the normalized iris image is 72×360.

Iris Enhancement

After normalization, the iris image sometimes has low contrast and non-uniform brightness that will affect the following feature extraction and matching. In order to obtain a more well-distributed texture image, following processing steps are implemented. (see Figure 4)

Figure 4. Iris image enhancement (a) original normalized iris image (b) Divided iris image (c) Estimated background illumination (d) Iris image with uniform brightness (e) Histogram equalized iris image (f) final enhanced iris image after mean filtering

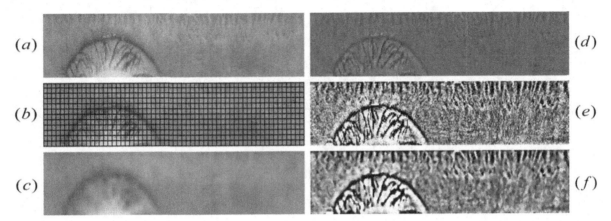

1. Divide iris image into 720 small blocks with a fixed size of 6×6 and calculate the mean of each block to estimate the background illumination (as shown in Figure 4b).
2. Extend the coarse estimation of illumination above to the same size as the normalized iris image using bicubic interpolation (as shown in Figure 4c).
3. Subtract the estimated background illumination from the iris image to get uniform brightness (as shown in Figure 4d).
4. Enhance the lighting correct image by means of histogram equalization (as shown in Figure 4e).
5. Using mean filter to eliminate the noises coming from capture device and circumstance (as shown in Figure 4f).

IRIS FEATURE EXTRACTION USING ICM NEURAL NETWORK AND IRIS MATCHING

Intersecting Cortical Model (ICM) Neural Network

From the image (b) in Figure 5, we can see that some distinctive features of the iris image such as furrows, ridges, and crypts are more visible than before. If they can be segmented out efficiently, the iris pattern can be described using them. But some iris features tend to be extremely soft in some areas of an iris image, even after enhancement. Some current segmentation methods are difficult to be implemented for iris features segmentation. So, in our research, the ICM neural network is selected as a segmentation tool for its special advantages. ICM neural network is a simple version of the Pulse Coupled Neural Network (PCNN) model of Eckhorn (Eckhorn, & Reitoeck, Arndt, & Dicke, 1990; Johnson & Padgett, 1999). This type of neural network doesn't need any training, and generates a sequence of binary images for the input digital image. These output images can be used for different image processing tasks, for example image segmentation and image smoothing.

The basic simplified structure of the ICM neuron for a two-dimensional input image is shown in Figure 5a. In the ICM neural network, the state oscillators of all the neurons are represented by a 2D

Figure 5. (a) The basic ICM neuron (b) Iris coding process

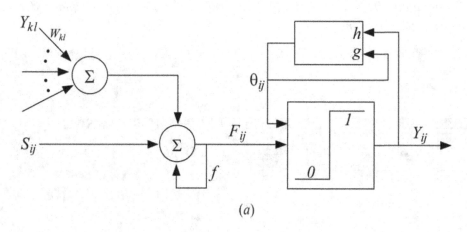

(a)

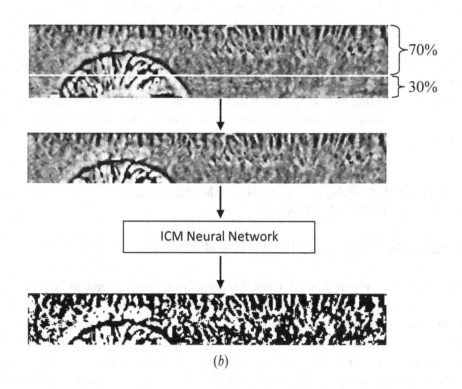

(b)

array F (the internal neuron states; initially $F_{ij} = 0$"i, j) and the threshold oscillators of all the neurons by a 2D array θ (initially $\theta_{ij} = 0$"i, j), Thus, the ijth neuron has state F_{ij} and threshold θ_{ij}. They are computed as follows:

$$F_{ij}[n+1] = fF_{ij}[n] + S_{ij} + \sum_{kl} W_{ijkl} Y_{kl}[n] \tag{18}$$

$$Y_{ij}[n+1] = \begin{cases} 1 & if \ F_{ij}[n+1] > \theta_{ij}[n] \\ 0 & otherwise \end{cases} \tag{19}$$

$$\theta_{ij}[n+1] = g\theta_{ij}[n] + hY_{ij}[n+1] \tag{20}$$

Where S_{ij} is the stimulus (the input image, scaled so that the largest pixel value is 1.0); Y_{ij} is the firing state of the neuron (Y is the output image); f, g and h are scalars (in our research, they are 0.4, 0.32 and 10 respectively); W_{ij} describes the inter-neuron communications (in our research, we consider only the 8-connected areas of the ijth pixel. So the W_{ij} is 0.125); and $n=1, 2,..., N$ is the iteration number. The scalars f and g are decay constants and thus less than 1. The outputs of the ICM neural network are the binary pulse images Y obtained after a number of neural pulse iterations (Ekblad. U., & Kinser, J.M., 2004).

Feature Extraction and Matching

In this part, the enhanced iris image is input into the ICM neural network mentioned above. The fourth output pulse image is used as the iris code in our algorithm with considering the time consumption. In our experiments, we extract features only in the top-most 70% section (corresponding to the regions closer to the pupil) of the fourth output impulse image because we find that the iris regions close to the sclera contain few texture characteristics and are easy to be occluded by eyelids and eyelashes. The Figure 5b illustrates the process.

In order to determine whether two iris images come from the same class, the Hamming Distance between the two corresponding iris codes is computed directly as follows:

$$HD = \frac{\left\| (CodeA \otimes CodeB) \right\|}{18000} \tag{21}$$

Where Code A and Code B are the two iris codes to be compared, and the *18000* is the number of bits to be compared. The *XOR* operator detects the disagreement between any pair of iris codes. And the resulting *HD* is a fractional measure of dissimilarity.

EXPERIMENTAL RESULTS AND DISCUSSION

Experimental Results

In order to evaluate the proposed iris recognition algorithm, the CASIA v1.0 iris image database (CASIA Iris Image Database v1.0) is used. CASIA v1.0 Iris Image Database contains 756 images from

Table 1. Iris location accuracy comparisons of some popular methods for CASIA v1.0 iris database

Algorithm	FAR/FRR	Overall Accuracy
Avila (de Martin-Roche, D., & Sanchez-Avila, C., & Sanchez-Reillo,.R. (2001))	0.03/2.08	97.89%
Li Ma (Ma, L., & Wang, Y., & Tan, T. (2002))	0.02/1.98	98.0%
Tisse (Tisse, C., & Martin, L., & Torres, L., & Robert, M. (2002))	1.84/8.79	89.37%
Daugman (Daugman, J. (2001))	0.01/0.09	99.90%
Proposed Method	0.02/1.87	98.11%

108 different objects. Each of the iris images is 8 bit gray scale with a resolution of *320x280*. In our experiments all the parameters of the iris recognition system were carefully selected through rigorous experimentations. The accuracy rate of iris location is 98.42%, so in our study, 744 images in CASIA v1.0 are used for identification experiments.

For CASIA v1.0, each eye has 7 images, which were captured in two sessions: three samples were collected in the first session and four in the second session. In iris matching stage, we have taken three images for training purpose and the rest four for testing which is as same as Vatsa's (2004). The performance results are based on error rates: False Acceptance Rate (FAR) and False Rejection Rate (FRR); and the overall accuracy. The comparison results of some different algorithms are shown in Table1 for CASIA v1.0. Here, the data of the reference (Vatsa, Singh, & Gupta, 2004) is cited to compare. The reason for choosing the data is that the reference (Vatsa et al., 2004) used the same image gallery and also divided the image database into two parts for training and matching. On the other hand, the reference is one paper special for comparing the performances of different iris recognition methods, so the data of it is more meaningful.

From Table 1 we can see that the proposed iris recognition method based on ICM neural network has encouraging performance. Figure 6a shows the Hamming distance distribution of inter-class and intra-class comparisons in CASIA v1.0 image database. Where *d'* (Daugman 1999) is one measure of the decidability, which is a function of the magnitude of difference between the mean of the intra-class distribution μ_s, and the mean of the inter-class distribution μ_d, and also the standard deviation of the intra-class and inter-class distributions, σ_s and σ_d respectively (as shown in Equation.22). The higher is the decidability *d'*, the greater is the separation of intra-class and inter-class distribution, which allows for more accurate recognition (Daugman, 1999). Figure 6b is the Receiver Operating Characteristic (ROC) curve (Park, Goo, & Jo, 2004) that is a graphical representation of the tradeoff between genuine acceptance and false acceptance rates. Points in this curve denote all possible system operating states in different tradeoffs. It shows the overall performance of a system.

$$d' = \frac{\left| \mu_S - \mu_D \right|}{\sqrt{(\sigma_s^2 + \sigma_D^2)/2}} \tag{22}$$

Discussion

CASIA v1.0 is one of the most used iris image database which has been released to more than 1,500 researchers and 70 countries. Its latest version is CASIA v3.0 (subset 1). Comparing with CASIA v3.0,

Figure 6. (a) Intra-class and Inter-class comparisons result (b) ROC curve

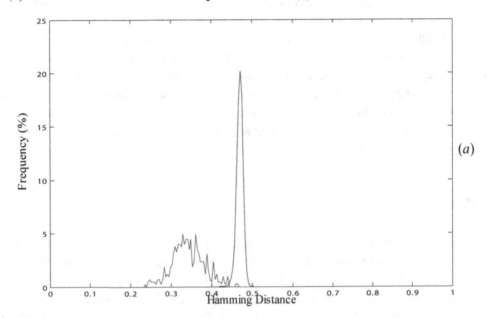

(a)

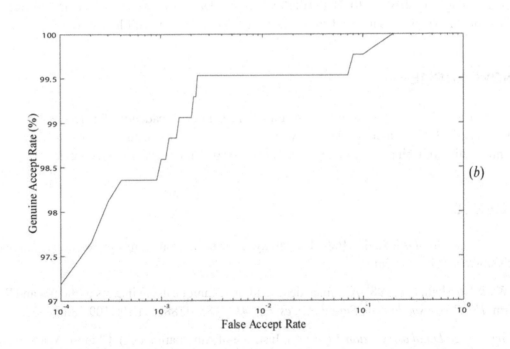

(b)

the pupil area of each eye image in CASIA v1.0 is automatically filled with a uniform black block to cover those bright spots coming from refection. This preprocessing makes pupil-iris boundary automatic detection simple. But CASIA v1.0 is still valuable on other components of iris recognition system, such as feature extraction and classification. The location method in our system is also fit for CASIA v3.0, because the morphological operations used in our method can fill the bright spots in pupil area. On the other hand, CASIA v1.0 is organized better than CASIA v3.0 though CASIA v1.0 is a subset of CASIA v3.0.

The reason for false rejection in CASIA v1.0 is that the iris regions are occluded so badly by eyelids and eyelashes that there is not enough useful information for matching. For false accept, the reasons come from two ways. One is that eyelids and eyelashes occluds the iris badly and the some eyelids/eyelashes areas are taken as the iris region in iris matching process. Another is that iris textures of some objects are not so clear that two different iris images are very similar especially when the pupil is extend too much. All above cases can be resolved at some level by using iris image quality evaluation and improving the capture device.

CONCLUSION

In this paper, an efficient method for iris recognition is proposed. After preprocessing, the enhanced iris image is put into ICM neural network, and the fourth output is used as the iris code. The ICM neural network is a simplified model of Pulse-Coupled Neural Network (PCNN), which has excellent performance for image segmentation, so the coding process is fast enough. The recognition results in CASIA v1.0 show that our iris recognition system has better identification performance. Except for CASIA v1.0 our method also can be used for some other public iris image database such as CASIA v3.0 (subset1) (CASIA Iris Image Database v3.0), Bath (Bath Iris Image Database), MMU v1.0 (MMU Image Database). But for some noisy iris image database as UBIRIS our system can't locate well.

ACKNOWLEDGMENT

Authors wish to acknowledge institute of Automation, Chinese Academy of Sciences for providing CASIA v1.0 and v3.0 iris database. Authors would also like to thank institute of Intelligent Vision and Image Information of China Three Gorges University for providing experimental devices.

REFERENCE

Bath Iris Image Database (n.d.). Bath University. Retrieved from http://www.bath.ac.uk/elec-eng/research/sipg/irisweb/index.htm

Boles, W., & Boashah, B. (1998). A human identification technique using images of the Iris and Wavelet transform. *IEEE Transactions on Signal Processing*, *46*, 1185–1188. doi:10.1109/78.668573

CASIA Iris Image Database version 1.0. (n.d.). Institute of Automation (IA), Chinese Academy of Sciences (CAS). Retrieved from http://www.sinobiometrics.com

CASIA Iris Image Database version 3.0. (n.d.). Institute of Automation (IA), Chinese Academy of Sciences (CAS). Retrieved from http://www.cbsr.ia.ac.cn/english/IrisDatabase.asp

Daugman, J. (1993). High confidence visual recognition of persons by a test of statistical independence. *IEEE Transactions on Pattern Analysis and Machine Intelligence, 15*(11), 1148–1161. doi:10.1109/34.244676

Daugman, J. (1999). *Biometric Decision Landscape* (Technical Report No. TR482).University of Cambridge Computer Laboratory.

Daugman, J. (2001). Statistical richness of visual phase information update on recognizing Persons by Iris Patterns. *International Journal of Computer Vision, 45*(1), 25–38. doi:10.1023/A:1012365806338

de Martin-Roche, D., Sanchez-Avila, C., & Sanchez-Reillo, R. (2001). Iris Recognition for Biometric Identification Using Dyadic. Wavelet Transform Zero-Crossing. *IEEE 35th International Carnahan Conference on Security Technology* (pp. 272-277).

Eckhorn, R., Reitoeck, H. J., Arndt, M., & Dicke, P. (1990). Feature Linking via Synchronisation among Distributed Assemblies: Simulation of Results from Cat Cortex. *Neural Computation, 2,* 293–307. doi:10.1162/neco.1990.2.3.293

Ekblad, U., & Kinser, J. M. (2004). The intersecting cortical model in image processing. *Nuclear Instruments & Methods in Physics Research. Section A, Accelerators, Spectrometers, Detectors and Associated Equipment,* 392–396. doi:10.1016/j.nima.2004.03.102

Jain, A. K., Bolle, R. M., & Pankanti, S. (1999). *Biometrics - Personal Identification in a Networked Society.* MA: Kluwer Academic.

Johnson, J. L., & Padgett, M. L. (1999). PCNN models and applications. *IEEE Transactions on Neural Networks, 10*(3), 480–498. doi:10.1109/72.761706

Liam, L. W., Chekima, A., Fan, L. C., & Dargham, J. A. (2002). Iris Recognition. Using Self- Organizing Neural Network. *Student Conference on. Research and Development* (pp. 169-172).

Lim, S., Lee, K., Byeon, O., & Kim, T. (2001). Efficient iris recognition through improvement of feature vector and Classifier. *ETRI J, 23*(2), 61–70. doi:10.4218/etrij.01.0101.0203

Ma, L., Wang, Y., & Tan, T. (2002). Iris Recognition Based on Multichannel Gabor Filtering. *the Fifth Asian Conference on Computer Vision, 1,* 279-283.

Masek, L. (2003). *Recognition of Human Iris Patterns for Biometric identification.* Retrieved from http://www.csse.uwa.edu.au/òpk/studentprojects/libor/ *MMU Image Database (version 1.0)* (n.d.). Multimedia University. Retrieved from http://pesona.mmu.edu.my/~ccteo/

Monro, D. M., Rakshit, S., & Zhang, D. (2007). DCT-Based Iris Recognition. *IEEE Transactions on Pattern Analysis and Machine Intelligence, 29*(4), 586–595. doi:10.1109/TPAMI.2007.1002

Muron, J., & Pospisil, J. (2000). The Human Iris Structure and its Usages. *Dept. of Experimental Physics, 39,* 87–95.

Park, S. H., Goo, J. M., & Jo, C. H. (2004). Receiver operating characteristic (roc) curve: Practical review for radiologists. *Korean Journal of Radiology, 5*(1), 11–18. doi:10.3348/kjr.2004.5.1.11

Proença, H., & Alexandre, L. A. (2005). UBIRIS: A noisy iris image database. *Proc International Conf. on Image Analysis and Processing, 1,* 970–977.

Tisse, C., Martin, L., Torres, L., & Robert, M. (2002). Person identification technique using human iris recognition. *Proc. of Vision Interface* (pp. 294-299).

Vatsa, M., Singh, R., & Gupta, P. (2004). Comparison of Iris Recognition Algorithms. *International Conference on Intelligent Sensing and Information Processing* (pp. 354-358).

Wayman, J. L. (2001). Fundamentals of Biometric Authentication Technologies. *International Journal of Image and Graphics, 1*(1), 93–113. doi:10.1142/S0219467801000086

Wildes, R. (1997). Iris recognition:An Emerging. Biometric Technology. *Proceedings of the IEEE, 85*(9), 1348–1363. doi:10.1109/5.628669

Chapter 25
Neural Networks for Language Independent Emotion Recognition in Speech

Yongjin Wang
University of Toronto, Canada

Muhammad Waqas Bhatti
University of Sydney, Australia

Ling Guan
Ryerson University, Canada

ABSTRACT

This chapter introduces a neural network based approach for the identification of human affective state in speech signals. A group of potential features are first identified and extracted to represent the characteristics of different emotions. To reduce the dimensionality of the feature space, whilst increasing the discriminatory power of the features, a systematic feature selection approach which involves the application of sequential forward selection (SFS) with a general regression neural network (GRNN) in conjunction with a consistency-based selection method is presented. The selected parameters are employed as inputs to the a modular neural network, consisting of sub-networks, where each sub-network specializes in a particular emotion class. Comparing with the standard neural network, this modular architecture allows decomposition of a complex classification problem into small subtasks such that the network may be tuned based on the characteristics of individual emotion. The performance of the proposed system is evaluated for various subjects, speaking different languages. The results show that the system produces quite satisfactory emotion detection performance, yet demonstrates a significant increase in versatility through its propensity for language independence.

DOI: 10.4018/978-1-60566-902-1.ch025

INTRODUCTION

General Background

As computers have become an integral part of our lives, the need has arisen for a more natural communication interface between humans and machines. To accomplish this goal, a computer would have to be able to perceive its present situation and respond differently depending on that perception. Part of this process involves understanding a user's emotional state. To make the **human-computer interaction (HCI)** more natural, it would be beneficial to give computers the ability to recognize situations the same way a human does.

A good reference model for emotion recognition is the human brain. Machine recognition of human emotion involves strong combination of informatics and cognitive science. The difficulty of this problem is rooted in the understanding of mechanisms of natural intelligence and cognitive processes of the brain, Cognitive Informatics (Wang, 2003). For effective recognition of human emotion, important information needs to be extracted from the captured emotional data to mimic the way human distinguish different emotions, while the processed information needs to be further classified by simulating that of human brain system for pattern recognition

In the field of HCI, speech is primary to the objectives of an emotion recognition system, as are facial expressions and gestures. It is considered as a powerful mode to communicate intentions and emotions. This chapter explores methods by which a computer can recognize human emotion in the speech signal. Such methods can contribute to human-computer communication and to applications such as learning environments, consumer relations, entertainment, and educational software (Picard, 1997).

A great deal of research has been done in the field of speech recognition, where the computer analyzes an acoustic signal and maps it into a set of lexical symbols. In this case, much of the emphasis is on the segmental aspect of speech, that is, looking at each individual sound segment of the input signal and comparing it with known patterns that correspond to different consonants, vowels and other lexical symbols. In emotion recognition, the lexical content of the utterance is insignificant because two sentences could have the same lexical meaning but different emotional information.

Emotions have been the object of intense interest in both Eastern and Western philosophy since before the time of Lao-Tzu (sixth century B.C.) in the east and of Socrates (470-399 B.C.) in the west, and most contemporary thinking about emotions in psychology can be linked to one Western philosophical tradition or another (Calhoun & Solomon, 1984). However, the beginning of modern, scientific inquiry into the nature of emotion is thought by many to have begun with Charles Darwin's study of emotional expression in animals and humans (Darwin, 1965). A survey of contemporary research on emotion in psychology reveals four general perspectives about defining, studying, and explaining emotion (Cornelius, 1996). These are the Darwinian, the Jamesian, the cognitive, and the social constructivist perspectives. Each of these perspectives represents a different way of thinking about emotions. Each has its own set of assumptions about how to define, construct theories about, and conduct research on emotion, and each has associated with its own tradition of research (Ekman & Sullivan, 1987; Levenson, Ekman, & Friesen 1990; Smith & Kleinman, 1989; Smith & Lazarus, 1993).

A wide investigation on the dimensions of emotions reveals that at least six emotions are universal. Several other emotions, and many combinations of emotions, have been studied but remain unconfirmed as universally distinguishable. A set of six principal emotions is *happiness, sadness, anger, fear, surprise, and disgust*, which is the focus of study in this chapter.

Previous Work

In the past few years a significant portion of research in speech has been conducted on machine recognition of human vocal emotions. Dellaert, Polzin, and Waibel (1996) used five human subjects and five emotional classes: anger, fear, happiness, sadness, and neutral. The project also explored several classification methods including the Maximum Likelihood Bayes classifier, Kernel Regression and K-nearest Neighbors (KNN), and feature selection methods such as Majority Voting of Specialists. The feature selection methods improved system performance, and recognition rate of up to 79.5 percent was achieved. However, the authors noted in their concluding remarks that the results were speaker dependent, and that the classification methods had to be validated on completely held-out databases.

Cowie and Douglas-Cowie (1996) broadened the view of emotion recognition by noting that speech features previously associated with emotion could also be associated with impairments such as schizophrenia and deafness. Their studies focused more on intensity and rhythm and also investigated the importance of unvoiced sounds.

Amir and Ron (1998) reported a method for identifying the emotions based on analysis of the signal over sliding windows. A set of basic emotions was defined and for each emotion a reference point was computed. At each instant the distance of the measured parameter set from the reference points was calculated, and used to compute a fuzzy membership index for each emotion.

Sato and Morishima (1996) demonstrated the use of neural networks in analyzing and synthesizing emotions in speech. Their paper also discussed the way emotion is encoded in speech. The authors categorized the emotions as "anger", "disgust", "happiness", "sadness" and "neutral". They briefly discussed the six speech parameters that were analyzed, and made some empirical observations about the relationship between these parameters and certain emotions. The sound samples used in the experiment were recorded by a professional actor, yet a group of human subjects could correctly recognize his emotions only 70% of the time.

Nicholson, Takabashi, and Nakatsu (2000) proposed a speaker and context independent system for emotion recognition in speech using neural networks (NN). The paper examined both prosodic and phonetic features. Based on these features, one-class-in-one (OCON) and all-class-in-one (ACON) neural networks were employed to classify emotions. However, no feature selection techniques were used, and the recognition rate was only around 50 percent.

Lee, Narayanan, and Pieraccini (2001) classified a corpus of human-machine dialogs recorded from a commercial application into two basic emotions: negative and non-negative. Two methods, namely Linear Discriminant Classifier and K-nearest Neighbors classifier, are used to classify the emotional utterances. The features used by the classifiers are utterance-level statistics of the fundamental frequency and energy of the speech signal. To improve classification performance, two specific feature selection methods: Promising First Selection and Forward feature Selection, are used. Principle Component Analysis (PCA) is used to reduce the dimensionality of the features while maximizing classification accuracy.

Nwe, Wei, and De Silva (2001) introduced a Discrete Hidden Markov Model (HMM) based recognizer using Mel frequency short time speech power coefficients. Six basic human emotions, anger, dislike, fear, happiness, sadness, and surprise are investigated. A universal codebook is constructed based on emotions under observation for each experiment. The database consists of 90 emotional utterances each from two speakers. The system gives an average accuracy of 72.22 percent and 60 percent respectively for the two speakers.

Kwon, Chan, Hao, and Lee (2003) used a group of prosodic and phonetic features as the input to a forward selection and backward elimination based method for feature selection. Different classification algorithms including Support Vector Machine (SVM), Discriminant Analysis (DA), and Hidden Markov Model are compared. However, this system only achieves 42.3% for 5-class emotion recognition.

Ververidis, Kotropoulos, and Pitas (2004) extracted 87 speech features from a corpus of 500 emotional utterance collected from 4 subjects. Sequential forward selection is used to discover significant features with cross-validation as the criterion. Principal component analysis is then applied to the selected features to further reduce the dimensionality. Two classifiers are used to classify the utterances into five classes. This system only achieves an overall accuracy of 51.6%. The authors also provide clues that the system can be improved by reducing classification to a two-class problem, due to the fact that the features which can separate two classes could be different from those which separate five classes.

You, Chen, Bu, Liu and Tao (2006) presented a support vector machine based method for emotion recognition from both clean and noisy speech inputs. A set of prosodic and formant frequency features were first extracted. The resulting feature vector is then embedded into a low dimensional manifold by using an enhanced Lipschitz embedding approach. The proposed method was compared with principal component analysis, linear discriminant analysis, as well as sequential forward selection for dimension reduction. Experimentation was performed on a data set that contains speech samples from 2 males and 2 females. The proposed method obtained a gender-dependent recognition rate of around 75% from noisy speech signals.

Kostoulas and Fakotakis (2006) presented a speaker-dependent emotion recognition architecture. The extracted features include the pitch, the first thirteen Mel frequency cepstral coefficients, the first four formants, energy, and harmonicity. The classification is based on a decision tree generating algorithm, C4.5. The proposed model was tested on a five-emotion scenario, and a mean accuracy of 80.46% was achieved for 8 speakers.

Sedaaghi, Kotropoulos, and Ververidis (2007) employed adaptive genetic algorithms in combination with sequential floating feature selection method for searching discriminant features from a set of extracted speech statistics including formats, pitch, energy, as well as spectral features. The recognition is based on Bayes classifier. The proposed method was tested on an emotional speech dataset that contains 1160 utterances from 2 male and 2 female subjects. Their system obtains an overall recognition rate of 48.91% on a five-class problem.

In this chapter, we present an approach to language-independent machine recognition of human emotion in speech. The system uses voice characteristics in the speech signal to determine the emotional state of the speaker. A corpus of emotional speech collection experiments have been successfully conducted to provide the necessary emotional speech data for developing and testing the feasibility of the system. In the first step, the potential prosodic features from the signal are identified and extracted for the computational mapping between emotions and speech patterns. The discriminatory power of these features is then analyzed using a systematic approach, which involves the application of sequential forward selection (Kittler, 1978) with a general regression neural network (Specht, 1991) in conjunction with a consistency-based selection method. These features are then used for training and testing a modular neural network. Standard neural network and K-nearest Neighbors classifier are also investigated for the purpose of comparative studies. The performance of the proposed system is evaluated for various subjects, speaking different languages. The results demonstrate that the system gives quite satisfactory emotion detection performance and works better than those techniques reported in the literature, which used only a single language. In addition to the increase in performance, our system also demonstrates a significant increase in versatility through its propensity for language independence.

The remainder of this chapter is organized as follows. In Section 2, we describe the acquisition of emotional speech database. Section 3 presents the emotion recognition system. Feature selection and classification approaches are described in Sections 4 and 5 respectively. In Section 6, experimental results are presented. Comparison of results is discussed in Section 7. Finally, conclusions are given in Section 8.

EMOTIONAL SPEECH ACQUISITION

In order to build an effective **language independent** emotion recognition system and test its feasibility, a speech corpus containing utterances that are truly representative of an emotion is needed. Since there is no such database available, we set up an emotional speech data collecting system to record a corpus containing emotional speech.

The performance of an emotion recognition system is highly dependent on the quality of emotional speech database on which it is trained. In working with emotions in speech, special care must be taken to ensure that the particular emotion being vocalized is correct. We set up a data collecting system to record emotional speech with adequately high accuracy. A digital video camera was used to record the utterances in a quiet environment. The background and machine noise are considered at the preprocessing stage. Our experimental subjects were provided with a list of emotional sentences and were directed to express their emotions as naturally as possible by recalling the emotional happening, which they had experienced in their lives. Examples of these sentences are as follows: I am so happy (Happy); I lost all my money (Sadness); Don't you ever say that again (Anger); Please don't kill me (Fear); What, am I the winner (Surprise)? I hate the smell of this perfume (Disgust). The list of emotional sentences was provided for reference only. While some subjects expressed their emotions by using the same sentence structure for each emotion class, others opted to use a combination of different sentences. Since our aim is to develop a language-independent system, we did not focus on the significance of specific verbal contents. Every language has a different set of rules that govern the construction and interpretation of words, phrases, and sentences. Furthermore, two sentences could have the same lexical meaning but different emotional information.

The data are recorded for six classes: happiness, sadness, anger, fear, surprise, and disgust. Since the objective is to develop a language-independent system, subjects from different language backgrounds are selected in this study. The seven subjects and four languages used in this study are as follows: two native speakers of English, two native speakers of Chinese (Mandarin), two native speakers of Urdu, and one native speaker of Indonesian. The speech samples were recorded at a sampling rate of 22050 Hz, using a single channel 16-bit digitization. To ensure the emotions are properly expressed in the speech samples, the recorded samples were evaluated using experimental human subjects that do not understand the corresponding language. This is consistent with our purpose of developing an emotion recognition system that is independent of language. A total of 580 samples were selected for training and testing.

Figure 1. Structure of the emotion recognition system

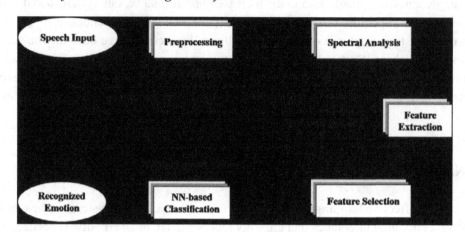

OVERVIEW OF THE RECOGNITION SYSTEM

The functional components of the language-independent emotion recognition system for the identification of a human emotional state are depicted in Figure 1. It consists of seven modules, reflecting the recognition process: speech data input, preprocessing, spectral analysis, feature extraction in multidimensional prosodic space, feature subset selection, modular neural network for classification, and the recognized emotion output.

Pre-Processing

The preprocessing prepares the input speech for recognition by eliminating the leading and trailing edge. The volume is then normalized to improve detection by the spectrogram generator. Unvoiced sounds are cut if they appear dominant in the signal. A noise gate with a delay time of 150ms, and a threshold of 0.05 is used to remove the small noise signal caused by digitization of the acoustic wave. Threshold is the amplitude level at which the noise gate starts to open and let sound pass. A value of 0.05 is selected empirically through the observation of background static "hiss" in the quiet parts of sections.

Spectral Analysis and Feature Extraction

Previous work has explored several features for classifying speaker affect: phoneme and silence duration, short-time energy, long-term power spectrum of an utterance, pitch statistics, formant ratios and so on (Kuwabara & Sagisaka, 1995; Protopapas & Lieberman, 1997; Cummings & Clements, 1995). We choose prosodic features of speech for emotion analysis, as **prosody** is believed to be the primary indicator of a speaker's emotional state (Hirst, 1992; Collier, 1992). Acoustic factors that represent prosodic characteristics of the speech are the fundamental frequency, intensity, and segmental duration. The fundamental frequency (f0) contour plots the rate over time at which the vocal cords vibrate.

The **spectral analysis** of speech utterances is performed and the pitch extraction is carried out by cepstral analysis. Figure 2 shows spectrograms and associated waveforms of the six emotions, as produced by one of the subjects. On the spectrogram, time is represented along the horizontal axis, whereas frequency is plotted along the vertical axis. For a given spectrogram S, the strength of a given frequency component f at a given time t in the speech signal is represented by the darkness of the corresponding point $S(t,f)$. It can be observed that each emotion class exhibits different patterns.

A total of 17 prosodic features are extracted, which carry the relevant information about the emotional class of the utterance. These 17 possible candidates that we have chosen are listed in Table 1.

Speaking rate was approximated by Dellaert ct al. (1996):

$$R_{spk} = \frac{1}{mean\_segment\_length}$$
$$= \frac{N}{\sum_{i}^{N} T_i}$$

(1)

where T_i is the length of voiced segment i and N is the number of voiced segments.

Pauses are of no use in calculating the other parameters, so they are discarded. Pitch (amplitude) range is determined by scanning the curve, finding the maximum and minimum pitch (amplitude), calculating the difference, and then normalizing to remove individual characteristics from the result. Mean values

Figure 2. Spectrograms of the six emotion

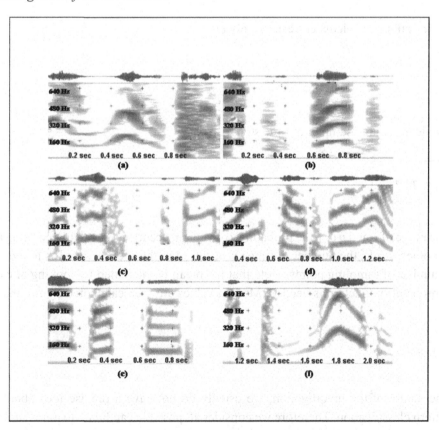

Table 1. List of 17 feature vectors

Feature	Description
1.	Pitch range (normalized)
2.	Pitch mean (normalized)
3.	Pitch standard deviation (normalized)
4.	Pitch median (normalized)
5.	Rising pitch slope maximum
6.	Rising pitch slope mean
7.	Falling pitch slope maximum
8.	Falling pitch slope mean
9.	Overall pitch slope mean
10.	Overall pitch slope standard deviation
11.	Overall pitch slope median
12.	Amplitude range (normalized)
13.	Amplitude mean (normalized)
14.	Amplitude standard deviation (normalized)
15.	Amplitude median (normalized)
16.	Mean pause length
17.	Speaking rate

and standard deviation are calculated respectively by:

$$\bar{x} = \frac{1}{N} \sum_{i}^{N} x_i \tag{2}$$

where N is the length of the sample (in time steps), and:

$$\sigma = \sqrt{\sum_{j=0}^{M} (x_j - \bar{x})^2 \, p(x_j)} \tag{3}$$

where M is the range of x_j and $p(x_j)$, the probability of value x_j occurring, is calculated using a normalized histogram. In other words, the number of times x_j occurred in the speech signal is found, then divided by the total number of sampling points. Note that the mean is calculated by looking at each sampling point, so no probability function is needed. Median values are then calculated by finding the value of x_i such that:

$$\sum_{i} p(x < x_i) \approx 0.5 \tag{4}$$

Due to the nature of the investigation, we usually do not have a precise idea about the features needed in pattern classification. Therefore we consider all possible candidate features in feature extraction. Some of the features may be redundant or irrelevant, and cause negative effects in learning and classification. Hence, we introduce a systematic feature selection approach to choose features that are relevant to language-independent emotion recognition application to achieve maximum performance with the minimum measurement effort.

FEATURE SELECTION

The performance of a pattern recognition system critically depends on how well the features chosen as the inputs separate patterns belonging to different classes in the feature space. The importance of selecting the relevant subset from the original feature set is closely related to the "curse of dimensionality" problem in function approximation, where sample data points become increasingly sparse when the dimensionality of the function domain increases, such that the finite set of samples may not be adequate for characterizing the original mapping (Haykin, 1999). In addition, the computational requirement is usually greater for implementing a high-dimensional mapping. To alleviate these problems, we reduce the dimensionality of the input domain by choosing a relevant subset of features from the original set.

The ultimate goal of **feature selection** is to choose a number of features from the extracted feature set that yields minimum classification error. There exist several popular feature selection algorithms, which can be roughly grouped into linear methods and non-linear methods. Linear methods normally are mathematically tractable and efficient; for example, principal component analysis is one of the best choices in transform-domain feature selection in the linear or minimum mean squared error sense. However, the nonlinearity inherent in emotional speech prompts us to consider methods that select features in a nonlinear fashion in order to achieve improved performance. The branch-and-bound feature selection algorithm can be used to find the optimal subset of feature, but it requires the feature selection criterion function to be monotone, which means the value of the criterion function can never be decreased by adding new features to a feature subset. This surely is not the case when the sample size is relatively small. The wrapper method (Kohavi & John, 1997) is another choice of selecting the feature subset. However, it is very slow and computationally expensive because the whole dataset needs to be analyzed repeatedly to evolve a feature set. In this section, we propose the adoption of an efficient nonlinear one-pass selection procedure, the **sequential forward selection** (SFS) approach (Kittler, 1978) that incrementally constructs a sequence of feature subsets by successively adding relevant features to those previously selected. Due to the need for evaluating the relevancy of the subsets, which normally requires iterative identification of multiple mappings between the corresponding reduced feature spaces, we adopt **the general regression neural network** (GRNN) (Specht, 1991) for this purpose. Unlike the popular feed-forward neural network models which require iterative learning, the parameters of the GRNN model can be directly determined in a single pass of training, which allows rapid evaluation of the individual feature subsets in terms of their relevance. Furthermore, because GRNN is a special example of Radial Basis Function Network (RBFN), this makes it more consistent with the module neural network which is used for classification than adopting any other classifiers to evaluate the feature relevance. In this section, we first analyze the discrimination power of the 17 features extracted from the emotional speech using the SFS method with GRNN. We then discuss some limitations of GRNN as the number of selected features grows, and adopt a **consistency-based selection** (Wu, Joyce, Wong, Guan, & Kung et al., 2000) as a complementary approach.

Sequential Forward Selection Method

The sequential forward selection procedure allows the construction of a suitable feature set starting from a single feature. In mathematical terms, the feature selection problem can be expressed in the following way. Let $\gamma = \{y_j, j = 1, 2, \ldots, N\}$ be a set of N possible features providing adequate representation of any pattern Z, belonging to one of m classes to be classified. Let $X_n \subset \gamma$ be a subset of n features ($n \leq N$) which contain more discriminatory power about Z than any other subset of features x_n of n features in γ. Let J be a measurement of the classification error by using the feature set for classification. Then the feature set X_n must satisfy

$$J(X_n) = \min (J(x_n)) \tag{5}$$

For a pattern recognition problem, the classification error measurement is usually the mean square classification error, which is defined as

$$E = \frac{1}{q} \frac{1}{q} \sum_{i=1}^{q} \sum_{i=1}^{q} (d_i - a_i)^2 \tag{6}$$

where i is the ith pattern to be classified, a_i is the actual output of the classifier, d_i is the desired output, and q is the total number of training samples.

The intuitive solution to determine the optimal subset of features is by exhaustive testing of all the possible combinations, which is equal to $\sum_{n=1}^{N} \binom{N}{n}$. However, even for moderate N and n, this is a large number and the approach is practically infeasible. Therefore, we adopt the sequential forward selection (SFS) method for incrementally constructing the relevant subset starting from a single feature. For this approach, a subset can be constructed rapidly without requiring a large number of possible subsets.

The SFS is a bottom–up search procedure where one feature at a time is added to the current feature set. At each stage, the feature to be included in the feature set is selected among the remaining available features from γ, which have not been added to the feature set. So the new enlarged feature set yields a minimum classification error compared to adding any other single feature.

Mathematically, suppose k features have been selected from a feature set X_k, then y_j features are selected from the remaining $N - k$ features to add to X_k so that

$$J(X_k \cup y_j) \leq J(X_k \cup y_i), \text{ for } i = 1, 2, \ldots N - k \; i \neq j \tag{7}$$

Then the enlarged feature set X_{k+1} is given as $X_{k+1} = X_k \cup y_j$. The procedure is initialized by setting $X_0 = \varnothing$.

If we want to find the most discriminatory feature set, the algorithm will stop at a point when adding more features to the current feature set increases the classification error. For finding the order of the discriminatory power of all N features, the algorithm will continue until all N features are added to the feature set. The order in which a feature is added is the rank of feature's discriminatory power.

General Regression Neural Network

The GRNN is then used to realize the feature selection criteria in measuring classification error. The main advantage of the GRNN over the conventional multilayer feed-forward neural network is that, unlike the multilayer feed-forward neural network which requires a large number of iterations in training to converge to a desired solution, GRNN needs only a single pass of learning to achieve optimal performance in classification. The GRNN is a memory-based neural network based on the estimation of a probability density function. Originally known as Nadaraya–Watson regression in statistics literature, it was re-discovered by Donald Specht (Specht, 1991).

Assume that $f(x,y)$ represents the known joint continuous probability density function of a vector random variable, x, and a scalar random variable, y. Let X be a particular measured value of the random variable x. The conditional mean of y given X can be represented as

$$E[y \mid X] = \frac{\int\limits_{-\infty}^{\infty} yf(X,y)dy}{\int\limits_{-\infty}^{\infty} f(X,y)dy}$$

(8)

where the density $f(x,y)$ is usually unknown, and in GRNN, this probability density function is usually estimated from samples of observations of x and y using nonparametric estimators. The estimator used in this study is the class of consistent estimators proposed by Parzen (Parzen, 1962). This probability estimator $\hat{f}(X,Y)$ is based upon sample values X_i, Y_i of the random variables x and y, where n is the number of sample observations and p is the dimension of the vector variable x:

$$\hat{f}(X,Y) = \frac{1}{(2\pi)^{(p+1)/2}\sigma^{(p+1)}} \times \frac{1}{n}\sum_{i=1}^{n} \exp[-\frac{(X-X_i)^T(X-X_i)}{2\sigma^2}] \times \exp[-\frac{(Y-Y_i)^2}{2\sigma^2}]$$

(9)

where n denotes the number of samples and p denotes the dimension of the vector variable x. A physical interpretation of the probability estimator $\hat{f}(X,Y)$ is that it assigns sample probability of width σ for each sample X_i, and Y_i, and the probability estimate is the sum of those sample probabilities. Substituting the joint probability estimate $\hat{f}(X,Y)$ into the conditional mean yields:

$$\hat{Y}(X) = \frac{\sum_{i=1}^{n} Y_i \exp(-\frac{D_i^2}{2\sigma^2})}{\sum_{i=1}^{n} \exp(-\frac{D_i^2}{2\sigma^2})}$$

(10)

where D_i^2 is defined as:

$$D_i^2 = (X - X_i)^T (X - X_i) \qquad\qquad (11)$$

The only known parameter in the above equation is the width of the estimating kernel, which can be selected by using a cross validation method called the leave-one-out method. The leave-one-out method works as follows. For a particular value of σ with a training data set of n samples, the leave-one-out method moves one sample at a time and constructs the GRNN using the remaining (n-1) samples. Then the GRNN is used to classify the removed sample. This is repeated n times, and each classification result is stored. Then the mean square classification error of this σ is calculated. The σ which minimizes the mean squared classification error is chosen for later studies.

The topology of a GRNN is shown in Figure 3. It consists of four layers: the input layer, the hidden layer, the summation layer, and the output layer. The function of the input layer is to pass the input vector variables X to all the units in the hidden layer. The hidden layer consists of all the training samples $X_1, ..., X_n$. When an unknown pattern X is presented, the squared distance D_i^2 between the unknown pattern and the training sample is calculated and passed through the kernel function. The summation layer has two units A and B, the unit A computes the summation of $\exp[-D_i^2 / (2\sigma^2)]$ multiplied by the Y_i associated with X_i. The B unit computes the summation of $\exp[-D_i^2 / (2\sigma^2)]$. The output unit divides A by B to provide the prediction result.

We apply the SFS technique to select feature subsets from the original set of 17 prosodic vectors, and the GRNN to evaluate the relevance of the feature subset. The order of the discriminatory power of the 17 features is shown in Table 2. The mean square error versus the feature index γ, is plotted in Figure 4. The abscissa in Figure 4 corresponds to feature order number. For example, for the curve generated by using the SFS method, six features included refer to the top six discriminatory features in Table 2, which are feature numbers 1, 13, 17, 4, 8, and 9. From Figure 4, the most discriminatory feature set, which gives the minimum mean square error, occurs at the point where the top 11 features are included.

Figure 3. Architecture of general regression neural network

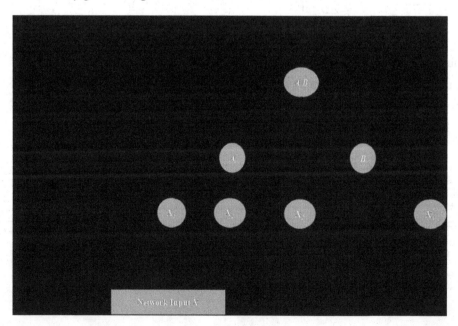

These 11 features correspond to the index subset {1, 3, 4, 6, 7, 8, 9, 13, 15, 16, 17}. In Figure 4, it is observed that the GRNN approximation error curve is almost flat for $\gamma \geq 9$. A possible interpretation of this outcome is that due to the approximation nature of the GRNN modeling process which does not incorporate any explicit trainable parameters, it will be increasingly difficult for the network to characterize the underlying mapping beyond a certain number of features due to the limited number of training samples and their increasing sparseness in high-dimensional spaces. Although the sequence of indices in Figure 4 is supposed to indicate the importance of the individual features but this may not be the case for those features around and beyond the minimum point. In other words, the order of features beyond the minimum point may not necessarily reflect their actual importance due to the increasing difficulties of characterizing mapping in high dimensional space using a finite training data set for the simple GRNN model. We therefore need to consider more carefully, the relevance of those features around and beyond the minimum. Hence, we use an alternative approach in the next section to review the effectiveness of features from the point where the error curve begins to flatten.

Consistency Based Feature Selection

In this section, we describe a consistency-based approach as a complementary selection mechanism to evaluate the relevance of features around and beyond the minimum error point. Consistency measure is originally used to formulate the class separability and to select features that are most effective for preserving class separability (Fukunaga, 1990).

The consistency measure c of each feature is computed by Bocheck and Chang (1998):

Table 2. The order of the discriminatory power of the 17 features obtained by using SFS/GRNN

Order	Feature Number, Feature Name
1.	1, Pitch range (normalized)
2.	13, Amplitude mean (normalized)
3.	17, Speaking rate
4.	4, Pitch median (normalized)
5.	8, Falling pitch slope mean
6.	9, Overall pitch slope mean
7.	3, Pitch standard deviation (normalized)
8.	16, Mean pause length
9.	6, Rising pitch slope mean
10.	7, Falling pitch slope maximum
11.	15, Amplitude median (normalized)
12.	14, Amplitude standard deviation (normalized)
13.	12, Amplitude range (normalized)
14.	5, Rising pitch slope maximum
15.	2, Pitch mean (normalized)
16.	11, Overall pitch slope median
17.	10, Overall pitch slope standard deviation

Figure 4. Error plot for SFS/GRNN

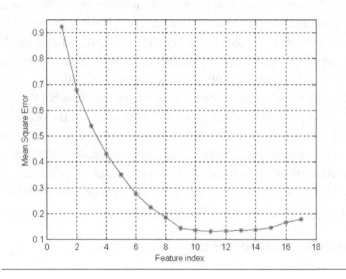

$$C = \frac{\text{mean inter-class distance}}{\text{mean intra-class distance}} \qquad (12)$$

where the distances are in the space of the features under consideration. A given feature is said to have a large discrimination power if its intra-class distance is small and inter-class distance is large. Thus, a greater value of the consistency implies a better feature.

We compute the consistency measure for the features ($\gamma 9 - \gamma 17$) according to Equation (12). The consistency measure versus the feature index is plotted in Figure 5. We find that feature 2 has the highest consistency measure. The consistency ranking of the next top three features is the same as achieved by SFS/GRNN approach. As a result, we choose four highly consistent features, namely {2, 6, 7, 15}.

Using the combined SFS/GRNN and consistency based approach, we get a total of 12 features, which are used as an input to the modular neural network, described in the next section. We will see later that the features selected by the combined approach have noteworthy influence on the emotion classification results.

RECOGNIZING EMOTIONS

To classify the extracted features into different human emotions, we propose a modular neural network architecture. It should be noted that although we use a GRNN for feature selection, but GRNN has the disadvantage of high computational complexity (Specht, 1991), and is, therefore not suitable for evaluating new samples. After the features are selected, no further adaptation is needed. Thus we apply a modular neural network based on back-propagation for classification which requires less computation. Furthermore, standard neural networks and a K-nearest Neighbors classifier are also investigated for the purpose of comparative studies.

Figure 5. Sorted consistency measures for features (γ 9− γ 17)

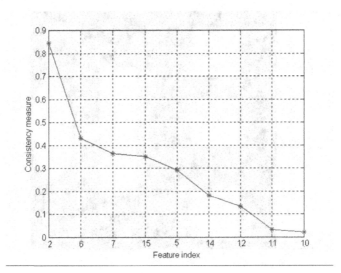

Neural Network Based Classification

In this section, we present **a modular neural network** (MNN) architecture, which effectively maps each set of input features to one of the six emotional categories. Artificial neural networks (ANN) have seen an explosion of interest over the last few years, and are being successfully applied across an extraordinary range of problem domains. Unlike the classical statistical classification methods such as the Bayes classifier, no knowledge of the underlying probability distribution is needed by a neural network. It can "learn" the free parameters (weights and biases) through training by using examples. This makes it suitable to deal with real problems, which are nonlinear, nonstationary and non-Gaussian.

While ANN have achieved success in many small-scale problems (mimicking the function of a piece of tissue), the generalization to practical, large-scale problems has not been impressively successful (mimicking the human thinking machine). Many networks fail to generalize because they have too many degrees of freedom. A large number of weights often allow a network to implement a look-up table that correctly calculates the response to the patterns in the training set, but does not implement the desired mapping function. With the help of modularity, we can decompose a large neural network into a network of smaller networks given a set of dependencies (or conditional independencies) amongst the variables (attributes) in the space. The MNN implementation is based on the principle of "divide and conquer," where a complex computational task is solved by dividing it into a number of computationally simple subtasks, and then combining their individual solutions. Modular architecture offers several advantages over a single neural network in terms of learning speed, representation capability, and the ability to deal with hardware constraints (Jocob & Jordon, 1991).

In this study, the motivation for adopting modular structure is based on the consideration that the complexity of recognizing emotions varies depending on the specific emotion. Thus, it would be appropriate to adopt a specific neural network for each emotion and tune each network depending on the characteristics of each emotion to be recognized. This basic consideration was confirmed by carrying out preliminary recognition experiments.

Figure 6. Modular neural network architecture

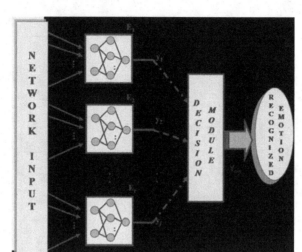

The proposed architecture is composed of hierarchical structure consisting of sub-networks, where each sub-network specializes in a particular emotion class. In the recognition stage, an arbitration process is applied to the outputs of the sub-networks to produce the final decision. The architecture of emotion detection network is shown in Figure 6. This architecture fuses the attributes of emotions acquired by experts to arrive at an overall decision which is superior to that attainable by any one of them acting alone. Consequently, the expert modules of the network tend to become specialized by learning different regions of input space. When the whole network is ready to operate, a decision-making strategy takes part in order to integrate different local decisions into a global one.

The network incorporates a set of experts representing the six emotion categories: happiness, sadness, anger, fear, surprise, and disgust. The outputs of all expert modules are connected to the decision module. Each expert E_r, $r = 1, \dots k$, is trained in parallel, independent of each other. The back-propagation algorithm is used to perform the training. Each expert E_r consists of 3-layered feed-forward neural networks with a 12 element input vector, 10 units in the hidden hyperbolic tangent sigmoid layer and one unit in the output linear layer.

The hyperbolic tangent sigmoid transfer function is defined as

where $\sigma(n)$ is the output of a neuron in terms of the induced local field n.

In the recognition phase, the network is required to identify the emotion class of the input patterns that were not part of the training data, thereby testing the generalization capability of the network.

We construct a mapping $f: D_F \subset \mathbf{R}^P \to \mathbf{R}^S$, where $\mathbf{x} = \{x^{(1)}, \dots, x^{(P)}\} \in D_F$ is the P-th dimension input vector, each corresponding to one of the J classes $\{\Omega_i, i, \dots, J\}$.

The mapping f can be decomposed into the concatenation of modular functional mapping M, and decision mapping N given by,

$$f = M \cup N, \text{ where } M: \mathbf{R}^P \to \mathbf{R}^O \text{ and } N: \mathbf{R}^O \to \mathbf{R}^S \tag{13}$$

Let $Y = \{y_j, j = 1, 2, \dots N\}$ be the output of the rth expert in response to the input vector $x^{(p)}$. The decision module classifies the input $x^{(p)}$ as a class Ω_r, if the jth element of E_r has the highest magnitude, that is,

$$Y_{net} = \arg\max_j y_j \tag{14}$$

K-Nearest Neighbors Classifier

K-nearest Neighbors is a non-parametric method for classification proposed by T. M. Cover and P. E. Hart (1967). It assigns a class label to the unknown classification by examining its k nearest neighbors of known classification. Let $\mathbf{x} = \{\mathbf{x}_j, j=1,2, \dots n\}$ denotes the known n feature vectors, p denotes the number of different classes, $l = \{l_j, j=1,2,\dots n \mid l_j \in (1,2,\dots p)\}$ be the correspondent class labels, the reference training samples can be written as:

$$S_n = \{(\mathbf{x}_1, l_1),(\mathbf{x}_2, l_2),\dots (\mathbf{x}_j, l_j),\dots(\mathbf{x}_n, l_n)\} \tag{15}$$

For a new input vector $\mathbf{y}$, the k-nearest Neighbors algorithm is to identify the subset of k feature vectors from S_n that lies closest to $\mathbf{y}$ with respect to the pattern similarity function $D(\mathbf{y}, \mathbf{x})$. If we use F_q to denote the frequency of each class label in the k nearest neighbors subset, the input vector can be classified by the following rule:

$$l_{out} = \arg\max\{F_q, q=1, 2,\dots p \} \tag{16}$$

RECOGNITION RESULTS

The experiments we performed are based on speech samples from seven subjects, speaking four different languages. A total of 580 speech utterances, each delivered with one of six emotions were used for training and testing. The six different emotion labels used are happiness, sadness, anger, fear, surprise, and disgust. From these samples, 435 utterances were selected for training the networks and the rest were used for testing.

We investigated several approaches to recognize emotions in speech. These methods were tested on English, Chinese, Urdu, and Indonesian speaking subjects. In our first experiment, a standard neural network was investigated. We employed the supervised classification for the 17 input nodes, corresponding to all the 17 extracted prosodic parameters. Six output nodes, associated with each emotion and a single hidden layer with 10 nodes were used. A learning process was performed by the back-propagation algorithm. This approach yields an average emotion recognition accuracy of 77.19 percent. The recognition rate is 76 percent for happiness, 76 percent for sadness, 79.17 percent for anger, 77.27 percent for fear, 80.77 percent for surprise and 73.91 percent for disgust.

In the second experiment, we examined the proposed modular neural network architecture. In this network, each expert Er consisted of 3-layered feed-forward neural networks with a 17 element input vector. Each expert was trained in parallel, independent of each other. It was noted that the modular network was able to learn faster than the standard NN. Furthermore, the classification performance was improved with the added benefit of computational simplicity. This technique gains an overall classification accuracy of 81.34 percent. With this approach, the system achieves a recognition rate of 84 percent for happiness, 84 percent for sadness, 79.17 percent for anger, 81.82 percent for fear, 80.77 percent for surprise and 78.26 percent for disgust. These results lead to the evidence that the use of modular neural networks implies a reasonable learning time and generalizing improvement compared to a single NN.

In our next experiment, we tested a MNN utilizing the 11 features selected by SFS/GRNN. This approach achieves an average recognition of 82.71 percent with the following distribution for emotional categories: 88 percent for happiness, 84 percent for sadness, 75 percent for anger, 86.36 percent for fear, 84.62 percent for surprise and 78.26 percent for disgust. From the experimental results, we can observe that the SFS/GRNN selection strategy is capable of identifying the most important features. As explained previously, there are increasing difficulties of characterizing mapping in high dimensional space using a finite training set for the simple GRNN model, and we have incorporated consistency-based selection to complement the SFS/GRNN process. To demonstrate the improvement, we used the 12 features selected by the combined approach and trained the MNN as described in Section 5. This technique yields the best overall classification accuracy of 83.31 percent. This verifies that incorporating the alternative selection approach can help enhance the recognition performance. The system achieves a recognition rate of 88 percent for happiness, 88 percent for sadness, 79.17 percent for anger, 81.82 percent for fear, 84.62 percent for surprise and 78.26 percent for disgust.

To further demonstrate the efficiency of the proposed system, we examine standard neural network and K-nearest Neighbors classifier on the 12 selected features. The architecture of the standard neural network is the same as the one used on 17 features except that the input nodes are reduced to 12. It gives an overall correct recognition rate of 80.59 percent with 84 percent for happiness, 80 percent for sadness, 79.17 percent for anger, 81.82 percent for fear, 84.62 percent for surprise and 73.91 percent for disgust. In the last experiment, we use K-nearest Neighbors to classify the 12 selected features. Leave-one-out cross validation was used to determine the appropriate k value. Experiments show that the classifier gives overall recognition rate of 79.34 percent while $k=4$. The recognition rate is 80 percent for happiness, 76 percent for sadness, 79.17 percent for anger, 81.82 percent for fear, 80.77 percent for surprise and 78.26 percent for disgust.

DISCUSSION

The performance of the recognition methods discussed in the previous section is depicted in Figure 7, while the details of the recognition results of individual emotional states are shown in Table 3. The NN17 and MNN17 represent an input vector of 17 elements to a standard neural network and a modular neural network respectively, where MNN11 uses eleven features selected by SFS/GRNN, and MNN12 consists of twelve highly discriminative features chosen by combined SFS/GRNN and consistency-based measure selection methods. NN12 and KNN12 represent using twelve selected features on standard neural networks and K-nearest Neighbors classifier respectively. The results demonstrate that a modular neural network produces noticeable improvement in emotion recognition over a single neural network and K-nearest Neighbors classifier. Moreover, modularity implied the reduction of a correspondingly large number of adjustable parameters. The time for training a set of experts was much less than the time for a large standard neural network, while the amount of computation was much less than the K-nearest

Figure 7. Comparison of the emotion recognition results

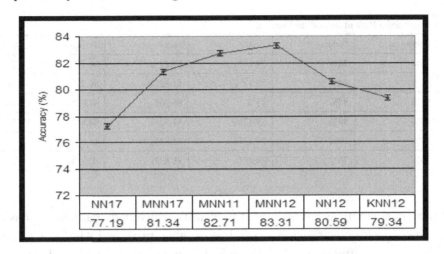

	NN17	MNN17	MNN11	MNN12	NN12	KNN12
	77.19	81.34	82.71	83.31	80.59	79.34

Neighbors classifier. This leads to efficient computation and better generalization. From the performance achieved by MNN11, we find that SFS/GRNN selection mechanism is capable of identifying most relevant features. Furthermore, the incorporation of an alternative approach for selection of important features exhibits enhanced emotion recognition results. In the experiments, the combination of SFS/GRNN with consistency based method produces best overall recognition rates, and highest recognition accuracy in five of the individual emotions.

It is interesting to note that "junking" all the extracted features into the decision making does not give the best performance, as we compare Experiment 2 and Experiment 4. Since the neural network addresses the problem by "learning," that is, being trained by the training data, if the feature does not indicate clearly the differences between the two groups, it will not contribute positively.

Table 4 provides a comparison of our methods with some of the works reported in the literature. Although the experiments were carried out on different databases, it is quite clear that even with different languages as the input, our system still works better than those techniques reported in the literature, which used only a single language. Compared with KNN based approaches (Dellaert et al., 1996; Lee et al., 2001), our system deals with more emotional states, and produces comparable results by using KNN classifier (see Table 3). The classification accuracy is improved by 4 percent by using the proposed modular neural network. Although Nicholson et al. (2000) tries to classify more emotional states, there was no feature selection performed, and their system only produces 50 percent accuracy, which is far below our system. Kostoulas and Fakotakis (2006) produce one of the best recognition results, but their paper focused on speaker dependent recognition. The other existing works used similar emotion space, but different approaches for feature extraction, selection, or classification. The experimental results demonstrate the efficiency of the proposed methods. As such, further to the increase in performance, our system also demonstrates a significant increase in versatility through its propensity for language independence.

In our experiments, the system showed some confusion in classifying emotions due to the acoustic similarities that exist between certain expressions of emotions. The confusion matrix in Table 5 shows that the obvious confusion in recognition occurred between the following pairs: anger and fear, anger and surprise, fear and surprise. This confusion pattern can be resolved by adding another modality to

Table 3. Recognition results of individual emotions

	Recognition Rate of Individual Emotion					
	Happiness	Sadness	Anger	Fear	Surprise	Disgust
NN17	76%	76%	79.17%	77.27%	80.77%	73.91%
MNN17	84%	84%	79.17%	81.82%	80.77%	78.26%
MNN11	88%	84%	75%	86.36%	84.62%	78.26%
MNN12	**88%**	**88%**	**79.17%**	81.82%	**84.62%**	**78.26%**
NN12	84%	80%	79.17%	81.82%	84.62%	73.91%
KNN12	80%	76%	79.17%	81.82%	80.77%	78.26%

the system. Research on emotions has attempted to identify which body parts or regions can operate as meaningful transmitters on their own, independent of other areas, and whether clusters of similar messages are conveyed by different areas of the body. It appears that the body and gesture play lesser roles in communicating affect than do the voice and the face. Therefore facial expressions also play an important role in communicating emotions because they are not only the most visible but they also provide sensitive cues about human emotional state. Figure 8 shows the video clips of facial expressions for anger, surprise, and fear, which are recorded for our further study of emotion recognition from both

Table 4. Comparison with existing works

Reference	Feature Extraction	Feature Selection	Classifier	# of Emotions	Average Accuracy
Dellaert, Polzin, & Waibel. 1996	Prosodic	Majority Voting of specialist	KNN	4	79.5%
Nicholson Takabashi, & Nakatsu. 2000	Prosodic, Phonetic		NN	8	50%
Lee, Narayanan, & Pieraccini 2001	Prosodic	Promising First Selection,	KNN	2	77.9%
Nwe, Wei, & Silva. 2001	Phonetic		HMM	6	72.22%
Kwon, Chan, Hao, & Lee. 2003	Prosodic, Phonetic	Forward selection, Backward elimination	SVM, DA, HMM	5	42.3%
Ververidis, Kotropoulos, & Pitas. 2004	Prosodic	Forward selection, PCA	Bayes classifier	5	51.6%
You, Chen, Bu, Liu & Tao. 2006	Acoustic	Lipschitz embedding,	SVM	6	75%
Kostoulas & Fakotakis. 2006	Prosodic, phonetic		C4.5 classifier	5	80.46%
Sedasghi, Kotropoulos, & Ververidis. 2007	Prosodic, Formant	Genetic algorithm, Sequential floating selection	Bayes classifier	5	48.91%
Proposed method	Prosodic	SFS/GRNN with consistency analysis	MNN	6	83.31%

Table 5. Performance confusion matrix for MNN12

		Desired					
		Happiness	Sadness	Anger	Fear	Surprise	Disgust
D E T E C T	**Happiness**	**88**	0	4.2	0	0	4.35
	Sadness	0	**88**	0	4.55	0	8.7
	Anger	4	0	**79.17**	4.55	7.69	4.35
	Fear	0	8	8.33	**81.82**	7.69	4.35
	Surprise	8	0	8.33	9.1	**84.62**	0
	Disgust	0	4	0	0	0	**78.26**

the video and the speech. It can be observed that the emotions that are difficult to investigate precisely from vocal cues due to similarities have significant visual differences. Integrating a dominant cue from one modality with a cue in another can create the blends for more robust results.

CONCLUSION

In this chapter, an approach to language-independent machine recognition of human emotion in speech is presented. We have investigated the universal nature of emotion and its vocal expression. Although language and cultural background have some influence on the way in which people express their emotions, our proposed system has demonstrated that the emotional expression in speech can be identified beyond the language boundaries.

Experiments for collecting the emotional speech have been designed and implemented successfully, which make it possible to develop the language-independent emotion recognition system and to test its feasibility. We examined the nonverbal aspects of the speech waveform and discreetly identified and extracted 17 prosodic features for the computational mapping between emotions and speech patterns. The problem of determining the relevant input features for an emotion recognition system is then addressed. For this purpose, we adopt the SFS method to construct a sequence of feature subsets, and the GRNN to allow the efficient evaluation of the relevancy of these subsets without requiring iterative training. As the confidence in the SFS/GRNN approach diminishes around and beyond the minimum MSE point, we adopt the complementary consistency-based approach. The selected parameters are then employed as an

Figure 8. Video clips of facial expressions portrayed by one subject

input to the modular neural network, consisting of sub-networks, where each sub-network specializes in a particular emotion class.

The results of these experiments are promising. Our study shows that prosodic cues are very powerful signals of human vocal emotions. The results obtained by the proposed MNN architecture exhibit superior recognition performance. Experiments show that the SFS/GRNN selection mechanism is capable of identifying a highly relevant subset of features, and incorporating alternative consistency-based selection method helps to further enhance the recognition performance. The recognition results demonstrate that the system can successfully extract non-lexical information from the speech signals and is capable of classifying the signals based on the selected prosodic parameters.

The performance of the system is evaluated for various subjects, speaking different languages. The results show that the system gives quite satisfactory emotion detection performance, yet demonstrates a significant increase in versatility through its propensity for language independence.

The approaches that are proposed in this work in combination with visual emotion analysis (Wang & Guan, 2005) are being applied to an industrial collaborative project with Dr Robot Inc., a Toronto based company specialized in intelligent mobile robots, for detecting human intention and activities in security and surveillance applications. The deliverable of the project aims at developing vision guided intelligent mobile robots in order to provide an effective solution for the ever increasing needs of security/surveillance at airports, banks, subway stations, and other places of national and military importance, thus representing a vast potential for improving the performance of the current security systems.

ACKNOWLEDGMENT

The authors wish to thank Dr. Hau-San Wong and Dr. Kim Hui Yap for their enlightening comments and suggestions. Special thanks are due to the members of Sydney University Signal and Multimedia Processing laboratory for their help in acquiring the emotional speech database.

REFERENCES

Amir, N., & Ron, S. (1998). Towards an automatic classification of emotions in speech. In *Proceedings of 5th International Conference on Spoken Language Processing ICSLP 98, Sydney, Australia, November/December* (Vol. 3, p. 555).

Bocheck, P., & Chang, S. F. (1998). *Contend-based VBR traffic modeling and its application to dynamic network resource allocation* (Research Report 48c-98-20). Columbia University.

Calhoun, C., & Solomon, R. C. (1984). *What is an emotion? Classic readings in philosophical psychology.* New York: Oxford University Press.

Collier, R. (1992). A comment of the prediction of prosody. In G. Bailly, C. Benoit, & T.R. Sawallis (Eds.), *Talking machines: Theories, models, and designs*. Amsterdam: Elsevier Science Publishers.

Cornelius, R. R. (1996). *The science of emotion. Research and tradition in the psychology of emotion.* Upper Saddle River, NJ: Prentice Hall.

Cover T. M. & Hart P. E. (1967). Nearest neighbor pattern classification. *IEEE Transactions on Information Theory, January*(IT-13), 21-27.

Cowie, R., & Douglas-Cowie, E. (1996). Automatic statistical analysis of the signal and prosodic signs of emotion in speech. In *Proceedings of Fourth International Conference on Spoken Language Processing ICSLP 96, Philadelphia PA, USA, October* (pp.1989-1992).

Cummings, K., & Clements, M. (1995). Analysis of the glottal excitation of emotionally styled and stressed speech. *The Journal of the Acoustical Society of America, 98*(1), 88–98. doi:10.1121/1.413664

Darwin, C. (1965). *The expression of emotions in man and animals.* John Murray, 1872, reprinted by University of Chicago Press.

Dellaert, F., Polzin, T., & Waibel, A. (1996). Recognizing emotion in speech. In *Proceedings of Fourth International Conference on Spoken Language Processing ICSLP 96, Philadelphia PA, USA, October* (pp.1970-1973).

Ekman, P., & Sullivan, M. O. (1987). The role of context in interpreting facial expression: Comment on Russell and Fehr. *Journal of Experimental Psychology, 117*, 86–88.

Fukunaga, K. (1990). *Introduction to statistical pattern recognition* (2nd ed.). Academic press.

Haykin, S. (1999). Neural networks: A comprehensive foundation. NJ: Prentice Hall.

Hirst, D. (1992). Prediction of prosody: An overview. In G. Bailly, C. Benoit, & T.R. Sawallis (Eds.), *Talking machines: Theories, models, and designs.* Amsterdam: Elsevier Science Publishers.

Jacobs, R. A., & Jordon, M. I. (1991). A competitive modular connectionist architecture. *Advances in Neural Information Processing Systems, 3*, 767–773.

Kittler, J. (1978). *Feature selection algorithm, pattern recognition and signal processing* (pp. 41-60). C. H. Chen (Ed.), Alphen aan den Rijin, Germany: Sijthoff & Noordhoof0.

Kohavi, R., & John, G. H. (1997). Wrappers for feature subset selection. *Artificial Intelligence, 97*(1-2), 273–324. doi:10.1016/S0004-3702(97)00043-X

Kostoulas, T., & Fakotakis, N. (2006). A speaker dependent emotion recognition framework. *CSNDSP Fifth International Symposium, Patras, July* (pp. 305-309).

Kuwabara, H., & Sagisaka, Y. (1995). Acoustic characteristics of speaker individuality: Control and conversion. *Speech Communication, 16*, 165–173. doi:10.1016/0167-6393(94)00053-D

Kwon, O., Chan, K., Hao, J., & Lee, T. (2003). Emotion recognition by speech signals. In *Proceedings of European Conference on Speech Communication and Technology, Geneva, Switzerland, September* (pp. 125-128).

Lee, C. M., Narayanan, S., & Pieraccini, R. (2001). Recognition of negative emotions from the speech signal. *Automatic Speech Recognition and Understanding, 2001. ASRU'01.*

Levenson, R. W., Ekman, P., & Friesen, W. V. (1990). Voluntary facial action generates emotion-specific autonomic nervous system activity. *Psychophysiology*, *27*, 363–384. doi:10.1111/j.1469-8986.1990. tb02330.x

Nicholson, J., Takabashi, K., & Nakatsu, R. (2000). Emotion recognition in speech using neural networks. *Neural Computing & Applications*, *9*(4), 290–296. doi:10.1007/s005210070006

Nwe, T. L., Wei, F. S., & De Silva, L. C. (2001). Speech based emotion classification. Electrical and Electronic Technology, 2001. TENCON. In *Proceedings of IEEE Region 10 International Conference on, August* (Vol. 1, pp. 19-22).

Parzen, E. (1962). On estimation of a probability density function and mode. *Annals of Mathematical Statistics*, *33*, 1065–1076. doi:10.1214/aoms/1177704472

Picard, R. W. (1997). *Affective computing*. Cambridge, MA: MIT Press.

Protopapas, A., & Lieberman, P. (1997). Fundamental frequency of phonation and perceived emotional stress. *The Journal of the Acoustical Society of America*, *101*(4), 2267–2277. doi:10.1121/1.418247

Sato, J., & Morishima, S. (1996). Emotion modeling in speech production using emotion space. In *Proceedings of IEEE International Workshop on Robot and Human Communication, Tsukaba, Japan, November* (pp.472-477).

Sedaaghi, M. H., Kotropoulos, C., & Ververidis, D. Using adaptive genetic algorithms to improve speech emotion recognition. *IEEE 9th Workshop on Multimedia Signal Processing* (pp. 461-464).

Smith, A. C., & Kleinman, S. (1989). Managing emotions in medical school: Students' contacts with the living and the dead. *Social Psychology Quarterly*, *52*, 56–59. doi:10.2307/2786904

Smith, C. A., & Lazarus, R. S. (1993). Appraisal components, core relational themes, and the emotions. *Cognition and Emotion*, 233–269. doi:10.1080/02699939308409189

Specht, D. F. (1991). A general regression neural network. *IEEE Transactions on Neural Networks*, *2*(6), 568–576. doi:10.1109/72.97934

Ververidis, D., Kotropoulos, C., & Pitas, I. Automatic emotional speech classification. In *Proceedings of IEEE International Conference on Acoustics, Speech, and Signal Processing, Montreal, Canada, May* (Vol. 1, pp. 593-596).

Wang, Y. (2003). Cognitive Informatics: A new transdisciplinary research field. *Brain and Mind: A Transdisciplinary Journal of Neuroscience and Neurophilosophy, 4*(2), 115-127.

Wang, Y., & Guan, L. (2005). Recognizing human emotion from audiovisual information. In *Proceedings of IEEE International Conference on Acoustics, Speech and Signal Processing* (Vol. II, pp. 1125-1128).

Wu, M., Joyce, R. A., Wong, H. S., Guan, L., & Kung, S. Y. (2000). Dynamic resource allocation via video content and short-term statistics. In . *Proceedings of IEEE International Conference on Image Processing, III*, 58–61.

You, M., Chen, C., Bu, J., Liu, J., & Tao, J. (2006). Emotion recognition from noisy speech. In *Proceedings of the IEEE International Conference on Multimedia and Expo, Toronto, Canada* (pp. 1653-1656).

Chapter 26
An Analysis of Internal Representations for Two Artificial Neural Networks that Classify Musical Chords

Vanessa Yaremchuk
McGill University, Canada

INTRODUCTION

Cognitive informatics is a field of research that is primarily concerned with the information processing of intelligent agents; it can be characterised in terms of an evolving notion of information (Wang, 2007). When it originated six decades ago, conventional accounts of information were concerned about using probability theory and statistics to measure the amount of information carried by an external signal. This, in turn, developed into the notion of modern informatics which studied information as "properties or attributes of the natural world that can be generally abstracted, quantitatively represented, and mentally processed" (Wang, 2007, p. iii). The current incarnation of cognitive informatics recognised that both information theory and modern informatics defined information in terms of factors that were external to brains, and has replaced this with an emphasis on exploring information as an internal property.

This emphasis on the internal processing of information raises fundamental questions about how such information can be represented. One approach to answering such questions — and for proposing new representational accounts — would be to train a brain-like system to perform an intelligent task, and then to analyse its internal structure to determine the types of representations that the system had developed to perform this intelligent behaviour. The logic behind this approach is that when artificial neural networks

DOI: 10.4018/978-1-60566-902-1.ch026

are trained to solve problems, there are few constraints placed upon the kinds of internal representations that they can develop. As a result, it is possible for a network to discover new forms of representation that were surprising to the researcher (Dawson & Boechler, 2007; Dawson & Zimmerman, 2003).

RELATED WORK

Cognitive informatics has been applied to a wide variety of domains, ranging from organisation of work in groups of individuals (Wang, 2007) to determining the capacity of human memory (Wang, Liu & Wang, 2003) to modelling neural function (Wang, Wang, Patel & Patel, 2006). The studies described in this chapter provide an example of this approach in a new domain, musical cognition. There is a growing interest in the cognitive science of musical cognition, ranging from neural accounts of musical processing (Jourdain, 1997; Peretz & Zatorre, 2003) through empirical accounts of the perceptual regularities of music (Deutsch, 1999; Krumhansl, 1990) to computational accounts of the formal properties of music (Assayag, Feichtinger, & Rodrigues, 2002; Lerdahl & Jackendoff, 1983). Because music is characterised by many formal and informal properties, there has been a rise in interest in using connectionist networks to study it (Griffith & Todd, 1999; Todd & Loy, 1991).

There are numerous types of connectionist networks, and multiple dimensions on which they can vary. A variety of both supervised and unsupervised approaches have been used in studying various aspects of musical cognition. In many instances it is impossible to provide a complete formal specification of a set of rules that define some property of music. For instance, not all of the rules of musical composition are known or definable (Loy, 1991). Unsupervised networks like self organising maps (SOMs) and adaptive resonance theory (ART) networks are well suited for studying musical tasks that cannot themselves be completely specified. A multitude of connectionist research uses unsupervised networks to attempt to capture informal, under-defined, or undefined properties of music, ranging from connectionist models for perception (J. J. Bharucha & Todd, 1989; Desain & Honing, 1991; Laden & Keefe, 1989; Large & Kolen, 1999; Sano & Jenkins, 1989; Scarborough et al., 1989; Taylor & Greenhough, 1999), models of the physical process of sound production (Casey, 1999; Sayegh, 1991), to composition (Mozer, 1991, 1999; Todd, 1991).

Leman (1991) used self organising maps (SOMs) to study the relationships between tones. SOMs were presented major triads, minor triads, and dominant seventh chords, using twelve input units which correspond to tones. In an initial study, chords were presented in the training data with equal frequency. A weak circle of fifths representation could be discerned in the arrangements of characteristic units on the map. The circle of fifths is a theoretical structure that contains all the keys, or all 12 of the notes used in the dodecaphonic set; each step clockwise along the circle is a perfect fifth or an interval of 7 semitones (see figure 2A). In a further study, statistical data regarding the presence of chords in western music was used to adjust the frequency with which input chords were presented, and the circle of fifths representation was significantly strengthened.

Tillmann et al. (2003) used a hierarchical self organising map (HSOM) with 12 inputs (one for each pitch class, or one for each of the dodecaphonic notes) each of which was connected to the SOM which was the second layer, which was connected to layer three — another SOM. Similar to the study by Leman, the goal was to demonstrate implicit learning of tonal regularities. This study explored two different variations on the format of the input. First a straight pitch class where inputs were activated if the corresponding note was present in the chord was tried. Subsequently, the weighted sum of subharmonics of relevant pitch classes, still using only the 12 input units already described was used. The presentation groupings of the training sets were also varied with the first training set made up of music chords that were presented separately, and the second set grouped according to key. Input style did not have a significant effect, while the training sets resulted in networks specialised at detecting chords and keys respectively.

There are several musical problems that have been studied using adaptive resonance theory (ART) networks, one of which is musical dictation (Gjerdingen, 1991). Musical dictation involves translating the pitches and durations heard during a musical event into formal musical notation. As it increases in complexity, musical dictation moves further away from being a task with strictly true or false outcome and a model with flexibility is desirable. This motivates the use of a connectionist network, training them with complex patterns from passages of Mozart. Each new note or tone in a musical score was treated as a discrete event, and represented to the network as a vector of values for the inputs which corresponded to attributes such as melodic inflection, melodic contour, melodic scale degrees, bass inflection, bass contour, etc. The resulting trained network encodes musical categorisations that resemble the harmonic-contrapuntal complexes known as voice-leading combinations. Voice-leading occurs when a harmonic relationship exists between two or more lines but the harmonies exist with one line (or voice) leading the other(s) in time rather than synchronously (as in a chord).

Griffith (1999) used ART networks for tonal classification, with an overall goal of determining the key of a piece of music. Input to the networks was made up of vectors representing the melodies of nursery rhymes. Once again, the circle of fifths appeared in the resulting organisation of the trained ART network, although it is worth noting that the weights were yoked together in a way that ensured the network would pick up similarities based on related intervals, such as tonic major chords. That is, chords were grouped into pools, and the chords in those pools were yoked together.

Unsupervised architectures are useful for uncovering similarity-based relations amongst input patterns. That is, input pattern regularities can be discovered by looking at levels of activation in the grid from the trained network. This reveals how the network has attuned to the structure of the data — as opposed to revealing a process by which the problem is solved. Supervised architectures, on the other hand, offer the latter as their internal structure can be interpreted to uncover a procedure or algorithm for the modelled cognitive task. Supervised learning has been used in a variety of areas including the study of spatial cognition (M.R.W. Dawson & Boechler, 2005), logical reasoning (M. R. W. Dawson & Zimmerman, 2003; Zimmerman, 1999), animal learning (V. Yaremchuk et al., 2005), medical diagnostics (M.R.W. Dawson et al., 1994b), language (Sejnowski & Rosenberg, 1988), optical character recognition (Le Cun et al., 1989), and driving (Jochem et al., 1993; Pomerleau, 1991). While supervised learning is quite popular in a wide range of cognitive science domains, it is less common in the study of music. Though unsupervised learning is more prevalent in this domain, supervised learning has been used in a variety of areas within music including physical models, perception, and composition.

Various architectures that use supervised learning have been used for modelling musical perception. Sano and Jenkins (1989) explored pitch perception by pre-processing nerve fibre data and feeding the result into a multilayer perceptron for classification. They performed several rounds of processing, tying a set of networks together. The first round of processing took as input data representing the excitation levels of 7000 nerve fibres corresponding to the approximately 8 octave range of human hearing. The network was trained to map this to 463 categories in that frequency range. This approximates the number of discriminations that humans can make in this range. These categories in turn were used as input for the next stage and were mapped to semitones based on the 12-tone scale of western music. The set of

96 semitones were then used as input for the next phase where they were reduced to the tone within an octave (one tone out of 12 possible tones), and the octave itself (one octave out of 8 possible octaves in the data range). The network then had perfect pitch, identifying both pitch and octave. The network assumed just one tone as input at a time initially, but was later extended to allow more than one tone as long as they were at least 1.5 semitones apart. It is worth noting that dividing up the processing into separate phases in this way, forces certain mid-point calculations. There may be some situations in which this is desired because such a calculation is felt to be essential, but it has the drawback of eliminating a potential for discovery of novel representations or algorithms.

Supervised learning has been used to create models of fingering and violin string position. Sayegh (1991) formulated fingering for string instruments as an optimisation problem in searching for the minimum path on a graph. A feed-forward network was used for estimating the connection weights of the graph, and weights on the best path were strengthened. Casey (1999) used inverse modelling to determine which physical parameters for sound generating models were mapped to by which representations of sound. More specifically, the physical parameters in question were violin string positions. A regular multilayer perceptron was used to model a single string, but for two strings a 2-layer multilayer perceptron was found to be inadequate. Casey used a composite method instead that equates to two 2-layer multilayer perceptron placed in series. While this may be easier to train, it does not actually possess any additional computational capabilities over the single network; technically, a single network should be able to solve this problem. Using two networks in place of a single network requires that the researcher decide how and where to split the task. Since the weights of the connections are initially random, the internal structure of the trained network is not known in advance. Splitting up the task into two networks means you have forced a certain midpoint calculation that may or may not have been a strictly necessary step.

There are several examples of networks for musical composition that are trained on examples, and then presented with input from outside the training set to exploit the generalisation properties of connectionist networks. Examples include melodic (Lewis, 1991), rhythmic (Dolson, 1991), and harmonic (Mozer, 1991) aspects of composition being treated in this way.

Lewis (1991) trained a multilayer perceptron network to critically rate melodies ranging from 0 (not music) to 1 (music), allowing values in between to indicate the subjective quality of music (e.g., 0.5 would be not very good music). After the network had successfully learned the training set, training was turned off and random starts were given to generate new melodies. These new melodies were refined and adjusted using back propagation until they met the criteria to qualify as music according to the network. This produced new compositions that were sufficiently similar to the high rated training examples to qualify as music, and possibly as good music. Clearly this approach required new compositions to be similar in style to the examples, but this limitation can be overcome to some extent by increasing the variety of musical styles in the training set.

Dolan (1991) used a temporally recurrent network for evaluating rhythm, using as few hidden units as possible to increase generalisability. Certain patterns of attacks and rests can be considered more aesthetically pleasing than others, and the networks were trained on patterns that have been classified according to the presence or absence of objectionable sequences. As a benefit to using connectionist networks, this process does not require an explicit knowledge of what makes a rhythm appealing; it only requires the ability to specify whether or not a rhythm is pleasing. New rhythms were generated by feeding the output values back in as input values until a rhythm of sufficient length was attained.

Mozer (1991) trained a recurrent network on simple scales, random walk sequences, and simple melodies drawn from J.S. Bach. The input was made up of the pitch height, 2-dimensional co-ordinates

Figure 1. Chromatic Circle

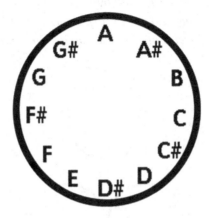

on the chromatic circle (figure 1) and 2-dimensional co-ordinated on the circle of fifths (figure 2a). After training, the network was given new fragments not seen in the training set, and generated patterns of its own. Mozer reported that the results were encouraging; for instance, when presented a note in a major scale, the network correctly determined the next note over 90 percent of the time.

Todd (1991) used a sequential network for modelling composition. It was a feed forward network with a decaying input function. One note at a time was input, producing a sequence of notes with a continuing effect via this manner. The network learned monophonic (only one note played at a time) melodies, and then recreated the same melodies, or similar ones depending on input settings.

Similarly, Bharucha and Todd (1989) used a decaying input function to investigate harmonic aspects of composition. They considered temporal representation in a multilayer perceptron by using a decaying input function to represent a time passing effect, much like in the study just mentioned. The inputs represented 6 different chord types corresponding to the 3 major and 3 minor chords in any given key, and ignored pitch by normalising all chords to a common tonic. The sequences in which the training data were presented were based on the probabilities of those particular transitions occurring in western music from the common practice era (circa 1725 – 1900), which is considered the period of the defining tradition of western music. Though the outputs corresponded to instance-based (veridical) expectancies, interpretation of the network revealed that it had learned culture-based (schematic) expectancies. That is, the network learned the probability information indirectly present in the sequencing of the training data, despite being explicitly trained only on the probabilities corresponding to specific instances as removed from the greater musical context.

It isn't truly accurate to refer to unsupervised and supervised learning as distinct approaches, as some architecture combine both. Taylor and Greenhough (1999) used an ARTMAP network (also called Predictive ART network) to model human pitch perception in which they pursued pitch extraction from complex sounds. The input to the ARTMAP network was pre-processed, using Fourier analysis, into 60 chromatic semitone bins corresponding to the range C3 (C an octave below middle C, 131 Hz) to B7 (the top B on a conventional piano keyboard, 3951 Hz). That is, in pre-processing, groups of frequencies within certain bandwidths were mapped to corresponding semitones. As it is not just a specific frequency but a small range of them that are labelled as the same semitone, they are thought of as bins that catch everything within a certain proximity of the characteristic frequency. The output was made

Figure 2. (A) The traditional circle of fifths used to demonstrate similarity relationships between different keys. (B) The four circles of major thirds used by Franklin (2004), and discovered in the networks of both studies presented here. See the text for an explanation. (C) The three circles of minor thirds used by Franklin (2004). (D) Two circles of major seconds. This representation was found in both of the trained networks.

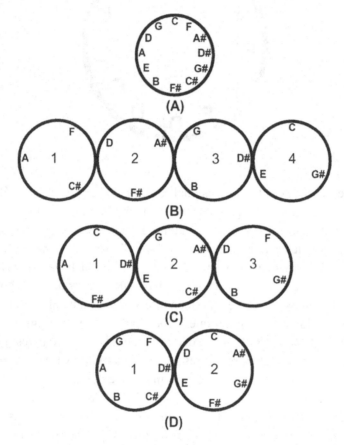

up of the pitch names of the C-major scale from C3 to C6. While these multi-step networks do offer the potential for greater speed of learning, every time a step is built directly into the architecture, it removes potential for surprises, as it is making an algorithmic design decision for the network. The simulation below illustrates in greater detail this potential for the discovery of previously unknown representations of formal musical structures. As such, it illustrates that artificial neural networks can be used as a medium to explore a synthetic approach to psychology and make important representational contributions to cognitive informatics and cognitive science (Dawson, 1998, 2004).

CHORD CLASSIFICATION BY NEURAL NETWORKS

In a pioneering study, artificial neural networks (ANNs) were trained to classify musical stimuli as being major chords, minor chords, or diminished chords (Laden & Keefe, 1989). Laden and Keefe's networks used 12 input units, where each unit represented a particular note or "piano key" in an octave range — called a pitch class representation. They created a training set consisting of 36 different chords: the major triad for each of the 12 different major key signatures, as well as the minor triad and a diminished seventh triad for each of the 12 different minor key signatures. They examined a number of different networks by manipulating the number of hidden units (three, six, eight, or nine), and by manipulating the pattern of network connectivity.

In general, Laden and Keefe (1989) found that the performance of their simple networks was disappointing. Their most successful simple network used three hidden units, and had direct connections between input and output units, but was still able to correctly classify only 72 percent of the presented chords. Other small networks had accuracy rates as low as 25 percent. Laden and Keefe improved network accuracy to a maximum level of 94 percent by using a more complex network that had 25 hidden units and which used output units to represent distances between musical notes (i.e., musical intervals) rather than chord types.

The study discussed here is an extension of Laden and Keefe's (1989) research. It examines two simple networks. The first network uses a pitch class representation like that used by Laden and Keefe. The second network uses a binary code variation on the representation that allows for distinct input encoding for different chord inversions (figure 3). This alternate input encoding makes an initial step towards exploring whether the internal representations that a network creates depend in any way upon the input encoding.

Instead of the traditional sigmoid-shaped activation function (the logistic equation) used by Laden and Keefe in the processing units of their networks, both networks in this study use Gaussian activation functions because previous research has demonstrated that networks that employ this activation function are adept at solving complex problems, and also lend themselves to detailed interpretation (Berkeley, Dawson, Medler, Schopflocher, & Hornsby, 1995; Dawson, 2004, 2005). The working hypothesis was that this change in network architecture would permit simple networks to classify chord types, and would also permit the internal structure of such networks to be interpreted in the search for new musical representations.

STUDY 1: CHORDS DEFINED WITH PITCH CLASS REPRESENTATION METHOD

Training Set

Networks were trained to identify four different types of musical chords: major, minor, dominant seventh, and diminished seventh. The training set was constructed as follows: First, a root note was selected (e.g., C). Second, the major chord based on this root note was created by activating the three input units that defined the component notes of this chord (e.g., C, E, and G). Third, the minor chord based on this root note was created by activating the three input units that defined its component notes (e.g., C, E ♭, and G). Fourth, the dominant seventh chord based on this root was defined by activating the four input units that represented its component notes (e.g., C, E, G, and B ♭). Fifth, the diminished seventh chord based on this root was defined by activating the four input units that represented its components (e.g., C, D#, F#, A). This process was repeated until four chords had been constructed for each of the 12 possible root notes in a dodecaphonic note system, resulting in a training set of 48 different chords.

Figure 3. The network used in the second simulation study. Each input unit corresponds to a note on a 24-note keyboard. Signals from these input units are passed along for processing by four different hidden units through sets of weighted connections. For simplicity's sake, only the connections involving two of the hidden units are depicted. Activations from the hidden units are then passed through a second layer of connections to produce activity in a set of four output units. After training, an input stimulus will only turn on one of the output units, which will classify the stimulus as being a particular type of chord.

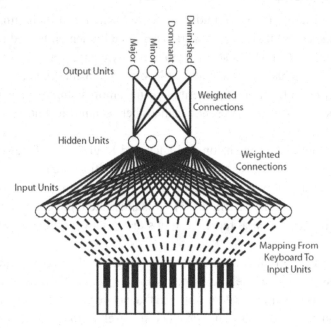

Network Architecture

The network had four output units, three hidden units, and 12 input units. Each of the output units represented one of the four types of musical chords, and each of the input units represented a particular musical note in a pitch class representation. Three hidden units were used because pilot simulations had indicated that this was the smallest number of hidden units that would permit a network to correctly classify the training stimuli. All of the output units and all of the hidden units were value units that used the Gaussian activation function described by Dawson and Schopflocher (1992): $G(net_i) = exp\ (-\pi(net_i - \mu_i)^2)$. In this equation, $G(net_i)$ is the activation being calculated for unit i, net_i is the net input for that unit, and μ_i is the Gaussian mean. When the net input to the equation is equal to the mean (i.e., equal to μ_i), the activity that is generated is equal to 1.0. As net input moves away from the mean in either direction, unit activity quickly drops off to near-zero levels.

Network Training

The network was trained to classify chords by turning the appropriate output unit "on," and the other three output units "off," for each stimulus in the training set. Training was conducted using a variation of the generalised delta rule for value units (Dawson, 2004, 2005; Dawson & Schopflocher, 1992). The software used to perform this training is available as freeware from http://www.bcp.psych.ualberta. ca/~mike/Software/Rumelhart/index.html.

Prior to training, all of the connection weights were randomly assigned values ranging from –0.10 to +0.10. The biases of processing units (i.e., the μs of the Gaussian activation functions) were all initially assigned a value of 0.00. The network was trained with a learning rate of 0.005 and zero momentum. During a single epoch of training each of the 48 chords was presented to the network in random order. Connection weights were updated after each stimulus presentation.

Training proceeded until the network generated a hit for every output unit on every pattern. A hit was defined as an activation of 0.90 or higher when the desired activation was 1.00, and as an activation of 0.10 or lower when the desired activation was 0.00. The network converged on a solution to the problem—generating a correct response for each of the 48 chords—after 3,964 epochs of training.

RESULTS

One of the potential contributions of artificial neural networks to the study of music is the ability of artificial neural networks to reveal novel or surprising regularities in musical stimuli (Bharucha, 1999). Connectionist architectures are able to not only memorise but to generalise, and provide the opportunity for researchers to discover new forms of representation (Dawson, 2004; Dawson & Boechler, 2007; Dawson, Medler, & Berkeley, 1997; Dawson, Medler, McCaughan, Willson, & Carbonaro, 2000; Dawson & Piercey, 2001). In order for such a contribution to be realised, the internal structure of a trained network must be interpreted. The sections below present the interpretation of the current network, and show that it developed a simple, elegant and surprising representation of the relationships between musical notes that could in turn be used to classify the chord types.

Interpretation of Weights from Input Units

The first step in interpreting the network was to examine the connection weights from the input units to the hidden units. Because each input unit was associated with a particular note, each of these connection weights could be viewed as a numerical "note name." An inspection of the first layer of connection weights (see Table 1) revealed that the network had converted the pitch class representation of the input units into a smaller set of equivalence classes that assigned the same connection weight or "name" to more than one note. For example, the notes A, C#, and F are all represented by different input units in the pitch class representation. However, the network assigned the same numerical "note name" (i.e., a weight of –1.27) to each of the connections between these input units and hidden unit 1. As a result, each of these three notes was treated as being the same by this hidden unit.

An examination of Table 1 reveals that both hidden units 1 and 3 convert the pitch class representation of 12 different notes into 4 equivalence classes that each contains 3 notes. Each of these equivalence classes can be described in formal musical terms as a circle of major thirds. That is, each of the notes in one of these classes differs from the other two by a musical interval of a major third, or four semitones. For instance, if one moves a major third up from A, then one reaches the note C#. If one then moves another major third up from C#, then one reaches the note F. If one finally moves yet another major third up from F, then one completes the circle and returns to the note A. The first four rows of Table 1 identify four different groups of three notes that can each be described as a circle of major thirds.

Hidden unit 2 also employs connection weights from input units that group notes into equivalence classes, but not according to circles of major thirds. Instead, notes are classified as belonging to one of

Table 1. Correspondence between note names and connection weight values for three hidden units in the first chord classification network. Note the correspondence between the first four rows of the first column and the circles of major thirds in Figure 2B, and the correspondence between the last two rows of the first column and the circles of major seconds in Figure 2D.

Note Name	Hidden Unit 1	Hidden Unit 3	Hidden Unit 2
A, C#, F	-1.27	-0.28	
A#, D, F#	-0.61	-0.10	
B, D#, G	1.28	0.28	
C, E, G#	0.63	0.10	
A, C#, F, B, D#, G			-0.76
A#, D, F#, C, E, G#			-0.68

two groups that correspond to circles of major seconds. In this representation, each note in the group is exactly two semitones apart from the next on a scale. The connection weights that define these two equivalence classes are also presented in Table 1; the final two rows of this table identify two groups of six notes that can each be described as a circle of major seconds.

Using Hidden Unit Responses To Classify Chords

How does the network use circles of thirds and seconds representations to classify chords? In examining hidden unit responses, it was found that each hidden unit responds to some stimuli, but not to others. For instance, hidden unit 1 generates a strong response (i.e., an activity level of 1.00) to all of the diminished seventh tetra-chords, as well as to half of the minor triads (i.e., those associated with the minor keys of a, b, c#, e♭, f, and g). It generates a very weak response to any other type of stimulus. The selective responding of the hidden units is directly related to the circles of thirds and seconds.

For example, any diminished seventh tetra-chord is defined by four notes. With respect to the four circles of major thirds that were presented in Table 1, each of these notes comes from a different circle of major thirds. That is, one note from each of the first four rows in Table 1 is required to define any diminished seventh chord. The connection weights that encode these classes for hidden unit 1 are such that when each class is represented in a stimulus, the resulting signal to the hidden unit causes it to generate a maximum response.

As well, every minor triad can be defined as having two notes belonging to the same circle of major thirds, and the third note belonging to one of the other circles of major thirds. Furthermore, the two circles of major thirds that are required to define the triads for the minor keys of a, b, c#, e♭, f, and g minor are associated with connection weights that also result in a signal being sent to hidden unit 1 that produces near maximum activity in it. However, the two circles of major thirds that are required to define the remaining minor triads (for the minor keys of b♭, c, d, e, f#, and a♭) are associated with weights that send a signal to hidden unit 1 that does not cause it to generate a strong response.

The fact that hidden units a) selectively respond to stimuli, but b) respond to more than one type of stimulus (e.g., diminished seventh tetra-chords and minor triads) indicates that the hidden units are representing stimuli using a coarse code. In general, coarse coding means that an individual processor is sensitive to a variety of features or feature values, and is not tuned to detect a single feature type (e.g.,

Churchland & Sejnowski, 1992). As a result, individual processors are not particularly accurate feature detectors. However, if different processors are sensitive to different feature varieties, then their outputs can be pooled, which often produces an accurate representation of a specific feature.

If hidden units are coarse coding musical chords, then the network's response to each stimulus requires considering the activity that it produces in all three hidden units at the same time. To explore this possibility, one can graph a hidden unit space of the patterns in the training set. In such a graph, each pattern is represented as a point in space, where the co-ordinates of the point are provided by the activity produced by the pattern in each hidden unit. Figure 4A presents the three-dimensional hidden unit space of the music chord patterns for the current network.

Figure 4A indicates that the hidden unit space provides a very simple representation of the 48 patterns in the training set. In particular, many different chords are mapped into the identical location in this graph. For example, all 12 diminished seventh tetra-chords are located at the same position in Figure 4A, the location indicated by the symbol d.

How is such a hidden unit space used to classify patterns? An ANN can be described as a tool that carves such a space into distinct decision regions (Lippmann, 1989). All of the stimuli (i.e., all of the points in a space) that fall into one decision region are classified as belonging to the same type, and lead the network to generate one kind of classification response. In order to solve a problem, the network must learn how to partition the hidden unit space in such a way that it makes the correct response for every stimulus.

Recall that the output units in the current network were all value units that used the Gaussian activation function. Value units partition spaces by making two parallel cuts to separate some patterns from others (e.g., Dawson, 2004; see also Figure 4B). This type of partitioning could easily be used to separate the hidden unit space of Figure 4A into four different decision regions that could be used to correctly classify all 48 of the stimuli. For example, Figure 4B illustrates the orientation of two straight cuts that could be used by the output unit to separate dominant seventh chords from the other three chord types. The other three output units could make similar cuts to separate their chord type from all of the others.

STUDY 2: CHORD CLASSIFICATION USING LOCAL REPRESENTATION

The first simulation demonstrated that when chords are encoded with the pitch class representation, an artificial neural network is capable of classifying them into different types. However, there are some issues with pitch class representation that motivate the exploration of other input encoding schemes.

One issue to consider is that the pitch class representation represents major and minor chords with a different number of notes than are used to represent dominant and diminished chords. This introduces the possibility that networks will solve chord classification problems by keying in on a feature of the training set (i.e., whether a stimulus is a triad or a tetra-chord) that is not a particularly interesting musical regularity.

Relatedly, a network that uses pitch class representation cannot be used to classify inversions of the same chord. This follows because inversions of a chord are made up of the same notes and are therefore represented with the same pattern of activation in the inputs.

The second simulation was an attempt to address the issues mentions here, by encoding the input with a representation does not force identical coding of notes an octave apart (Figure 3). This change in encoding allowed for all of the stimuli to be represented as tetra-chords. It also allowed for the network

Figure 4. (A) The hidden unit space for the first network. Major chords are represented by M, minor chords are represented by m, dominant seventh chords are represented by D, and diminished seventh chords are represented by d. (B) An example of how an output value unit could partition the space of Figure 4A in such a way to separate the dominant seventh chords from all others. The other output units classify chords by adopting a similar partitioning of the hidden unit space.

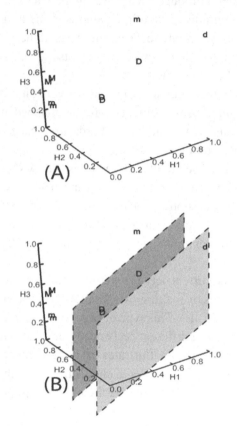

to be trained to not only to find sets of equivalent chords across keys, but also across chord inversions. That is, the network was presented with major and minor chords in root form, as well as their first and second inversions. Dominant and diminished chords were presented in root form, as well as their first, second, and third inversions. The corresponding training set was composed of 168 distinct input patterns. The results below show that a relatively simple network — consisting of four hidden units — was trained to correctly classify all of these chords. It was found that this network was able to do so by relying on circles of thirds and circles of seconds representations.

METHOD

Training Set

As was the case in the first simulation, the network in the second simulation was trained to classify input chords into four different chord types. Each chord was presented in root form, as well as each of the chord's possible inversions, as different stimulus patterns. Figure 5 presents the musical notation for some of the stimuli that were presented to the network: three different versions of the A major tetra-chord, and four different versions of the dominant 7th tetra-chord for the key of A major in the upper staff, as well as three different versions of the A minor tetra-chord, and four different versions of the diminished 7th tetra-chord for the key of A minor in the lower staff.

Network Architecture

The network had 4 output units, 4 hidden units, and 24 input units. All of the output units and all of the hidden units were value units that used the Gaussian activation function that was described by Dawson and Schopflocher (1992).

The representation of the input patterns for this network can be described by imagining a small piano keyboard consisting of only 24 keys, black and white, starting on the note A and ending on the note G#. Let each of 24 input units represent one of the keys of this keyboard (see figure 3). If a particular note was included in the stimulus pattern, then the input unit associated with this note was turned "On" (i.e., it was given an activation value of 1). If the note was not included, then the input unit was turned "Off" (i.e., it was assigned an activation value of 0).

The network was trained to classify input patterns into one of four different chord types, regardless of the key of the chord or of its inversion. This was done using the same representation of responses in the output units as was employed in the first simulation. Four hidden value units were included in this network because pilot tests had shown that this was the smallest number of hidden units that could be used by the network to discover a method for classifying all of the input chords.

Network Training

This second network was also trained using the variation of the generalised delta rule which was used in the first simulation. Prior to training, all of the connection weights were randomly assigned values ranging from –0.10 to +0.10. The biases of processing units were assigned initial values of 0.00. The network was trained with a learning rate of 0.005 and zero momentum. During each epoch of training,

Figure 5. Musical notation for some of the stimuli that were presented to the network in the second simulation study. The first line presents three different versions of the A-major chord, and four different versions of the dominant seventh tetrachord for the key of A-major. The second line presents three different versions of the a-minor chord, and four different versions of the diminished seventh tetrachord for the key of a-minor.

each of the 168 chords was presented to the network, with the order of presentation of the set of 168 patterns randomised prior to beginning the epoch.

Training proceeded until the network generated a hit for every output unit on every pattern. A hit was defined as an activation of 0.90 or higher when the desired activation was 1.00, and as an activation of 0.10 or lower when the desired activation was 0.00. The network converged on a solution to the problem after 5230 sweeps of training.

RESULTS

Interpretation of Weights from Input Unit

In the first simulation it was found that the connection weights between the input units and the hidden units were used to convert stimulus information from pitch class to circles of thirds and seconds. The first step in analysing the network from the second simulation was the examination of its first layer of weights for evidence for a similar style of processing.

The 24 connection weights from the input units to hidden unit 2 and hidden unit 3 are presented in Figure 6. This figure reveals that both of these hidden units were converting the local, binary representation of the input units into circles of major thirds representations. The connection weights into each unit can be classified as belonging to one of four categories: strong negative, weak negative, strong positive, and weak positive. All of the notes belonging to one of the circles of major thirds from Figure 2B are assigned the same type of connection weight. For example, the three notes belonging to the first circle (A, F, C#) are all assigned strong negative connection weights by hidden unit 2, and are all assigned weak positive connection weights by hidden unit 3.

The connection weights that feed into hidden unit 1 are represented in Figure 7A. As can be seen from this figure, hidden unit 1 organises the input according to circles of major seconds, a representation that was also observed in the first simulation. All of the notes that fall into the first circle of Figure 2D are assigned positive weights, and all of the notes that fall into the second circle of Figure 2D are assigned negative weights. However, unlike hidden unit 2 in the first simulation (see Table 1), there is an additional modulation to this representation, because the weights vary in magnitude across the graph.

The connection weights connecting the input units to hidden unit 4 are graphed in Figure 7B. This set of connection weights appears quite unsystematic in comparison with those of the other hidden units, because the fourth hidden unit is highly specialised. It only generates a strong response (i.e., an activation of 0.88 or higher) to a small number of stimuli. As will be elaborated upon in the following section, the primary role of this unit is to separate the second inversions of a small number of major chords from the set of minor chords.

Using Hidden Unit Responses to Classify Chords

The results above indicate that hidden units 2 and 3 transform the local signals coming from the input units into two circles of major thirds representations. One result of this transformation is that both of these hidden units generate distinguishable patterns of activity to different classes of input chords. A general account of how each of these two hidden units responds to different types of chords is provided in Table 2.

Figure 6. (A) The connection weight values from each of the input units to Hidden Unit 2. (B) The connection weight values from each of the input units to Hidden Unit 3. Note that both sets of connection weights are organized into the four circles of major thirds.

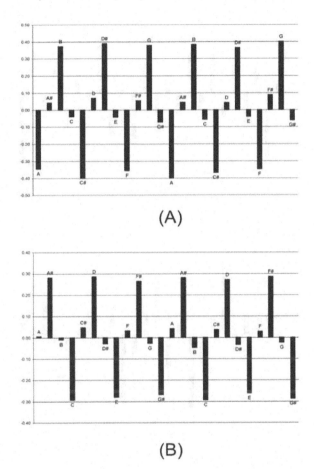

(A)

(B)

Table 2 reveals three important properties of hidden units 2 and 3. First, the two hidden units act in such a way that they distinguish between two different subsets of key signatures. The first set of key signatures is A, B, C#, E, F, and G, in both their major and minor form. The second set of key signatures (again in both major and minor form) is A, B, C, D, E, and F#. These two sets of key signatures correspond to the two circles of major seconds in Figure 2D. While hidden units 2 and 3 represent notes using circles of major thirds, their more extreme positive and negative weights pick out the two circles of major seconds. It is this characteristic of their connection weights that leads these hidden units to activate in such a way that they differentiate chords from these two sets of keys.

The second property of these two hidden units is that they provide complementary response patterns to stimuli belonging to these two different sets of key signatures. For example, consider the responses of these two hidden units to major chords in either root position or the first inversion. For chords associated with keys that belong to the first circle of major seconds (A, B, C#, E, F, and G), hidden unit 2 generates a weak response, but it generates a very strong response to chords associated with keys that belong to the second circle of major seconds (A, B, C, D, E, and F#). Hidden unit 3 compliments this

Figure 7. (A) The connection weight values from each of the input units to Hidden Unit 1. Note that the sign of the connection weight organizes the notes into the two circles of major seconds. (B) The connection weight values from each of the input units to Hidden Unit 4.

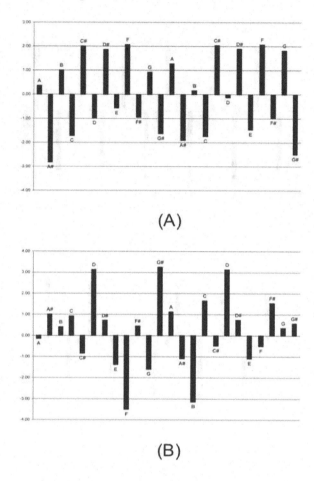

(A)

(B)

by providing the opposite pattern of activity: it generates strong activity to the chords associated with the first circle of major seconds, and weak activity to the chords associated with the second circle of major seconds. Several other examples of this relationship between the two hidden units are evident in Table 2. This is due to the fact that one hidden unit has its more extreme connection weights associated with one circle of major seconds, while the other hidden unit has its more extreme connection weights associated with the other.

The third property of these two hidden units is that, in combination, they provide a unique pattern of activity to all but a very select subset of the chords. An examination of Table 2 suggests that the only chords that are not provided a unique set of activation patterns to distinguish these chords from others are the second inversions of the 12 different major chords. These 12 chords generate very weak activity in both hidden units 2 and 3, which is also the case for all of the minor chords associated with the keys a, b, c#, e, f, and g. In other words, the out of phase circles of major thirds representations used by these two hidden units appears to be capable of identifying any type of chord except the second inversion of a major chord, which will be mistakenly identified as a minor chord in this representation.

Figure 8. The hidden unit space spanned by Hidden Units 2 and 3 of the second network. The dashed lines indicate how the space can be partitioned by the output units to classify different chord types. The dashed circles indicate regions in this space in which second inversion major chords cannot be distinguished from minor chords.

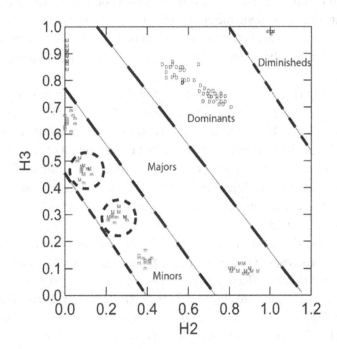

Table 2. Responses of Hidden Units 2 and 3 in the second network to different classes and subclasses of chords. See text for details.

Stimulus	Stimulus Subcategory	Hidden Unit 2	Hidden Unit 3
All Diminished Seventh Chords		On (0.99 -1.00)	On (0.99 -1.00)
Major Chords – root position and first inversion	Keys of A ♭ , B ♭ , C, D, E, F#	High (0.79-0.92)	Weak (0.08-0.10)
	Keys of A, B, C#, E ♭ , F, G	Weak (0.01-0.12)	High (0.86-0.93)
All Dominant Seventh Chords	Keys of A ♭ , B ♭ , C, D, E, F#	Medium (0.49-0.68))	Medium (0.79-0.86)
	Keys of A, B, C#, E ♭ , F, G	Medium (0.69-0.79)	Medium (0.70-0.78)
All Minor Chords and 12 Major chords	Keys of a ♭ , b ♭ , c, d, e, f#	Low (0.38-0.44)	Low (0.62-0.67)
	Keys of a, b, c#, e ♭ , f, g	Weak (0.02-0.32	Weak (0.12-0.51)
	Second inversion of major chord from each of the 12 major keys	Weak (0.01)	Weak (0.08-0.12)

This third property of these two hidden units was confirmed by using discriminant analysis to classify the four types of input chords using the activity generated by an input chord in hidden units 2 and 3 as the only predictor variables. The resulting discriminant analysis was capable of correctly classifying all minor, diminished, and dominant chords. 24 of the 36 major chords were also correctly classified. The discriminant analysis incorrectly classified the remaining 12 major chords as minors. These 12 chords, as would be expected from Table 2, were the second inversions.

Earlier it was noted that hidden unit 1 uses its incoming connection weights to convert the binary input representation into one based upon the circles of major seconds, although the particular form of this representation was more complicated than the one observed in the first simulation. One consequence of these incoming connection weights is that hidden unit 1 generates distinct patterns of activity to fairly broad classes of chords.

First, it generates strong activity (0.69-0.99) to half of the second inversion major chords (A, B, C#, D, F, and G). Second, it generates medium activity (0.48-0.49) to all of the diminished chords. Third, it generates medium activity (0.46) to the second inversion of the C major chord. Fourth, it generates low activity (0.00 – 0.24) to all of the minor chords, all of the dominant chords, and all of the remaining major chords. In the context of the responses of hidden units 2 and 3, one of the key properties of this pattern of activity is the fact that it differentiates some of the second inversion major chords from all of the minor chords. Thus, this hidden unit can help deal with the one kind of classification that was posing problems for hidden units 2 and 3.

It was noted earlier that the connection weights between the input units and hidden unit 4 did not resemble any of the previous types of representations, and indicated that this unit was highly specialised. The degree of its specialisation is reflected in the kinds of responses that it makes to input chords.

First, this hidden unit only generates high activity (0.88-0.93) to a handful of major chords: those in root position and in first inversion for the keys of A, B, C#, E, F, and G. Importantly, these keys all belong to the first circle of major seconds in Figure 2D, which suggest that the representation used by this hidden unit is sensitive to a circles of major seconds regularity, even though this regularity is not apparent from a first glance at its connection weights (Figure 6B). Second, it generates low to medium activity (0.17-0.60) to the second inversion major chords of the keys A, B, C, E, E, and F#. This is the subset of second inversion major chords that hidden unit 1 did not respond to. Third, it generates low to medium activity to a handful of dominant chords. Fourth, it turns off (activity of 0.00) to all remaining chords. Importantly, this final set of chords includes all of the minor chords. So, in the context of the previous analysis of the other three hidden units, hidden unit 4 generates a response that distinguishes the remaining second inversion major chords from the minor chords. Again, this is property is important to compensate for the one kind of classification that hidden units 2 and 3 were unable to mediate.

DISCUSSION

In their original study of chord classification, Laden and Keefe (1989) were unable to train a network to correctly classify 100 percent of their training set of 36 major, minor, and diminished seventh triads. One important result of the simulations reported here was that the networks were able to classify all of the chords in the training set, including 12 dominant seventh chords that were not studied by Laden and Keefe. This result was achieved even though the network was simpler than the best performing network that Laden and Keefe reported.

There are several likely explanations for this result. As was noted earlier, while the simulations were conducted in the spirit of Laden and Keefe's (1989) research, there were a number of differences.

First, value units were used, instead sigmoid-shaped activation functions. Because value units carve up pattern spaces in a different fashion than do these latter units, they are likely more suited to the chord classification problem. Second, the diminished seventh and dominant seventh stimuli were defined as tetra-chords instead of triads. As was shown in the analysis of the behaviour of both hidden units 1 and 3, the network was able to take advantage of the "balancing" of four incoming signals to respond to stimuli (e.g., to generate high responses to diminished seventh tetra-chords). In short, moderate changes to the network architecture and to stimulus representation produced conditions that made the chord classification problem easier for the network than was the case in Laden and Keefe's earlier simulations.

A more important result concerns the interpretation of network structure. One of connectionism's potential contributions to the psychology of music is its ability to reveal novel regularities in stimulus structure, or to suggest new approaches to represent musical patterns. In order for this potential to be realised, it must be possible to analyse the internal structure of a network after it has been trained.

This study demonstrated that the internal structure of the chord classification networks could be interpreted. It revealed that the first network classified chord structure first by representing individual notes in terms of circles of major thirds and major seconds, and then by combining these representations to position chords in a three-dimensional hidden unit space. Despite use of a different local representation of input chords, interpretation of the second network revealed a very strong tendency to adopt a transformation of input similar to that observed in the first network. While there is a growing body of evidence concerning specialised neural processing of tones and chords (e.g., Peretz & Zatorre, 2005), this evidence is not yet sufficiently precise to indicate whether distributed representations based on tone circles are used by the brain. A search for examples of an ANN reorganising an input encoding scheme into this type of representation, was not successful. This raises the question of whether circles of thirds and seconds are pertinent to human subjects' representation of musical stimuli.

ACKNOWLEDGMENT

The author is funded by an NSERC PGS scholarship.

This chapter is an extended version of an earlier publication by Yaremchuk and Dawson (2008). The reported research was conducted at the Biological Computation Project University of Alberta and was funded by NSERC and SSHRC grants awarded to M.R.W. Dawson.

REFERENCES

Assayag, G., Feichtinger, H. G., & Rodrigues, J.-F. (2002). *Mathematics and music: A Diderot mathematical forum*. Berlin/New York: Springer.

Berkeley, I. S. N., Dawson, M. R. W., Medler, D. A., Schopflocher, D. P., & Hornsby, L. (1995). Density plots of hidden value unit activations reveal interpretable bands. *Connection Science, 7*, 167–186. doi:10.1080/09540099550039336

Bharucha, J. J. (1999). Neural nets, temporal composites, and tonality. In D. Deutsch (Ed.), *The Psychology Of music* (2nd ed., pp. 413-440). San Diego, CA: Academic Press.

Bharucha, J. J., & Todd, P. M. (1989). Modeling the perception of tonal structure with neural nets. *Computer Music Journal, 13*(4), 44–53. doi:10.2307/3679552

Casey, M. A. (1999). Understanding musical sound with forward models and physical models. In N. Griffith & P. M. Todd (Eds.), *Musical networks: Parallel distributed perception and performace* (pp. 45-61). London: MIT Press.

Churchland, P. S., & Sejnowski, T. J. (1992). *The computational brain*. Cambridge, MA: MIT Press.

Dawson, M. R. W. (1998). *Understanding cognitive science*. Malden, MA: Blackwell.

Dawson, M. R. W. (2004). *Minds and machines: Connectionism and Psychological modelling*. Malden, MA: Blackwell.

Dawson, M. R. W. (2005). *Connectionism: A hands-on approach* (1st ed.). Oxford, UK/Malden, MA: Blackwell.

Dawson, M. R. W., & Boechler, P. M. (2007). Representing an intrinsically nonmetric space of compass directions in an artificial neural network. *International Journal of Cognitive Informatics and Natural Intelligence, 1*, 53–65.

Dawson, M. R. W., Medler, D. A., & Berkeley, I. S. N. (1997). PDP networks can provide models that are not mere implementations of classical theories. *Philosophical Psychology, 10*, 25–40. doi:10.1080/09515089708573202

Dawson, M. R. W., Medler, D. A., McCaughan, D. B., Willson, L., & Carbonaro, M. (2000). Using extra output learning to insert a symbolic theory into a connectionist network. *Minds and Machines, 10*, 171–201. doi:10.1023/A:1008313828824

Dawson, M. R. W., & Piercey, C. D. (2001). On the subsymbolic nature of a PDP architecture that uses a nonmonotonic activation function. *Minds and Machines, 11*, 197–218. doi:10.1023/A:1011237306312

Dawson, M. R. W., & Schopflocher, D. P. (1992). Modifying the generalised delta rule to train networks of nonmonotonic processors for pattern classification. *Connection Science, 4*, 19–31. doi:10.1080/09540099208946601

Dawson, M. R. W., & Zimmerman, C. (2003). Interpreting the internal structure of a connectionist model of the balance scale task. *Brain and Mind, 4*, 129–149. doi:10.1023/A:1025449410732

Desain, P., & Honing, H. (1991). The quantization of musical time: A connectionist approach. In P. M. Todd & D. G. Loy (Eds.), *Music and connectionism*. London: The MIT Press.

Deutsch, D. (1999). *The Psychology of music* (2nd ed.). San Diego: Academic Press.

Dolson, M. (1991). Machine tongues xii: neural networks. In P. M. Todd & D. G. Loy (Eds.), Music and connectionism (pp. 3 - 19). London: The MIT Press.

Franklin, J. A. (2004). *Recurrent neural networks and pitch representations for music tasks*. Paper presented at the Seventeenth International Florida Artificial Intelligence Research Symposium Conference, Miami Beach, FA.

Gjerdingen, R. O. (1991). Using connectionist models to explore complex musical patterns. In P. M. Todd & D. G. Loy (Eds.), *Music and connectionism* (pp. 138 - 148). London: The MIT Press.

Griffith, N. (1999). Development of tonal centres and abstract pitch as categorizations of pitch use. In N. Griffith & P. M. Todd (Eds.), *Musical networks: Parallel distributed perception and performac*e (pp. 23-43). London: MIT Press.

Griffith, N., & Todd, P. M. (1999*). Musical networks: Parallel distributed perception and performance.* Cambridge, MA: MIT Press.

Jochem, T., Pomerleau, D. A., & Thorpe, C. (1993). Maniac: A next generation neurally based autonomous road follower. In *Proceedings of the International Conference on Intelligent Autonomous Systems*.

Jourdain, R. (1997). *Music, the brain, and ecstasy*. New York: William Morrow & Co.

Krumhansl, C. L. (1990). *Cognitive foundations of musical pitch*. New York: Oxford University Press.

Laden, B., & Keefe, B. H. (1989). The representation of pitch in a neural net model of pitch classification. *Computer Music Journal, 13*, 12–26. doi:10.2307/3679550

Large, E. W., & Kolen, J. F. (1999). Resonance and the perception of musical meter. In N. Griffith & P. M. Todd (Eds.), *Musical networks: Parallel distributed perception and performace* (pp. 65 - 96). London: MIT Press.

Le Cun, Y., Jackel, L. D., Boser, B., & Denker, J. S. (1989). Handwritten digit recognition: Applications of neural network chips and automatic learning. *IEEE Communications Magazine, 27*(11), 41–46. doi:10.1109/35.41400

Leman, M. (1991). The ontogenesis of tonal semantics: Results of a computer study. In P. M. Todd & D. G. Loy (Eds.), *Music and connectionism* (pp. 100 - 127). London: The MIT Press.

Lerdahl, F., & Jackendoff, R. (1983). *A generative theory of tonal music*. Cambridge, MA: MIT Press.

Lewis, J. P. (1991). Creation by refinement and the problem of algorithmic music composition. In P. M. Todd & D. G. Loy (Eds.), *Music and conncectionism*. London: The MIT Press.

Lippmann, R. P. (1989). Pattern classification using neural networks. *IEEE Communications Magazine*, (November): 47–64. doi:10.1109/35.41401

Loy, D. G. (1991). Connectionism and musiconomy. In P. M. Todd & D. G. Loy (Eds.), *Music and connectionism* (pp. 20 - 36). London: The MIT Press.

Mozer, M. C. (1991). Connectionist music composition based on melodic, stylistic, and psychophysical constraints. In P. M. Todd & D. G. Log (Eds.), *Music and connectionism*. London: The MIT Press.

Mozer, M. C. (1999). Neural network music composition by prediction: Exploring the benefits of psychoacoustic constraints and multi-scale processing. In N. Griffith & P. M. Todd (Eds.), *Musical networks: Parallel distributed perception and performace* (pp. 227-260). London: MIT Press.

Peretz, I., & Zatorre, R. J. (2003). *The cognitive neuroscience of music*. Oxford/New York: Oxford University Press.

Peretz, I., & Zatorre, R. J. (2005). Brain organization for music processing. *Annual Review of Psychology, 56*, 1–26. doi:10.1146/annurev.psych.56.091103.070225

Pomerleau, D. A. (1991). Efficient training of artificial neural networks for autonomous navigation. *Neural Computation, 3*, 88–97. doi:10.1162/neco.1991.3.1.88

Sano, H., & Jenkins, B. K. (1989). A neural network model for pitch perception. *Computer Music Journal, 13*(3), 41–48. doi:10.2307/3680010

Sayegh, S. I. (1991). Fingering for string instruments with the optimum path paradigm. In P. M. Todd & D. G. Loy (Eds.), *Music and connectionism* (pp. 243-255). London: The MIT Press.

Scarborough, D. L., Miller, B. O., & Jones, J. A. (1989). Connectionist models for tonal analysis. *Computer Music Journal, 13*(3), 49–55. doi:10.2307/3680011

Sejnowski, T. J., & Rosenberg, C. R. (1988). Nettalk: A parallel network that learns to read aloud. In J. A. Anderson & E. Rosenfeld (Eds.), *Neurocomputing: Foundations of research* (pp. 663-672). Cambridge, MA: MIT Press.

Taylor, I., & Greenhough, M. (1999). Modelling pitch perception with adaptive resonance theory artificial neural networks. In N. Griffith & P. M. Todd (Eds.), *Musical networks: Parallel distributed perception and performance* (pp. 3-22). London: The MIT Press.

Tillmann, B., Bharucha, J. J., & Bigand, E. (2003). Learning and perceiving musical structures: Further insights from artificial neural networks. In I. Peretz & R. Zatorre (Eds.), *The cognitive neuroscience of music* (pp. 109 - 126). Oxford; New York: Oxford University Press.

Todd, P. M., & Loy, D. G. (1991). *Music and connectionism.* Cambridge, MA: MIT Press.

Wang, Y. (2003). Cognitive informatics: A new transdisciplinary research field. *Brain and Mind, 4*, 115–127. doi:10.1023/A:1025419826662

Wang, Y. (2007a). Cognitive informatics: Exploring the theoretical foundations for natural intelligence, neural informatics, autonomic computing, and agent systems. *International Journal of Cognitive Informatics and Natural Intelligence, 1*, i–x.

Wang, Y. (2007b). On laws of work organization in human cooperation. *International Journal of Cognitive Informatics and Natural Intelligence, 1*(2), 1–15.

Wang, Y., Liu, D., & Wang, Y. (2003). Discovering the capacity of human memory. *Brain and Mind, 4*(2), 189–198. doi:10.1023/A:1025405628479

Wang, Y., Wang, Y., Patel, S., & Patel, D. (2006). A layered reference model of the brain. *IEEE Transactions on Systems, Man, and Cybernetics, 36*(2), 124–133. doi:10.1109/TSMCC.2006.871126

Yaremchuk, V., & Dawson, M. R. W. (2008). Artificial neural networks that classify musical chords. *International Journal of Cognitive Informatics and Natural Intelligence, 2*(3), 22–30.

Yaremchuk, V., Willson, L. R., Spetch, M. L., & Dawson, M. R. W. (2005). The implications of null patterns and output unit activation functions on simulation studies of learning: A case study of patterning. *Learning and Motivation, 36*(1), 88–103. doi:10.1016/j.lmot.2004.10.001

Zimmerman, C. L. (1999). *A network interpretation approach to the balance scale task.* Unpublished Ph.D., University of Alberta, Edmonton.

Chapter 27
Foundation and Classification of Nonconventional Neural Units and Paradigm of Nonsynaptic Neural Interaction

I. Bukovsky
Czech Technical University, Czech Republic

J. Bila
Czech Technical University, Czech Republic

M. M. Gupta
University of Saskatchewan, Canada

Z-G Hou
The Chinese Academy of Sciences, P.R. China

N. Homma
Tohoku University, Japan

ABSTRACT

This chapter introduces basic types of nonconventional neural units and focuses their mathematical notation and classification. Namely, the notation and classification of higher-order nonlinear neural units, time-delay dynamic neural units, and time-delay higher-order nonlinear neural units is introduced. The classification of nonconventional neural units is founded first according to nonlinearity of aggregating function, second according to the dynamic order, third according to time-delay implementation within neural units. Introduction into the simplified parallel of the higher-order nonlinear aggregating function of higher-order neural units revealing both the synaptic and nonsynaptic neural interaction is made; thus, a new parallel between the mathematical notation of nonconventional neural units and the neural signal processing of biological neurons and is drawn. Based on the mathematical notation of neural input inter-correlations of higher-order neural units, it is shown that higher-order polynomial aggregating

DOI: 10.4018/978-1-60566-902-1.ch027

function of neural inputs can be naturally understood as a single-equation representation consisting of synaptic neural operation plus nonsynaptic neural operation. Thus it unravels new simplified yet universal mathematical insight into understanding the higher computational power of neurons that also conforms to biological neuronal morphology according to nowadays achievements of biomedical sciences.

INTRODUCTION

Neural networks are powerful cognitive tools with learning and generalization capability; however, the black-box or sometimes gray-box effect of neural networks is a well known drawback that often prevents researchers from further network analysis and utilization of learned knowledge hidden in the network, e.g. to analyze generalization capabilities of the network for a particular real system. In neural computation oriented literature, the focus is usually put on a neural network as whole and the computational strength is naturally to be induced by neuronal networking. The network complexity and the number of neural parameters should be minimized while its maximum computational power and generalization capability has to be maintained in order to minimize the black-box effect of neural networks. As seen from the multidisciplinary point of view, there are three major attributes that establish complex behavior of systems and that can be used to mathematically describe complex system behavior. These attributes are the nonlinearity, dynamics, and time delays; these attributes also appear in neurons and neural networks. These three attributes can be simultaneously implemented in individual neurons to maximize their individual approximation capability and thus to minimize neural network complexity and to maximize its cognitive capabilities. In this paper we propose (or highlight) new emerging notation and classification of neural units that emerges from neural network discipline as well as from concepts common to various fields of science. We also propose a discussion on a plausible neurological aspect of a full polynomial notation of neural aggregation function in the next subsection.

An important nonlinearity attribute in neural network was significantly proposed in neural networks using higher–order polynomials as neural activation function (Ivakchnenko, 1971; Ivakchenko & Iba, 2003). An exhaustive survey has been made by Duch & Jankowski (1999) where various neural activation functions and neural output functions are investigated and summarized. For simple demonstration of our proposed classification approach and also for their universal approximating and correlating capabilities, only the polynomials are considered as neural input aggregating functions (activation functions) optionally including neural states (in case of dynamic neural units). An alternative concept of higher-order nonlinear neural units (HONNU) was recently published by M.M. Gupta et al. (2003, pp.279-286). Therefore, the conception and terminology used by M.M. Gupta et al. in their book on neural networks (Gupta et al., 2003) is followed in this work. Typical representatives of HONNU are namely the quadratic neural unit (QNU) and the cubic neural unit (CNU) that were consequently investigated. The results were published by the research group of M.M. Gupta (Redlapalli et al., 2003), where a higher-order polynomial nonlinear aggregating function has been originally understood as a merely synaptic neural operation, i.e., as a synaptic neural input preprocessor. More recently, an application of HONNU to robot image processing was published by Hou et al. (2007) with similar interpretation of a synaptic neural operation of HONNU. Except the proposed classification of nonconventional neural units in this paper, then next section shows that polynomial aggregating functions of neural inputs includes in principle also nonsynaptic and possibly somatic neural transmissions.

Figure 1. A conventional artificial dynamic neural unit with linear aggregation (summation) of neural inputs and neural state feedback (Hopfield, Pineda 1980', Gupta et al. 2003, p. 302)

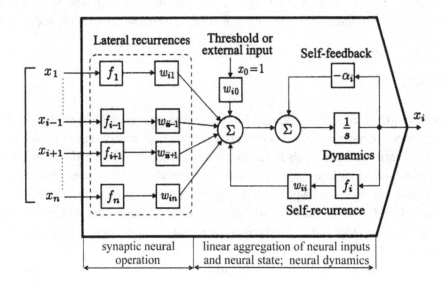

In parallel to development of HONNU, another class of continuous-time dynamic neural units with linear aggregating function that are called time-delay dynamic neural units (TmD-DNU) was proposed recently by Bukovsky et al. (2005, 2006). The idea of neural networks utilizing adaptable time delays also in individual neural state variables has also simultaneously appeared in fuzzy neurons by Oysal (2005) and more recently in work of Becerikli & Oysal (2007). TmD-DNU are distinguished by the implementation of adaptable time delays in order to increase computational and approximating capability of a single neural unit, to minimize the number of neural parameters, and thus to simplify the neural architecture. Originally, the neural architecture of TmD-DNU was inspired by conventional linear dynamic neural units (DNU) as by research work namely of Pineda (1982) and Hopfield (1988), e.g. Figure 1, and recently Gupta et al. (2003). Similarly to conventional linear neural units, the TmD-DNU shown in Figure 2 has a linear aggregating function (weighted summation) of neural inputs and the neural state; then it has either nonlinear or linear function on the neural output. Contrary to conventional dynamic neural units, the neural structure of TmD-DNU contains continuous time delays as adaptable neural parameters. These adaptable time delays can be implemented in neural inputs as T_j where $j=1...n$ (Figure 2), and as T_j in the internal state variable as shown later in Figure 8, Figure 9, and Figure 10. Consequently, the concept of time-delay dynamic higher-order nonlinear neural units (TmD-HONNU) was introduced recently by Bukovsky (2007) in parallel to the research of TmD-DNU and HONNU.

As regards linear synaptic operation of conventional neural units as in Figure 1, the neural weighted summation of neural inputs has been commonly accepted paradigm of mathematical representation of simple neuronal models since the foundation of artificial neural networks in their earliest stages such as in the work of McCulloch and Pitts in 1943. Nowadays, the paradigm of the human brain being viewed as purely via-synapse wired network is being revolutionary moved forward according to the recent discoveries of also nonsynaptic neuronal communication. For example, Vizi (2000) concludes that

Figure 2. Linear type-1 time-delay dynamic neural unit (TmD₁-DNU); w_j is j^{th} neural weight, T_j is j^{th} adaptable time-delay in j^{th} neural input u_j (u_0 is neural bias, v is aggregated variable, ξ is neural state variable, $\varphi()$ belongs to somatic neural operation, y is neural output, τ is adaptable dynamic parameter, t is continuous parameter of time, and s is the Laplace operator

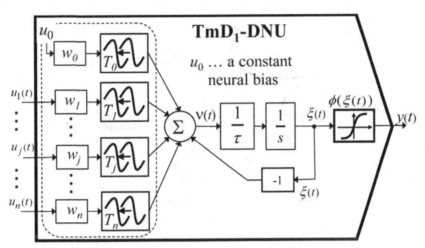

"...The formerly more restricted view of chemical signal transmission within the synapse has to be extended, because considerable evidence has accumulated to show that although the brain is a wired instrument, its neurons, besides cabled information signaling (through synapses), are able to talk to each other without synaptic contact (i.e., "wireless")... ...Gone is our understanding of hard-wired neuronal circuitry created for the amplification of digital information in the synapse, with the use of very fast transmitters able to produce "on" and "off" signals within us; we have to change our mentality and accept there is a nonsynaptic communication system that in the brain, an analog information transfer, whose time constant may be seconds or even minutes..."(p.81).

Our paper shows that the nonsynaptic neural interaction is, in principle, already present in nonlinear neural input aggregation function of nonconventional neural units, esp. higher-order neural units and also of time-delay higher-order neural units.

This paper is further organized as follows. The introduction and new classification of nonconventional neural units are introduced. Then the principle of fundamental notion of nonsynaptic neural interaction is introduced as a part of the mathematical structure of the nonlinear aggregation function of nonconventional neural units esp. HONNU and TmD-HONNU. The summary follows then.

CLASSIFICATION OF NONCONVENTIONAL NEURAL UNITS

Classification of Neural Units by Nonlinear Aggregating Function

The systematic classification of HONNU, designed by the research group of M.M. Gupta et al. (Figure 3, Figure 4), is naturally based upon the order of polynomial neural aggregating function $v = f_{HONNU}$. Second-order HONNU are naturally called quadratic neural units (QNU), and third-order HONNU are

Figure 3. Comparison of the sketch of a biological neuron with the structure of static QNU. The quadratic (nonlinear) terms of the polynomial of HONNU have been originally understood as being the synaptic nonlinear preprocessor of the neural inputs since originally proposed by the research group of M.M. Gupta (Song, Redlapalli, Bukovsky, 2003) and recently also in (Hou et al. 2007)

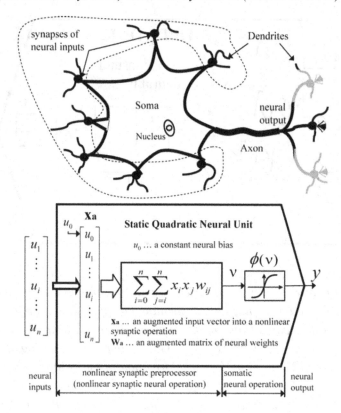

called cubic neural units (CNU). Our proposed generalized classification of neural units is shown later in Figure 7, Figure 11, and Figure 15 in this paper.

Classification of Neural Units by Neural Dynamics

Next to the major classification of dynamic neural units into either discrete dynamic neural units or continuous dynamic neural units, another significant attribute is their dynamics approximating capability represented by the dynamic order of a neural unit. According to the general concept of continuous dynamic systems, the dynamic order is understood as the number of integrations of neural aggregated variable $v(t)$ resulting in internal neural state variable $\xi(t)$, i.e. the dynamic order is the number of time derivatives of internal neural state variable $\xi(t)$. Moreover, according to the common conception of dynamic systems described by integral calculus, the attribute of the dynamic order of a system is viewed as distinct from the attribute of system nonlinearity, i.e., distinct from the nonlinearity of the aggregating operation discussed in the previous subsection. Then each of these two attributes, the dynamic order and the order of the nonlinearity (basically the order of a polynomial f_{HONNU}), allows as to classify HONNU as well as the other neural units from the point of these two attributes, while their classes and subclasses can be modified and combined (Figure 7).

Figure 4. Structure of the static cubic neural unit where cubic polynomial used to be understood pure synaptic nonlinear preprocessor of the neural inputs (CNU)

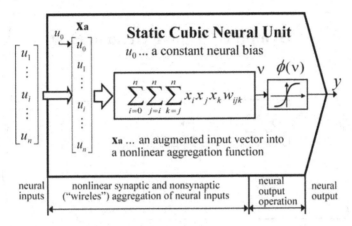

Figure 5. Continuous-time dynamic cubic neural unit

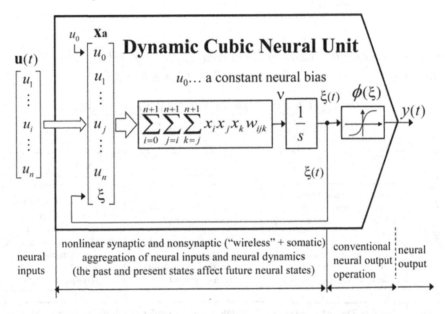

The combinations may then result in, e.g., the dynamic cubic neural unit (Figure 5), the dynamic-order extended QNU (Figure 6), and so on. Basically, it shall be distinguished between the first-order (such as the single-integrator) dynamic HONNU (Figure 5) and the dynamic-order extended HONNU (Figure 6) that could be possibly considered as rather more suitable for standalone system identification rather than for the network implementations.

So far, neural units were classified by the nonlinearity of the neural aggregated variable v and by the number of its time integrations as shown in Figure 7. Note that discrete-time dynamic neural units are not considered in this paper; however, the proposed classification is similar and applicable also to discrete neural units (when instead of time integrations we may think of step delays of neural state variable). Next, further classification of neural units is shown according to the implementation of time-

Figure 6. Dynamic-order extended quadratic neural unit (with multiple integration of neural aggregated variable v)

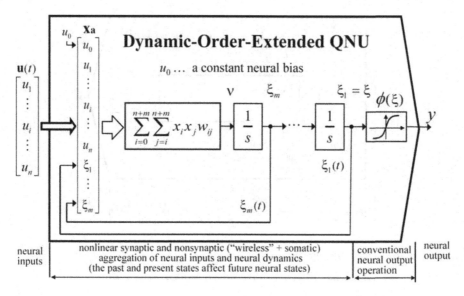

Figure 7. Classification of basic nonconventional continuous artificial neural units according to aggregating nonlinearity $f_{HONNU}=v$ and its time integrations (dynamic order)

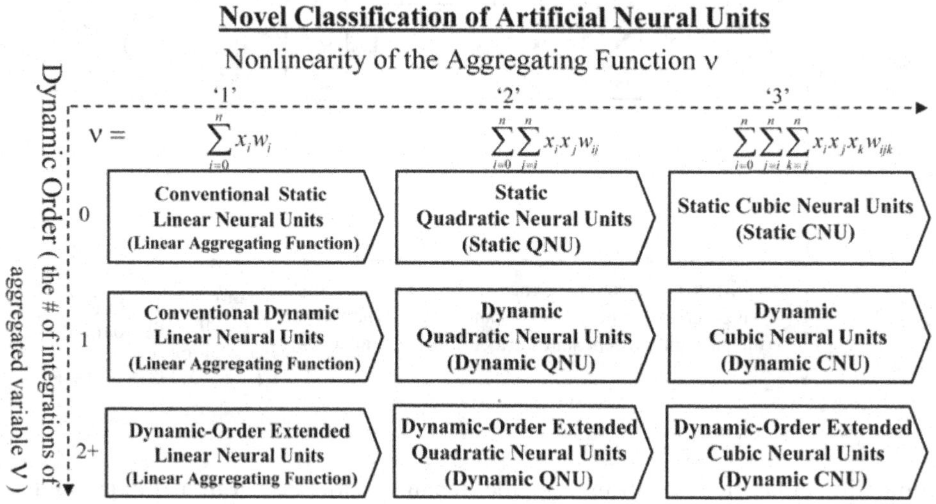

delays in internal neural dynamics, i.e., according to adaptable time-delays in neural inputs and neural state feedback of a unit.

Classification of Neural Units by Implementation of Time Delays

Delays are natural phenomenon to many real systems and the concept of continuous-time delays is well known in engineering problems as theoretically quite complex phenomenon. It is well known that simple linear dynamic systems become systems with theoretically infinity number of poles and zeros once enhanced with time delays. Practically, the implementation of time delays results in higher number of significant zeros and poles of a linear dynamic system. Therefore, adaptable time delays can be used as a very powerful tool for high dynamic-order system approximation and can be implemented into neural architectures (Bukovsky et al., 2005, 2006). Analogically to linear systems, the approximating capability of nonlinear dynamic systems can be significantly increased once nonlinear systems become enhanced with time delays. Therefore, the third of the most significant and general attributes useful for classifying of the new neural units is the type of implementation of adaptable continuous time delays within a neural unit. Such a nonconventional neural unit with linear aggregating function is generally called time-delay dynamic neural unit (TmD-DNU) (Bukovsky et al., 2005, 2006). The simplest class of these units is denoted as type-1 time-delay dynamic neural unit (TmD_1-DNU) and is shown already in Figure 2. TmD_1-DNU has implemented adaptable time-delays only in neural inputs. The second basic type of time-delay dynamic neural units is determined by implementation of adaptable time delays both in neural inputs as well as in the neural state feedback of a unit. The unit is denoted type-2 time-delay dynamic neural unit (TmD_2-DNU) and is shown in Figure 8.

Similarly to the classification of non-delay dynamic neural units (dynamic HONNU) discussed in previous subsection, the time-delay dynamic neural units can be also classified according to the non-linearity of the aggregating function f_{HONNU} (i.e. $v(t)$) as it is shown in Figure 11. The particular example of type-2 time delay HONNU with time integration of quadratic neural aggregation is shown in Figure 9. Moreover, similarly to the classification of non-delay dynamic neural units (dynamic HONNU) discussed in previous subsection, the time-delay dynamic neural units can be furthermore classified according to the number of time integrations of neural aggregated variable v. So far, TmD-DNU and TmD-HONNU (i.e. TmD-QNU, TmD-CNU,...) with more than one integration of neural aggregated variable v are generally called dynamic-order extended TmD-DNU or dynamic-order extended TmD-HONNU (Bukovsky, 2007). An example of the type-2 dynamic-order extended TmD-DNU (i.e. with linear aggregating function) is shown in Figure 10 (Bukovsky et al., 2006).

Figure 8. Linear type-2 time-delay dynamic neural unit (TmD_2-DNU)

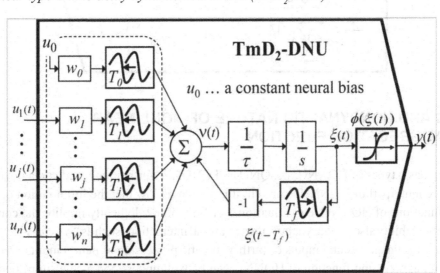

Figure 9. Time-delay dynamic HONNU: Type-2 time-delay quadratic neural unit (TmD₂-QNU)

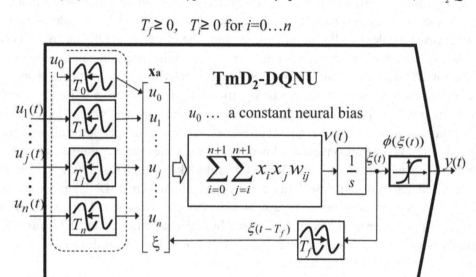

Figure 10. Type-2 dynamic-order extended time-delay dynamic neural unit; where s is the Laplace operator

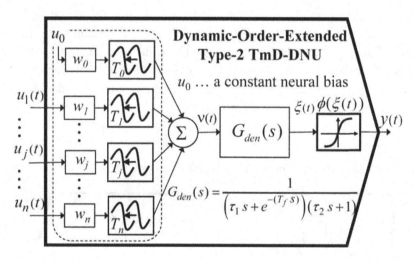

SYNAPTIC AND NONSYNAPTIC NATURE OF NONLINEAR NEURAL AGGREGATION FUNCTION

In this section, basic types of HONNU, i.e. QNU and CNU, are further analyzed and a novel parallel to the biological counterpart of HONNU is drawn; it is shown bellow that the full notation of polynomial aggregating functions of HONNU, e.g. Equation 1 or Equation 2, logically implies the contribution of computational capability also of nonsynaptic inter-neuronal interactions such as "wireless" or "gas mixing" interference of nonsynaptic neural inputs or further somatic processing of neural inputs. In other words, the neural input aggregating function of HONNU can be well understood as the simplified interaction

Figure 11. *Classification of basic time-delay dynamic neural units according to aggregating nonlinearity v and the type of delay implementation*

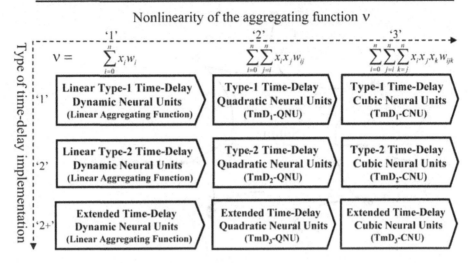

of both neural synapses and partial neural nonsynaptic activity according to the mathematical notation of input inter-correlations of HONNU, e.g. Equation1 or Equation 2, and with respect to the biological nature of neurons (Figure 12, Figure 13, & Figure 14). This mathematical single-equation representation of synaptic neural operation plus nonsynaptic neural operation is not deducible from conventional linearly aggregating neural units such as in Figure 1. First recall that the conventional neural units have usually incorporated single-argument nonlinear functions on neural inputs; the argument is the particular only neural input (dendrite), e.g. Figure 1, and neural inputs are further linearly aggregated by weighted summation. Second recall that HONNU, e.g. QNU or CNU, have a full quadratic Equation1 or cubic Equation 2 polynomial as their aggregating function f_{HONNU} (Figure 14); such design of static HONNU is still simple but crucially increases computational power, i.e. approximating capability and neural input correlation and autocorrelation of a single artificial neuron. The proposal of a single-equation representation of both synaptic neural input aggregation and nonsynaptic neural operation within aggregating function f_{HONNU} is made on theoretical deduction and conforms to the mathematical concept of static HONNU and biological neuronal morphology. Static HONNU are good universal approximators of complex functions due to their polynomial aggregating function v. Let's start with a simplified imagination as if the aggregating function v resulted from a neuron in Figure 12, i.e., a neuron with single dendrites on synaptic junctions. The mathematical notation of neural input aggregating function of a simplified single-dendrite neuron shown in Figure 12 can be then logically understood as being composed for the case of quadratic neural unit in Equation 1

$$\nu = f_{QNU} = \nu_{synaptic} + \nu_{nonsynaptic} = \sum_{i=0}^{n}\sum_{j\geq i}^{n} u_i u_j w_{ij} =$$

$$= \sum_{i=1}^{n}\left(w_{0i}u_i + w_{ii}u_i^2\right) + w_{00} + \sum_{i=1}^{n}\sum_{j>i}^{n}\left(w_{ij}u_i u_j\right) =$$

$$(1)$$

Figure 12. A simplified neuron with single dendrites on synaptic junctions with somatic operation incorporating further interactions of neural inputs; the biological parallel of the decomposition of the aggregating function into synaptic and somatic part for quadratic neural unit (QNU) is shown in Equation1

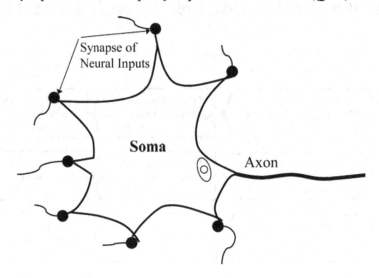

= nonlinear aggregation of neural inputs on synaptic junctions +

+ nonlinear nonsynaptic aggregation (simplified effect of "wireles"

    neural input interferences and further interactions inside soma

    that affect the signal transmitted into axons)

where w_{ij} are neural weights, u_i are neural inputs (dendrites of other neurons), and u_0 is neural bias. The neural operation is simplified to a higher-order polynomial function, and other optional nonlinearity can be involved as well.

To become closer to reality, a synaptic neural junction of course incorporates more neural inputs in case of real neurons as shown in Figure 13 (and Figure 14). In addition to the aggregation of neural inputs on synaptic junctions, the full polynomial notation of f_{HONNU} (the example of cubic neural unit is shown in Equation 2 implies logically the effect also of nonsynaptic aggregation of those combinations of neural inputs that have not been already aggregated apparently in synaptic junctions (Figure 13).

$$\nu = \nu_{synaptic} + \nu_{nonsynaptic} = \sum_{i=0}^{n}\sum_{j=i}^{n}\sum_{k=j}^{n} w_{ijk} u_i u_j u_k \tag{2}$$

This section focused the nonlinearity of the aggregating function of the higher-order nonlinear neural units HONNU which is also common to time-delay dynamic higher order nonlinear neural units (TmD-HONNU). The aggregating nonlinear operation f_{HONNU} is the most significant feature of nonlinearity for classification of static HONNU, and its mathematical notation is well comparable to the structure of a biological neuron as in Figure 13 and in Figure 14. By comparison with the general morphology of biological neurons, the nonlinear aggregating operation of HONNU was shown to be partially related also to the nonsynaptic aggregation of neural inputs and possible somatic processing and not only to

Figure 13. A simplified sketch of a neuron with nonlinear aggregation of neural inputs; the biological parallel of the decomposition of the polynomial aggregating function into synaptic and nonsynaptic part for mathematical notation of the cubic neural unit (CNU) is indicated

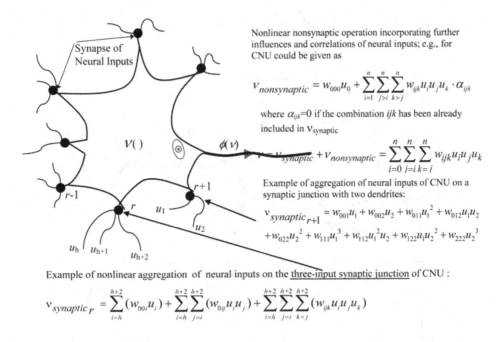

Nonlinear nonsynaptic operation incorporating further influences and correlations of neural inputs; e.g., for CNU could be given as

$$v_{nonsynaptic} = w_{000}u_0 + \sum_{i=1}^{n}\sum_{j>i}^{n}\sum_{k>j}^{n} w_{ijk}u_i u_j u_k \cdot \alpha_{ijk}$$

where $\alpha_{ijk}=0$ if the combination ijk has been already included in $v_{synaptic}$

$$v_{synaptic} + v_{nonsynaptic} = \sum_{i=0}^{n}\sum_{j=i}^{n}\sum_{k=j}^{n} w_{ijk}u_i u_j u_k$$

Example of aggregation of neural inputs of CNU on a synaptic junction with two dendrites:

$$v_{synaptic_{r+1}} = w_{001}u_1 + w_{002}u_2 + w_{011}u_1^2 + w_{012}u_1 u_2$$
$$+ w_{022}u_2^2 + w_{111}u_1^3 + w_{112}u_1^2 u_2 + w_{122}u_1 u_2^2 + w_{222}u_2^3$$

Example of nonlinear aggregation of neural inputs on the three-input synaptic junction of CNU :

$$v_{synaptic_r} = \sum_{i=h}^{h+2}(w_{00i}u_i) + \sum_{i=h}^{h+2}\sum_{j=i}^{h+2}(w_{0ij}u_i u_j) + \sum_{i=h}^{h+2}\sum_{j=i}^{h+2}\sum_{k=j}^{h+2}(w_{ijk}u_i u_j u_k)$$

the conventionally understood pure synaptic neural operation as in case of conventional linearly aggregating neural units.

SUMMARY

Novel artificial neural units called higher-order nonlinear neural units (HONNU), linear time-delay dynamic neural units (TmD-DNU), and time-delay higher-order nonlinear neural units (TmD-HONNU) were briefly introduced as they can be classified according to three distinct attributes discussed in this paper. These attributes are the nonlinearity of the neural aggregating function v, the dynamic order of a unit (i.e. the number of time integrations of v), and the type of implementation of adaptable time delays within a neural unit. All these three attributes are generally distinct and their application-dependent combinations create distinct subclasses of artificial neural units. This novel universal classification of artificial neural units is summarized in Figure 15 where each of the axes represents each of the three attributes. The new neural units introduced in this paper were developed as new cognitive tools that have maximized computational capability, minimized number of neural parameters, and comprehensible mathematical structure allowing researchers to further analyze the knowledge learned by a neural architecture. Some very recent examples, such as results on image processing (Hou et al., 2007) and approximation, control, and evaluation of complex systems (Bukovsky, 2007), show that this new direction in the field of cognitive science, esp. neural networks, is a very promising way.

Figure 14. General structure of a static higher-order nonlinear neural unit (HONNU); where interaction of both synaptic preprocessor of neural inputs and nonsynaptic neural operation is simplified to a higher-order polynomial function f_{HONNU}

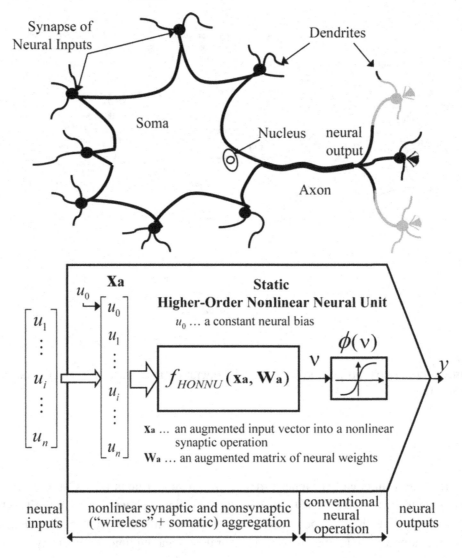

By comparison of the biological neuronal morphology with the full higher-order polynomial neural-input aggregating function, it can be concluded that the mathematic notation of aggregating function of higher-order neural units, i.e. HONNU such as QNU, CNU, TmD-QNU, TmD-CNU, DOE-QNU, DOE-CNU,..., can be understood as both synaptic and nonsynaptic neural interaction. It was shown that polynomial inter-correlation of neural inputs of HONNU can be understood simultaneously as both synaptic and nonsynaptic neural operation also for static higher-order nonlinear neural units (i.e. for HONNU in general). The nonconventional neural architectures, i.e., the higher-order nonlinear neural units, time-delay dynamic neural units and their modifications and combinations, such as time-delay higher-order nonlinear neural units, represent a fresh wind into the field of artificial neural networks, and these new neural units allow us to find some parallels to recent biomedical and neurological discoveries.

Figure 15. Novel classification of basic artificial neural units according to aggregating nonlinearity v, its time integrations (i.e. the dynamic order), and adaptable time-delay implementation; only some of most general types are shown for simplicity; (not all types are shown for simplicity of the picture)

Classification of Basic Types of Nonconventional Neural Units in the Design Space

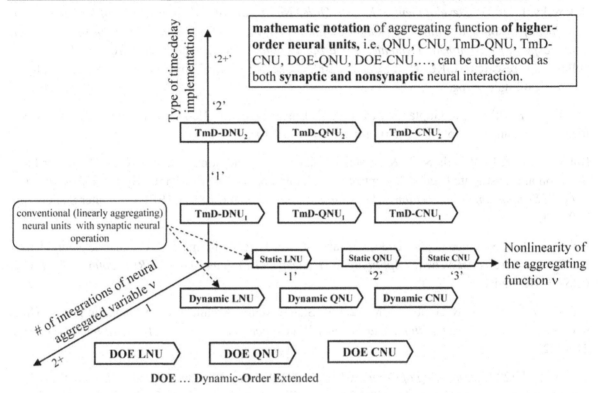

DOE ... Dynamic-Order Extended

It is just a matter of time when recent biological discoveries about nonsynaptic neuronal communications in the human brain will arrive into new widely accepted paradigms that will affect engineering fields and mainly the field of (artificial) neural networks; this paper introduced notation and new generalized classification of nonconventional neural units and is to be one of the first founding works on the new paradigm regarding artificial neurons and mathematical notation of both synaptic and nonsynaptic neural interactions.

ACKNOWLEDGMENT

The work of I. Bukovsky and J. Bila was supported by grant No. MSMT 2B06023. Z.-G. Hou's work was supported in part by the National Natural Science Foundation of China (Grant 60775043). M.M. Gupta's work was supported in part by NSERC of Canada. The work of Noriyasu Homma was supported in part by The Ministry of Education, Culture, Sports, Science and Technology, Japanese Government under Grant-in-Aid for Scientific Research \#19500413 and Okawa Foundation.

REFERENCES

Becerikli, Y., & Oysal, Y. (2007). Modeling and Prediction with a Class of Time Delay Dynamic Neural Networks. *Applied Soft Computing, 7*(4), 1164–1169. doi:10.1016/j.asoc.2006.01.012

Bukovsky, I. (2003). *Development of Higher-Order Nonlinear Neural Units as a Tool for Approximation, Identification and Control of Complex Nonlinear Dynamic Systems and Study of their Application Prospects for Nonlinear Dynamics of Cardiovascular System.* Final Report from NATO Science Fellowships research. (ISRL, UofS, Canada 2003). Czech Technical University in Prague. Faculty of Mechanical Engineering.

Bukovsky, I., Bila, J., & Gupta, M., M. (2005). Linear Dynamic Neural Units with Time Delay for Identification and Control [in Czech]. *Automatizace, 48*(10), 628–635.

Bukovsky, I., & Redlapalli, S. S., & Gupta, M. M. (2003). Quadratic and Cubic Neural Units for Identification and Fast State Feedback Control of Unknown Non-Linear Dynamic Systems. *Fourth International Symposium on Uncertainty Modeling and Analysis ISUMA 2003*, IEEE Computer Society (pp. 330-334).

Bukovsky, I., & Simeunovic, G. (2006). Dynamic-Order-Extended Time-Delay Dynamic Neural Units. *8th Seminar on Neural Network Applications in Electrical Engineering NEUREL-2006, IEEE (SCG) CAS-SP.* Belgrade.

Bukovsky, I., Bila, J., & Gupta, M. M. (2006). Stable Neural Architecture of Dynamic Neural Units with Adaptive Time Delays. *7th International FLINS Conference on Applied Artificial Intelligence* (pp. 215-222).

Bukovsky, I. (2007). *Modeling of Complex Dynamic Systems by Nonconventional Artificial Neural Architectures and Adaptive Approach to Evaluation of Chaotic Time Series.* Ph.D. Thesis. Czech Technical University in Prague. The Faculty of Mechanical Engineering. Czech Republic. Prague.

Duch, W., & Jankowski, N. (1999). Survey of neural transfer functions. *Neural Computing Surveys, 2,* 163–212.

Gupta, M. M., Liang, J., & Homma, N. (2003). *Static and Dynamic Neural Networks: From Fundamentals to Advanced Theory.* IEEE Press and Wiley-Interscience, John Wiley & Sons, Inc.

Hopfield, J. (1982). Neural Networks and Physical Systems with Emergent Collective Computational Abilities. *Proceedings of the National Academy of Sciences of the United States of America, 79,* 2554–2558. doi:10.1073/pnas.79.8.2554

Hou, Z.-G., Song, K.-Y., Gupta, M. M., & Tan, M. (2007). Neural Units with Higher-Order Synaptic Operations for Robotic Image Processing Applications. *Soft Computing, 11*(3), 221–228. doi:10.1007/s00500-006-0064-8

Ivakhnenko, A. G. (1971). Polynomial Theory of Complex Systems. *IEEE Transactions on Systems, Man, and Cybernetics, 1*(4), 364–378. doi:10.1109/TSMC.1971.4308320

McCulloch, W., & Pitts, W. (1943). A logical calculus of the ideas immanent in nervous activity. *The Bulletin of Mathematical Biophysics*, *7*, 115–133. doi:10.1007/BF02478259

Nikolaev, N. Y., & Iba, H. (2003). Learning Polynomial Feedforward Neural Networks by Genetic Programming and Backpropagation. *IEEE Transactions on Neural Networks*, *14*(2), 337–350. doi:10.1109/TNN.2003.809405

Oysal, Y., Sunderam, V. S., van Albada, G. D., Sloot, P. M. A., & Dongarra, J. J. (2005). Time Delay Dynamic Fuzzy Networks for Time Series Prediction. In *ICCS: International Conference on Computational Science*. (Vol. 3516, pp.775-782).

Pineda, F. J. (1988). Dynamics and Architecture for Neural Computation. *Journal of Complexity*, *4*, 216–245. doi:10.1016/0885-064X(88)90021-0

Redlapalli, S., Song, K.-Y., & Gupta, M. M. (2003). Development of Quadratic Neural Unit with Applications to Pattern Classification. *Fourth International Symposium on Uncertainty Modeling and Analysis ISUMA 2003* (pp. 141-146). IEEE Computer Society. Maryland USA.

Song, K.-Y., Redlapalli, S., & Gupta, M. M. (2003). Cubic Neural Units for Control Applications. *Fourth International Symposium on Uncertainty Modeling and Analysis ISUMA 2003*. IEEE Computer Society (pp. 324-329). Maryland. USA.

Vizi, E. S. (2000). Role of High-Affinity Receptors and Membrane Transporters in Nonsynaptic Communication and Drug Action in the Central Nervous System. *Pharmacological Reviews*, *52*(1), 63–90.

Chapter 28
Scaling Behavior of Maximal Repeat Distributions in Genomic Sequences:
A Randomize Test Follow Up Study

J.D. Wang
Asia University, Taiwan

Ka-Lok Ng
Asia University, Taiwan

ABSTRACT

The maximal repeat distribution analysis is redone by plotting the relative frequency of maximal repeat patterns against the rank of the appearance. In almost all of the cases, the rank plots give a better coefficient of determination values than the authors' previous work, i.e. frequency plot was used. A randomized version is repeated for the maximal repeat study; it is found that rank plot regression analysis did not support scaling behavior; hence, the validity of the findings is not due to an artifact.

INTRODUCTION

In our previous study (Wang et al., 2008) it is found that the relative frequency distribution of **maximal repeat sequences** $Log(P(k))$ versus the frequency of appearance $Log(k)$ exhibits **scaling behavior**, i.e. $P(k) \sim k^{\gamma}$. In order to valid the above findings are not due to an artifact, we redone the study by performing the randomize test, and reanalysis the results by plotting the relative frequency of maximal repeat patterns against the rank of the appearance. The rank plots give a better coefficient of determination values than our previous work, i.e. using frequency plot. The **rank plot study** is motivated by Li et al. (Li et al. 2005). The work gave a rigorous presentation on the theory of **scale-free graphs**, and it is pointed out that size-rank plot is more reliable than size-frequency plot.

In section 2, we give a description of the randomize test procedures. Section 3 is the **power-law** study results. Section 4 is the summary and discussion.

DOI: 10.4018/978-1-60566-902-1.ch028

METHOD

The randomize test proceed as the following; (i) the nucleotides positions are randomized while keeping the nucleotide composition fixed, that is the percentage of nucleotides A, T, C and G in the randomize sequence is the same as the original sequence, and (ii) the maximum repeat distribution analysis is repeated five times via the external memory approach (Wang 2006), the average scaling exponent and coefficient of determination are computed.

RESULTS

In this section, we present the maximal repeats frequencies study in different **genomic sequences**. To implement our analysis using the power-law model, we first record the total number of identified maximal repeats (N) that are appear in the genomic sequence under study. For each frequency of appearance of maximal repeat, a, we record the total number ($N(a)$) of maximal repeat patterns that have such a frequency of appearance in that genomic sequence. The frequency of appearance of maximal repeat a is ranked in descending order, for example, the frequency of appearance of maximal repeat two ($a=2$) is ranked number one, that is k equals to one. We divide number $N(a)$ by N and call it $P(k)$, and then plot $Log\,P(k)$ against $Log(k)$, where k denotes the rank of a with non-zero $P(k)$. Power law states that $P(k) \sim k^\gamma$. $P(k)$ is the fraction of the total number of maximal repeats with rank k ($1 \leq k \leq 999$) in the genomic sequence under study, for example, $P(902)$ is the fraction of maximal repeat patterns among the total number of maximal repeat patterns that appears in the genomic sequence one thousand times, and 1000 is ranked 902. The length of the maximal repeat pattern we search ranges from 3 to 50 bps.

Table 1 is the results of the regression analysis of the genomic sequences chosen from different groups of taxa. For each of the genomic sequences, we give the result for the total genomic sequence length, exponent of the power-law and r^2. GenBank ID column label with 'chromosomes' means the power-law result obtained with the species' chromosomes length assembled together. Regression analysis determines that the exponent γ ranges from 1.81 to 2.06 (the same range as our previous work [1]), and all the 56 species' data are well fitted by the power-law distributions (the date reject the null hypothesis of uniform distribution with $p\text{-}value \ll 10^{-6}$). All the 56 species have a r^2 value larger than 0.938.

Table 2 is the results of the regression analysis of plant chloroplast genome sequences. Regression analysis determines that γ lies between 1.79 and 1.88, and all the 17 species' data are well fitted by the power-law distributions ($r^2 > 0.930$).

Results of the maximal repeat distributions regression analysis of plant mitochondria genome sequences is the same as our previous work (Wang et al. 2008) reported, so it is omitted.

In order to valid the above findings are not due to an artifact, twelve genome sequences are picked (ten from nucleus, one from chloroplast, and one from mitochondria) to perform the randomize test, and the results are reported in Table 3. It is found that randomized studies do not provide consistent results for the frequency-rank plot regression analysis, that is, some sequences give poor r^2 values while reasonable values are obtained in other cases. For instance, the average exponent of the randomized *E.coli* K-12 sequence is 2.13 with an average r^2 value of 0.490, whereas the yeast chromosome IV has an average exponent of 1.99 with an average r^2 value of 0.840.

Table 1. Results of the maximal repeat power-law distributions study for genomic sequences chosen from different groups of taxa (with their GenBank accession numbers listed). For each of the genomic sequence, results for the length of the chromosome (bp), exponent of the power-law (γ) and the coefficient of determination (r²) are listed

Species	GenBank ID	bp	γ	r^2
Fungi				
S. cerevisiae	NC_001133	230207	1.84	0.951
	NC_001134	813138	1.94	0.949
	NC_001135	316617	1.86	0.948
	NC_001136	1531912	1.99	0.959
	NC_001137	576869	1.90	0.953
	NC_001138	270148	1.85	0.946
	NC_001139	1090944	1.97	0.953
	NC_001140	562639	1.90	0.946
	NC_001141	439885	1.88	0.943
	NC_001142	745445	1.93	0.947
	NC_001143	666445	1.91	0.947
	NC_001144	1078173	1.97	0.953
	NC_001145	924430	1.95	0.951
	NC_001146	784328	1.93	0.948
	NC_001147	1091285	1.96	0.955
	NC_001148	940061	1.95	0.951
S. cerevisiae	16 chromosomes	12070527	2.00	0.988
S. pombe	NC_003421	5570797	2.01	0.957
	NC_003423	4468099	2.03	0.968
	NC_003424	2456786	2.02	0.974
S. pombe	3 chromosomes	12495682	1.99	0.990
Eremothecium gossypii	NC_005782-9 (8 chromosomes)	8741434	2.02	0.954
Candida glabrata	NC_005967	485192	1.88	0.938
Kluyveromyces lactis	NC_006037	1062590	1.97	0.956
Debaryomyces hansenii	NC_006043-49	1249565	1.97	0.953
Yarrowia lipolytica	NC_006067-72	2303261	1.93	0.940
Encephalitozoon cuniculi	NC_003229	197426	1.82	0.948
Encephalitozoon cuniculi	NC_003230	194439	1.81	0.944

continued on the following page

Table 1. continued

Species	GenBank ID	bp	γ	r²
Encephalito-zoon cuniculi	NC_003229-38,42 (11 chromo-somes)	2497519	1.99	0.956
Algae				
Cryptomonas (Guillardia theta)	NC_002751-53 (3 chromo-somes)	551264	1.91	0.944
Protozoa				
Plasmodium falciparum 3D7	NC_000521, 910, 4314-18, 4325-31 (14 chromo-somes)	22820308	1.97	0.994
Archaea				
	NC_003901	4096345	2.03	0.965
	NC_003552	5751492	2.04	0.974
	NC_003551	1694969	1.99	0.951
	NC_003413	1908256	2.00	0.958
	NC_000868	1765118	2.01	0.959
	NC_002689	1584804	1.98	0.952
Bacteria - Gram nega-tives				
Chlamydiae	NC_005043	1225935	1.98	0.955
	NC_002491	1226565	1.98	0.953
	NC_002620	1072950	1.98	0.953
	NC_002179	1229858	1.99	0.953
	NC_000922	1230230	1.98	0.955
	NC_005861	2414465	2.01	0.956
Cyanobacte-ria	NC_005125	4659019	2.02	0.972
	NC_005072	1657990	1.99	0.956
	NC_005071	2410873	2.00	0.953
	NC_005070	2434428	1.98	0.957
	NC_005042	1751080	2.00	0.953
	NC_004113	2593857	1.99	0.961
Spirochaetes	NC_006156	904246	1.95	0.951
	NC_005823	4277185	2.04	0.967
	NC_002967	2843201	2.01	0.959
	NC_000919	1138011	2.00	0.943

continued on the following page

Table 1. continued

Species	GenBank ID	bp		γ		r^2	
	NC_001318	910724		1.95		0.952	
Bacteria - Gram positives							
Firmicutes (low G+C)	NC_002662	2365589		2.01		0.961	
	NC_002758	2878040		2.01		0.961	
	NC_002745	2814816		2.02		0.961	
	NC_002737	1852441		1.99		0.957	
	NC_002162	751719		1.94		0.949	
	NC_002570	4202353		2.02		0.966	
Actinobacteridae (high G+C)	NC_002945	4345492		2.03		0.969	
	NC_002935	2488635		1.95		0.950	
	NC_006085	2560265		2.00		0.956	
	NC_006087	2584158		2.03		0.962	
	NC_000962	4411529		2.03		0.971	
Proteobacteria							
α-Proteobacteria	NC_003103	1268755		1.98		0.949	
	NC_002696	4016947		2.02		0.973	
S. Meliloti	NC_003037	1354226		1.99		0.957	
	NC_003047	3654135		2.02		0.965	
γ-Proteobacteria	NC_003198	4809037		2.04		0.970	
	NC_003143	4653728		2.06		0.965	
	NC_000907	1830138		2.00		0.954	
ε-Proteobacteria	NC_000915	1667867		2.00		0.952	
Bacteria							
E.coli K-12	NC_000913	4639675		2.05		0.968	
Plant							
Arabidopsis thaliana	NC_003070, 71, 74-76 (5 chromosomes)	119186497		1.99		0.998	
	NC_3070	30432563		1.92		0.949	
	NC_3071	19705359		1.99		0.993	

continued on the following page

Table 1. continued

Species	GenBank ID	bp		γ		r^2
	NC_3074	23470805	1.99		0.994	
	NC_3075	18585042	2.00		0.994	
	NC_3076	26992728	2.02		0.991	
Nematodes						
C. elegan	NC_003279-84 (6 chromosomes)	100096025	1.99		0.998	
	NC_003279	15072419	2.01		0.991	
	NC_003280	15279316	2.01		0.992	
	NC_003281	13783681	2.01		0.989	
	NC_003282	17493784	2.01		0.991	
	NC_003283	20919398	2.01		0.994	
	NC_003284	17718852	2.02		0.991	

Table 2. Results of the maximal repeat power-law distributions study for plant chloroplast genomic sequences (with their GenBank accession numbers listed). For each of the genomic sequence, results for the length of the chromosome (bp), exponent of the power-law (γ) and the coefficient of determination (r^2) are listed

Species	GenBank ID	bp	γ	r^2
Psilotum nudum	NC_003386	138829	1.79	0.934
Medicago truncatula	NC_003119	124033	1.80	0.944
Arabidopsis thaliana	NC_000932	154478	1.81	0.938
Marchantia polymorpha	NC_001319	121024	1.79	0.939
Oryza sativa	NC_001320	134525	1.80	0.943
Pinus thunbergii	NC_001631	119707	1.79	0.942
Zea mays	NC_001666	140384	1.81	0.944
Nicotiana tabacum	NC_001879	155939	1.82	0.949
Spinacia oleracea	NC_002202	150725	1.81	0.938
Oenothera elata subsp. hookeri	NC_002693	163935	1.82	0.931
Lotus japonicus	NC_002694	150519	1.81	0.936
Triticum aestivum	NC_002762	134545	1.80	0.939
Porphyra purpurea	NC_000925	191028	1.83	0.941
Nephroselmis olivacea	NC_000927	200799	1.82	0.945
Chlamydomonas reinhardtii	NC_005353	203828	1.88	0.948
Gracilaria tenuistipitata var. liui	NC_006137	183883	1.85	0.930
Panax ginseng	NC_006290	156318	1.81	0.935

Table 3. Results of the maximal repeat power-law distributions study for randomized sequences. For each of the genomic sequence, results for the average exponent of the power-law (γ) and the coefficient of determination (r^2), maximal length of the maximal repeats in randomize sequence, L_{rand}, and the maximal length of the maximal repeats in raw genome sequence, L, are listed in the last four columns respectively

Species	GenBank ID	$\gamma\gamma$	r^2	L_{rand}	L
E. coli K-12	NC_000913	2.13	0.490	22	50
Arabidopsis thaliana	NC_003070	2.26	0.581	26	50
C.elegan	NC_003279	1.97	0.610	21	50
S.pombe	NC_003421	2.00	0.713	21	50
Firmicutes	NC_002662	2.00	0.746	22	50
α-Proteobacteria	NC_002696	2.02	0.787	24	50
Actinobacteridae	NC_000962	2.01	0.818	22	50
Archaea	NC_003901	2.12	0.835	23	50
Cyanobacteria	NC_00 5125	1.98	0.830	22	50
S. cerevisiae (IV)	NC_001136	1.99	0.840	21	50
Arabidopsis thaliana (chloroplast)	NC_00932	1.45	0.807	19	33
Nicotiana tabacum (mitochondria)	NC_006581	1.86	0.845	19	50

Figure 1 shows the randomize version of the frequency-rank plot for *E.coli* K-12, which obviously suggested that it did not support scaling behavior.

Another difference between randomized sequence and the raw sequence is the distribution of the length of maximum repeat patterns. Distributions of the length of maximum repeat patterns of raw genome sequences have a longer tail when compare to their randomized counterparts. The maximum of the lengths of maximal repeats, L, in any particular species is at least 50 bps long (our study only search for pattern up to 50 bps long) except chloroplast genomes, whereas the maximum of the lengths of maximal repeats in randomized sequences, L_{rand}, is least than 26 bps long (Table 3). This is a reasonable finding because one would expect that it is unlikely to find maximum repeat with a very long length in randomized sequence.

SUMMARY AND DISCUSSION

We re-analyze the maximal repeat patterns for a wide range of species and find that the relative frequency distribution of maximal repeat sequences *P(k)* versus the rank of appearance *k* exhibits scaling behavior ($P(k) \sim k^\gamma$). Regression analysis provides very good evidence ($r^2 > 0.938$ for the nucleus chromosome sequences) supporting the relative frequency-rank distributions of maximal repeats are well described by the power law with an exponent $1.81 \sim 2.06$. Furthermore, this scaling behavior also holds for plant chloroplast and mitochondria genome sequences with a slightly smaller exponent, which is $1.79 \sim 1.88$

Figure 1. Randomize version of the logarithm of the probability of the frequency of maximal repeats P(k) vs the logarithm of rank of appearance Log(k) for E.coli K-12

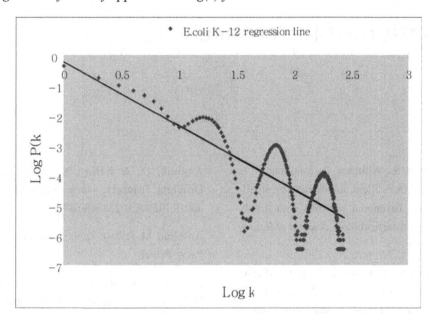

$(r^2 > 0.930)$ and $1.60 \sim 1.82$ $(r^2 > 0.898)$ respectively. Randomized studies do not provide consistent results, hence, valid the maximal repeat rank distribution findings are not due to an artifact.

ACKNOWLEDGMENT

Dr. Ka-Lok Ng would like to thank the National Science Council (NSC) for financial support. Dr .Ng's work is supported by NSC grant number NSC 97-2221-E-468-010. Dr. Wang would express thanks to the financial support by the Asia University research project grant number 97-I-07.

REFERENCES

Li, L., Alderson, D., Doyle, J. C., & Willinger, W. (2005). Towards a Theory of Scale-Free Graphs: Definition, Properties, and Implications. *Internet Math*, *2*(4), 431–523.

Wang, J. D. (2006). External memory approach to compute the maximal repeats across classes from DNA sequences. *Asian Journal of Health and Information Sciences*, *1*(3), 276–295.

Wang, J. D., Liu, H.-C., Tsai, J., & Ng, K.-L. (2008). Scaling Behavior of Maximal Repeat Distributions in Genomic Sequences. *International Journal of Cognitive Informatics and Natural Intelligence*, *2*(3), 31–42.

Compilation of References

Achard, S., Salvador, R., Whitcher, B., Suckling, J., & Bullmore, E. (2006). A resilient, low-frequency, small-world human brain functional network with highly connected association cortical hubs. *Journal of Neuroscience, 26*(1), 63-72.

Agrawal, R., Imielinsky, T., & Swami, A. (1993). Mining association rules between sets of items in large databases. In *Proceedings of the 1993 International Conference on Management of Data (SIGMOD 93)*(pp. 207-216).

Aho, A. V., Sethi, R. & Ullman, J. D. (1985). *Compilers: Principles, techniques, and tools.* New York: Addison-Wesley.

Alexandros, K., & Melanie, H. (2001). Model selection via meta-learning: A comparative study. *International Journal on AI Tools, 10*(4), 444–455.

Amir, N., & Ron, S. (1998). Towards an automatic classification of emotions in speech. In *Proceedings of 5th International Conference on Spoken Language Processing ICSLP 98, Sydney, Australia, November/December* (Vol. 3, p. 555).

Anderson, J. R. (1983). *The architecture of cognition.* Cambridge, MA: Harvard University Press.

Anderson, J. R. (1991). Is human cognition adaptive? *Behavioral and Brain Science, 14,* 71-517.

Angluin, D. (1988). Queries and concept learning. *Machine Learning, 2,* 319–342.

Angluin, D. (2004). Queries revisited. *Theoretical Computer Science, 313,* 175–194. doi:10.1016/j.tcs.2003.11.004

Angluin, D., & Krikis, M. (2003). Learning from Different Teachers. *Machine Learning, 51,* 137–163. doi:10.1023/A:1022854802097

Anselme, M. (1989). *Après la morale, quelles valeurs?* Paris: Privat.

Aronson, R. B., Edmunds, P. J., Precht, W. F., Swanson, D. W., & Levitan, D. R. (1994). Large-scale, long-term monitoring of Caribbean coral reefs: Simple, quick, inexpensive techniques. *Atoll Research Bulletin, 421,* 1-19.

Ashby, W. R. (1958). Requisite variety and implications for control of complex systems. *Cybernetica, 1,* 83-99.

Ashby, W. R. (1962) Principles of the self-organizing system. In von H. Foerster & G. Zopf (Eds.), *Principles of self-organization* (pp. 255-278). Oxford, England: Pergamon.

Assayag, G., Feichtinger, H. G., & Rodrigues, J.-F. (2002). *Mathematics and music: A Diderot mathematical forum.* Berlin/New York: Springer.

Astolfi, J.-P., Giordan, A., Gohau, G., Host, V., & Martinand, J.-L. Rumelhard, G., et al. (1978). *Quelle éducation scientifique pour quelle société?* Paris: Puf l'éducateur.

Baader, F., Calvanese, D., McGuinness, D. L., Nardi, D., & Patel-Schneider, P. F. (2003). *The description logic handbook: Theory, implementation, applications.* Cambridge, UK: Cambridge University Press.

Bachelard, G. (1934). *Le Nouvel Esprit Scientifique.* Paris: Broché (2003).

Backhouse, R. C. (1968). *Program construction and verification.* London: Prentice Hall International.

Backus, J. (1978). Can programming be liberated from the van Neumann Style? *Communications of the ACM, 21*(8), 613-641.

Baeten, J. C. M., Bergstra, J. A. (1991). Real time process algebra. *Formal Aspects of Computing, 3,* 142-188.

Barber, B., & Hamilton, H. (2003). Extracting share frequent itemsets with infrequent subsets. *Data Mining and Knowledge Discovery, 7,* 153–185. doi:10.1023/A:1022419032620

Barr, A. & Feigenbaum, E. (1982). *The handbook of artificial intelligence.* William Kaufmann.

Barr, A. (1981). Superquadrics and angle-preserving transformations. *IEEE Transactions on Computer Graphics and Applications, 1*(1), 11-23.

Bath Iris Image Database (n.d.). Bath University. Retrieved from http://www.bath.ac.uk/elec-eng/research/sipg/irisweb/index.htm

Battle, J., Ridao, P., Garcia, R., Carreras, M., Cufi, X., El-Fakdi, A., et al. (2004). *URIS: Underwater robotic intelligent system.* In Automar, Instiuto de Automatica Industrial, CSIC, J. Aranda, M. A. Armada, & J. M. de la Cruz (Eds.) pp 177-203.

Bazan, J. G. (1998). A comparison of dynamic and non-dynamic rough set methods for extracting laws from decision tables. In L. Polkowski & A. Skowron (Eds.), *Rough sets in knowledge discovery 1* (pp. 321-365). Heidelberg, Germany: Physica-Verlag.

Bazan, J. G., Nguyen, H. S., Nguyen, S. H., Synak, P., & Wróblewski, J.(2000). Rough set algorithms in classification problems. In L. Polkowski, S. Tsumoto, & T. Y. Lin (Eds.), *Rough set methods and applications* (pp. 49-88). Heidelberg, Germany: Physica-Verlag.

Becerikli, Y., & Oysal, Y. (2007). Modeling and Prediction with a Class of Time Delay Dynamic Neural Networks. *Applied Soft Computing, 7*(4), 1164–1169. doi:10.1016/j.asoc.2006.01.012

Beck, K., Coplien, J. O., Crocker, R., & Dominick, L. (1996, March). Industrial experience with design patterns. In *Proceedings of the 19ᵗʰ Intel. Conf. on Software Engineering,* (pp. 103-114). Berlin: IEEE CS Press.

Beinlich, I., Suermondt, G., Chavez, R., & Cooper, G. (1989). The ALARM monitoring system: A case study with two probabilistic inference techniques for belief networks. In *Proceedings of the 2nd European Conference on AI and Medicine,* (Vol. 38, pp. 247-256). Berlin: Springer-Verlag.

Bell, A., & Sejnowski, T. (1995). An information-maximization approach to blind separation and blind deconvolution. *Neural Computation, 7,* 1129-1159.

Bender, E. A. (1996). *Mathematical methods in artificial intelligence.* Los Alamitos, CA: IEEE CS Press.

Bergevin, R., & Levine, M. (1993). Generic object recognition: Building and matching coarse descriptions from line drawings. *IEEE Transactions on Pattern Analysis and Machine Intelligence, 15*(1), 19-36.

Berkeley, I. S. N., Dawson, M. R. W., Medler, D. A., Schopflocher, D. P., & Hornsby, L. (1995). Density plots of hidden value unit activations reveal interpretable bands. *Connection Science, 7,* 167–186. doi:10.1080/09540099550039336

Bernstein, A., & Provost, F. (2001). An intelligent assistant for the knowledge discovery process. In *Proceedings of IJCAI-01 workshop on wrappers for performance enhancement in kdd.*

Berrer, H., & Keller, I. P. J. (2000). Evaluation of machine-learning algorithm ranking advisors. In *Proceedings of the PKDD 2000 workshop on data mining, decision support, meta-learning and ilp* (pp. 1-13). Forum for Practical Problem Presentation and Prospective Solutions.

Bharucha, J. J. (1999). Neural nets, temporal composites, and tonality. In D. Deutsch (Ed.), *The Psychology Of music* (2ⁿᵈ ed., pp. 413-440). San Diego, CA: Academic Press.

Bharucha, J. J., & Todd, P. M. (1989). Modeling the perception of tonal structure with neural nets. *Computer Music Journal, 13*(4), 44–53. doi:10.2307/3679552

Biederma, I., & Gerhardstein, P. (1993). Recognizing depth-rotated objects: Evidence for 3D viewpoint invariance. *Journal of Experimental Psychology: Human Perception and Performance, 19*, 1162-1182.

Biederman, I. (1987). Recognition-by-components: A theory of human image understanding. *Psychological Review, 94*, 115-147.

Bjorner, D. (2000, November). Pinnacles of software engineering: 25 years of formal methods. In Y. Wang & D. Patel (Eds.), *Annals of software engineering: An international journal, 10*, 11-66.

Bjorner, D., & Jones, C. B. (1982). *Formal specification and software development*. Englewood Cliffs, NJ: Prentice Hall.

Bocheck, P., & Chang, S. F. (1998). *Contend-based VBR traffic modeling and its application to dynamic network resource allocation* (Research Report 48c-98-20). Columbia University.

Boehm, B. W. (1987). Improving software productivity. *IEEE Computer, 20*(9), 43.

Boles, W., & Boashah, B. (1998). A human identification technique using images of the Iris and Wavelet transform. *IEEE Transactions on Signal Processing, 46*, 1185–1188. doi:10.1109/78.668573

Borges, D. L., & Fisher, R. B. (1997). Class-based recognition of 3D objects represented by volumetric primitives. *Image and Vision Computing, 15*(8), 655-664.

Bosch, J. (1996). Relations as object model components. *Journal of Programming Languages, 4*(1), 39-61.

Boucher, A., & Gerth, R. (1987). A timed model for extended communicating sequential processes. In *Proceedings of ICALP'87* (LNCS 267). Springer.

Boulton-Lewis, G., Smith, D., McCrindle, A., Burnett, P., & Campbell, K. (2001). Secondary teachers' conceptions of teaching and learning. *Learning and Instruction, 11*, 35–51. doi:10.1016/S0959-4752(00)00014-1

Boykov, Y., & Kolmogorov, V. (2004). An experimental comparison of min-cut/max-flow algorithms for energy minimization in vision. In IEEE PAMI, 26, 1124-1137.

Brachmann, R., & Anand, T. (1996). The process of knowledge discovery in databases: a human- centered approach. *Advances in Knowledge Discovery and Data Mining* (pp. 37-57). Menlo Park, CA: AAAI Press and MIT Press.

Brazdil, P., & Soares, C. (2000). A comparison of ranking methods for classification algorithm selection. In *Ecml '00: Proceedings of the 11th European conference on machine learning* (pp. 63–74). London, UK: Springer-Verlag.

Brin, S., Motwani, R., & Silverstein, C. (1997). Beyond market baskets: generalizing association rules to correlations. In *Proceedings of ACM SIGMOD International Conference on Management of Data* (pp. 265-276).

Broek, E. L., van den, Rikxoort, E. M. van, & Schouten, Th.E. (2005). Human-centered object-based image retrieval. *Lecture Notes in Computer Science* (Advances in Pattern Recognition), (Vol. 3687, pp. 492-501).

Brooks, R. A. (1990). Intelligence without representation. *Artificial Intelligence, 47*, 139-159.

Brooks, R. A. (1991). Intelligence without reasoning. In *Proceedings of IJCAI'91*, Sydney.

Brown, L. E., Tsamardinos, I., & Aliferis, C. F. (2005). A comparison of novel and state-of-the-art polynomial bayesian network learning algorithms. *AAAI* 2005, 739-745.

Bruner, J. S., Goodnow, J. J., & Austin, G. A. (1956). *A study of thinking*. New York: Wiley.

Bukovsky, I. (2003). *Development of Higher-Order Nonlinear Neural Units as a Tool for Approximation, Identification and Control of Complex Nonlinear Dynamic Systems and Study of their Application Prospects for Nonlinear Dynamics of Cardiovascular System*. Final Report from NATO Science Fellowships research. (ISRL, UofS, Canada 2003). Czech Technical University in Prague. Faculty of Mechanical Engineering.

Bukovsky, I. (2007). *Modeling of Complex Dynamic Systems by Nonconventional Artificial Neural Architectures and Adaptive Approach to Evaluation of Chaotic*

Time Series. Ph.D. Thesis. Czech Technical University in Prague. The Faculty of Mechanical Engineering. Czech Republic. Prague.

Bukovsky, I., & Redlapalli, S. S., & Gupta, M. M. (2003). Quadratic and Cubic Neural Units for Identification and Fast State Feedback Control of Unknown Non-Linear Dynamic Systems. *Fourth International Symposium on Uncertainty Modeling and Analysis ISUMA 2003*, IEEE Computer Society (pp. 330-334).

Bukovsky, I., & Simeunovic, G. (2006). Dynamic-Order-Extended Time-Delay Dynamic Neural Units. *8th Seminar on Neural Network Applications in Electrical Engineering NEUREL-2006, IEEE (SCG) CAS-SP.* Belgrade.

Bukovsky, I., Bila, J., & Gupta, M. M. (2006). Stable Neural Architecture of Dynamic Neural Units with Adaptive Time Delays. *7th International FLINS Conference on Applied Artificial Intelligence* (pp. 215-222).

Bukovsky, I., Bila, J., & Gupta, M., M. (2005). Linear Dynamic Neural Units with Time Delay for Identification and Control [in Czech]. *Automatizace, 48*(10), 628–635.

Buntine, W. (1993). Learning classification trees. In *Artificial intelligence frontiers in statistics* (pp. 182-201). London: Chapman and Hall.

Buschmann, F. (1995). *The MasterSlave Pattern, pattern languages of program design.* Addison-Wesley.

Bziau, J. Y. (2006). Many-valued and Kripke Semantics. In J. van Benthem (Ed.), *The Age of Alternative Logics* (pp. 89-101). Dordrecht: Springer.

Calhoun, C., & Solomon, R. C. (1984). *What is an emotion? Classic readings in philosophical psychology.* New York: Oxford University Press.

Cardelli, L. & Wegner, P. (1985). On understanding types, data abstraction and polymorphism. *ACM Computing Surveys, 17*(4), 471-522.

Cardoso, J. F. (1999). Higher-order contrasts for independent component analysis. *Neural Computation, 11*, 157-192.

Cardoso, J. F. (n.d.). JADE for Matlab (Version 1.5) [Computer software]. Retrieved February 2, 2005, from http://www.tsi.enst.fr/~cardoso/Algo/Jade/jadeR.m

Casey, M. A. (1999). Understanding musical sound with forward models and physical models. In N. Griffith & P. M. Todd (Eds.), *Musical networks: Parallel distributed perception and performace* (pp. 45-61). London: MIT Press.

CASIA Iris Image Database version 1.0. (n.d.). Institute of Automation (IA), Chinese Academy of Sciences (CAS). Retrieved from http://www.sinobiometrics.com

Cerone, A. (2000). *Process algebra versus axiomatic specification of a real-time protocol* (LNCS 1816, pp. 57-67). Berlin, Germany: Springer.

Chalmers, A. F. (1976). Qu'est-ce que la science? (translated from *What is this Thing Called Science? An Assessment of the Nature and Status of Science and its* []). Paris: La Découverte.]. *Methods (San Diego, Calif.)*, 1988.

Chan, C., Kinsner, W., Wang, Y., & Miller, M. (Eds.). (2004, August). *Proceedings of the Third IEEE International Conference on Cognitive Informatics (ICCI'04).* Los Alamitos, CA: IEEE Computer Society Press.

Chan, K.-W., & Elliott, R. (2004). Relational analysis of personal epistemology and conceptions about teaching and learning. *Teaching and Teacher Education, 20*, 817–831. doi:10.1016/j.tate.2004.09.002

Chavalarias, D. (1997). *La thèse de popper est-elle réfutable?* Unpublished doctoral dissertation, CREA - CNRS/Ecole Polytechnique.

Chen, Y. H., & Yao, Y. Y. (2007). A multiview approach for intelligent data analysis based on data operators. *Information Sciences, 178*(1), 1–20. doi:10.1016/j.ins.2007.08.011

Chen, Y., & Yao, Y. Y. (2005). Formal concept analysis based on hierarchical class analysis. In *Proceedings of the Fourth IEEE International Conference on Cognitive Informatics (ICCI'05)* (pp. 285-292). Irvin, CA: IEEE CS Press.

Chickering, D., Meek, C., & Heckerman, D. (2003). Large-sample learning of bayesian networks is np-hard. In *Proceedings of the 19th Annual Conference on Uncertainty in Artificial Intelligence* (UAI-03), (pp. 124–133).

Choe, Y. (2001). *Perceptual grouping in a self-organizing map of spiking neurons*. Doctoral dissertation thesis, Department of Computer Sciences, The University of Texas at Austin.

Chomsky, N. (1956). Three models for the description of languages. *I.R.E. Transactions on Information Theory, 2*(3), 113-124.

Chomsky, N. (1957). *Syntactic structures*. The Hague, The Netherlands: Mouton.

Chomsky, N. (1982). *Some concepts and consequences of the theory of government and binding*. Cambridge, MA: MIT Press

Churchland, P. S., & Sejnowski, T. J. (1992). *The computational brain*. Cambridge, MA: MIT Press.

Codin, R., Missaoui, R., & Alaoui, H. (1995). Incremental concept formation algorithms based on Galois (concept) lattices. *Computational Intelligence, 11*(2), 246-267.

Colins, A. M., & Loftus, E. F. (1975). A Spreading-activation theory of semantic memory. *Psychological Review, 82,* 407-428.

Collier, R. (1992). A comment of the prediction of prosody. In G. Bailly, C. Benoit, & T.R. Sawallis (Eds.), *Talking machines: Theories, models, and designs*. Amsterdam: Elsevier Science Publishers.

Compton, P., & Jansen, B. (1988). Knowledge in context: a strategy for expert system maintenance. In *Proceedings of the Second Australian Joint Conference of Artificial Intelligence* (pp. 292-306).

Cornelius, R. R. (1996). *The science of emotion. Research and tradition in the psychology of emotion*. Upper Saddle River, NJ: Prentice Hall.

Corsetti E., Montanari, A., & Ratto, E. (1991). Dealing with different time granularities in formal specifications of real-time systems. *The Journal of Real-Time Systems, 3*(2), 191-215.

Cover T. M. & Hart P. E. (1967). Nearest neighbor pattern classification. *IEEE Transactions on Information Theory, January*(IT-13), 21-27.

Cover, T. M., & Thomas, J. A. (1991). *Elements of information theory*. New York: Wiley.

Cowie, R., & Douglas-Cowie, E. (1996). Automatic statistical analysis of the signal and prosodic signs of emotion in speech. In *Proceedings of Fourth International Conference on Spoken Language Processing ICSLP 96, Philadelphia PA, USA, October* (pp.1989-1992).

Craik, K. (1943). *The Nature of Explanation*. New York: Cambridge University Press.

Cries, D. (1981). *The science of programming*. New York: Springer-Verlag.

Csákány, P., & Wallace A. M. (2003). Representation and Classification of 3-D Objects. *IEEE Transactions on Systems, Man, and Cybernetics - Part B: Cybernetics, 33*(4), 638-647.

Cummings, K., & Clements, M. (1995). Analysis of the glottal excitation of emotionally styled and stressed speech. *The Journal of the Acoustical Society of America, 98*(1), 88–98. doi:10.1121/1.413664

Dagum, P., & Luby, M. (1993). Approximating probabilistic inference in bayesian belief networks is np-hard. *Artificial Intelligence, 60,* 141-153.

Dale, C. J., & Zee, H. (1992). Software productivity metrics: Who needs them? *Information and Software Technology, 34*(11), 731-738.

Dansereau, R. (2001, May). *Progressive image transmission using fractal and wavelet complexity measures*. Doctoral Thesis, Department of Electrical & Computer Engineering, University of Manitoba, Winnipeg.

Dansereau, R., & Kinsner, W. (1998, May). Progressive transmission of images using wavelets: Evaluation using the Rényi generalized entropy. In *Proceedings of the IEEE Canadian Conference on Elec. and Comp. Eng. (CCECE98)*, (pp. 273-276).

Dansereau, R., & Kinsner, W. (1999, May). Rényi generalized entropy analysis of images from a progressive wavelet image transmission. In *Proceedings of the IEEE Canadian Conf. on Elec. and Comp. Eng. (CCECE99)*.

Dansereau, R., & Kinsner, W. (2000, May). Progressive image transmission using wavelet packets guided by metrics. In *Proceedings of the Mathematical Modelling and Scientific Computing*.

Dansereau, R., & Kinsner, W. (2001, May) New relative multifractal dimension measures. In *Proceedings of the IEEE International Conference Acoustics, Speech and Signal Processing, ICASSP2001*, (Vol. 3, pp. 1741-1744).

Dartnell, C. (2008). *Conception d'un Cadre Formel d'Interaction pour la Découverte Scientifique Computationelle*. Ph.D. thesis, Université Montpellier 2.

Dartnell, C., & Sallantin, J. (2005). Assisting scientific discovery with an adaptive problem solver. Springer Berlin / Heidelberg: *Discovery science*, 99-112.

Dartnell, C., Martin, E., & Sallantin, J. (2008). Learning from Each Other. Springer Berlin / Heidelberg: *Discovery science*, 148-159.

Dartnell, C., Martin, E., Hagège, H., & Sallantin, J. (2008). Human Discovery and Machine Learning. *International Journal of Cognitive Informatics and Natural Intelligence*, 2, 55–69.

Darwin, C. (1965). *The expression of emotions in man and animals*. John Murray, 1872, reprinted by University of Chicago Press.

Dash, M., & Liu, H. (2003). Consistency-based search in feature selection. *Artificial Intelligence*, *151*(1-2), 155–176. doi:10.1016/S0004-3702(03)00079-1

Daubechies, I. (1990, September). Orthonormal bases of compactly supported wavelets. *IEEE Trans. Inform. Theory, 36*(5), 961-1005.

Daugman, J. (1993). High confidence visual recognition of persons by a test of statistical independence. *IEEE Transactions on Pattern Analysis and Machine Intelligence*, *15*(11), 1148–1161. doi:10.1109/34.244676

Daugman, J. (1999). *Biometric Decision Landscape* (Technical Report No. TR482).University of Cambridge Computer Laboratory.

Daugman, J. (2001). Statistical richness of visual phase information update on recognizing Persons by Iris Patterns. *International Journal of Computer Vision*, *45*(1), 25–38. doi:10.1023/A:1012365806338

David-Néel, A. (1977). *Le bouddhisme du Bouddha*. Paris: Pocket (1989)

Dawson, M. R. W. (1998). *Understanding cognitive science*. Malden, MA: Blackwell.

Dawson, M. R. W. (2004). *Minds and machines: Connectionism and Psychological modelling*. Malden, MA: Blackwell.

Dawson, M. R. W. (2005). *Connectionism: A hands-on approach* (1st ed.). Oxford, UK/Malden, MA: Blackwell.

Dawson, M. R. W., & Boechler, P. M. (2007). Representing an intrinsically nonmetric space of compass directions in an artificial neural network. *International Journal of Cognitive Informatics and Natural Intelligence*, *1*, 53–65.

Dawson, M. R. W., & Piercey, C. D. (2001). On the subsymbolic nature of a PDP architecture that uses a nonmonotonic activation function. *Minds and Machines*, *11*, 197–218. doi:10.1023/A:1011237306312

Dawson, M. R. W., & Schopflocher, D. P. (1992). Modifying the generalised delta rule to train networks of nonmonotonic processors for pattern classification. *Connection Science*, *4*, 19–31. doi:10.1080/09540099208946601

Dawson, M. R. W., & Zimmerman, C. (2003). Interpreting the internal structure of a connectionist model of the balance scale task. *Brain and Mind*, *4*, 129–149. doi:10.1023/A:1025449410732

Dawson, M. R. W., Medler, D. A., & Berkeley, I. S. N. (1997). PDP networks can provide models that are not mere implementations of classical theories. *Philosophical Psychology*, *10*, 25–40. doi:10.1080/09515089708573202

Dawson, M. R. W., Medler, D. A., McCaughan, D. B., Willson, L., & Carbonaro, M. (2000). Using extra output learning to insert a symbolic theory into a connectionist network. *Minds and Machines, 10*, 171–201. doi:10.1023/A:1008313828824

de Bakker, J. W. (1980). *Mathematical theory of program correctness*. London: Prentice Hall International.

de Martin-Roche, D., Sanchez-Avila, C., & Sanchez-Reillo, R. (2001). Iris Recognition for Biometric Identification Using Dyadic. Wavelet Transform Zero-Crossing. *IEEE 35th International Carnahan Conference on Security Technology* (pp. 272-277).

Dean, T. (2005). A computational model of the cerebral cortex. In *The Proceedings of the 20th National Conference on Artificial Intelligence (AAAI-05)* (pp. 938-943). Cambridge, MA.

Dellaert, F., Polzin, T., & Waibel, A. (1996). Recognizing emotion in speech. In *Proceedings of Fourth International Conference on Spoken Language Processing ICSLP 96, Philadelphia PA, USA, October* (pp.1970-1973).

Dempster, A. P., Laird, N. M., & Rubin, D. B. (1977). Maximum likelihood from incomplete data via the em algorithm. *Journal of the Royal Statistical Society. Series B. Methodological, 39*, 1–38.

Demri, S., & Orlowska, E. (1997). Logical analysis of indiscernibility. In E. Orlowska (Ed.), *Incomplete Information: Rough Set Analysis* (pp. 347-380). Heidelberg: Physica Verlag.

Desain, P., & Honing, H. (1991). The quantization of musical time: A connectionist approach. In P. M. Todd & D. G. Loy (Eds.), *Music and connectionism*. London: The MIT Press.

Descartes, R. (1637). *Discours de la Méthode*. Paris: Maxi-poche (1995)

Deutsch, D. (1999). *The Psychology of music* (2nd ed.). San Diego: Academic Press.

Dhaliwal, J. S., & Benbasat, I. (1996). The use and effects of knowledge-based system explanations: theoretical foundations and a framework for empirical evaluation.

Information Systems Research, 7, 342–362. doi:10.1287/isre.7.3.342

Dickinson S.J., Bergevin R., Biederman I., Eklundh J. O., Munck-Fairwood R., Jain A.K., Pentland A. (1997). Panel report: The potential of geons for generic 3-D object recognition. *Image and Vision Computing, 15*(4), 277-292.

Dierks, H. (2000). A process algebra for real-time programs (LNCS 1783, pp. 66/76). Berlin, Germany: Springer.

Dijkstra, E. W. (1975). Guarded commands, nondeterminacy, and the formal derivation of programs. *Communications of the ACM, 18*(8), 453-457.

Dijkstra, E. W. (1976). *A discipline of programming*. Englewood Cliffs, NJ: Prentice Hall.

Dinstein, I., Thomas, C., Behrmann, M., & Heeger, D. J. (2008). A mirror up to nature. *Current Biology, 18*, 13–18. doi:10.1016/j.cub.2007.11.004

Doise, W., & Mugny, G. (1997). *Psychologie sociale et développement cognitif*. Paris: Armand Colin

Dolson, M. (1991). Machine tongues xii: neural networks. In P. M. Todd & D. G. Loy (Eds.), Music and connectionism (pp. 3 - 19). London: The MIT Press.

Doyle, J. (1992). Rationality and its role in reasoning. *Computational Intelligence, 8*, 376–409. doi:10.1111/j.1467-8640.1992.tb00371.x

Duch, W., & Jankowski, N. (1999). Survey of neural transfer functions. *Neural Computing Surveys, 2*, 163–212.

Duda, R. O., Hart, P. E., & Stork, D. G. (2000). *Pattern classification* (2nd ed.). Wiley-Interscience.

Dudek, G., Giguere, P., Prahacs, C., Saunderson, S., Sattar, J., Torres, L., et al. (2007). AQUA: An amphibious autonomous robot. *IEEE Computer, 40*, 46-53.

Dudek, G., Sattar, J., & Xu, A. (2007). A visual language for robot control and programming: A human-interface study. In *Proceedings of IEEE ICRA, Rome* (pp. 2507-2513).

Dzeroski, S., & Zenko, B. (2002). Is combining classifiers better than selecting the best one. In *Icml '02: Proceedings of 19th international conference on machine learning* (pp. 123–130). San Francisco, CA, USA: Morgan Kaufmann Publishers Inc.

Eagly, A. H., & Chaiken, S. (1992). *The psychology of attitudes*. San Diego, CA: Harcourt Brace.

Eckhorn, R., Reitoeck, H. J., Arndt, M., & Dicke, P. (1990). Feature Linking via Synchronisation among Distributed Assemblies: Simulation of Results from Cat Cortex. *Neural Computation, 2,* 293–307. doi:10.1162/neco.1990.2.3.293

Eden, A. H., Gil, J., Hirshfeld, Y., & Yehudai, A. (2005). *Towards a mathematical foundation for design patterns* (Tech. Rep.). Dept. of Computer Science, Concordia University, Montreal, Canada.

Eigen, M., & Schuster, P. (1979). *The hypercycle: A principle of natural self-organization*. Berlin, Germany: Springer.

Ekblad, U., & Kinser, J. M. (2004). The intersecting cortical model in image processing. *Nuclear Instruments & Methods in Physics Research. Section A, Accelerators, Spectrometers, Detectors and Associated Equipment,* 392–396. doi:10.1016/j.nima.2004.03.102

Ekman, P., & Sullivan, M. O. (1987). The role of context in interpreting facial expression: Comment on Russell and Fehr. *Journal of Experimental Psychology, 117,* 86–88.

Ellis, D. O., & Fred, J. L. (1962). *Systems philosophy*. Prentice Hall.

Elm, W. C., Cook, M. J., Greitzer, F. L., Hoffman, R. R., Moon, B., & Hutchins, S. G. (2004). Designing support for intelligence analysis. In *Proceedings of the Human Factors and Ergonomics Society,* pp. 20-24.

Elman, J. L. (1995). Language as a dynamical system. In R. F. Port & T. van Gelder (Eds.), *Mind as motion* (pp. 195-225). MIT Press.

Embry, D. E. (1986). *SHERPA: A systematic human error reduction and prediction approach*. Paper presented at the International Topical Meeting on Advances in Human Factors in Nuclear Power Systems, Knoxville, TN.

Encina, A., Llana, L., & Rubio, F. (2005). Formalizing the debugging process in Haskell. In *Proceedings of International Conference on Theoretical Aspects of Computing, (ICTAC'05)* (LNCS 3772, pp. 211–226). Springer-Verlag.

Encina, A., Llana, L., & Rubio, F. (2006). Introducing debugging capabilities to natural semantics. In *Proceedings of 6th International Andrei Ershov Memorial Conference, Perspectives of System Informatics, (PSI'06)* (LNCS 4378, pp. 195–208). Springer-Verlag.

Encina, A., Llana, L., Rubio, F., & Hidalgo-Herrero, M. (2007). Observing intermediate structures in a parallel lazy functional language. In *Proceedings of 9th International ACM SIGPLAN Conference on Principles and Practice of Declarative Programming, (PPDP'07),* (pp. 109-120). ACM Press.

Encina, A., Rodríguez, I., & Rubio, F. (2008). A debugger for parallel Haskell dialects. In *Proceedings of 8th International Conference on Algorithms and Architectures for Parallel Processing, (ICA3PP'08)* (LNCS 5022, pp. 282–293). Springer-Verlag.

Engel, A. K., Fries, P., & Singer, W. (2001). Dynamic predictions: Oscillations and synchrony in top-down processing. *Nature Reviews Neuroscience, 2,* 704-716.

Eustice, R. (2005). *Large-area visually augmented navigation for autonomous underwater vehicles*. Unpublished doctoral dissertation, Woods Hole Oceanographic Institute, Massachusetts Institute of Technology, Cambridge.

Eustice, R., Singh, H., Leonard, J., Walter, M., & Ballard, R. (2005). Visually navigating the RMS Titanic with SLAM information filters. *In Proceedings of Robotics: Science and Systems (RSS),* Cambridge, MA. (pp 57-64).

Falmagne, J.-C., Koppen, M., Villano, M., Doignon, J.-P., & Johannesen, L. (1990). Introduction to knowledge spaces: how to build, test and search them. *Psychological Review,* 201–224. doi:10.1037/0033-295X.97.2.201

Favre, D. (2006). Émotion et cognition: un couple inséparable. *Cahiers Pédagogiques, 448*, 66–68.

Favre, D. (2007). *Transformer la violence des élèves.* Paris: Dunod.

Fecher, H. (2001). A real-time process algebra with open intervals and maximal progress. *Nordic Journal of Computing, 8*(3), 346-360.

Feigenbaum, E. A., & Feldman, J. (Eds.). (1963). *Computers and thought.* McGraw-Hill.

Ferber, J., & Gutknecht, O. (1998). A meta-model for the analysis and design of organizations in multi-agent systems. In *Third international conference on multi-agent systems (icmas98)* (p.128-135).

Fischer, K.W., Shaver, P. R., & Carnochan, P. (1990). How emotions develop and how they organize development. *Cognition and Emotion, 4*, 81-127.

Fischler, M., & Bolles, R. (1981). Random sample consensus: A paradigm for model fitting with application to image analysis and automated cartography. *Communications of the ACM, 24*, 381-385.

Fishburn, P. C. (1970). *Utility Theory for Decision-Making.* New York: John Wiley and Sons.

Florijn, G., Meijers, M., & Wionsen, P. V. (1997). Tool support for object-oriented patterns. In *Proceedings of the 11th European Conference on Object-Oriented Programming* (ECOOP'97)(pp. 472-495), Jyvaskyla, Finland.

Ford, J. (1986). Chaos: Solving the Unsolvable, predicting the unpredictable. In *Chaotic dynamics and fractals.* Academic Press.

Foulin, J.-N., & Mouchon, S. (1998). Psychologie de l'éducation. Paris: Nathan (2005)

Fourez, G. (2002). *La construction des sciences.* Paris: DeBoeck Université.

Fourez, G., Englebert-Lecomte, V., & Mathy, P. (1997). *Nos savoirs sont nos savoirs.* Paris: DeBoeck Université.

Franklin, J. A. (2004). *Recurrent neural networks and pitch representations for music tasks.* Paper presented at the Seventeenth International Florida Artificial Intelligence Research Symposium Conference, Miami Beach, FA.

Freud, S. (1966). Project for a scientific psychology. In J. Strachey (Ed.), *The standard edition the complete psychological works of Sigmund Freud* (Vol. 1). London: Hogarth Press. (Original work published 1895)

Friedman, N. (1997). Learning belief networks in the presence of missing values and hidden variables. In *Proceedings of the Fourteenth International Conference on Machine Learning*, San Francisco, CA, USA, (pp.125-133).

Friedman, N., Linial, M., Nachman, I., & Pe'er, D. (2000). Using bayesian networks to analyze expression data. *Computational Biology, 7*, 601-620.

Fukunaga, K. (1990). *Introduction to statistical pattern recognition* (2nd ed.). Academic press.

Gadhok, N. (2006). *A study of outliers for robust independent component analysis.* Unpublished master's thesis, Department of Electrical and Computer Engineering, University of Manitoba, Winnipeg, Canada.

Gadhok, N., & Kinsner, W. (n.d.). ICA by Beta Divergence for Matlab (Version 1.0) [Computer software]. Retrieved October 16, 2006, from http://www.ee.umanitoba.ca/~kinsner/projects

Gago, P., & Bento, C. (1998). A metric for selection of the most promising rules. In *Proceedings of PKDD* (pp. 19-27).

Gamma, E., Helm, R., Johnson, R., & Vlissides, J. (1995). *Design patterns: Elements of reusable object oriented software.* Reading, MA: Addison-Wesley.

Ganter, B., & Wille, R. (1999). *Formal Concept Analysis, Mathematical Foundations.* Berlin: Springer.

Gardner, H. (1984) *Frames of Mind: The Theory of Multiple Intelligences.* Basic Books.

Gävert, H., Hurri, J., Särelä, J., & Hyvärinen A. (n.d.). FastICA for Matlab (Version 2.3) [Computer software]. Retrieved February 2, 2005, from http://www.cis.hut.fi/projects/ica/fastica

Geisler, W., & Diehl, R. L. (2003). A Bayesian approach to the evolution of perceptual and cognitive systems. *Cognitive Science, 27*, 379-402.

Geisler, W., & Murray, R. (2003). Practice doesn't make perfect. *Nature, 423*, 696-697.

Geist, A., Beguelin, A., Dongarra, J., & Jiang, W. (1994). *PVM: Parallel Virtual Machine*. MIT Press.

George, D., & Hawkins, J. (2005). A hierarchical Bayesian model of invariant pattern recognition in the visual cortex. In *Proceedings of the International Joint Conference on Neural Networks.*

Gerber, R., Gunter, E. L., & Lee, I. (1992). Implementing a real-time process algebra In M. Archer, J. J. Joyce, K. N. Levitt, & P. J. Windley (Eds.), *Proceedings of the International Workshop on the Theorem Proving System and its Applications* (pp. 144-145). Los Alamitos, CA: IEEE Computer Society Press.

Gilbert, C. D., & Wiesel, T. N. (1989). Columnar specificity of intrinsic horizontal and corticocortical connections in cat visual cortex. *Journal of Neuroscience, 9*, 2432-2442.

Gill, A. (2000). Debugging Haskell by observing intermediate data structures. In *Proceedings of the 4th Haskell Workshop*. Technical Report of the University of Nottingham.

Gintert, B. E., Madijdi, H., Reid, R. P., Boynton, G. C., Negahdaripour, S., Miller, M., et al. (2007). Documenting hurricane impacts on coral reefs using two-dimensional video-mosaic technology. *Marine Ecology, 28*, 254-258.

Gjerdingen, R. O. (1991). Using connectionist models to explore complex musical patterns. In P. M. Todd & D. G. Loy (Eds.), *Music and connectionism* (pp. 138 - 148). London: The MIT Press.

Goguen, J. A., & Malcolm, G. (1996). *Algebraic semantics of imperative programming*. Cambridge, MA: MIT Press.

Goguen, J.A., Thatcher, J. W., Wagner, E. G., & Wright, J. B. (1977). Initial algebra semantics and continuous algebras. *Journal of the ACM, 24*(1), 68-59.

Gold, E. M. (1967). Language identification in the limit. *Information and Control, 10*, 447–474. doi:10.1016/S0019-9958(67)91165-5

Goleman, D. (1997). *L'Intelligence émotionnelle: Comment transformer ses émotions en intelligence*. Paris: R. Laffont

Gray, P. (1994). *Psychology* (2nd ed.). New York: Worth Publishers, Inc.

Gries, D. (1981). *The science of programming*. Berlin, Germany: Spinger Verlag

Griffith, N., & Todd, P. M. (1999*). Musical networks: Parallel distributed perception and performance*. Cambridge, MA: MIT Press.

Grimson, W. E. L. (1990). *Object recognition by computer: The role of geometric constraints*. USA: MIT Press.

Grzymala-Busse, J. W. (2005). Incomplete data and generalization of indiscernibility relation, definability, and approximations. *Rough Sets, Fuzzy Sets, Data Mining, and Granular Computing. Proceedings of 10th International Conference* (LNAI 3641, pp. 244-253).

Gunter, C. A. (1992). Semantics of programming languages: Structures and techniques. In M. Garey & A. Meyer (Eds.), *Foundations of computing*. Cambridge, MA: MIT Press.

Gupta, A., & Bajcsy R. (1993). Volumetric segmentation of range images of 3-D objects using superquadric models. *Computer Vision, Graphics, and Image Processing, 58*(3), 302-326.

Gupta, M. M., Liang, J., & Homma, N. (2003). *Static and Dynamic Neural Networks: From Fundamentals to Advanced Theory*. IEEE Press and Wiley-Interscience, John Wiley & Sons, Inc.

Gutknecht, O., & Ferber, J. (1997, December). *MadKit: Organizing heterogeneity with groups in a platform for multiple multiagent systems* (Tech. Rep. No. 97188). LIRMM, 161, rue Ada - Montpellier - France.

Guttag, J. V., & Horning, J. J. (1978). The algebraic specification of abstract data types. *Acta Informatica, 10,* 27-52.

Ha'jek, P. (1998). *Metamathematics of fuzzy logic.* Dordrecht, Germany: Kluwer.

Hagège, H. (2004). *Emergence et évolution de la notion d'information génétique.* Unpublished doctoral dissertation, LIRDEF – Université Montpellier 2.

Hagège, H. (2007). Jugement de valeurs, affects et conceptions sur l'élaboration du savoir scientifique: la recherche d'obstacles l'enseignement des questions vives. In A. Giordan & J.-L. Martinand (Eds.), *XXVIIIᵉᵐᵉˢ journées internationales sur la communication, l'éducation et la culture scientifiques, techniques et industrielles. Ecole, culture et actualite' des sciences techniques*

Hagège, H., Dartnell, C., & Sallantin, J. (2007). Positivism against constructivism: A network game to learn epistemology. Springer Berlin / Heidelberg: *Discovery science,* 91-103.

Haken, H. (1977). *Synergetics.* New York: Springer-Verlag.

Halsey, T. C., Jensen, M. H., Kadanoff, L. P., Procaccia, I., & Shraiman, B. I. (1986, February). Fractal measures and their singularities: The characterization of strange sets. *Phys. Rev.,* A33, 1141-1151. (See also Halsey, T. C., Jensen, M. H., Kadanoff, L. P., Procaccia, I., & Shraiman, B. I. (1986, August). Erratum: Fractal measures and their singularities: The characterization of strange sets. *Phys. Rev.,* A34, 1601).

Hampel, F. R., Ronchetti, E. M., Rousseeuw, P. J., & Stahel, W. A. (1986). *Robust statistics: The approach based on influence functions.* New York: John Wiley & Sons.

Hampton, J. A. (1997). *Psychological representation of concepts of memory* (pp. 81-11). Hove, England: Psychology Press

Han, J., Hu, X., & Cercone, N. (2003). A visualization model of interactive knowledge discovery systems and its implementations. *Information Visualization, 2,* 105–125. doi:10.1057/palgrave.ivs.9500045

Hancock, P. A., & Scallen, S. F. (1996). The future of function allocation. *Ergonomics in Design, 4,* 24–29.

Harrison, M. A. (1978). *Introduction to Formal Language Theory.* Addison-Wesley.

Hawkins, J., & Blackeslee, S. (2004). *On intelligence.* Times Books. New York: Henry Holt and Company.

Haykin, S. (1998). *Neural Networks: A Comprehensive Foundation.* Upper Saddle River, NJ: Prentice Hall.

Haykin, S. (1999). Neural networks: A comprehensive foundation. NJ: Prentice Hall.

He, H. (2006). Principles of universal logic. Beijing, China: Science Press.

Heckerman, D. (1996). *A tutorial on learning with Bayesian networks* (Tech. Rep. No. MSR-TR-95-06). Microsoft Research.

Heckerman, D., Geiger, D., & Chickering, D. M. (1995). *Learning Bayesian networks: The combination of knowledge and statistical data.* Springer.

Hehner, E. C. R. (1984). Predicative programming, parts I and II. *Communications of the ACM, 27*(2), 134-151.

Hentschel, H. G. E., & Procaccia, I. (1983, July). The infinite number of generalized dimensions of fractals and strange attractors. *Physica D: Nonlinear Phenomena, D8*(3), 435-444.

Hermes, H. (1969). *Enumerability, decidability, computability.* New York: Springer-Verlag.

Heylighen, F. (1989). Self-organization, emergence and the architecture of complexity. In *Proceedings of the First European Conference on System Science (AFCET)* (pp. 23-32). Paris.

Hidalgo-Herrero, M., Rodríguez, I., & Rubio, F. (2005). Testing learning strategies. In *Proceedings of the 4th*

IEEE International Conference on Cognitive Informatics (ICCI'05) (pp. 212–221). IEEE-CS Press.

Hidalgo-Herrero, Ortega-Mallén, Y., & Rubio, F. (2006). Analyzing the influence of mixed evaluation on the performance of Eden skeletons. *Parallel Computing, 32,* 528–538.

Higman, B. (1977). *A comparative study of programming languages* (2nd ed.). MacDonald.

Hilderman, R. J., & Hamilton, H. J. (2000). Knowledge Discovery and Measures of Interest. Boston: Kluwer Academic Publishers.

Hirst, D. (1992). Prediction of prosody: An overview. In G. Bailly, C. Benoit, & T.R. Sawallis (Eds.), *Talking machines: Theories, models, and designs.* Amsterdam: Elsevier Science Publishers.

Hoare, C. A. R. (1969). An axiomatic basis for computer programming. *Communications of the ACM, 12*(10), 576-580.

Hoare, C. A. R. (1978). Communicating sequential processes. *Communications of the ACM, 21*(8), 666-677.

Hoare, C. A. R. (1985). *Communicating sequential processes.* London: Prentice Hall International.

Hoare, C. A. R., Hayes, I. J., He, J., Morgan, C. C., Roscoe, A. W., Sanders, J. W., et al. (1987, August). Laws of programming. *Communications of the ACM, 30(*8), 672-686.

Hogue, A., & Jenkin, M. (2006). *Development of an underwater vision sensor for 3D reef mapping.* Paper presented at IEEE/RSJ IROS, Beijing, China.

Hogue, A., German, A., & Jenkin, M. (2007). Underwater environment reconstruction using stereo and inertial data. In *Proceedings of IEEE SMC,* Montreal, Canada.

Hogue, A., German, A., Zacher, J., & Jenkin, M. (2006). Underwater 3D mapping: Experiences and lessons learned. In *Proceedings of the Third Canadian Conference on Computer and Robot Vision (CRV).* Quebec City, Canada.

Hopfield, J. (1982). Neural Networks and Physical Systems with Emergent Collective Computational Abilities. *Proceedings of the National Academy of Sciences of the United States of America, 79,* 2554–2558. doi:10.1073/pnas.79.8.2554

Hopfield, J. J. (1982). Neural networks and physical systems with emergent collective computational abilities. In *Proceedings of the National Academy of Science* (Vol. 79, pp. 2554-2558).

Horn, B. (1987). Closed-form solution of absolute orientation using unit quaternions. *AI Magazine, A,* 629.

Horstmann, C., & Budd, T. (2004). *Big C++.* Danvers, MA: John Wiley & Sons.

Hou, Z.-G., Song, K.-Y., Gupta, M. M., & Tan, M. (2007). Neural Units with Higher-Order Synaptic Operations for Robotic Image Processing Applications. *Soft Computing, 11*(3), 221–228. doi:10.1007/s00500-006-0064-8

Hughes, R. (1989). Why Functional Programming Matters. *The Computer Journal, 32*(2), 98–107. doi:10.1093/comjnl/32.2.98

Hull, C. L. (1943). *Principles of behavior: An introduction to behavior theory.* New York: Oxford University Press.

Hurley, P. J. (1997), *A concise introduction to logic* (6th ed.). Belmony, CA: Wadsworth.

Hyvärinen, A., & Oja, E. (1997). A fast fixed-point algorithm for independent component analysis. *Neural Computation, 9*(7), 1483-1492.

Hyvärinen, A., Karhunen, J., & Oja, E. (2001). *Independent component analysis.* New York: John Wiley & Sons.

Itti, L., & Koch, C. (2001). Computational modelling of visual attention. *Nature Reviews Neuroscience, 2*(3), 194-203.

Ivakhnenko, A. G. (1971). Polynomial Theory of Complex Systems. *IEEE Transactions on Systems, Man, and Cybernetics, 1*(4), 364–378. doi:10.1109/TSMC.1971.4308320

Jacobs, R. A., & Jordon, M. I. (1991). A competitive modular connectionist architecture. *Advances in Neural Information Processing Systems, 3*, 767–773.

Jacobs, R.A. (2002 August). What determines visual cue reliability? *TRENDS in Cognitive Sciences, 6*(8), 345-350.

Jain, A. K., Bolle, R. M., & Pankanti, S. (1999). *Biometrics - Personal Identification in a Networked Society.* MA: Kluwer Academic.

Jaklic, A., Leonardis, A., & Solina F. (2000). *Segmentation and recovery of superquadrics.* The Netherlands: Kluwer Academic Publishers.

Jeffrey, A. (1992). Translating timed process algebra into prioritized process algebra. In J. Vytopil (Ed.), *Proceedings of the Second International Symposium on Formal Techniques in Real-Time and Fault-Tolerant Systems* (LNCS 571, pp. 493-506). Nijmegen, The Netherlands: Springer-Verlag.

Jenkins, J. B., & Dallenbach, K. M. (1924). Oblivescence during sleep and waking. *American Journal of Psychology, 35*, 605-612.

Jochem, T., Pomerleau, D. A., & Thorpe, C. (1993). Maniac: A next generation neurally based autonomous road follower. In *Proceedings of the International Conference on Intelligent Autonomous Systems.*

Johnson, E. A., Jr. (2002). *Unmanned undersea vehicles and guided missile submarines: Technological and operational synergies* (Occasional Paper No. 27). AL: Center for Strategy and Technology, Air War College, Air University.

Johnson, J. L., & Padgett, M. L. (1999). PCNN models and applications. *IEEE Transactions on Neural Networks, 10*(3), 480–498. doi:10.1109/72.761706

Jones, C. (1986). *Programming productivity.* New York: McGraw-Hill Book Co.

Jones, C. B. (1980). *Software development: A rigorous approach.* London: Prentice Hall International.

Jones, C. B. (2003). Operational semantics: Concepts and their expression. *Information Processing Letters, 88*(1-2), 27 – 32.

Jones, S. L. P. (1996). Compiling Haskell by program transformation: A report from the trenches. In *ESOP'96 —European Symposium on Programming* (LNCS 1058, pp. 18–44). Springer-Verlag.

Jones, S. L. P., & Hughes, J. (1999, February). *Report on the programming language Haskell 98.* (Tech. Rep.).

Jones, S. L. P., Hall, C. V., Hammond, K., & Partain, W. (1992). *The Glasgow Haskell compiler: a technical overview.* Computer Science Dept., Glasgow University.

Jorge, P. M., Marques, J. S., & Abrantes, A. J. (2004). Estimation of the bayesian network architecture for object tracking in video sequences. In *Proceedings of the 17th International Conference on Pattern Recognition* (ICPR'04), (Vol. 2, pp. 732-735).

Jourdain, R. (1997). *Music, the brain, and ecstasy.* New York: William Morrow & Co.

Kang, H.-B., & Cho, S.-H. (2004). Adaptive object tracking using bayesian network and memory. In *Proceedings of the ACM 2nd International Workshop on Video Surveillance & Sensor Networks*, New York (pp. 104-113).

Kaufman, L., & Rousseeuw, P. J. (1990). *Finding groups in data: an introduction to cluster analysis.* Wiley, New York.

Kim, H. D. (2003). Complementary occurrence and disjunctive rules for market basket analysis in data mining. In *Proceedings of Information and Knowledge Sharing.*

Kinsner, W. (1994, June 15). *Batch and real-time computation of a fractal dimension based on variance of a time series* (Tech. Rep. *DEL94-6).* Winnipeg, MB: University of Manitoba.

Kinsner, W. (1994, June 20). *The Hausdorff-Besicovitch Dimension Formulation for Fractals and Multifractals* (Tech. Rep. *DEL94-7).* Winnipeg, MB: University of Manitoba.

Kinsner, W. (1994, May). *Fractal dimensions: Morphological, entropy, spectral and variance classes* (Tech. Rep. DEL94-4). Winnipeg, MB: University of Manitoba.

Kinsner, W. (2002, August). Compression and its metrics for multimedia. In *Proceedings f the IEEE 2002 International Conference on Cognitive Informatics (ICCI02),* (pp. 107-121).

Kinsner, W. (2003, August). Characterizing chaos through Lyapunov metrics. In *Proceedings of the IEEE 2003 International Conference On Cognitive Informatics (ICCI03),* (pp. 189-201).

Kinsner, W. (2004, August). Is entropy suitable to characterize data and signals for cognitive informatics? In *Proceedings of the IEEE 2004 International Conference on Cognitive Informatics (ICCI04),* (pp. 6-21).

Kinsner, W. (2005). Signal processing for autonomic computing. In *Record Can. Applied & Industrial Mathematical Sciences (CAIMS05).*

Kinsner, W. (2005). A unified approach to fractal dimensions. In *Proceedings of the IEEE 2005 International Conference on Cognitive Informatics (ICCI05),* (pp. 58-72).

Kinsner, W. (2008). Complexity and its measures in cognitive and other complex systems. In *Proceedings of the 7th IEEE International Conference on Cognitive Informatics, (ICCI'08)* (pp.121-123). IEEE-CS Press.

Kinsner, W., & Dansereau, R. (2006, August). A relative fractal dimension spectrum as a complexity measure. In *Proceedings of the IEEE 2006 International Conference on Cognitive Informatics (ICCI06)* (pp. 200-208).

Kinsner, W., Zhang, D., Wang, Y., & Tsai, J. (Eds.). (2005, August). *Proceedings of the Fourth IEEE International Conference on Cognitive Informatics (ICCI'05).* Los Alamitos, CA: IEEE Computer Society Press.

Kirsh, D. (2000). A few thoughts on cognitive overload. *Intellectica, 1*(30), 19–51.

Kittler, J. (1978). *Feature selection algorithm, pattern recognition and signal processing* (pp. 41-60). C. H.

Chen (Ed.), Alphen aan den Rijin, Germany: Sijthoff & Noordhoof0.

Kleene, S. C. (1952). *Introduction to meta-mathematics.* North Holland, Amsterdam.

Klir, G. J. (1992). *Facets of systems science.* New York: Plenum Press.

Klir, R. G. (1988). Systems profile: the emergence of systems science. *Systems Research, 5*(2), 145-156.

Kloesgen, W., & Żytkow, J. (Eds.). (2002). *Handbook of data mining and knowledge discovery.* Oxford, England: Oxford University Press.

Klusener, A. S. (1992). Abstraction in real time process algebra. In J. W. de Bakker, C. Huizing, W. P. de Roever, & G. Rozenberg (Eds.), *Proceedings of Real-Time: Theory in Practice* (LNCS, pp. 325-352). Berlin, Germany: Springer.

Klusik, U., Loogen, R., Priebe, S., & Rubio, F. (2001). Implementation skeletons in Eden: Low-effort parallel programming. In *Proceedings of the Implementation of Functional Languages (IFL'00)* (LNCS 2011, pp. 71–88). Springer-Verlag.

Kohavi, R., & John, G. H. (1997). Wrappers for feature subset selection. *Artificial Intelligence, 97*(1-2), 273–324. doi:10.1016/S0004-3702(97)00043-X

Kostoulas, T., & Fakotakis, N. (2006). A speaker dependent emotion recognition framework. *CSNDSP Fifth International Symposium, Patras, July* (pp. 305-309).

Kotsiantis, S., & Kanellopoulos, (2006). Association rules mining: a recent overview. *GESTS international transactions on computer science and engineering, 32*(1), 71-82.

Krantz, D. H., Luce, R. D., Suppes, P., & Tversky, A. (1971). *Foundations of Measurement.* New York: Academic Press.

Krivic, J., & Solina, F. (2004). Part-level object recognition using superquadrics. *Computer Vision and Image Understanding, 95*(1), 105-126.

Krumhansl, C. L. (1990). *Cognitive foundations of musical pitch*. New York: Oxford University Press.

Kuhn, T. (1962). *La structure des révolutions scientifiques*. (Translated from *The Structure of Scientific Revolutions*, 1972). Champs Flammarion.

Kullback, S., & Leibler, R. A. (1951). On information and sufficiency. *Annals of Math. Stats.*, *22*(1), 79-86.

Kuwabara, H., & Sagisaka, Y. (1995). Acoustic characteristics of speaker individuality: Control and conversion. *Speech Communication, 16*, 165–173. doi:10.1016/0167-6393(94)00053-D

Kwon, O., Chan, K., Hao, J., & Lee, T. (2003). Emotion recognition by speech signals. In *Proceedings of European Conference on Speech Communication and Technology, Geneva, Switzerland, September* (pp. 125-128).

Laden, B., & Keefe, B. H. (1989). The representation of pitch in a neural net model of pitch classification. *Computer Music Journal, 13*, 12–26. doi:10.2307/3679550

Lai, W.-C., Chang, C., Chang, E., Cheng, K.-T., & Crandell, M. (2002). Pbir-mm: Multimodal image retrieval and annotation. In *Proceedings of the Tenth ACM International Conference on Multimedia*, (pp. 421-422).

Lakatos, I. (1976). *Proofs and refutations*. Cambridge University Press.

Lam, W., Low, K. F., & Ho, C. Y. (1997). Using a Bayesian network induction approach for text categorization. In *Proceedings of IJCAI97, 15th International Joint Conference on Artificial Intelligence*, Nagoya, Japan, (pp. 745-750).

Langley, P. Simon, H. A., & Zytkow, J. M. (1987). *Scientific discovery: Computational explorations of the creative processes*. Cambridge: The MIT Press

Langley, P., Bradshaw, G. L., & Simon, H. A. (1981). Bacon5: The discovery of conservation laws. *IJCAI'81*.

Lano, K., Goldsack, S., & Bicarregui, J. (1996). Formalizing design patterns. In *Proceedings of the 1st BCS-FACS Northern Formal Methods Workshop* (p. 1).

Lanterman, A. D., O'Sullivan, J. A., & Miller, M. I. (1999, December). Kullback-Leibler distances for quantifying clutter and models. *Optical Engineering, 38*(12), 2134-2146.

Large, E. W., & Kolen, J. F. (1999). Resonance and the perception of musical meter. In N. Griffith & P. M. Todd (Eds.), *Musical networks: Parallel distributed perception and performace* (pp. 65 - 96). London: MIT Press.

Lauder, A., & Kent, S. (1998). Precise visual specification of design patterns. In *Proceedings of the 12th European Conference on Object-Oriented Programming (ECOOP'98)*, (LNCS, 1445, pp. 114-134). Springer-Verlag.

Le Cun, Y., Jackel, L. D., Boser, B., & Denker, J. S. (1989). Handwritten digit recognition: Applications of neural network chips and automatic learning. *IEEE Communications Magazine, 27*(11), 41–46. doi:10.1109/35.41400

Le Moigne, J.-L. (1995). *Les épistémologies constructivistes*. Paris: Puf, Que sais-je? Lenat, D. B. (1983). The role of heuristics in learning by discovery. In *Machine Learning: An Artificial Intelligence Approach*.

Leahey, T. H. (1997). *A history of psychology: Main currents in psychological thought* (4th ed.). Upper Saddle River, NJ: Prentice- Hall Inc.

Learned-Miller, E. (n.d.). RADICAL for Matlab (Version 1.1) [Computer software]. Retrieved February 2, 2005, from http://www.cs.umass.edu/~elm/ICA

Learned-Miller, E., & Fisher, J., III. (2003). ICA using spacing estimates of entropy. *Journal of Machine Learning Research, 4*, 1271-1295.

Lecourt, D. (2001). *La philosophie des sciences*. Paris: Puf Que sais-je? Lemberger, N., Hewson, P., & Park, H.-J. (1999). Relationships between prospective secondary teachers' classroom practice and their conceptions of biology and of teaching science. *Science Education, 83*, 347–371.

Lee, C. M., Narayanan, S., & Pieraccini, R. (2001). Recognition of negative emotions from the speech signal. *Automatic Speech Recognition and Understanding, 2001. ASRU'01*.

Lee, T. S., & Mumford, D. (2003). Hierarchical Bayesian inference in the visual cortex. *Journal of the Optical Society of America, 20*(7), 1434-1448.

Lee, T. T. (1987). An information-theoretic analysis of relational databases - part I: data dependencies and information metric. *IEEE Transactions on Software Engineering, 13*, 1049–1061. doi:10.1109/TSE.1987.232847

Lee, T., Girolami, M., & Sejnowski, T. (1999). Independent component analysis using an extended infomax algorithm for mixed subgaussian and supergaussian sources. *Neural Computation, 11*, 417-441.

Leman, M. (1991). The ontogenesis of tonal semantics: Results of a computer study. In P. M. Todd & D. G. Loy (Eds.), *Music and connectionism* (pp. 100 - 127). London: The MIT Press.

Lerdahl, F., & Jackendoff, R. (1983). *A generative theory of tonal music.* Cambridge, MA: MIT Press.

Leśniewski, S. (1916). *Podstawy ogólnej teoryi mnogosci* [On the foundations of set theory]. Moscow: The Polish Scientific Circle.

Levenson, R. W., Ekman, P., & Friesen, W. V. (1990). Voluntary facial action generates emotion-specific autonomic nervous system activity. *Psychophysiology, 27*, 363–384. doi:10.1111/j.1469-8986.1990.tb02330.x

Lewis, J. P. (1991). Creation by refinement and the problem of algorithmic music composition. In P. M. Todd & D. G. Loy (Eds.), *Music and conncectionism.* London: The MIT Press.

Li, L., Alderson, D., Doyle, J. C., & Willinger, W. (2005). Towards a Theory of Scale-Free Graphs: Definition, Properties, and Implications. *Internet Math, 2*(4), 431–523.

Li, Y., Sun, J., Tang, C., & Shum, N. (2004). Lazy snapping. *ACM Transactions on Graphics, 23*, 303-308.

Liam, L. W., Chekima, A., Fan, L. C., & Dargham, J. A. (2002). Iris Recognition. Using Self- Organizing Neural Network. *Student Conference on. Research and Development* (pp. 169-172).

Lim, S., Lee, K., Byeon, O., & Kim, T. (2001). Efficient iris recognition through improvement of feature vector and Classifier. *ETRI J, 23*(2), 61–70. doi:10.4218/etrij.01.0101.0203

Lin, T .Y. (2005). Granular computing: Examples, intuitions, and modeling. In *Proceedings of IEEE 2006 Conference on Granular Computing GrC06* (pp. 40-44).

Lin, T. Y. (1997). From rough sets and neighborhood systems to information granulation and computing with words. In *Proceedings of the European Congress on Intelligent Techniques and Soft Computing* (pp. 1602-1606).

Lin, T. Y., Yao, Y. Y., & Zadeh, L. A. (Eds.). (2002). *Data Mining, Rough Sets and Granular Computing.* Heidelberg: Physica-Verlag.

Lindner, G., & Studer, R. (1999). AST: support for algorithm selection with a CBR approach. In *Proceedings of the 3rd European conference on principles and practice of knowledge discovery in databases* (pp.418-423).

Lippmann, R. P. (1989). Pattern classification using neural networks. *IEEE Communications Magazine,* (November): 47–64. doi:10.1109/35.41401

Lipschutz, S. (1964). *Schaum's outline of theories and problems of set theory and related topics.* New York: McGraw-Hill Inc.

Liquiere, M., & Sallantin, J. (1998). *Structural machine learning with galois lattice and graphs.* 5th International Conference on Machine Learning.

Liu, B., Hsu, W., & Chen, S. (1997). Using general impressions to analyze discovered classification rules. In *Proceedings of ACM SIGKDD International Conference on Knowledge Discovery and Data Mining* (pp. 31-36).

Liu, W. B., & Yuan, B. Z. (2001). Superquadric based hierarchical reconstruction for virtualizing free form objects from 3D data. *Chinese Journal of Electronics, 10*(1), 100-105.

Livermore, J. (2005). *Measuring programmer productivity.* Retrieved from http://home.sprynet.com/~jgarriso/jlpaper.htm

Lonka, K., Joram, E., & Brysin, M. (1996). Conceptions of learning and knowledge: Does training make a difference. *Contemporary Educational Psychology, 21*, 347–371. doi:10.1006/ceps.1996.0021

Loogen, R., Ortega-Mallén, Y., Peña, R., Priebe, S., & Rubio, F. (2002). Parallelism abstractions in Eden. In *Proceedings of the Patterns and Skeletons for Parallel and Distributed Computing* (pp. 95-128). Springer-Verlag.

López, N., Núñez, M., & Rubio, F. (2004). An integrated framework for the performance analysis of asynchronous communicating stochastic processes. In *Formal Aspects of Computing 16*(3), 238-262. Springer-Verlag.

Lorenson, W. E., & Cline, H. E. (1987). Marching cubes: A high resolution 3D surface construction algorithm. In *Proceedings of the 14th Annual Conference on Computer Graphics and Interactive Techniques* (pp. 163-169).

Louden K.C. (1993). *Programming languages: Principles and practice.* Boston: PWS-Kent Publishing Co.

Loy, D. G. (1991). Connectionism and musiconomy. In P. M. Todd & D. G. Loy (Eds.), *Music and connectionism* (pp. 20 - 36). London: The MIT Press.

Luchins, A. S., & Luchins, E. H. (1999). Isomorphism in Gestalt Theory: Comparison of Wertheimer's and Köhler's concepts. *GESTALT THEORY, 21*(3), 208-234.

Ma, L., Wang, Y., & Tan, T. (2002). Iris Recognition Based on Multichannel Gabor Filtering. *the Fifth Asian Conference on Computer Vision, 1*, 279-283.

MacKay, D. (1992). Bayesian interpolation. *Neural Computation, 4*, 415-477.

Makeig, S., et al. (n.d.). EEGLAB: ICA toolbox for psychophysiological research (Version 4.5) [Computer software]. Retrieved February 2, 2005, from http://sccn.ucsd.edu/eeglab

Makeig, S., Westerfield, M., Jung, T., Enghoff, S., Townsend, J., Courchesene, E., et al. (2002). Dynamic brain sources of visual evoked responses. *Science, 295*(5555), 690-694.

Mallat, S. G. (1989, July). A theory for multiresolution signal decomposition: The wavelet representation. *IEEE Trans. Pattern Anal. Machine Intell., 11*(7), 674-693.

Manjunath B. S., & Ma, W. Y. (1996). Texture features for browsing and retrieval of image data. *IEEE Transactions on Pattern Analysis and Machine Intelligence, 18*(8), 837-842.

Mapelsden, D., Hosking, J., & Grundy, J. (1992). *Design pattern modeling and instantiation using DPML*, (Tech. Rep.). Department of Computer Science, University of Auckland.

Marchand, D., & Chaline, J. (2002). *Les merveilles de l'évolution*. Paris: Broché.

Marcotty, M., & Ledgard. H. (1986). *Programming language landscape* (2nd ed.). Chicago: SRA.

Marr, D. (1982). *Vision, A Computational Investigation into Human Representation and Processing of Visual Informatio*. San Francisco: W.H. Freeman and Company.

Martin-Lof, P. (1975). *An intuitionistic theory of types: Predicative part*. In H. Rose & J. C. Shepherdson (Eds.), Logic Colloquium 1973, North Holland.

Masek, L. (2003). *Recognition of Human Iris Patterns for Biometric identification*. Retrieved from http://www.csse.uwa.edu.au/òpk/studentprojects/libor/ *MMU Image Database (version 1.0)* (n.d.). Multimedia University. Retrieved from http://pesona.mmu.edu.my/~ccteo/

Maslow, A. H. (1962). *Towards a psychology of being*. Princeton, NJ: Van Nostrand.

Maslow, A. H. (1970). *Motivation and personality* (2nd ed.). New York: Harper & Row.

Matlin, M. W. (1998). *Cognition* (4th ed.). New York: Harcourt Brace.

McCulloch, W. S. et al. (1943). A logical calculus of the ideas imminent in nervous activity. *Bull. Math. Biophy., 5*, 115-135.

McCulloch, W., & Pitts, W. (1943). A logical calculus of the ideas immanent in nervous activity. *The Bulletin of Mathematical Biophysics, 7*, 115–133. doi:10.1007/BF02478259

McDermid, J. (Ed.)(1991). *Software engineer's reference book*. Oxford, UK: Butterworth Heinemann Ltd.

McKeown, M., Jung, T., Makeig, S., Brown, G., Kindermann, S., Lee, T., et al. (1998). Spatially independent activity patterns in functional MRI data during the Stroop color-naming task. In *Proceedings of the National Academy of Science U.S.A.* (Vol. 95, pp. 803-810).

Medin, D. L., & Shoben, E. J. (1988). Context and structure in conceptual combination. *Cognitive Psychology, 20*, 158-190.

Medioni, G., & François, A. (2000). 3-D structures for generic object recognition. In *Proceedings of the 15th International Conference on Pattern Recognition (ICPR'00)*, Barcelona, Spain, (pp. 1030-1037).

Meek, B. L. (1991). Early high-level languages (Chapter 43). In J. McDermid (Ed.), *Software engineer's reference book*. Oxford: Butterworth Heinemann.

Mendelson, E. (1964). *Introduction to mathematical logic*. New York: Van Nostrand Reinhold.

Meyer, B. (1990). *Introduction to the theory of programming languages*. Englewood Cliffs, NJ: Prentice Hall

Michie, D., & Spiegelhalter, D. (1996). Book review: Machine learning, neural and statistical classification (Edited by. Michie, D.J. Spiegelhalter and C.C. Taylor; Ellis Horwood Limited, 1994). *SIGART Bull, 7*(1), 16–17.

Mihoko, M., & Eguchi, S. (2002). Robust blind source separation by beta divergence. *Neural Computation, 14*, 1859-1886.

Milner, R. (1980). *A calculus of communicating systems* (LNCS 92). Springer-Verlag.

Milner, R. (1989). *Communication and concurrency*. Englewood Cliffs, NJ: Prentice Hall.

Minami, M., & Eguchi, S. (2003). Adaptive selection for minimum β-divergence method. In *Fourth International Symposium on Independent Component Analysis and Blind Signal Separation (ICA 2003)* (pp. 475-480).

Mitchell, J. C. (1990). Type systems for programming languages. In J. van Leeuwen (Ed.), *Handbook of theoretical computer science* (pp.365-458). North-Holland.

Mitchell, T. (1997). *Machine learning*. New York: McGraw-Hill.

Miyashita, Y. (2004). Cognitive memory: Cellular and network machineries and their top-down control. *Science, 306*(5695), 435-440.

Molnár, G., Oláh, S., Komlósi, G., Füle, M., & Szabadics, J., Varga, et al. (2008). Complex Events Initiated by Individual Spikes in the Human Cerebral Cortex. *PLoS Biology, 6*, 1842–1849. doi:10.1371/journal.pbio.0060222

Monro, D. M., Rakshit, S., & Zhang, D. (2007). DCT-Based Iris Recognition. *IEEE Transactions on Pattern Analysis and Machine Intelligence, 29*(4), 586–595. doi:10.1109/TPAMI.2007.1002

Montemerlo, M., Thrun, S., Koller, D., & Wegbreit, B. (2003). FastSLAM 2.0: An improved particle filtering algorithm for simultaneous localization and mapping that provably converges. In *Proceedings of the 18th International Joint Conference on Artificial Intelligence (IJCAI)*.

Morin, E. (1973). *Le paradigme perdu*. Paris: Seuil (1979)

Mozer, M. C. (1991). Connectionist music composition based on melodic, stylistic, and psychophysical constraints. In P. M. Todd & D. G. Log (Eds.), *Music and connectionism*. London: The MIT Press.

Mozer, M. C. (1999). Neural network music composition by prediction: Exploring the benefits of psychoacoustic constraints and multi-scale processing. In N. Griffith & P. M. Todd (Eds.), *Musical networks: Parallel distributed perception and performace* (pp. 227-260). London: MIT Press.

MPI. (1994). A message passing interface standard. *International Journal of Supercomputer Applications, 8*(3) & *8*(4).

Muron, J., & Pospisil, J. (2000). The Human Iris Structure and its Usages. *Dept. of Experimental Physics, 39*, 87–95.

Murphy, G. L. (1993). Theories and concept formation. In I. V. Mechelen et al. (Eds.), *Categories and concepts, theoretical views and inductive data analysis* (pp. 173-200). New York: Academic Press.

Murphy, K., Torralba, A., & Freeman, W. T. (2004). Using the forest to see the trees: A graphical model relating features, objects, and scenes. *Advances in neural information processing systems* 16 (NIPS). Vancouver, British Columbia: MIT Press.

Negahdaripour, S., & Firoozfam, P. (2006). An ROV stereovision system for ship-hull inspection. *IEEE Journal of Oceanic Engineering, 31*, 551-564.

Nettleton, E., Gibbens, P., & Durrant-Whyte, H. (2000). Closed form solutions to the multiple platform simultaneous localisation and map building SLAM problem. In B. Dasarathy (Ed.), *Sensor fusion: Architectures, algorithms, and applications IV* (pp. 428-437).

Newell, A., & Simon, H. A. (1972). *Human problem solving.* Englewood Cliffs, NJ: Prentice Hall.

Nguyen, H. S., Skowron, A., & Stepaniuk, J. (2001). Granular computing: a rough set approach. *Computational Intelligence, 17*, 514–544. doi:10.1111/0824-7935.00161

Nguyen, S. H. (2000). Regularity analysis and its applications in data mining. In L. Polkowski, S. Tsumoto, & T. Y. Lin (Eds.), *Rough set methods and applications* (pp. 289-378). Heidelberg, Germany: Physica-Verlag.

Nicholson, J., Takabashi, K., & Nakatsu, R. (2000). Emotion recognition in speech using neural networks. *Neural Computing & Applications, 9*(4), 290–296. doi:10.1007/s005210070006

Nicollin, X., & Sifakis, J. (1991). An overview and synthesis on timed process algebras. In *Proceedings of the Third International Computer Aided Verification Conference* (pp. 376-398).

Nikolaev, N. Y., & Iba, H. (2003). Learning Polynomial Feedforward Neural Networks by Genetic Programming and Backpropagation. *IEEE Transactions on Neural Networks, 14*(2), 337–350. doi:10.1109/TNN.2003.809405

Nwe, T. L., Wei, F. S., & De Silva, L. C. (2001). Speech based emotion classification. Electrical and Electronic Technology, 2001. TENCON. In *Proceedings of IEEE Region 10 International Conference on, August* (Vol. 1, pp. 19-22).

Ollongren, A. (1974). *Definition of programming languages by interpreting automata.* New York: Academic Press.

OMG. (1997). *Object Constraint Language Specification 1.1.*

OMG. (2002, July). *IDL syntax and semantics.* 1-74.

Oysal, Y., Sunderam, V. S., van Albada, G. D., Sloot, P. M. A., & Dongarra, J. J. (2005). Time Delay Dynamic Fuzzy Networks for Time Series Prediction. In *ICCS: International Conference on Computational Science.* (Vol. 3516, pp.775-782).

Pagan, F. G. (1981). *Semantics of programming languages: A panoramic primer.* Englewood Cliffs, NJ: Prentice Hall.

Pagel, B. U., & Winter, M. (1996). Towards pattern-based tools. In *Proceedings of the EuropLop'96,* (pp. 3.1-3.11).

Pal, S. K. (2004). Soft data mining, computational theory of perception and rough-fuzzy approach. *Information Sciences, 163*(1/3), 5-12.

Pal, S. K., Polkowski, L., & Skowron, A. (Eds.). (2004). *Rough-neural computing: Techniques for computing with words.* Berlin, Germany: Springer Verlag.

Papageorgiou, C., & Poggio, T. (2000). A trainable system for object detection. *International Journal of Computer Vision, 38*(1), 15-33.

Papoulis, A. (1991). *Probability, random variables, and stochastic processes* (3rd ed.). New York: McGraw Hill.

Park, S. H., Goo, J. M., & Jo, C. H. (2004). Receiver operating characteristic (roc) curve: Practical review for radiologists. *Korean Journal of Radiology, 5*(1), 11–18. doi:10.3348/kjr.2004.5.1.11

Parzen, E. (1962). On estimation of a probability density function and mode. *Annals of Mathematical Statistics, 33*, 1065–1076. doi:10.1214/aoms/1177704472

Patel, D., Patel, S., & Wang, Y. (Eds.). (2003, August). In *Proceedings of the Second IEEE International Conference on Cognitive Informatics (ICCI'03.* Los Alamitos, CA: IEEE Computer Society Press.

Pawlak, Z. (1982). Rough sets. *International Journal of Computer Information and Science, 11*(5), 341–356. doi:10.1007/BF01001956

Pawlak, Z. (1991). *Rough Sets: Theoretical aspects of reasoning about data.* Dordrecht: Kluwer Academic Publishers.

Pawlak, Z. (1994). Decision analysis using rough sets. *International Trans. Oper. Res. ,1*(1), 107-114.

Pawlak, Z., & Skowron, A. (1994). Rough membership functions. In R. R. Yager, M. Fedrizzi, & J. Kasprzyk (Eds.), *Advances in the Dempster-Shafer theory of evidence* (pp. 251-271). New York: Wiley.

Pawlak, Z., & Skowron, A. (2007). Rough sets: some extensions. *Information Science, 177*, 28–40. doi:10.1016/j.ins.2006.06.006

Payne, D. G., & Wenger, M. J. (1998). *Cognitive psychology.* Boston: Houghton Mifflin Co.

Pearl, J. (1988). *Probabilistic reasoning in intelligent systems.* San Mateo, CA: Morgan Kaufmannn.

Peitgen, H.-O., Jürgens, H., & Saupe, D. (1992). *Chaos and fractals: New frontiers of science.* New York: Springer-Verlag.

Peng, Y., Flach, P. A., Brazdil, P., & Soares, C. (2002, August). Decision tree-based characterization for meta-learning. In M. Bohanec, B. Kasek, N. Lavrac, & D. Mladenic (Eds.), *Ecml/Pkdd'02 Workshop on Integration and Collaboration Aspects of Data Mining, Decision Support and Meta-Learning* (pp. 111-122). University of Helsinki.

Pentland, A. (1987). Recognition by parts, In *Proceedings of the First International Conference on Computer Vision (ICCV'87),* London, England, (pp. 612-620).

Perelman, C., & Olbrechts-Tyteca, L. (1970). *Traité de l'argumentation. La nouvelle rhétorique.* Paris: Vrin.

Peretz, I., & Zatorre, R. J. (2003). *The cognitive neuroscience of music.* Oxford/New York: Oxford University Press.

Peretz, I., & Zatorre, R. J. (2005). Brain organization for music processing. *Annual Review of Psychology, 56*, 1–26. doi:10.1146/annurev.psych.56.091103.070225

Pestre, D. (2006). *Introduction aux Science Studies.* Paris: La Découverte.

Peter, R. (1967). *Recursive functions.* New York: Academic Press.

Piaget, J. (1973). *Introduction à l'Épistemologie Genetique.* PUF, Paris.

Picard, R. W. (1997). *Affective computing.* Cambridge, MA: MIT Press.

Pineda, F. J. (1988). Dynamics and Architecture for Neural Computation. *Journal of Complexity, 4*, 216–245. doi:10.1016/0885-064X(88)90021-0

Pinel, J. P. J. (1997). *Biopsychology* (3rd ed.). Needham Heights, MA: Allyn and Bacon.

Pizarro, O., Eustice, R., & Singh, H. (2004). Large area 3D reconstructions from underwater surveys. In *Proceedings of the MTS/IEEE OCEANS Conference and Exhibition,* Kobe, Japan (pp. 678-687).

Plotkin, G. (1981). A structural approach to operational semantics. *Technical Report DAIMI FN-19,* Aarhus University, Denmark.

Point Grey Research. (2003). *TRICLOPS: Software Development KIT (SDK) version 3.1 user's guide and command reference.*

Poldrack, R. A., et al. (2001, November 29). Interactive memory systems in the human brain. *Nature,* 546-50.

Polkowski, L. (2002). *Rough sets. Mathematical foundations.* Heidelberg, Germany: Physica-Verlag.

Polkowski, L. (2003). A rough set paradigm for unifying rough set theory and fuzzy set theory (a plenary talk).

In *Proceedings RSFDGrC03*, Chongqing, China (LNAI 2639, pp. 70-78).

Polkowski, L. (2004). A note on 3-valued rough logic accepting decision rules. *Fundamenta Informaticae, 61*, 37-45.

Polkowski, L. (2004). A rough-neural computation model based on rough mereology. In Pal et al. (Eds.), (pp. 85-108).

Polkowski, L. (2004). Toward rough set foundations. Mereological approach (a plenary talk). In *Proceedings of RSCTC04*, Uppsala, Sweden (LNAI 3066, pp. 8-25). Berlin, Germany: Springer Verlag.

Polkowski, L. (2005). Formal granular calculi based on rough inclusions (a feature talk). In *Proceedings of the IEEE 2005 Conference on Granular Computing (GrC05)* (pp. 57-62).

Polkowski, L. (2005). Rough-fuzzy-neurocomputing based on rough mereological calculus of granules. *International Journal of Hybrid Intelligent Systems, 2*, 91-108.

Polkowski, L. (2006). A model of granular computing with applications (a feature talk). In *Proceedings of IEEE 2006 Conference on Granular Computing (GrC06)* (pp. 9-16).

Polkowski, L. (2007). Granulation of knowledge in decision systems: The approach based on rough inclusions. The method and its applications (a plenary talk). In *Proceedings of RSEISP 07*, Warsaw, Poland (LNAI 4585). Berlin, Germany: Springer Verlag.

Polkowski, L., & Artiemjew, P. (2007). On granular rough computing: Factoring classifiers through granulated structures. In *Proceedings of RSEISP07* (LNAI 4585, pp. 280-289). Berlin, Germany: Springer Verlag.

Polkowski, L., & Artiemjew, P. (2007). On granular rough computing with missing values. In *Proceedings of RSEISP07* (LNAI 4585, pp. 271-279). Berlin, Germany: Springer Verlag.

Polkowski, L., & Semeniuk-Polkowska, M. (2005). On rough set logics based on similarity relations. *Fundamenta Informaticae, 64*, 379-390.

Polkowski, L., & Skowron, A. (1997). Rough mereology: A new paradigm for approximate reasoning. *International Journal of Approximate Reasoning, 15*(4), 333-365.

Polkowski, L., & Skowron, A. (1999). Grammar systems for distributed synthesis of approximate solutions extracted from experience. In Gh. Paun & A. Salomaa (Eds.), *Grammatical models of multi-agent systems* (pp. , 316-333). Amsterdam: Gordon & Breach.

Polkowski, L., & Skowron, A. (1999). Towards an adaptive calculus of granules. In L. A. Zadeh & J. Kacprzyk (Eds.), *Computing with words in information/intelligent systems, 1*, (pp. 201-228). Heidelberg, Germany: Physica-Verlag.

Polkowski, L., & Skowron, A. (2001). Rough mereological calculi of granules: A rough set approach to computation. *Computational Intelligence: An International Journal, 17*(3), 472-492.

Pomerleau, D. A. (1991). Efficient training of artificial neural networks for autonomous navigation. *Neural Computation, 3*, 88–97. doi:10.1162/neco.1991.3.1.88

Popper, K. R. (1934). *Logique de la découverte scientifique.* Paris: Broché (2002).

Porter, J. W., & Meier, O. W. (1992). Quantification of loss and change in Floridian reef coral populations. *American Zoologist, 32*, 625-640.

Potter, M., & Kinsner, W. (2007, August). Direct calculation of the fractal singularity spectrum. In *Proceedings of the IEEE 2007 International Conference on Cognitive Informatics (ICCI07)*, (pp. 7).

Potter, M., Gadhok, N., & Kinsner, W. (2002). Separation performance of ICA on simulated EEG and ECG signals contaminated by noise. *Canadian Journal of Electrical and Computer Engineering, 27*(3), 123-127.

Press, W., Teukolsky, S., Vetterling, W., & Flannery, B. (2002). *Numerical recipes in C.* Cambridge University Press.

Prigogine, I., & Nicolis, G. (1972). Thermodynamics of evolution. *Physics Today, 25*, 23-28.

Prince, M. (2004). Does Active Learning Work? A Review of the Research. *Journal of Engineering Education, 93*, 223–231.

Proença, H., & Alexandre, L. A. (2005). UBIRIS: A noisy iris image database. *Proc International Conf. on Image Analysis and Processing, 1*, 970–977.

Protopapas, A., & Lieberman, P. (1997). Fundamental frequency of phonation and perceived emotional stress. *The Journal of the Acoustical Society of America, 101*(4), 2267–2277. doi:10.1121/1.418247

Qing, L., & Hui, S. (2006). Theoretical study of granular computing. In *Proceedings of the RSKT06*, Chongqing, China (LNAI 4062, pp. 92-102). Berlin, Germany: Springer Verlag.

Quillian, M. R. (1968). Semantic memory. In M. Minsky (Ed.), *Semantic information processing.* Cambridge, MA: MIT Press.

Quinlan, J. R. (1983). Learning efficient classification procedures and their application to chess end-games. In J.S. Michalski et al.(Eds.), *Machine Learning: An Artificial Intelligence Approach* (pp. 463-482). Morgan Kaufmann.

Rabanal, P., Rubio, F., & Rodríguez, I. (2007). Using River Formation Dynamics to Design Heuristic Algorithms. In *Proceedings of the 6th International Conference on Unconventional Computation, (UC'07)* (LNCS 4618, pp. 163-177). Springer-Verlag.

Rabanal, P., Rubio, F., & Rodríguez, I. (2008). Finding Minimum Spanning/Distances Trees by Using River Formation Dynamics. In *Proceedings of the 6th International Conference on Ant Colony Optimization and Swarm Intelligence, (ANTS'08)* (LNCS 5217, pp. 60-71). Springer-Verlag.

RAISE (1992). *The RAISE specification language.* London: Prentice Hall.

Raja, N., & Jain, A. (1992). Recognizing geons from superquadrics fitted to range data. *Image and Vision Computing, 10*(3), 179-190.

Ramoni, M., & Sebastiani, P. (2001). Robust learning with missing data. *Machine Learning, 45*(2), 147-170.

Rao, R. P. N., & Ballard, D. H. (1996). Dynamic model of visual recognition predicts neural response properties in the visual cortex. *Neural Computation, 9*, 721-763.

Rao, R. P. N., Olshausen, B., & Lewicki, M. (2002). *Probabilistic models of the brain: Perception and neural function.* Cambridge, MA: The MIT Press.

Rapoport, A. (1962). Mathematical aspects of general systems theory. *General Systems Yearbook, 11,* 3-11.

Ras, Z., & Wieczorkowska, A. (2000). Action rules: how to increase profit of a company. In *Proceedings of PKDD* (pp. 587-592).

Rayward-Smith, V. J. (1986). *A first course in computability.* Oxford: Blackwell Scientific.

Reason, J. (1987). Generic error-modeling system (GEMS): A cognitive framework for locating common human error forms. In J. Rasmussen et al. (Eds.), *New technology and human error.* New York: Wiley.

Reason, J. (1990). *Human error.* Cambridge, United Kingdom: Cambridge University Press.

Redlapalli, S., Song, K.-Y., & Gupta, M. M. (2003). Development of Quadratic Neural Unit with Applications to Pattern Classification. *Fourth International Symposium on Uncertainty Modeling and Analysis ISUMA 2003* (pp. 141-146). IEEE Computer Society. Maryland USA.

Reed, G. M., & Roscoe, A. W. (1986). A timed model for communicating sequential processes. In *Proceedings of ICALP'86* (LNCS 226). Berlin, Germany: Springer-Verlag.

Reisberg, D. (2001). *Cognition: Exploring the science of the mind* (2nd ed.). W. W. Norton & Company, Inc.

Reisberg, D. (2001). *Cognition: Exploring the science of the mind* (2nd ed.). New York: Norton.

Ren, X. (2006). *Neural computation science.* National Defense Industry Press.

Rendell, L., Seshu, R., & Tcheng, D. (1987). Layered concept-learning and dynamically-variable bias management. In . *Proceedings of, IJCAI-87*, 308–314.

Rényi, A. A. (1955). On a new axiomatic theory of probability. *Acta Mathematica Hungarica, 6*, 285-335.

Rényi, A. A. (1959). On the dimension and entropy of probability distributions. *Acta Mathematica Hungarica, 10*, 193-236.

Rényi, A. A. (1960). On measures of entropy and information. In *Proceedings of the Fourth Berkeley Symposium on Math. Statist. Probab.*, (Vol. 1, pp. 547-561).

Reppy, J. H. (1991). CML: A higher-order concurrent language. In *Proceedings of the ACM SIGPLAN Conference on Programing Language Design and Implementation* (pp. 293-305). ACM Press.

Ribes, P., & Borrelly, J.-J. (1997). Underwater pipe inspection task using visual serving techniques. In *Proceedings of IEEE/RSJ IROS* (pp. 63-68).

Riedi, R.H., & Scheuring, I. (1997). Conditional and relative multifractal spectra. *Fractals, 5*(1), 153-168.

Ringach, D. (2002). Spatial structure and symmetry of simple-cell receptive fields in macaque primary visual cortex, *Journal of Neurophysiology, 88*, 455-463.

Robinson, E. S. (1920). Studies from the psychological laboratory of the University of Chicago: Some factors determining the degree of retroactive inhibition. *Psychological Monographs, 28*(128), 1-57.

Rosenblatt, F. (1958). The perceptrom: A probabilistic model for information storage and organization in the brain. *Psychology Review, 65*, 386-408.

Rubio, F., & Rodríguez, I. (2003). A parallel framework for computational science. In *Proceedings of the International Conference on Computational Science (ICCS'03)* (LNCS 2658, pp. 1002-1011). Springer-Verlag.

Rubio, F., & Rodríguez, I. (2004). A parallel language for cognitive informatics. In *Proceedings of the 3rd IEEE International Conference on Cognitive Informatics (ICCI'04)* (pp. 32-41). IEEE-CS Press.

Rumelhart, D. E. (1990). Brain style computation: Leaning and generalization. *Introduction to neural and electronic networks.* New York: Academic Press.

Ruppert, D. (1987). What is kurtosis? An influence function approach. *American Statistician, 41*(1), 1-5.

Russell S., & Norvig, P. (2006). *Artificial intelligence: A modern approach* (2nd ed.). Pearson Education Asia Limited and Tsinghua University Press.

Russell, B. (1961). *Basic writings of Bertrand Russell.* London: George Allen & Unwin Ltd.

Rydeheard, D., & Burstall, R. (1988). *Computational category theory.* Prentice Hall.

Saez, J., Hogue, A., Escolano, F., & Jenkin, M. (2006). Underwater 3D SLAM through entropy minimization. In *Proceedings of the IEEE International Conference on Robotics and Automation (ICRA)* (pp. 3562-3567).

Sano, H., & Jenkins, B. K. (1989). A neural network model for pitch perception. *Computer Music Journal, 13*(3), 41–48. doi:10.2307/3680010

Sato, J., & Morishima, S. (1996). Emotion modeling in speech production using emotion space. In *Proceedings of IEEE International Workshop on Robot and Human Communication, Tsukaba, Japan, November* (pp.472-477).

Sattar, J., Bourque, E., Giguere, P., & Dudek, G. (2007). Fourier tags: Smoothly degradable fiducial markers for use in human-robot interaction. In *Proceedings of the Canadian Conference on Computer and Robot Vision (CRV)*, (pp 165-174) Montreal, Canada.

Sayegh, S. I. (1991). Fingering for string instruments with the optimum path paradigm. In P. M. Todd & D. G. Loy (Eds.), *Music and connectionism* (pp. 243-255). London: The MIT Press.

Saygin, A., Cicekli, I., & Akman, V. (2000). Turing test: 50 years later. *MANDMS: Minds and Machines, 10*, 463–518. doi:10.1023/A:1011288000451

Scarborough, D. L., Miller, B. O., & Jones, J. A. (1989). Connectionist models for tonal analysis. *Computer Music Journal, 13*(3), 49–55. doi:10.2307/3680011

Scheurmann, E. (1920). *Le Papalagui, Les étonnants propos de Touiavii, chef de tribu, sur les hommes blancs.* Paris: Pocket (2001)

Schilpp, P. A. (1946). The philosophy of Bertrand Russell. *American Mathematical Monthly, 53*(4), 7210.

Schmidt, D. (1988). *Denotational semantics: A methodology for language development.* Dubuque, IA: Brown.

Schmidt, D. (1996, March). Programming language semantics. *ACM Computing Surveys, 28*(1).

Schmidt, D. A. (1994). *The structure of typed programming languages.* Cambridge, MA: MIT Press.

Schneider, S. (1995). An operational semantics for timed CSP. *Information and Computation, 116*(2), 193-213.

Schneider, S. (2000). *Concurrent and real-time systems: The CSP approach.* Wiley.

Schneider, S. A. (1991). *An operational semantics for timed CSP* (Programming Research Group Tech. Rep. TR-1-91). Oxford University.

Schneiderman, H. (2004). Learning a restricted bayesian network for object detection. In *Proceedings of the IEEE Computer Society Conference on Computer Vision and Pattern Recognition* (CVPR'04) (Vol. 2, pp. 639-646).

Schneiderman, H., & Kanade, T. (2000). A statistical model for 3d object detection applied to faces and cars. In *Proceedings of the IEEE Conference on Computer Vision and Pattern Recognition.*

Scott, D. (1982). Domains for denotational semantics. In *Automata, languages and programming IX* (pp. 577-613). Berlin, Germany: Springer Verlag.

Scott, D. S., & Strachey, C. (1971). *Towards a mathematical semantics for computer languages.* (Programming Research Group Tech. Rep. PRG-1-6). Oxford University.

Searles, H. (1960). *L'environnement non humain* (translated from *The Nonhuman Environment*, 1986). Paris: nrf Gallimard.

Sedaaghi, M. H., Kotropoulos, C., & Ververidis, D. Using adaptive genetic algorithms to improve speech emotion recognition. *IEEE 9th Workshop on Multimedia Signal Processing* (pp. 461-464).

Segal, J. (2003). *Le zéro et le un, histoire de la notion scientifique d'information au 20e siècle.* Paris: Syllepse.

Sejnowski, T. J., & Rosenberg, C. R. (1988). Nettalk: A parallel network that learns to read aloud. In J. A. Anderson & E. Rosenfeld (Eds.), *Neurocomputing: Foundations of research* (pp. 663-672). Cambridge, MA: MIT Press.

Shannon, C. E. (1948, July & October). A mathematical theory of communications. *Bell Syst. Tech. J., 27,* 379-423 & 623-656.

Shastri, L. (2001). A computational model of episodic memory formation in the hippocampal system. *Neurocomputing, 38-40,* 889-897.

Shastri, L., & Wendelken, C. (1999). Knowledge fusion in the large—Taking cues from the brain. In *Proceedings of FUSION'99.*

Shi, J., & Tomasi, C. (1994). Good features to track. In *Proceedings of the IEEE Conference on Computer Vision and Pattern Recognition (CVPR)* (pp. 593-600).

Shi, Z. Z. (2006). *On intelligence science.* Beijing, China: Tsinghua University Press.

Shi, Z., & Shi, Z. (2005). Constructing fast linear classifier with mutual information. In *Proceedings of the Second International Conference of Neural Network and Brain (ICNN&B2005)*, Beijing, China (pp. 1611-1615).

Shi, Z., Shi, Z., & Hu, H. (2006). A novel plausible model for visual perception. In *Proceedings of ICCI 2006*, Beijing, China (pp. 19-24).

Shneiderman, B. (1998). *Designing the User Interface: Strategies for Effective Human-Computer Interaction* (3rd ed.). Addison-Wesley.

Silberschatz, A., & Tuzhilin, A. (1995). On subjective measures of interestingness in knowledge discovery. In *Proceedings of ACM SIGKDD International Confer-*

ence on Knowledge Discovery and Data Mining (pp. 275-281).

Silberschatz, A., & Tuzhilin, A. (1996). What makes patterns interesting in knowledge discovery systems? *IEEE Transactions on Knowledge and Data Engineering, 8*, 970–974. doi:10.1109/69.553165

Simon, H. A. (1969). *The sciences of artificial.* Cambridge, MA: The MIT Press.

Simon, H. A., & Kaplan, C. A. (1989). Foundations of cognitive science. In M. I. Posner (Ed.), *Foundations of Cognitive Science* (pp. 1-47). Cambridge, MA: MIT Press.

Simon, H., Valdés-Pérez, R. E., & Sleeman, D. H. (1997). Scientific discovery and simplicity of method. *Artificial Intelligence, 91*, 177–181. doi:10.1016/S0004-3702(97)00019-2

Simon, R. (1993). *Ethique de la responsabilité.* Paris: Cerf.

Skarda, C. A., & Freeman, W. J. (1987). How brains make chaos into order. *Behavioral and Brain Sciences, 10.*

Skowron, A., & Stepaniuk, J. (2001). Information granules: Towards foundations of granular computing. *International Journal of Intelligent Systems, 16,* 57-85.

Skowron, A., et al. (1994). RSES: A system for data analysis. Retrieved from www.logic.mimuw.edu.pl/ rses/

Sleeman, D., Rissakis, M., Craw, S., Graner, N., & Sharma, S. (1995). Consultant-2: pre and post-processing of machine learning applications. *International Journal of Human-Computer Interaction, 43*(1), 43–63.

Slonneg, K., & Kurts, B. (1995). *Formal syntax and semantics of programming languages.* Addison-Wesley.

Slonneger, K., & Barry, L.K. (1995). *Formal syntax and semantics of programming languages: A laboratory based approach,* (Chapter 8), Reading, MA: Addison-Wesley Publishing Company.

Smith, A. C., & Kleinman, S. (1989). Managing emotions in medical school: Students' contacts with the living and the dead. *Social Psychology Quarterly, 52,* 56–59. doi:10.2307/2786904

Smith, C. A., & Lazarus, R. S. (1993). Appraisal components, core relational themes, and the emotions. *Cognition and Emotion,* 233–269. doi:10.1080/02699939308409189

Smith, E. E. (1989). Concepts and induction. In M. I. Posner (Ed.), *Foundations of Cognitive Science* (pp. 501-526). Cambridge, MA: MIT Press.

Smith, E. E., & Medin, D. L. (1981). *Categories and concepts.* Cambridge, MA: Harvard University Press.

Smith, R. E. (1993). *Psychology.* St. Paul, MN: West Publishing Co.

Smith, R., & Cheeseman, P. (1987). On the representation and estimation of spatial uncertainty. *International Journal of Robotics Research, 5,* 56-68.

Smith, R., Self, M., & Cheeseman, P. (1990). Estimating uncertain spatial relationships in robotics. In I. Cox, and G. Wilfong (Eds) *Autonomous Robot Vehicles,* 167-193.

Smyth, P., & Goodman, R. An information theoretic approach to rule induction from databases. *IEEE Transactions on Knowledge and Data Engineering, 4,* 301–316. doi:10.1109/69.149926

Soares, C., & Brazdil, P. (2000). Zoomed ranking: Selection of classification algorithms based on relevant performance information. In *Pkdd '00: Proceedings of the 4th European conference on principles of data mining and knowledge discovery* (pp. 126–135). London, UK: Springer-Verlag.

Solina, F., & Bajcsy, R. (1990). Recovery of parametric models from range images: The case for superquadrics with global deformations. *IEEE Transactions on Pattern Analysis and Machine Intelligence, 12*(2), 131-147.

Song, K.-Y., Redlapalli, S., & Gupta, M. M. (2003). Cubic Neural Units for Control Applications. *Fourth International Symposium on Uncertainty Modeling and Analysis ISUMA 2003.* IEEE Computer Society (pp. 324-329). Maryland. USA.

Southall, B., Buxton, B., Marchant, J., & Hague, T. (2000). On the performance characterisation of image segmentation algorithms: A case study. In *Proceedings of ECCV 2000*, Dublin, Ireland (Vol. 2, pp. 351-365).

Sowa, J. F. (1984). *Conceptual Structures, Information Processing in Mind and Machine*. Reading, MA: Addison-Wesley

Specht, D. F. (1991). A general regression neural network. *IEEE Transactions on Neural Networks, 2*(6), 568–576. doi:10.1109/72.97934

Stefanowski, J. (1998). On rough set based approaches to induction of decision rules. In L. Polkowski & A. Skowron (Eds.), *Rough sets in knowledge discovery 1*, (pp. 500-529). Heidelberg, Germany: Physica-Verlag.

Sternberg, R. J. (1998). *In search of the human mind* (2nd ed.). New York: Harcourt Brace & Co.

Strike, K., & Posner, G. (1992). A revisionist theory of conceptual change. *Philosophy of Science, Cognitive Psychology, and Educational Theory and Practice*, 147-176.

Stubbs, D.F. & Webre, N.W. (1985). *Data structures with abstract data types and Pascal*. Monterey, CA: Brooks/Cole Publishing Co.

Sunye, G., Guennec, A. L., & Jezequel, J. M. (2000). Design patterns application in UML. In *Proceedings of the 14th European Conference on Object-Oriented Programming* (ECOOP'00)(pp. 44-62), Sophia Antipolis, France.

Taibi, T., & Ngo, D. C. L. (2003). Formal specification of design patterns–a balanced approach. *Journal of Object Technology, 2*(4), 127-140.

Tamminen, T., & Lampinen, J. (2003). Bayesian object matching with hierarchical priors and Markov chain Monte Carlo. *Bayesian statistics 7*. Oxford University Press.

Tan, P. N., Kumar, V., & Srivastava, J. (2000). Selecting the right interestingness measure for association patterns. In *Proceedings of the Eighth ACM SIGKDD International Conference on Knowledge Discovery and Data Mining*(pp. 32-41).

Tan, X. & Wang, Y. (2008). A denotational semantics of real-time process algebra (RTPA). *The International Journal of Cognitive Informatics and Natural Intelligence (IJCINI), 2*(3).

Tan, X. (2006). Toward automatic code generation based on real-time process algebra (RTPA). PhD Thesis, University of Calgary, Canada.

Tan, X., Wang, Y. & Ngolah, C.F. (2004). Specification of the RTPA grammar and its recognition. *Proceedings of the 2004 IEEE International Conference on Cognitive Informatics (ICCI'04)*, IEEE CS Press, Victoria, Canada, August, pp. 54-63.

Tan, X., Wang, Y., & Ngolah, C. F. (2004). A novel type checker for software system specifications in RTPA. In *Proceedings of the 17th Canadian Conference on Electrical and Computer Engineering (CCECE'04)*. (pp. 1549-1552). Niagara Falls, Ontario, Canada: IEEE CS Press.

Tan, X., Wang, Y., & Ngolah, C. F. (2006). Design and implementation of an automatic RTPA code generator. In *Proceedings of the 19th Canadian Conference on Electrical and Computer Engineering (CCECE'06)* (pp. 1605-1608). Ottawa, Ontario, Canada: IEEE CS Press.

Tarski, A. (1944). The semantic conception of truth. *Philosophic Phenomenological Research, 4*, 13-47.

Tarski, A. (1955). A lattice-theoretic fixed point theorem and its applications. *Pacific Journal of Mathematics, 5*, 285-309.

Tarski, A. (1956). *Logic, Semantics, Metamathematics: Papers from 1923 to 1938*. Oxford: Clarendon Press.

Taylor, I., & Greenhough, M. (1999). Modelling pitch perception with adaptive resonance theory artificial neural networks. In N. Griffith & P. M. Todd (Eds.), *Musical networks: Parallel distributed perception and performance* (pp. 3-22). London: The MIT Press.

Tcheng, D., & Lambert, B. (1989). Building robust learning systems by combining induction and optimization. In *11th International Joint Conference on AI*.

Tillmann, B., Bharucha, J. J., & Bigand, E. (2003). Learning and perceiving musical structures: Further insights from artificial neural networks. In I. Peretz & R. Zatorre (Eds.), *The cognitive neuroscience of* music (pp. 109 - 126). Oxford; New York: Oxford University Press.

Tisse, C., Martin, L., Torres, L., & Robert, M. (2002). Person identification technique using human iris recognition. *Proc. of Vision Interface* (pp. 294-299).

Todd, P. M., & Loy, D. G. (1991). *Music and connectionism*. Cambridge, MA: MIT Press.

Todorovski, L., Blockeel, H., & Dzeroski, S. (2002). Ranking with predictive clustering trees. In *Ecml '02: Proceedings of the 13th European conference on machine learning* (pp. 444–455). London, UK: Springer-Verlag.

Triggs, B., McLauchlan, P., Hartley, R., & Fitzgibbon, A. (2000). Bundle adjustment: A modern synthesis. In *Lecture notes in computer science* (pp. 278-375). Springer-Verlag.

Trinder, P. W., Hammond, K., Loidl, H. W., & Jones, S. L. P. (1998). Algorithm + strategy = parallelism. *Journal of Functional Programming, 8*(1). doi:10.1017/S0956796897002967

Trinder, P. W., Hammond, K., Partridge, A. S., & Jones, S. L. P. (1996). GUM: A portable parallel implementation of Haskell. In *Proceedings of Programming Language Design and Implementation (PLDI'96)* (pp. 79-88). ACM Press.

Tsumoto, S. (1999). Automated discovery of plausible rules based on rough sets and rough inclusion. In *Proceedings of PAKDD'99* (LNAI 1574, pp. 210-219).

Turing, A. (1950). Computing machinery and intelligence. *Mind, 59*(236), 433–460. doi:10.1093/mind/LIX.236.433

Valiant, L. (1984). A theory of the learnable. *Communications of the ACM, 27*, 1134–1142. doi:10.1145/1968.1972

van Heijenoort, J. (1997). *From Frege to Godel, a source book in mathematical logic 1879-1931*. Cambridge, MA: Harvard University Press.

Van Rullen, R., & Thorpe, S. (2001). Is it a bird? Is it a plane? Ultra-rapid visual categorization of natural and artificial objects. *Perception, 30*, 655-668.

Van, M. I., Hampton, J., Michalski, R.S., & Theuns, P. (Eds.) (1993). *Categories and Concepts, Theoretical Views and Inductive Data Analysis*. New York: Academic Press.

Vatsa, M., Singh, R., & Gupta, P. (2004). Comparison of Iris Recognition Algorithms. *International Conference on Intelligent Sensing and Information Processing* (pp. 354-358).

Vereijken, J. J. (1995). A process algebra for hybrid systems. In A. Bouajjani & O. Maler (Eds.), In *Proceedings of the Second European Workshop on Real-Time and Hybrid Systems*. Grenoble: France.

Vernon, D. T., & Blake, R. L. (1993). Does problem-based learning work? A meta-analysis of evaluative research. *Academic Medicine, 68*, 542–544. doi:10.1097/00001888-199307000-00015

Ververidis, D., Kotropoulos, C., & Pitas, I. Automatic emotional speech classification. In *Proceedings of IEEE International Conference on Acoustics, Speech, and Signal Processing, Montreal, Canada, May* (Vol. 1, pp. 593-596).

Vignaux, G. (1991). *Les sciences cognitives*. Paris: La Découverte.

Vilalta, R., & Drissi, Y. (2002). A perspective view and survey of metalearning. *Artificial Intelligence Review, 18*(2), 77–95. doi:10.1023/A:1019956318069

Viola, P., & Jones, M. (2004). Robust real-time object detection. *International Journal of Computer Vision, 57*(2), 137-154.

Vizi, E. S. (2000). Role of High-Affinity Receptors and Membrane Transporters in Nonsynaptic Communication and Drug Action in the Central Nervous System. *Pharmacological Reviews, 52*(1), 63–90.

von Bertalanffy, L. (1952). *Problems of life: An evolution of modern biological and scientific thought*. London: C. A. Watts.

Vu, N. C., & Wang, Y. (2004, May). Specification of design patterns using real-time process algebra (RTPA). In *Proceedings of the 2004 Canadian Conference on*

Electrical and Computer Engineering (CCECE'04), (pp. 1545-1548). Niagara, Falls, Ontario: IEEE CS Press.

Vygotsky, L. S. (1934). *Pensée et langage.* Paris: La Dispute (1997).

Waeytens, K., Lens, W., & Vandenberghe, R. (2002). Learning to learn: Teachers conceptions of their supporting role. *Learning and Instruction, 12,* 305–322. doi:10.1016/S0959-4752(01)00024-X

Wang Y., Johnston, R. H., & Smith, M. R. (Eds.). (2002, August). *Proceedings of the First IEEE International Conference on Cognitive Informatics (ICCI'02),* Calgary, Canada. Los Alamitos, CA: IEEE Computer Society Press.

Wang, J. D. (2006). External memory approach to compute the maximal repeats across classes from DNA sequences. *Asian Journal of Health and Information Sciences, 1*(3), 276–295.

Wang, J. D., Liu, H.-C., Tsai, J., & Ng, K.-L. (2008). Scaling Behavior of Maximal Repeat Distributions in Genomic Sequences. *International Journal of Cognitive Informatics and Natural Intelligence, 2*(3), 31–42.

Wang, K., & He, Y. (2001). User-defined association mining. In *Proceedings of 5th Pacific-Asia Conference on Knowledge Discovery and Data Mining* (pp. 387-399).

Wang, K., Zhou, S., & Han, J. (2002). Profit mining: from patterns to actions. In *Proceedings of International Conference on Extending Database Technology* (pp. 70-87).

Wang, Y. & King, G. (2000). Software engineering processes: Principles and applications, CRC series in software engineering, Vol. I. CRC Press.

Wang, Y. & Ngolah, C.F. (2008). An operational semantics of real-time process algebra (RTPA). *International Journal of Cognitive Informatics and Natural Intelligence* (IJCINI), *2*(3), July.

Wang, Y. (2002). On cognitive informatics. In *Proceedings of the 1st IEEE International Conference on Cognitive Informatics (ICCI'02)* (pp. 34-42). IEEE-CS Press.

Wang, Y. (2002). The real-time process algebra (RTPA). *The International Journal of Annals of Software Engineering, 14,* 235-274.

Wang, Y. (2002, August). On cognitive informatics (Keynote Speech). In *Proceedings of the 1st IEEE International Conference on Cognitive Informatics* (ICCI'02) (pp. 34-42). Calgary, Canada: IEEE CS Press.

Wang, Y. (2003). Cognitive informatics: A new transdisciplinary research field. *Brain and Mind, 4,* 115–127. doi:10.1023/A:1025419826662

Wang, Y. (2003). On cognitive informatics. *Brain and Mind: A Transdisciplinary Journal of Neuroscience and Neurophilosophy, 4*(2), 151-167.

Wang, Y. (2003). Using process algebra to describe human and software system behaviors. *Brain and Mind: A Transdisciplinary Journal of Neuroscience and Neurophilosophy, 4*(2), 199-213.

Wang, Y. (2003, August). Cognitive informatics models of software agent systems and autonomic computing (Keynote Speech). In *Proceedings of the International Conference on Agent-Based Technologies and Systems* (ATS'03) (p. 25). Calgary Canada: University of Calgary Press.

Wang, Y. (2004, August). On autonomic computing and cognitive processes (Keynote Speech). In *Proceedings of the 3rd IEEE International Conference on Cognitive Informatics* (ICCI'04) (pp. 3-4). Victoria: Canada. IEEE CS Press.

Wang, Y. (2005). System science models of software engineering. In *Proceedings of the Eighteenth Canadian Conference on Electrical and Computer Engineering (CCECE'05)* (pp. 1802-1805). Saskatoon, Saskatchewan, Canada: IEEE CS Press.

Wang, Y. (2005, August). On the cognitive processes of human perceptions. In *Proceedings of the 4th IEEE International Conference on Cognitive Informatics* (ICCI'05) (pp. 203-211). Irvin, CA: IEEE CS Press.

Wang, Y. (2005, August). The cognitive processes of abstraction and formal inferences. In *Proceedings of the 4th*

IEEE International Conference on Cognitive Informatics (ICCI'05), (pp. 18-26), Irvin, CA: IEEE CS Press.

Wang, Y. (2006). On the informatics laws and deductive semantics of software. *IEEE Transactions on Systems, Man, and Cybernetics (Part C), 36(2)*, 161-171.

Wang, Y. (2006). *Software engineering foundations: A transdisciplinary and rigorous perspective* (CRC Book Series in Software Engineering 2). Boca Raton, FL: CRC Press.

Wang, Y. (2006, May). The OAR model for knowledge representation. In *Proceedings of the 19th IEEE Canadian Conference on Electrical and Computer Engineering* (CCECE'06). Ottawa, Canada, (pp. 1696-1699).

Wang, Y. (2006). Cognitive informatics and contemporary mathematics for knowledge representation and manipulation (Invited plenary talk). In *Proceedings of the First International Conference on Rough Set and Knowledge Technology (RSKT'06)* (LNAI 4062, pp. 69-78). Chongqing, China: Springer.

Wang, Y. (2006, July). Cognitive informatics: Towards the future generation computers that think and feel (keynote speech). In *Proceedings of the Fifth IEEE International Conference on Cognitive Informatics (ICCI'06)*, Beijing, China (pp. 3-7). IEEE CS Press.

Wang, Y. (2006a, July). On concept algebra and knowledge representation. In *Proceedings of the 5th IEEE International Conference on Cognitive Informatics (ICCI'06)*, (pp. 320-331). Beijing, China: IEEE CS Press.

Wang, Y. (2006). Cognitive informatics—Towards the future generation computers that think and feel (Keynote speech). In *Proceedings of the Fifth IEEE International Conference on Cognitive Informatics (ICCI'06)* (pp. 3-7). Beijing, China: IEEE CS Press.

Wang, Y. (2006b). On abstract systems and system algebra. In *Proceedings of the Fifth IEEE International Conference on Cognitive Informatics (ICCI'06)* (pp. 332-343), Beijing, China: IEEE CS Press.

Wang, Y. (2006b, May 8-10). A unified mathematical model of programs. In *Proceedings of the 19th Canadian Conference on Electrical and Computer Engineering* (CCECE'06), Ottawa, ON, Canada, (pp. 2346-2349).

Wang, Y. (2007). The theoretical framework of cognitive informatics. *The International Journal of Cognitive Informatics and Natural Intelligence (IJCiNi), 1*(1), 1-27. Hershey, PA: IGI Publishing.

Wang, Y. (2007). Cognitive informatics: Exploring the theoretical foundations for natural intelligence, neural informatics, autonomic computing, and agent systems. *International Journal of Cognitive Informatics and Natural Intelligence, 1*, i–x.

Wang, Y. (2007). Formal description of the cognitive process of memorization. In *Proceedings of the Sixth International Conference on Cognitive Informatics (ICCI'07)* (pp. 284-293). Lake Tahoe, CA: IEEE CS Press.

Wang, Y. (2007). Formal description of the cognitive processes of perceptions with emotions, motivations, and attitudes. *International Journal of Cognitive Informatics and Natural Intelligence, 1*(4), 1-13.

Wang, Y. (2007). Keynote speech, on theoretical foundations of software engineering and denotational mathematics. In *Proceedings of the Fifth Asian Workshop on Foundations of Software* (pp. 99-102). Xiamen, China: BHU Press.

Wang, Y. (2007). Software engineering foundations: A software science perspective. *CRC book series on software engineering* (Vol. II). Boca Raton, FL: CRC Press.

Wang, Y. (2007). The Cognitive Processes of Formal Inferences. *The International Journal of Cognitive Informatics and Natural Intelligence, 1*(4), 75-86.

Wang, Y. (2007). On laws of work organization in human cooperation. *International Journal of Cognitive Informatics and Natural Intelligence, 1*(2), 1–15.

Wang, Y. (2007). The OAR model of neural informatics for internal knowledge representation in the brain. *The International Journal of Cognitive Informatics and Natural Intelligence, 1*(3), 64-75.

Wang, Y. (2007, August). Formal description of the cognitive process of memorization. In *Proceedings of the Sixth International Conference on Cognitive Informatics (ICCI'07)*. CA: IEEE CS Press.

Wang, Y. (2007). The theoretical framework and cognitive process of learning. In *Proceedings of the Sixth International Conference on Cognitive Informatics (ICCI'07)* (pp. 470-479). Lake Tahoe, CA: IEEE CS Press.

Wang, Y. (2008). Deductive semantics of RTPA. *The International Journal of Cognitive Informatics and Natural Intelligence, 2*(2), 95-121.

Wang, Y. (2008). On the big-R notation for describing iterative and recursive behaviors. *The International Journal of Cognitive Informatics and Natural Intelligence, 2*(1),17-28.

Wang, Y. (2008). RTPA: A denotational mathematics for manipulating intelligent and computational behaviors. *International Journal of Cognitive Informatics and Natural Intelligence* (IJCINI), *2*(2), 44-62.

Wang, Y. (2008, August). On cognitive foundations of creativity and the cognitive process of creation. In *Proceedings of the Seventh International Conference on Cognitive Informatics (ICCI'08)*, Stanford, CA.

Wang, Y. (2008, April). On concept algebra: A denotational mathematical structure for knowledge and software modeling. *The International Journal of Cognitive Informatics and Natural Intelligence, 2*(2), 1-19.

Wang, Y. (2008, April). On system algebra: A denotational mathematical structure for abstract system modeling. *The International Journal of Cognitive Informatics and Natural Intelligence, 2*(2), 20-43.

Wang, Y. (2008, August). A cognitive informatics theory for visual information processing. In *Proceedings of the Seventh International Conference on Cognitive Informatics (ICCI'08)*, Stanford, CA.

Wang, Y. (2008). Mathematical laws of software. *Transactions of Computational Science, 2*(2).

Wang, Y. (2008e, June). On contemporary denotational mathematics for computational intelligence. *Transactions on Computational Science, 2*(3), 6-29.

Wang, Y. X. (2004). On autonomous computing and cognitive processes. In *Proceedings of the Third IEEE International Conference on Cognitive Informatics* (pp. 3-4).

Wang, Y., & Guan, L. (2005). Recognizing human emotion from audiovisual information. In *Proceedings of IEEE International Conference on Acoustics, Speech and Signal Processing* (Vol. II, pp. 1125-1128).

Wang, Y., & Huang, J. (2005, May). Formal models of object-oriented patterns using RTPA. In *Proceedings of the 2005 Canadian Conference on Electrical and Computer Engineering* (CCECE'05), Saskatoon, Canada, (pp. 1822-1825). IEEE CS Press.

Wang, Y., & King, G. (2000). Software engineering processes: Principles and applications. In *CRC Series in Software Engineering: Vol. I.*. CRC Press.

Wang, Y., & Kinsner, W. (2006). Recent advances in cognitive informatics. *IEEE Transactions on Systems, Man, and Cybernetics (C), 36*(2), 121-123.

Wang, Y., & Noglah, C. F. (2002). Formal specification of a real-time lift dispatching system. In *Proceedings of the 2002 IEEE Canadian Conference on Electrical and Computer Engineering (CCECE'02)* (pp.669-674). Winnipeg, Manitoba, Canada.

Wang, Y., & Noglah, C. F. (2003). Formal description of real-time operating systems using RTPA. In *Proceedings of the 2003 Canadian Conference on Electrical and Computer Engineering (CCECE'03)* (pp.1247-1250). Montreal, Canada: IEEE CS Press

Wang, Y., & Ruhe, G. (2007). The cognitive process of decision making. *International Journal of Cognitive Informatics and Natural Intelligence, 1*(2), 73-85.

Wang, Y., & Wang, Y. (2006). Cognitive informatics models of the brain. *IEEE Transactions on Systems, Man, and Cybernetics (C), 36*(2), 203-207.

Wang, Y., & Zhang, Y. (2003). Formal description of an ATM system by RTPA. In *Proceedings of the 16th Canadian Conference on Electrical and Computer Engineering* (CCECE'03) (pp. 1255-1258). Montreal, Canada: IEEE CS Press.

Wang, Y., Liu, D., & Wang, Y. (2003). Discovering the capacity of human memory. *Brain and Mind, 4*(2), 189–198. doi:10.1023/A:1025405628479

Wang, Y., Wang, Y., Patel, S., & Patel, D. (2006). A layered reference model of the brain (LRMB). *IEEE Transactions on Systems, Man, and Cybernetics (C), 36*(2), 124-133.

Wasserman, P. D. (1989). *Neural computing theory and practice*. Van Nostrand Reinhold.

Watkins, C., & Watkins, M. J. (1975). Buildup of proactive inhibition as a cue-overload effect. *Journal of Experimental Psychology: Human Learning and Memory, 1*(4), 442-452.

Wayman, J. L. (2001). Fundamentals of Biometric Authentication Technologies. *International Journal of Image and Graphics, 1*(1), 93–113. doi:10.1142/S0219467801000086

Wegner, P. (1972). The Vienna definition language. *ACM Computing Surveys, 4*(1), 5-63.

Westen, D. (1999). *Psychology: Mind, brain, and culture* (2nd ed.). New York: John Wiley & Sons, Inc.

Wickens, C. D., Gordon, S. E., & Liu, Y. (1998). *An introduction to human factors engineering*. New York: Addison Wesley Longman, Inc.

Wiggins, J. A., Eiggins, B. B., & Zanden, J. V. (1994). *Social psychology* (5th ed.). New York: McGraw-Hill, Inc.

Wikstrom, A. (1987). *Functional programming using standard ML*. Englewood Cliffs, NJ: Prentice Hall.

Wildes, R. (1997). Iris recognition: An Emerging. Biometric Technology. *Proceedings of the IEEE, 85*(9), 1348–1363. doi:10.1109/5.628669

Wille, R. (1982). Restructuring lattice theory: an approach based on hierarchies of concepts. In I. Rival (Ed.), *Ordered Sets* (pp. 445-470). Boston/Dordrecht: Reidel.

Wille, R. (1992). Concept lattices and conceptual knowledge systems. *Computers & Mathematics with Applications (Oxford, England), 23*, 493–515. doi:10.1016/0898-1221(92)90120-7

Williams, S., & Mahon, I. (2004). Simultaneous localisation and mapping on the Great Barrier Reef. In *Proceedings of the IEEE International Conference on Robotics and Automation (ICRA)* (pp. 1771-1776).

Wilson, L. B., & Clark, R. G. (1988). *Comparative programming language*. Wokingham, England: Addison-Wesley.

Wilson, R. A., & Keil, F. C. (Eds.). (1999). *The MIT encyclopedia of the cognitive sciences*. Cambridge, MA: The MIT Press.

Winskel, G. (1993). *The formal semantics of programming languages*. MIT Press.

Wirjadi, O. (2007). *Survey of 3D image segmentation methods* (Tvech. Rep. No. 123). Fraunhofer Institut, Techno- und Wirtschaftsmathematik.

Wixted, J. T. (2005). A theory about why we forget what we once knew. *Current Directions in Psychological Science, 14*(1), 6-9.

Wojna, A. (2005). Analogy-based reasoning in classifier construction. *Transactions on Rough Sets IV* (LNCS 3700, pp. 277-374). Berlin, Germany: Springer Verlag.

Woodcock, J. & Davies, J. (1996). *Using Z: Specification, refinement, and proof*. London: Prentice Hall International.

Woods, D. D., Patterson, E. S., & Roth, E. M. (2002). Can we ever escape from data overload? A cognitive systems diagnosis. *Cognition Technology and Work, 4*, 22–36. doi:10.1007/s101110200002

Wroblewski, J. (2000). Adaptive aspects of combining approximation space. In S. K. Pal et al. (Eds.), (2004) (pp. 139-156).

Wu, C.-H., Wun, C.-H., & Chou, H.-J. (2004). Using association rules for completing missing data. In *Proceedings of the Fourth International Conference on Hybrid Intelligent Systems* (HIS'04), (pp. 236-241).

Wu, M., Joyce, R. A., Wong, H. S., Guan, L., & Kung, S. Y. (2000). Dynamic resource allocation via video content and short-term statistics. In . *Proceedings of*

IEEE International Conference on Image Processing, III, 58–61.

Xing, W. W., Liu, W. B., & Yuan, B. Z. (2005). Superquadric similarity measure with spherical harmonics in 3D object recognition. *Chinese Journal of Electronics, 14*(3), 529-534.

Yao, J. T. (2007). A ten-year review of granular computing. In *Proceedings of the 3rd IEEE International Conference on Granular Computing* (pp. 299-302).

Yao, Y. Y. (2000). Granular computing: Basic issues and possible solutions. In *Proceedings of the Fifth Joint Conference Information Sciences I*, (pp. 186-189). Atlantic, NJ: Assoc. Intell. Machinery.

Yao, Y. Y. (2001). On modeling data mining with granular computing. In *Proceedings of COMPSAC* (pp. 638-643).

Yao, Y. Y. (2001). Information granulation and rough set approximation. *International Journal of Intelligent Systems, 16*, 87–104. doi:10.1002/1098-111X(200101)16:1<87::AID-INT7>3.0.CO;2-S

Yao, Y. Y. (2001). Modeling data mining with granular computing. In *Proceedings of the 25th Annual International Computer Software and Applications Conference* (pp. 638-643).

Yao, Y. Y. (2003). Information-theoretic measures for knowledge discovery and data mining. In Karmeshu (Ed.) *Entropy Measures, Maximum Entropy and Emerging Applications* (pp. 115-136). Berlin: Springer.

Yao, Y. Y. (2003). Mining high order decision rules. In M. Inuiguchi, S. Hirano & S. Tsumoto (Eds.), *Rough Set Theory and Granular Computing* (pp. 125-135). Berlin: Springer.

Yao, Y. Y. (2004). Concept formation and learning: A cognitive informatics perspective. In *Proceedings of the Third IEEE International Conference on Cognitive Informatics (ICCI'04)* (pp. 42-51). Victoria, British Columbia, Canada: IEEE CS Press.

Yao, Y. Y. (2004). Information granulation and approximation in a decision-theoretic model of rough sets. In S. K. Pal et al. (Eds.), (2004), (pp. 491-516).

Yao, Y. Y. (2004). A comparative study of formal concept analysis and rough set theory in data analysis. In *International Conference on Rough Sets and Current Trends in Computing (RSCTC'2004)*, pp. 59-68.

Yao, Y. Y. (2004). Concept formation and learning: A cognitive informatics perspective. In *Proceedings of the Third IEEE International Conference on Cognitive Informatics*.

Yao, Y. Y. (2004). Granular computing. In *Proceedings of the Fourth Chinese National Conference on Rough Sets and Soft Computing* (pp. 1-5).

Yao, Y. Y. (2004). A partition model of granular computing. *LNCS transactions on rough sets* (. *LNCS, 3100*, 232–253.

Yao, Y. Y. (2005). Perspectives of granular computing. In *Proceedings of the IEEE 2005 Conference on Granular Computing (GrC05)* (pp. 85-90).

Yao, Y. Y. (2005, May). Web intelligence: New frontiers of exploration. In *Proceedings of the 2005 International Conference on Active Media Technology*, Takamatsu, Japan, (pp. 3-8).

Yao, Y. Y. (2006). Granular computing and cognitive informatics. In *Proceedings of the Fifth IEEE International Conference on Cognitive Informatics* (pp. 17-18).

Yao, Y. Y. (2006). Three perspectives of granular computing. In *Proceedings, International Forum on Theory of GrC from Rough Set Perspective, Journal of Nanchang Institute of Technology* (pp. 16-21).

Yao, Y. Y. (2007). The art of granular computing. In *Proceeding of the International Conference on Rough Sets and Emerging Intelligent Systems Paradigms* (LNAI 4585, pp. 101-112).

Yao, Y. Y. (2007). Granular computing for web intelligence and brain informatics. *The 2007 IEEE/WIC/ACM International Conference on Web Intelligence* (pp.1-20).

Yao, Y. Y., & Liau, C.-J. (2002). A generalized decision logic language for granular computing. *FUZZ-IEEE'02 in The 2002 IEEE World Congress on Computational Intelligence* (pp. 1092-1097).

Yao, Y. Y., & Wong, S. K. M. (1992). A decision theoretic framework for approximating concepts. *International Journal of Man-Machine Studies, 37*, 793–809. doi:10.1016/0020-7373(92)90069-W

Yao, Y. Y., & Zhong, N. (1999). An analysis of quantitative measures associated with rules. In *Proceedings of the Third Pacific-Asia Conference on Knowledge Discovery and Data Mining* (pp. 479-488).

Yao, Y. Y., & Zhou, B. (2007). A logic language of granular computing. In *Proceedings of the 6th IEEE International Conference on Cognitive Informatics* (pp. 178-185).

Yao, Y. Y., Chen, Y. H., & Yang, X. D. (2003). A measurement-theoretic foundation for rule interestingness evaluation. In *Proceedings of the Workshop on Foundations and New Directions in Data Mining in the 3rd IEEE International Conference on Data Mining* (pp. 221-227).

Yao, Y. Y., Wang, F. Y., Wang, J., & Zeng, D. (2005). Rule + exception strategies for security information analysis. *IEEE Intelligent Systems, 20*, 52–57. doi:10.1109/MIS.2005.93

Yao, Y. Y., Zhao, Y., & Maguire, R. B. (2003). Explanation-oriented association mining using rough set theory. In *Proceedings of Rough Sets, Fuzzy Sets and Granular Computing* (pp. 165-172).

Yao, Y. Y., Zhou, B., & Chen, Y. H. (2007). Interpreting low and high order rules: a granular computing approach. In *Proceedings of International Conference on Rough Sets and Emerging Intelligent System Paradigms (RSEISP'07), Lecture Notes in Artificial Intelligence* (LNAI 4585, pp. 371-380).

Yao, Y.Y. (2007b). A note on definability and approximations. *Transactions on Rough Sets*, 274-282.

Yaremchuk, V., & Dawson, M. R. W. (2008). Artificial neural networks that classify musical chords. *International Journal of Cognitive Informatics and Natural Intelligence, 2*(3), 22–30.

Yaremchuk, V., Willson, L. R., Spetch, M. L., & Dawson, M. R. W. (2005). The implications of null patterns and output unit activation functions on simulation studies of learning: A case study of patterning. *Learning and Motivation, 36*(1), 88–103. doi:10.1016/j.lmot.2004.10.001

You, M., Chen, C., Bu, J., Liu, J., & Tao, J. (2006). Emotion recognition from noisy speech. In *Proceedings of the IEEE International Conference on Multimedia and Expo, Toronto, Canada* (pp. 1653-1656).

Zadeh, L. A. (1965). Fuzzy sets and systems. In J. Fox (Ed.), *Systems theory* (pp. 29-37). Brooklyn, NY: Polytechnic Press.

Zadeh, L. A. (1965). Fuzzy Sets. *Information and Control, 8*, 338-353.

Zadeh, L. A. (1973). Outline of a new approach to analysis of complex systems. *IEEE Trans. on Sys., Man and Cyb., 1*(1), 28-44.

Zadeh, L. A. (1979). Fuzzy sets and information granularity. In M. Gupta, R. Ragade, & R. Yager (Eds.), *Advances in fuzzy set theory and applications* (pp. 3-18). Amsterdam: NorthHolland.

Zadeh, L. A. (1997). Towards a theory of fuzzy information granulation and its centrality in human reasoning and fuzzy logic. *Fuzzy Sets and Systems, 19*, 111–127. doi:10.1016/S0165-0114(97)00077-8

Zadeh, L. A. (2001). A new direction in AI – toward a computational theory of perception. *AI Magazine, 22*(1), 73-84.

Zadeh, L. A. (2005). Graduation and granulation are keys to computation with information described in natural language. In *Proceedings of the IEEE 2005 Conference on Granular Computing (GrC05)* (p. 30).

Zhang, D., Kinsner, W., Tsai, J., Wang, Y., Sheu, P., & Wang, T. (2007). Cognitive informatics in practice – a report of IEEE ICCI 2005. *International Journal of Cognitive Informatics and Natural Intelligence, 1*(1), 79–83.

Zhang, D., Wang, Y., & Kinsner, W. (Eds.). (2007). *Proceedings of the Sixth IEEE International Conference on Cognitive Informatics.*

Zhao, Y. (2007). *Interactive Data Mining.* Ph.D. Thesis, University of Regina.

Zhao, Y., & Yao, Y. Y. (2005). Interactive user-driven classification using a granule network. In *Proceedings of the Fourth IEEE International Conference on Cognitive Informatics* (pp. 250-259).

Zhong, N., Yao, Y. Y., & Ohshima, M. (2003). Peculiarity oriented multi-database mining. *IEEE Transactions on Knowledge and Data Engineering, 15,* 952–960. doi:10.1109/TKDE.2003.1209011

Zhong, N., Yao, Y. Y., Ohshima, M., & Ohsuga, S. (2001). Interestingness, peculiarity, and multi-database mining.

In *Proceedings of IEEE International Conference on Data Mining* (pp. 566-573).

Zhong, Y.X. (2000). A framework of knowledge theory. *China Engineering Science, 2*(9), 50-64.

Zhong, Y.X. (2002). *Principles of information science* (3rd ed. in Chinese). Beijing. China: BUPT Press.

Ziarko, W., & Shan, N. (1995). Discovering attribute relationships, dependencies and rules by using rough sets. In *Proceedings of the 28th annual Hawaii international conference on system sciences* (pp. 293–299).

Zimmerman, C. L. (1999). *A network interpretation approach to the balance scale task.* Unpublished Ph.D., University of Alberta, Edmonton.

About the Contributors

Yingxu Wang (yingxu@ucalgary.ca) is Professor of Cognitive Informatics and Software Engineering, Director of International Center for Cognitive Informatics (ICfCI), and Director of Theoretical and Empirical Software Engineering Research Center (TESERC) at the University of Calgary. He is a Fellow of WIF, a P.Eng of Canada, a senior member of IEEE and ACM, and a member of ISO/IEC JTC1 and the Canadian Advisory Committee (CAC) for ISO. He received a PhD in software engineering from The Nottingham Trent University (UK, 1997) and a BSc in electrical engineering from Shanghai Tiedao University (1983). He has industrial experience since 1972 and has been a full professor since 1994. He was a visiting professor in the Computing Laboratory at Oxford University in 1995, the Deptartment of Computer Science at Stanford University in 2008, and the Berkeley Initiative in Soft Computing (BISC) Lab at University of California, Berkeley in 2008, respectively. He is the Founder and Steering Committee Chair of the annual IEEE International Conference on Cognitive Informatics (ICCI). He is founding Editor-in-Chief of International Journal of Cognitive Informatics and Natural Intelligence (IJCINI), founding Editor-in-Chief of International Journal of Software Science and Computational Intelligence (IJSSCI), Associate Editor of IEEE Trans on System, Man, and Cybernetics (A), and Editor-in-Chief of CRC Book Series in Software Engineering. He is an initiator of a number of cutting-edge research fields such as cognitive informatics, abstract intelligence, denotational mathematics, theoretical software engineering, and built-in tests. He has published over 105 peer reviewed journal papers, 193 peer reviewed full conference papers, and 12 books in cognitive informatics, software engineering, and computational intelligence. He is the recipient of dozens international awards on academic leadership, outstanding contribution, research achievement, best paper, and teaching in the last thirty years.

***

Jiri Bila graduated in 1969 in Automatic Control, Faculty of Mechanical Engineering, from the Czech Technical University in Prague. In 1977 he defended his dissertation thesis and in 1987 the doctoral dissertation thesis in the field Technical Cybernetics at the CTU in Prague. Besides his university stages he was employed in a few research institutes in Czech Republic and in Germany. He collaborated (study stays and research projects) with departments and institutes of universities in Sweden (1989-1990), Italy (1993) and in France (1994). His scientific fields are Automatic Control, Artificial Intelligence, Neural Networks, Qualitative Modelling of ill-defined systems, Detection of Unexpected Situations and Modelling of Emergent phenomena in Conceptual Design.

Muhammad Waqas Bhatti received his BSc degree in Mathematics and Physics from the University of Punjab in 1992, his BSc degree in Electronics and Communication Engineering from Adamson

University in 1996, and his ME (Research) degree in Signal Processing from the University of Sydney in 2001. His research interests include human-computer interaction, artificial intelligence, pattern recognition, and neural networks.

Ivo Bukovsky graduated from Czech Technical University in Prague where he received his Ph.D. in the field of Control and System Engineering in 2007. He spent seven months working as a visiting researcher under supervision of Dr. M.M. Gupta at the Intelligent Systems Research Laboratory at the University of Saskatchewan within the frame of the NATO Science Fellowships Award in 2003. His Ph.D. thesis on nonconventional neural units and adaptive approach to evaluation of complex systems was recognized by the Verner von Siemens Excellence Award 2007. He is an associate researcher at the Czech Technical University in Prague and his major research interest is the development of new neural architectures and their applications to complex real dynamic systems.

Christopher Dartnell is a doctor in computer sciences. He defended his PhD concerning the conception of a formal interaction framework for scientific discovery in June 2008, in the university Montpellier II. He was part of the Intermed project, which aim is to provide electronic democratic tools to assist debates and the redaction of legal documents such as charters on water regulation, and to empower local structures with adapted governance tools. His main interest lies in the appartition of culture in artificial communities.

Alberto de la Encina is a Lecturer in the Computer Systems and Computation Department, Universidad Complutense de Madrid (Spain). He obtained his MS degree in Mathematics in 1999 and his PhD in the same subject in 2008. Dr. de la Encina has published more than 20 papers in international refereed conferences and journals. His research interests cover functional programming, learning strategies, debugging techniques, and formal methods.

Lisa Fan is an associate professor at Department of Computer Science, Faculty of Science, University of Regina. She received her Ph.D. from the University of London, U.K. Dr. Fan's main research areas include Web Intelligence, Intelligent Learning Systems, Web-based Adaptive Learning, Cognitive Modeling. She is also interested in intelligent systems applications in engineering (intelligent manufacturing system and intelligent transportation system).

Ling Guan is a Tier I Canada Research Chair in Multimedia and a Professor of Electrical and Computer Engineering at Ryerson University, Toronto, Canada. He received his Bachelor's Degree from Tianjin University, China, Master's Degree from University of Waterloo and Ph.D. Degree from University of British Columbia. Dr. Guan has made several seminal contributions to image, video and multimedia signal processing and published extensively in the field. He currently serves on the editorial boards of IEEE Transactions on Multimedia and IEEE Transactions on Circuits and Systems for Video Technology, and chaired the 2006 IEEE International Conference on Multimedia and Expo in Toronto. Dr. Guan is a Fellow of the IEEE and a co-recipient of the 2005 IEEE Transactions on Circuits and Systems for Video Technology Best Paper Award.

Madan M. Gupta is a Professor (Emeritus) and Director of the Intelligent Systems Research Laboratory, College of Engineering, University of Saskatchewan. Dr. Gupta received his B.E. (Hons.) and

M.E. degrees in electronics-communications engineering from the Birla Engineering College (now the Birla Institute of Technology & Science), Pilani, India in 1961 and 1962, respectively. He received his Ph.D. degree from the University of Warwick, United Kingdom in 1967 in adaptive control systems. In 1998, for his extensive contributions in neuro-control, neuro-vision, and fuzzy-neural systems, Dr. Gupta was awarded an earned doctor of science (D.Sc.) degree by the University of Saskatchewan. Dr. Gupta has published over 800 research papers and many books. Dr. Gupta was elected fellow of the Institute of Electrical and Electronics Engineers (IEEE), fellow of the International Society for Optical Engineering (SPIE) and the fellow of the International Fuzzy Systems Association (IFSA). In 1991, Dr. Gupta was co-recipient of the Institute of Electrical Engineering Kelvin Premium. In 1998, Dr. Gupta received the Kaufmann Prize Gold Medal for Research in the field of fuzzy logic.

Hélène Hagège is a young academic at the Université Montpellier 2, France. She graduated from the prestigious Ecole Normale Supérieure of Lyon where she studied molecular and cellular biology. She holds an agrégation in general life and earth sciences and a Ph.D in functional genomics. Part of the work of her PhD has been published in Nature protocol. She has a strong interest in epistemology, which attracted her to human sciences, as well as to the field of teaching and education, where she conducted innovative work on environment and sustainable development education using quantitative methods from psychosociology. She now works in the department of Education sciences, where she is leading a research program on epistemological education, particularly aimed at forming primary and high school teachers to epistemology principles; Jean Sallantin is one of the many researchers who have been collaborating to this project. She is also developing a very ambitious research program on education to responsibility with far reaching consequences on the education system.

Mercedes Hidalgo-Herrero is a Lecturer in the Mathematics Education Department, Universidad Complutense de Madrid (Spain). She obtained her MS degree in Mathematics in 1997 and her PhD in the same subject in 2004. Dr. Hidalgo-Herrero has published more than 20 papers in international refereed conferences and journals. Her research interests cover functional programming, learning strategies, and formal methods.

Noriyasu Homma received a BA, MA, and PhD in electrical and communication engineering from Tohoku University, Japan, in 1990, 1992, and 1995, respectively. From 1995 to 1998, he was a lecturer at the Tohoku University, Japan. He is currently an associate professor of the Faculty of Medicine at the Tohoku University. From 2000 to 2001, he was a visiting professor at the Intelligent Systems Research Laboratory, University of Saskatchewan, Canada. His current research interests include neural networks, complex and chaotic systems, soft-computing, cognitive sciences, actual brain functions. He has published over 70 papers, and co-authored book.

Zeng-Guang Hou received the B.E. and M.E. degrees in electrical engineering from Yanshan University, Qinhuangdao, China, in 1991 and 1993, respectively, and the Ph.D. degree in electrical engineering from Beijing Institute of Technology, Beijing, China, in 1997. From May 1997 to June 1999, he was a Postdoctoral Research Fellow at the Laboratory of Systems and Control, Institute of Systems Science, Chinese Academy of Sciences, Beijing. He was a Research Assistant at the Hong Kong Polytechnic University, Hong Kong, China, from May 2000 to January 2001. From July 1999 to May 2004, he was an Associate Professor at the Institute of Automation, Chinese Academy of Sciences, and has been a

Full Professor since June 2004. From September 2003 to October 2004, he was a Visiting Professor at the Intelligent Systems Research Laboratory, College of Engineering, University of Saskatchewan, Saskatoon, SK, Canada. His current research interests include neural networks, optimization algorithms, robotics, and intelligent control systems.

Minxiao Lei is a graduate student at Department of Computer Science, University of Regina. She received her bachelor degree in Guangxi University in China and has more than two years industry experiences in software development. Data Mining, Web Mining, and Intelligent System Applications are her current research areas and interests.

Yide Ma received the B.Sc. and M.Sc. degrees in radio technology from ChengDu University of Engineering Science and Technology, China, in 1984 and 1988, respectively. In 2001, he received the Ph.D. degree from the Department of Life Science, Lanzhou University, China. He is a current professor in School of Information Science and Engineering of Lanzhou University and published more than 40 papers on major journals and international conferences. His current research interests include artificial neural network, digital image processing, pattern recognition, digital signal processing, computer vision, etc.

Eric Martin is a Senior lecturer at the School of Computer Science and Engineering in the University of New South Wales, Sydney, Australia. He obtained his PhD from the University of Paris VII in 1993 in theoretical computer science. His research mainly focuses on the logical foundations of Artificial intelligence. He developed a general framework, Parametric logic, that unifies various modes of reasoning, including deduction and induction, and relates them to concepts from the field of inductive inference and to topological hierarchies. His work has been applied to extensions of systems of logic programming that can answer more complex queries than traditional systems do, and can be used in the context of automated scientific discovery. Together with one of his students, Ori Allon, he has patented a technique used in the implementation of Orion, a system that analyses web pages and answers discovery queries. The system has attracted the interest of many companies, including Google and Yahoo, with Google acquiring the rights to the patent.

Ka-Lok Ng (corresponding author) received the Honours diploma from Hong Kong Baptist College in 1983, and the Ph.D. degree in theoretical physics from the Vanderbilt University at USA in 1990. He is a professor at the Department of Bioinformatics, Asia University since February 2008. He has funded research and published articles in the areas of protein-protein interaction network, topological and robustness study of biological network, modeling of DNA sequences, cosmic microwave background radiation and neutrino study. His research interests include protein-protein interaction network, cancer-related microRNA genes and cancerous protein domain-domain interactions study.

Pablo Rabanal is a Teaching Assistant in the Computer Systems and Computation Department, Universidad Complutense de Madrid (Spain). He obtained his MS degree in Computer Science in 2004 and he is currently working on his PhD Thesis, devoted to the development of nature-inspired techniques to solve NP-complete problems. His research interests cover heuristic methods, testing techniques, and machine learning.

Ismael Rodríguez is an Associate Professor in the Computer Systems and Computation Department, Universidad Complutense de Madrid (Spain). He obtained his MS degree in Computer Science in 2001 and his PhD in the same subject in 2004. Dr. Rodríguez received the Best Thesis Award of his faculty in 2004. He also received the Best Paper Award in the IFIP WG 6.1 FORTE 2001 conference. Dr. Rodríguez has published more than 60 papers in international refereed conferences and journals. His research interests cover formal methods, testing techniques, e-learning environments, and heuristic methods.

Fernando Rubio is an Associate Professor in the Computer Systems and Computation Department, Universidad Complutense de Madrid (Spain). He obtained his MS degree in Computer Science in 1997 and his PhD in the same subject in 2001. Dr. Rubio received the National Degree Award on the subject of Computer Science from the Spanish Ministry of Education in 1997, as well as the Best Thesis Award of his faculty in 2001. Dr. Rubio has published more than 50 papers in international refereed conferences and journals. His research interests cover functional programming, testing techniques, e-learning environments, and heuristic methods.

Jean Sallantin is a Director of Research at the LIRMM Laboratoire dInformatique, de Robotique et de Micro-électronique de Montpellier of the CNRS in Montpellier, France. Phd from University Paris VI in Theoretical Physic (1972) and professor thesis in Computer Science (1979). He currently heads the Rationality and machine learning team that develops and studies the applications of machine learning techniques in a scientific discovery environment. One of the pioneers of bioinformatics in France, Jean Sallantin established the bioinformatics laboratory at the Curie Institute Paris (1983-85) and was the director of the GSDIARL research consortium (1985-89).

Jing-Doo Wang received the B.S. degree in Computer Science and Information Engineering from the Tatung Institute of Technology in 1989, and the M.S. and Ph.D. degrees Computer Science and Information Engineering from the University of Chung Cheng in 1993 and 2002 respectively. He has been with Asia University (formerly Taichung Healthcare and Management University) since spring 2003, where he is currently an assistant professor in the Department of Computer Science and Information Engineering, and also holds a joint appointment with the Department of Bioinformatics. His research interests were in the areas of Chinese text categorization, information extraction before 2003. Recently, he focused on the bioinformatics, such as DNA sequence classification, significant pattern extraction and genomic sequences comparison.

Yongjin Wang received his M. A. Sc degree in Electrical and Computer Engineering from Ryerson University, Canada in 2005. He is currently a Ph. D. candidate at the Edward S. Rogers Sr. Department of Electrical and Computer Engineering, University of Toronto, Canada. From January to August 2005, he was a research assistant at Ryerson Multimedia Research Lab. He is a recipient of Natural Sciences and Engineering Research Council (NSERC) Canadian Graduate Scholarships Doctoral (CGSD) award from 2007 to 2009. His research interests include speech and image processing, computer vision, biometrics, and pattern recognition.

Guangzhu Xu received the B.Sc. degree and Ph.D. degree in radio physics from Lanzhou University, China, in 2002 and 2007, respectively. He is a current assistant professor in the College of Electrical Engineering and Information Technology. His major research interests include biometrics, neural network, digital image processing and analysis, pattern recognition.

Yiyu Yao is a professor of computer science in the Department of Computer Science, University of Regina, Regina, Saskatchewan, Canada. His research interests include information retrieval, rough sets, interval sets, granular computing, web intelligence, data mining and fuzzy sets. He has published over 200 journal and conference papers. He is an area editor of International Journal of Approximate Reasoning, a member of the editorial boards of the Web Intelligence and Agent Systems journal, Transactions on Rough Sets, Journal of Intelligent Information Systems, Journal of Chongqing University of Posts and Telecommunication, The International Journal of Cognitive Informatics & Natural Intelligence (IJCiNi), International Journal of Software Science and Computational Intelligence (IJSSCI). He has served and is serving as a program co-chair of several international conferences. He is a member of ACM and IEEE.

Vanessa Yaremchuk is a PhD student in the McGill Music Technology program and a member of the Input Devices and Music Interaction Laboratory at Mcgill University. Her research has involved application of artificial neural networks to modelling musical cognition. Her earlier background is in computing science and artificial intelligence, and she has published in the areas of animal learning and musical cognition. She is currently using artificial neural networks to explore issues concerning mapping between gesture and music generation. She also works semi-professionally as a photographer.

Zaifeng Zhang received the B.Sc. degree in mechanism manufacture and equipments from Lanzhou institute of technology, China, in 1990. In 2002, he received the M.Sc. degree in communication and information system from Lanzhou University, China. He is currently pursuing the Ph.D. degree in biometrics in the school of information science and engineering of Lanzhou University, China. His current research interests include biometrics, digital signal processing, digital watermark, pattern recognition, etc.

Yan Zhao received her B. Eng. from the Shanghai University of Engineering and Science, People's Republic of China, in 1994, and her M.Sc. and Ph.D. from the University of Regina, Regina, Saskatchewan, Canada in 2003 and 2007. She is a current Post Doctoral Research Fellow at the University of Regina. Her research interests include data mining and machine learning.

Bing Zhou received her B. Eng. from the Shandong University of Technology, People's Republic of China, in 1998, and her M.Sc. from the University of Regina, Regina, Saskatchewan, Canada in 2008. She is currently pursuing her Ph.D. degree in computer science under the supervision of Professor Yiyu Yao in the University of Regina. Her research interests include granular computing, cognitive informatics, rough sets, formal concept analysis and information retrieval.

Index

U

V